Third Edition

Clinical Social Work Practice in Behavioral Mental Health

TOWARD EVIDENCE-BASED PRACTICE

Roberta G. Sands
University of Pennsylvania

Zvi D. Gellis
University of Pennsylvania

Allyn & Bacon

Boston   Columbus   Indianapolis   New York   San Francisco   Upper Saddle River
Amsterdam   Cape Town   Dubai   London   Madrid Milan Munich   Paris   Montreal   Toronto
Delhi   Mexico City   São Paulo   Sydney   Hong Kong   Seoul   Singapore   Taipei   Tokyo

Executive Editor: Ashley Dodge
Editorial Product Manager: Carly Czech
Senior Marketing Manager: Wendy Albert
Marketing Assistant: Shauna Fishweicher
Production Editor: Shelly Kupperman
Editorial Production Service: PreMediaGlobal
Manufacturing Buyer: Fran Russello
Cover Administrator: Jayne Conte
Editorial Production and Composition Service: Chitra Ganesan/PreMediaGlobal
Cover Designer: Bruce Kenselaar
Printer/Binder: RR Donnelley and Sons Company

Library of Congress Cataloging-in-Publication Data
Sands, Roberta G.
  Clinical social work practice in behavioral mental health : toward evidence-based practice / Roberta G. Sands, Zvi D. Gellis.—3rd ed.
    p. cm.
  Includes index.
  ISBN-13: 978-0-205-82016-0
  ISBN-10: 0-205-82016-6

1. Psychiatric social work—United States.   2. Community mental health services—United States.   3. Chronic diseases—Psychological aspects.   I. Gellis, Zvi D.   II. Title.
  HV690.U6S26 2012
  362.2'20973—dc22

                                                                                          2010048113

10 9 8 7 6 5 4 3 2   15 14 13

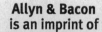
Allyn & Bacon
is an imprint of

www.pearsonhighered.com

ISBN-10: 0-205-82016-6
ISBN-13: 978-0-205-82016-0

TABLE OF CONTENTS

PREFACE

We are in the dawn of a new era in the field of mental health. Expanded biopsychosocial knowledge and increased experience applying this knowledge to practice have resulted in new, evidence-based methods of intervening with clients for whom there was little hope in the past. The growing presence of clients with serious and moderately disabling conditions that can be helped and clients from diverse cultures has heightened the need for clinical and cultural competence. Public policy has called for "transforming mental health care in America."[1] Through *Clinical Social Work Practice in Behavioral Mental Health: Toward Evidence-Based Practice*, third edition, we hope to prepare social workers to use advances in knowledge to contribute to this transformation.

Social workers are one of the principal providers of mental health services in the United States. They are ubiquitous in mental health centers, psychiatric rehabilitation programs, emergency services, hospitals, housing and residential programs, and other behavioral health entities. Social workers provide clinical services to clients who need time-limited psychotherapy and those who require continuing supportive care. They work in both the pubic sector and private settings. Members of a profession that sees itself at the interface between the person and the environment, social workers offer a critical link between the client, the behavioral health treatment team, and the community.

This book is written for those who wish to gain specialized knowledge of social work practice with adults in the field of mental health/behavioral health. One of the book's audiences is social work graduate students who are taking courses in or are specializing in mental health. Advanced undergraduate students who are interested in mental health or are preparing for a career in this field constitute another audience. A third audience is mental health practitioners. Although this book was written from a social work perspective, clinicians and students of related professions, such as nursing and psychosocial rehabilitation, may benefit from reading this volume. This book does, however, assume prior foundation knowledge of human behavior and social work practice theory, counseling skills, and some familiarity with the *Diagnostic and Statistical Manual of Mental Disorders (DSM-IV-TR)*.[2]

The third, substantially revised edition of this book has some new features that are especially relevant to the contemporary behavioral health environment. First, this book has a new focus on recovery and recovery models for consumers with serious and persistent mental illness. Second, it highlights evidence-based practices with clients with depressive disorders, anxiety disorders, serious mental illness, and dual disorders (severe mental illness and substance abuse) and has an updated focus on best and promising practices. A third novel feature is that it gives increased attention to the mental health of older adults.

Other special features of this volume are that it:

1. describes research evidence supporting practice interventions.
2. gives special attention to SAMHSA's evidence-based toolkits for interventions with clients with severe and persistent mental illness.
3. addresses cultural disparities in the chapter on cultural competence.
4. discusses feminist theories and violence perpetrated against women and human trafficking in the chapter on feminist mental health practice.
5. explains legal and ethical issues related to mental health, including documentation.

6. provides a historical context for understanding mental health policies.
7. describes interventions and provides stimulating case examples.
8. includes four chapters on working with adults with severe and persistent mental illness (including one on co-occurring severe mental illness and substance abuse).
9. suggests instruments that can be used to monitor progress and evaluate outcomes of treatment of clients with particular mental health problems.
10. provides extensive information about medication.
11. uses a postmodern lens to critically examine the contents of chapters.
12. includes case studies within and at the conclusions of chapters.

The mental/behavioral health practice described in this book is with adults with moderate to severe mental health difficulties. These difficulties include depression, anxiety, severe mental illness, and substance abuse (including dual diagnoses). Consistent with today's practice environment, the locus of treatment that is emphasized is the community and outpatient settings, but many of the interventions that are described can be used within hospitals and other institutions. Although efforts have been made to be comprehensive, certain boundaries had to be drawn. This book does not discuss intervention with persons who simply have "problems in living" or difficulties that are principally environmental. Moreover, it does not give attention to treatment of children and adolescents, persons with personality disorders and dementia, and adults with co-occurring mental illness and mental retardation/developmental disabilities and co-occurring severe mental illness and anxiety and personality disorders.

The book is organized as follows. It begins with an orienting chapter, in which the reader is introduced to the leading concepts, themes, and contexts that are addressed in the field of mental/behavioral health and in the book. The book then is divided into two parts. Part One, "A Framework for Practice," consists of six chapters. The first (Chapter 2) looks at the historical context of social work practice in the field of mental health. The next, the conceptual framework, describes the terms, theories, and perspectives related to the book's integrated biopsychosocial perspective. In keeping with the conceptual framework, Chapter 4 describes components of a comprehensive biopsychosocial assessment. Here the mental status examination, a functional assessment, and the biopsychosocial summary are described, and model formats are provided. Chapter 5 is concerned with legal and ethical issues that social workers face when they practice within the framework of their professional values and the legal system, and includes background on the decisions and information on record keeping. The next two chapters address culture and gender. Chapter 6 provides a framework for culturally competent mental health practice and gives attention to practice with African Americans, American Indians/Alaska Natives, Asian Americans and Pacific Islanders, and Hispanics/Latinos/Latinas. Chapter 7 describes feminist theories and practice and discusses violence and trauma, particularly in relation to intimate partner violence and human trafficking.

Part Two contains six chapters on intervention. Although the primary emphasis here is on psychosocial modalities, information on psychotropic medication is provided as well. Chapters 8 and 9 describe evidence-based practices with persons suffering from depression and anxiety, respectively, provide illustrative case examples, and identify medications that are used. Because persons with severe and persistent mental disorders constitute a prominent population in the field of mental health, four chapters are devoted to their treatment. Chapter 10 defines terminology and describes various concepts and perspectives, including recovery, psychosocial (psychiatric) rehabilitation, stress-diathesis, and community integration. Chapter 11 discusses evidence-based and best practices that operate on the community level, including case management and the

Assertive Community Treatment (ACT) model. This chapter also describes a range of community resources appropriate for persons with severe and persistent psychiatric disorders and a couple of best practices. The third chapter on treatment with this population (Chapter 12) focuses on the evidence-based practices of "Illness and Recovery" and "Family Psychoeducation," but also discusses other family interventions, cognitive rehabilitation, and medication. Chapter 13, which was written by Kathleen J. Farkas of Case Western Reserve University, Mandel School of Applied Social Sciences, is on clinical practice with clients with the co-occurring severe mental illness and an addictive disorder. This chapter provides definitions, reviews epidemiological research, and describes two evidence-based practices with this population. Notably, this chapter has rich case examples.

The authors gratefully acknowledge the help of a number of individuals who made this revision possible. Both of us would like to thank Phyllis Solomon, our colleague at the University of Pennsylvania School of Social Policy and Practice, who helped clarify many of the points we are making in this book. Other colleagues at Penn who have been part of our "support team" include Yin-Ling Irene Wong and Joretha Bourjolly. Roberta Sands would like to thank members of the PRIME (Partners Reaching to Improve Multicultural Education) for furthering her knowledge of culture. She thanks Laurene Finley for her suggestions on revising this chapter and Anita Pernell-Arnold for the insights that she provided through PRIME and collaborative writing projects. Roberta Sands would especially like to thank Samuel Klausner, whose support has been constant throughout this project. Zvi Gellis would like to thank Stan McCracken for his insights and assistance on the topic of mental health and older adults. Finally, we gratefully acknowledge the assistance of staff of Allyn & Bacon for their contributions to this publication.

NOTES

1. Substance Abuse and Mental Health Services Administration (SAMHSA), U.S. Department of Health and Human Services. (2005). *Transforming mental health care in America: The federal action agenda: First steps* (DHHS Publication No. SMA 05-4060). Rockville, MD: Department of Health and Human Services. See also President's New Freedom Commission on Mental Health. (2003). *Achieving the promise: Transforming mental health care in America. Final report* (DHHS Publication No. SMA 03-3832). Rockville, MD: U.S. Government Printing Office.
2. American Psychiatric Association. (2000). *Diagnostic and statistical manual of mental disorders* (4th ed., text rev). Washington, DC: Author.

Getting Oriented
Themes and Contexts

*Social workers should base practice on recognized
knowledge, including empirically based knowledge relevant to
social work and social work ethics.*

—NATIONAL ASSOCIATION OF SOCIAL WORKERS,
"NASW CODE OF ETHICS," 1996/2008

Clinical social workers are one of the foremost professionals in the field of mental health. They are the most numerous clinically trained mental health personnel working in mental health settings, with a preponderance in direct service roles (Duffy et al., 2006). Among members of the National Association of Social Workers, mental health is the leading field of practice, with close to 40 percent indicating that this is their primary area (Gibelman & Schervish, 1997). Mirroring practitioners, more students in master's programs that offer concentrations in fields of practice or social problems are enrolled in mental health or community mental health than any other specific area and more master's degree students are situated in mental health field placements than any other practicum types (Council on Social Work Education [CSWE], 2007). The Bureau of Labor Statistics of the U.S. Department of Labor (2010–2011) projects that social workers in mental health and substance abuse will be in increasing demand in the future.

This book aims to equip social workers with up-to-date contextualized knowledge about scientific developments, theories, and methods of social work practice in mental health settings. In the decade preceding the publication of this edition, federal initiatives such as the report of the President's New Freedom Commission on Mental Health (2003) have put forth a new agenda for the field of mental health. The agenda includes evidence-based practices, consumer- and family-centered services and treatment, the promotion of recovery, and the elimination of ethnic, racial, and gender-based disparities in the delivery of mental health services. The third edition of this book is responsive to this report as well as the federal action agenda, *Transforming Mental Health Care in America* (Substance Abuse and Mental Health Services Administration [SAMHSA], 2005), which endorsed culturally competent services, prevention and treatment of co-occurring psychiatric and substance abuse disorders, and "promising" as well as evidence-based practices (EBPs). Consistent with these documents and the Surgeon General's (U.S. Department of Health and Human Services, 1999) report on mental health and the Institute of Medicine's (2001) report on health care reform and accessibility, this book also encompasses the mental health of older as well as younger adults.

This book is directed at social work students and practitioners who wish to advance their knowledge and skills in clinical practice in the field of mental health. Clinical social workers practice with and on behalf of individuals, families, and small groups to help reduce their distress and improve their psychological and social functioning. Knowledgeable about human behavior theories, as well as a variety of modes of intervention, clinical social workers make psychosocial assessments, formulate goals, and provide psychotherapeutic interventions or treatment. Although professionals of other disciplines share some of the same knowledge and engage in similar activities, clinical social workers have a broader perspective than their colleagues in other disciplines. Social workers view clients and their problems in relation to the contexts in which these difficulties occur and intervene in the social environment as well as the psychological and interpersonal domains. They are especially committed to enhancing clients' strengths and fostering connections between clients and the community. When interpersonal and institutional barriers interfere with clients' ability to obtain resources, clinical social workers promote changes to eliminate obstacles, ensure clients' rights, and create linkages and resources. Professionals with a mission to promote human welfare and social justice, clinical social workers are particularly concerned with the plight of vulnerable populations.

This description of clinical social work encompasses what is also called *direct social work practice*, a general term that applies to practice in a wide range of field settings among various populations and problem areas. Direct practitioners in most specialized fields draw from diverse sources of knowledge, theories, and methods. They work with clients and systems to prevent and/or solve problems, change maladaptive behaviors, resolve psychological issues, develop social networks, and use community resources. Intervention is psychological and social and adapted to the needs of the client or client system.

In the field of mental health, clinicians' therapeutic and case management roles predominate and are interconnected. As therapists, clinical social workers use their knowledge of practice theories, differential diagnosis, and treatment modalities, as well as empirically supported and evidence-based methods of practice, to promote psychological and/or behavioral changes, enhance clients' psychosocial functioning, and improve their situations. They foster clients' decision making and promote their recovery from the effects of mental illness and/or substance abuse. As case managers, clinical social workers link consumers with resources, monitor their treatment plans, and engage in advocacy. Those who work as case managers for individuals with severe mental illness promote clients' use of personal and community supports and provide that support themselves. (See Chapter 11 for a discussion of case management in relation to the severely mentally ill.) Within these two roles, clinical social workers take on numerous functions, which include diagnosis, mediation, crisis intervention, skills training, collaboration on interdisciplinary and interagency teams, family and consumer consultation, and education (Bentley, 2002). They have extensive contacts with colleagues in related disciplines, staff of a variety of human service agencies, landlords, physicians, lawyers, clergy, and others. Through these contacts, clinical social workers connect clients with community resources and work to reduce barriers to mental health services.

Social work practice in mental or behavioral health takes place in a number of different settings. Among these are community mental health centers, outpatient clinics, psychiatric hospitals or units within general hospitals, assertive community treatment teams, psychosocial rehabilitation services, substance abuse treatment programs, supported apartments, group homes, and managed behavioral care carve-outs, as well as Veterans Affairs hospitals and employee assistance programs (Gibelman, 2004). Aside from services that specialize in mental health, family service and child welfare agencies, homeless shelters, and private practices also serve clients with mental health and substance abuse issues. This book was written with the former set of treatment centers in mind, but much of what is described here applies to other settings as well.

This chapter aims to orient readers to the context of behavioral or mental health practice today and the themes that run through this book. It begins with a description of community mental health, the predecessor of today's system of behavioral health under managed care. It explains the ideology of behavioral or mental health, its relation to deinstitutionalization, and its public health model. Next, behavioral health under managed care is described. The third topic that is introduced in this chapter is scientific knowledge and EBP, which include knowledge of psychiatric epidemiology, biological research, and EBP research. This is followed by definitions that are important to understanding the field. The chapter concludes with an explanation of the postmodern perspective that is used as a critical framework for chapters in this book.

COMMUNITY MENTAL HEALTH

Community mental health is a concept, philosophy of intervention, social movement, ideology, and policy that dominated the field of mental health during the last few decades of the twentieth century. In its initial conceptualization by Gerald Caplan (1961), the community was thought to generate stress that, in turn, produced psychopathology. Public policies in keeping with the community mental health concept supported the creation and expansion of services close to consumers in their local communities.

Caplan (1964) incorporated a public health model of prevention into his philosophy. Accordingly, intervention on three levels would reduce the incidence, duration, and degree of impairment associated with mental illness.

Three Levels of Prevention

The first level of mental health prevention, *primary prevention*, has the goal of reducing the incidence (rate of new cases) of mental disorders by addressing their causes. This level focuses on the community and the conditions within it that may be toxic. Primary prevention invites research into potential biological, environmental, and psychological causes. When this research identifies groups that are at a high risk of developing a particular problem, preventive interventions, such as education, can be directed at that sector of the population. Primary prevention focuses on providing supports, which may be physical (food, housing), psychosocial (relationships), and sociocultural (cultural values, customs, and expectations), and preventing barriers to the flow of supports, such as racism (Caplan, 1964).

The second level, *secondary prevention*, has the goals of reducing the prevalence of actual cases (old and new) in the community and shortening the duration of time in which individuals experience problems, thus preventing existing problems from getting worse. Early identification (case finding), assessment, and intervention (crisis intervention and short-term therapy) are some ways in which this level of prevention is implemented. Prompt and effective individual, family, and group psychotherapies also apply to the secondary level.

The third level, *tertiary prevention*, has the goal of reducing the rate of mental disability in the community through rehabilitation. This level focuses on restoring individuals with serious psychiatric problems to as high a level of functioning as possible and on preventing complications (Langsley, 1985b). Tertiary prevention is directed at the community as well as at clients and their social networks (Caplan, 1964). On the community level, efforts are made to prevent or reduce stigma, ignorance, and other barriers to recovery through advocacy and community education. When applied to individuals with severe mental disabilities, tertiary prevention aims to thwart decompensation, homicide, and suicide.

In addition to the three levels of prevention, several principles guided the community mental health practice from the beginning. Many of these principles also operate in today's behavioral health/managed care environment.

Principles of Community Mental Health Practice

The community mental health movement embraced a set of principles that constituted a belief system or ideology. These include comprehensiveness, continuity of care, accessibility, multidisciplinary teams, and accountability. One of the foremost principles was that services should be *comprehensive* (Langsley, 1985a). This meant that communities should provide a wide range of mental health services at various levels of intensity from outreach programs to outpatient clinical services to day treatment to hospitalization. Within these services, alternatives such as psychotherapies (individual, family, and group), social skills training, and vocational rehabilitation were to be offered. The community itself was to have a diverse range of residential settings, such as halfway houses and supported housing, in which clients may live (Bachrach, 1986). Community treatment was to be responsive to all age groups (including children and older adults), to be available around the clock and on an emergency basis, and to address special problems such as substance abuse. Services were to be flexible and adapted to the needs of the populations served (Bachrach, 1986).

A related principle was that *continuity of care* was to be assured (Langsley, 1985a). This was a way to prevent clients from falling through the cracks in the context of a service delivery system that was complex, fragmented, and bureaucratic. It meant that services should be linked—"a system of services with easy flow of patients among its component parts" (Bloom, 1984, p. 4). For example, clients leaving psychiatric facilities were to be connected to treatment services when they were discharged. The case manager made sure that linkages were made and acted on.

Community mental health services were supposed to be *accessible* to those who sought treatment (Langsley, 1985a). This meant that they were to be located near clients' residences or places of work, reachable by public transportation, and available during evenings (at least for emergencies) and weekends. To assure this, community mental health services were distributed into *catchment areas* or service units that served residents in a particular geographic area. Facilities were also to be accessible to persons with physical disabilities, and provisions were to be made for communicating with those who could not hear. Furthermore, services were to be culturally and gender sensitive.

Another principle of community mental health was that treatment providers should organize into *multidisciplinary teams* (Langsley, 1985a). Teams were comprised of psychiatrists, psychologists, community mental health nurses, social workers, recreation therapists, and counselors, among others. Indigenous mental health workers (paraprofessional), who lived in the neighborhood, also participated (Bloom, 1984). Multidisciplinary teams make it possible for the knowledge, skills, and perspectives of diverse members to contribute to a holistic understanding of the client and the provision of multidimensional treatment or rehabilitation.

A further principle was *accountability* (Langsley, 1985a). The citizen board members who governed mental health agencies were responsible not only to those who sought treatment but also to those who were well (Langsley, 1985a). Accountability also applied to consumers, who participated increasingly in the governance of community mental health agencies. As consumers recognized their potential power, they asserted themselves increasingly over time.

Although community mental health and deinstitutionalization were distinct movements within the mental health field, their ideologies converged. Community mental health practitioners identified with some of the attitudes toward hospitalization assumed by advocates of deinstitutionalization.

Deinstitutionalization

Deinstitutionalization is a philosophy, process, and ideology (Bachrach, 1976; Mechanic, 2008) that began to unfold in the United States in the late 1950s when the principal locus of treatment began to change from hospitals to the community. In 1955, the number of patients residing in state and county psychiatric hospitals peaked at 559,000. After that time, these facilities were substantially (but not completely) depopulated. By 2002, the inpatient population was down to 57,263 residents (Duffy et al., 2006), a substantial reduction. This process was facilitated by the development of medications that could be prescribed and taken in the community. Another condition that supported deinstitutionalization was a switching of costs from the state to the federal level in the 1960s, which made it possible for persons who were formerly long-term hospital residents to live in the community (Mechanic, 2008).

Although some advocates of deinstitutionalization hoped that hospitals could be entirely eliminated, the philosophy in practice revolved around the appropriate use of hospitals. Instead of maintaining a large cadre of persons with severe mental illness in custodial care, hospitals would care for persons with acute exacerbations (flare-ups) for a brief period of time in which they would be stabilized. Short-term hospitalizations could be provided in psychiatric units of local general hospitals (rather than state facilities located some distance from clients' homes), with follow-up treatment to help them maintain their gains provided in the community.

Deinstitutionalization was supposed to involve two processes—(a) the avoidance of hospitalization and (b) the concurrent development of community services that would serve as alternatives to institutionalization (Bachrach, 1976). The first process meant that community treatment strategies, such as placement in a day treatment program, were to be pursued before considering hospitalization. This mechanism of diversion was dependent on the second process, the existence or creation of community alternatives such as crisis and emergency services, group homes, supported residential programs, outpatient treatment centers, vocational rehabilitation programs, and other options (for today's options, see Chapter 11). Unfortunately, many communities did not develop community alternatives. Many discharged patients were "dumped" on city streets without a place in which to live and without outpatient care. Another consequence of deinstitutionalization was the development of a *revolving door syndrome*, with the same individuals flowing in and out of the hospitals on a regular basis. The increase in admission rates that followed deinstitutionalization suggests that brief hospitalizations were not long enough to allow recovery to take place and/or that some clients did not receive or follow up on referrals to agencies providing aftercare. A further flaw in the implementation of this policy was that some residents of psychiatric hospitals were reinstitutionalized in nursing homes and prisons. With the passage of time it has become clear that state hospitals continue to be needed in some areas to care for persons who are poor community risks, "revolving door" patients, and those who require long-term hospitalization (Bachrach, 1996).

Deinstitutionalization evolved as a public policy during the 1960s, a period of heightened social consciousness and advocacy for the rights of marginalized populations. In the 1960s and 1970s, practices such as involuntary commitment, custodial care without treatment, and coercive forms of intervention were successfully challenged in courts on constitutional grounds. (See Chapter 2 for a review of this history and Chapter 5 for a discussion of legal issues.) But deinstitutionalization was also an ideology that was associated with certain values (Mechanic, 1989). First, hospitalization was considered undesirable, adversely affecting patients (Mechanic, 2008). Second, it was considered desirable for persons with mental health difficulties to be free to live normal lives, integrated as fully as possible into the fabric of the community (cf. Wolfensberger, Nirje, Olshansky, Perske, & Roos, 1972).

Although proponents of deinstitutionalization and community mental health identified with these values, there were others who saw in the emergence of deinstitutionalization an opportunity for taxpayers to save money. Hospitalization is the most expensive form of psychiatric treatment that there is. States had been bearing a significant economic burden for long-term hospital care. When liberal thinkers depicted institutionalization as undesirable, conservatives responded by closing state hospitals. Other policies such as limiting admissions to those who were a danger to themselves and others and retaining people in the hospital over relatively short periods of time also appeared to be economically advantageous to taxpayers. Cost-mindedness continues to drive policy under managed care.

Behavioral Health under Managed Care

The term *behavioral health* is used in today's managed care environments to describe the prevention and treatment of mental health and substance abuse. Managed care is a means of structuring, financing, and administering health care that aims to be cost-effective, efficient, and high in quality. It came to the fore at a time when health care costs in the United States were skyrocketing and appeared to be out of control. It has changed the face of health care and mental health practice and introduced certain terms and concepts that require explanation.

In contrast to the fee-for-service, *indemnity* model in which third-party payers, such as health insurance companies, pay for each medical visit or procedure, with managed care, physicians are paid for services at a negotiated rate. A primary care physician (PCP) coordinates services and makes decisions about the need for outside referrals and procedures. Under managed care, interventions must be preapproved, reauthorized at intervals, and evaluated in terms of outcomes.

Behavioral health services may be provided under a managed health care insurance plan. There are two main types: health maintenance organizations (HMOs) and preferred provider organizations (PPOs). HMOs are prepaid plans in which the member uses specific health providers that are part of the organization's network. These providers may be employed directly by the HMO or may be groups or individuals who contract with the HMO. In a PPO, the member has the option of using the organization's preferred network or going outside the network, in which case there are additional costs. Consumers in PPOs pay a modest copayment for each visit (Jackson, 1995). One can use providers outside HMO and PPO networks in an emergency. A third type, the point-of-service (POS) plan, which may be a separate alternative or part of an HMO or PPO, also allows consumers flexibility in using network and nonnetwork providers, with different terms applying to different sets of providers (Corcoran & Vandiver, 1996). Behavioral health care in HMOs and PPOs may be provided through a kind of carve-out arrangement, a contract with a managed behavioral healthcare organization (MBHO) that provides mental health and/or substance abuse services (Edmunds et al., 1997). Alternatively, behavioral health may be integrated into the health care provider system. Providers of behavioral health services under any of these managed care arrangements usually agree to accept what is called a *capitated* rate. This is a specific amount per user that the provider is given for a particular time period (e.g., per month).

In 1995, about 60 percent of people living in the United States were in some kind of managed health care plan (Health Insurance Association of America, 1996). About 25 percent had other kinds of coverage. Many states have obtained waivers from the Health Care Financing Administration, making it possible for some people on Medicaid to enroll in managed care plans (McGuirk, Keller, & Croze, 1995). Similarly, Medicare beneficiaries may receive their benefits through a managed care arrangement. Full-time employees of relatively large companies provide individual (and sometimes family) coverage as a fringe benefit, with some or no cost sharing between the employer and the employee. In 2007, 15.3 percent of the U.S. population had no health insurance (DeNavas-Walt, Proctor, & Smith, 2008). With the passage of President Obama's Patient Protection and Affordable Care Act in March of 2010, it is expected that the proportion of uninsured will be substantially reduced after the act is put into operation.

Clients in need of mental health or behavioral health services may or may not have health insurance. Some lose their private insurance when mental health problems make it difficult for them to maintain their jobs. For those who are insured, behavioral health benefits may be limited. The Health Maintenance Organization Act of 1973 (Pub. L. No. 93-222) established a minimal level of behavioral health coverage by HMOs at twenty outpatient visits and thirty days of inpatient treatment a year (Jackson, 1995). The Mental Health Parity Act of 1996 required equity in insurance coverage between physical and mental health problems, but this legislation had a number of loopholes. The Mental Health Parity and Addiction Equity Act (MHPAEA) of 2008 strengthened the previous act.

The introduction of managed care into mental health and substance abuse practice has centered attention on cost-effectiveness and prevention. *Cost-effectiveness* refers to the need to assess the connection between cost and outcomes to assure the best outcome at the least cost. Expensive treatment strategies, such as hospitalization and long-term psychotherapy, are avoided if alternative, less expensive approaches are feasible, available, and sound. When more expensive treatment is authorized, it is monitored to determine whether it is working and the amount of time this level of intensity of intervention is required. In general, brief, time-limited treatment or crisis intervention is preferred. Managed care organizations do not support time- and money-consuming psychotherapy that aims to restructure the personality (Furman, 2003; Poynter, 1998). Reduction of symptomatology, restoration of functioning, and behavioral change are the primary goals (Poynter, 1998). Effectiveness is measured through the use of indicators determined by the managed care organization, an external group that conducts a utilization review, the provider, and/or the behavioral health delivery system. Although outcomes are usually measured on a system basis, individual practitioners can use instruments that measure the outcome of treatment, the extent to which goals are attained, and (in the case of clients with long-term problems) intermittent progress. (Suggestions for practitioner instruments are offered elsewhere in this volume.) Another means of assessing effectiveness is to ask consumers how they found services. Managed care organizations use client satisfaction surveys that they tailor to the needs of the particular program (Corcoran & Vandiver, 1996).

Prevention is an integral part of managed care. Managed health care plans in the private sector emphasize wellness and health promotion strategies such as giving up smoking and drinking, and stress management. Public managed care, which will be described next, uses prevention approaches such as family education, peer support groups, and psychosocial rehabilitation (Corcoran & Vandiver, 1996).

Clients on Medicaid in most areas of the country can receive health and mental health care under a managed care arrangement. States may arrange to use existing HMOs, contract with community mental health centers, or contract with a behavioral health care company (Mechanic, 2008). Local mental health authorities or boards, which have administrative and financial oversight of their districts, have an important role in the provision of care for these public sector clients (Hoge, Davidson, Griffith, Sledge, & Howenstine, 1994). Although public sector managed care arrangements in different parts of the country vary (Hoge, Jacobs, Thakur, & Griffith, 1999), the following six core functions are needed to provide comprehensive treatment for clients who are recipients of public support (Hoge et al., 1994):

1. *Gatekeeping.* At points of entry into the system, efforts are made to admit clients that the mental health authorities define as target populations, to limit admission to more expensive services by adhering to restrictive criteria, and to divert clients to alternative, less expensive forms of treatment.
2. *The community is the locus of activity.* Treatment is to be in the local community where clients, their support networks, and services are located.
3. *Provision of comprehensive services.* Local mental health authorities and service providers are to assess needs, allocate resources, and overcome barriers to access, so that the needs of the target population can be met.
4. *Continuity of care* is to be facilitated by coordinating services that are currently needed and those that will be needed over time.
5. *Maximizing economic efficiency* can be realized by consolidating funding streams, using these funds flexibly, and introducing incentives to providers to deliver efficient, effective services.
6. *Accountability* should be established at the delivery level by assigning a particular staff member, such as a case manager, as the point person. Local mental health authorities are accountable to the public for the effective operation of the mental health service delivery system.

Notably, several of these functions (2, 3, 4, and 6) were tenets of the community mental health movement. In addition, the three levels of prevention under community mental health continue to be relevant. It also remains important that services are *accessible* to consumers by having twenty-four-hour coverage, being nearby, posing no architectural barriers, and being responsive to diverse cultures.

The Committee on Quality Assurance and Accreditation Guidelines for Managed Behavioral Care, which developed a framework to guide the evaluation of behavioral health care arrangements, found that *arranging wraparound* or *enabling services* to address clients' social needs was also an important function. The committee recommended services such as social welfare, housing, vocational, and other rehabilitative services for persons with severe mental illness and chronic substance abuse problems (Edmunds et al., 1997). Another recommendation was that behavioral health programs should be responsive to racial and ethnic minorities and persons with co-occurring mental illness and substance abuse. The committee stated that efforts should be made to employ providers who are culturally competent and use innovative and alternative treatments, even if research on the effectiveness of these strategies has not as yet been conducted (Edmunds et al., 1997). Elsewhere in this book, services for persons with severe mental illness (Chapter 11), culturally competent practice (Chapter 6), and treatment of persons with co-occurring disorders (Chapter 13) are discussed.

IMPLICATIONS OF BEHAVIORAL HEALTH FOR CLINICAL SOCIAL WORK

Behavioral health under managed care introduces some procedures and expectations that affect social workers. In some agencies and practices, clinical social workers are extensively involved in requests for authorization and reauthorization of services. These may involve telephone calls and/or the submission of paperwork. Social workers may experience requests to justify continued work with a client as intrusive and object to an outside party's weighing of cost saving over what they consider the best interest of the client. Differences in judgment and values can raise troubling ethical issues for social workers. In addition, the introduction of administrative requirements and paperwork can complicate the client–worker relationship (Poynter, 1998). Although utilization reviews and quality assurance have been part of mental health delivery for some time, documentation requirements have increased.

At the very least, behavioral health care has made the already complicated mental health scene more complex. Interactions with clients need to be considered in the context of their behavioral health insurance, the agency, the availability and accessibility of services, and the best interest of the clients. Mental health agencies are funded by multiple sources, public and private, including sponsors of supportive services. With so many parties that expect accountability, it is a challenge for social workers to maintain a primary focus on the needs of clients.

Another consideration for clinical social workers is that the behavioral health scene has become increasingly competitive. Managed care organizations may be biased toward physicians and providers with Ph.D.s, although social workers can provide similar services at a lower rate (Jackson, 1995). The best way to overcome these biases is for social workers to be knowledgeable and competent. We turn next to some areas of research knowledge that inform competent social work practice.

SCIENTIFIC KNOWLEDGE AND EVIDENCE-BASED PRACTICE

The knowledge that informs social work practice comes from a variety of sources and disciplines. The sources that will be highlighted in this book are multidisciplinary—psychiatric epidemiology, biology, and EBP research. Research findings from these sources have an impact on priorities within the mental health field and the practitioner's selection of interventions. (From this point on, the terms *mental health*, *behavioral health*, and *behavioral mental health*, which combines the two concepts, will be used interchangeably.)

Psychiatric Epidemiology

Clinical social work practice in behavioral mental health is informed by psychiatric epidemiological research. *Epidemiology* is "the study of the distribution, incidence, prevalence, and duration of disease" (Sadock & Sadock, 2007, p. 170). A project of significance to public health, it looks at biological, social, and environmental conditions that might point to the origin, cause, and distribution of pathology, such as the transmission of body fluids and acquired immunodeficiency syndrome. Epidemiological research involves the use of sophisticated methods of sampling and statistical methods of analysis.

Epidemiological research is predicated on the paradigm of "host/agent/environment" (Kellam, 1987). The host is the person with the disease; the agent is the causal factor. When epidemiology has been applied to psychopathology, research has rarely been able to identify a specific agent that causes a mental disorder. Unlike physical diseases, psychological disorders are not infectious. Their causes are multiple and interactive. Epidemiological studies have found varying levels of association among a number of social, environmental, and demographic variables and the disorder.

Two terms that are widely used in epidemiological research are *incidence* and *prevalence*. Incidence refers to the number of new cases of a particular disorder that occur in a given period of time (e.g., in a year). Prevalence refers to the total number of cases (new cases and existing cases) in a population. *Point prevalence* refers to the prevalence at a particular point of time (e.g., today), *period prevalence* to a period of time longer than a day (e.g., six-month prevalence), and *lifetime prevalence* to any time in a person's life (Sadock & Sadock, 2007). Epidemiologists also look at variables that may be associated with the incidence and prevalence of particular disorders such as age, race, gender, and socioeconomic status.

Psychiatric epidemiology refers to "the study of the distribution of mental illness and positive mental health and related factors in human populations" (Sadock & Sadock, 2007, p. 170). Research in this area has advanced tremendously in the last 60 years. Early research looked at both aggregated data of cases in treatment and large community samples, but each of these strategies had methodological problems. The focus on cases in treatment, usually in public facilities, resulted in the exclusion of people who did not seek help (for various social and cultural reasons) and those who were treated privately. Epidemiological studies of communities have the advantage of being more inclusive, but early studies were hampered by their collection of mental status data by lay interviewers and by the difficulty of converting findings about symptoms into diagnoses. Among the classic early investigations were Hollingshead and Redlich's (1958) study of the community and persons in treatment in the area of New Haven, Connecticut, which found a relationship between social class and diagnosis and treatment; Leighton's (1959) Stirling County study of a rural county in Nova Scotia, which found around one third of the population significantly impaired; and Srole's Midtown Manhattan Study (Srole & Fischer, 1986; Srole, Langer, Michael, Kirkpatrick, & Rennie, 1962), which found that 14 percent of the population studied were considered impaired in 1954 and 12 percent in 1974.

During the last two decades of the twentieth century, psychiatric epidemiological research benefited from the development of instruments that were capable of generating diagnostic information and could be administered by nonprofessional interviewers (Weissman, Myers, & Ross, 1986). Among these are the Diagnostic Interview Schedule (DIS) (Robins; Helzer, Croughan, & Ratcliff, 1981), the Composite International Diagnostic Interview (CIDI) (World Health Organization, 1990), and, in this century, the World Mental Health Survey Initiative Version of the World Health Organization Composite International Diagnostic Interview (WMH-CIDI) (Kessler & Ustun, 2004).

The DIS was used in the National Institute of Mental Health (NIMH) Epidemiological Catchment Area (ECA) Program, a group of studies implemented in the late 1970s and early 1980s (Regier et al., 1984). These extensive studies took place in five urban areas—New Haven, Connecticut; Baltimore, Maryland; Durham, North Carolina; St. Louis, Missouri; and Los Angeles, California. Both institutionalized and noninstitutionalized residents of these communities were surveyed once and then again a year later, thus providing comprehensive and longitudinal data (Freedman, 1984). These studies gathered information on the prevalence of specific psychiatric disorders, associated demographic factors, and patterns of usage of physical and mental health services for mental health problems. This ambitious program of research has provided fruitful information about the distribution of mental disorders in the United States. The findings are limited, however, because the five surveys took place in urban areas with university-based psychiatric facilities; it is not clear to what extent the results apply to people who live in rural areas and other locations where mental health services are not so accessible (Kessler, Abelson, & Zhao, 1998).

The National Comorbidity Survey (NCS), also funded by NIMH, attempted to remedy limitations of the ECA studies (Kessler et al., 1994). The NCS sample was more representative of the United States, but the age range was limited to persons between the ages of 15 and 54. This study used the CIDI to assess diagnoses. Whereas the DIS was compatible with the *Diagnostic and Statistical Manual of Mental Disorders* (*DSM-III*) (American Psychiatric Association [APA], 1980), the CIDI converted to the *DSM-III-R* (APA, 1987). Neither the NCS nor the ECA Study included personality disorders other than the antisocial type (Kessler et al., 1998). Subsequently (2001–2003), the National Comorbidity Survey Replication (NCS-R) expanded the age parameters of the CIDI by including individuals who were 55 years of age and older. The findings of the NCS-R were converted to *DSM-IV* diagnoses (Kessler, Berglund, et al., 2005; Kessler, Chiu, Demler, & Walters, 2005). The replication excluded schizophrenia and autism (Kessler, Berglund, et al., 2005; Kessler, Chiu, et al., 2005).

Regardless of the limitations of the ECA and the two NCSs, these epidemiological studies have contributed substantially to knowledge about the distribution of the disorders that are included, as well as knowledge about the use of treatment facilities. For example, the NCS produced two startling findings. First, the twelve-month and lifetime prevalences of any CIDI disorder among persons ages 15 to 54 are 30.9 and 49.7 percent, respectively. Second, comorbidity (the co-occurrence of two or more disorders) was the rule rather than the exception for twelve-month and lifetime prevalences (Kessler et al., 1994). The NCS-R arrived at similar findings, clarifying that comorbidity was associated with greater severity (Kessler, Berglund, et al., 2005; Kessler, Chiu, et al., 2005). Other results of these studies will be referred to elsewhere in this book.

Biological Research

Another avenue that informs mental health practice is biological research. With increasing evidence that many mental disorders are diseases of the brain, attention has been focused on understanding how the brain works, the causes of brain dysfunction, and the use of pharmacological means to overcome biochemical deficiencies. This has resulted in a vast body of research on neuroanatomy, genetics (including molecular biology), brain imaging, and psychopharmacology. For example, the Human Genome Project has succeeded in sequencing the human genome, which has the potential of contributing to understanding and treatment of mental disorders.

During the twentieth century, there was considerable dissension within the mental health field about the role of biology in the etiology of mental disorders. Freud's seminal work on the role of early life experiences in generating mental conflict directed attention to developmental, family environmental, and personality factors that contribute to mental illness (particularly neuroses). One consequence of Freud's work and that of others who focused on early life experiences was that families were blamed for causing mental illness in their progeny. It was not until after the breakthroughs in psychopharmacology that began to occur in the middle of the twentieth century and spurred the process of deinstitutionalization that the biological viewpoint became prominent. During and following the 1990s, a new generation of medications has shown promise to enhance the functioning and quality of life of persons with mental illnesses.

With its focus on person–environment interactions, the field of social work has been reluctant to incorporate biological knowledge into its own knowledge base, even though the biopsychosocial perspective is recognized as central to understanding practice (Johnson et al., 1990; Saleebey, 1992). But increasingly, social workers in the field of mental health have been writing about the importance of biological knowledge (Johnson, 1996) and, in particular, the need for practitioners to understand the structure of the brain and psychopharmacology (Bentley & Walsh, 2006). Chapter 3 of this volume provides an introduction to some important information drawn from biology and related scientific disciplines (neurophysiology, psychopharmacology, genetics). Later chapters on intervention show how this knowledge applies to understanding and intervening with clients with different kinds of mental health problems.

In this book, biological and psychosocial dimensions are viewed as integrally related. Although professions may carve knowledge into spheres that each claims as its own, individuals are complex biopsychosocial (and spiritual) wholes whose lives are constituted and created through varied relationships and experiences. The integrative biopsychosocial conceptualization that is used in this book is described in Chapter 3.

Evidence-Based Practice

In the 1990s, the social work profession was concerned with promoting a more scientifically based practice and appeared to have shifted from the practitioner-as-scientist using single-subject design (SSD) methods to the utilization of empirically tested interventions. A decline in interest in SSD has been attributed to feasibility problems in agency application and criticisms of its usefulness. The application of intervention research findings to actual social work practice had begun to emerge as the catalyst for advancing the movement of science in social work. As the foregoing has suggested, a critical mass of experimentally tested interventions began to take shape in social work and related fields during the past two decades—sufficient to provide a basis for forms of clinical practice that have been variously called "scientifically based," "empirically supported," or "evidence-based." The current trend is to refer to such practice as EBP—that is, practice based on tested interventions.

In the social work field, two major conceptions of EBP have emerged. The first of these was developed by Gambrill (2003) and Gibbs (2003), who derived their view from Sackett and his colleagues (Sackett, Rosenberg, Gray, Haynes, & Richardson, 1996; Sackett, Straus, Richardson, Rosenberg, & Haynes, 2000) and Gray (2001), who have been among the prime movers of the EBP movement in medicine. Accordingly, EBP consists of five steps: (a) needs for knowledge are translated into answerable questions; (b) track down scientifically based evidence that can answer the questions, primarily through a search of computerized databases; (c) the evidence is critically appraised; (d) review results with client and then apply to the clinical decision at hand; and (e) the outcome of the application is recorded and evaluated. The emphasis rests on the client's concerns and expectations, the sharing of evidence with the client, and the collaborative decision making about the course of action suggested by the evidence (Gambrill, 2003; Gibbs & Gambrill, 2002).

The other major conception of EBP generally refers to practice that uses knowledge and interventions with research validation but leaves open the question regarding how to implement this practice. For example, Rubin (2008) suggests that EBP is a "process for making practice decisions in which practitioners integrate the best research evidence available with their practice expertise and with client attributes, values, preferences, and circumstances" (p. 7). Drake et al. (2001) and

Torrey et al. (2001) discuss implementation of EBP on the assumption that such practice consists of service practitioners using research-supported treatment guidelines. Both of these notions of EBP are equivalent to empirically supported practice; in fact, the terms are often used interchangeably. This second conception of EBP has become dominant in the mental health services literature. Current EBP paradigms stress the role of the practitioner as a user of scientific findings as is seen in the book by Corrigan, Mueser, Bond, Drake, and Solomon (2008) on the practice of psychiatric rehabilitation. In these paradigms, interventions are tested through randomized controlled trials (RCTs). Those interventions that prove to be efficacious are then "transported" to service programs for implementation by line practitioners. The evidence in this form of EBP is generated by group experiments. Little attention is given to the evidence that practitioners might obtain in the application of these presumably efficacious interventions. Largely set aside is the conception of the scientifically oriented practitioner using single-subject methods to test and guide implementation of these interventions. An alternative definition of EBP would result from broadening the notion of evidence to include not only evidence obtained from research studies but also evidence garnered by practitioners in their work with clients, that is, practice-based evidence. A key idea in this conception would be an integration of the two kinds of evidence in ways that would provide a stronger scientific base for practice than would be the case if only one kind were used.

Evidence-based practice in mental health has been influenced by many approaches adapted from current service models, some of which were developed by demonstration grants or other government or private funding streams. During the past three decades, major advances have been made in the development of clinical practices and service interventions for the seriously mentally ill (SMI). Robust research evidence demonstrates that there is abundant empirical evidence to suggest the availability of interventions with positive outcomes that can be termed EBPs. The most compelling of these practices is delineated in a report by the Schizophrenia Patient Outcomes Research Team (PORT) with thirty-five recommendations for psychosocial and pharmacological interventions for individuals with schizophrenia (Lehman, Steinwachs, and PORT Co-Investigators, 1998) with subsequent updates (Kreyenbuhl, Buchanan, Dickerson, & Dixon, 2010; Lehman et al., 2004). In 1998, the Robert Woods Johnson Foundation held a national consensus meeting of experts, researchers, administrators, consumers, family caregivers, and providers who described six EBPs for individuals with SMI (Drake et al., 2001). These practices include (a) assertive community treatment, (b) illness management and recovery, (c) family education, (d) supported employment, (e) medication management, and (f) integrated dual disorders interventions.

This book describes several such evidence-based interventions, as well as others that are exemplars of best practices and those that are promising. The criteria for inclusion come from quantitative and qualitative reports of results, meta-analyses, meta-syntheses, frequent references to them in the literature, and their congruence with social work values. Examples are introduced in the intervention chapters (8 to 13). Before becoming conversant with research findings of epidemiological, biological, and practice-effectiveness research, it is necessary to become grounded in the basics. The next section will describe some of the definitional issues that are fundamental to understanding mental health.

DEFINITIONAL ISSUES

Many of the terms used in the field of mental health are not transparent. Fundamental concepts such as *normality*, *mental health*, and *mental illness* have been contested (e.g., Szasz, 1961). The centrality of diagnosis of mental illness and the *DSM* obscures personal *strengths* and the potential for *recovery*.

Normality, Mental Health, and Mental Illness

The terms *normality*, *mental health*, and *mental illness* are value-laden Western constructs. Normality and mental health suggest positive psychological functioning, whereas mental illness suggests dysfunctioning. Mental health and mental illness indicate a medical model, whereas normality implies a statistical one. Mental health is frequently used as a euphemism for mental illness—as illustrated by mental health centers that treat mental illness. The relatively new term, *behavioral health*, adds to the confusion.

NORMALITY   The terms *normality* and *mental health* have similar meanings but different connotations. On the surface, normality suggests a statistical criterion (Frances, Widiger, & Sabshin, 1991)—the average or mean; the most common behavior, the mode; or one or two standard deviations from the mean. Studies employing statistical measures, however, have produced surprising results. Psychiatric epidemiological studies of normal community samples have found that a substantial proportion of the population had symptoms of psychological problems, with a minority rated as "well" (Kessler et al., 1994; Kessler, Chiu, et al., 2005; Leighton, Harding, Macklin, Macmillan, & Leighton, 1963; Srole et al., 1962). Accordingly, mental illness seems to be "normal."

The term *normality* also suggests adaptation to the social context (Frances et al., 1991). Normal persons accommodate to the demands of society, meet legal and social obligations, and generally fit in with the contours of society. Although such persons are not troublesome, they are not necessarily creative or self-actualized. Persons who merely adapt to situational demands generally do not have the "peak experiences" of insight, self-awareness, or integration described by Maslow (1968). Furthermore, they do not necessarily have integrity, independence, or courage. Indeed, they may acquiesce to injustices, exploitation, and persecution.

In his paper, "The Myth of Normality," Jackson (1977) asserted, "There is no standard of psychological 'normality' or 'good health' " (p. 157). The dichotomy between the normal and abnormal is false and based on the assumption that psychopathology is fixed and tangible. Recognizing human variability, he said, "How a person acts varies with the culture, the subculture, the ethnic group, and the family group in which he lives" (p. 162). Accordingly, normality is context-related. Assessment requires knowledge of the cultural and other contexts.

MENTAL HEALTH   On the simplest level, mental health is characterized by the *absence of mental illness* (Jahoda, 1958). Thus, mentally healthy individuals do not have psychiatric disorders, such as those described in the *DSM-IV-TR* (APA, 2000). Gross psychopathology (e.g., delusions, hallucinations) is not present or observed. Such persons do not communicate feelings of distress or present evidence of mental illness. Ordinarily, they are not receiving mental health treatment.

The problem with this definition is that there is a sociocultural process that intervenes between the presence of symptoms and diagnosis. Many individuals have signs of psychiatric disorders that neither they nor others consider indicators of mental disorder. Individuals comprising the person's intimate network may view the person's behavior as a personal idiosyncrasy, a sign of divine powers, or an expression of a developmental stage. The group's ideas about what is normal may contrast with what mental health professionals consider mental illness. In order for diagnosis to take place, someone or some system will have to establish that what was previously considered normal is abnormal (Scheff, 1984).

Mental health also represents an *optimal* or *ideal state*. Jahoda's (1958) concept of "positive mental health" includes attitudes toward oneself; growth, development, or self-actualization;

personality integration; autonomy; environmental mastery; and perception of reality. This definition emphasizes high levels of functioning, which go beyond well-being or the absence of disease. A contemporary development of this perspective is positive psychology, a "science of positive subjective experience, positive individual traits, and positive institutions" (Seligman & Csikszentmihalyi, 2000), which provides an alternative to the psychopathological perspective. Akin to social work's "strengths perspective" (Saleebey, 2006), positive individual traits include the capacity to love, interpersonal skills, perseverance, courage, spirituality, and wisdom (Seligman & Csikszentmihalyi, 2000).

Mental health can also be viewed as an *aspect of health*. The constitution of the World Health Organization (WHO, 1948) defines health as "the state of complete physical, mental and social well-being and not merely the absence of disease or infirmity." This definition includes mental health as an aspect of health and suggests positive mental health. Table 1.1 presents an elaboration of the WHO's (2007) conceptualization of mental health, based on a statement on

---

TABLE 1.1   Conceptualizing Mental Health

Mental health is more than the absence of mental disorders

- Mental health can be conceptualized as a state of well-being in which the individual realizes his or her own abilities, can cope with the normal stresses of life, can work productively and fruitfully, and is able to make a contribution to his or her community.
- In this positive sense, mental health is the foundation for well-being and effective functioning for an individual and for a community. This core concept of mental health is consistent with its wide and varied interpretation across cultures. . . .

Mental health is determined by socio-economic and environmental factors

- Mental health and mental health disorders are determined by multiple and interacting social, psychological, and biological factors, just as health and illness in general.
- The clearest evidence is associated with indicators of poverty, including low levels of education, and in some studies with poor housing and poor income. Increasing and persisting socio-economic disadvantages for individuals and for communities are recognized risks to mental health.
- The greater vulnerability of disadvantaged people in each community to mental health disorders may be explained by such factors as the experience of insecurity and hopelessness, rapid social change, and the risks of violence and physical ill-health.
- A climate that respects and protects basic civil, political, socio-economic and cultural rights is also fundamental to mental health promotion. Without the security and freedom provided by these rights, it is very difficult to maintain a high level of mental health.

Mental health is linked to behaviour

- Mental, social, and behavioural health problems may interact to intensify their effects on behaviour and well-being.
- Substance abuse, violence, and abuse of women and children on the one hand, and health problems such as HIV/AIDS, depression, and anxiety on the other, are more prevalent and more difficult to cope with in conditions of high unemployment, low income, limited education, stressful work conditions, gender discrimination, social exclusion, unhealthy lifestyle, and human rights violations.

Source: World Health Organization, *Mental health: strengthening mental health promotion*, Fact sheet N° 220, September 2007. Retrieved and excerpted from http://www.who.int/mediacentre/factsheets/fs220/en/print.html. Reproduced with permission from the World Health Organization.

mental health promotion. It recognizes that multiple interacting factors—biological, psychological, social, economic, political, and behavioral—determine mental health and mental health disorders.

In this volume, mental health will be considered a state of psychosocial functioning that ranges from optimal to functional to dysfunctional. Optimal captures qualities of positive mental health as defined by the individual's own culture. Functional refers to the ability to take care of oneself, assume social roles, and participate in community life purposefully and constructively. Dysfunctional describes impairment in the capacity to take care of oneself and participate in the community and includes patterns that are destructive of one's self and others.

Mental health is a phenomenon of the individual, family, group, community, culture, and nation. What affects one of these systems affects others. On the individual level, mental health encompasses the expression of emotions, cognitions, and behavior; coping with life challenges; and the social, occupational, and management skills needed for survival. Biological, psychological, and social dimensions are connected.

MENTAL ILLNESS   During the early 1960s, Thomas Szasz (1960, 1961) launched an attack on the usage of the concept of mental illness. To Szasz, the term *mental illness* applied appropriately to brain (organic) or neurological diseases but not to discrepant beliefs, values, behaviors, social relationships, and the like, which were commonly viewed as symptoms of mental disease. Many persons adjudged mentally ill hold unusual beliefs (e.g., "I am Napoleon") or violate legal norms (the criminally insane), but they do not have objective bodily illnesses. Although these individuals may be troubled, Szasz said, they are experiencing "problems in living," not mental illness. Because the term *mental illness* is applied where there is no evidence of medical pathology, Szasz said, mental illness is a "myth." Szasz was not alone in his criticism of concepts of mental illness and related social practices. Scheff (1984) described a social process in which deviant behavior gets defined as mental illness.

Behaviorists objected to the medical vocabulary, labeling, and assumption that there was an inner cause of psychological problems. They preferred to look at environmental contingencies that support the presentation of maladaptive behavior. Existential phenomenologists were critical of the use of the scientific method in the study of mental illness. According to their thinking (see, e.g., Esterson, 1970), it was not possible to be objective in assessing mental illness because such determinations are made in the course of interacting with a client. In addition, many social factors (family, environment) surrounding the client contribute to what is socially defined as mental illness.

Some of the criticism was in response to inappropriate labeling of mental illness. During the 1960s, for example, some young political activists who went south to register African American voters were incarcerated in mental hospitals for alleged paranoia (Coles, 1970). Labeling behaviors or practices that deviate from those valued by mainstream society (e.g., homosexuality, substance abuse, illegal acts) as symptoms of mental illness is a means of invalidating persons who are different.

The authors of the last four editions of the *DSM* (APA, 1980, 1987, 1994, 2000) have attempted to address some of the definitional problems that have been described, as well as questions that had been raised about the scientific merits of previous editions. First, they assigned specific criteria to each psychiatric diagnosis. This should deter labeling and other inappropriate uses of psychiatric diagnoses. Second, they ran extensive field tests in an attempt to arrive at reliable diagnoses and compare alternative criteria (APA, 1980, 1994). Third, they acknowledged that the boundaries between physical and mental disorders, among different mental disorders, and between a particular mental disorder and no mental disorder are nebulous (APA, 1994). Finally, they came up with their own definition of *mental disorder*, the term which they use for *mental illness*. The definition in the *DSM-IV-TR* (APA, 2000), which repeats that used in the *DSM-III*, *DSM-III-R*, and *DSM-IV*, is as follows:

> In *DSM-IV* each of the mental disorders is conceptualized as a clinically significant behavioral or psychological syndrome or pattern that occurs in an individual and that is associated with present distress (e.g., a painful symptom) or disability (i.e., impairment in one or more areas of functioning) or with a significantly increased risk of suffering death, pain, disability, or an important loss of freedom. In addition, this syndrome or pattern must not be merely an expectable response to a particular event, for example, the death of a loved one. Whatever its original cause, it must currently be considered a manifestation of a behavioral, psychological, or biological dysfunction in the individual. Neither deviant behavior (e.g., political, religious, or sexual) nor conflicts that are primarily between the individual and society are mental disorders unless the deviance or conflict is a symptom of a dysfunction in the person, as described above. (p. xxxi)

This definition clearly places the disorder *inside the person*. It excludes individual reactions to painful life events (e.g., bereavement) unless these events are accompanied by an inordinate degree of distress. Furthermore, it discounts unhappiness, which often prompts people to seek psychotherapy. Although the definition draws a distinction between mental disorders and moral deviance, the *DSM-IV-TR* does not require that mental illnesses represent organic disorders. Behavioral, affective, and cognitive evidence of distress and impairment in psychosocial functioning are usually assessed through a diagnostic interview, not biological tests. Clinicians make judgments about whether certain behaviors, emotions, and beliefs are to be viewed as symptoms of mental disorders. Inevitably, these judgments are made by referring to a vague normative model. As Wakefield (1992) asserts, the concept of mental illness lies "on the boundary between biological facts and social values" (p. 373).

Another word used to describe mental illness is *psychopathology*—a medical term that refers to the scientific study of diseases of the mind, including their etiology (origin or cause), their nature, and the course the diseases take. This term is used in the literature interchangeably with mental disorder, mental disease, mental illness, and abnormality. This book considers knowledge of psychopathology, mental illness, and mental disorders to be linked with the values of Western culture and its naming practices. Because practitioners need to work within the constructions of the culture in which they live, the terms *psychopathology*, *mental illness*, and *mental disorder* and the definition in the *DSM-IV-TR* will be accepted as cultural givens. With this in mind, the following criteria are indicators of mental disorders:

1. *Subjective distress.* The individual must report emotional pain, somatic distress, discomfort, lack of control, or volitions that contradict personal values.
2. *Impaired psychosocial functioning.* The individual is unable to take care of personal needs (bathing, dressing, grooming, eating) or cannot fulfill ordinary social functions (working, going to school, household management, caring for dependents, reciprocating in interpersonal relationships), or is destructive or self-destructive. Other expressions of impaired psychosocial functioning include indirect strategies of problem solving (e.g., time-consuming rituals, approach-avoidance patterns, and passive-aggressive behavior).

3. *Markedly deviant behavior.*   The individual initiates actions that have no instrumental purpose and that substantially deviate from behavior that is functional within the individual's subculture (e.g., smearing the walls with feces in mainstream U.S. society).
4. *Sensory dysfunctioning.*   The individual's sensory mechanisms are deficient; that is, the senses of vision, hearing, taste, touch, or smell do not correspond with stimuli emanating from the shared social environment.
5. *Disturbed thinking.*   The individual has cognitions that are false, unrealistic, intrusive, or incongruent with those that are shared by the individual's subculture.

Individuals with severe mental illness are likely to meet all of these criteria. Others will meet only a few. Clients who present concerns, symptoms, or behaviors that involve none of these, or only the first criterion, probably have problems in living or display socially deviant behavior.

The polemics over what normality, mental health, and mental illness are, which have been described, underscore how difficult it is to define and classify human experiences. Preferences for particular terms over others seem to be rooted in differences in theoretical orientation, which in turn are linked to ideology and power. The following discussion on definitions of recovery and strengths represents a discourse that is an alternative to the dominant Western medical discourse.

Recovery and Strengths

Recovery is a concept of mental health in which consumers strive to improve their lives in keeping with their own values, interests, and goals (Gagne, White, & Anthony, 2007). A positive, consumer-driven concept, it is a guiding principle for transforming the mental health system, described in the document, *Transforming Mental Health Care in America: The Federal Action Agenda: First Steps* (SAMHSA, 2005).

The concept of recovery came out of the experiences of consumers who saw themselves as having survived, healed, or coped successfully with symptoms of mental illness (U.S. Department of Health and Human Services, 1999). It is supported by empirical research indicating a positive trajectory (Gagne et al., 2007). Definitions of recovery are abundant, with some depicting it as a process and others seeing it as an outcome or vision (Onken, Craig, Ridgway, Ralph, & Cook, 2007). Used largely in relation to severe mental illness, it also applies to addiction, as in both cases the goal is to assist people who are affected "by reducing the impairment and disability, and improve quality of life" (Gagne et al., 2007, p. 34). To clarify the meaning of recovery, a national consensus conference held in 2004 came up with this statement:

> Mental health recovery is a journey of healing and transformation enabling a person with a mental health problem to live a meaningful life in a community of his or her choice while striving to achieve his or her full potential. (U.S. Department of Health and Human Services, 2004)

The concept of recovery offers hope to consumers, who, in a previous era, were written off as incurable. Today, they can anticipate better mental health care, improved psychosocial functioning, and the opportunity to take charge of their own lives. (Recovery will be explained in more detail in Chapter 10 and will be integrated into Chapters 11 through 13.)

One of the components of recovery is that it is *strengths-based*. The strengths perspective offers a standpoint that is affirmative rather than psychopathological. As explained by Saleebey (2005), it describes possibilities, promises, and hopes that can be obscured by a label of mental illness. Saleebey envisions a "Diagnostic Strengths Manual" in which personal qualities such as trustworthiness and patience are described. Although a book on mental health unavoidably addresses vulnerabilities, this volume will recognize and, where relevant, highlight strengths of individuals.

As indicated, the mental health field is characterized by the discourses of Western medicine, which emphasize psychopathology, and discourses of strength and recovery, which highlight the humanness of consumers. Multiple discourses are characteristic of postmodernism, which will be used as a critical framework for this book.

POSTMODERNISM AS A CRITICAL FRAMEWORK

Postmodernism is an intellectual movement that has swept across academic disciplines and fields of professional practice over the last few decades. It is associated with the rapid changes that have emerged—particularly mass communication, information systems, globalization, and technology—which paradoxically have brought people closer together and farther apart. Postmodernism challenges basic assumptions about the nature of knowledge and thought that have characterized modern Western societies since the Enlightenment. The concerns that are associated with this movement undermine the belief that categories are fixed, reality is real, and knowledge is certain. Postmodernism questions the modernist project of arriving at universal, explanatory systems of thought (including scientific ones). Because the field of mental health is predicated on the ideas that categories of illness are determinate, misperception of reality is symptomatic of mental illness, and mental disorders can be understood scientifically, postmodernism raises serious questions about the validity of the entire realm of mental health.

Post*modern* thought is a development of post*structuralist* thought, the latter of which is associated with European figures such as Derrida (1978) and Foucault (1965). Poststructuralists are critical of structuralists such as Freud and Marx, who had developed grand theories describing universal, lawful, underlying structures. Some of the philosophers associated with postmodernism are Baudrillard (1988), Lyotard (1984), and Rorty (1979). The boundaries between poststructuralism and postmodernism are hazy.

Poststructuralist/postmodern thought begins with a critique of language. At question is the relationship between the sign (a written or spoken symbol, such as a word) and the signified (what the sign means). Challenging the idea that language *reflects* a pregiven true reality, poststructuralism asserts that language *constitutes* a reality that is historically and socially contingent and, thus, fluid (Weedon, 1987). Another way of describing the reality constituted in language is that it is "socially constructed" (Berger & Luckmann, 1966). As a consequence of the mutability of what is immediately perceived as real, meanings become *multiple*, unstable, and subject to diverse interpretations.

Poststructuralists are critical of *logocentrism*, the idea that there is a logical, rational, unified order that is neutral and objective (Grosz, 1989). The logocentrism, which characterizes Western, post-Enlightenment thought, is problematic because it ignores the complexity that is embedded in language (Derrida, 1976). First, logocentrism assumes that categories that constitute knowledge are essential; that is, they are inherent. Derrida (1978) asserts that the meanings of these categories change in relation to context. Logocentrism is also problematic in its characteristic dependence on *binary categories*, terms that are defined in relation to their polar opposites. Derrida notes whenever there are binaries, there is an implicit hierarchy, with one term valued over the other (e.g., male over female, white over black). Viewing categories as binary opposites is misleading because the two terms are not entirely different or opposite. To capture the idea that the meanings of the binary terms may overlap and there may be meanings associated with one term that are not captured by the other, Derrida used the term *différence* (Grosz, 1989). Accordingly, one can have a situation of *both/and* where both meanings of terms that are commonly viewed as opposites are applicable.

Although binary terms have multiple meanings, diverse interpretations are not immediately accessible. Language is a site in which political interests struggle for dominance (Weedon, 1987). Foucault's (1975, 1980) writings highlight the ways in which those who have power are able to establish their meanings as *the* meanings and impose these on others. Postmodernists use the terms *master narratives* and *dominant discourses* to describe ideas that overshadow other coexisting narratives in the public domain. Mental illness, patriarchy, and progress are examples of master narratives.

Even though knowledge of master narratives allows one to understand the values of dominant sectors of society, it obscures the narratives of disenfranchised or "subjugated" populations, such as persons with severe mental illness or those who are poor, members of ethnic minority groups, or women. Postmodernists and poststructuralists have developed a method called *deconstruction* to uncover meanings that are not immediately apparent because they are those of persons who lack the power to directly voice their concerns. This is done by situating the text (a body of written or spoken language) in the political, social, and historical contexts in which it occurs; identifying biases and moving them to the periphery of the text; and treating marginal perspectives as if they are central. In this way, subjugated voices (i.e., those of vulnerable groups) can be heard. "The term 'deconstruction' has also come to mean more generally any exposure of a concept as ideological or culturally constructed rather than natural or a simple reflection of reality" (Alcoff, 1997, p. 353 n. 24). Here our concern is with ideology, subjugated voices, and concealed power relations.

As is evident in deconstruction, postmodernism is attentive to the contexts in which knowledge is constructed and communicated. Clinicians need to be knowledgeable about local contexts—the norms of their particular agency and the managed care entities with which they interact, the functions of different professions working there, and the situations of each client with whom they work. In addition, they need to understand other contexts such as mental health policies and concepts that are used in the behavioral health field. One of the goals of this book is to communicate specialized knowledge that will help social workers interpret what is happening in their agencies and with clients who come for help.

There are many implications of postmodernism for the mental health field, some of which will be mentioned here. Clearly, the categories of mental disorders that are described so carefully in the *DSM-IV-TR* (APA, 2000) and its predecessors are problematic. There is no "essential" schizophrenia or any other label used to designate that a person's mind is out of order. Schizophrenia, like other categories, is heterogeneous and diverse. Every person with schizophrenia is unique. Diagnoses are prototypes, not essences, and the diversity among them needs to be acknowledged. And, of course, these are categories of disorders, not people.

Furthermore, the meanings of the binary terms within the field of mental health need to be unpacked. For example, the terms *mental health* and *mental illness*, often construed as opposites, may overlap. One may have been diagnosed with a particular mental disorder, yet function exceedingly well in a number of areas of life (e.g., work, friendships, self-sufficiency skills). Accordingly, one may have both strengths and vulnerabilities.

In the field of mental health, voices of modernism—as expressed through EBP, diagnosis, and psychopharmacology—coexist with voices of postmodernism—as expressed by consumers in the process of recovery and professionals who direct their attention to clients' strengths. To offset the possibility that the voices of modernism dominate this text at the expense of the voices of clients, a postmodern critique will conclude the chapters that follow this one. These sections will summarize the chapter, identify the various voices, and deconstruct the text.

References

Alcoff, L. (1997). Cultural feminism versus post-structuralism: The identity crisis in feminist theory. In L. Nicholson (Ed.), *The second wave: A reader in feminist theory* (pp. 330–355). New York: Routledge.

American Psychiatric Association. (1980). *Diagnostic and statistical manual of mental disorders* (3rd ed.). Washington, DC: Author.

American Psychiatric Association. (1987). *Diagnostic and statistical manual of mental disorders* (3rd ed., rev.). Washington, DC: Author.

American Psychiatric Association. (1994). *Diagnostic and statistical manual of mental disorders* (4th ed.). Washington, DC: Author.

American Psychiatric Association. (2000). *Diagnostic and statistical manual of mental disorders* (4th ed., text rev.). Washington, DC: Author.

Bachrach, L. L. (1976). *Deinstitutionalization: An analytical review and sociological perspective* (DHEW Publication No. ADM 76-351). Washington, DC: U.S. Government Printing Office.

Bachrach, L. L. (1986). The challenge of service planning for chronic mental patients. *Community Mental Health Journal, 22,* 170–174.

Bachrach, L. (1996). The state of the state mental hospital in 1996. *Psychiatric Services, 47*(10), 1071–1078.

Baudrillard, J. (1988). *Jean Baudrillard: Selected writings* (M. Poster, Ed.). Stanford, CA: Stanford University Press.

Bentley, K. J. (Ed.). (2002). *Social work practice in mental health: Contemporary roles, tasks, and techniques.* Pacific Grove, CA: Brooks/Cole.

Bentley, K. J., & Walsh, J. (2006). *The social worker and psychotropic medication: Toward effective collaboration with mental health clients, families, and providers* (3rd ed.). Belmont, CA: Thomson Brooks/Cole.

Berger, P. L., & Luckmann, T. (1966). *The social construction of reality: A treatise in the sociology of knowledge.* New York: Doubleday/Anchor.

Bloom, B. L. (1984). *Community mental health: A general introduction* (2nd ed.). Monterey, CA: Brooks/Cole.

Bureau of Labor Statistics, U.S. Department of Labor. (2010–2011). *Occupational outlook handbook, 2010–2011 edition. Social Workers.* Retrieved August 18, 2010, from http://www.bls.gov/oco/pdf/ocos060.pdf

Caplan, G. (1961). *An approach to community mental health.* New York: Grune & Stratton.

Caplan, G. (1964). *Principles of preventive psychiatry.* New York: Basic Books.

Coles, R. (1970, November). A fashionable kind of slander. *The Atlantic,* 53–55.

Corcoran, K., & Vandiver, V. (1996). *Maneuvering the maze of managed care: Skills for mental health practitioners.* New York: The Free Press.

Corrigan, P. W., Mueser, K., Bond, G. R., Drake, R. E., & Solomon, P. (2008). *Principles and practice of psychiatric rehabilitation.* New York: Guilford.

Council on Social Work Education. (2007). *Statistics on social work education in the United States: 2004.* Alexandria, VA: Author.

DeNavas-Walt, C., Proctor, B. D., & Smith, J. C. (2008). *Income, poverty, and health insurance coverage in the United States: 2007.* U.S. Census Bureau, Current Population Reports, P60-235. Washington, DC: U.S. Government Printing Office.

Derrida, J. (1976). *On grammatology* (G. C. Spivak, Trans.). Baltimore: Johns Hopkins University Press.

Derrida, J. (1978). *Writing and difference* (A. Bass, Trans.). Chicago: University of Chicago Press.

Drake, R. E., Goldman, H. H., Leff, H. S., Lehman, A. F., Dixon, L., Mueser, K. T., et al. (2001). Implementing evidence-based practices in routine mental health service settings. *Psychiatric Services, 52*(2), 179–182.

Duffy, F. F., Wilk, J., West, J. C., Narrow, W. E., Rae, D. S., Hall, R., et al. (2006). Mental health practitioners and trainees. In R. W. Manderscheid & J. T. Berry (Eds.), *Mental health, United States, 2004* (pp. 256–309). DHHS Publication No. SMA 06-4195). Rockville, MD: Substance Abuse and Mental Health Services Administration.

Edmunds, M., Frank, R., Hogan, M., McCarty, D., Robinson-Beale, R., & Weisner, C. (Eds.). (1997). *Managing managed care: Quality improvement in behavioral health* [Summary]. Washington, DC: National Academy Press.

Esterson, A. (1970). *The leaves of spring*. Middlesex, UK: Penguin Books.

Frances, A. J., Widiger, T. A., & Sabshin, M. (1991). Psychiatric diagnosis and normality. In D. Offer & M. Sabshin (Eds.), *The diversity of normal behavior* (pp. 3–38). New York: Basic Books.

Foucault, M. (1965). *Madness and civilization*. New York: Vintage Books.

Foucault, M. (1975). *Discipline and punish: The birth of the prison*. New York: Vintage Books.

Foucault, M. (1980). *Power/knowledge: Selected interviews and other writings 1972–1977* (C. Gordon, Ed.; C. Gordon, L. Marshall, J. Mepham, & K. Soper, Trans.). New York: Pantheon Books.

Freedman, D. X. (1984). Psychiatric epidemiology counts. *Archives of General Psychiatry, 41,* 931–933.

Furman, R. (2003). Frameworks for understanding value discrepancies and ethical dilemmas in managed mental health for social work in the United States. *International Social Work, 43,* 37–52.

Gagne, C., White, W., & Anthony, W. A. (2007). Recovery: A common vision for the fields of mental health and addictions. *Psychiatric Rehabilitation Journal, 31*(1), 32–37.

Gambrill, E. (2003). Evidence-based practice: Implications for knowledge development and use in social work empirical foundations for practice guidelines in current social work knowledge. In A. Rosen and E. Proctor (Eds.), *Developing practice guidelines for social work intervention: Issues, methods, and research agenda* (pp. 37–58). New York: Columbia University Press.

Gibbs, L. E. (2003). *Evidence-based practice for the helping professions*. Pacific Grove, CA: Brooks/Cole.

Gibbs, L., & Gambrill, E. (2002). Evidence-based practice: Counterarguments to objections. *Research on Social Work Practice, 12*(1), 452–476.

Gibelman, M. (2004). *What social workers do* (2nd ed.). Washington, DC: National Association of Social Workers.

Gibelman, M., & Schervish, P. H. (1997). *Who we are: A second look*. Washington, DC: National Association of Social Workers.

Gray, J. A. M. (2001). *Evidence-based health care: How to make health policy and management decisions* (2nd ed.). New York: Churchill Livingston.

Grosz, R. (1989). *Sexual subversions*. Sydney, Australia: Allen & Unwin.

Health Insurance Association of America. (1996). *Sourcebook of health insurance data, 1995*. Washington, DC: Author.

Hoge, M. A., Davidson, L., Griffith, E. E. H., Sledge, W. H., & Howenstine, R. A. (1994). Defining managed care in public-sector psychiatry. *Hospital and Community Psychiatry, 45*(11), 1085–1089.

Hoge, M. A., Jacobs, S., Thakur, N. M., & Griffith, E. E. H. (1999). Ten dimensions of public-sector managed care. *Psychiatric Services, 50*(1), 51–55.

Hollingshead, A. B., & Redlich, F. L. (1958). *Social class and mental illness*. New York: Wiley.

Institute of Medicine. (2001). *Crossing the quality chasm: A new health system for the 21st century*. New York: Institute of Medicine, National Academy of Sciences.

Jackson, D. (1977). The myth of normality. In P. Watzlawick & J. H. Weakland (Eds.), *The interactional view* (pp. 157–163). New York: Norton.

Jackson, V. H. (Ed.). (1995). *Managed care resource guide for social workers in agency settings*. Washington, DC: National Association of Social Workers.

Jahoda, M. (1958). *Current concepts of positive mental health*. New York: Basic Books.

Johnson, H. C. (1996). Violence and biology. *Families in Society, 77*(1), 3–18.

Johnson, H. C., Atkins, S. P., Battle, S. F., Hernandez-Arata, L., Hesselbrock, M., Libassi, M. F., et al. (1990). Strengthening the "bio" in the biopsychosocial paradigm. *Journal of Social Work Education, 26*(2), 109–123.

Kellam, S. G. (1987). Families and mental illness: Current interpersonal and biological approaches (Part 1). *Psychiatry, 50,* 303–307.

Kessler, R. C., Abelson, J. M., & Zhao, S. (1998). The epidemiology of mental disorders. In J. B. W. Williams & K. Ell (Eds.), *Advances in mental health research: Implications for practice* (pp. 3–24). Washington, DC: NASW Press.

Kessler, R. C., Berglund, P., Demler, O., Jin, R., Merlkangas, K. R., & Walters, E. E. (2005). Lifetime prevalence and age-of-onset distributions of DSM-IV disorders in the National Comorbidity Survey Replication. *Archives of General Psychiatry, 62,* 593–603.

Kessler, R. C., Chiu, W. T., Demler, O., & Walters, E. E. (2005). Prevalence, severity, and comorbidity of 12-month DSM-IV disorders in the National Comorbidity Survey Replication. *Archives of General Psychiatry, 62,* 617–627.

Kessler, R. C., McGonagle, K. A., Zhao, S., Nelson, C. B., Hughes, M., Eshleman, S., et al. (1994). Lifetime and 12-month prevalence of DSM-III-R psychiatric disorders in the United States: Results from the National Comorbidity Survey. *Archives of General Psychiatry, 51,* 8–19.

Kessler, R. C., & Ustun, T. B. (2004). The World Mental Health (WMH) survey initiative version of the World

Health Organization (WHO) Composite International Diagnostic Interview (CIDI). *International Journal of Methods of Psychiatric Research, 13*, 93–121.

Kreyenbuhl, J., Buchanan, R. W., Dickerson, F. B., & Dixon, L. B. (2010). The Schizophrenia Patient Outcomes Research Team (PORT): Updated treatment recommendations 2009. *Schizophrenia Bulletin, 36*(1), 94–103.

Langsley, D. G. (1985a). Community psychiatry. In H. I. Kaplan & B. J. Sadock (Eds.), *Comprehensive textbook of psychiatry/IV* (4th ed., pp. 1878–1884). Baltimore, MD: Williams & Wilkins.

Langsley, D. G. (1985b). Prevention in psychiatry: Primary, secondary, and tertiary. In H. I. Kaplan & B. J. Sadock (Eds.), *Comprehensive textbook of psychiatry/IV* (4th ed., pp. 1885–1888). Baltimore, MD: Williams & Wilkins.

Lehman, A. F., Kreyenbuhl, J., Buchanan, R., Dickerson, F. B., Dixon, L., Goldberg, R. W., et al. (2004). The Schizophrenia Patient Outcomes Research Team (PORT): Updated treatment recommendations 2003. *Schizophrenia Bulletin, 30*, 193–217.

Lehman, A. F., Steinwachs, D. M., & PORT Co-Investigators. (1998). At issue: Translating research into practice: The Schizophrenia Patient Outcomes Research Team (PORT) treatment recommendations. *Schizophrenia Bulletin, 24*, 1–10.

Leighton, A. H. (1959). *My name is legion: Foundations for a theory of man in relation to culture.* New York: Basic Books.

Leighton, D. C., Harding, J. S., Macklin, D. B., Macmillan, A. M., & Leighton, A. H. (1963). *The Stirling County study of psychiatric disorder and sociocultural environment: Vol. 3. The character of danger: Psychiatric symptoms in selected communities.* New York: Basic Books.

Lyotard, J.-F. (1984). *The post-modern condition: A report on knowledge.* Minneapolis: University of Minnesota Press.

Maslow, A. H. (1968). *Toward a psychology of being.* New York: Van Nostrand Reinhold.

McGuirk, F. D., Keller, A. B., & Croze, C. (1995). *Blueprints for managed care: Mental healthcare concepts and structure.* Boulder, CO: Western Interstate Commission for Higher Education.

Mechanic, D. (1989). *Mental health and social policy* (3rd ed.). Englewood Cliffs, NJ: Prentice-Hall.

Mechanic, D. (2008). *Mental health and social policy: Beyond managed care* (5th ed.). Boston: Allyn & Bacon.

Onken, S. J., Craig, C. M., Ridgway, P., Ralph, R. O., & Cook, J. A. (2007). An analysis of the definitions and elements of recovery: A review of the literature. *Psychiatric Rehabilitation Journal, 31*(1), 9–22.

Poynter, W. L. (1998). *The textbook of behavioral managed care: From concept through management to treatment.* Bristol, PA: Brunner/Mazel.

President's New Freedom Commission on Mental Health. (2003). *Achieving the promise: Transforming mental health care in America. Final report.* (DHHS Publication No. SMA 03-3832). Rockville, MD: U.S. Government Printing Office.

Regier, D. A., Myers, J. K., Kramer, M., Robins, L. N., Blazer, D. G., Hough, R. L., et al. (1984). The NIMH Epidemiologic Catchment Area Program: Historical context, major objectives, and study population characteristics. *Archives of General Psychiatry, 41,* 934–941.

Robins, L. N., Helzer, J. E., Croughan, J. L., & Ratcliff, K. S. (1981). National Institute of Mental Health Diagnostic Interview Schedule: Its history, characteristics and validity. *Archives of General Psychiatry, 38,* 381–389.

Rorty, R. (1979). *Philosophy and the mirror of nature.* Princeton, NJ: Princeton University Press.

Rubin, A. (2008). *Practitioner's guide to using research for evidence-based practice.* Hoboken, NJ: John Wiley.

Sackett, D. L., Rosenberg, W., Gray, J. A. M., Haynes, R. B., & Richardson, W. S. (1996). Evidence-based medicine: What it is and what it isn't. *British Medical Journal, 312,* 71–72.

Sackett, D. L., Straus, S. E., Richardson, W. S., Rosenberg, W., & Haynes, R. B. (2000). *Evidence-based medicine: How to practice and teach EBM* (2nd ed.). New York: Churchill Livingston.

Sadock, B. J., & Sadock, V. A. (2007). *Synopsis of psychiatry: Behavioral sciences/clinical psychiatry* (10th ed.). Philadelphia, PA: Wolters Klumer Lippincott Williams & Wilkins.

Saleebey, D. (1992). Biology's challenge to social work: Embodying the person-in-environment perspective. *Social Work, 37*(2), 112–125.

Saleebey, D. (2005). Balancing act: Assessing strengths in mental health practice. In S. A. Kirk (Ed.), *Mental disorders in the social environment: Critical perspectives* (pp. 23–44). New York: Columbia University Press.

Saleebey, D. (Ed.). (2006). *The strengths perspective in social work practice.* Boston: Pearson/Allyn & Bacon.

Scheff, T. (1984). *Being mentally ill* (2nd ed.). New York: Aldine.

Seligman, M. E. P., & Csikszentmihalyi, M. (2000). Positive psychology: An introduction. *American Psychologist, 55*(1), 5–14.

Srole, L., & Fischer, A. K. (1986). The midtown Manhattan longitudinal study: Aging, generations, and genders.

In M. M. Weissman, J. K. Myers, & C. E. Ross (Eds.), *Community surveys of psychiatric disorders* (pp. 77–107). New Brunswick, NJ: Rutgers University Press.

Srole, L., Langer, T. S., Michael, S. T., Kirkpatrick, P., & Rennie, T. A. C. (1962). *Mental health in the metropolis: The midtown Manhattan study.* New York: McGraw-Hill.

Substance Abuse and Mental Health Services Administration, U.S. Department of Health and Human Services. (2005). *Transforming mental health care in America: The federal action agenda: First steps.* (DHHS Publication No. SMA 05-4060). Rockville, MD: Author.

Szasz, T. S. (1960). The myth of mental illness. *American Psychologist, 15,* 113–118.

Szasz, T. S. (1961). *The myth of mental illness.* New York: Delta.

Torrey, W. C., Drake, R. E., Dixon, L., Burns, B. J., Flynn, L., Rush, A. J., et al. (2001). Implementing evidence-based practices for persons with severe mental illnesses. *Psychiatric Services, 52*(1), 45–50.

U.S. Department of Health and Human Services. (1999). *Mental health: A report of the surgeon general.* Rockville, MD: U.S. Department of Health and Human Services, Substance Abuse and Mental Health Services Administration, Center for Mental Health Services, National Institutes of Health, National Institute of Mental Health.

U.S. Department of Health and Human Services. (2004). *National consensus statement on mental health recovery.*

SAMHSA's National Mental Health Information Center, Rockville, MD. Retrieved August 18, 2010, from http://mentalhealth.samhsa.gov/publications/allpubs/sma05-4129/

Wakefield, J. C. (1992). The concept of mental disorder: On the boundary between biological facts and social values. *American Psychologist, 47*(3), 373–388.

Weedon, C. (1987). *Feminist practice and poststructuralist theory.* Oxford, UK: Basil Blackwell Ltd.

Weissman, M. M., Myers, J. K., & Ross, C. E. (1986). Community studies in psychiatric epidemiology: An introduction. In M. M. Weissman, J. K. Myers, & C. E. Ross (Eds.), *Community surveys of psychiatric disorders* (pp. 1–19). New Brunswick, NJ: Rutgers University Press.

Wolfensberger, W., Nirje, B., Olshansky, S., Perske, R., & Roos, P. (1972). *The principle of normalization in human services.* Toronto, Ontario, Canada: National Institute on Mental Retardation.

World Health Organization. (1948). *Constitution and basic documents.* Geneva, Switzerland: Author.

World Health Organization. (1990). *Composite International Diagnostic Interview (CIDI), Version 1.0.* Geneva, Switzerland: Author.

World Health Organization. (2007, September). *Mental health: Strengthening mental health promotion.* Fact sheet N° 220. Retrieved July 11, 2009, from http://www.who.int/mediacenter/factsheets/fs220/en

Historical Context
Changes in Mental Health Policies
and Social Work Practice

> *If a knowledge of the past does not offer a precise prescription*
> *for the future, it can nevertheless yield insights and knowledge*
> *that provide a context against which to measure and to evaluate*
> *contemporary policies and issues.*
>
> —GROB, *THE MAD AMONG US*, 1994, P. 3

Social work practice in mental health evolved from the history of care of persons with identified mental health problems and from the history of the profession. This chapter visits the history of the mental health field in the United States, social work's part in that history, and the profession's own evolution. These histories are affected by changing in the social, economic, and political landscapes of various eras.

Mental health treatment in the colonial period and early years of the United States was influenced by ideas and practices from Europe. This includes treatment methods such as bloodletting and purging to restore a balance among the "humors" (body fluids); the use of chains and straitjackets; and "moral treatment," the humanitarian response to the previous methods during the Enlightenment (Dain, 1964; Grob, 1994; Katz, 1985). As the United States became transformed from an agrarian to an industrial country, it adapted ideas from Europe and its own early experiences to conditions in this country.

Changes in mental health policy have been dramatic. During colonial times, public policies addressing the needs of persons with mental health difficulties were virtually nonexistent. Instead those who would be later be characterized as mentally ill were maintained at home, in private settings run by physicians, or in almshouses, or they became vagrants (Leiby, 1978). There were a couple of early institutions. The Quaker-run Pennsylvania Hospital was the first to accept patients (1756). Another in Williamsburg, Virginia (founded 1773), was the first public institution for this population. Later policy has vacillated between institutionalization and community care. After social work emerged as a profession early in the twentieth century, social work practitioners worked in both hospital and community settings. During most of this time, physicians, particularly psychiatrists, took the lead in the development of mental health treatment in the United States.

THE BEGINNINGS OF PSYCHIATRY IN THE UNITED STATES

The U.S. physician credited with fathering psychiatry in the United States was *Benjamin Rush* (1745–1813), a signer of the Declaration of Independence. Considered a proponent of moral treatment, Rush believed that although insanity was physiological, intense intellectual activity or emotional shock ("moral" influences) could damage the brain (Caplan, 1969). The brain was considered "malleable" and, thus, experiences that promote health can alter the brain:

> The essence of moral treatment was the belief that, because of this great malleability of the brain surface, because of its susceptibility to environmental stimuli, pathological conditions could be erased or modified by corrective experience. Therefore, insanity, whether the result of direct or indirect injury or disease, or of overwrought emotions or strained intellectual faculties, would be cured in almost every case. (p. 9)

This interpretation of moral treatment shows that Rush recognized the impact of the environment on psychological experiences. Yet, as a medical practitioner who believed that mental diseases were physiological, Rush did not adequately explain the linkage between environmental and organic factors (Dain, 1964). Furthermore, his ideas and practices were inconsistent. On the one hand, he believed in kindness and humane care. On the other, he used techniques such as bleeding, purges, restraining devices, and shock (Caplan, 1969). Those who succeeded him in the nineteenth century, however, developed a purer form of moral treatment.

NINETEENTH CENTURY

Moral Treatment

During the early part of the nineteenth century, a number of other influential U.S. physicians of the mind (called *alienists* at that time) embraced moral treatment. Eschewing many of the physical methods used in Europe and by Rush, these physicians created in both private and public hospitals an environment that was intimate, caring, and beneficent. The Quaker model of moral treatment—which emphasized self-restraint, stability, and social harmony (Grob, 1994)—was adopted by four of the eight U.S. asylums built prior to 1824 (Dain, 1964).

Medical superintendents, who lived on the hospital grounds and shared meals and activities with residents, administered moral treatment personally. They encouraged patients to work, play, read, and, if interested, attend religious services. Hospitals that were guided by a philosophy of moral treatment recognized environmental causes of mental illness, which they attempted to counter:

> [B]y manipulation of the physical and social milieu of the asylum. This was done in large measure by mobilizing staff and patients into small groups to support and control the individual strictly but without undue coercion. . . . There were attempts to involve other care-giving groups, such as teachers and clergymen, in the treatment of the insane. And, in spite of geographic isolation, violent dislocation of the patient from the community was avoided because the undesirability of long-term institution-alization was recognized and because the entire therapeutic program was designed to inculcate normative cultural values and modalities so that the individual could return to society better able to cope with its demands. (Caplan, 1969, pp. 37–38)

Furthermore, physicians established relationships with nearby communities by educating the public about insanity, inviting the community residents to events at the hospital, and sending patients to live or work in these communities (Caplan, 1969). Many of the ideas and practices of the community mental health movement of the twentieth century have roots in moral treatment as it was interpreted in the nineteenth-century United States (Caplan, 1969).

Although some persons with psychiatric problems were treated in benign hospitals that provided moral treatment, such facilities were few and far between and many were private. Other institutions did not distinguish between the mentally ill and other populations, such as the mentally retarded, epileptics, criminals, and the homeless. Consequently, many of the poor mentally disabled were confined in almshouses and prisons (Rothman, 1971).

It was in this context that *Dorothea Lynde Dix* (1802–1887) began her campaign. Dix was a schoolteacher who retired when she was in her thirties, following an emotional and physical collapse (Kreisler & Lieberman, 1986; Marshall, 1937). After returning home from a trip to Europe, where she had gone to recover her strength, she was uncertain about what to do with her life. In 1841, she was asked to teach a Sunday school class in a jail in East Cambridge, Massachusetts. Upon assuming this volunteer work, she found poor women who seemed to be suffering from mental disorders imprisoned together with criminals.

> She was shocked to see them among hardened criminals, and entirely devoid of medical and moral treatment. Upon inquiry she learned that their only crime against society was their affliction. She inspected their quarters and to her horror found them bare, cold, and unheated. She asked the jailer why there was no stove or other heat in the part of the jail reserved for the insane, and why nothing was done to make their living as comfortable as that furnished for persons who had committed actual crimes against society. The jailer tried to dismiss the matter by saying that "lunatics" did not feel the cold as others, and that a fire would be very unsafe. (Marshall, 1937, p. 61)

Subsequently, Dix visited other prisons, almshouses, and other places in which persons with mental disabilities were confined in Massachusetts and reported her findings of widespread inhumane care and neglect in a "memorial" to the state legislature. For thirty years, Dix traveled from state to state, investigating conditions of the poor mentally ill and advocating for more humane care in public institutions. She traveled 60,000 miles by train, stagecoach, and riverboat, paying personal visits to over 9,000 individuals (Marshall, 1937). Dix is credited with the expansion or creation of thirty-two mental hospitals (Katz, 1985). In contrast with late twentieth-century mental health reformers, however, Dix worked for the creation of more or expanded state hospitals rather than for their reduction or elimination.

One of Dix's goals was that the federal government would assume some responsibility for the care of the mentally ill. As a result of vigorous lobbying activities, Dix got Congress to introduce a bill that would have had the federal government appropriate land to the states for the benefit of indigent persons with mental illness. In 1854, the bill was passed by both houses of Congress but was vetoed by President Franklin Pierce, who said that the federal government would be overstepping its powers if it were to provide for the poor in the states. An attempt to override the veto failed (Marshall, 1937). Nevertheless, Dix served as a model for future social workers to emulate.

Decline of Moral Treatment

During the second half of the nineteenth century, the practice of moral treatment declined. Success stories told by early advocates of moral treatment were not borne out by later experience (Caplan, 1969). The population of public asylums expanded and now included large numbers of alcoholics, violent persons, and immigrants, who did not seem to adapt to the benign regime of moral treatment. With overcrowded conditions and a population that was difficult to manage, methods of restraint from previous eras were resurrected, and programs that primarily provided custodial care became the norm (Caplan, 1969; Rothman, 1971). Thus, the institutions became warehouses for poor social rejects.

During this period, the ideas of Darwin and the organic viewpoint in medicine pervaded thinking. Persons with mental illness were considered genetically defective inferior beings, who were unfit for survival. In view of their assumed deficiencies, treatment was deemed irrelevant (Williams, Bellis, & Wellington, 1980). Although some received medication, medical attention was largely given to conducting pathological research on the brains of deceased patients (Caplan, 1969).

Still some community treatment took place during the latter part of the nineteenth century. According to the *Social Work Year Book 1935,* family care was in use in the state of Massachusetts as early as 1885 (Pollock, 1935). The same year an outpatient mental hygiene clinic was established at the Pennsylvania Hospital, and two years later a similar clinic opened at the Boston Dispensary (French, 1940).

Reform Begins Again

During the last few decades of the nineteenth century, another reform movement developed. One issue that provoked interest was the false commitment of individuals to mental asylums. Some of the victims of this practice were women, the most well known being *Elizabeth (E. P. W.) Packard* (1816–1897). Packard's husband was able to commit her to the state mental hospital in Jacksonville, Illinois, against her will because the law at that time did not protect the rights of married women. Packard (1865/1974) argued that she was falsely imprisoned because her religious values differed from those of her husband, a Calvinist minister. After Packard succeeded in suing her husband and the superintendent of the hospital in which she had been confined, she led a national movement to promote legislation protecting individuals from commitment without a jury trial and to assure that those who are hospitalized receive humane treatment. Some states responded by authorizing committees of visitors who could investigate conditions in mental hospitals. Others gave patients the right to send uncensored letters outside the hospital (Grob, 1983; Wrench, 1985).

Another manifestation of reform was the establishment of the National Association for the Protection of the Insane and the Prevention of Insanity, which advocated better treatment and protection of the rights of patients in public asylums. A forerunner of the mental hygiene movement that was to follow early in the twentieth century, this organization was founded simultaneously with the annual meeting of the National Conference of Charities and Corrections that convened in Cleveland in 1880 and was initiated largely by social workers, psychiatrists, neurologists, and lay reformers. Unfortunately, this organization died after only four years of existence (Deutsch, 1949; Grob, 1983).

Another organization that was critical of the prevailing practices in mental institutions (asylums) was the New York Society of Neurology. This group had concerns about the medical qualifications of physicians as well as the supervision, treatment, and rights of patients. Nevertheless, neither the lay reformers nor the members of the National Conference of Charities and Corrections or the Society of Neurology were able to overcome the power of the Association of Medical Superintendents of American Institutions of the Insane, which ran the principal psychiatric establishments and functioned as a self-contained guild that did not listen to criticism from outside its ranks (Caplan, 1969). Its control over psychiatric institutions continued until it was challenged by stronger forces in the twentieth century.

THE EARLY YEARS OF THE TWENTIETH CENTURY

The Progressive Era

The years between the turn of the century and 1920 encompass what is known as the *Progressive Era* in U.S. history. This was a period of reaction to the consequences of unregulated free enterprise and industrialism—poverty, onerous working conditions, and corrupt politics. During this era of reform, reports about child labor, sweatshops, prisons, and mental hospitals appeared in the print media. This stimulated a reassessment of the responsibility of the federal government to the people and of people to each other.

During the Progressive Era, environmental and psychological perspectives on the cause and nature of mental illness were dominant (Rothman, 1979). The social sciences looked at the impact of social class and economic conditions on individual well-being. The social work scholars Sophonisba Breckinridge and Edith Abbott (1912) incorporated a social environmental perspective in their influential book, *The Delinquent Child and the Home*. Meanwhile new psychological theories were introduced. Pioneer social workers and reformers whose thinking was consonant with the emerging social work profession assimilated these ideas.

Mental Hygiene Movement

An individual who, like Elizabeth Packard, became a social reformer following his institutionalization was *Clifford W. Beers* (1876–1943), a graduate of Yale University. Following three years of confinement in public and private mental asylums, Beers recovered and published *A Mind That Found Itself,* an autobiographical account of his experiences. Beers (1907/1923) described his suicide attempt, delusions, depression, and mania in vivid detail and reported the abusive and punitive treatment to which he had been subjected when he was hospitalized:

After fifteen interminable hours the strait-jacket was removed. Whereas just prior to its putting on I had been in vigorous enough condition to offer stout resistance when wantonly assaulted, now, on coming out of it, I was helpless. When my arms were released from their constricted position, the pain was intense. Every joint had been racked. I had no control over the fingers of either hand, and could not have dressed myself had I been promised my freedom for doing so. (p. 133)

Beers's book was praised by leading figures in psychology and psychiatry of that time and was widely read. The same year that the book came out, Beers founded the Connecticut Society of Mental Hygiene, and in 1909, he started the National Committee for Mental Hygiene, the predecessor of the National Mental Health Association. Thus began the mental hygiene movement, which "has generally been seen as a turning point in psychiatric history" (Caplan, 1969, p. 179).

The mental hygiene movement, in which lay citizens and professionals participated, laid the groundwork for the later community mental health movement. Although Beers's original goal was the reform of conditions in psychiatric institutions, prevention became the mental hygiene movement's primary mission. The National Committee for Mental Hygiene collected data, studied legislation, conducted surveys of institutions, encouraged research and publications, and educated the public (Bassett, 1933), tasks that are associated with macro social work practice today.

One of the early supporters of the mental hygiene movement was the neurologist and psychiatrist, *Adolf Meyer* (1866–1950). An immigrant from Switzerland, Meyer held positions in several state hospitals before becoming director of the Phipps Psychiatric Clinic at Johns Hopkins University in Baltimore, Maryland, in 1909. Meyer's conception of mental health was holistic, encompassing the mind, the body, and the environment. He viewed individuals as social beings whose life situations influence their psychological reactions. Accordingly, Meyer required that his staff of physicians collect data on the patient's life history, family, economic circumstances, and neighborhood—a process that required visits to the patient's home, work, and community (Deutsch, 1949). Meyer envisioned the development of a comprehensive mental hygiene system in the community with psychiatric centers that are linked to state hospitals (Lubove, 1965). Not surprisingly, his ideas were attractive to pioneer mental health social workers.

Early Social Workers in Mental Health

Julia Lathrop was a social work reformer who worked with Meyer when both were employed at the state hospital in Kankakee, Illinois. A resident of the settlement house, Hull House, in its early years, she was a strong advocate for the mentally ill (Costin, 1986). Upon reading the proof of Beers's *A Mind That Found Itself,* Lathrop wrote the following statement of endorsement of the author's proposed national organization:

I have felt for some time that a national society for the study of insanity and its treatment, from the social as well as the merely medical standpoint, should be formed. I am glad to follow in the line you have indicated and to have my name appear as one of the honorary trustees. I have talked with Miss Addams and she has agreed to the use of her name and will so inform you soon by letter. (Beers, 1907/1923, p. 271)

Lathrop became a founder of the National Committee for Mental Hygiene. She later served as chief of the U.S. Children's Bureau.

During the first decade of the twentieth century, several social workers held positions in hospitals for the psychiatrically impaired. Adolf Meyer's wife, *Mary Potter Brooks Meyer,* appears to have been the first such worker. A volunteer recruited by her husband, she visited psychiatric patients in the wards of Manhattan State Hospital and in their homes (Deutsch, 1949; Lubove, 1965). Mary Meyer assumed this responsibility in 1904, after a need for special personnel who would make linkages with the community was recognized (Deutsch, 1949).

Elsewhere other social workers were employed in similar capacities. *Edith N. Burleigh,* who began working in the Neurological Clinic of Massachusetts General Hospital in 1905, was responsible for conducting social investigations and treatment (Southard & Jarrett, 1922). In 1906, a social worker was assigned to the psychiatric wards of Bellevue Hospital in New York City (Southard & Jarrett, 1922). The same year, the New York State Charities Aid Association hired *E. H. Horton,* a trained social worker, as an aftercare agent, who helped patients find housing, employment, and other resources in the community. Her employment was a significant moment for the aftercare movement that had been promoting assistance to discharged psychiatric patients since the 1890s (Deutsch, 1949). In 1911, Charities Aid convinced the State of New York to have Manhattan State Hospital hire an aftercare worker. Within a few years, other states (Massachusetts, Illinois, Pennsylvania, New Jersey) appointed social workers in inpatient psychiatric facilities.

The social worker who, together with E. E. Southard, coined the term *psychiatric social work* and pioneered the field's development was *Mary C. Jarrett.* Jarrett was a caseworker who in 1913 became chief of social service of the Boston Psychopathic Hospital, of which Southard was medical director. This formal psychiatric social work department was designed to be an integral part of the hospital. Southard and Jarrett described the social work function in their classic book, *The Kingdom of Evils* (1922). They stated therein that the social worker's primary responsibility was social investigation—gathering facts regarding the patient's medical and social history from the patient and others in the community—a function that was viewed as extremely helpful to the diagnostic process in certain cases. Another important social work responsibility was individual casework, through which patients and families were helped "to secure the largest measure of social well being possible" (p. 526). Social workers also mediated relationships among doctors, social workers outside the hospital, patients, families, and friends. The social service department assumed responsibility for research and the training of social work students. Southard and Jarrett's description of the functions of the psychiatric social worker and the social work department provided a model for others to follow.

WORLD WAR I AND ITS AFTERMATH

World War I created conditions that promoted the development of social work practice in mental health. During the war, the American Red Cross organized a Home Service Bureau that looked after the families of soldiers and sailors. Trained Charity Organization Society workers, working for this bureau and providing psychosocial services to military families, departed from their earlier focus on the poor; similarly, middle-class families who did not have previous exposure to social workers became recipients of a new kind of service (Briar & Miller, 1971; Robinson, 1930).

Meanwhile many soldiers were experiencing "shell shock" or "war neurosis." In response to the emergency needs of soldiers in army hospitals and those who would be returning, Boston Psychopathic Hospital, together with the National Committee for Mental Hygiene and Smith College, developed the first training program for psychiatric social workers at Smith College in

1918. Mary Jarrett, who was responsible for the curriculum of this eight-week summer program, later became associate director of Smith College Training School for Social Work (Clark, 1966; Deutsch, 1949). Around the same time, other schools of social work—The New York School, Chicago School of Civics and Philanthropy, and Pennsylvania School of Social and Health Work—began to include psychiatric studies in their educational programs (Fink, Anderson, & Conover, 1968).

Although interest in the psychological aspects of human functioning was growing, social work of the first two decades of the twentieth century adhered primarily to economic and socio-logical perspectives (Robinson, 1930). This was evident in two parallel social work movements of that time. The settlement house movement drew attention to the effects of poverty and environmental deprivation on human lives; the charity organization movement tried to remedy poverty through almsgiving and friendly visiting.

Mary Richmond, who came out of the charity organization movement, was the author of a key social work publication of this period, *Social Diagnosis* (1917), which outlined a way in which to collect social data from a variety of sources and examine evidence before coming to conclusions. Richmond contributed to the development of a professional (i.e., scientific) approach to casework. Although she asserted the importance of personality in her later book, *What Is Social Case Work?* (1922), her focus was primarily on the person in relation to the environment (Clarke, 1947).

Emergence of the Psychological Perspective in Social Work

The 1919 National Conference of Social Work was the scene of a turning point in the history of clinical social work in mental health. Mary Jarrett (1919) presented a paper, "The Psychiatric Thread Running through All Social Case Work," in which she argued that the psychiatric thread "constitutes the entire *warp* of the fabric of case work" (p. 587). In this significant presentation, Jarrett noted that half the cases cited by Mary Richmond in *Social Diagnosis* were characterized by psychiatric problems. Jarrett urged that the mastery of psychiatric knowledge be required of all social workers, not only those who specialize in psychiatric social work. Other speakers at this historic conference (Jessie Taft, Southard, Sheldon Glueck) echoed Jarrett's promotion of the psychiatric perspective.

The state of knowledge of the mind, meanwhile, was expanding. In 1909, Freud came to the United States to give a series of lectures on psychoanalysis at Clark University in Worcester, Massachusetts. Freud was interested in neuroses, which could be treated through intensive analysis of the individual. Although his views about childhood sexuality were viewed as shocking at the time, his ideas about the impact of early life experiences on adult personality and his "talking cure" were intriguing.

By the 1920s, psychoanalysis acquired a following among intellectuals and medical professionals (Lubove, 1965). It appealed to social workers for a number of reasons. Despite Richmond's "scientific" casework, many clients were not responding to the approach she outlined. Psychoanalysis recognized that unconscious, irrational, intrapsychic dynamics comprise forces that resist treatment. "The client had to be enlisted in the struggle against his difficulties—caseworker and client were to be allies against the enemy within" (Briar & Miller, 1971, p. 13). Freudian theory provided both a framework for understanding the personality and a means to intervene. Social workers who underwent psychoanalysis themselves recognized the benefits of understanding oneself.

In the third decade of the twentieth century, however, psychoanalysis was only one of a number of theories that were under discussion. Behavioral psychology was developed in this country by J. D. Watson (1878–1958) and E. L. Thorndike (1874–1949). A U.S. psychiatrist, William Healy (1869–1963), was concerned with the psychological problems related to juvenile delinquency. Although he acknowledged the influences of genetics, the family, and environmental conditions, Healy was interested primarily in the psychology of the individual. His focus on "mental imagery" anticipates cognitive therapy:

> Hence it is clear that *whatever* influences the individual towards offense must influence first the mind of the individual. It is only because the bad companion puts dynamically significant pictures into the mind, or because the physical activity becomes a sensation with representation in psychic life, or the environmental conditions produce low mental perceptions of one's duty towards others, that there is any inclination at all towards delinquency. (1915/1924, p. 28)

With the impetus provided by the mental hygiene movement, interest in prevention grew during the 1920s. Not surprisingly, children—especially "delinquents"—became the population of concern. The Commonwealth Fund supported the establishment of seven child guidance clinics throughout the country, ushering in the child guidance movement. The focus on children appears to have some relation to the emphasis in Freudian psychology on the formative role of the early years of life. Moreover, the writings of Healy, which were read by social workers, emphasized early intervention.

Robinson (1930) considered the 1920s a period in which the psychological perspective became important to social work. Two schools of thought—psychiatric interpretation and behavioristic psychology—were dominant. The former was based on the psychoanalytic ideas of Freud, and the latter on social behaviorism. Psychiatric interpretation at that time looked at symptoms as responses to inner needs and encouraged a search for cause–effect relationships. In contrast, behavioristic psychology looked at external factors and emphasized "habit training, conditioning and reconditioning in treatment" and saw "the interview as a stimulus–response situation where the behavior of the interviewer sets the response of the interviewee" (pp. 83–84). Robinson was interested in interactive patterns, rather than a history of social facts, as well as the relationship between worker and client.

According to some scholars (Grinker, Macgretor, Selan, Klein, & Kohrman, 1961), the psychiatric knowledge that practicing psychiatric social workers of that time had was primarily of the diagnostic categories developed by the psychiatrist Emil Kraepelin. Still social workers employed in psychiatric settings began to think of themselves as specialists. In 1926, they formed the American Association of Psychiatric Social Workers (French, 1940).

The trend toward specialization within social work aroused concern that the profession would become splintered. The Milford Conference of Social Work Professionals attempted to reconcile differences in its 1929 report, *Social Case Work: Generic and Specific* (1929/1974). This document outlined common features of all fields of social work and unique features of special fields. The psychiatric social worker was to work in hospitals and agencies that gave special consideration to personality deviations. Psychiatric social casework included participation in diagnostic activity and individual therapy.

The extent to which social workers employed in psychiatric settings actually did participate in diagnosis and treatment in the 1920s is not entirely clear. Grinker et al. (1961) identified several functions of inpatient psychiatric social workers—history taking; providing information about resources to psychiatrists and patients; making visits to homes, schools, and employers; and contacting relatives and other relevant persons. In these capacities, the social worker functioned as a "handmaiden" to the psychiatrist, carrying out medical recommendations "without developing an independent relationship with patients" (p. 118). In the next two decades, however, changes in the economy and in the field of social work paved the way for more professional autonomy.

THE 1930s

During the 1930s, when the country was overwhelmed by the Great Depression, the federal government sponsored an array of services to relieve mass poverty and unemployment. Meanwhile psychiatric hospitals were becoming overcrowded (Deutsch, 1949), challenging inpatient facilities to come up with alternative ways to take care of residents. One alternative was the placement of patients in family care homes (Pollock, 1935). Social workers were to arrange and supervise these community placements. Furthermore, they became members of disciplinary mental health teams in outpatient services including child guidance centers (Stevenson, 1935).

By the late 1930s, psychiatric social workers had established themselves in Red Cross and Veterans' Administration services, public and private hospitals, child guidance clinics, mental hygiene clinics (some of these "traveling clinics"), general hospital clinics, educational institutions, mental hygiene societies, state departments of mental hygiene, public health nursing organizations, family welfare agencies, and private practice (French, 1940). Functions varied by setting. Psychiatric social workers employed by hospitals gathered social histories, worked with inpatients and their families from the time of admission to the completion of parole (period of supervision following discharge), promoted adjustment and environmental changes, and participated in programs of community education. Outpatient social workers working with adults performed similar functions, whereas child guidance social workers were principally psychotherapists. Social workers employed by mental hygiene societies engaged in community organization, program planning, and data gathering.

WORLD WAR II AND ITS AFTERMATH

Experiences related to World War II raised the consciousness of the nation about mental health problems and the need for expanded services. The high rate of rejection of prospective soldiers by the selective service system highlighted the prevalence of mental health problems among civilians. The psychiatric difficulties experienced by inducted soldiers who had passed the psychological screening examinations demonstrated that mental health difficulties could be experienced by healthy individuals who are exposed to stress (Klerman, 1986).

During the war, psychiatric social work services became part of the complex of military medical services—hospitals, mental health clinics, convalescent centers, and the like. The introduction of psychiatric services into the Veterans' Administration facilities stimulated the growth of mental health social work (Knee & Lamson, 1971).

In 1946, the National Mental Health Act was passed, ushering in a period of federal responsibility for mental health. This significant piece of legislation authorized federal funds for training mental health professionals (including social workers), research, and the development of community-based psychiatric services. Three years later, the National Institute of Mental Health

(NIMH) of the Public Health Service of the Department of Health, Education, and Welfare was established, and Robert Felix became its first director. The function of NIMH was to administer programs outlined in the 1946 act and to promote mental health education and prevention.

During the 1940s and 1950s, social workers in mental health settings expanded their roles. The social data that they gathered on clients' families and home environments were used to help establish the diagnosis. Social workers had increased contacts with the community because of the placement of discharged patients on parole or convalescent care with their own or foster families (Fink et al., 1968). The shortage of psychiatrists at this time necessitated the use of social workers as psychotherapists (Nacman, 1977).

Meanwhile, the knowledge base of social work was changing. Following the publication of Anna Freud's *The Ego and the Mechanisms of Defense* in 1946 in the United States, psychoanalysis was reworked by a group of U.S. psychiatrists. The ego psychology that emerged was more palatable to social workers because it was less deterministic than Freud's psychoanalysis and gave more emphasis to reality and conscious processes. Ego psychology was absorbed by social workers, who began to emphasize reality relationships, adaptation, coping, and mastery. Meanwhile, new developments in the field of mental health, as well as national and international events, paved the way social workers would be practicing community mental health.

CHANGING APPROACHES TO MENTAL HEALTH TREATMENT: 1950–1980

From the middle of the twentieth century through 1980, dramatic changes occurred in mental health policies and practices. Table 2.1 lists the numerous federal mental health acts that were passed during this period. Change in practice began in the early 1950s with the discovery of the therapeutic effects of the drug chlorpromazine on patients with schizophrenia (Grob, 1994). The symptom control this medication produced made it possible for hospitals to discharge some of their residents. Around the same time, reports from England about a therapeutic community (Jones, 1953) stimulated thoughts about community alternatives to hospitalization.

Community Mental Health

During the 1950s, an ideology centered around community mental health was taking shape. In Boston, Erich Lindemann and Gerald Caplan developed preventive strategies such as strengthening social networks, providing mental health education, and restructuring communities (Klerman, 1986). Lindemann developed theory and practice approaches about grief as he worked with survivors of the Coconut Grove nightclub fire. Both men contributed to the theoretical development of crisis intervention.

During World War II and the Korean War, effective strategies to treat shell shock and related reactions were developed in the military. Wartime experience revealed that psychiatric disability related to combat could be reduced by adhering to the principles of *immediacy*, *proximity*, *centrality*, *expectancy*, and *simplicity* (Ursano & Holloway, 1985). Soldiers who were seen soon after they were affected and in close proximity to the combat zone had a better chance of recovering and returning to their units than those who were sent to remote hospitals. A central coordinating system (called *triage*) was used to identify those individuals with emotional problems and to give priority to those with the most urgent needs. Treatment was simple and was accompanied by a high expectation that the soldier would recover. These principles are compatible with crisis intervention theory.

TABLE 2.1	Major Federal Mental Health Legislation: 1955–1980

Year	Act
1955	Mental Health Study Act (Pub. L. No. 84-182) authorized the establishment of the Joint Commission on Mental Illness and Mental Health
1963	Mental Retardation Facilities and Community Mental Health Center Construction Act (Pub. L. No. 88-164) outlined five community mental health services and authorized expenditures for construction only
1965	Community Mental Health Centers Construction Amendments (Pub. L. No. 89-105): construction and staffing Medicare Act (Pub. L. No. 89-97) Medicaid established in Title XIX of the Social Security Act
1967	Amendment to the community mental health center law (Pub. L. No. 90-31), providing an extension of the staffing and construction funding
1968	Alcohol and Narcotic Addict Rehabilitation Amendments (Pub. L. No. 90-574): funding for facilities providing treatment of drug and alcohol addiction
1970	Reauthorization of community mental health center program (Pub. L. No. 91-211): continuing staffing grants, providing for services for children and adolescents, supporting services in poverty areas, and including consultation and education
1972	Supplemental Security Income (SSI) program (Pub. L. No. 92-603) established
1975	Amendments to community mental health center program (Pub. L. No. 94-63), expanding number of required services, including drug and alcohol rehabilitation and prevention and services for the severely mentally disabled
1977	Reauthorization of the community mental health center program (Pub. L. No. 95-83) for one year
1978	Reauthorization of the community mental health center program (Pub. L. No. 95-622) for two years
1980	Mental Health Systems Act (Pub. L. No. 96-398) gave priority to services for vulnerable populations such as persons with severe mental disabilities; increased emphasis on advocacy; authorized for four years

In 1955, Congress passed and President Eisenhower signed the Mental Health Study Act (see Table 2.1), which authorized a national study of mental health treatment. The need for a study grew out of concern about the high numbers of patients residing in public psychiatric hospitals and the cost of their care (Klerman, 1986). The Joint Commission on Mental Illness and Mental Health that was subsequently established undertook a comprehensive study of the domain of mental health, the results of which were reported in *Action for Mental Health* (1961). The Commission recommended comprehensive mental health services in local communities, the continuation of state hospitals, and increased federal funding.

On February 5, 1963, President John F. Kennedy delivered an address to the 88th Congress on the issues of mental illness and mental retardation. This was the first time a U.S. president gave a special speech on these issues. Kennedy recommended a "bold new approach"—community care:

This approach is designed, in large measure, to use Federal resources to stimulate State, local, and private action. When carried out, reliance on the cold mercy of custodial isolation will be supplanted by the open warmth of community concern and capability. Emphasis on prevention, treatment, and rehabilitation will be substituted for a desultory interest in confining patients in an institution to wither away. (p. 3)

In October 1963, Kennedy signed the Mental Retardation Facilities and Community Mental Health Center Construction Act.

Between 1965 and 1980, a series of federal mental health bills fostering the implementation of community mental health systems was passed (see Table 2.1). In 1965, funds were allocated for the construction and staffing of community mental health centers. The federal government outlined the kinds of services that should be included in a community mental health system—inpatient, outpatient, community education, partial hospitalization, and emergency services. Later acts identified specific services (e.g., alcohol and drugs) to be offered and populations (children, older adults) that should be served. Medicare, Medicaid, and Supplemental Security Income (SSI) provided sources of financial support for persons with mental disabilities.

In 1977, the NIMH initiated the pilot Community Support Program (CSP) to stimulate states to develop support systems for the severely mentally ill who were living in the community. Not a specific piece of legislation, this was under NIMH's authorization to sponsor research and other activities and was funded (Grob, 1994).

Soon after he was inaugurated, President Carter issued an executive order creating a Presidential Commission on Mental Health that was to review national mental health needs (Grob, 1994; Mechanic, 2008). Although the Commission's final report "offered at best a potpourri of diverse and conflicting recommendations," it did recognize the dire needs of persons with severe psychiatric disabilities (Grob, p. 285), who were being released from hospitals only to be readmitted because of a lack of follow-up services. Even though the original intent of the report, *Action for Mental Health* (Joint Commission, 1961), was to provide community support for persons with severe mental disabilities, the programs that were implemented in the 1960s and 1970s were for a wide spectrum of populations, many of whom had less serious difficulties (Klerman, 1986). The legislation that came out of Carter's efforts was the Mental Health Systems Act of 1980, which recognized the needs of the severely mentally ill and other vulnerable, underserved populations, who were increasingly visible on city streets as a consequence of deinstitutionalization.

Deinstitutionalization

Deinstitutionalization refers to the ideology, policy, and practice of moving patients with severe mental illnesses from hospitals to the community. Liberal advocates believed that institutionalization—especially long-term hospitalization—was damaging to the self and a violation of civil rights, whereas conservative proponents wished to save taxpayer expenses by eliminating state hospitals. Deinstitutionalization constitutes a paradigm shift that converged with the goals of the community mental health movement.

Deinstitutionalization was supported by a series of judicial decisions that, in effect, reconstructed mental health policy. *Wyatt v. Stickney* (1971/1972), a case in Alabama, concluded that patients who had been involuntarily committed had a right to treatment and that adequate standards of treatment should be defined. The decision stipulated that the institution should have sufficient, qualified staff and that each patient should have an individualized treatment plan. Several cases (*Lake v. Cameron*, 1966; *Covington v. Harris*, 1969; *Dixon v. Weinberger*, 1975; *Welsch v.*

Likins, 1974) affirmed that treatment should take place in the least restrictive environment that was compatible with a client's needs. These cases gave recognition to the individual's capacity for autonomy and promoted discharge planning for community alternatives to hospitalization, such as halfway houses, group homes, and family care homes. In the case of *O'Connor v. Donaldson* (1975), the Supreme Court ruled that unless an individual was dangerous (to self or others), a state hospital could not retain the person involuntarily (Budson, 1978; Levine, 1981; Perlin, 1986).

The preceding court cases supported the rights of clients. They are reflective of a shift in the national climate from an ideology of "state as parent" that looks after human needs, which was characteristic of the Progressive Era, to a civil rights orientation (Rothman, 1978). Although the earlier perspective was paternalistic, it promoted care. During the 1960s and 1970s, however, reformists held the state responsible for coercive practices and social control (Rothman, 1978). (For a discussion of legal and ethical issues, see Chapter 5.)

During the 1960s and 1970s, the practices of involuntary commitment, cruel or nonexistent treatment, and inhumane methods of control became the subject of critical discourse (Cooper, 1967; Laing, 1967; Scheff, 1966; Szasz, 1970). Kesey (1962) dramatized the concerns of an emerging antipsychiatry movement in *One Flew over the Cuckoo's Nest*, a play in which a spirited hospital patient is subjugated by the staff. Participants in the antipsychiatry movement, which included former patients, raised questions about the use of shock treatment, lobotomies, and restraints, as well as the authority of psychiatrists (see, e.g., Chamberlin, 1978). Many sought the liberation of psychiatric patients from the oppressive mental health system. This movement was concurrent with the Vietnam War, during which time some conscientious objectors performed alternative service as aides in psychiatric hospitals.

During this period of social upheaval, social work texts demonstrated an openness to diverse theoretical perspectives (e.g., Turner, 1974). The systems approach, which facilitates the identification of problems in the social environment, emerged as a perspective that could be adapted to social work practice (Pincus & Minahan, 1973; Siporin, 1975). With increased recognition that problems do not reside exclusively within the individual, attention was also given to family and group processes. Social workers in mental health settings became aware of systemic impediments to the clients' ability to realize their rights to treatment and discharge and advocated on behalf of clients.

At the same time, as social workers were broadening their understanding of social functioning and modes of intervention, graduate-level social workers who worked directly and therapeutically with clients began to call themselves clinical social workers. In 1971, the National Federation of Societies for Clinical Social Work was founded. The National Association of Social Workers and the National Federation worked vigorously to help pass licensing laws in the states and advocated for insurance coverage for the services of social workers. Licensure and vendorship made it possible for mental health agencies to obtain insurance reimbursement for clinical social work services and for social workers to engage in private practice.

CHANGES IN MENTAL HEALTH POLICIES: 1981–2010

During the last two decades of the twentieth century, the mental health paradigm changed again. The federal government stopped providing direct funding of community mental health programs. The block grant strategy, which will be described next, routed federal funding through the states. The development of managed care of behavioral health during this period also affected the context of practice.

In 1981, under the Reagan administration, the Omnibus Budget Reconciliation Act (Pub. L. No. 97-35) passed. This legislation established block grants to states, which would determine how these funds would be used. This act replaced the progressive Mental Health Systems Act and promoted a shift of responsibility from the federal government to the states. The implementation of the Omnibus Budget Reconciliation Act during the 1980s was accompanied by a decline in federal funding. During the Reagan administration, too, many psychiatric clients lost their SSI when stricter criteria for disability were applied. Many such cases were successfully appealed (Mechanic, 2008).

Although federal leadership in mental health faltered during the Reagan years, a couple of developments during this administration aroused attention to mental health needs. During Reagan's first term, John Hinckley attempted to kill the president and seriously injured White House Press Secretary James Brady. Hinckley, who was diagnosed with schizophrenia, had not been receiving proper mental health treatment. Another development during this administration was Nancy Reagan's "just say no to drugs" campaign, which stimulated primary prevention of substance abuse among youth.

In the late 1980s, community mental health systems faced financial constraints and increasing demands to serve the indigent seriously mentally ill and other vulnerable populations. Advocacy groups such as the National Mental Health Association, the National Alliance for the Mentally Ill (now called the National Alliance on Mental Illness), the National Depressive and Manic-Depressive Association, as well as various local consumer groups, became a significant force in the field of mental health.

Since the Omnibus Budget Reconciliation Act of 1981, additional federal laws have provided direction to the implementation of services funded to the states through block grants. The State Comprehensive Mental Health Services Plan Act (Pub. L. No. 99-660) of 1986 required that states draw up plans that would describe the community-based system of services for individuals with severe mental illness that they would establish and implement, and come up with a target number of clients they expected to serve. The law stipulated that states had to provide case management if they were to receive federal funding. This act was reauthorized four years later under the Mental Health Amendments (Pub. L. No. 101-639) of 1990 (Rochefort, 1993). In 1986, the Protection and Advocacy Services Act, which offered protection to consumers, became law. A year later, the Stewart B. McKinney Homeless Assistance Act (Pub. L. No. 100-77), which included funds for special services to the homeless with mental illness, was passed. This act was reauthorized in 1988 and 1990 (Rochefort, 1993). In 1990, the National Affordable Housing Act (Pub. L. No. 101-625) authorized funds for housing and services for the homeless with mental health and substance abuse problems.

In 1990, the Americans with Disabilities Act (ADA, Pub. L. No. 101-336) was passed. The ADA prohibited discrimination in employment, education, public accommodations, public services, and transportation against persons with mental as well as physical disabilities. The protections against discrimination in employment in the ADA were more extensive than those in the previous Rehabilitation Act of 1973, which only applied to employment in federal agencies or organizations with federal contracts of more than $2,500. The ADA of 1990 extended protection against discrimination to private employers of fifteen or more persons (Hermann, 1997). Although some conditions remain excluded from coverage, the passage of the ADA was a tremendous victory for advocates of rights of persons with mental disabilities. In 2002, the U.S. Supreme Court issued a unanimous opinion that made it more difficult for employees to triumph in work-related claims under the ADA. In the case of *Toyota Motor Manufacturing, Kentucky, Inc. v. Williams* (2002), the Court clarified the legal principles governing the determination of disability under the statute. In doing so, it continued a trend toward a more conservative interpretation of the ADA. In general, the Court's decision made it more difficult for people with mental illnesses to successfully pursue claims under the ADA.

During the 1980s and 1990s, managed health care became increasingly widespread as a cost-effective means to provide employees with a health care benefit. The term *behavioral health* came to describe mental health and substance abuse treatment within managed care programs or carved out through a contract with a separate entity. Still persons who were employed by an organization that did not provide a health care benefit, those who were unemployed, and those who were not beneficiaries of Medicare or recipients of Medicaid remained uncovered. During Clinton's first term, he tried and failed to pass legislation that would assure universal health insurance.

One law that was passed around that time (1996) was the Mental Health Parity Act (MHPA), which went into effect in January 1998. This law called for equal coverage for physical and mental illness in annual and lifetime limits under group health insurance plans with mental health benefits in organizations serving more than fifty employees. The MHPA had many loopholes, including exclusion of coverage for substance abuse treatment.

It took another decade for a more complete parity legislation to be passed. On October 3, 2008, President Bush signed the Mental Health Parity and Addiction Equity Act (MHPAEA) of 2008. This legislation entitles 113 million more people across the country to nondiscriminatory mental health coverage (Centers for Medicare and Medicaid Services, 2009). It is intended to take effect on January 1, 2010. A person is ensured equity if he or she is enrolled in a group health plan of fifty or more employees that provides both medical and surgical benefits and mental health or substance use disorder benefits. Insurance plans are not allowed to require different deductibles or copayments, or limit frequency of treatment and days of coverage for mental health care as compared with treatment for physical illnesses. Building on the original 1996 parity act, the new law requires parity coverage for annual and lifetime dollar limits. A recent trend in primary care practice settings is to provide care for behavioral health and psychological problems. As such, this act is to provide access to mental health care for many individuals who are in need.

Two momentous federal reports were issued around the turn of the century. One was *Mental Health: A Report of the Surgeon General* (U.S. Department of Health and Human Services, 1999), the first Surgeon General's report on the state of mental health in the United States. A culmination of scientific advances in the last half of the twentieth century and, in particular, the 1990s, the "decade of the brain," the report describes current knowledge and speaks to the need to use this knowledge to respond to the needs of adults (including older adults) and children with mental illnesses. The second federal report, *Mental Health: Culture, Race, and Ethnicity: A Supplement to Mental Health: A Report of the Surgeon General* (U.S. Department of Health and Human Services, 2001), identifies disparities in mental health care and acknowledges a greater burden of disability among certain racial and ethnic groups. This report calls for changes on the systems level and increased cultural competence among mental health providers.

In 2002, President Bush signed an executive order that set up the New Freedom Commission on Mental Health. The commission was established due to continued access barriers to obtaining high-quality mental health care including (a) stigma, (b) financial requirements and treatment limitations placed on mental health benefits, and (c) a fragmented mental health care delivery system. The Commission's final report, *Achieving the Promise: Transforming Mental Health Care in America* (2003), identified several goals as a foundation for fundamental transformation of the delivery of mental health care in the United States. These goals delineated the importance of family and consumer-driven care; eliminating disparities in mental health services; early screening, assessment, and referral to services; and the use of technology to access care and information. The follow-up document, *Transforming Mental Health Care in America: The Federal Action Agenda: First Steps* (Substance Abuse and Mental Health Services Administration, 2005), outlined principles and action steps that need to be taken to achieve these goals.

On March 23, 2010, President Obama signed the Patient Protection and Affordable Care Act, a major piece of health legislation. Together with the MHPAEA of 2008, the 2010 legislation should enable millions of previously uninsured Americans to have health insurance for mental health services.

During the decade of 2000–2010, many of the mental health initiatives that were described were supported by the accelerated research and technology in mental health care and service delivery. The evidence-based practice (EBP) movement has made a quantum leap in providing new ways of thinking about and treating mental illnesses. The philosophical shift toward a hopeful *recovery* for every individual with a mental illness has also shaped the landscape of mental health delivery systems. A number of practice principles of EBP that have been identified in mental health require that the practice be targeted to a specific group for whom it is intended, that it have demonstrated effectiveness, that the practice must be clearly defined, and that it have generalizability to a wide variety of mental health settings (Bond & Campbell, 2008). Increasingly, social work has been embracing EBP in mental health and other fields of practice.

Summary and Deconstruction

This chapter described the history of mental health treatment in the United States and social work's place in that history. The chapter highlighted the role played by noted individuals, the world wars, and federal public policies, as well as ideologies. Some of the reformers who were depicted suffered themselves from mental illness (Clifford Beers) or from institutionalization for an alleged illness (Elizabeth Packard). Besides these prominent figures were persons at the margins who were hidden away in attics by their families, chained in prisons or mental hospitals, sheltered in poorhouses, or incarcerated against their will in mental hospitals. Some of those who were hospitalized were immigrants who did not speak English and people of color whose differences were constructed as symptoms of mental illness. Little is known about the suffering of individuals such as these.

Paradigms of mental illness and its treatment have changed many times over the course of U.S. history. For example, the reformer Dix in the nineteenth century viewed hospitalization as desirable, but civil rights advocates in the 1960s and 1970s saw hospitalization as detrimental. At various times, the approach to treatment was viewed through the standpoint of morality. Furthermore, the role of the federal government has changed over time. A constant feature, however, has been the marginalization of those with severe mental illness who were living in poverty. Although events, such as medical discoveries, the Great Depression, and war, appear to have influenced social changes, unequal power relations and economic factors underlie the reforms. It remains to be seen whether today's EBP will be regarded as a reform or the consequence of political influences.

Social workers employed in mental health settings began as "helpmates" to psychiatrists, gaining increasing autonomy over time. During the last few decades, however, they have been grappling with the influence of managed care entities. Meanwhile the social work profession has expanded its knowledge base, debating internally about theoretical frameworks, how clinical it wants to be, and to whom it is accountable. Furthermore, there are differences of opinion about the value of scientific practice. Rather than being divisive, these debates can result in new constructions about addressing the behavioral or mental health problems of the future.

Websites

http://special.lib.umn.edu/swha/index.html
http://www.surgeongeneral.gov/library/mentalhealth/

https://www.cms.gov/HealthInsReformforConsume/
    04_TheMentalHealthParityAct.asp

References

Bassett, C. (1933). Mental hygiene. In F. S. Hall (Ed.), *Social work yearbook 1933* (pp. 297–301). New York: Russell Sage Foundation.

Beers, C. W. (1907/1923). *A mind that found itself: An autobiography*. Garden City, NY: Doubleday, Page.

Bond, G. R., & Campbell, K. (2008). Evidence-based practices for individuals with severe mental illness. *Journal of Rehabilitation, 74*(2), 33–44.

Breckinridge, S. P., & Abbott, E. (1912). *The delinquent child and the home*. New York: Charities Publication Committee.

Briar, S., & Miller, H. (1971). *Problems and issues in social casework*. New York: Columbia University Press.

Budson, R. D. (1978). In J. Goldmeir, F. V. Mannino, & M. F. Shore (Eds.), *New directions in mental health care* (chap. 1). (DHEW Publication No. ADM 78–685). Adelphi, MD: National Institute of Mental Health.

Caplan, R. B., in collaboration with Caplan, G. (1969). *Psychiatry and the community in nineteenth-century America*. New York: Basic Books.

Centers for Medicare and Medicaid Services. (2009). *The Mental Health Parity and Addiction Equity Act*. Retrieved October 5, 2008, from http://www.cms.hhs.gov/healthinsreformforconsume/04_thementalhealth-parityact.asp

Chamberlin, J. (1978). *On our own: Patient-controlled alternatives to the mental health system*. New York: McGraw-Hill.

Clark, E. (1966). The development of psychiatric social work. *Bulletin of the Menninger Foundation, 30*, 161–173.

Clarke, H. I. (1947). *Principles and practice of social work*. New York: Appleton-Century.

Cooper, D. (1967). *Psychiatry and antipsychiatry*. London: Tavistock.

Costin, L. (1986). Lathrop, Julia Clifford. In W. I. Trattner (Ed.), *Biographical dictionary of social welfare in America* (pp. 478–481). New York: Greenwood Press.

Covington v. Harris, 419 F.2d 617 (D.C. Cir. 1969).

Dain, N. (1964). *Concepts of insanity in the United States, 1789–1865*. New Brunswick, NJ: Rutgers University Press.

Deutsch, A. (1949). *The mentally ill in America*. New York: Columbia University Press.

Dixon v. Weinberger, 405 F. Supp. 974 (D.D.C. 1975).

Fink, A. E., Anderson, C. W., & Conover, M. B. (1968). *The field of social work*. New York: Holt, Rinehart and Winston.

French, L. M. (1940). *Psychiatric social work*. New York: Commonwealth Fund.

Freud, A. (1946). *The ego and the mechanisms of defense* (C. Baines, Trans.). New York: International Universities Press.

Grinker, R. R., Macgretor, H., Selan, K., Klein, A., & Kohrman, J. (1961). The early years of psychiatric social work. *Social Service Review, 35*(2), 111–126.

Grob, G. N. (1983). *Mental illness and American society, 1875–1940*. Princeton, NJ: Princeton University Press.

Grob, G. N. (1994). *The mad among us: A history of the care of America's mentally ill*. Cambridge, MA: Harvard University Press.

Healy, W. (1915/1924). *The individual delinquent*. Boston: Little, Brown.

Hermann, D. H. J. (1997). *Mental health and disability law in a nutshell*. St. Paul, MN: West Publishing Co.

Jarrett, M. C. (1919). The psychiatric thread running through all social case work. *Proceedings of the National Conference of Social Work*, Atlantic City, NJ.

Joint Commission on Mental Illness and Mental Health. (1961). *Action for mental health*. New York: Basic Books.

Jones, M. (1953). *The therapeutic community*. New York: Basic Books.

Katz, S. E. (1985). Psychiatric hospitalization. In H. I. Kaplan & B. J. Sadock (Eds.), *Comprehensive textbook of psychiatry/IV* (pp. 1576–1582). Baltimore, MD: Williams & Wilkins.

Kennedy, J. F. (1963). *Message from the President of the United States relative to mental illness and mental retardation*. (88th Congress, House of Representatives Document No. 58, pp. 1–14).

Kesey, K. (1962). *One flew over the cuckoo's nest: A novel*. New York: Viking Press.

Klerman, G. L. (1986). The scope of social and community psychiatry. In G. L. Klerman, M. M. Weissman, P. S. Appelbaum, & L. H. Roth (Eds.), *Social, epidemiologic, and legal psychiatry* (pp. 1–14). New York: Basic Books.

Knee, R. I., & Lamson, W. C. (1971). Mental health services. In R. Morris (Ed.), *Encyclopedia of social work* (16th ed., Vol. 1, pp. 802–813). New York: National Association of Social Workers.

Kreisler, J. D., & Lieberman, A. A. (1986). Dorothea Lynde Dix. In W. I. Trattner (Ed.), *Biographical dictionary of social welfare in America* (pp. 241–244). New York: Greenwood Press.

Laing, R. D. (1967). *The politics of experience.* New York: Ballantine.

Lake v. Cameron, 364 F.2d (D.C. Cir. 1966).

Leiby, J. (1978). *A history of social welfare and social work in the United States.* New York: Columbia University Press.

Levine, M. (1981). *The history and politics of community mental health.* New York: Oxford University Press.

Lubove, R. (1965). *The professional altruist: The emergence of social work as a career 1880–1930.* Cambridge, MA: Harvard University Press.

Marshall, H. (1937). *Dorothea Dix: Forgotten samaritan.* Chapel Hill: University of North Carolina Press.

Mechanic, D. (2008). *Mental health and social policy: Beyond managed care* (5th ed.). Boston: Allyn & Bacon.

Nacman, M. (1977). Mental health services: Social workers. In *Encyclopedia of social work* (17th ed., Vol. 2). Washington, DC: National Association of Social Workers.

O'Connor v. Donaldson, 422 U.S. 563 (1975), 1 MDLR 336.

Packard, E. P. W. (1974). *Great disclosure of spiritual wickedness!! in high places. With an appeal to the government to protect the inalienable rights of married women.* New York: Arno Press. (Original work published 1865)

Perlin, M. L. (1986). Patients' rights. In G. L. Klerman, M. M. Weissman, P. S. Appelbaum, & L. H. Roth (Eds.), *Social, epidemiologic, and legal psychiatry* (pp. 401–422). New York: Basic Books.

Pincus, A., & Minahan, A. (1973). *Social work practice: Model and method.* Itasca, IL: R. E. Peacock.

Pollock, H. M. (1935). Mental diseases. In F. S. Hall (Ed.), *Social work year book 1935* (pp. 273–277). New York: Russell Sage Foundation.

President's New Freedom Commission on Mental Health. (2003). *Achieving the promise: Transforming mental health care in America. Final report.* (DHHS Publication No. SMA-03-3832). Rockville, MD: U.S. Government Printing Office.

Richmond, M. (1917). *Social diagnosis.* New York: Russell Sage Foundation.

Richmond, M. E. (1922). *What is social case work? An introductory description.* New York: Russell Sage Foundation.

Robinson, V. P. (1930). *A changing psychology of social case work.* Chapel Hill: University of North Carolina Press.

Rochefort, D. A. (1993). *From poorhouses to homelessness.* Westport, CT: Auburn House.

Rothman, D. J. (1971). *The discovery of the asylum. Social order and disorder in the new republic.* Boston: Little, Brown.

Rothman, D. J. (1978). The state as parent: Social policy in the Progressive Era. In W. Gaylin, I. Glasser, S. Marcus, & D. Rothman (Eds.), *Doing good: The limits of benevolence* (pp. 67–96). New York: Pantheon Books.

Rothman, D. J. (1979). *Incarceration and its alternatives in 20th century America.* Washington, DC: U.S. Department of Justice.

Scheff, T. (1966). *Being mentally ill.* Chicago: Aldine Atherton.

Siporin, M. (1975). *Introduction to social work practice.* New York: Macmillan.

Social case work: Generic and specific. (1974). A report of the Milford Conference. Washington, DC: National Association of Social Workers. (Original work published 1929)

Southard, E. E., & Jarrett, M. C. (1922). *The kingdom of evils.* New York: Macmillan.

Stevenson, G. S. (1935). Psychiatric clinics for children. In F. S. Hall (Ed.), *Social work year book 1935* (pp. 350–353). New York: Russell Sage Foundation.

Substance Abuse and Mental Health Services Administration, U.S. Department of Health and Human Services. (2005). *Transforming mental health care in America: The federal action agenda: First Steps.* (DHHS Publication No. SMA 05-4060). Rockville, MD: U.S. Department of Health and Human Services.

Szasz, T. (1970). *Ideology and insanity.* Garden City, NY: Anchor Books.

Toyota Motor Manufacturing, Kentucky, Inc. v. Williams, 2002 LEXIS 400 (2002).

Turner, F. J. (Ed.). (1974). *Social work treatment: Interlocking theoretical approaches.* New York: Free Press.

U.S. Department of Health and Human Services. (1999). *Mental health: A report of the surgeon general.* Rockville, MD: U.S. Department of Health and Human Services, Substance Abuse and Mental Health Services Administration, Center for Mental Health Services, National Institutes of Health, National Institute of Mental Health.

U.S. Department of Health and Human Services. (2001). *Mental health: Culture, race, and ethnicity: A supplement to Mental health: A report of the surgeon general.* Rockville, MD: U.S. Department of Health and Human Services, Substance Abuse and Mental Health Services Administration, Center for Mental Health Services.

Ursano, R. J., & Holloway, H. C. (1985). Military psychiatry. In H. I. Kaplan & B. J. Sadock (Eds.), *Comprehensive textbook of psychiatry/IV* (4th ed., pp. 1900–1909). Baltimore, MD: Williams & Wilkins.

Welsch v. Likins, 373 F. Supp. 487 (D. Minn. 1974).

Williams, D. H., Bellis, E. C., & Wellington, S. W. (1980). Deinstitutionalization and social policy: Historical perspectives and present dilemmas. *American Journal of Orthopsychiatry, 50,* 54–64.

Wrench, S. B. (1985). Packard, Elizabeth Parsons Ware. In A. Whitman (Ed.), *American Reformers* (pp. 627–628). New York: H. W. Wilson.

Wyatt v. Stickney, 325 F. Supp. 781, aff'd, 334 F. Supp. 1341 (M.D. Ala. 1971) and 344 F. Supp. 373 (M.D. Ala. 1972), aff'd sub nom.

Biopsychosocial Conceptual Framework

*[I]t is evident that human experience is not driven solely from
the bottom up by neurobiology and genetics. Instead there is growing
evidence that psychosocial experience can exert a macrodeterministic,
top-down force on our biology.*

—GARLAND & HOWARD, "NEUROPLASTICITY, PSYCHOSOCIAL GENOMICS,
AND THE BIOPSYCHOSOCIAL PARADIGM IN THE 21ST CENTURY," 2009, P. 197

Traditional approaches to understanding human behavior have highlighted competing paradigms such as nature *versus* nurture, mind *versus* body, and biology *versus* the environment. Another standard approach is to identify distinct psychological, social, and biological factors that are thought to be determinants of human behavior. These dualistic and linear strategies to knowledge formation have limited applicability to behavioral health today. Today's understanding of human behavior requires an integrated understanding of biological, psychological, and social environmental perspectives. The emphasis is on reciprocal influences, interactions, and the interpenetration of one with the other. The mind and body are inseparable. Moreover, individual mindbodies are part of and connected with the social worlds that sustain or neglect them and serve as a context for creating meaning.

The biopsychosocial conceptual framework of this book encompasses the understanding that there are *mutual influences* among biological functions, mental life, and social processes in their effects on adaptive functioning, which are realized in the integrated use of medical, psychological, and social approaches to intervention. This framework is in keeping with the person–environment, person-in-situation, and psychosocial perspectives that have been integral to the social work profession since its early days (Hamilton, 1940; Hollis, 1964; Richmond, 1917), which have been augmented with biological knowledge (Bentley & Walsh, 2006; Saleebey, 1992).

At the same time that the field of social work adopted psychosocial and biopsychosocial frameworks, medicine, including psychiatry, championed a biomedical model. Change began after George Engel (1977) asserted that the biomedical model was "reductionist" and "exclusionist" (p. 196), proposing instead a biopsychosocial model. Since then, psychiatrists, psychologists, and family medicine practitioners have given increased attention to the biopsychosocial model (see, e.g., Astin, Shapiro, Eisenberg, & Forys, 2003; Gatchel, 2004; Kandel, 1998).

The integration of biopsychosocial knowledge and treatment is supported by emerging scientific research. For example, Kumari (2006) found evidence that psychological therapies such as interpersonal (IPT), cognitive-behavioral (CBT), and exposure produce neurobiological effects, and Astin et al. (2003) found evidence for the efficacy of a number of mind–body therapies (e.g., relaxation techniques, meditation, and guided imagery) in the treatment of particular medical diseases. Research findings have led to the hypothesis that psychotherapy produces changes in gene expression that in turn brings about changes in the structure of the brain (Kandel, 1998).

Reviewing emerging research for social work readers, Garland and Howard (2009) discuss the concepts of *neuroplasticity* and *psychosocial genomics*:

> Neuroplasticity research describes how neurons within the brain proliferate and grow new connections across the life span, whereas psychosocial genomics describes the processes by which psychological and social experiences activate or deactivate genes, thereby driving the development of new neural pathways. (p. 191)

This research offers hope that with increased credible research, clients can change not only their emotions, cognition, and behavior, but also their neurobiology (Garland & Howard, 2009).

The integrative biopsychosocial framework used in this book was influenced by the idea of mutual influence from these emerging developments, an integrative health model (to be explained next), and concepts from social work. Weiner (1984) and Weiner and Fawzy's (1989) integrative health model incorporates the concepts of *health*, *illness*, and *disease*. Accordingly, health refers to adaptive biopsychosocial functioning, that is, functioning that promotes, assists, and fosters the ability to live fruitfully in the social environment. Health is a positive goal that depends on bio-genetic, psychological, and social factors and is maintained by proper nutrition, good sanitation, stable political conditions, and an adequate standard of living (Weiner & Fawzy, 1989). Health can change as the person matures and acquires social experience over time. Disease is associated with biochemical, immunological, structural, functional, or genetic impairment, whereas illness is a psychosocial state characterized by malaise, dissatisfaction, or pain (Weiner, 1984).

In contrast with the Western biomedical model, the integrative health model views illness and disease as *multifaceted and complex* rather than as well-defined entities that have a single physical cause (Weiner, 1984). Diseases are *heterogeneous* (varied) and have diverse, multiple, and complex causes and manifestations. This model is not deterministic, that is, *no assumption of linear cause–effect* influences is being made (Zimmerman, 1989). Thus, disease and illness are not necessarily related causally or sequentially. One can feel ill without having a disease, and one

TABLE 3.1	Characteristics of the Integrative Biopsychosocial Perspective	
Mutual influences of biological, psychological, and social	Mental health as health	
Neuroplasticity and psychosocial genomics	Individualization	
Concepts of health, disease, and illness	Multiple contexts	
Multifaceted and complex	Strengths perspective	
Heterogeneity/diversity	Client as active participant	
Nonlinear causality	Client empowerment	
Proclivity toward healing	Meaning-making	

can have a disease without feeling ill (Weiner & Fawzy, 1989). Social supports can protect a person with a genetic predisposition from developing a disease, whereas poverty and other stressors can foster an outbreak or exacerbation of a disease (Weiner, 1984). Regardless of whether one is ill or has a disease, or both, one has a natural *proclivity toward healing* (Weiner, 1984). Table 3.1 summarizes the characteristics of the integrative biopsychosocial framework we are using.

In this book, we view *mental health as health.* Thus, psychopathology is seen as a disturbance in biopsychosocial integration and is manifested by inner difficulties as well as challenges adapting to the demands of the environment. The person with a psychiatric disorder may have difficulty with cognition (or cognitive processing), performing adaptive behavior, coping with emotions, or perceiving the demands of the environment. The individual may experience or have symptoms of distress (illness) or manifest through laboratory examinations signs of structural or genetic impairment (disease).

During the last few decades, biological research has produced evidence of neurological and genetic explanations for substance abuse and major mental disorders that has led to improved means of treatment. Biological knowledge does not, however, replace other sources of knowledge that contribute to understanding of a particular client experiencing particular difficulties in particular social contexts. Individual clients express their subjective pain through cognitive, behavioral, somatic, and emotional symptoms as well as the ways in which they function in particular environments. They manifest symptoms in unique ways. Accordingly, clients must be *individualized* and viewed in the *multiple contexts* of their lives.

The biopsychosocial framework used in this book is consistent with the *strengths perspective* (Weick, Rapp, Sullivan, & Kisthardt, 1989), that is:

All people possess a wide range of talents, abilities, capacities, skills, resources, and aspirations. No matter how little or how much may be expressed at one time, a belief in human potential is tied to the notion that people have untapped, undetermined reservoirs of mental, physical, emotional, social, and spiritual abilities that can be expressed. (p. 352)

Nevertheless, it is recognized that individuals with behavioral health problems have vulnerabilities that can interfere with their biopsychosocial functioning and result in decompensation.

Furthermore, the client is viewed as an *active participant* in his or her own care, not a passive recipient of services. The client has legal and ethical rights (e.g., least restrictive environment, self-determination) that should be protected (see Chapter 5) as well as the right to competent, informed, effective service. The social worker assures that the client participates in the development of the treatment plan and goal setting and that the client makes his or her own decisions to the extent possible. The clinical social worker recognizes that the client has the capacity for growth or self-transformation based on a perceived inner sense of his or her own needs (Weick, 1987). The social worker helps clients who are discriminated against because of sexism, racism, ableism, heterosexism, ageism, or classism in their struggles, promoting their *empowerment*.

A further characteristic of the biopsychosocial framework used here is the assumption that clients actively engage in a process of *meaning-making*. As humans, they have some awareness of their place in the cosmos and their relationship to themselves, others, the material environment, and, if they so believe, a higher power. They seek a purpose in life, wholeness, connectedness, self-actualization, and growth as they and their respective cultures define these qualities. Meaning-making can be viewed as a process that is developmental (Kegan, 1982) and spiritual.

In this chapter, interdisciplinary knowledge that is relevant to behavioral health practice is described. Although the biopsychosocial conceptual framework is integrative, this chapter will discuss biological and psychosocial perspectives separately. Separate treatment of these topics, as well as subtopics within each of them, is a consequence of the division of knowledge into areas that are developed by different academic and professional disciplines.

BIOLOGICAL KNOWLEDGE

During the last few decades, major mental disorders such as schizophrenia and bipolar disorder came to be understood as diseases of the brain. Researchers have learned much about genetics, the structure and functioning of the brain, and psychopharmacology. Because this knowledge is applied to clients with whom social workers practice, social workers need to understand these developments and how they translate into treatment.

Genetics

Inherited potential is believed to be involved in the etiology (cause or origin) of a number of mental disorders. A large body of research examines genetic patterns associated with schizophrenia and mood disorders. Some studies have explored the genetics of alcoholism, anxiety disorders, and personality disorders, among other disorders. Traditional approaches to research include family risk, twin studies, and adoption studies. Today the spotlight is on molecular genetics.

FAMILY RISK   One means of looking at genetic influences has been to study the prevalence of a particular disease in families with the disease and compare rates in genetically linked groups with the rate in the general population. Such research requires intensive investigation of the families of persons with an identified mental disorder through a standardized interview of relatives or from records. This research begins with an individual with an identified disorder (*proband* or *index case*) and proceeds to first-degree relatives (parents, siblings, children) and more distant family members (Rainer, 1985). A genetic hypothesis is supported when the prevalence of a psychiatric disorder is higher among first-degree than more distant relatives and when the rate among relatives is higher than that of the general population. Population prevalence rates obtained from large-scale psychiatric epidemiological studies can be compared with data from family risk studies (Choudary & Knowles, 2008). Another approach is to compare the prevalence among the first-degree relatives with that of a control group (Andreasen & Black, 2006). Studies of family risk indicate that schizophrenia, bipolar disorder, alcoholism, social phobia, obsessive-compulsive disorder, and panic disorder run in families (Andreasen & Black, 2006; Choudary & Knowles, 2008). Furthermore, they show that relatives often develop similar but not the same disorders. For example, relatives of individuals with schizophrenia may have an increased rate of schizotypal or paranoid personality disorder, schizoaffective disorder, and atypical psychosis, whereas relatives of persons with bipolar I disorder may have increased cyclothymia, bipolar II disorder, schizoaffective disorder, dysthymia, and recurrent major depression. This finding, also found in other types of genetic studies, has stimulated discussion about *spectrums* of related disorders (Choudary & Knowles, 2008).

TWIN STUDIES Another approach has been to study identical *(monozygotic)* and fraternal *(dizygotic)* twins. Clinical cases identified as afflicted twins are the basis for investigating whether the cotwin or other family members have had a similar mental illness. The rate of co-occurrence is called the *concordance rate*. Research studies of schizophrenia in twins have revealed a higher rate among monozygotic than dizygotic twins (Gottesman & Shields, 1972; Kendler, 1988). The rate for dizygotic twins and siblings is similar. Furthermore, research has found that the closer the biological relationship, the higher the rate (Sadock & Sadock, 2007). Research on the offspring of monozygotic cotwins where only one twin developed schizophrenia found that the risk for the offspring of both twins was equal (Gottesman & Bertelson, 1989).

Twin studies have been undertaken for mood and anxiety disorders, too. With respect to bipolar psychotic mood disorders, the concordance rate for same-sex dizygotic twins is 23 percent, whereas the rate for monozygotic twins is 68 percent (Klerman, 1988). For anxiety disorder, the rate for dizygotic twins is 5 to 10 percent; for monozygotic twins, it is 30 to 40 percent (Andreasen, 1984). These rates indicate that genetics is a factor in anxiety and bipolar disorders and that its role in bipolar disorder is stronger than it is in anxiety disorders.

However illuminating these findings may be, they also raise questions about the social environment. If genetic factors were the only influence, the concordance rates between monozygotic twins would be 100 percent. Clearly other factors are involved. Twins share a similar prenatal environment; within the family, however, one of a pair of twins may be treated differently from the other (Rainer, 1985). Because it is difficult to separate the contributions of social, environmental, and genetic factors in the etiology of the disease, another approach has been used—adoption studies.

ADOPTION STUDIES Adoption studies may take a variety of forms. Some compare adopted children whose biological mothers are afflicted with a mental disorder with a control group of adopted children with normal parents; others compare children with and without a family history of a mental disorder with children raised by afflicted foster parents. The incidence of mental disorders among the children raised in different homes and the characteristics of parents are compared.

Studies of adoptees have been undertaken largely to determine the differential roles of genetics and environment in schizophrenia. Results indicate a higher prevalence of schizophrenia and schizophrenia spectrum disorders among children of schizophrenics than among controls (Rainer, 1985). Studies using the reverse strategy, that is, first identifying adopted adults with schizophrenia spectrum disorders and then interviewing relatives, have found an excess of schizophrenia and schizophrenia spectrum disorders among relatives (Kendler, 1988). The small number of adoption studies undertaken in relation to mood disorders has produced inconsistent results (Sadock & Sadock, 2007).

Overall, the twin and adoption studies suggest that genetics and the environment affect persons with schizophrenia, with genetics exercising a stronger effect. Kendler (1988) estimates that inheritance contributes between 60 and 70 percent to the variance in liability of schizophrenia, whereas environment contributes less than 20 percent. Nevertheless, these studies have their limitations. Controlled adoption studies require random assignment of children to adoptive homes, an ethical impossibility. Many of the adoption studies include different disorders under schizophrenia spectrum disorders, thus affecting the comparability between studies (Rainer, 1985). Moreover, family association does not mean that there are genetic markers for schizophrenia and related disorders. Genetic information can be more clearly acquired through molecular genetic studies.

MOLECULAR GENETIC STUDIES   The discovery of DNA (deoxyribonucleic acid, the substance of chromosomes) and technological developments in the field of molecular genetics have made it possible to study genetics more directly than the previously described methods. Now that the international Human Genome Project has met its goal of mapping the sequencing of genes of human organisms, hope lies in learning more about the contribution of genetics to psychiatric disorders.

Two strategies that molecular genetic researchers use are *linkage* and *association* studies. Linkage studies investigate DNA markers in families in which a number of individuals have a disease; association studies compare unrelated individuals who have the disease with controls (Craddock, 1996). These two strategies make it possible for scientists to map chromosomal regions of the disease genes and explore candidate genes within these areas (Craddock & Owen, 1996; Mowry, Nancarrow, & Levinson, 1997).

Although molecular genetics promises to identify abnormal proteins and genetic markers (Kaplan & Sadock, 1988), thus far the search for single genes responsible for specific mental disorders has not produced conclusive results. There are, however, promising genetic loci and candidate genes for schizophrenia and bipolar disorder, with the loci of several candidates for these two psychiatric disorders overlapping (Choudary & Knowles, 2008).

Psychiatric disorders are considered "complex" genetic disorders in that they do not follow Mendelian or sex-linked patterns (Choudary & Knowles, 2008). One explanation is that multiple genes that interact with each other and environmental factors are involved (Craddock, 1996; Moldin & Gottesman, 1997; Mowry et al., 1997). Also contributing to the complexity is the fact that some individuals with the disorder lack a genetic predisposition, whereas others with a genetic predisposition do not become ill (Choudary & Knowles, 2008).

It is anticipated that aggregated genetic information on psychiatric disorders will lend itself to more definitive findings in the future (Craddock & Owen, 1996). If abnormal genes are identified, new strategies of intervention will be necessary. These could include gene replacement therapy, new medication, and genetic counseling (Moldin & Gottesman, 1997). Furthermore, ethical issues around genetic testing and the social problem of genetic discrimination are likely to follow (Moldin & Gottesman, 1997). It is incumbent on social workers to be knowledgeable about genetic research findings and their implications for families, as social workers may be engaging in genetic counseling.

The Brain

Another direction of biological research has been on the brain. The brain is a complex organ that plays a central role in sensory, cognitive, perceptual, and emotional experiences and in information processing. Although it depends on oxygen and glucose to function, it cannot store either of these (Palfai & Jankiewicz, 1991). The brain is described as having three structures—the hindbrain, the midbrain, and the forebrain (Bentley & Walsh, 2006). From an evolutionary perspective, the *hindbrain* or "reptilian brain" is the oldest. It consists of the brain stem, the cerebellum, and the pons. The *brain stem* is responsible for maintaining automatic life support processes.

Behind the brain stem is the *cerebellum,* which coordinates the body's movement and receives information from joints and muscles. The *pons* connects parts of the brain with each other. The *midbrain* mediates hearing, seeing, and movement. The largest section, the *forebrain,* consists of the *hypothalamus,* the *limbic system,* and *thalamus,* which regulate biological functions, emotions and homeostasis, and sensory information, respectively (Bentley & Walsh, 2006).

The brain has also been described structurally as consisting of two hemispheres. The *left hemisphere* is responsible for language and analytic thinking, whereas the *right hemisphere* is the source of nonverbal, emotional, holistic thinking in right-handed individuals (Hedaya, 1996). Another way in which the brain structure has been viewed is in terms of *lobes,* each located in a different region of the brain, each with its own functions. The four lobes are as follows:

1. *frontal*   (in the front; responsible for self-awareness and decision making, motivation, regulation of emotional expression and motor behavior)
2. *parietal*   (above the ear; responsible for coordination of sensation and motor behavior, spatial orientation, recognition of people and objects)
3. *temporal*   (near the temples; responsible for memory formation, emotion, language comprehension, and learning)
4. *occipital*   (in the rear; responsible for vision, visual perception, and visual memory). (Hedaya, 1996; Sadock & Sadock, 2007)

An alternative way to think about the brain is in terms of anatomical (cf. structural) and functional systems, all of which interact with each other (Andreasen & Black, 2006). Among the former is the large *prefrontal system,* the part of the cerebral cortex that integrates information from different sources to facilitate decision making and planning, generates insight, and executes complex and novel behaviors (Andreasen & Black, 2006; Hedaya, 1996). These high-level cognitive activities are known as executive functions. Other anatomical systems are the *limbic,* which seems to play a role in assigning meaning to sensory information and memories (Sadock & Sadock, 2007), and the *basal ganglia* system, which regulates motor activity and the expression of cognition and emotion. The functional systems include memory, language, and attention, as well as the executive functions that are associated with the prefrontal system (Andreasen & Black, 2006).

The significance of these various systems emerged in research on individuals with brain impairment, such as aphasia, head injuries, and brain tumors. Associations have been made between the person's clinical presentation of self and the location of the structural damage (or lesion). In the past, the brains of persons with potential lesions could only be studied after death. Through modern technology, it is now possible to study the neurophysiology of living individuals.

Neuroimaging

A number of neuroimaging techniques are now used to obtain pictures of the brain. These techniques make it possible to determine if and where there are structural abnormalities and the parts of the brain in which mental activity takes place. Some techniques, such as the CT (computerized tomography) scan and the MRI (magnetic resonance imaging), are used to assess the *structure* of the brain. Other techniques, such as the fMR (functional magnetic resonance), the PET (positron emission tomography) scan, the SPECT (single photon emission computed tomography), and the MRS (magnetic resonance spectroscopy), show brain *functioning,* that is, where brain activity is taking place (where the blood flows) while the person performs cognitive and perceptual tasks.

Developments in neuroimaging have provided evidence of structural abnormalities in schizophrenia, dementia, anorexia nervosa, alcoholism, and some mood disorders (Andreasen, 2001).

Although neuroimaging cannot be used for screening or to make definitive diagnoses, it does contribute to research knowledge and is helpful in tracking changes in individuals over time (Andreasen, 2001). Neuroimaging can also be used to observe the activity of neurotransmitters, which have become important in understanding the action of psychopharmacological agents used to treat mental disorders. We turn next to neurons and neurotransmitters.

Neurons and Neurotransmitters

Neurons are nerve cells that receive and transmit messages or signals from and to other neurons. The signals that they process within themselves are electrical, but those that they transmit are chemical (Hedaya, 1996).

The neuron has a number of parts. The *cell body* is its interior, which is composed of fatty material, the nucleus, and protein synthetic material. The *cell nucleus* contains the cell's DNA and plays an important role in the cell's growth and activities. The cell is covered with a *cell membrane.* Jutting out from the cell body are numerous branchlike extensions called *dendrites,* which receive signals from other neurons and transmit them to the cell body. Another extension of the cell body is the *axon,* which transmits electrical signals from this neuron to others. Axons vary in length; some extend a few feet. Normally axons are covered with a fatty *myelin sheath,* which protects it, and *nodes* (or openings) that facilitate the transmission of signals. At the end of the axon are one or more *presynaptic terminals,* where *synaptic vesicles* are located. *Neurotransmitters,* chemicals produced by the neuron, are released (or fired) from these vesicles into the *synapse* where they interact and bind with dendrites from other neurons. Whatever chemical neurotransmitters are not taken by the other neuron is taken back by the initial cell by a "reuptake pump" (Hedaya, 1996).

There are numerous types of neurotransmitters produced by neurons. Among those that are most relevant to the study of mental disorders are dopamine, norepinephrine, serotonin, and GABA (gamma-aminobutyric acid). Dopamine seems to play a role in the production of psychoses; norepinephrine is related to mood disorders; serotonin is connected with depression, schizophrenia, and other psychoses; and GABA may be related to anxiety (Andreasen & Black, 2006). Psychopharmacological agents regulate the release of neurotransmitters by slowing, activating, blocking, and reversing the production process (Andreasen & Black, 2006; Hedaya, 1996).

Psychopharmacology

The development of pharmacological agents that reduce disturbing symptoms has resulted in important changes in the understanding and treatment of persons with psychiatric problems. With the improvement of these treatments, individuals have been able to obtain symptomatic relief and improve their psychosocial functioning.

The discovery in the middle of the twentieth century of the effectiveness of chlorpromazine (Thorazine) in tranquilizing and reducing psychotic symptoms of schizophrenia was a major scientific breakthrough. This was followed by the development of other *neuroleptic* (antipsychotic) drugs and an increased understanding of brain functioning. Although these drugs reduced the prominence of psychotic symptoms, they did have deleterious side effects and did not address negative symptoms such as apathy. As Chapter 12 will explain, second-generation antipsychotics such as risperdal (Risperidone) and clozapine (Clozaril) have remedied some of the deficiencies of the earlier drugs.

Medications for mood disorders have also been introduced and refined. During the late 1940s, Cade discovered that lithium carbonate could control manic symptoms in bipolar disorder.

Although this drug was not tested in the United States until the late 1950s and 1960s (Fieve, 1975), lithium soon became a major drug prescribed for bipolar and related mood disorders. Today other mood stabilizers are prescribed as an alternative to or in conjunction with lithium. Additional pharmacological agents that treat depression have also been used with success. At first the older drugs, heterocyclic antidepressants and monoamine oxidase inhibitors, were routinely used, but like the older neuroleptics, they had troublesome side effects. Today, selective serotonin reuptake inhibitors (SSRIs) and atypical antidepressants are prominent. Some of the antidepressant agents are also effective in treating anxiety. Medication used to treat depression will be discussed in Chapter 8, anxiety in Chapter 9, and schizophrenia and bipolar disorder in Chapter 12.

Although medication can treat symptoms, it does not eliminate the psychosocial problems of individuals who take the medication, clients' feelings about being dependent on drugs, or the side effects of the drugs. Medications such as neuroleptics do not cure the disease and only partially eliminate symptoms. Some prescribed drugs, especially those that treat anxiety and sleep disorders, are addictive. Some medications affect sexual potency or desire.

Even though social workers do not prescribe medication, they work with clients who receive or need psychopharmacotherapy. Social workers have become increasingly aware of their need to be knowledgeable about psychotropic drugs, their expected effects, and their deleterious side effects (Bentley & Walsh, 2006). Often social workers refer clients to psychiatrists for an evaluation for medication. For those clients who are already on medication, social workers are able to observe the extent to which medications are working, client adherence, potential interactions with other substances, and other complications. Social workers should be able to recognize physical, psychological, and social side effects of drugs and work with the client and others involved in the client's care (Bentley & Walsh, 2006). Psychosocial interventions, based on psychosocial knowledge, are often implemented in conjunction with medication.

PSYCHOLOGICAL AND PSYCHOSOCIAL KNOWLEDGE: THEORIES, FRAMEWORKS, AND THERAPIES

Just as it is difficult to separate the biological from the psychological and social, it is also problematical to separate the psychological from the social. Psychological theories provide explanations for the inner workings of the mind, that is, the underlying motivations that drive human behavior. Because these explanations often involve socially valued goals (e.g., love), social interactions, and transactions with the environment, the psychological and social are interrelated. This section will discuss two theories that are primarily psychological but also have social dimensions—ego psychology and cognitive theory. Both provide frameworks for understanding normal and psychopathological behavior. Next behavioral theory and therapy will be discussed. This will be followed by interactional perspectives. This section will begin with ego psychology.

Ego Psychology

Ego psychology is a reconstruction of Freud's psychoanalytic theory, particularly his structural theory. Initially developed by Hartmann (1958) and his colleagues (Kris and Loewenstein), it has been enriched by the writings of Anna Freud (1946), Erikson (1950, 1959), and White (1959), as well as object relations theorists. Its departures from classical, doctrinaire psychoanalysis (especially the drive theory and psychic determinism) and its emphasis on the reciprocal relationship between the person and the environment make ego psychology particularly compatible with social work.

In psychoanalysis and ego psychology, three hypothetical structures—the ego, id, and superego—comprise the psychic system. The id represents impulses, desires, and wishes that know no boundaries; the superego encompasses the conscience and ego ideal; and the ego is responsible for perception, reality testing, and mediation. In ego psychology, the ego is vested with more independence than it had in classical psychoanalysis. In psychoanalysis, the ego derives from the id and attempts to achieve the aims of the id in realistic ways. In ego psychology, both ego and id arise from an undifferentiated matrix that is present at birth; ego and id become differentiated from this matrix and develop separately and in concert with each other. The ego develops apparatuses of primary autonomy, inborn capacities for perception, intelligence, thinking, motility, and the like, which can develop outside psychic conflict. In addition, the ego develops apparatuses of secondary autonomy, defenses that are associated with conflict early in life that are later transformed through a process change of function to interests, goals, and preferences. With the expansion and increased autonomy of ego functions in ego psychology, the ego has come to be viewed as more than a mediator among the three parts of the psychic system and between the psyche and the external reality. The ego in ego psychology organizes, forms object relations, and promotes adaptation (Blanck & Blanck, 1974, 1979; Hartmann, 1958).

Adaptation refers to the capacity to achieve a state of equilibrium with the environment. It includes the ability to survive, respond, make one's needs known to others, and solve problems. An active process, it depends partially on the possession of biological equipment and partially on the capacity of the environment to respond. According to Hartmann (1958), people are born with a capacity to adapt to an "average expectable environment," that is, an environment that is safe, provides food and warmth, and is reasonably nurturing. A child cannot be expected to cope with an abusive environment. Hartmann also posits that there is a reciprocal relationship between the person and the environment. Strengths and deficits in the person and the environment affect each other.

Ego psychology builds on, reinterprets, and makes modifications of Freud's drive theory. Freud postulated that there are two primary drives that motivate human behavior—libido and aggression. Blanck and Blanck (1979) assert that these drives should be distinguished from affects; that is, libido and love are not equivalent, nor are aggression and hostility. On the basis of Freud's later work, Blanck and Blanck conclude that libido refers to the drive to unite or bond with others and that aggression refers to undoing connections (and, consequently, destroying them). This interpretation permits aggression to include the separation-individuation process, which was described by Mahler, Pine, and Bergman (1975). The two drives, as revised, are complementary rather than polar opposites. Like the ego and id, they are innate capacities latent in the undifferentiated matrix. In early life, the libido is dominant, fostering the development of object relations. Soon the drive to be separate and individuated becomes dominant. But both drives coexist and function in concert with each other (Blanck & Blanck, 1979).

Building on the ideas of Hartmann and other ego psychologists, White (1959) postulated that there is a source of motivation for human behavior that does not emanate from the two drives. Rather than seeking tension reduction, as Freud proposed, the ego is motivated by the desire for competence that is exemplified in exploration, manipulating objects, and mastery—activities that are pursued for its own sake. He stated further that participation in activities such as these may, in fact, increase tension rather than reduce it. Competence motivation, which is associated with the ego, engages the person with the environment. White came up with the term, *effectance,* to capture the feeling of efficacy (having an impact on the environment), which comes from the exercise of competence. He suggested that independent ego energies provide fuel for effectance. The emphasis on mastery of the environment through effective activity (i.e., coping) is an important contribution to ego theory.

Ego psychology also includes a *developmental perspective*. It acknowledges that early life experiences, such as losses and other traumatic events, can impede healthy development. On the other hand, it recognizes Erikson's (1950, 1959) contribution that human growth is a continuous activity that occurs throughout the life span. Although his eight developmental stages are presented as polar opposites *(trust versus mistrust, autonomy versus shame and doubt, initiative versus guilt, industry versus inferiority, identity versus identity diffusion, intimacy versus isolation, generativity versus stagnation*, and *integrity versus despair)*, Erikson viewed each stage on a continuum and considered all stages to exist in some form concurrently. In this book, we focus on young, middle-aged, and older adults, who normatively are at the last three stages but vary in their development.

Ego psychology has also been enriched by the contributions of neoanalytic and object relations theorists in the United States and England who are interested in childhood development. Although there is considerable diversity among individual thinkers, they share an emphasis on the development of object relations. Objects are persons, the self and others, who take on a life of their own as structures that are introjected within the psyche. The infant develops into a social human being in the context of social interactions with significant others. Through an emotionally charged interpersonal relational process, the ego incorporates representations of the self and significant others into the self. At first infants fuse with their principal caregivers. In time and with some ambivalence, they become aware of differences and they become more independent. As they develop, they form mental images (internalized representations) of themselves and others, which allow them to carry significant others and others' images of themselves with them as they become separate. Successful negotiation of early developmental stages promotes the formation of permanent, stable personality structures (Blanck & Blanck, 1986).

The cumulative contributions of ego psychologists and object relations theorists make it possible to obtain a more expansive view of the role of the ego in adaptive functioning. The ego promotes personality organization and object relations (Blanck & Blanck, 1979, 1986). It regulates internal processes, links the person with the environment, and promotes mastery. The ego helps the individual distinguish between internal and external demands, control impulses, and develop interpersonal relationships. It fosters growth throughout the life cycle through a process of bonding (libido) and separation-individuation. The defense mechanisms described by Anna Freud (1946) and others are also associated with the ego.

THE THERAPEUTIC RELATIONSHIP IN EGO PSYCHOLOGY   The psychoanalytic school—which includes ego psychology, neoanalytic, and object relations theory, as well as feminist theory within this framework—has made a tremendous contribution to understanding the therapeutic relationship. This relationship provides a context in which a client can receive nurturance and acceptance that he or she may not have had as a child. The process of working through issues from the past that are transferred to the therapist makes it possible for clients to correct distortions in the structure of their personalities and develop more realistic relationships with others. As described in feminist theory that has emerged from the Stone Center, relationships are central to personal growth and self-realization (Jordan, 1997a). Empathetic understanding from a clinician can reduce a client's isolation and promote his or her feelings of connectedness (Jordan, 1997b). Although many managed care plans restrict the time period in which relationship issues can be worked through, the quality of the therapeutic relationship (or alliance) remains important.

EGO PSYCHOLOGICAL TREATMENT   Ego psychology is implemented in the context of a therapeutic relationship in which the social worker conveys empathy, acceptance, and support. The therapist serves as an auxiliary ego to the client. Goldstein (1995) describes two types of ego psychological treatment: ego supportive and ego modifying. The ego-supportive approach aims to help the client adapt or achieve mastery over an immediate problem, crisis, or stressful situation. Intervention focuses on a current situation and engages the client's conscious thoughts and feelings. Change is directed at the person, the environment, and/or the interaction between the person and the environment. The therapist works with the existing and latent strengths of the client's ego and builds on these. Through understanding, reflecting on, and utilizing these capacities, the client comes to resolve an immediate problem and attain a sense of satisfaction in utilizing internal capacities and external supports. Ego-supportive treatment may be brief or long term.

The ego-modifying strategy emphasizes the development of insight and the resolution of intrapsychic conflict. Accordingly, past historical material is utilized and the transference that arises in the therapeutic relationship is interpreted. The client is engaged in a process of self-disclosure, uncovering, and working through recurrent maladaptive patterns. Generally ego-modifying treatment is long term and appropriate only for certain clients. Goldstein (1995) recommends this strategy primarily for clients with good ego strengths but some maladaptive patterns and says that it can be used selectively with clients with more severe pathology. For the client who has developmental deficits that interfere with object constancy, the social worker becomes an object for the client and facilitates the development of object constancy. Ego psychological concepts, however, are difficult to operationalize, resulting in more limited evidence of effectiveness of ego psychological intervention compared with cognitive and cognitive-behavioral theory and therapy.

Cognitive and Cognitive-Behavioral Theory and Therapy

Cognitive theory focuses on thinking, beliefs, interpretations, and images. Associated with diverse theorists, most hold that emotional reactions and maladaptive behavior are mediated by thoughts. Cognitive theory has been intellectually traced to the Greek stoic philosophers (Beck, 1985). Beck credits his formulation to the cognitive revolution in psychology and the writings of George Kelly (1963) and Albert Ellis (Beck, 2005). Today a cognitive perspective, from which many evidence-based treatments emanate, is used by therapists of diverse disciplines. It is common for therapists to integrate behavioral methods, to be discussed in the next section, within cognitive therapy, that is, CBT.

Cognitive theories have introduced a number of concepts that guide understanding. One is the term *scheme* or *schema*, which refers to the individual's units of thought or mental constructs that provide rules for sorting through and coding information from environment (Wright, Thase, & Beck, 2008). These may be adaptive or maladaptive. For example, a person may have a positive scheme about his or her friends ("they care about me") or a maladaptive one ("they do not care enough about me"). Another term used in cognitive theory is *automatic thoughts* (Beck, 1976). These are messages one gives oneself, often in a telegraphic form, which precede an experience of emotional arousal. The messages may be instructional, interpretive, self-praising, or self-critical. Persons experiencing depression, for example, may have thoughts about their own worthlessness; those with anxiety may think about unrealistic dangers that lurk in the environment. Automatic thoughts are evident in verbal self-statements and mental images. According to Beck (1976), automatic thoughts influence emotions and behavior.

Albert Ellis (1913–2007) and Aaron Beck (1921–) are considered founders of cognitive therapy . Ellis developed a therapy called *rational emotive therapy* (RET) and later refined it as *rational emotive behavioral therapy* (REBT). He holds that irrational beliefs (B), aroused by activating events (A), are responsible for the development of neurotic symptoms or dysfunctional behaviors (C). Beliefs that engender these consequences are generally grandiose, narcissistic, and unrealistic, such as the ideas that one must be loved by all people one considers significant; that one must be thoroughly competent; and that when one gets frustrated, the situation in which one finds oneself is awful (Ellis & Harper, 1975). These beliefs have an exaggerated quality and often use the words *should* and *must*. Irrational beliefs represent logical fallacies in which one misconstrues oneself, others, and situations.

Ellis recognized that behaviors, beliefs, and emotions are related. By changing irrational beliefs through a course of therapy, dysfunctional emotions and behaviors dissipate and are replaced by constructive ones. Therapy consists of identifying irrational ideas, refuting them through logical argument, and replacing irrational with rational self-talk. RET is didactic and experiential. It utilizes homework assignments, role play, practice exercises, and imagery. Generally it is short term and concerned with conscious, current experiences (Ellis, 1979).

Beck's cognitive theory and therapy are similar to Ellis's. Beck (1976, 1985) asserts that automatic thoughts trigger emotions (anxiety, sadness, anger, affection) and behavior (flight, withdrawal, attack, approach). Characteristic of normal and psychopathological reactions, automatic thoughts can become so distorted that they result in dysfunctional responses. These thoughts are endowed with meaning that is idiosyncratic to the individual and specific to the psychopathological syndrome.

Beck (1985) identified several cognitive errors made by depressed and anxious people. One, called *selective abstraction,* is a generalization that accounts for only one aspect of a situation, while at the same time other components of the situation are ignored (e.g., "I am a bad mother because my child got a C"). This is similar to another error, *overgeneralization,* in which an inference resting on one experience is applied to all like situations ("I can't do anything right"). Another logical error is *arbitrary inference.* Here an inaccurate conclusion is drawn from a neutral experience (e.g., "Jack is avoiding me" when Jack, in fact, did not see anyone). With *personalization*, one endows events with meaning related to oneself. In this case, others' statements or affective responses ("mother looks perturbed") are viewed as causally related to one's own behavior ("I hurt her feelings"). Another cognitive error is *dichotomous* (or *polarized*) *thinking.* Here the individual perceives only two contrasting and extreme alternatives—a phenomenon that is often described as tunnel vision. With *magnification* or *minimization*, one exaggerates the difficulty of a task or underestimates one's ability to accomplish it.

Depressed persons make cognitive errors to support negative pictures of themselves, their experiences, and the outlook for the future—three dimensions that Beck (1985) describes as the *cognitive triad.* They may, for example, generalize from a single experience (e.g., "I was turned down for a job") to prospects in the distant future ("no one will ever hire me"). They see themselves as totally worthless and attribute others' neutral actions as indicators of their low evaluation of themselves. Anxious persons err in their interpretation of signals of danger. Accordingly, they become apprehensive in situations that are objectively safe. Thoughts focus on an anticipated catastrophe, such as death, losing control, or failure.

In Beck's treatment model, the therapist and client are viewed as partners. The therapist conveys warmth, acceptance, and understanding. Educating the client about cognitive therapy, Beck's therapist conveys to the client an understanding that his or her belief system is related to the problem and shows clients how they can make changes in their thinking and behavior. Together they develop hypotheses about the soundness of the client's schemas and automatic thoughts, a process known as "collaborative empiricism" (Wright et al., 2008).

Cognitive treatment is generally short term, present-oriented, and structured (Wright et al., 2008). The client and therapist collaboratively set an agenda and prioritize the issues they will deal with in the session. The process usually proceeds with helping the client identify automatic thoughts (Beck, 1985). The client may be asked to describe a stressful situation to recognize the thought that precipitated it, or to keep a diary of fleeting thoughts. After the thoughts are identified, the cognitive errors underlying the thoughts are discussed. Distortions in thinking are identified and alternative explanations are proposed. This process, *reattribution training,* opens up alternative ways of thinking (schemes) to the client. Next cognitive distortions, such as overgeneralizations, are subjected to an empirical test in the outside world (Beck, 1985). The client is given the task of testing false expectations (e.g., "no one wants to talk to me") by initiating new activities (e.g., talking to a number of people and documenting their responses). These exercises may be rehearsed in advance and are discussed after they are performed. Afterward the client's distortions are reexamined in light of empirical findings. Other techniques that are used include Socratic questioning, imagery exercises, generating alternatives, listing of advantages and disadvantages, and the charting of events, automatic thoughts, emotional responses, and alternative rational responses and outcomes (Wright et al., 2008). Quantitative measures are used to monitor the client's level of stress during the course of treatment (Beck, 1985).

Cognitive therapy has been shown to be effective in modifying the thoughts and behaviors of individuals with anxiety disorders and depression and has had some success in the treatment of eating disorders, personality disorders, suicidal behavior, and schizophrenia and bipolar disorder (Beck, 2005; Wright et al., 2008). Table 3.2 shows how cognitive therapy is applied to various symptoms. In this volume, special attention will be given to Beck's method of treating depression (see Chapter 8).

Aside from Ellis's and Beck's models, there are several other cognitive and cognitive-behavioral-related therapeutic approaches. Among these are constructivist, coping skills therapies, and problem-solving therapy (Dobson, Backs-Dermott, & Dozois, 2000). We turn to problem-solving therapy next.

PROBLEM-SOLVING THERAPY Problem-solving therapy (PST) is an evidenced-based, cognitive-behavioral-derived treatment, based on studies demonstrating a strong link between social problem solving (SPS) and psychological distress (Nezu, 2004). The main treatment goal of PST is to foster adoption and implementation of adaptive positive problem-solving attitudes and

TABLE 3.2 Application of Cognitive Therapies

Concepts	Targeted Symptoms	Techniques
Schemes	Depression	Identify irrational ideas
Automatic thoughts	Anxiety	or automatic thoughts
Appraisal	Phobias	Refutation
Attributions	Obsessions	Reattribution training
Cognitive errors	Compulsions	Empirical testing
	Substance abuse	Charting
	Personality disorders	Imagery
	Eating disorders	Listing advantages and disadvantages
		Generating alternatives

Sources: Based on Bandura (1982); Beck (1976, 1985); Ellis (1979); Lazarus & Folkman (1984); Wright et al. (2009).

behaviors as a means of decreasing emotional distress and improving one's overall quality of life (D'Zurilla & Nezu, 2007). Originally developed by D'Zurilla and Goldfried (1971), Nezu and his colleagues (Nezu, 1987; Nezu, Nezu, & Perri, 1989) revised and adapted PST for the treatment of major depression in adults. Early work by Nezu and colleagues (e.g., Nezu, 1986; Nezu et al., 1989) established PST as an effective approach for the treatment of major depressive disorder (MDD).

Problem-solving therapy has also been tested as an intervention for substance abuse, smoking addiction, anxiety disorders, and the seriously mentally ill population. Several early studies have examined the efficacy of PST for substance abuse, specifically, adult alcoholic inpatients, with demonstrated superior outcomes in comparison with standard substance abuse care (Chaney, O'Leary, & Marlatt, 1978; Intagliata, 1978). In a different study, the addition of PST to a standard behavioral intervention to reduce smoking demonstrated superior effects compared with behavioral intervention alone (Karol & Richards, 1978). There has been little attention in the use of PST for anxiety-related disorders. However, early research has demonstrated some evidence for anxiety disorders, specifically for agoraphobia and social phobia (DiGiuseppe, Simon, McGowan, & Gardner, 1990; Jannoun, Munby, Catalan, & Gelder, 1980). Research on PST with the seriously mentally ill has found robust evidence for the superiority of PST to various attention-placebo control conditions (Coche, Cooper, & Petermann, 1984; Coche & Flick, 1975; Medalia, Revheim, & Casey, 2001), although one study did not find any treatment differences between PST and coping skills training (Bradshaw, 1993).

Empirical work has found PST to be effective for the treatment of minor depressive disorder in community-based home health care settings (Gellis et al., 2008) and MDD in primary care settings (e.g., Mynors-Wallis, Gath, Day, & Baker, 2000), as well as for individuals suffering from a medical illness such as cancer (e.g., Nezu, Nezu, Felgoise, McClure, & Houts, 2003), heart disease (Gellis & Bruce, 2010), and diabetes (e.g., Williams et al., 2004) that are concomitant with clinical depression. In fact, three recent systematic reviews provide significant quantitative support for the efficacy of this approach for reducing depression (Bell & D'Zurilla, 2009; Cuijpers, van Straten, & Warmerdam, 2007; Gellis & Kenaley, 2008). PST has also been adapted to treat depression among community-based older adults (Areán et al., 1993; Gellis, McGinty, Horowitz, Bruce, & Misener, 2007), including depressed elderly patients with executive functioning difficulties (Alexopoulus, Raue, & Areán, 2003).

Problem-solving therapy helps to reduce depression by increasing an individual's optimism, self-efficacy, and skill levels in effectively coping with stressful problems. In addition, it focuses on a more realistic (as compared to catastrophic) appraisal and evaluation of specific daily living problems linked to depression, as well as developing and choosing the best-possible solution alternatives and implementing action plans to solve these problems. PST can also address anhedonia (inability to experience pleasure) and psychomotor retardation (slow physical and mental responsiveness), common symptoms of depression through increased exposure to daily pleasurable activities (behavioral activation) by the individual. Scheduling and implementation of daily pleasurable activities can be used as a pathway to problem-solving strategies and skills. Thus, PST is conceptually relevant for depression treatment due to its robust evidence base (Cuijpers, van Straten, & Smit, 2006; Gellis & Kenaley, 2008).

Problem-solving conceptual framework.   PST for depression is based on a model of depression that characterizes SPS as serving both mediating (e.g., Kant, D'Zurilla, & Maydeu-Olivares, 1997) and moderating (e.g., Nezu, Nezu, Saraydarian, Kalmar, & Ronan, 1986; Nezu & Ronan, 1985) roles regarding the relationship between stressful life events and depression. SPS is the multidimensional psychosocial factor that has been repeatedly identified as an important feature in the pathway of both mental health and health problems resulting from poor adjustment to stress (Nezu, 2004). More specifically, SPS has been defined as the cognitive-behavioral process by which a person attempts to identify or discover effective or adaptive means of coping with stressful problems encountered during everyday living (D'Zurilla & Nezu, 2007). In this context, it involves the process whereby individuals attempt to direct their coping efforts at altering the problematic nature of a stressful situation itself, their reactions to such situations, or both. SPS refers more to the meta-process of understanding, appraising, and adapting to stressful life events, such as those related to the experience of a chronic illness, rather than representing a singular coping strategy or activity (D'Zurilla & Nezu, 2007).

Contemporary models of problem solving indicate that it is composed of two general, but partially, independent processes—(a) problem orientation and (b) problem-solving style (D'Zurilla, Nezu, & Maydeu-Olivares, 2004). *Problem orientation* involves the set of generalized appraisals and emotional reactions concerning problems in living, as well as one's ability to successfully resolve them. It can either be *positive* (e.g., viewing problems as opportunities to benefit in some way; perceiving oneself as able to solve problems effectively), which serves to enhance subsequent problem-solving efforts, or *negative* (e.g., viewing problems as a major threat to one's well-being; overreacting emotionally when problems occur), which functions to inhibit attempts to solve problems. Problem-solving style will be discussed next.

Problem-solving style. A key concept in PST is the process in which individuals attempt to solve their daily problems. *Problem-solving style* refers to specific cognitive-behavioral activities aimed at coping with stressful daily living problems. Two overarching types of problem-solving styles are derived from problem-solving theory. These activities can be either adaptive, leading to successful problem resolution, or dysfunctional, leading to negative consequences, such as emotional distress and depressive symptoms. Individuals use different kinds of problem-solving styles. *Rational problem solving* is the practical style aimed at identifying a realistic and effective solution to the problem and involves the systematic application of various specific problem-solving tasks. These tasks include accurately identifying obstacles that need to be overcome to achieve reasonable goals, generating alternative solutions to cope with such difficult problems, making effective decisions regarding which coping strategies to engage in, and monitoring the consequences of one's coping attempts to determine the need to engage in additional problem solving. *Dysfunctional problem-solving* styles include (a) *impulsivity/carelessness* (i.e., the tendency to engage in impulsive, hurried, and/or incomplete attempts to solve a problem) and (b) *avoidance* (i.e., the tendency to circumvent problems, procrastinate, and/or depend on others to solve one's problems).

This problem-solving conceptualization suggests that symptoms of depression can result from deficiencies, or decreased effectiveness, in these problem orientation and problem-solving style dimensions (Nezu, 1987, 2004). For example, depressed individuals are often characterized by a strong negative orientation, having little faith in their ability to cope with stressful problems, frequently blaming themselves for causing the problem, often believing that problems are catastrophes, and becoming distressed when problems occur. Collectively, negative beliefs decrease one's desire or motivation to engage in any meaningful coping attempts. One's ability to effectively define and formulate problems and to set realistic goals is also decreased when depressed, thus, making it very difficult to identify effective solutions. Often depressed individuals set unrealistically high goals, and when they are not achieved, self-blame, frustration, and decreased motivation are likely to occur. Depressed individuals also tend to generate both fewer and less effective alternatives to problem situations. A negative problem orientation and lack of alternatives biases the depressed person to selectively attend to negative versus positive events and to immediate versus long-term consequences. The depressed individual may also have difficulty actually carrying out his or her plan due to specific behavioral and social skill deficits. Further, a negative problem orientation may impact on an individual's ability to be objective about the outcome of solution implementation. Thus, the depressed individual is unsatisfied with the coping attempt and may feel that the goals have not been achieved. In addition, poor problem solving has been found to be related to feelings of hopelessness and suicidal intent (D'Zurilla, Chang, Nottingham, & Faccini, 1998).

Problem-solving therapy, then, is geared to teach adults specific skills to (a) enhance their positive problem orientation, (b) decrease their negative orientation, (c) improve their rational problem-solving ability, (d) decrease their tendency to be avoidant, and (e) minimize their tendency to be impulsive and careless when attempting to cope with stressful problems in daily living. The PST model specifically targets the skills of solving daily living problems. Through modeling and reinforcement of cognitive and behavioral skills, PST can also increase the individual's sense of self-efficacy in taking responsibility for day-to-day management of their problems. Improved problem-solving and coping skills along with resulting self-efficacy are potential active components thus likely to buffer against the effect of risk factors on depression disorders (Gellis et al., 2007). The PST model described here will be expanded upon in Chapter 8 in relation to treatment of depression. Problem solving is also an important component of two evidence-based practices, the Illness Management and Recovery Model and McFarlane's Psychoeducational Multifamily Group approach, both of which are described in Chapter 12.

Behavioral Theories and Therapies

Whereas ego psychology and cognitive theory have to do largely with the inner life, behavior theory focuses on what can be observed. Behavioral theories are concerned with events or conditions that surround behaviors. An underlying assumption is that regardless of whether behaviors are adaptive or maladaptive, they are learned. Through an understanding of scientific principles of learning, one can implement procedures that extinguish, maintain, or modify existing behaviors and foster the development of new ones.

Behavioral theories are empirically grounded. Originally based on animal research, they have been carefully applied to and researched in relation to human individuals and groups. Behavioral therapies employ rigorous scientific procedures in the assessment process, during implementation, and in evaluation. In each case, specific, observed, problematic behaviors are identified, and changes are implemented, monitored, and measured.

Within the behavioral school, there are three major approaches, each of which has contributed to an understanding of the person in relation to the environment and to therapeutic approaches. These are respondent (classical) conditioning, operant (instrumental) conditioning, and social learning theory. Although these schools emerged sequentially, in practice their boundaries have come to be blurred. As mentioned earlier, some behavioral therapies are informed by and integrated with the cognitive perspective.

RESPONDENT CONDITIONING   *Respondent conditioning* was the earliest of the behavioral theories to appear. Also called *classical conditioning* and *stimulus-response* (S-R) theory, it was discovered by the Russian physiologist, Ivan Pavlov, who, in the course of his work with dogs, noticed that the dogs produced saliva automatically when they were given meat, a reaction he called an *unconditioned reflex.* He also observed that salivation occurred in response to a bell that had been previously presented together with the meat but was later presented alone. Pavlov concluded that the bell, a neutral stimulus, acquired the capacity of the meat, a natural stimulus, to evoke the response after the two were paired together a few times. Pavlov called the meat an *unconditioned stimulus* (US) and the salivation an *unconditioned response* (UR) and determined that these were connected through a biological, reflexive process. He described the bell as a *conditioned stimulus* (CS) and the saliva produced by the bell alone a *conditioned response* (CR) and concluded that these became connected through a process of pairing or association (Chance, 1979).

Three therapeutic procedures are based on respondent conditioning. One, *extinction,* is based on Pavlov's discovery that a conditioned response could be eliminated. If the conditioned stimulus is presented repeatedly without the unconditioned stimulus, the association between conditioned and unconditioned stimuli weakens. The result is *extinction.* The principle of extinction is used to eliminate undesirable behaviors. Another therapeutic technique that is based on principles of respondent conditioning is *systematic desensitization.* Developed by Wolpe (1982), systematic desensitization pairs an unconditioned stimulus, such as relaxation exercises, with a conditioned stimulus (e.g., a mental image of a situation about which one is phobic). A client who begins the session with relaxation exercises is presented with a hierarchy of situations, from the least anxiety provoking to the most, to imagine. The client participates in this exercise up to the point of experiencing anxiety. In subsequent sessions, the client proceeds through the hierarchy of situations, increasing tolerance along the way. Subsequently the client applies this to real-life situations, relaxing in advance and proceeding in small steps. Systematic desensitization is based on the principle of *reciprocal inhibition* (Wolpe, 1982). By pairing relaxation, an inhibiting stimulus, with mental images of situations producing a phobia, the bond between the phobic situation and the anxiety loosens. A related therapeutic technique, *exposure,* involves repeatedly facing the anxiety-generating situation through guided imagery or in vivo (Angell, 2008).

OPERANT CONDITIONING With *operant conditioning,* the emphasis is on the *consequences* (or what follows) behavior, that is, the *reinforcement.* Also called *instrumental conditioning,* it is associated with B. F. Skinner. Skinner's theory is considered radical behaviorism because its attention to environmental contingencies minimizes the role of cognitive processes (Maddi, 1980).

According to operant conditioning, a behavior is strengthened (i.e., it is likely to recur) when it is followed by a reinforcement (Salkind, 1985). The reinforcement may be a reward or some action, consequence, or occurrence that increases the likelihood that the previous behavior will recur. *Positive reinforcements* are actions, stimuli, or consequences that follow the occurrence of a behavior, and which usually result in increased satisfaction. These may be primary (of biological importance, such as food) or secondary (of acquired value, such as a gold star). *Negative reinforcements* are consequences that allow one to escape or avoid an unpleasant situation (Salkind, 1985). Regardless of whether the reinforcements are positive or negative, they promote the continuance of the preceding behavior.

Punishment is also used in operant conditioning (Crain, 1992). Punishment is an unpleasant or aversive consequence that results in decreasing a behavior. Punishments may be positive (add an unpleasant experience) or negative (something desired is taken away). Spanking, losing privileges, and having to pay fines are examples of punishments. Punishments (as well as reinforcements) should be tailored to the individual. Sometimes what may appear to be a punishment (e.g., yelling at someone) becomes a reinforcement (increased attention).

A variety of behavior modification techniques can be used to create desirable behaviors as well as extinguish undesirable ones. *Shaping* consists of progressively reinforcing behaviors as they come closer and closer to what is desired (Crain, 1992). At first behaviors that are in the ballpark of the desired behavior are reinforced (e.g., a child's sound "mm"). Later behaviors that more closely resemble what is desired (e.g., "mum") are reinforced until the desired outcome is achieved (e.g., "mama"). Persons with phobias can eliminate fears by gradually approaching the object feared. Close approximations are reinforced. Another technique that is used is *time-out*. A kind of negative punishment, it is implemented by removing an individual from a pleasant situation to an unpleasant one. A third approach is the *token economy*. Tokens are items such as chips that can be traded in for products or privileges. Some residential and community programs utilize this mechanism. Clients are able to earn tokens for desirable behaviors but can lose them when they violate rules. This way, clients can work toward goals that they choose and learn the consequences of not abiding by rules of the program.

SOCIAL LEARNING THEORY   *Social learning theory* is a theory in which observational learning is emphasized. Associated with Rotter (1954) and Bandura (1977), it also uses principles of classical and operant conditioning. Because of its recognition of mental processes that mediate between behaviors that are observed and those that are performed, social learning theory may be considered a cognitive-behavioral theory.

According to social learning theory, behavior is acquired by observing other persons or events. Observers can learn or acquire new behaviors by watching, listening to, or reading about models. Observation encompasses the process (what models do, how they perform) and the consequences (rewards or punishments provided to the model or observer) that are perceived to occur. Inferences are made about what can be anticipated *(expectancy)* and rules that guide the model's behavior *(abstract modeling)* (Bandura, 1977). Observers develop inner symbolic representations of what they have seen and match their own behaviors with these.

Social learning theory is guided by the principle of *reciprocal determinism* (Bandura, 1978). Accordingly there is a three-way interaction among the behavior, the external environment, and internal events (including cognition). The environment affects the individual's behavior through the mediation of cognition; the individual's behavior and cognition in turn affect the environment.

Behavioral change, maintenance, or control can occur through the use of reinforcements, punishment, and self-regulation. Reinforcements and punishments can be applied to the participant or observer or to oneself. Individuals can regulate their own behaviors by observing and assessing their own behaviors and cognitions and by responding and correcting their own behaviors. Through self-regulation, the self (through its cognitive faculties) takes on the function of the environment of providing rewards and punishments (Lundin, 1983). The self develops a feeling of *self-efficacy,* or competence (Bandura, 1982).

Clinical social workers can use principles of social learning theory in their practice with clients by modeling prosocial behaviors for clients with asocial or antisocial tendencies. In working with clients diagnosed with schizophrenia who may have difficulty in social relationships, social workers can teach positive skills in an incremental fashion. Social workers can model for the client the desired behavior first, and then have clients practice and perform what was observed in a safe environment and then try the skill in the community where they live. Similarly social workers can demonstrate the performance of other social skills, assume the client's role in role plays, and otherwise model desirable behaviors. Social skills training that includes modeling is integrated into the evidence-based Illness Management and Recovery program that is described in Chapter 12. Table 3.3 portrays the various behavioral therapies that are applied.

TABLE 3.3	Application of Behavioral Therapies	
Types*	**Target Symptoms**	**Techniques and Procedures**
Respondent	Maladaptive behavior patterns	Extinction
Operant		Systematic desensitization
Social learning	Anxiety (including phobias and obsessive-compulsive behavior)	Exposure
		Reinforcement (positive and negative)
	Depression	Punishment
	Addictions	Shaping
		Token economy
		Role modeling
		Role rehearsal
		Role-playing
		Social skills training

*Although the types listed were once discrete, today techniques and concepts from the various schools overlap.

Theories and Perspectives on Social Interactions and Transactions

Another set of theories relevant to working in the mental health field focuses on the interactions between individuals and transactions between persons and their environments. Some of these approaches, such as the ecological perspective, were developed within the field of social work. Others have been developed by other disciplines. The ecological perspective, family, and group intervention approaches will be discussed next. This will be followed by interpersonal theory.

THE ECOLOGICAL PERSPECTIVE The *ecological framework or perspective* uses ecological concepts from biology as a metaphor with which to describe the simultaneous focus and reciprocity between people and their environments (Germain & Gitterman, 1995; Gitterman & Germain, 2008). Attention is on the goodness of the fit between an individual or group and the places in which they live out their lives (Germain & Gitterman, 1995). The ecological perspective's emphasis on health, potentiality, and competence highlights human adaptability and problems in living rather than psychopathology (Germain & Gitterman, 1987). Furthermore, it looks at life stressors, stress, coping methods, and resources from formal and informal networks (Gitterman & Germain, 2008).

The ecological perspective is social and interactional in its focus on human relatedness, attachment, and person–environment transactions. The need for relatedness, support, and affiliation is regarded as essential to human functioning (Germain & Gitterman, 1987). Individual problems may be rooted in maladaptive relationships with other persons or institutions—problems that may be remedied through social environmental interventions as well as an individual approach. Accordingly, the ecological perspective and its related life model support efforts to change individuals, their social contexts, and the interface between them. In recent years, the ecological perspective has been augmented with the concept of *resilience*, which refers to the capacity to survive despite obstacles, and the related concept, *protective factors*, processes that lessen the impact of life stressors (Gitterman & Germain, 2008).

FAMILY THERAPY THEORIES   *Family therapy theories* also address social interactions, particularly those among members of family units. Depending on the theoretical perspective used (e.g., Bowenian, behavioral, structural, contextual, strategic), problematic interactions are viewed as patterns acquired from previous generations, learned behaviors that are reinforced, or some other interpretation. Clinicians work with the nuclear family unit or household, with subunits (parents, children), and with multiple generations of family members, helping them change dysfunctional patterns to more constructive modes of interaction.

Therapeutic intervention with a family aims to change structure, communication patterns, organization, and behaviors. Roles and responsibilities may be reallocated; boundaries between members and between the family and others may be redefined; feelings may be expressed, shared, and understood; and dysfunctional behaviors may be identified and changed. The newer narrative and constructionist approaches to family therapy (see especially White & Epston, 1990) engage the family in a collaborative process of meaning-making. Families are encouraged to tell their stories, deconstruct them so that they hear how they have incorporated narratives of the dominant culture within these stories, and rewrite them (Diamond, 1998).

In behavioral health practice, the individual is usually identified as the client. Nevertheless, the family may be contributing to or reinforcing maladaptive individual patterns or have interactional patterns that are problematic. In such instances, the family should have some involvement in treatment. In work with families with a member with a severe mental disorder, the family needs to be educated about the nature of the family member's disorder and how to respond. In such cases, evidence-based family-focused or family group-oriented psychoeducational approaches can be used (see Chapter 12).

GROUP THEORIES AND THERAPIES   *Groups,* like families, comprise a context in which interpersonal interactions take place. The group format lends itself to therapies in which interactional processes are used to help people in various ways. Groups are used widely in outpatient behavioral health settings to provide psychotherapy, support, and psychoeducation. They are also used in inpatient substance abuse and mental health residential treatment, as well as in intensive outpatient treatment programs.

Like family therapy theory, group theory has a variety of schools, each with its own perspective. Some of the therapeutic groups incorporate behavioral, psychodynamic, and cognitive theories into practice. Most groups incorporate concepts from small group theory. Group intervention techniques vary according to the goals and purpose of the group and the theory that drives it. The Illness Management and Recovery program, which is described in Chapter 12, can be conducted on the individual or group level.

Groups provide a context in which clients can express their feelings, identify problematic behaviors, gain insight into their problems, and make changes. With the support of a peer group and clinical social workers, clients can talk about or nonverbally act out problems that they ordinarily would keep to themselves. The group serves as a point of reference and support for the client to achieve autonomy, self-determination, and a feeling of competence and worth. The acceptance the group provides enables the client to achieve self-acceptance.

INTERPERSONAL THEORY AND THERAPY   Interpersonal therapy was originally developed in the late 1970s by Klerman, Weissman, and colleagues as a manualized psychotherapy intervention for depression in research studies comparing the efficacy of medication and psychotherapeutic approaches for MDD (Klerman, Weissman, Rounsaville, & Chevron, 1984; Weissman, Markowitz, & Klerman, 2007). IPT as a psychosocial intervention was subsequently included in the NIMH Treatment of Depression Collaborative Research Program (Elkin et al., 1989).

Since that time, IPT has been adapted for depressed adolescents (Mufson et al., 2004), depressed older adults (Hinrichsen & Clougherty, 2006), and medical patients with cancer, coronary artery disease, and HIV (Donnelly et al., 2000; Lesperance et al., 2007; Markowitz et al., 1998) with varied success. More research is needed to establish effectiveness for these and other disorders.

Interpersonal therapy is a short-term (12–16 sessions), evidence-based intervention for outpatients with depression and other depressive subtypes and psychiatric disorders. The theoretical framework is based on the constructs of the interpersonal school (Sullivan, 1953) and the demonstrated relationship between mood and life events (Klerman et al., 1984). This school of therapy recognizes that depressive symptoms such as depressed mood interfere with how individuals cope with and manage their social roles, likely resulting in negative life events. Thus, in IPT sessions, therapists assist clients to identify current interpersonal issues and negative life events that are related to the onset and maintenance of their depressive symptoms. These associations are then used as part of the psychoeducational process of helping clients manage their social roles by building the connection between one's mood and life circumstances (environment). By changing their interpersonal situations, clients can be taught to improve mood and reduce depressive symptoms (Klerman et al., 1984). Research has demonstrated that depression frequently develops following the loss of a loved one (bereavement depression), diagnosis of medical illness, isolation or lack of social supports, marital problems, and job loss.

Interpersonal therapy focuses on current interpersonal issues, life events, and the social environment in which the client interacts and makes meaning of their social role, rather than on internal processes and conflicts common to a psychodynamic framework. Interpersonal issues/conflicts may have had origins in the past, yet the focus of the intervention is on present relationship issues to improve depression symptoms. According to the clinician's guide to IPT, problem areas that the intervention focuses on include (a) complicated bereavement, (b) interpersonal role disputes, (c) interpersonal role transitions, and (d) interpersonal deficits (Weissman et al., 2007).

Other Dimensions of Context

Today's clinical social workers practice in behavioral health environments in which diversity is the norm. Thus, it is incumbent upon them to feel comfortable with people from different cultural groups, genders, gender identities, sexual orientations, religions, age groups, and racial groups. Furthermore, social workers need to be sensitive to and counteract disparities in mental health treatment of clients from diverse cultures and other groupings.

Cultures are communities that have a common history, knowledge, language, values, experience, and/or identity. Their shared ways of viewing experience enter into their daily interactions among themselves and with outsiders and are transmitted through socialization processes from one member to another. Persons who are socialized in a particular culture—through family, community, or social ties—often have distinct worldviews. For example, the concepts of mental health, mental illness, and treatment that are dominant in today's mainstream U.S. culture may be strange to clients whose cultures do not share these notions. Cultures vary in their definitions of emotional problems, where they place responsibility (the person, the community, previous generation, etc.), and how emotional problems should be treated. The importance of culture to mental health practice will be discussed in Chapter 6.

Gender is another dimension of the individual and society that inevitably enters into behavioral health practice. Some of the psychological theories that were used in the twentieth century defined normal human development and personality in terms of male behavior. New knowledge about women's ways of knowing has made it possible for men and women to live more fully on their own terms. Chapter 7 will discuss gender in relation to mental health.

In addition to culture and gender, there are other areas of difference that require knowledge and sensitivity. This includes, but is not limited to, sexual orientation, gender identity, religious or spiritual orientation, place of origin (a rural area, another country, etc.), prior trauma, and physical disability. References will be made to such areas of difference throughout the book.

Nonspecific Common Therapeutic Factors

Psychotherapy research has demonstrated that aside from therapeutic techniques used in various clinical therapies (e.g., cognitive, problem solving, ego psychology, PST), nonspecific common therapeutic factors are also important ingredients in any clinical relationship that may affect the client's readiness for change, insight, and optimism for ameliorating life problems. Individual differences in relation to therapeutic factors should always be taken into consideration during counseling sessions.

First discussed by Rosenzweig (1936), common nonspecific therapeutic factors can be significant mediators of client outcomes in counseling. Some of these factors may be related to the therapist and others to the client. Lambert and Ogles (2004) list a variety of nonspecific therapeutic factors common in all therapies that are ascribed to the therapist, therapist process, and the client. These factors can be defined as supportive, learning, and action factors. For example, some supportive factors include reassurance, therapeutic alliance, warmth, respect, empathy, trust, positive regard, and genuineness. Some learning factors include feedback, rationale, exploration, and cognitive learning, and action factors may include cognitive mastery, modeling, practice, working through, and reality testing (Lambert & Ogles, 2004). These factors in conjunction with a broad range of psychotherapies can produce positive outcomes in clients that are clinically meaningful, many of which have been shown to produce statistically significant results as compared to no treatment or placebo.

INTEGRATING BIOLOGICAL, PSYCHOLOGICAL, AND SOCIAL FACTORS

It was stated earlier in this chapter that the division of areas of knowledge into separate disciplines has made it necessary to present biological and psychosocial perspectives as separate sections. Because the practitioner works with clients who are biopsychosocial wholes, there is a need to understand how these perspectives converge in the individual client.

One occasion when these elements come into play is in the development of a psychiatric episode. Even though an individual may have a genetic predisposition for a mental disorder, he or she may not develop the disorder. When a person who is vulnerable to stress is surrounded by people who are patient, protective, and caring, these significant others may offer support and guidance that can prevent the individual from becoming overwhelmed. When persons like this who buffer stress are not available, life occurrences that tax the person's capacity to cope can precipitate a psychiatric episode. Accordingly, environmental stressors can arouse a latent biological phenomenon, while environmental supports can impede it. The role of stressors and supports in the genesis of schizophrenia will be developed further in the discussion of the stress-vulnerability-coping model in Chapter 10.

This book addresses four groups of mental disorders—severe and persistent mental illness (schizophrenia, major mood disorders, and related disorders), depression, anxiety, and substance abuse co-occurring with a severe mental illness. In the chapters on intervention with persons with these disorders, the biological, psychological, and social environmental dimensions are described and applied to treatment. With an integrated understanding of how these elements converge in the individual client, social workers can implement interventions that account for the client's complexity.

Case Study

Mrs. Marilyn Holden is a well-groomed, white, 40-year-old woman of average height who came to the outpatient mental health center at the suggestion of the admissions director at a nursing home where her husband was recently placed following a stay in the state psychiatric hospital. Mrs. Holden had told the director that ever since she had her husband committed to the state hospital, she has felt depressed.

Mrs. Holden told the clinical social worker at the mental health center that she had her husband committed because he was "acting up" at home. He was drinking a keg of beer every three or four days, cursing loudly, and hitting her and the children (a boy and a girl who are 12 and 14, respectively). In the past, he has choked her, pulled out her hair, doused her with beer, and has threatened to hurt the children. When he raised a knife at their son recently, she called the police, who brought him to the state hospital. Mrs. Holden explained that her husband was given the diagnosis of Huntington's disease several years ago, but he refused to take the medication that was prescribed after he was told that he could not drink alcohol while taking the medicine. He has not worked for five years because of difficulties he had holding a job. He has been receiving Social Security and Medicare. She has been working part time.

Mrs. Holden said that she and her husband have been married twenty-two years. They met in high school and married after they graduated. Mrs. Holden said that during the first two years of their marriage they lived with her parents, who supported them until she and her husband were able to obtain stable jobs and save money for housing. During that period, her parents were critical of her for marrying when she was young. Later the couple was able to buy a home, where Mrs. Holden and the children live now. Mrs. Holden expressed affection for her husband "the way he used to be" but said that he has changed. During the last few years, he has followed her around the house and has made her account for her every move. Although his sexual demands have increased, she has felt increasingly repelled. Mrs. Holden expressed feelings of guilt about "dumping him" in the state hospital and a nursing home, at the same time she admitted feeling relieved.

Mrs. Holden said that during the past few years, the children have taken "breaks" from the family by staying with her mother and friends. They have spoken of "hating" their father and fearing that they would inherit the same disease. Mrs. Holden said that she had no idea when she married him that this disease ran in his family; she learned about it only after her husband was diagnosed and she began to ask questions. Since then she learned that his mother and uncle died of the disease and that cousins have the disease today. His family does not like to talk about it.

Mrs. Holden said that when Mr. Holden was living at home, she thought about killing him with a billy club. Since he has been out of the home, however, she has thought about killing herself. She said that she felt confused about "what she owed her husband and what she owed the children" and believes that over the years she has been a "bad mother" and now she is a "bad wife." She said that she had been ignoring his abusive behavior and drinking in the past, even though these behaviors affected her and the children. She reported feeling like a failure and wished that she could feel better about herself.

Mrs. Holden said that her mother continues to provide support to her family. Her mother believes that Mrs. Holden did "the right thing" in placing him in a nursing home but did "the wrong thing" over the years in ignoring the feelings of the children. Mrs. Holden has frequent contact with her mother, a widow in poor health, whom Mrs. Holden helps with household chores and shopping. Other supports include friends and a Huntington's disease support group. There are relatives on her husband's side who are critical of her for placing him in the nursing home. Nevertheless, none of them was willing to have him stay with them. Mrs. Holden requested support from the social worker in sticking with her decision to leave her husband in the nursing home and asked for help dealing with the children. She also expressed bewilderment at how she would live her life without her husband at home.

Summary and Deconstruction

Clinical practice in behavioral health is informed by an integrative biopsychosocial perspective. Accordingly, neither biological, nor psychological, nor social dimensions determine mental health. Instead, knowledge and theories arising from these perspectives infuse each other and are interrelated. The integrative model proposed here is nonlinear and multifaceted. It is predicated on a view of the person as an active agent who strives for empowerment and meaning. Health and mental health are viewed as positive goals. Clients' strengths and vulnerabilities are recognized and respected.

Advances in biological knowledge during the last few decades can be viewed from the perspectives of those at the margins, particularly clients, but also social workers, who are largely informed by psychological and social knowledge. The ascendancy of the biological narrative has reinforced the dominant position of psychiatrists and medicine. As a consequence, psychiatrists are "providing care" in the form of pre-

scriptions, which clients are "receiving." This promotes a relationship of inequality in knowledge and power, which is an impediment to the goal of client empowerment. Furthermore, psychiatrists' knowledge has become "the" knowledge that has the potential of obscuring clients' self-knowledge and awareness of what they want to know.

Similarly but in a different vein, social workers' knowledge and skill in relationship building can become underestimated while biological knowledge is overvalued. Although social workers' expertise in the person–environment interaction is integral to behavioral health practice, as well as the ordinary, daily lives of clients, in an atmosphere of biological hegemony, this knowledge can be overlooked.

In this postmodern era in which information is freely available in cyberspace, the ownership of knowledge is becoming anachronistic. A day may arrive when clients insist on certain treatments and mental health professionals become the respondents.

References

Alexopoulus, G. S., Raue, P., & Areán, P. A. (2003). Problem-solving therapy versus supportive therapy in geriatric major depression with executive dysfunction. *American Journal of Geriatric Psychiatry, 11,* 46–52.

Andreasen, N. C. (1984). *The broken brain: The biological revolution in psychiatry.* New York: Harper & Row.

Andreasen, N. C. (2001). *Brave new brain: Conquering mental illness in the era of the genome.* New York: Oxford University Press.

Andreasen, N. C., & Black, D. W. (2006). *Introductory textbook of psychiatry* (4th ed.). Washington, DC: American Psychiatric Publishing.

Angell, B. (2008). Behavioral theory. In T. Mizrahi & L. E. Davis (Eds.), *Encyclopedia of social work* (e-reference edition). Oxford: Oxford University Press. Retrieved November 15, 2009, from http://www.oxford-naswsocialwork.com/entry?entry+t203.e30

Areán, P. A., Perri, M. G., Nezu, A. M., Schein, R. L., Christopher, F., & Joseph, T. X. (1993). Comparative effectiveness of social problem-solving therapy and reminiscence therapy as treatments for depression in older adults. *Journal of Consulting and Clinical Psychology, 61,* 1003–1010.

Astin, J. A., Shapiro, S. L., Eisenberg, D. M., & Forys, K. L. (2003). Mind-body medicine: State of the science, implications for practice. *Journal of the American Board of Family Medicine, 16*(2), 131–147.

Bandura, A. (1977). *Social learning theory.* Englewood Cliffs, NJ: Prentice-Hall.

Bandura, A. (1978). The self system in reciprocal determinism. *American Psychologist, 33,* 344–358.

Bandura, A. (1982). Self-efficacy mechanism in human agency. *American Psychologist, 37,* 122–147.

Beck, A. (1976). *Cognitive therapy and the emotional disorders.* Madison, CT: International Universities Press.

Beck, A. (1985). Cognitive therapy. In H. I. Kaplan & B. J. Sadock (Eds.), *Comprehensive textbook of psychiatry/IV* (pp. 1432–1438). Baltimore, MD: Williams & Wilkins.

Beck, A. (2005). The current state of cognitive therapy: A 40-year retrospective. *Archives of General Psychiatry, 62,* 953–958.

Bell, A. C., & D'Zurilla, T. J. (2009). Problem-solving therapy for depression: A meta-analysis. *Clinical Psychology Review, 29,* 348–353.

Bentley, K. J., & Walsh, J. (2006). *The social worker and psychotropic medication: Toward effective collaboration with mental health clients, families, and providers* (3rd ed.). Belmont, CA: Thomson Brooks/Cole.

Blanck, G., & Blanck, R. (1974). *Ego psychology: Theory and practice.* New York: Columbia University Press.

Blanck, G., & Blanck, R. (1979). *Ego psychology II: Psychoanalytic developmental psychology.* New York: Columbia University Press.

Blanck, R., & Blanck, G. (1986). *Beyond ego psychology: Developmental object relations theory.* New York: Columbia University Press.

Bradshaw, W. (1993). Coping skills training versus a problem solving approach with schizophrenic patients. *Hospital and Community Psychiatry, 44,* 1102–1104.

Chance, P. (1979). *Learning and behavior.* Belmont, CA: Wadsworth.

Chaney, E. F., O'Leary, M., & Marlatt, G. (1978). Skill training with alcoholics. *Journal of Consulting and Clinical Psychology, 46,* 1092–1104.

Choudary, P. V., & Knowles, J. A. (2008). Genetics. In R. E. Hales, S. C. Yudofsky, & G. O. Gabbard (Eds.), *The American Psychiatric Publishing textbook of psychiatry* (5th ed.). Arlington, VA: American Psychiatric Publishing. DOI: 10.1176/appi.books.9781585623402.303582

Coche, E., Cooper, J., & Petermann, K. (1984). Differential outcomes of cognitive and interactional group therapies. *Small Group Behavior, 15,* 497–509.

Coche, E., & Flick, A. (1975). Problem solving training groups for hospitalized psychiatric patients. *Journal of Psychology, 91,* 19–29.

Craddock, N. (1996). Psychiatric genetics. *British Journal of Psychiatry, 169,* 386–392.

Craddock, N., & Owen, M. J. (1996). Modern molecular genetic approaches to psychiatric disease. *British Medical Bulletin, 52,* 434–452.

Crain, W. (1992). *Theories of development: Concepts and applications* (3rd ed.). Englewood Cliffs, NJ: Prentice Hall.

Cuijpers, P., van Straten, A., & Smit, F. (2006). Psychological treatment of late-life depression: A meta-analysis of randomized controlled trial. *International Journal of Geriatric Psychiatry, 21,* 1139–1149.

Cuijpers, P., van Straten, A., & Warmerdam, L. (2007). Problem solving therapies for depression: A meta-analysis. *European Psychiatry, 22,* 9–15.

Diamond, J. (1998). Postmodern family therapy: New voices in clinical social work. In R. A. Dorfman (Ed.), *Paradigms of clinical social work* (pp. 185–224). New York: Brunner/Mazel.

DiGiuseppe, R., Simon, K., McGowan, L., & Gardner, F. (1990). A comparative outcome study of four cognitive therapies in the treatment of social anxiety. *Journal of Rationale-Emotive and Cognitive Behavior Therapy, 8,* 129–146.

Dobson, K. S., Backs-Dermott, B. J., & Dozois, D. J. A. (2000). Cognitive and cognitive-behavioral therapies. In C. R. Snyder and R. E. Ingram (Eds.), *Handbook of psychological change* (pp. 209–228). New York: John Wiley & Sons.

Donnelly, J. M., Kornblith, A. B., Fleishman, S., Zuckerman, E., Raptis, G., Hudis, C. A., et al. (2000). A pilot study of interpersonal psychotherapy by telephone with cancer patients and their partners. *Psycho-Oncology, 9*(1), 44–56.

D'Zurilla, T. J., Chang, E. C., Nottingham IV, E. J., & Faccini, L. (1998). Social problem-solving deficits and hopelessness, depression, and suicidal risk in college students and psychiatric inpatients. *Journal of Clinical Psychology, 54,* 1–17.

D'Zurilla, T. J., & Goldfried, M. R. (1971). Problem solving and behavior modification. *Journal of Abnormal Psychology, 78,* 107–126.

D'Zurilla, T. J., & Nezu, A. M. (2007). *Problem-solving therapy: A positive approach to clinical intervention* (3rd ed.). New York: Springer Publishing.

D'Zurilla, T. J., Nezu, A. M., & Maydeu-Olivares, A. (2004). Social problem solving: Theory and assessment. In E. C. Chang, T. J. D'Zurilla, & L. Sanna (Eds.), *Social problem solving: theory, research, and training* (pp. 11–27). Washington, DC: American Psychological Association.

Elkin, I., Shea, M., Watkins, J., Imber, S., Sotsky, S., Collins, J., et al. (1989). National Institute of Mental Health treatment of depression collaborative research program: General effectiveness of treatments. *Archives of General Psychiatry, 46,* 971–982.

Ellis, A. (1979). Rational-emotive therapy as a new theory of personality and therapy. In A. Ellis & J. M. Whiteley (Eds.),*Theoretical and empirical foundations of rational emotive therapy* (pp. 1–60). Monterey, CA: Brooks/Cole.

Ellis, A., & Harper, R. A. (1975). *A new guide to rational living.* North Hollywood, CA: Wilshire Book.

Engel, G. L. (1977). The need for a new medical model: A challenge for biomedicine. *Science*, New Series, *196*(4286), 129–136.

Erikson, E. (1950). *Childhood and society.* New York: Norton.

Erikson, E. (1959). Identity and the life cycle. *Psychological Issues, 1,* 50–100.

Fieve, R. (1975). *Moodswing: The third revolution in psychiatry.* New York: William Morrow.

Freud, A. (1946). *The ego and mechanisms of defense.* New York: International Universities Press.

Garland, E. L., & Howard, M. O. (2009). Neuroplasticity, psychosocial genomics, and the biopsychosocial paradigm in the 21ˢᵗ century. *Health and Social Work, 34*(3), 191–199.

Gatchel, R. J. (2004). Comorbidity of chronic pain and mental health disorders: The biopsychosocial perspective. *American Psychologist, 59*(8), 795–805.

Gellis, Z. D., & Bruce, M. B. (2010). Problem solving therapy for depression for subthreshold in home healthcare patients with cardiovascular disease. *American Journal of Geriatric Psychiatry, 18,* 464–474.

Gellis, Z. D., & Kenaley, B. (2008). Problem solving therapy for depression in adults: A systematic review. *Research on Social Work Practice, 18,* 117–131.

Gellis, Z. D., McGinty, J., Horowitz, A., Bruce, M., & Misener, E. (2007). Problem solving therapy for late life depression in home care elderly: A randomized controlled trial. *American Journal of Geriatric Psychiatry, 15*(11), 968–978.

Gellis, Z. D., McGinty, J., Tierney, L., Burton, J., Jordan, C., & Misener, E. (2008). Randomized controlled trial of problem-solving therapy for minor depression in home care. *Research on Social Work Practice, 18*(6), 596–606.

Germain, C., & Gitterman, A. (1987). Ecological perspective. In A. Minahan et al. (Eds.), *Encyclopedia of social work* (18th ed., Vol. 1, pp. 488–499). Silver Spring, MD: National Association of Social Workers.

Germain, C. B., & Gitterman, A. (1995). Ecological perspective. In R. L. Edwards & J. G. Hopps (Eds.), *Encyclopedia of social work* (19th ed., Vol. 1, pp. 816–824). Washington, DC: NASW Press.

Gitterman, A., & Germain, C. B. (2008). Ecological framework. In T. Mizrahi & L. E. Davis (Eds.), *Encyclopedia of social work* (e-reference edition). Oxford: Oxford University Press. Retrieved November 15, 2009, from http://www.oxford-naswsocialwork.com/entry?entry+t203.e118

Goldstein, E. (1995). *Ego psychology and social work practice* (2nd ed.). New York: Free Press.

Gottesman, I. I., & Bertelsen, A. (1989). Confirming unexpressed genotypes for schizophrenia. Risks in the offspring of Fischer's Danish identical and fraternal discordant twins. *Archives of General Psychiatry, 46,* 867–872.

Gottesman, I. I., & Shields, J. (1972). *Schizophrenia and genetics: A twin study vantage point.* New York: Academic Press.

Hamilton, G. (1940). *Theory and practice of social case work.* New York: Columbia University Press.

Hartmann, H. (1958). *Ego psychology and the problem of adaptation.* New York: International Universities Press.

Hedaya, R. J. (1996). *Understanding biological psychiatry.* New York: W. W. Norton.

Hinrichsen, G. A., & Clougherty, K. F. (2006). *Interpersonal therapy for depressed older adults*. Washington, DC: American Psychiatric Association.

Hollis, F. (1964). *Casework: A psychosocial therapy*. New York: Random House.

Intagliata, J. C. (1978). Increasing the interpersonal problem solving skills of an alcoholic population. *Journal of Consulting and Clinical Psychology, 46*, 489–498.

Jannoun, L., Munby, M., Catalan, J., & Gelder, M. (1980). A home-based treatment program for agoraphobia: Replication and controlled evaluation. *Behavior Therapy, 11*, 194–305.

Jordan, J. V. (Ed.). (1997a). *Women's growth in diversity: More writings from the Stone Center*. New York: The Guilford Press.

Jordan, J. V. (1997b). A relational perspective for understanding women's development. In J. V. Jordan (Ed.), *Women's growth in diversity: More writings from the Stone Center* (pp. 9–24). New York: The Guilford Press.

Kandel, E. R. (1998). A new intellectual framework for psychiatry. *American Journal of Psychiatry, 155*(4), 457–469.

Kant, G. L., D'Zurilla, T. J., & Maydeu-Olivares, A. (1997). Social problem solving as a mediator of stress-related depression and anxiety in middle-aged and elderly community residents.*Cognitive Therapy and Research, 21*, 73–96.

Kaplan, H. I., & Sadock, B. J. (1988). *Synopsis of psychiatry: Behavioral sciences/clinical psychiatry* (5th ed.). Baltimore, MD: Williams & Wilkins.

Karol, R., & Richards, C. (1978). *Making it last: An investigation of maintenance strategies for smoking reduction*. Paper presented to the Association for Advancement of Behavior Therapy, Chicago.

Kegan, R. (1982). *The evolving self: Problems and process in human development*. Cambridge, MA: Harvard University Press.

Kelly, G. A. (1963). *A theory of personality*. New York: Norton.

Kendler, K. S. (1988). The genetics of schizophrenia and related disorders. In D. L. Dunner, E. S. Gershon, & J. E. Barrett (Eds.), *Relatives at risk for mental disorder* (pp. 247–263). New York: Raven Press.

Klerman, G. (1988). Depression and related disorders of mood (affective disorders). In A. M. Nicholi, Jr. (Ed.), *The new Harvard guide to psychiatry* (pp. 309–336). Cambridge, MA: Belknap Press of Harvard University Press.

Klerman, G., Weissman, M., Rounsaville, B., & Chevron, E. (1984). *Interpersonal psychotherapy of depression*. New York: Basic Books.

Kumari, V. (2006). Do psychotherapies produce neurobiological effects? *Acta Neuropsychiatrica, 18*, 61–70.

Lambert, M., & Ogles, K. (2004). The efficacy and effectiveness of psychotherapy. In M. Lambert (Ed.), *Bergin's and Garfield's handbook of psychotherapy and behavior change* (pp. 139–193). New York: Wiley.

Lesperance, F., Frasure-Smith, N., Koszycki, D., Latiberte, M.-A., van Zyl, L. T., Baker, B., et al. (2007). Effects of citalopram and interpersonal psychotherapy on depression in patients with coronary artery disease: The Canadian Cardiac Randomized Evaluation of Antidepressant and Psychotherapy Efficacy (CREATE) trial. *JAMA, 297*(4), 367–379.

Lundin, R. W. (1983). Learning theories: Operant reinforcement theories and social learning theories of B. F. Skinner and Albert Bandura. In R. J. Corsini & A. J. Marsella (Eds.), *Personality theories, research and assessment* (pp. 287–330). Itasca, IL: Peacock Press.

Maddi, S. (1980). *Personality theories: A comparative analysis* (4th ed.). Homewood, IL: Dorsey Press.

Mahler, M., Pine, F., & Bergman, A. (1975) *The psychological birth of the human infant*. New York: Basic Books.

Markowitz, J. C., Kocsis, J. H., Fishman, B., Spielman, L. A., Jacobsberg, L. B., Francis, A. J., et al. (1998). Treatment of depressive symptoms in human immunodeficiency virus-positive patients. *Archives of General Psychiatry, 55*, 452–457.

Medalia, A., Revheim, N., & Casey, M. (2001). The remediation of problem solving skills in schizophrenia. *Schizophrenia Bulletin, 27*, 259–267.

Moldin, S. O., & Gottesman, I. I. (1997). At issue: Genes, experience, and chance in schizophrenia—Positioning for the 21st century. *Schizophrenia Bulletin, 23*(4), 547–561.

Mowry, B. J., Nancarrow, D. J., & Levinson, D. F. (1997). The molecular genetics of schizophrenia: An update. *Australian and New Zealand Journal of Psychiatry, 31*(5), 704–713.

Mufson, L., Pollack, D. K., Wickramaratne, P., Nomura, Y., Olfson, M., & Weissman, M. M. (2004). A randomized effectiveness trial of interpersonal psychotherapy for depressed adolescents. *Archives of General Medicine, 61*, 577–584.

Mynors-Wallis, L., Gath, D., Day, A., & Baker, F. (2000). Randomized controlled trial of problem solving treatment, antidepressant medication, and combined treatment for major depression in primary care. *British Journal of Medicine, 320*, 26–30.

Nezu, A. M. (1986). Efficacy of a social problem-solving therapy approach for unipolar depression. *Journal of Consulting and Clinical Psychology, 54*, 196–202.

Nezu, A. M. (1987). A problem-solving formulation of depression: A literature review and proposal of a pluralistic model.*Clinical Psychology Review, 7*, 122–144.

Nezu, A. M. (2004). Problem solving and behavior therapy revisited. *Behavior Therapy, 35,* 1–33.

Nezu, A. M., Nezu, C. M., Felgoise, S. H., McClure, K. S., & Houts, P. S. (2003). Project genesis: Assessing the efficacy of problem-solving therapy for distressed adult cancer patients. *Journal of Consulting and Clinical Psychology, 71,* 1036–1048.

Nezu, A. M., Nezu, C. M., & Perri, M. G. (1989). *Problem-solving therapy for depression: Therapy, research, and clinical guidelines.* New York: Wiley.

Nezu, A. M., Nezu, C. M., Saraydarian, L., Kalmar, K., & Ronan, G. F. (1986). Social problem solving as a moderator variable between negative life stress and depressive symptoms. *Cognitive Therapy and Research, 10,* 489–498.

Nezu, A. M., & Ronan, G. F. (1985). Life stress, current problems, problem solving, and depressive symptomatology: An integrative model. *Journal of Consulting and Clinical Psychology, 53,* 693–697.

Palfai, T., & Jankiewicz, H. (1991). *Drugs and human behavior.* Dubuque, IA: William C. Brown Publishers.

Rainer, J. D. (1985). Genetics and psychiatry. In H. I. Kaplan & B. J. Sadock (Eds.), *Comprehensive textbook of psychiatry/IV* (4th ed., pp. 25–42). Baltimore, MD: Williams & Wilkins.

Richmond, M. (1917). *Social diagnosis.* New York: Russell Sage Foundation.

Rosenzweig, S. (1936). Some implicit common factors in diverse methods of psychotherapy. *American Journal of Orthopsychiatry, 6,* 412–415.

Rotter, J. (1954). *Social learning and clinical psychology.* Englewood Cliffs, NJ: Prentice-Hall.

Sadock, B. J., & Sadock, V. A. (2007). *Kaplan & Sadock's synopsis of psychiatry: Behavioral sciences/clinical psychiatry* (10th ed.). Philadelphia, PA: Wolters Klumer Lippincott Williams & Wilkins.

Salkind, N. J. (1985). *Theories of human development* (2nd ed.). New York: Wiley.

Saleebey, D. (1992). Biology's challenge to social work: Embodying the person-in-environment perspective. *Social Work, 37*(2), 112–125.

Sullivan, H. S. (1953). *The interpersonal theory of psychiatry.* New York: Norton.

Weick, A. (1987). Reconceptualizing the philosophical perspective of social work. *Social Service Review, 61,* 218–230.

Weick, A., Rapp, C., Sullivan, W. P., & Kisthardt, W. (1989). A strength perspective for social work practice. *Social Work, 34,* 350–354.

Weiner, H. (1984). An integrative model of health, illness, and disease. *Health and Social Work, 9,* 253–260.

Weiner, H., & Fawzy, F. I. (1989). An integrative model of health, disease, and illness. In S. Cheron (Ed.), *Psychosomatic medicine: Theory, physiology, and practice* (Vol. 1, pp. 9–44). Madison, CT: International Universities Press.

Weissman, M., Markowitz, J., & Klerman, G. (2007). *Clinician's quick guide to interpersonal psychotherapy.* New York: Oxford Press.

White, M., & Epston, D. (1990). *Narrative means to therapeutic ends.* New York: W. W. Norton.

White, R. F. (1959). Motivation reconsidered: The concept of competence. *Psychological Review, 66,* 297–333.

Williams, J., Katon, W., Lin, E., Noel, P., Worchel, J., Cornell, J., et al. (2004). The effectiveness of depression care management on diabetes-related outcomes in older patients. *Annals of Internal Medicine, 140,* 1015–1024.

Wolpe, J. (1982). *The practice of behavior therapy* (3rd ed.). New York: Pergamon.

Wright, J. H., Thase, M. E., & Beck, A. T. (2008). Cognitive therapy. In R. E. Hales, S. C. Yudofsky, & G. O. Gabbard (Eds.), *The American Psychiatric Publishing textbook of psychiatry* (5th ed.). Arlington, VA: American Psychiatric Publishing. DOI: 10.1176/appi.books.9781585623402.313094

Zimmerman, J. H. (1989). Determinism, science, and social work. *Social Service Review, 63,* 52–62.

CHAPTER

4

The Biopsychosocial Assessment

Although assessment has been recognized as a core skill in social work and should underpin social work interventions, there is no singular theory or understanding as to what the purpose of assessment is and what the process should entail.

—CRISP, ANDERSON, ORME, & LISTER, "LEARNING AND TEACHING ASSESSMENT: REVIEWING THE EVIDENCE," 2004, P. 199

The biopsychosocial assessment refers to the process of acquiring an understanding of a client's situation and difficulties and the analysis of the meaning of the information that is gathered. Professionals elicit the client's narrative and observe his or her emotions, cognitions, and behavior. Although they view the client's report as primary data, they also take into account the findings from medical and psychiatric evaluations and information provided by family members and the staff of social agencies. They draw from biological and psychosocial sources of knowledge, described in Chapter 3, to assess each unique individual (otherwise known as a *case*). Professional social work assessments highlight clients' strengths, but in behavioral health practice, mental health problems need to be recognized. Assessments are largely professional constructions in which the client's system of meaning may or may not be addressed (Kleinman, 1988).

In this volume, the term *biopsychosocial assessment* will be used to denote a broad understanding of the client's situation, biological, psychological, and social functioning, risks, and needs. The assessment includes but goes beyond the specific *DSM-IV-TR* (American Psychiatric Association [APA], 2000) diagnosis. The biopsychosocial assessment will be viewed as a process *and* a product (Hepworth & Larsen, 1982). Because understanding changes from week to week, the process is dynamic, always subject to revision. At a given moment, the participants in the assessment process inscribe the results of their thinking in a written report, which also may be called a *biopsychosocial assessment*. The written assessment, however, is a snapshot, frozen in time.

In the contemporary managed care environment, the assessment is a critical component of behavioral health care. The clinician is expected to document the client's presenting problems and symptoms and arrive at an accurate diagnosis and treatment plan. Third parties use this information to decide whether the problems that are described and the proposed treatment call for reimbursement (Franklin & Jordan, 2003). The assessment should also indicate the anticipated time frame for treatment, keeping in mind today's emphasis on short-term intervention. For identified problems, the goals and means of measuring goal attainment or symptom reduction are further elements used by third parties. The initial assessment is revisited over time in continuation or utilization reviews.

The assessment described here will focus on the individual. Although family and group modes of intervention are prevalent in clinical practice today, case records, as well as reimbursement policies, are predominantly based on individuals. This is not to say that an individual's family and social milieu are excluded. In the assessment described here, the multiple contexts of an individual's life are described.

This chapter includes the following topics: (a) components of a comprehensive interdisciplinary assessment, (b) assessing the client's psychiatric symptoms, (c) components of a written biopsychosocial assessment, (d) the written biopsychosocial report, and (e) case review with an interdisciplinary treatment planning team.

COMPONENTS OF A COMPREHENSIVE INTERDISCIPLINARY ASSESSMENT

Ideally, an assessment of a client is developed by an interdisciplinary team of mental health professionals, all of whom have some direct contact with the client. Such a team might include a psychiatrist, social worker, psychiatric nurse, physician, psychologist, recreation therapist, and vocational rehabilitation specialist. A team has the resources of diverse specialties, each of which has a unique lens through which to perceive the client. The team uses the expertise of different professionals to gather and make sense of data, which are pooled and integrated. The inclusion of multiple professionals promotes a more comprehensive understanding of the client and client system.

The major components of an interdisciplinary assessment are as follows:

1. Medical assessment
2. Psychological testing
3. Rapid assessment instruments
4. Functional assessment
5. Biopsychosocial assessment
6. Psychiatric evaluation, mental status examination, and diagnosis

A given client's assessment may include some or all of these components or additional elements related to the agency's function. The following sections will describe each of the components listed and will indicate which discipline usually performs each task.

Medical Assessment

Behavioral health clients should initially and routinely have complete medical examinations. Physical evaluations can determine the client's overall state of health and the presence of particular medical problems. Findings from physical evaluations can inform decisions about psychiatric diagnoses, guide psychiatrists in the prescription of medications, and provide information that social workers can take into account in their work with clients.

Medical assessments usually involve an interview in which the physician asks the client to describe his or her chief complaints and medical history, after which the doctor conducts a physical examination and, in some cases, orders or runs particular tests. Psychiatrists, mental health teams, or individual practitioners who refer clients to physicians may request specific laboratory tests such as the dexamethasone-suppression test (DST) for depression or a urine screening test for substance use. Sometimes the physician who conducts the physical examination will refer the client to a specialist in other medical disciplines such as a neurologist.

The physical examination helps mental health practitioners clarify the psychiatric diagnosis. Many medical conditions, such as those listed in Table 4.1, as well as substance abuse, produce symptoms that resemble those associated with some psychiatric disorders. The general practice has been to rule out physical disorders before determining that a psychiatric disorder is responsible for these symptoms. It is possible, however, that a client has one of these physical disorders or conditions or others not listed *and* a psychiatric disorder, so it is important to determine whether a physical disorder is present, whether the two coexist, and the extent to which they affect each other. Current medication and past surgery may also be associated with psychiatric symptoms. In addition, certain physical conditions (including pregnancy) and age signal that some kinds of psychiatric medication are contraindicated or that the dosage should be reduced. A further advantage of a client having a medical evaluation is that this information can be inserted on Axis III of the multiaxial *DSM-IV-TR* diagnosis.

Psychological Testing

Psychological testing may be called for under some circumstances. Such examinations help clarify the diagnosis, assess intellectual ability, and uncover unconscious material. Some psychological tests are capable of diagnosing organic brain damage. A social worker who is the first professional who sees a client should refer the client to a psychologist if clarification seems to be needed.

Psychologists have a wide repertoire of tests, which can be administered as a package. Such batteries of tests require interpretation as a whole. Among the personality tests, the one that is most

TABLE 4.1	Examples of Medical Conditions in Which Psychiatric Symptoms May be Presented
Huntington's disease	Nutritional deficiency disease
Multiple sclerosis	Systemic lupus erythematosus
Cardiovascular disease	Amyotrophic lateral sclerosis
Hypoglycemia	Human immunodeficiency virus (HIV) infection
Parkinson's disease	Viral hepatitis
Diabetes	

Source: Adapted from Sadock & Sadock (2007).

commonly used in mental health settings is the *Minnesota Multiphasic Personality Inventory*, which is usually referred to by its acronym, MMPI. This test contains true and false questions describing emotional states, attitudes, and behaviors, such as "I have trouble making friends." Today, the more up-to-date MMPI-2 and the MMPI-2-RF (restructured form) are used. Psychologists use the MMPI to assist with diagnosis, identify problem areas, and develop a treatment plan.

Projective tests encourage subjects to reveal indirectly what they may find difficult to state directly. For these tests, clients are presented with ambiguous stimuli about which they are asked to talk. One well-established projective test is the *Rorschach Test*, which has subjects respond to a set of inkblots. Another is the *Thematic Apperception Test* (TAT), which contains a set of pictures about which clients are asked to develop a story. A third type of projective test is the *Sentence Completion Test* (SCT), which consists of a series of statements with blanks for the subject to complete, for example, "I am afraid of...." These tests reveal areas of conflict or anxiety.

Another test is the *Bender Visual Motor Gestalt* test. This test is used for adults and children primarily to detect organic dysfunction (Sadock & Sadock, 2007) but also as a projective tool (Graham & Lilly, 1984). Subjects are asked to reproduce designs printed on cards, such as a circle and a square that touch.

Psychologists also administer intelligence tests to some clients who receive mental health services. Testing may be required for a vocational or rehabilitation program the client wishes to enter, or to clarify the client's potential. The best known of these tests is the *Wechsler Adult Intelligence Scale* (WAIS). There are other versions of this test for children.

Psychological testing has certain advantages. First, the findings are empirically based. Many of the instruments used are reliable and valid. Tests provide measured scores on specific dimensions. Many psychological tests are sensitive to personality dimensions that are not revealed in face-to-face conversations and in behavior.

As valuable as psychological tests may be, they do not replace understanding the person in his or her natural environment. Testing is usually performed in a clinical environment, the demands of which differ from those of the everyday life of the client. Questions are presented in a standardized way and do not account for the diverse social, cultural, and literacy levels of individual clients. Tests may be biased toward norms of the white middle-class population. Results that are distorted or reflect a transient state can become reified in a diagnosis that can remain with a client over time.

Rapid Assessment Instruments

In addition to the diagnostic tests performed by psychologists, there is a vast array of rapid assessment instruments that can be administered by social workers in clinical practice. These instruments can be used to assess a variety of individual, family, marital, or child-related problems or issues. These quickly administered tools provide information that clinicians can use to support a particular diagnosis, justify treatment, and assess intervention progress. The client's baseline score at the beginning of treatment can be compared with community norms (based on instrument validity testing) and with scores of individuals whose responses fall within the clinical range. A score within the clinical range provides a baseline level of the problem and justification for treatment. A client's scores at the beginning, during, and end of treatment can be compared to monitor and assess the client's progress and provide quality assurance information to agencies and managed care organizations (Franklin & Jordan, 2003). Fischer and Corcoran (2007) have compiled many of these assessment tools in their two-volume book, *Measures for Clinical Practice and Research: A Sourcebook.*

Many of the rapid assessment instruments in use are adapted to particular problems (e.g., marital issues, parenting, poor assertiveness, loneliness, anger) or clinical states (e.g., depression, anxiety). On the basis of information gathered during early sessions, the social worker determines which areas to assess and monitor during treatment. Usually it is the client who completes the instrument, but there are some that can be filled in by family members, caregivers, and the clinician. Tools relevant to the topics addressed in Part Two of this book will be mentioned where they apply.

Functional Assessment

A further area for assessment is the extent of the client's ability to conduct his or her life independently in the community. An assessment of functioning is of particular relevance to those with severe mental illness, those with mental retardation or developmental disabilities, or those with physical, aging-related, and/or psychiatric disabilities that affect the performance of activities of daily life. In many mental health services, the nurse is responsible for the functional assessment, but the social worker may be the one who performs this evaluation.

Among the areas that may be addressed in a functional assessment are the following:

1. Ability to communicate his or her needs to others. What language(s) does the client use (English, Spanish, sign language, gestures, none)?
2. Ability to use public transportation.
3. Ability to drive a car.
4. Ability to take care of physical needs independently—eating, bathing, grooming, dressing, use toilet unaided.
5. Ability to handle and manage money—budgeting, counting change, shopping.
6. Literacy: ability to read, reading level, language(s) of literacy.
7. Physical mobility: walking, climbing stairs, ability to transfer from wheelchair to bed, need for cane, walker, or wheelchair.
8. Social skills: ability to interact with others, ability to initiate, develop, and maintain relationships.
9. Ability to manage a household independently—cooking, cleaning, laundry, dishes, making bed.
10. Occupational/employment skills and experience: work skills, ability to follow directions and accept supervision, ability to get to work on time.
11. Ability to assume responsibility for taking own medication consistently.
12. Sensory functions: sight, hearing, and so on.
13. Ability to protect self and others from fire.
14. Ability to protect oneself from involuntary sex, assault, and other kinds of exploitation.
15. Use of leisure time.

Scales that assess adaptive behavior skills, such as the Independent Living Skills Survey (Wallace, 1986) and the Instrumental Activities of Daily Living Scale (Lawton & Brody, 1969) for older adults, can be used.

The functional assessment contributes to identifying the client's strengths, needs, and problem areas. The client's strengths and the resources of the client, agency, and community are used to address the client's needs.

Biopsychosocial Evaluation

The biopsychosocial evaluation is a comprehensive report on the client's current problem and symptoms, life history, and situation. It is gleaned from a number of sources—the client, client system (family, partner, friends, neighbors, any significant others), reports from other agencies, the case record, and so forth—provided that the client consents to the participation of others. Although the production of a written psychosocial evaluation is frequently assigned to the clinical social worker, in some settings professionals and students of any of the mental health disciplines develop the written document.

In this volume, the written biopsychosocial evaluation will be referred to as a *biopsychosocial assessment*. The report will include a summary of medical findings obtained from the physician, as well as psychological and social findings. This is consistent with the biopsychosocial conceptual framework described in Chapter 3. The written assessment includes a description of the client, the presenting problem, the client's life circumstances, medical history, psychiatric history, financial/occupational information, and family/relationships. It also includes mental status information and the diagnosis. A recommended means to organize this assessment is presented later in this chapter.

Psychiatric Evaluation, Mental Status Examination, and Diagnosis

The evaluation performed by the psychiatrist can include the client's developmental, psychiatric, medical, and social history and current symptoms. The process resembles the history taking of the social worker but reflects the medical training of the psychiatrist. The psychiatrist may explore the client's psychiatric history more closely than the social worker but pay less attention to social environmental factors. The term that psychiatrists use for the psychiatric history is *anamnesis*.

In the process of explaining his or her current difficulties and history, the client reveals the symptoms. The client's reported complaints, as well as the verbal and nonverbal behavior accompanying the report, provide clues to the client's diagnosis. Further clarification of the nature of the client's psychiatric problem can be obtained by performing a *mental status examination* during the history gathering. The mental status examination is to the psychiatrist what the physical examination is to the physician. Each is a clinical means to assess the presence of *pathology* (i.e., disease) in the client and to come to an accurate diagnosis. Although psychiatrists are frequently the professionals who perform these evaluations, social workers and psychologists are also capable of conducting them. Suggested formats for reporting findings of this examination are presented in the next section of this chapter.

The psychiatric examination also includes an evaluation of the need for further medical testing and current medical needs. The psychiatrist may recommend a neurological examination, laboratory tests, or a referral for additional medical evaluations. The psychiatrist has particular expertise about psychotropic medication. Some clients can benefit from psychotherapy without medication. Others require medication along with psychosocial treatment. The psychiatrist explores the client's medication history and any indications of an inclination to abuse drugs. The medication that is prescribed is related to the client's symptoms, diagnosis, and health status.

Assessing the Client's Psychiatric Symptoms

Psychiatric symptoms are human expressions of emotion and thought that are sometimes viewed as indicators of mental illness. They include universal feelings such as sadness, anger, anxiety, and elation, as well as more unusual experiences such as hallucinations and delusions. Although some psychiatrists differentiate between signs (objective indicators of a psychiatric disorder) and symptoms (subjective reports by the client) (Trzepacz & Baker, 1993), the objective and subjective are not always distinguishable. Here we will use the term *symptoms* for both concepts. As discussed in Chapter 1, mental health professionals view symptoms as indicators of psychopathology when the symptoms appear to be intense, long in duration, extreme, and psychologically painful, and they interfere with psychosocial functioning.

Symptoms can be observed directly during an interview, or a client (or someone who sees the client in other contexts) may describe them. Individuals reveal their feelings in the way they present themselves to the clinician and how they respond to questions. When clients are asked to tell their story ("what brings you here today?"), they frequently share what happened, under what circumstances, how they felt, and what they thought about their experiences. For example, clients may cry while telling of a loss or express anger over someone's trying to poison them. Depending on what was said and observed, the clinician will identify symptoms from the content of the client's account and the way in which the client expresses himself or herself.

Usually a client will present with more than one psychiatric symptom. The presence of a collection of symptoms that co-occur suggests one or more diagnoses. The *DSM-IV-TR* (APA, 2000) describes those combinations of symptoms that psychiatrists and other mental health practitioners regard as indicators of specific mental disorders. The *DSM-IV-TR* is the standard manual used in the United States for diagnosis. Managed care organizations usually require, as a condition for reimbursement, that behavioral health providers apply a *DSM-IV-TR* diagnosis to every client. It is recommended that social workers employed in such settings become familiar with the manual, how it is used, and the major diagnostic categories. Some of them will be reviewed in the intervention chapters in Part Two of this book. It should be noted that an updated version of the *DSM* (*DSM-V*) is currently being developed.

One way in which mental health professionals arrive at a diagnosis is to conduct a *mental status examination* as mentioned earlier. This face-to-face evaluation explores the client's complaints, symptoms, and demeanor to determine the nature of the difficulty, how it expresses itself, and potential diagnoses. The client is assessed in many areas to identify problematic domains and the extent of the dysfunction. The focus of the mental status examination is on *current functioning* that is evidenced during the examination.

There are various tools that are used to conduct mental status examinations. In some settings (e.g., psychiatry, services to older adults), practitioners use the brief Mini-Mental State Examination (MMSE) (Folstein, Folstein, & McHugh, 1975) to screen for cognitive functioning. This examination tests the individual's short-term memory, ability to perform calculations (like subtracting 7 from 100 several times), and ability to follow a series of commands.

A more comprehensive diagnostic tool is the Structured Clinical Interview (SCID) (Spitzer, Williams, Gibbon, & First, 1989), which produces *DSM* diagnoses. The SCID consists of questions about particular symptoms, followed by probes, which help the clinician arrive at a diagnosis. The SCID is a more lengthy examination than the typical mental status examination. Used frequently in research studies, both clinical and research versions are available (see http://www.scid4.org/ and http://www.appi.org/group.cfm?groupid=SCID-I).

Although fixed formats for interviewing clients can be helpful, many practitioners gain their impressions through an interview (psychosocial interview or *anamnesis*). At the same time the client is describing the presenting problems or complaints, the examiner is able to observe the client's affect, interpersonal behavior, mood, and so forth. As the troubling symptoms become visible, the clinician can ask questions that elicit more detailed information about specific symptoms. As the interview draws to an end, the examiner probes further into dimensions of psychosocial functioning that were either glossed over or not revealed by the client.

There are many ways to report the results of the mental status examination. Traditionally, examiners have written narrative reports that describe observed psychological functioning along multiple dimensions. Table 4.2 outlines these dimensions and provides an example of

TABLE 4.2	Areas Addressed in a Mental Status Examination (narrative type)	
Dimension	**Description**	**Example**
General Appearance and Attitude	Appearance includes physical characteristics, mannerisms, facial expression, clothing, and grooming. Attitude refers to how the client relates to the examiner and how the client comes across.	John is tall and slender and looks young for his age (40). He was neatly dressed in khaki pants and a striped, long-sleeved shirt. He was cooperative except for a few questions that he dodged.
Behavior and Motor Activity	This includes physical activity, body movements, gestures, posture, and gait. Note the quantity and quality of activity.	John appeared restless in the waiting room but calmed down during the interview. He rubbed his hands together at times.
Speech and Language	This addresses knowledge and fluency in English and whether this or another language is primary. Determine whether loudness and speed are congruent with client's primary cultural group. Note any unusual speech patterns and how talkative the client is.	John spoke fluently, loudly, and rapidly in English, his primary language. He used puns and laughed at his own humor. At times the interviewer had to break into John's profuse talk.
Feeling, Affect, and Mood	This concerns the emotions and mood that the client verbalizes and that the clinician observes and the observed affect. Determine whether affect matches the content of the feelings (i.e., whether it is appropriate). Does the client shift quickly from one feeling state to another (lability)?	John came across primarily as happy and enthusiastic but at times he shifted into a sad state. His affect was consistent with his reported mood and was appropriate. He seemed irritated with some of the interviewer's questions.
Thought Content and Processes	This addresses the themes and preoccupations evident in the client's talk. Note unusual or unrealistic ideas. Describe the quality of the client's thinking in his or her speech.	John revealed plans to start his own travel agency but said that he lacked capital and experience in this business. He displayed flight of ideas and grandiosity.
Intelligence and Cognition	This addresses the client's general level of intelligence and intellectual functioning. Assess abstract thinking apart from education and culture. Evaluate orientation, memory, and consciousness.	John seemed to be highly intelligent and was able to interpret the saying, "A rolling stone gathers no moss" abstractly. He was oriented to time, place, and person; had no apparent impairments in immediate, recent, and long-term memory; and was alert.
Perception or Sensory Experiences	This refers to the client's ability to accurately perceive and process environmental stimuli. It explores whether the client has hallucinations, illusions, depersonalization, and/or derealization.	The client described voices telling him that he was brilliant and destined to be a millionaire. These auditory hallucinations were congruent with his grandiose mood.
Impulsivity	This refers to the ability to control aggressive, sexual, and other impulses.	The client reported that his wife was complaining about his high sexual energy. He denied having extramarital affairs. He appears to have some control over his impulses.

(Continued)

TABLE 4.2	Areas Addressed in a Mental Status Examination (narrative type) *(Continued)*	
Dimension	**Description**	**Example**
Judgment and Insight	This addresses the client's ability to distinguish among thoughts, feelings, and actions; to examine alternative solutions to a problem; and assume responsibility for and understand the consequences of his or her own behavior. Inquire whether the client has suicidal or homicidal ideations; and the extent to which the client acknowledges the presence of problems and his or her own role in their development.	John does not seem to have realistic ideas about how one goes about starting a business. Thus far, however, he has not borrowed or spent money toward developing a travel agency. John denied mental health problems. He said that his wife is the one who thinks he needs help. He reported having fleeting thoughts of suicide but because the thoughts disappear rapidly, he has not done anything about them. He lacked insight into his own difficulty.

Source: Adapted from Sadock & Sadock (2007) with modifications. The example was developed by Roberta Sands.

a professional mental status report on each area on "John," who was exhibiting symptoms of bipolar disorder, manic episode. As one can see in this example, John functions well in some respects but has difficulties in other respects.

In recent years, it has become common for behavioral health providers to use checklists such as the one in Table 4.3. Completing forms such as this places lower demands on the examiner's time than writing narratives. Checklists, however, portray the client as a bundle of symptoms; narratives describe individual responses.

Regardless of whether clinicians write narratives, use checklists, or write an abbreviated report, they need to ask questions that operationalize the various dimensions of the mental status examination. One way to do this is to review instruments such as the SCID for sample questions. There are some questions that are frequently used in behavioral health settings to tap symptoms related to some of these dimensions. Here are some examples:

Orientation:	What's today's date? Where are you?
Hallucination:	Do you ever see things that other people do not see? (If yes) What do they look like? Do you ever hear things that other people do not hear? (If yes) What do they sound like? When you hear these sounds, where do they come from?
Delusion of Persecution:	Do you ever think that people are planning to hurt you in some way?
Mood:	How are you feeling today? Is this feeling typical of the way you have been feeling lately? How is your appetite? How much energy do you have?

When the client's responses to a particular question are positive, the clinician asks follow-up questions, as illustrated in some of the preceding examples.

On the basis of the information that is formulated in the mental status report, the clinician should be able to arrive at one or more diagnoses described in the *DSM-IV-TR*. Nevertheless, this

TABLE 4.3   Mental Status Checklist

I. Appearance and Attitude
- _____ appropriate dress
- _____ well groomed
- _____ poor hygiene
- _____ poor eye contact
- _____ bizarre appearance
- _____ cooperative
- _____ guarded

II. Behavior and Motor Activity
- _____ retarded motor activity
- _____ agitated motor activity
- _____ tremors
- _____ tics
- _____ stereotyped movements

III. Characteristics of Speech
- _____ English is not primary language
- _____ normal speech
- _____ flight of ideas
- _____ speaks slowly
- _____ mute
- _____ thought blocking
- _____ circumstantiality
- _____ loose associations
- _____ tangential thoughts
- _____ perseveration
- _____ irrelevance
- _____ incoherence
- _____ loud

IV. Orientation
- _____ time
- _____ place
- _____ person
- _____ reason for being here

V. Affect
- _____ appropriate
- _____ inappropriate
- _____ flat
- _____ blunted
- _____ affect lability

VI. Mood/Feeling Tone
- _____ normal
- _____ depressed
- _____ elated
- _____ angry
- _____ afraid
- _____ optimistic
- _____ pessimistic

VII. Thought Content
- _____ delusions
- _____ paranoid
- _____ grandiose
- _____ somatic
- _____ ideas of reference
- _____ ideas of influence
- _____ obsessive and phobic ideas

VIII. Cognition

Memory
- _____ long-term memory poor
- _____ intermediate memory poor
- _____ short-term memory poor

Attention and Concentration
- _____ attention cannot be aroused
- _____ attention cannot be sustained

Fund of Information/ Intelligence
- _____ average
- _____ below normal

IX. Perception
- _____ hallucinations
- _____ auditory
- _____ visual
- _____ other
- _____ illusions

X. Insight and Judgment
- _____ suicidal
- _____ homicidal
- _____ poor judgment
- _____ denial of mental health problems

is not always possible. Despite the specificity of diagnostic categories in the manual, the same symptoms characterize a number of disorders. Rather than affix a definite category, the clinician may defer the diagnosis, pending further evaluation (including physical examinations, laboratory tests, psychological tests, interviews with significant others), or designate a provisional diagnosis and alternative categories to consider (APA, 2000).

COMPONENTS OF THE WRITTEN BIOPSYCHOSOCIAL ASSESSMENT

The biopsychosocial assessment is constructed from the elements that have been described previously. In interdisciplinary settings, information from team members and others who have conducted evaluations or provided reports are assembled, examined, and discussed. This section describes the kind of information that clinical social workers think about, gather, and include in a written biopsychosocial report. In keeping with the biopsychosocial framework of this book, the report incorporates biological, social, and psychological information.

Biological Information

Biological information is obtained from the physician and from the client's self-report. Social workers can also assess the client's health by inquiring about the client's nutrition, exercise, sleep, and substance use. The quality, quantity, and consistency of the client's health behaviors suggest healthy or maladaptive self-care. The social worker should also ask clients about their use of health care services and determine whether there are barriers (e.g., lack of health insurance) that impede service use. Just as it is difficult to separate health from mental health, one cannot easily separate health and mental health status from the use of services, which is a social process. Because social workers' expertise is in the social domain, particular emphasis will be given here to the social dimensions of the client's life.

Social Information

The social aspects of the biopsychosocial assessment require that one understand the interpersonal relationships that are part of a person's life. This includes the family and other significant relationships. The cultures that permeate the client's life affect individual and social functioning as well.

To understand the social dimension of a person's life, several interrelated topics should be addressed in the assessment. Although these are discussed separately for the sake of clarity, it should be recognized that they are coexistent in the person's life. The topics to be discussed are (a) the family or household, (b) the culture or cultural group, (c) other social supports, (d) social environmental stressors and resources, and (e) tools to assess the social context.

THE FAMILY OR HOUSEHOLD The persons with whom a client lives or is otherwise closely connected consist of the family of origin (parents, siblings), the current, immediate family (spouse or partner, children), extended family (relatives such as grandparents, aunts, cousins), friends, and/or coresidents of a group home.

In making an assessment of the family or household, one is interested in determining who is in the household, the quality of the relationships (emotionally supportive, conflictual, competitive) of the household as a whole and of component parts, the nature of the interactions (domineering, reciprocal), the strength of the bonds, and sensitive family issues. This can best be done by meeting with the family.

The problems of the behavioral health client should be looked at in relation to his or her household or family. It should be determined how the family views and responds to the client, and how the client sees the family. The family's concern about the client, the members' willingness to be involved in treatment, and their resourcefulness should be assessed. Many of the dimensions described in family systems theory—boundaries (openness, permeability), communication patterns, organizational structure (roles, rules, subsystems), linkage with other systems (extended family, community), and power relations—can be assessed.

The family or household may or may not provide support to the client. The social worker should determine who is supportive in what ways, and the obstacles presented by those who are not supportive. If there are obstacles, their nature and purpose should be explored so that a strategy to overcome them can be developed.

On the other hand, the family may be burdened with the care of their relative or with crises that emerge. Family members can experience burden whether the client lives with them or separately. It is important to assess the ability of the family to provide support and care to the client. Often family caregivers themselves need support.

THE CULTURE(S)   The individual and family may be part of an ethnic, religious, or ethno-religious culture that influences the client's identity, values, feelings of belonging, as well as individual behavior and family patterns of interaction. Cultures provide structure and meaning. For some people, however, association with a cultural group that is not valued by the larger society may be a source of conflict or ambivalence.

The clinical social worker has a responsibility to understand clients in relation to their respective culture(s). Workers who are not familiar with the client's particular ethnic group or religion should ask questions of the client so as to encourage him or her to explain the cultural meanings. Culturally sensitive practice is discussed in Chapter 6.

The assessment should identify significant ethnic groups and describe the nature of the client's ties and identification. Cultural patterns, such as ideas about sharing private feelings, modes of decision making, valued goals, and the role of kin in their lives, should be assessed. The cultural group, with its sense of community, shared life-cycle events, and holidays, is a potential resource for the client. The client's mental health problems should be viewed in terms of normative values and behaviors of the cultural group; what is psychopathological in one culture may be normal in another.

OTHER SOCIAL SUPPORTS   Clients may have additional relationships that provide them with emotional support. These persons and groups provide friendship, personal help in time of need, concrete services (e.g., baby-sitting, transportation), or the like. The "supporters" may be personal friends, work associates, or neighbors. Doctors, lawyers, and ministers also provide social support, as do church or synagogue members. Barbers and beauticians, bartenders, and grocers may also be part of a client's social network.

Besides these informal social supports, clients may belong to peer support groups. On the other hand, they may have peers who provide friendship at the same time they foster problematic behaviors such as "drinking buddies" and collaborators in antisocial activity. If such peers are significant to the individual and comprise a large proportion of the client's social relationships, they may present an obstacle to treatment.

Some individuals are estranged from their families and have few friends. For whatever reason, it may be difficult for them to make or keep friends. In these cases, human service workers from a number of agencies may constitute the client's social support network.

Social supports may also be in the form of organized community groups and activities. Self-help and advocacy groups that focus on particular issues (e.g., alcoholism, rape, child abuse, loss of a child) provide a network of individuals who can support each other. Settlement houses, YMCAs, and Jewish Community Centers offer social programs, recreational activities, cultural events, and classes that can contribute to the well-being of clients.

SOCIAL ENVIRONMENTAL RESOURCES AND STRESSORS   Clients live in environmental contexts that may provide protection from or promote stress. Resources such as savings, financial support from others, receipt of Supplemental Security Income (SSI) and/or food stamps, housing, and employment can buffer stress, whereas poverty and inadequate housing can generate or exacerbate stress.

Conflict between the individual and social systems can be threatening. Legal problems over child support, debts, and driving while intoxicated involve individuals with lawyers and courts, the rules and practices of which are mystifying to those who are not familiar with the system. Defending oneself under such circumstances is costly and takes time away from employment. Trouble with the law and difficulties with other systems are taxing, making one vulnerable to physical and mental disorders.

Discrimination based on race, sex, class, age, sexual orientation, gender identity, and disability can create emotional stress and interfere with obtaining employment. On the other hand, holding more than one job, being a single parent, or caring for a mentally disabled person or an older parent makes extra demands on a person.

Changes in one's circumstances or roles can also create stress. Accordingly, graduating, getting married, changing jobs, receiving a promotion, and retiring can be anxiety provoking. Even though the client may not complain of these changes, it is expected that he or she will be making adjustments in adapting to the new circumstances.

A biopsychosocial assessment should identify the social environmental stressors in a person's life and evaluate the adequacy of supports and resources. What looks like symptoms of psychopathology may be a reaction to stressful life events or conditions.

TOOLS TO ASSESS THE SOCIAL CONTEXT   A number of tools can be used to assess social supports, resources, and stressors. Among these is the *ecomap* (Hartman, 1978), a drawing of social systems with which family members interact. With the ecomap, the household members are drawn in the center of a circle that is surrounded by other systems such as the behavioral health agency, extended family, the church, and a child welfare agency. The ecomap portrays the quality of the relationship between individuals and these systems (e.g., conflictual, supportive). Another tool, the *genogram* (McGoldrick, Gerson, & Petry, 2008), is a diagram of the family over a few generations. It is used to depict the quality of family relationships, potential "supporters," family members who generate stress, and patterns that recur within and across generations. Both the genogram and the ecomap can be used productively in early interviews with clients to learn about their family and other potential social supports.

The *DSM-IV-TR* (APA, 2000) itself has axes that account for social and environmental stressors. Axis IV is the place in which clinicians list problems with a primary support group, occupational difficulties, economic problems, trouble with the legal system, and other problems that have been present in the previous year (or before that time if they are relevant). The Axis III diagnosis (health problems) is also of concern because health problems have social as well as psychological consequences. The Axis V diagnosis, Global Assessment of Functioning (GAF), is made by rating the client's psychological, social, and occupational functioning according to a scale that goes from 1 (extremely low) to 100 (superior). This scale requires that the clinician consider the overall impact of the client's psychological problems on his or her ability to enact social roles. By listing the highest GAF score in the last year as well as the current one, the clinician can estimate the client's prognosis. The Axis V diagnosis can also be used in behavioral health settings as a tool with which to monitor a client's progress.

Psychological Information

Psychological information is also an important component of the biopsychosocial assessment. This includes the client's symptoms and reported results of psychological testing, both of which have already been discussed. Some of these findings suggest areas in which the client is *vulnerable* to mental health crises. The client may also be vulnerable in the face of life changes, environmental stressors, or when someone he or she has counted on for support in the past is not available or helpful, or leaves.

The clinical social worker gives particular attention to the client's psychological *strengths*. These may be personal attributes or positive coping mechanisms. Examples of personal characteristics that can be identified and included in a biopsychosocial assessment are the following:

1. completed an educational course of study (high school, college, technical training, business school)
2. good problem-solving skills
3. good analytic skills
4. ability to make friends; social skills
5. well groomed
6. good sense of humor
7. keeps appointments; is able to get places on time
8. has work experience and work skills
9. has a special talent (art, music, writing, storytelling)
10. prepares nutritious meals
11. maintains a neat apartment

Strengths are unique to the individual. Everyone has his or her own complex of strengths. Besides these personal strengths, the strengths of the individual's culture can be brought to bear in the amelioration of problems.

Coping mechanisms are strategies individuals use to deal with ordinary, everyday problems and more challenging difficulties that come their way. In contrast with defense mechanisms, which are unconscious and automatic, coping mechanisms are conscious and deliberate. The following is a list of coping mechanisms that can be included in the assessment:

1. seeking out information
2. asking for support from others (e.g., friends, family, or professionals)
3. analyzing a problem and coming up with alternative solutions
4. exercising to relieve stress
5. going to a movie
6. reading a book
7. listening to music
8. thinking about the consequences if the worst-case scenario would occur
9. using religious resources or praying alone

10. minimizing the seriousness of the problem
11. keeping a journal and reflecting on the experience

Like strengths, coping mechanisms are diverse and individualized. They help individuals manage their feelings, prevent them from becoming overwhelmed, and empower them to do something.

THE WRITTEN BIOPSYCHOSOCIAL ASSESSMENT

The preliminary biopsychosocial report pulls together, summarizes, and analyzes the findings of the initial interview(s) with the client and significant others, medical findings, reports from other agencies and professionals (if available), results of psychological and rapid assessment tests (if performed), and the findings of social assessment tools (if used). The report should be comprehensive and provide a view of the person and problem in the context of the client's life. Care should be given to present the client as an individual who is experiencing a difficulty—not as a diagnostic category.

Recommended Format

Many behavioral or mental health organizations have a preferred format for collecting and writing the biopsychosocial assessment. Often these formats reflect the purpose of the agency and its philosophy of treatment. The one presented here is broad and may not apply to the specific function of every agency. Furthermore, it is more detailed than what is generally required by managed care entities. Some of the information included here can be incorporated in summary sheets or transformed into checklists.

I. Identifying Information
   A. Demographic information: age, sex, ethnic group, current student/employment/household roles, marital status, and so on.
   B. Referral information: referral source (self or another), reason for referral.
   C. Data sources used in writing this report: interviews with identified persons (list dates and persons), examinations and tests performed, other data used.
II. Presenting Problem
   A. Detailed description of the problem, situation, and symptoms for which help is sought *as presented by the client.* Use the client's words, if possible. What precipitated the current difficulty? What feelings and thoughts have been aroused? How has the client coped so far?
   B. Who else is involved in the problem? How are they involved? How do they view the problem? How have they reacted? How have they contributed to the problem or solution?
   C. Past experiences related to current difficulty. Has something like this ever happened before? If so, how was it handled then? What were the consequences then?
   D. Other recent problems. Identify stressful life events or circumstances that have occurred in the last year, how they were managed, and what they have meant to the client.
III. Current Situation
   A. Description of family or household: who is in the household (names, ages) and relationship (natural child, stepparent, friend), quality of relationships, caregivers inside and outside the household.
   B. Social network: extended family, friends, peer groups, community affiliations.
   C. Guardianship information (if applicable).

    D. Economic situation: who is working; nature of employment; receiving public assistance, social security, SSI, or retirement income; adequacy of income; state of indebtedness. Identify economic needs, if applicable, and money management practices.

    E. Physical environment/housing: nature of living circumstances (apartment, group home or other shared living arrangement, crowded conditions, homeless shelter); neighborhood.

    F. Significant issues, roles, or activities: student, retired, military, health problems, disabled, substance abuse, legal problems.

 IV. Previous Mental Health Problems and Treatment: nature of difficulties (including suicide attempts) and treatment, kind of treatment (outpatient, hospitalization), outcome of treatment, attitude toward medication and psychotherapy.

  V. Background Information

    A. Family background: description of family of origin and family of procreation (if applicable).

    B. Marital/intimate relationship history.

    C. Education and/or vocational training.

    D. Employment history.

    E. Military history (if applicable).

    F. Use and abuse of alcohol or drugs, self, and family.

    G. Health issues: accidents, disabilities, diseases, health problems in family, nutrition, sleep, exercise, dietary restrictions.

    H. Cultural background: ethnic group(s), identification and association with ethnic and/or religious group. Immigration issues, if applicable. Cultural beliefs about mental health problems and their treatment.

    I. Other historical information (violence, conflict with the law)

 VI. Results of Mental Status Examination and Diagnosis

VII. Analysis

    A. What is the key issue or problem from your perspective? How does your perspective compare with the client's? How serious is the problem?

    B. How effectively is the client functioning?

    C. What factors (thoughts, behaviors, personality issues, circumstances) seem to be contributing to the problems? Are these factors within the client, in the client system, from the social environment, or from social interactions?

    D. Identify the personal and cultural strengths, sources of meaning, coping ability, and resources that can be mobilized to help the client.

    E. Identify stressors, obstacles, vulnerabilities, and needs.

    F. Assess the extent to which the client is at risk (Is he or she suicidal? At risk of homelessness?). Are others close to the client at risk of being harmed?

    G. Assess client's motivation and potential to benefit from intervention.

VIII. Recommendations/Intervention Plan

    A. What course of action do you recommend? Specify:

       1. Type(s) of intervention (case management; individual, family, or group therapy; environmental intervention). If a specific evidence-based intervention is appropriate and available, specify what this is.

       2. Referral to psychiatrist for assessment for medication.

       3. Referral for special program within agency (ACT program, medication group).

       4. Referral to other agencies for services.

       5. Advocacy on a particular issue.

       6. Further testing.

B. What are the goals of intervention? How will you evaluate goal attainment or symptom reduction? (Which rapid assessment or clinical instrument[s] do you recommend?)

C. What are the short-term and long-term goals? Are they realistic and manageable? How long do you think it will take to achieve the goals?

Name of social worker, degree, and license

Job title

Date

Section VII, analysis, will reflect the clinician's theoretical orientation. An assessment from an ego psychology perspective, for example, will assess the ego functions, developmental issues, situational stress, role performance, and environmental insufficiencies and analyze the extent to which the client's problems are related to difficulties in each of these areas (Goldstein, 1995). An assessment using cognitive theory will highlight thinking patterns that are related to current difficulties, as well as clients' perceptions of themselves, others, the environment, and their future (Beck, 1976).

The intervention plan that is described in a preliminary form in section VIII of the outline is negotiated between the client and the social worker. Clinical social workers should offer their own perception of the client's problem and needs but should give the client the opportunity to do the same. In keeping with the values of self-determination (as well as client empowerment), the client's priorities should be reflected in the intervention plan.

Goals are evaluated in a number of ways. When they are behaviorally specific enough (e.g., "Mary will leave the home one hour a day for the next week"), they can be checked off on an agency form developed for this purpose as "accomplished," "partially accomplished," or "not accomplished" after the time period passes. Alternatively, various instruments can be used to monitor goal attainment. Some practitioners assess goals that they negotiate with the client using Goal Attainment Scaling (GAS) techniques. To do this, they measure achievement of each goal along an ordinal scale in a continuum of outcomes in which the worst to the most positive are described. Goal Attainment Scales are described in numerous social work texts (e.g., Sheafor, Horejsi, & Horejsi, 1994). The GAS is completed by the social worker. If the goal is to reduce the severity of symptoms, the client can complete many of the rapid assessment tools described earlier during each visit or at intervals. When goals are not accomplished, the social worker should reflect about and discuss with clients and colleagues possible reasons for this. On the one hand, it may be that the goals are not appropriate, there are barriers toward achieving them, or the client is not motivated to change. In such cases, the obstacles should be addressed and, in some cases, the goals should be changed. Similarly, if symptoms do not lessen, the social worker should reflect on the adequacy of the intervention plan. The intervention strategy may not be appropriate and should be reexamined or revised.

Many agencies have a form that staff members complete collaboratively with clients, in which the problems, needs, goals, and objectives are outlined, usually in behaviorally specific language. The items that are included are designed to conform to the requirements of the Joint Commission (formerly called the Joint Commission on Accreditation of Healthcare Organizations), medical assistance programs, and behavioral managed care entities. The following is a list of the kinds of items that are generally included in the intervention plan:

Description of problem areas and needs

Problem list (in priority order)

Strengths/assets

Obstacles/needs

Goals (short term, long term)

Objectives—list objectives for each problem and indicate:

What is to be done (action proposed) by whom (client, staff person, etc.)

How objective is to be accomplished (methods)

Target date for achieving objective

Criteria for assessing accomplishment of goal and tools to be used

Review date

Goals are usually global ("Jack will improve his social skills"), whereas objectives are more concrete and specific ("Jack will join a bowling league in the next month"). Some agencies use a method of recording called *problem-oriented record keeping;* for such agencies, progress notes will reflect the problems that are listed. Other agencies use a goal-oriented system, in which they record accomplishments achieving goals or objectives. *SOAP* (subjective information, objective information, assessment, and plan) comprise another approach to record keeping; this is used by some behavioral health agencies.

In today's managed behavioral care settings, it is very important to construct clear, behaviorally specific, measurable objectives that are linked to dealing with particular problems or symptoms. This information is needed not only during a formal intake or assessment stage but throughout the treatment or intervention process. Utilization reviews, which use this information, can occur prospectively (to show that treatment and a particular type of intervention are needed), concurrently (while treatment is taking place), and retrospectively (after treatment is completed) (Corcoran & Vandiver, 1996). Clinicians need to advance a rational case for what they want to do, what they are doing, and what they did. On the other hand, it is important that social workers avoid using standardized, mechanical language that is more reflective of agency goals than what is happening with the individual client (cf. Floersch, 2000).

CASE REVIEW WITH AN INTERDISCIPLINARY TREATMENT PLANNING TEAM

Although agencies vary in their interdisciplinary practices, it is valuable to have the team participate in the assessment and treatment planning of clients. To the mental health professional, group meetings provide an opportunity to obtain perspectives of colleagues of other disciplines; to learn from group discussion and deliberation; to obtain consultation and advice from others. Social work students can gain knowledge from hearing and participating in such discussions. It is beneficial to clients to have multiple voices contributing to their recommended treatment.

Some agencies follow a procedure in which all cases that have gone through an intake procedure (preliminary screening and development of the written psychosocial assessment) are discussed in an open meeting of a team of professionals. The team listens to a description of the case, deliberates over the diagnosis, and develops an initial treatment plan collaboratively. Some agencies invite the client, significant others, the case manager, and others to the meeting. At this time, cases may be assigned to another worker, assigned to a special program, or referred to the psychiatrist or psychologist.

Many agencies also have the team conduct periodic reviews of the client's progress. The primary therapist may, for example, present a report on the client's progress in psychotherapy and in obtaining resources at periodic intervals—for example, after sixty days, ninety days, six months. In this way, the diagnosis and the treatment plan can be reviewed and modified as more information is obtained and circumstances change. Moreover, the professional staff is monitoring cases corporately—thus fulfilling their responsibility to clients, the agency, and the funding sources.

Other teams meet on a daily basis to report on new developments and to come to a consensus about consistent strategies of intervention to be used in relation to particular clients. Such teams are continually revising their assessment and intervention plan to address the immediate needs of clients.

The participation of the client and significant others in the periodic reviews of the client's progress is a valuable component of this process. Treatment is not a regimen one imposes on someone. The client should be working on problems that are of personal relevance and import. Goals and objectives should reflect the client's wishes and priorities. More than paperwork required by "the system," the review provides a means to evaluate and revise the plan so that it reflects the client's voice.

Summary and Deconstruction

The biopsychosocial assessment is an open-ended, ongoing activity in clinical work with clients; it is also a written summary, frozen in time, which summarizes and analyzes information about the client that is available at the time the report is written. A number of professionals may participate in the construction of the assessment—the social worker, psychiatrist, psychologist, nurse, and other members of the agency's behavioral mental health team, as well as physicians who examine or conduct tests on the client. Significant others such as family members may also provide information about the client.

The key participant in the assessment process is the client. The client's story and responses to clinical interviews comprise primary data that professionals examine and analyze. Although the client clearly plays a role in the construction of the assessment, the biopsychosocial assessment is a professional activity that is biased toward categories that the professionals and their funding sources consider meaningful. Even terms such as *stressors*, *supports*, and *strengths* are professional constructions.

This chapter provided recommended formats for the mental status examination and the biopsychosocial assessment. These are constructed from interactions with the client. However useful they are for contemporary practice, there is a need to understand the ways clients perceive themselves, others, and treatment and to work toward goals that are meaningful to them and their recovery. This requires going beyond diagnosis and the other components of the biopsychosocial assessment.

Websites

http://www.jointcommission.org/Standards/Requirements/
http://www.appi.org/group.cfm?groupid=SCID-I

http://www.scid4.org/

References

American Psychiatric Association. (2000). *Diagnostic and statistical manual of mental disorders* (4th ed., text rev.). Washington, DC: Author.

Beck, A. T. (1976). *Cognitive therapy and the emotional disorders*. Madison, CT: International Universities Press.

Corcoran, K., & Vandiver, V. (1996). *Maneuvering the maze of managed care: Skills for mental health practitioners*. New York: The Free Press.

Crisp, B. R., Anderson, M. R., Orme, J., & Lister, P. G. (2004). Learning and teaching assessment: Reviewing the evidence. *Social Work Education, 23*(2), 199–215.

Fischer, J., & Corcoran, K. (2007). *Measures for clinical practice: A sourcebook* (4th ed., Vols. 1 and 2). Oxford and New York: Oxford University Press.

Floersch, J. (2000). Reading the case record: The oral and written narratives of social workers. *Social Service Review, 74*(2), 169–192.

Folstein, M. F., Folstein, S. F., & McHugh, P. R. (1975). Mini-mental state: A practical method for coding the cognitive state of patients for the clinician. *Journal of Psychiatric Research, 12,* 189–198.

Franklin, C., & Jordan, C. (2003). A integrative skills assessment approach. In C. Jordan & C. Franklin (Eds.),

Clinical assessment for social workers (pp. 1–52). Chicago: Lyceum.

Goldstein, E. (1995). *Ego psychology and social work practice* (2nd ed.). New York: The Free Press.

Graham, J. R., & Lilly, R. S. (1984). *Psychological testing.* Englewood Cliffs, NJ: Prentice-Hall.

Hartman, A. (1978). Diagrammatic assessment of family relationships. *Social Casework, 59,* 465–476.

Hepworth, D. I., & Larsen, J. (1982). *Direct social work practice.* Homewood, IL: Dorsey Press.

Kleinman, A. (1988). *The illness narratives: Suffering, healing, and the human condition.* New York: Basic Books.

Lawton, M. P., & Brody, E. M. (1969). Assessment of older people: self-maintaining and instrumental activities of daily living. *Gerontologist, 9,* 179–186.

McGoldrick, M., Gerson, R., & Petry, S. (2008). *Genograms: Assessment and intervention* (3rd ed.). New York: W. W. Norton.

Sadock, B. J., & Sadock, V. A. (2007). *Kaplan & Sadock's synopsis of psychiatry: Behavioral sciences/cinical psychiatry* (10th ed.). Philadelphia, PA: Wolters Klumer Lippincott Williams & Wilkins.

Sheafor, B. W., Horejsi, C. R., & Horejsi, G. A. (1994). *Techniques and guidelines for social work practice* (3rd ed.). Boston: Allyn & Bacon.

Spitzer, R. L., Williams, J. B. W., Gibbon, M., & First, M. B. (1989). *Structured clinical interview for DSM-III-R SCID.* New York: New York State Psychiatric Institute.

Trzepacz, P. T., & Baker, R. W. (1993). *The psychiatric mental status examination.* New York: Oxford University Press.

Wallace, C. J. (1986). Functional assessment in rehabilitation. *Schizophrenia Bulletin, 12,* 625–629.

Legal and Ethical Issues

On April 16, 2007, Seung-Hui Cho, an undergraduate at
Virginia Polytechnic Institute (Virginia Tech), fatally shot 32 people
and himself and injured others. Despite a history of mental illness prior
to his admission to college, a court order that he seek outpatient
treatment, and warning signs observed by faculty and other students,
he was not hospitalized and was able to purchase guns.

The shooting at Virginia Tech was a national tragedy that raised complex legal and ethical questions for legal scholars, policy makers, universities, and mental health providers. How was it that a person with a documented mental illness was able to purchase guns? Why was Cho's mental illness not treated before it reached this point? Why was he ordered to seek outpatient rather than inpatient treatment? This chapter examines how legal and ethical issues such as these affect the provision of mental health care by clinical social workers.

As Dolgoff, Loewenberg, and Harrington (2009) explain, ethics has to do with what is correct and right. Ethical principles are based on values, which are beliefs about what is good and desirable (Dolgoff et al., 2009). In social work, professional values and ethics tend to converge (Levy, 1979). Both are encompassed in the National Association of Social Workers (NASW) Code of Ethics. The core professional values stated in the Code of Ethics are (a) service, (b) social justice, (c) dignity and worth of the person, (d) the importance of human relationships, (e) integrity, and (f) competence (NASW, 1996/1999/2008). A social worker's primary responsibility is to promote the well-being and interests of his or her clients and to respect clients' self-determination and privacy (NASW, 1996/1999/2008). Nevertheless, social workers are subject to laws that can supersede their accountability to clients. In addition to being responsible to clients, professional social workers are accountable to colleagues, practice settings, the social work profession (NASW, 1996/1999/2008), and the larger society. Thus, there are many layers of coexisting obligations and demands, any or many of which may be mobilized in a given situation.

Clinical social work practice in mental health is also affected by the law, which may or may not coincide with social work values and ethics. There are differences between legal and ethical principles. Whereas it is obligatory to comply with the law and punishment for noncompliance may follow, observance of ethical principles is voluntary (Dolgoff et al., 2009). Unethical professional practice, however, is subject to sanctions by professional organizations, peers, and agencies. Laws, which may be based on ethical principles, can be changed, but ethical rules tend to be resistant to change (Dolgoff et al., 2009).

Clinical social workers in mental health operate in environments in which the law and quasi-legal authorities are influential. The law includes state and federal court decisions, laws enacted by legislatures, public policies, and regulations interpreting public policies. Supreme Court decisions and federal laws that have evolved and continue to evolve apply to the entire nation. Legislation and decisions of state and federal district courts in one's own state affect practice in these areas. Although decisions that are made in higher courts of other states are not binding elsewhere, lawyers who argue in state and federal courts on cases involving similar issues often use these decisions as examples of appropriate decisions. State laws are sometimes consistent with decisions made in other states or with model laws created by special interest groups. Similarly, quasi-legal authorities such as managed care entities manifest themselves differently in different localities, but there are commonalities.

This chapter begins with a discussion of ethical theories. Then it addresses the topics of involuntary civil commitment, least restrictive alternative, clients' rights, confidentiality and the duty to protect, and documentation and record keeping.

ETHICAL THEORIES

Ethical theories are approaches to ethical questions that have been developed by philosophers of ethics. Reamer (2006) describes two types of normative ethical theories that social workers can apply to situations in which different ethical principles conflict. *Deontological* theory, based on Kant's universal principles, claims that certain actions are inherently right or wrong or good or bad. A person following this theory believes that there are fixed moral rules that one follows regardless of the consequences. The other theory Reamer describes is called *teleological*. Here actions are considered right or good depending on their consequences. Because one does not know the consequences in advance, one must think through possible outcomes and weigh the advantages of different options. *Utilitarianism*, associated with Jeremy Bentham and John Stuart Mill, is a teleological school. According to this way of thinking, an action is considered good if it promotes the maximum good (Reamer, 2006).

In addition to these, several other ethical theories have been introduced. Rooted in Greek philosophy, *virtue ethics* is concerned with character makeup, which refers to being a morally good person who wants to do the right thing (Beauchamp, 1999). *Ethics of care*, a term developed by Gilligan (1982), refers to ethical decision making that considers the relationship with a loved one. *Casuistry* refers to decision making in which a new situation is considered in relation to previous cases (Beauchamp, 1999). Another contemporary theory is *communitarianism*, in which what is best for the community and the community's values is given primacy in ethical decision making (Reamer, 2006).

Ethical theories can be helpful to the clinician when there are conflicts between different values or ethical principles or between a law and a professional value or ethical principles. In situations of conflict, social workers can use these theories to help them make decisions (Reamer, 2006). One issue that social workers face in mental health practice that can provoke an ethical conflict is involuntary civil commitment. We turn to this topic next.

INVOLUNTARY CIVIL COMMITMENT

Involuntary civil commitment refers to a legal procedure in which a person is required to be confined to an inpatient psychiatric facility or to conditional community outpatient treatment. Commitment to a psychiatric hospital is a serious step as it deprives individuals of their liberty, privacy, and freedom to pursue their own interests (Hermann, 1997). The state derives its right to commit people through its historical role as parent (*parens patriae*) and through its *police power* to protect the public from danger. As parent, the state takes a benevolent interest in the welfare of vulnerable citizens, whom it tries to protect. When the state assumes the parental role, it acts in what it perceives to be the best interest of the individual. "The police power is the authority of the state to maintain peace and order and to take action to punish or confine those whose behavior threatens the persons or property of others" (p. 146). When the state assumes police power, its focus is on the interests of the community (Brakel, Parry, & Weiner, 1985). Thus, the state is empowered to protect either the individual or the community or, at times, both.

Although states vary in their statutory requirements for involuntary civil commitment, most recognize two criteria that apply to the client. First, a diagnosis of a psychiatric disorder is necessary. Second, individuals must be considered dangerous to themselves or others. In recent years, criteria have widened to include need for treatment and probability, risk, or likelihood of harm (Pfeffer, 2008). Another criterion is the client's inability to provide for his or her basic needs, sometimes described as being gravely disabled. This standard, however, usually is not the sole requirement that must be met (Brakel et al., 1985). A civil commitment should be differentiated from a criminal one in which an individual is punished for a crime and, consequently, loses some of his or her civil rights.

Additional information that may be needed could pertain to dangerousness. A Wisconsin case, *Lessard v. Schmidt* (1974), ruled that commitment was justified only if it is likely that a person would do "immediate harm to himself or others." Although this case called for a "recent overt act, attempt or threat to do substantial harm" (p. 1093), many other states do not have such a requirement (Hermann, 1997). Even if there is evidence of aggressive behavior from the recent past, the assessment of dangerousness is a judgment call because behavior in the future cannot be accurately predicted. In *O'Connor v. Donaldson* (1975), which went to the Supreme Court, a man who was institutionalized for years was said to be wrongfully confined because he was *not* dangerous (Brakel et al., 1985). Another Supreme Court case, *Addington v. Texas* (1979), held that the state's criteria must be based on "clear and convincing evidence," thus requiring dangerousness to be documented. Generally psychiatrists determine whether an individual is mentally ill and make decisions around emergency admissions, but in formal hearings judicial officers, a jury, an administrative board, or a psychiatric board is authorized by different states to decide whether an individual is to be committed (Hermann, 1997). In the commitment hearing of Seung-Hui Cho (Virginia Tech shooting), he was found to be dangerous, but another standard, "least restrictive environment" (described in the next section), was used to justify his treatment on an outpatient basis (Pfeffer, 2008). Since the Virginia Tech shooting, the criteria for involuntary civil commitment have broadened in Virginia (Pfeffer, 2008).

Involuntary outpatient commitment (IOU) is an alternative to involuntary inpatient commitment in which clients are legally committed to a community treatment center rather than to a hospital (American Bar Association, 1988). Under regulations, community residence may be tied to compliance with the treatment plan. IOU may occur in place of hospitalization or upon discharge from a psychiatric facility. The outpatient treatment law in New York, known as "Kendra's Law," in memory of a woman who was pushed onto subway tracks by a man with schizophrenia, appropriates funds to pay for case management and other outpatient services (Appelbaum, 2005), but this stipulation is not necessarily included in laws of other states. A parallel law in Florida is underutilized (Petrila & Christy, 2008). Variations of IOU include *conditional release*, whereby a patient is discharged from the hospital but can be returned during the release period, and *preventive commitment,* which has been instituted by some states to protect persons who look as if they might deteriorate (Monahan, Swartz, & Bonnie, 2003).

Although most states have some sort of outpatient civil commitment, the policy is controversial (Monahan et al., 2003). On the one hand, it allows individuals who would otherwise be hospitalized to live relatively freely in the community. Moreover, it can be argued that it protects third parties from potential violence (Monahan et al., 2003). Furthermore, it makes it possible to treat individuals who are not likely to comply with their treatment plan. Gott (1997) noted that research has found that outpatient commitment has a positive effect on treatment outcome and that it provides an opportunity for a client to receive help. Swartz and Swanson (2004) concluded from their review of the literature that outpatient commitment is most effective for people with psychotic disorders who are treated for six months or more.

Despite potential benefits, IOU is coercive as it treats people without their consent (Monahan, 2008; Monahan et al., 2003). It uses tools such as inclusion in subsidized housing, management of their money, threat of incarceration, and hospitalization as leverage to compel individuals to comply with treatment (Monahan et al., 2003). As such, it puts social workers and other mental health professionals in the role of "mental health police," to say nothing of the liability it imposes on social workers whose caseloads include individuals who are considered "dangerous" (Wilk, 1997). Another approach is to assure that a client receives the least restrictive treatment that is consistent with his or her needs.

LEAST RESTRICTIVE ALTERNATIVE

The least restrictive alternative is a legal principle that has been the basis for discharging or not hospitalizing clients with mental illness who can function in a less intrusive environment, and for selecting an appropriate level of care in the community. Several court cases have affirmed that clients have a right to treatment in the least restrictive alternative (*Lake v. Cameron*, 1966; *Covington v. Harris*, 1969; *Wyatt v. Stickney*, 1971/1972; *Dixon v. Weinberger*, 1975). The *Wyatt* case, for example, ruled that clients in Alabama institutions for the mentally ill and mentally retarded have a right to humane treatment in conditions that introduce the least restrictions necessary to achieve the goals of treatment.

The least restrictive alternative applies to the treatment environment and the modes of intervention that are employed. Both are evaluated in relation to the treatment objectives for the individual client (Brakel et al., 1985) and eliminate the threat of dangerousness (Hermann, 1997). The *most* restrictive environment is the most confining and intrusive (Rinas & Clyne-Jackson, 1988); for example, an institution that maintains clients behind locked doors. The *least* is a community setting in which the client has little supervision. At the point of screening for admission, the client's treatment needs should be assessed in relation to alternative settings in which these needs can be met. For example, if an individual can be treated effectively in a community mental health center and with an intensive outpatient treatment program while living at home, hospitalization may be avoided. Similarly clients who are hospitalized should not be placed in constricting units, such as maximum-security wards, if this degree of restriction is not therapeutic. Clients who are transferred from less to more confining units or treatment facilities are entitled to a hearing (Brakel et al., 1985).

A 1999 Supreme Court case, *Olmstead v. L.C. and E.W.*, expanded the legal basis for favoring less restrictive settings. This case, filed on behalf of two women with mental illness and mental retardation, found that maintaining individuals with disabilities isolated in state institutions when they are capable of living more independently in the community discriminated against them under Title II of the Americans with Disabilities Act (ADA) of 1990 (Greenhouse, 1999). In a later application of the *Olmstead* decision and the ADA, a federal district judge ruled in 2009 in *DAI v. Paterson* that placement in board-and-care homes used to house thousands of adults with mental illnesses in New York State violated the ADA because they did not enable residents' integration with nondisabled individuals in the community (Bazelton Center for Mental Health Law, 2009).

The kinds of interventions employed are also encompassed under the least restrictive alternative. Those therapies that affect physical functioning (e.g., medication, shock treatment) are more intrusive than "talk" therapies; aversive treatment is more coercive than systematic desensitization; physical restraints are more confining than calm coaxing. Mental health practitioners are encouraged to use the lesser alternative that promises to help the client (Rinas & Clyne-Jackson, 1988). The client's medication also falls under the rubric of the least restrictive alternative (Brooks, 1988). Clients who object to a medication for a particular reason, such as its side effects, can be offered alternative medication that does not have these effects or a treatment strategy other than medication that is therapeutic.

Social workers are in positions in which they put the least restrictive alternative standard into effect. Whether they work in community mental health centers, behavioral health carve-outs, hospital admissions or emergency departments, step-down programs, residential programs, or inpatient facilities, they play an important role in determining which among a range of alternative treatment settings and services are most appropriate and beneficial and least limiting for particular clients. The social worker has a responsibility to be familiar with the particular settings, what they have to offer, the climate within each alternative, and whether there are openings at a particular time. Furthermore, they should explore with the client the kinds of living situation and treatment that he or she wants based on an empowerment and recovery process.

CLIENTS' RIGHTS AND PROTECTIONS

Ordinarily, clients have the same rights as other citizens, such as the rights to vote, due process, and legal representation. Among the rights that pertain to their mental health status are the right to treatment, the right to refuse treatment (including medication), and the right to informed consent. Consumers of mental health services have the right to make choices on their own behalf unless they are found to be incompetent.

Technically, the term *incompetence* denotes a legal status that is to be established by a court, whereas the term *incapacity* denotes a clinical judgment, but these two terms are not used in their strict sense in practice (Appelbaum, 2007). Criteria used to evaluate a client's capacity to make decisions include the following: (a) is able to communicate a choice, (b) understands relevant information, (c) appreciates the problem or situation and its likely consequences, and (d) is able to reason about treatment options (Appelbaum, 2007). Even persons who are formally adjudged incompetent and have legal guardians or conservators who look out for their interests do not surrender all their rights. These guardians may have limited areas in which they make decisions on behalf of the client (e.g., money management), leaving the client with rights in other areas.

As for the client's right to refuse treatment, many states make a distinction between clients' rights in emergency as opposed to nonemergency situations, denying clients their rights in the former instances. Similarly, clients who are determined to be incompetent can be given a treatment (such as medication) that they do not want. In *Rennie v. Klein* (1983), the U.S. Court of Appeals for the Third Circuit ruled that although involuntary patients can refuse to take antipsychotic medication in nonemergency situations, hospital staff could administer medication if they determine that patients present a danger to themselves or others (Hermann, 1997). In such cases, professional judgment (usually supported in an in-hospital procedure to establish due process) supersedes the client's wishes (Hermann, 1997).

The client's right to refuse treatment is based on his or her right to autonomy or self-determination (Caplan, 2008). From the perspective of a family member or clinician, however, the client is not acting in his or her best interest. Arguing against the client's right of refusal in some circumstances, Caplan states that those "who are truly addicted to alcohol or drugs really do not have the full capacity to be self-determining or autonomous" (p. 1919). He suggests that it is worth thinking about mandating the temporary use of a safe medication such as naltrexone to treat addiction. This is similar to the use of rehabilitation methods against a patient's will, in instances where the patient experiencing great pain asks to be allowed to die, or mandating treatment of medication for addiction under some circumstances would restore autonomy (Caplan, 2008).

Nevertheless, clients may have good reason to refuse treatment. Many medications have side effects (see Chapters 8, 9, and 12) that are difficult to tolerate. In those cases, other medications and psychotherapeutic interventions may be more suitable. Where possible, practitioners should explore the feasibility of these alternatives before the situation escalates into one in which treatment is forced. For clients who are willing to be treated but want to have a voice in how they are treated, drawing up advance directives may be appropriate.

Psychiatric Advance Directives

Advance directives are legal documents, written when an individual is competent, specifying "how decisions about treatment should be made if the person becomes incompetent" (Appelbaum, 1991, p. 983). They are widely used in health care by individuals who wish to express in advance their wishes about the use of specific, life-preserving measures (e.g., ventilators, feeding tubes). Psychiatric advance directives (PADs) specify the kinds of treatments clients want and do not want at a future time when they might decompensate or experience a mental health crisis. Because PADs enable consumers to spell out their choices, they are both empowering and consistent with the philosophy of recovery (Scheyett & Kim, 2007).

The two types of PADs that are generally used in the United States are *instructional* and *proxy*. The former is comparable to living wills, whereas the latter is something like power of attorney (Srebnik & La Fond, 1999). The instructional directives may include choices around types of medication and administration methods, use of restraints, preferred hospital, persons who should be notified, individuals who should be asked to assume child care, and the use of particular treatment methods (e.g., electric shock therapy) (Srebnik & La Fond, 1999). Proxy directives nominate a third party who is authorized to make decisions on behalf of the client in the event that the client becomes incompetent (Appelbaum, 1991). The proxy may be a family member or friend—someone who is trusted. An advance directive may include both instructional and proxy types. Some directives include a section signed by a psychiatrist attesting that the client is competent at the time the directive is made (Vogel-Scibilia, 1999). Other types of advance statements that are used in the United States and Europe are known as joint crisis plans, facilitated PADs, crisis cards, treatment plans, and wellness recovery action plans (Henderson, Swanson, Szmukler, Thornicroft, & Zinkler, 2008). Model forms specific to requirements of particular states in the United States can be obtained from the National Resource Center on Psychiatric Advance Directives (http://www.nrc-pad.org/).

Advance directives preserve clients' rights and preferences even when their functioning is compromised. Nevertheless, the instructions cannot compel a mental health provider to follow treatment methods that he or she considers undesirable, unethical, or unaffordable and tend to allow the clinician's judgment to supersede that of the client (Srebnik & La Fond, 1999; Swanson, Van McCrary, Swartz, Elbogen, & Van Dorn, 2006). A further complication is that if the advance directive is written as irrevocable, it can be construed as a Ulysses contract that limits an individual's future freedom, a contract that many states are reluctant to uphold (Srebnik & La Fond, 1999).

Up until now we have been considering the rights of clients and the constraints on these rights. Next we will look at constraints and obligations that are placed on the social worker.

CONFIDENTIALITY AND THE DUTY TO PROTECT

Confidentiality

Confidentiality is a core social work value and an ethical principle. Social workers are bound to maintain the privacy of communications shared by clients by not disclosing that the individual is a client and the particular information shared by the client without the client's consent, and by taking precautions to assure the security of case records. According to the NASW Code of Ethics (1996/1999/2008), "Once private information is shared, standards of confidentiality apply" (Section 1.07(a)).

Confidentiality should be distinguished from the closely related concept of privileged communication. Information shared in confidence with mental health professionals, lawyers, clergy, and physicians is protected from inquiry by the court ("privileged") where state laws stipulate that those particular professions have that status. In *Jaffee v. Redmond* (1996), the Supreme Court found that records and notes of licensed clinical social workers "written in the course of diagnosis and treatment are protected against involuntary disclosure by a psychotherapist-client privilege" (Gelman, Pollack, & Weiner, 1999, p. 244). Under these circumstances, the client has the right to have protected information withheld in legal proceedings. There are, however, instances in which privileged communication is disregarded. If a client signs a waiver or provides informed consent, the information can be revealed to the court or the party named in the waiver or consent form. On other occasions, such as suspected child abuse, involuntary commitment, and dangerous behavior (Rinas & Clyne-Jackson, 1988), social workers are required by law to testify.

Confidentiality is a critical feature of a therapeutic relationship. It is a way in which clients are able to feel that it is safe to share their feelings. In promising confidentiality, the social worker conveys a willingness to protect the interests of the client. Thus, confidentiality contributes to the quality of the therapeutic alliance. Nevertheless, confidentiality cannot be fully guaranteed.

There are circumstances in which the social worker is obliged to violate confidentiality. Exceptions to maintaining confidentiality are recognized in the NASW Code of Ethics (1996/1999/2008):

> Social workers should protect the confidentiality of all information obtained in the course of professional service, except for *compelling professional reasons* [emphasis added]. The general expectation that social workers will keep information confidential does not apply when disclosure is necessary to prevent serious, foreseeable, and imminent harm to a client or other identifiable person. In all instances, social workers should disclose the least amount of confidential information necessary to achieve the desired purpose; only information that is directly relevant to the purpose for which the disclosure is made should be revealed. (Section 1.07(c))

Tarasoff Decisions and the Obligation to Protect

The quotation that was just cited from the NASW Code of Ethics is relevant to discussions surrounding the *Tarasoff* case. This California case entailed confidentiality and "compelling professional reasons" to violate this principle.

Two *Tarasoff* rulings and subsequent court decisions lay out the obligations of psychotherapists to protect others from possible harm. The initial case arose under the following circumstances. Prosenjit Poddar, a graduate student who was receiving psychotherapy at the University of California Student Health Service in Berkeley, told his therapist that he intended to kill a female student who had indicated that she was not romantically interested in him. At the time, the student, Tatiana Tarasoff, was on vacation in Brazil. The therapist responded by (a) getting Poddar to promise that he would not act on his desires and (b) informing the campus police. The police investigated the matter and were assured by Poddar that nothing would happen. After Tarasoff returned from vacation, however, Poddar killed her (Brakel et al., 1985).

On the basis of information revealed at Poddar's trial, Tarasoff's family sued two of Poddar's therapists, the University of California, and the campus police, stating that Tarasoff should have been warned that she was in danger. The state supreme court said that the therapist and police could be liable for failing to warn Tatiana (*Tarasoff v. Regents of the University of California*, 1974). The case was later reargued before the court (in a case heard in 1976 that is referred to as *Tarasoff II*). This time the court said that the therapist could be culpable if he did not "exercise reasonable care" to protect the victim. Steps such as warning the victim or others who could warn the victim, notifying the police, or other reasonable actions were recommended (*Tarasoff v. Regents of the University of California*, 1976). The court did not have the opportunity to determine whether the therapists in this case were negligent, as an out-of-court settlement was reached and Poddar returned to India. Subsequent rulings on a number of other cases have stipulated that the victim should be a specific and identifiable person or group of persons (Brakel et al.,1985).

Since *Tarasoff II*, the focus has moved from the "duty to warn" to the "duty to protect" third parties from violent acts (Appelbaum, 1985) with the duty to warn viewed as one of several options one can use to protect a potential victim (Weinstock, Vari, Leong, & Silva, 2006). Interpreting *Tarasoff* and court decisions based on it, Appelbaum (1985) described a three-stage process for clinicians to undertake. During the first stage, *assessment*, one gathers information relevant to the individual's dangerousness and uses that data to evaluate his or her dangerousness. The second stage, *selection of a course of action*, may include steps other than or besides warning third parties, such as hospitalizing the client, beginning medication, or some other actions. The third step, *implementation*, entails carrying out the action plan and monitoring it.

The *Tarasoff* decisions pose a dilemma to clinical social workers. As mentioned, the NASW Code of Ethics specifies that confidentiality can be violated only for "compelling professional reasons." Although clients' statements about violent actions they want to direct toward another may appear to be compelling, these pronouncements may be made in anger with no intention to carry them out. Conversely, violent intentions that are communicated indirectly can be overlooked. The social worker, however, needs to make a judgment about how serious the client is about carrying out such an act, whether there is a specific victim, and whether the intended victim is in danger. If the act seems likely to occur, the social worker (or other mental health professional) is obligated to warn or take some other reasonable step to protect the victim.

The *Tarasoff* rulings put pressure on mental health workers not only to make assessments about a client's dangerousness but to *predict* whether an individual poses a threat to another. A task force of the American Psychiatric Association reported serious reservations about the ability of therapists to foresee violent behavior; mistakes can be made. Moreover, warning a victim or other appropriate parties can jeopardize the therapeutic relationship (Brakel et al., 1985). In warning another, a therapist is violating the client's trust. The resulting sense of betrayal may make it virtually impossible for the therapeutic relationship to continue.

Several channels are open to the social worker faced with such a case. First, one should obtain legal information about how the *Tarasoff* rulings are interpreted in one's own state. State cases and statutes triggered by the California cases are diverse, with some more encompassing than *Tarasoff* and others more limiting (Kachigian & Felthous, 2004; Simone & Fulero, 2005). State rulings change over time, even in California since *Tarasoff II* (Weinstock et al., 2006). In states that do not provide immunity (and even those that do), one should consider a range of options regarding means of protecting third parties and who, if anyone, should be warned. Consultation with another staff member, especially a psychiatrist, is desirable (Brooks, 1988). Similarly, the agency's attorney might be contacted.

This section has discussed confidentiality and the duty to protect potential victims of violence. In today's health and mental health care environment, where records are increasingly electronic, legal issues and confidentiality are of paramount importance to social workers and clients. These issues are addressed in the next section.

DOCUMENTATION AND RECORD KEEPING

Recording of the social worker's contacts with clients has been integral to practice since the profession's inception. Mary Richmond (1917) used case records both as research data and to illustrate the processes of inquiry and analysis described in *Social Diagnosis*. As the profession evolved, documentation in case records was used to help workers think about the client and his or her situation, as an aid to teaching and supervision, and for purposes of accountability (Kagle & Kopels, 2008).

Nowadays case records serve many functions. Among them are the following: (a) identify and describe the client situation and the reason for service, (b) document and provide a basis for evaluating use of available resources, (c) provide a rationale for the goals, plans, and interventions, (d) document compliance with agency policies, practice guidelines, legal standards, and professional ethics, (e) provide a basis for monitoring progress, (f) provide a basis for claims for reimbursement, (g) maintain case continuity in the event of the absence or departure of a worker, (h) provide information needed for external oversight, (i) serve as evidence in court, and (j) provide data for research (Kagle & Kopels, 2008).

Judicious documentation is particularly relevant to social work practice in behavioral health settings. First, mental illness continues to be a stigma that can interfere with clients' ability to obtain work and gain acceptance in social situations. Second, persons with mental health issues may reveal other problems that threaten their well-being such as being diagnosed with HIV/AIDS, involvement in an abusive relationship, substance abuse, trouble with the law, and eviction from a home. All of these situations denote private information that, if documented, needs protection. Third, as discussed in the section on the duty to protect, some clients receiving mental health services are at risk of harming themselves and others. It is prudent for social workers to document threats, actions, and professional responses in their records (Reamer, 2005).

Clinical practice in mental health today requires knowledge of professional ethical obligations and changes in the law as they apply to documentation and record keeping. This section examines contemporary issues around mental health records in relation to social work ethics and legal regulations.

Social Work Ethics and Documentation

The multiple functions of case recording result in threats to client confidentiality and privacy. As Reamer (2005) states, "there is no such thing as a truly confidential case record" (p. 332). Numerous individuals and organizations such as managed care entities, accrediting groups, utilization review teams, and billing organizations have access to client records (Kane, Houston-Vega, & Nuehring, 2002). In addition, computers and electronic communication pose risks to the safety of client records.

The NASW Code of Ethics shows sensitivity to such threats. It includes explicit statements about client records:

3.04 Client Records

(a) Social workers should take reasonable steps to ensure that documentation in records is accurate and reflects the services provided.

(b) Social workers should include sufficient and timely documentation in records to facilitate the delivery of services and to ensure continuity of services provided to clients in the future.

(c) Social workers' documentation should protect clients' privacy to the extent that is possible and appropriate and should include only information that is directly relevant to the delivery of services. (NASW, 1996/1999/2008)

As subsection 3.04(a) in the preceding excerpt affirms, social workers are obligated to be truthful about the activities that they describe in the record and, as stated in 3.04(b), they should enter their notes as soon as possible. On the other hand, as explained in 3.04(c), social workers should not provide more information than what is needed. It is considered a violation of a client's privacy rights to disclose issues that depart from the purpose of the social worker–client contact. Thus, for example, if a client's sexual orientation is not relevant to treatment, this information should not be recorded.

The Code has additional provisions about the social worker's obligation to protect the client's privacy and confidentiality:

1.07 Privacy and Confidentiality

(a) Social workers should respect clients' right to privacy. Social workers should not solicit private information from clients unless it is essential to providing services or conducting social work evaluation or research. Once private information is shared, standards of confidentiality apply....

(l) Social workers should protect the confidentiality of clients' written and electronic records and other sensitive information. Social workers should take reasonable steps to ensure that clients' records are stored in a secure location and that clients' records are not available to others who are not authorized to have access.

(m) Social workers should take precautions to ensure and maintain the confidentiality of information transmitted to other parties through the use of computers, electronic mail, facsimile machines, telephones and telephone answering machines, and other electronic or computer technology. Disclosure of identifying information should be avoided whenever possible. (NASW, 1996/1999/2008)

In highlighting disclosure of only that which is relevant, subsection 1.07(a) is consistent with 3.04(c). Subsections 1.07(l) and 1.07(m) explain that records are not limited to the hard copy, paper "case record." Advances in technology over the last few decades have stimulated the production of electronic records with communication expanded to include e-mail correspondence with clients, faxes, and other kinds of records. More will be said about electronic records later in this section.

An additional ethical requirement included in the Code of Ethics has to do with clients' access to their records.

1.08 Access to Records

(a) Social workers should provide clients with reasonable access to records concerning the clients. Social workers who are concerned that clients' access to their records could cause serious misunderstanding or harm to the client should provide assistance in interpreting the records and consultation with the client regarding the records. Social workers should limit clients' access to their records, or portions of their records, only in exceptional circumstances when there is compelling evidence that such access would cause serious harm to the client. Both clients' requests and the rationale for withholding some or all of the record should be documented in clients' files.

(b) When providing clients with access to their records, social workers should take steps to protect the confidentiality of other individuals identified or discussed in such records. (NASW, 1996/1999/2008)

Clients have a right to know what is being said about them in records. The term *reasonable access* in subsection 1.08(a) is subject to interpretation. One approach is for the social worker to review the record with the client. This way, the social worker can deal with the client's reaction to what he or she reads. Knowing about clients' rights to access, social workers should not write anything in the record that they would not want clients to see. It is also important that the confidentiality of others mentioned in the record be protected. That supports having the social worker review the record selectively with the client.

Legal Regulations and Documentation

Over the past few decades, additions to and changes in the legal regulations and the law have had an impact of social work documentation. Clinicians need to be particularly aware of the federal regulations known as Confidentiality of Alcohol and Drug Abuse Patient Records (2007) and the Health Insurance Portability and Accountability Act (HIPAA) of 1996.

The federal regulations on Confidentiality of Alcohol and Drug Abuse Patient Records, also known as Part 2 regulations, provide extra protection to individuals with substance abuse problems who are receiving treatment in a federally assisted program (Kagle & Kopels, 2008). For most instances, the regulations call for the client's written consent to reveal information that would identify the client. One exception is when social workers, who are mandated reporters, suspect child abuse or neglect, and another is where there is a medical emergency (Kagle & Kopels, 2008). The regulations also outline how personal information is to be handled when there is a court order or request for a court appearance (Kagle & Kopels, 2008).

The Health Insurance Portability and Accountability Act, which applies to health and mental health entities, consists of two major sections, Parts I and II, and a regulation under Part II called the Privacy Rule. Part I establishes that health insurance is portable, enabling employees and their families to maintain insurance coverage in the event that they lose or change their job, and Title II has to do with the administration of health care (Kagle & Kopels, 2008). The Privacy Rule provides minimal standards of protection for the privacy of medical records, particularly electronic ones, for health care entities (health care clearinghouses, health plans, health care providers who transmit health information electronically, and business associates who have a contract with the former entities) as well as protections for individuals to control the use of health information. The health information that is to be protected is described as *protected health information* (PHI). The concern is primarily with information that points to a particular individual (e.g., his or her name, address, Social Security number, birthdate). The data are available to analysts (e.g., researchers) when the health information is de-identified. (See *Summary of the HIPAA Privacy Rule*, 2003. More specific information can be found at http://www.hhs.gov/ocr/hipaa.) If a state has more stringent requirements, the state's requirements supersede those of the federal government. The American Recovery and Reinvestment Act of 2009 (part of the Stimulus Law enacted by Congress) contained additional provisions and allocated funds to further electronic health records by 2014.

Electronic records are viewed as advantageous in a number of ways. First, they are thought to reduce medication errors (Richards, 2009). Second, the federal government is able to realize tax savings (Kuczynski & Gibbs-Wahlberg, 2005). Third, they are thought to increase the efficient flow of health information and allow for greater patient participation and privacy (Richards, 2009; *Summary of the HIPAA Privacy Rule*, 2003). On the other hand, questions remain about the security of personal health information that is available on the internet (Kuczynski & Gibbs-Wahlberg, 2005) and about the availability of past health and mental health information that a patient would like to be kept private (Privacy Rights Clearinghouse, 2010).

Summary and Deconstruction

Clinical social workers practicing in behavioral health settings today are situated among numerous sources of power—clients, the agency, managed care entities, the profession of social work and its Code of Ethics, and the law. Not to be underestimated, a great deal of power lies within social workers to advocate for what they believe is right. Social workers have a professional obligation under the Code of Ethics to give primacy to clients—to respect their dignity and worth, their rights to self-determination, and the confidentiality of what they revealed in the client–worker relationship. Social workers are also obligated to obey the law and at times must breach confidentiality because it is required by law that they protect someone from harm. Besides meeting their professional obligations, practitioners must be knowledgeable about the rights of clients to live in the least restrictive environment and receive the least restrictive but most beneficial care.

Today's mental health environment poses risks to clients' confidentiality. Despite legal protections of privacy, numerous individuals and organizations have access to personal client data. Besides agency personnel, managed care organizations, billing agencies, quality assurance personnel, and others see or handle personally identifiable client information. Risks to

privacy are associated with electronic records, as well as electronic mail, voice mail, and cellular telephones.

Conversely, at times personal information that could endanger others is withheld. Returning to the case of Seung-Hui Cho, his prior mental health history and ongoing concerns about his behavior were kept private, endangering others. As this case shows, protection of privacy and respect for confidential information can turn out to help perpetrators of violence.

References

Addington v. Texas, 441 U.S. 418, 3MDLR 164 (1979).

American Bar Association. (1988). *Mental disability law primer* (3rd ed.). Chicago: Author.

Appelbaum, P. S. (1985). Tarasoff and the clinician: Problems in fulfilling the duty to protect. *American Journal of Psychiatry, 142*(4), 425–429.

Appelbaum, P. S. (1991). Advance directives for psychiatric treatment. *Hospital and Community Psychiatry, 42*(10), 983–984.

Appelbaum, P. S. (2005). Assessing Kendra's Law: Five years of outpatient commitment in New York. *Psychiatric Services, 56*(7), 791–792.

Appelbaum, P. S. (2007). Assessment of patients' competence to consent to treatment. *New England Journal of Medicine, 357*(18), 1834–1840.

Bazelton Center for Mental Health Law. (September 8, 2009). *Disability groups win landmark case affirming rights of people with mental disabilities in state-funded adult homes.* Retrieved January 9, 2010, from http://www.bazelton.org/ newsroom/2009/DAIruling9-9-09.htm

Beauchamp, T. L. (1999). The philosophic basis of psychiatric ethics. In S. Bloch, P. Chodoff, & S. A. Green (Eds.), *Psychiatric ethics* (3rd ed., pp. 25–48). New York: Oxford University Press.

Brakel, S. J., Parry, J., & Weiner, B. (1985). *The mentally disabled and the law* (3rd ed.). Chicago: American Bar Foundation.

Brooks, A. D. (1988). Law and the chronically mentally ill. In A. D. Brooks, K. S. Brown, L. F. Davis, P. Fellin, U. C. Gerhart, & A. B. Hatfield (Eds.), *Services for the chronically mentally ill: New approaches for mental health professionals* (Vol. 1, pp. 62–75). Washington, DC: Council on Social Work Education.

Caplan, A. (2008). Denying autonomy in order to create it: The paradox of forcing treatment upon addicts. *Addiction, 103*, 1919–1921.

Covington v. Harris, 419 F.2d 617 (D.C. Cir. 1969).

Dixon v. Weinberger, 405 F. Supp. (D.D.C. 1975).

Dolgoff, R., Loewenberg, F. M., & Harrington, D. (2009). *Ethical decisions for social work practice* (8th ed.). Belmont, CA: Thomson Brooks/Cole.

Gelman, S. R., Pollack, D., & Weiner, A. (1999). Confidentiality of social work records in the computer age. *Social Work, 44*(3), 243–252.

Gilligan, C. (1982). *In a different voice: Psychological theory and women's development.* Cambridge, MA: Harvard University Press.

Gott, W. (1997). Should clinical social workers support the use of outpatient commitment to mental health treatment? Yes. In B. A. Thyer (Ed.), *Controversial issues in social work practice* (pp. 110–115, 121–123). Boston: Allyn and Bacon.

Greenhouse, L. (1999, June 23). High court limits who is protected by disability law. *New York Times,* pp. A1, A16.

Henderson, C., Swanson, J. W., Szmukler, G., Thornicroft, G., & Zinkler, M. (2008). A typology of advance statements in mental health care. *Psychiatric Services, 59*(1), 63–71.

Hermann, D. H. J. (1997). *Mental health and disability law in a nutshell.* St. Paul, MN: West Publishing Co.

Kachigian, C., & Felthous, A. R. (2004). Court responses to Tarasoff statutes. *Journal of the American Academy of Psychiatry and Law, 32*, 263–273.

Kagle, J. D., & Kopels, S. (2008). *Social work records* (3rd ed.). Long Grove, IL: Waveland Press.

Kane, M., Houston-Vega, M. K., & Nuehring, E. M. (2002). Documentation in managed care: Challenges in social work education. *Journal of Teaching in Social Work, 22*(1/2), 199–212.

Kuczynski, K., & Gibbs-Wahlberg, P. (2005). HIPAA and the health care hippo: Despite the rhetoric, is privacy still an issue? *Social Work, 50*(3), 283–287.

Lake v. Cameron, 364 F.2d 657 (D.C. Cir. 1966).

Lessard v. Schmidt, 349 F. Supp. 1078 (E.D. Wis. 1972), vacated and remanded on other grounds, 414 U.S. 473 (1974), redecided, 379 F. Supp. 1376 (E.D. Wis. 1974), vacated and remanded on other grounds, 421 U.S. 957 (1975), redecided, 413 F. Supp. 1318 (E.D. Wis. 1976), LMDLR 32.

Levy, C. S. (1979). *Values and ethics for social work practice.* Washington, DC: National Association of Social Workers.

Monahan, J. (2008). Mandated community treatment: Applying leverage to achieve adherence. *Journal of the American Academy of Psychiatry and the Law, 36*(3), 282–285.

Monahan, J., Swartz, M., & Bonnie, R. J. (2003). Mandated treatment in the community for people with mental disorders. *Health Affairs, 22*(5), 28–38.

National Association of Social Workers. (1996/1999/2008). *Code of ethics of the National Association of Social Workers.* Retrieved January 23, 2010, from http://www.socialworkers.org/pubs/Code/code.asp?print=1

O'Connor v. Donaldson, 442 U.S. 563 (1975).

Olmstead v. L.C. and E.W., 527 U.S. 581 (1999).

Petrila, J., & Christy, A. (2008). Law & psychiatry: Florida's outpatient commitment law: A lesson in failed reform? *Psychiatric Services, 59,* 21–23.

Pfeffer, A. (2008). "Imminent danger" and inconsistency: The need for national reform of the "imminent danger" standard for involuntary civil commitment in the wake of the Virginia Tech tragedy. *Cardozo Law Review, 30,* 277–315.

Privacy Rights Clearinghouse. (2010). Fact sheet 8a: HIPAA basics: Medical privacy in the electronic age. Retrieved from http://www.privacyrights.org/fs/fs8a-hipaa.htm

Reamer, F. G. (2005). Documentation in social work: Evolving ethical and risk-management standards. *Social Work, 50*(4), 325–334.

Reamer, F. G. (2006). *Social work values and ethics* (3rd ed.). New York: Columbia University Press.

Richards, M. M. (2009). Electronic medical records: Confidentiality issues in the time of HIPAA. *Professional Psychology: Research and Practice, 40*(6), 550–556.

Richmond, M. E. (1917). *Social diagnosis.* New York: Russell Sage Foundation.

Rinas, J., & Clyne-Jackson, S. (1988). *Professional conduct and legal concerns in mental health practice.* Norwalk, CT: Appleton & Lange.

Scheyett, A. M., & Kim, M. M. (2007). Psychiatric advance directives: A tool for consumer empowerment and recovery. *Psychiatric Rehabilitation Journal, 31*(1), 70–75.

Simone, S., & Fulero, S. M. (2005). Tarasoff and the duty to protect. *Journal of Aggression, Maltreatment & Trauma, 11*(1), 145–168.

Srebnik, D. S., & La Fond, J. Q. (1999). Advance directives for mental health treatment. *Psychiatric Services, 50*(7), 919–925.

Summary of the HIPAA Privacy Rule. (2003). U.S. Department of Health and Human Services. Retrieved from http://www.hhs.gov/ocr/privacy/hipaa/understanding/summary/privacysummary.pdf

Swanson, J. W., Van McCrary, S., Swartz, M. S., Elbogen, E. B., & Van Dorn, R. A. (2006). Superseding psychiatric advance directives: Ethical and legal considerations. *Journal of the American Academy of Psychiatry and the Law, 34*(3), 385–394.

Swartz, M. S., & Swanson, J. W. (2004). Involuntary outpatient commitment, community treatment orders, and assisted outpatient treatment: What's in the data? *Canadian Journal of Psychiatry, 49*(9), 585–591.

Tarasoff v. Regents of the University of California, 529 P.2d 553 (Cal. Sup. Ct.) (1974).

Tarasoff v. Regents of the University of California, 551 P.2d 334 (Cal. Sup. Ct.) (*Tarasoff II*) (1976).

Vogel-Scibilia, S. (1999, Winter). Preparing an advance directive. *Alliance,* NAMI Pennsylvania, pp. 5, 11.

Weinstock, R., Vari, G., Leong, G. B., & Silva, J. A. (2006). Back to the past in California: A temporary retreat to a Tarasoff duty to warn. *Journal of the American Academy of Psychiatry and the Law, 34,* 523–528.

Wilk, R. (1997). Should clinical social workers support the use of outpatient commitment to mental health treatment? No. In B. A. Thyer (Ed.), *Controversial issues in social work practice* (pp. 115–121). Boston: Allyn and Bacon.

Wyatt v. Stickney, 325 F. Supp. 781, aff'd, 344 F. Supp. 1341 (M.D. Ala. 1971), and 344 F. Supp. 373 (M.D. Ala. 1972), aff'd sub nom.

Culturally Competent Mental Health Practice

[T]he mental health system has not kept pace with the diverse needs of racial and ethnic minorities, often underserving or inappropriately serving them. Specifically, the system has neglected to incorporate respect or understanding of the histories, traditions, beliefs, languages, and value systems of culturally diverse groups. Misunderstanding and misinterpreting behaviors have led to tragic consequences.

—PRESIDENT'S NEW FREEDOM COMMISSION ON
MENTAL HEALTH, *ACHIEVING THE PROMISE*, 2003, P. 49

The United States is a multicultural society in which the historically dominant white majority has regarded persons from dissimilar racial, ethnic, and cultural groups as "other." In the field of mental health, "others" have received disparate treatment, resulting in misdiagnosis, inadequate or inappropriate treatment, and neglect. Even though the lifetime prevalence of mental disorders for Caribbean and African American, most Latino groups, and Asian Americans has been found to be lower than that of whites in the United States, the former groups, as well as American Indians and Alaska Natives (AIANs), have less access to and receive poorer quality mental health services than their white counterparts (McGuire & Miranda, 2008).

To address these disparities in mental health service delivery, extensive multilevel, consumer-oriented system changes are needed (Dougherty, 2004). A way of addressing this situation on the provider level is for mental health professionals to develop increased cultural competence (Lum, 2007; McGoldrick, Giordano, & Garcia-Preto, 2005; Sue, 2006). Cultural competence refers to the development of awareness of others whose life experiences, worldview, language, ethnicity, or social location is different from that of the practitioner, and consciousness of one's own culture and cultural biases, and to translate this awareness into practice. Accordingly, the clinical social work practitioner needs to be knowledgeable about different cultural values and traditions; sensitive to the impact of discrimination; and skillful in building relationships with, assessing, and adapting interventions to individuals from different racial and ethnic communities. Besides contributing to the reduction of disparate treatment, cultural competence is crucial to ethical social work practice (National Association of Social Workers, 1996/1999/2008).

This chapter provides a framework for the development of culturally competent practice in mental health. The diverse populations that are the focus of attention are racial/ethnic groups that have been and continue to be disparately treated. Included among them are immigrants, documented and undocumented, many of whom lack health insurance, speak different languages, and maintain diverse cultural practices. To begin with, it is important to understand the terminology.

DEFINITIONS

Race, *ethnicity*, and *culture* are social constructions that intersect with social and economic status and political power in U.S. society. All these terms refer to ascribed differences that have various meanings, depending on whether one is an insider or outsider to the group designated.

The term *race* has been used traditionally to refer to a population characterized by biological or physical traits that are genetically transmitted. Skin color is one of many traits that have been considered inherent in a racial group. The use of the term *race* to refer to biological characteristics, however, is problematic. As asserted in a statement by the American Anthropological Association (1998):

> With the vast expansion of scientific knowledge in this century, however, it has become clear that human populations are not unambiguous, clearly demarcated, biologically distinct groups. Evidence from the analysis of genetics (e.g., DNA) indicates that most physical variation, about 94%, lies *within* so-called racial groups. Conventional geographic "racial" groupings differ from one another only in about 6% of their genes. This means that there is greater variation within "racial" groups than between them. In neighboring populations there is much overlapping of genes and their phenotypic (physical) expressions. Throughout history whenever different groups have come into contact, they have interbred. The continued sharing of genetic materials has maintained all of humankind as a single species. (http://www.aaanet.org/stmts/racepp.htm)

In view of scientific evidence, questions can be raised about why the concept of "race" has persisted as a category. Most likely it is because this term helps maintain a system in which the dominant white "race" is able to assert that the differences are based on the "other" group's inferiority and to thereby claim their own group's privileges. *Racism* is intolerance directed against a group based on socially constructed racial differences. It is expressed in institutional arrangements, the opportunity structure, and interpersonal behavior.

The term *ethnicity* makes it possible for one to avoid the biological fallacy associated with [...] ethnicity refers to the history, culture, and national origin that form a basis for group identity, beliefs, customs, and political organization. Based on nationality and ancestry, ethnicity is transmitted intergenerationally through the family (Lum, 2007). Ethnic groups have a common heritage, language, beliefs, customs, rituals, food preferences, and interactional patterns that infuse their family and intragroup lives. There are numerous white ethnic groups such as the Irish, Italians, Greeks, Amish, and Jews (who are also a religious group). Knowledge of the particular ethnic groups (tribes or clans) from which many African Americans originated has been lost, overshadowed by the slave experience that followed their passage to the United States. The Hispanic/Latino ethnic group consists of people of Latin American or Spanish origins from a variety of ethnic, racial, and national groups.

The term *culture*—defined by early social scientists at least 164 ways (Kroeber & Kluckhohn, 1952)—is used here to refer to a system of knowledge, values, symbols, ways of perceiving, customs, and behaviors that is learned and passed on to others. A particular way of knowing, evaluating, and perceiving may be referred to as a specific culture. The term *worldview* is frequently used to characterize an outlook or set of perspectives particular to a certain cultural group. Ethnicity is related to culture, but ethnicity is also the basis for identity and political action (i.e., identity politics). Some ethnics view themselves in relation to their group's history, religion, folkways, and values, whereas others find meaning in uniting in political activities. Accordingly, ethnicity may be behavioral (cultural) or ideological (political) (Harwood, 1981a).

A set of terms that is related to culture, ethnicity, and race consists of *cultural identity*, *ethnic identity*, and *racial identity*. Individuals connect with and identify with their respective culture, ethnicity, or race with varying degrees of self-acceptance and varying identification with the dominant culture. Some deny or minimize their culture as a way of assimilating into the mainstream, whereas others take pride in their cultural group and enjoy expressing its distinct cultural practices. More will be said about these identities in another section of this chapter.

Multiculturalism and *cultural diversity* are also used to describe cultural, ethnic, and racial differences. These terms encompass numerous types of differences (e.g., sexual orientation, gender, gender identity, age, disability, religion) representing a variety of aspects of human diversity. Because these terms dilute the significance of race, they tend to be disempowering to racial and ethnic groups (Helms & Cook, 1999). Hopps (1982, 1987) identified a similar problem with broad application of *ethnicity* and *minority*. Although the term *minority* suggests that a group is numerically small, it also indicates lower status or inferiority (L. Y. Finley, personal communication). Furthermore, the term belies the fact that many groups that are numerically underrepresented in the United States exist in large numbers worldwide (Finley, personal communication).

Historically, certain cultural groups in the United States—African Americans, Hispanics/Latinos, American Indians/Alaskan Natives, and Asian Americans—have been subjected to discriminatory practices that have interfered with their ability to survive and succeed in the larger society. These groups have histories of being subjugated and exploited, resulting in high vulnerability to poverty, infant mortality, malnutrition, underemployment, and unemployment. Because of their skin color or ethnicity, they have been treated like outsiders and systematically excluded from living in particular residential environments, pursuing advanced educational opportunities, and obtaining well-paid jobs. The obstacles they have faced in meeting the demands of living in a hostile environment generate stress and tax their coping resources.

As Table 6.1 illustrates, disproportionate numbers of racial and ethnic groups are classified as living at the poverty level. The per capita income of African American and Hispanics is

Group	Number of Poor (in millions)	Percentage of Poor	Per Capita Income (in dollars)
African Americans	9.4	24.7	18,406
Hispanics (any race)	11.0	23.2	15,674
Asian and Pacific Islanders	1.6	11.8	30,292
White non-Hispanics	17.0	8.6	31,313
All racial/ethnic groups	39.8	13.2	26,964

TABLE 6.1 Poverty Status among Different Populations

Source: U.S. Bureau of the Census (2009, Tables 1 and 4). Numbers reported are for the year 2008.

substantially below that of white non-Hispanics. Close to one-quarter of these ethnic and racial groups lived below the poverty line in 2008. AIANs, who were not listed in this table because data for the same year were not available, also have a high level of poverty. According to a 2006 analysis of census data (Ogunwole, 2006), in 2000, 25 percent of them were living at the poverty level. In 2008, 17.8 percent of foreign-born residents of the United States lived below the poverty line (U.S. Bureau of the Census, 2009).

Just as race, ethnicity, and class intersect in ways that increase the economic, social, and psychological burden on marginalized groups, so does gender intersect with race and class. As a consequence, women of color "are in multiple jeopardy, facing as they do the combined forces of racism, sexism, and, in many cases, poverty" (Hopps, 1982, p. 4). The feminization of poverty among single women and their children is especially pronounced among African American and Hispanic mother-headed families (Sands & Nuccio, 1989). Other factors that intersect with race, ethnicity, and class include sexual orientation, gender identity, age, disability (physical, psychiatric, intellectual), religion, and immigration status, among other characteristics. Living in a rural environment is disadvantageous when behavioral health services are not available.

This chapter discusses cultural issues that should be understood in order to provide culturally competent clinical social work services in behavioral health. The chapter gives prominence to racial and cultural groups that have been subjected to discrimination in the United States—African Americans, Asian Americans/Pacific Islanders, Hispanics/Latinos, and American Indians/Alaskan Natives. Although these groups are often characterized as nonwhite racial groups or people of color, some individuals within these categories self-identify as white. Others who are of mixed backgrounds identify with one group or see themselves as biracial, bicultural, or multiethnic. Nevertheless, it should be understood that everyone springs from and is part of one or more cultures. Diverse white ethnicities such as Irish, Italian, Greek, Swedish, and German influence the lives of people with these origins and need to be considered in clinical practice.

CONTEXT-RELATED CONCEPTS

Members of culturally diverse groups that are not part of the dominant white majority navigate familiar and at times unfamiliar contexts. Chestang (1976) identified two salient systems—the nurturing system and the sustaining system—that provide emotional support and economic livelihood to African Americans. The nurturing system consists of family and friends in the ethnic community, who provide warmth and support and facilitate expressiveness; the sustaining represents the material, political, and social provisions of the external society. African ___ns, as well as other native cultural groups, live within, negotiate with, and need both ___s. Emigrants from other countries and migrants (e.g., from Puerto Rico) face similar ___allenges as they try to accommodate to the economic and social demands of the new country while retaining values and customs of their sustaining culture. Regardless of whether one was born and raised in the United States or migrated here, the perceptions, demands, and attitudes of the two systems may conflict. This is evident in the ways in which the dominant culture has conceptualized race and ethnicity and in ways in which the various cultural groups view themselves.

Conceptualizations

Social scientists of the past espoused ideas that were consistent with the experiences of white people of European derivation, but not those of racial and cultural groups whose descent was different. Accordingly, it was believed that anyone who worked diligently could achieve the "American dream." The idea that the United States was a *melting pot* into which all ethnic groups can mix was relevant and appealing to poor, white ethnic European immigrants, who were better able to accommodate to the similar U.S. culture than racially different groups (de Anda, 1984). Even though some white ethnic and religious groups faced discrimination when they first immigrated, over time they were able to surmount obstacles and become "white folks" (e.g., Brodkin, 1998; Ignatiev, 1995).

During the 1960s, the melting pot concept lost credibility. This was the period of the civil rights movement in which African Americans in particular were politically active. Their political activities, as well as increasing evidence that people of color remained poor, were misinterpreted, leading to the development of the *cultural deficit* model, which viewed poor people of color as culturally deprived (de Anda, 1984). During this period of the War on Poverty, educational and social programs to address these "deficits" were developed. The cultural deficit model was later discredited because it evaluated diverse cultures from the perspective of middle-class norms (de Anda, 1984).

Another concept that was introduced emphasized *cultural differences* among diverse populations (de Anda, 1984). This model, however, went overboard in emphasizing the separateness of each cultural group. Instead de Anda (1984) recommends the *bicultural socialization* model, which recognizes that there are differences as well as areas of overlap between cultures and that one can function effectively in different cultural environments (Sue & Sue, 2008). Another notion, *cultural pluralism*, refers to the acceptance within society of coexisting diverse cultures. The metaphor *salad bowl* is currently used instead of *melting pot* to depict preserving practices from the culture of origin while adapting to American culture (Alessandria, 2002).

Identities

Besides these external conceptualizations of diversity, there are ways in which members of diverse racial, ethnic, and cultural groups view themselves. Scholars of multicultural counseling describe a developmental process in which the identity in relation to race and ethnicity changes as they gain awareness. The change for members of marginalized racial groups is in the direction of less dependence on the dominant society's definition of oneself and greater acceptance of oneself as a member of a particular racial group. The change process, which is not necessarily linear, applies not only to clients but also to providers.

According to the Racial/Cultural Identity Development (R/CID) model, summarized by Sue and Sue (2008), members of oppressed populations go through five stages of development— (a) conformity, (b) dissonance, (c) resistance and immersion, (d) introspection, and (e) integrative awareness. During *conformity*, the individual prefers the values of the dominant culture over those of his or her own racial or cultural group. This includes identification with and internalization of the dominant culture's racism. The second stage, *dissonance*, develops after one has a personal experience or an encounter that conflicts with dominant culture views, raising awareness of racism or bigotry directed at oneself or one's group. During this period, the individual becomes uncomfortable and begins to question his or her values and beliefs. The next stage, *resistance and immersion*, entails the espousal of the views of one's own culture and rejection of the values of the dominant society. The focus is on exploring, learning about, and identifying with one's own racial or cultural group and may involve feeling angry at white society. During the fourth stage, *introspection*, the individual reflects on limitations of the previous stage, such as the energy it takes to maintain anger, and thinks about being proactive. The fifth stage, *integrative awareness*, is one in which the individual accepts and appreciates his or her own culture as well as the U.S. culture, selecting aspects of each to embrace.

Models of racial identity development have also been created for white people, who tend to deny that they have a race and what being white means in U.S. society (Sue & Sue, 2008). White people are socialized into a society that holds racist attitudes, biases, and stereotyped ideas about nonwhites (Sue & Sue, 2008). In working with people of other races and ethnicities, it is important that white social workers be conscious of their privileges, potential biases, and the ways in which they may be viewed by clients who are not from the dominant race. Sue and Sue describe models of white racial identity development developed by Hardiman; Helms; Rowe, Bennett, and Atkinson; and their own. Sue and Sue's own model has stages that, with one exception, correspond with those of the R/CID, described earlier, but have a different focus. The exception is the addition of an initial stage, the *naïveté* phase, that occurs during the first few years of life, when one lacks awareness of race. After that the white child begins to absorb the idea that whiteness is positive. Next comes the *conformity* phase, when the white person believes that his or her culture is superior based on social stereotypes of other racial groups. The individual at this point may believe that there are no differences between groups and that he or she is unbiased. The move into the *dissonance* phase is precipitated by a personal experience in which the individual's belief that he or she is not racist is challenged. For example, an individual may feel uncomfortable about his or her child's friendship with a child of another racial background. This experience can propel the person to revert to the previous phase or to move to the *resistance and immersion* phase, when he or she becomes increasingly aware of racism externally and internally. This phase is characterized by anger, guilt, and self-hatred. The next phase, *introspection*, involves recognition of the privileges that he or she has had as a white person. In the final phase, *integrative awareness*, the individual understands his or her self as a racial/cultural being, is aware of the social and political factors in racism, appreciates diversity, and has an increased commitment to act toward eliminating oppression.

Identity theories call attention to the growth of awareness of oneself as a cultural being, whether one is a member of a culture that is marginalized in the U.S. context or one is white. Social workers, who are predominantly white, are likely to be working with clients of diverse racial, ethnic, and cultural groups. Self-awareness is a crucial step for all social workers, for even social workers from marginalized cultural groups work across differences. It is also important to recognize that most people have memberships in multiple cultural groups that affect how they view themselves in a variety of ways.

Explanatory Models

Cultures offer a framework for understanding life experiences. Medical anthropologist-psychiatrist Kleinman (1988) uses the term *explanatory models* to depict the ways in which cultures provide a lens for interpreting an illness. As Kleinman elucidates:

> Explanatory models are the notions that patients, families, and practitioners have about a specific illness episode. These informal descriptions of what an illness is about have enormous clinical significance; to ignore them may be fatal. They respond to such questions as: What is the nature of this problem? Why has it affected me? Why now? What course will it follow? How does it affect my body? What treatment do I desire? What do I most fear about this illness and its treatment? (p. 120)

Applied to mental health, a social worker may view a behavior as a manifestation of a psychiatric disorder while the client sees it as a commonplace response to a life event. Similarly, a provider and client may attribute a different cause to the same behavior. Cultures also offer their own treatments and provide expectations for the future. Culturally competent social work practice involves exploring questions like those posed by Kleinman.

Help-Seeking Behavior

Medical sociologists use a number of terms that are helpful in understanding help seeking among diverse racial and ethnic groups. Among these are *sick role*, *health behavior*, and *illness behavior*. Parsons (1964) defined the sick role as a legitimized social status in which sick persons have the right to be free of blame and to abdicate their usual responsibilities at the same time they have the obligation to desire to get well and to cooperate with treatment. Health behavior refers to activities of presumably healthy persons to prevent disease or detect it prior to the development of symptoms, whereas illness behavior refers to activities of persons who feel ill to determine the state of their health and find an appropriate remedy (Kasl & Cobb, 1966). A semiannual dental checkup is an example of health behavior; a medical appointment for a cold is illustrative of illness behavior.

Sociocultural variables influence the assumption of the sick role and the practice of health and illness behaviors. To legitimately engage in sick role behavior, one's culture must recognize that the person is sick and sanction appropriate rights and obligations. This requires the perception of the symptoms as meaningful and the view that release from social obligations is appropriate. If the culture does not have a category that corresponds to the symptoms, it is unlikely that the person will be considered sick. Similarly health behavior is culturally relative. Although preventive dentistry and regular checkups may be normative among middle-class U.S. citizens, these practices are not congruent with ideas of other cultures. Illness behaviors are activities that follow from the perception that one is ill. When applied to mental health, illness behavior refers to the use of informal supports or formal mental health services.

Cultural explanations and responses contribute to the receptivity of diverse cultures to the mental health service delivery system. Cultural differences are sometimes misunderstood by service providers and defined as resistance. The response of the service delivery system has contributed in part to cultural disparities.

CULTURAL DISPARITIES IN MENTAL HEALTH

Recognized since the 1960s, disparities in the quality and delivery of mental health services to culturally diverse groups is a national problem (U.S. Department of Health and Human Services [DHHS], 1999, 2001). Marginalized cultural groups underutilize services and face access barriers, and when they receive services they drop out or terminate early (Snowden & Yamada, 2005).

According to *Mental Health: Culture, Race, and Ethnicity: A Supplement to Mental Health: A Report of the Surgeon General* (DHHS, 2001), in which a large body of research was reviewed and analyzed, there are serious cultural disparities in the utilization and delivery of mental health services. As summarized in this document:

> Most minority groups are less likely than whites to use services, and they receive poorer quality mental health care, despite having similar community rates of mental disorders. Similar prevalence, combined with lower utilization and poorer quality of care, means that minority communities have a higher proportion of individuals with unmet mental health needs. (DHHS, 2001, p. 3)

The National Comorbidity Survey Replication Survey found that vulnerable groups—African Americans, Hispanics, older adults, and those with low income, low levels of education, and lack of health insurance—do not use mental health services as much as adults who are white, are younger, and have higher income and education (Wang et al., 2005). Other studies have arrived at similar conclusions (e.g., Alegría et al., 2002; Wells, Klap, Koike, & Sherbourne, 2001). A study of service utilization by African Americans and whites with co-occurring mental health (mood or anxiety disorders) and substance abuse disorders found that a higher proportion of whites than African Americans received outpatient mental health services (Hatzenbuehler, Keyes, Narrow, Grant, & Hasin, 2008). An epidemiological study of Chinese from Los Angeles found that only about 15 percent of those who needed mental health treatment, based on their meeting diagnostic criteria, were receiving it (Kung, 2003).

Several barriers impede the ability to use services. Consumers who do not speak English cannot communicate with mental health workers unless providers speak their language or arrange to have an interpreter. Cultural mistrust, stigma, and lack of health insurance may also hinder access to services (Snowden & Yamada, 2005). In a study of low-income U.S.-born black and Latina women and low-income immigrant women screened for depression, logistical barriers (e.g., lack of insurance, no child care) and stigma concerns (e.g., afraid of what others might think) turned out to be significant issues (Nadeem et al., 2007). A qualitative study exploring West Indian immigrants' reluctance to use mental health services in Montreal identified three issues: (a) objection to doctors' overreliance on medication, (b) treated in a dismissive way, and (c) belief in nonmedical healing such as divine intervention and use of folk medicine (Whitley, Kirmayer, & Groleau, 2006).

The quality of mental health care is another area of disparity. Among the factors that contribute to poor treatment is misdiagnosis.

Misdiagnosis

The clinical diagnostic system that is used in the United States today is based on a Western medical model, in which the individual is viewed as having a disease and scientific methods are used to understand and treat the disease (DHHS, 2001). Furthermore, the Western model emphasizes the separation between mind and body, a view that is inconsistent with that held by Asian cultures (Lin & Cheung, 1999). Because most social workers educated in Western societies have assimilated this model, they risk misinterpreting the thoughts, behaviors, and feelings of clients from different cultural systems and arriving at inappropriate diagnoses. Furthermore, white social workers who are not familiar with other cultures may misread clients' verbal and nonverbal communication. Symptoms of mental illness appear differently in individuals from different cultures and have different meanings (Kleinman, 1988).

Without knowledge of other cultures, the practitioner is likely to rely on stereotypical ideas or project his or her biases, which can result in misdiagnosis. Clients of diverse cultures may present symptoms in ways that are consistent with their cultures but incongruent with the categories of mental illness that are described in the *DSM-IV-TR*. Because of differences in worldviews and behaviors, the client and the clinician may interpret the same symptoms differently.

Over the years, the symptoms of African Americans have been misinterpreted, resulting in overdiagnosis of schizophrenia and underdiagnosis of mood disorders (DHHS, 2001). Although both schizophrenia and affective disorders have associated psychotic symptoms, U.S. psychiatrists have interpreted these symptoms as manifestations of schizophrenia, especially when clients were African American (Jones & Gray, 1986). Misdiagnosis is partially attributable to a misinterpretation of African Americans' presentations of themselves in clinical settings. Some symptoms, such as paranoia and flat affect, are adaptive strategies adopted by African Americans to survive in an alien culture. Grier and Cobbs (1968) speak of a "'healthy' cultural paranoia" that is essential for adaptive functioning. However adaptive paranoia may be, it is often regarded as a symptom of paranoid schizophrenia or paranoid personality disorder, both of which are also overdiagnosed among African Americans (Steinberg, Pardes, Bjork, & Sporty, 1977). Similarly, controlled emotional expression in response to a white therapist who is not trusted may be misinterpreted as blunted or flat affect, which are symptoms of schizophrenia (Jones & Gray, 1986). To prevent misinterpreting presentations of emotions and behaviors, "contextually based" mental health care is recommended (Suite, La Bril, Primm, & Harrison-Ross, 2007). The contexts to consider are the historical, cultural, social, spiritual, philosophical, and political bases of racism and how these factors affect the identities of the individuals and their communities (Suite et al., 2007).

Diagnostic problems have been reported for other ethnic groups. Escobar (1987) discusses the prevalent presentation of somatic complaints by Hispanics. These symptoms accompany depressive and schizophrenic disorders but rarely are of sufficient scope to indicate a *DSM* diagnosis of somatization disorder. Asian Americans also present somatic complaints (Lim & Lin, 1996; Lin & Cheung, 1999). Furthermore, symptoms presented by Asian Americans may not correspond to *DSM* nomenclature (Lin & Cheung, 1999). A deeper understanding of cultural factors and culture-bound syndromes can help prevent diagnostic confusion or misdiagnosis.

CULTURAL DIMENSIONS OF DIAGNOSIS, ASSESSMENT, AND TREATMENT

Culture in the *DSM-IV-TR*

In contrast with previous diagnostic manuals, the *DSM-IV* and *DSM-IV-TR* (American Psychiatric Association [APA], 1994, 2000) have given attention to the impact of culture on the expression of psychopathology. In the introductions to both editions, clinicians are advised not to use norms from their own culture to evaluate behaviors, experiences, or beliefs that come from another culture. Chapters in the *DSM* on groups of disorders have a section on specific culture, age, and gender features that describe cultural variations that one might see. In addition, two V-coded conditions—Acculturation Problem (V62.4) and Religious or Spiritual Problem (V62.89) (APA, 2000)—address culturally related issues. One of the appendices includes an Outline for Cultural Formulation and a Glossary of Culture-Bound Syndromes. It is expected that the Outline will be revised in the *DSM-V* (Lewis-Fernández, 2009).

Culture-Bound Syndromes

Culture-bound syndromes are sets of behaviors and experiences that are specific to certain cultures. They are recognized within certain sociocultural contexts, which have culturally assigned explanations and remedies (Sadock & Sadock, 2007). With the migration of refugees from around the world, such syndromes appear in U.S. mental health practice. Although most of the culture-bound syndromes in the glossary of the *DSM-IV-TR* originated in non-Western cultures, there are several syndromes, not listed, such as anorexia nervosa and Type A behavior, that are particular to North America (Flaskerud, 2000).

Culturally Sanctioned Healers

Just as cultures have specific syndromes, there are also certain persons among them who are sanctioned to treat identified conditions. Although mainstream U.S. society has assigned this role to psychiatrists, psychologists, and social workers, some ethnic groups have indigenous healers who treat ailments in ways that are congruent with the beliefs and norms of the culture. Folk healers, or *shamen*, are the equivalents of therapists. They are described by Mexican Americans as *curanderos* and by Puerto Ricans as *espiritismos* or spiritists. American Indians, Asians, and Haitians are also known to have their own healers. Shamen may prescribe herbs, a special diet, exercise, or a healing ritual. Some therapists work collaboratively with indigenous healers (Sadock & Sadock, 2007).

Cultural Assessment

Culturally competent social work practice calls for assessments that take into account the various aspects of culture, including its intersectionality with race, gender, social class, religion or spirituality, age, sexual orientation, and gender identity, among other aspects. As suggested, practitioners need to explore explanatory frameworks, determine whether there are indigenous healers, and assess for potential culture-bound syndromes. Regardless of whether the client is a member of the nondominant or majority culture, his or her sociocultural context should be given foremost attention because both cultures "express distress in culturally embedded ways" (Alarcón et al., 2009, p. 559).

To understand a client culturally, it would be helpful if the social worker would meet with other members of the client's family and social network who can contribute their cultural knowledge and understanding of the client. For some cultures, it is natural that family members accompany a client when he or she receives services.

The following outline includes recommended dimensions of a cultural assessment that should be explored with all clients:

  I. **Sociocultural Descriptors:** Briefly mention one or more relevant characteristics that locate the individual socially and culturally (e.g., racial or ethnic group, country of origin, socioeconomic status, education, sexual orientation, religion, language(s), occupation).

II. **Developmental Stage:**   Note the individual's age, age group, or stage in his or her life cycle as defined by the individual's culture.

III. **Family/Support System:**   Whom does the individual consider family? Whom does the individual consider supportive (family, friends, health or mental health providers, etc.)? Whom does the individual's culture define as its support system (including religious or spiritual leaders)?

IV. **Cultural and Community Resources:**   Identify groups, social service agencies, and organizations that offer less intimate and more formal support to the individual. These may be within or external to the individual's culture.

V. **Gender Roles:**   How does the client's culture define male and female roles in the private and public spheres? Who is responsible for parenting? Who is considered "head" of the household? Who works? Who is the primary financial provider? How are decisions made?

VI. **Acculturation/Adaptation:**   How does the individual navigate transitions between his or her native culture and the dominant culture (e.g., does the individual remain exclusively within his or her own cultural group, balance demands between groups, or assimilate to the dominant culture?)?

VII. **Cultural Beliefs, Values, and Behaviors:**   How do the individual's cultural beliefs, values, and behaviors shape his or her understanding and communication about his or her health and mental health? (This includes communication style, beliefs about physical and mental illness and health and wellness, help-seeking behavior, spirituality and religious beliefs, ideas about death and dying, means of problem solving, values related to independence and entitlement, etc.)

VIII. **Historic and Current Socio-political Factors:**   These are past events and present conditions that have an impact on the individual or family's well-being and feelings of comfort or acceptance in the host society. (This includes the circumstances around migration, immigration, or a geographic move, including traumatic events; history of discrimination against this culture by the host society; political climate of the host or dominant culture; social policies within the host culture; specific discriminatory experiences; and internalized discrimination.)

IX. **Cultural Identity:**   How does the individual see himself or herself in relation to his or her ethnic, cultural, or racial group, sexual orientation, religion, and so on? (Determine the extent to which the individual identifies with his or her own cultural group and groups outside his or her own group. How does the individual express his or her cultural identity?) (Based on conceptualizations by Finley, 1995, 2005, and Finley & Shake, 2000. Revised by Bourjolly et al., 2006–2007.)

This outline, together with the recommended practice strategies in Box 6.1 and culturally specific information, should help the practitioner practice in a more culturally competent way.

CULTURALLY COMPETENT PRACTICE WITH SPECIFIC CULTURAL GROUPS

As indicated in the cultural assessment outline, culturally competent social work practice considers a range of cultural dimensions and experiences that could be applied to anyone. Here we will consider cultures that have struggled with discrimination in the U.S. context. The specific cultures

Box 6.1

Recommended Practice Strategies

- Take time to nurture a trusting therapeutic alliance;
- Listen attentively and show respect;
- Assess English literacy, bilingual ability, and preferred language for communication;
- Determine whether there is a need for an interpreter;
- Assess external barriers to service delivery (e.g., lack of insurance, transportation, child care responsibilities) and remedy them to the extent possible;
- Inquire about attitudes of the client, his or her family, and his or her culture about mental illness;

- Explore explanatory models, cultural beliefs, and culturally related healing methods;
- Recognize culturally related presentation of emotional pain (e.g., somatization);
- Explore the possibility that the client is presenting a culture-bound syndrome;
- Inquire about culturally sanctioned healers;
- Develop a comprehensive cultural assessment; and
- Learn about the client's specific culture and its norms.

are affected by histories of injustice, economic and social inequality, and local ecologies. Those clients who live principally among their own people in isolated communities have less contact (and possibly less conflict) than those who are thrust into a competitive urban environment. Those who live in ethnic enclaves within larger multicultural communities experience the push and pull of different worldviews on a regular basis. New immigrants deal with the loss of their homeland and its culture, as well as adaptation to a new culture.

This section will provide descriptive information and suggested strategies for social work practice with individuals of African American, Asian American/Pacific Island, Latino/Hispanic, and American Indian/Alaskan Native cultures. The danger in presenting this material is that it will create or affirm stereotypes. In examining this section, the reader is advised to keep in mind that there is as much diversity within cultures as between cultures, and to recognize that although persons who are socialized in a particular culture generally have knowledge of the beliefs and practices of their group, individuals do not uniformly accept these beliefs or engage in these practices. In no way are the values and behaviors that are described here to be viewed as inherent, universal, "essential" characteristics of everyone associated with the group.

Furthermore, cultural ways are viewed as resources that can aid clients in their resolution of mental health problems. Accordingly, indigenous definitions and categories (what is called the *emic* perspective) are the ways in which the clients and their cultures view their problems. Indigenous categories encompass the subjective experience of the illness rather than the disease. As such they are an important source of meaning to the particular culture. Concepts of mental health and constructs of illness that are specific to a culture are just as valid as Western disease constructs. The clinical social worker starts from the client's perspective, helping him or her work through the problem in culturally congruent ways.

Social workers who identify with the dominant culture may have certain biases that interfere with their work with clients of diverse cultures. For example, the European American values of individualism, independence, competitiveness, and achievement are different from the values of sharing, modesty, and intergenerational connectedness that are held by some cultural groups. Similarly certain interpersonal behaviors that are valued by the dominant culture (e.g., assertiveness, eye contact, informality) are considered improper among persons of other cultures, while other behaviors (e.g., silence, deference) may be preferred. Expectations that clients verbalize their feelings, admit their weaknesses, and confront persons who arouse their anger are based on European American therapeutic models. To work with ethnically different clients, social workers must control their biases and accept clients on their own terms.

Because of potential differences between clinicians and clients, two approaches to behavioral health service delivery have been recommended: "(i) increasing cultural competence of mental health staff by training existing personnel or hiring ethnic minorities; and (ii) the need for culturally sensitive programs" (Takeuchi, Uehara, & Maramba, 1999, p. 555). Ethnic-specific service centers with clinicians who speak the same language and share the same culture or mainstream centers with clinicians from the same cultural group who are bilingual are particularly ethnic sensitive. Programs such as these, however, are few and far between. An alternative strategy is to hire interpreters as needed. The choice of an interpreter, however, should be culturally congruent and consistent with the client's preferences. Because of the personal nature of therapeutic conversations, interpreters who are young (particularly children), family members, or of a different gender may not be appropriate. In any case, mental health providers need to be knowledgeable about the characteristics of different ethnic groups, keeping in mind within-group diversity and the degree to which the clinician and client identify with their own group (Helms & Cook, 1999).

African Americans

Soon after Europeans settled in what is now the United States of America, they imported Africans to serve as slaves to the colonists. Considered property, the Africans were sold for use as plantation laborers and "bred" for their progeny. Plantation owners further subjugated African women by raping them. The forced immigration, exploitation, and separation of Africans from the same African societies resulted in the destruction of indigenous African cultures. Restrictions against marriage and the sale of family members undermined the establishment of stable African American families.

Although the Civil War was fought primarily to preserve the Union, conflict over the spread of slavery into newly acquired territories was one of the issues that divided the North and the South before the Civil War. The war did, nevertheless, result in the abolition of slavery and the granting of the rights of citizenship and the right to vote to African Americans. After the Civil War, public policies, such as poll taxes and grandfather clauses, as well as illegal and malevolent activities, such as lynchings, impeded African Americans from participating in civic life. The Supreme Court case *Plessy v. Ferguson* of 1896 endorsed segregation in establishing the principle of separate but equal education for African Americans and whites. Even after this decision was overturned in *Brown v. Board of Education of Topeka, Kansas* in 1954 and subsequent legislation outlawed segregated housing and employment discrimination, racism and poverty have kept African Americans oppressed (Kitano, 1985).

With close to 38 million persons, African Americans represent 12.4 percent of the general population in the United States (U.S. Census Bureau, 2008). These numbers and percentages would be higher if they included individuals with two or more races and those African Americans who do not get counted because they are institutionalized or homeless. Most are descendants of slaves but some came voluntarily as immigrants from the Caribbean, South America, and more recently, Africa (Kamya, 1997). Like immigrants of other racial and ethnic groups, they are faced with the challenges of learning a new language and social norms, securing a means of livelihood, and adapting to a new culture.

Black experience of life in the United States has been marked by domination, exploitation, and economic hardship. From the time the first Africans came here, they were regarded as chattel, whose value came from their usefulness in the white-dominated U.S. economy. The master–subject relationship that was established early in the United States' history relegated African Americans to a subhuman status in which their worth, rights, and dignity were denied (Bosmajian, 1974). Even after laws were changed to include African Americans as citizens with rights, inequality has been maintained through institutional racism.

Institutional racism directed at African Americans is reflected in census data. As shown in Table 6.1, 24.7 percent of African Americans are poor (U.S. Bureau of the Census, 2009). The median income of African American households in 2008 was $34,218 and per capita income was $18,406 (U.S. Bureau of the Census, 2009). Despite the high rate of poverty among African Americans, many are educated and employed as professionals and skilled laborers. According to census data from a number of sources, it was estimated that in 2007, 80.1 percent graduated high school or more and 17.3 percent had a bachelor's degree or more (Crissey, 2009). As a whole, African Americans are a heterogeneous population that has shown tremendous strength in coping with adversity.

CULTURAL VALUES AND NORMS African American cultural values and norms derive from residues of African culture, values of the mainstream United States, and responses and adaptations to the victim system that arose from oppression, poverty, and racism (Pinderhughes, 1982). Variation among individuals reflects these diverse sources of identification, as well as differences in social class, education, urban/rural environment, region of the country, and individual differences.

Nobles (1976) describes the African worldview as one that values cooperation, collective responsibility, and interdependence and is expressed psychobehaviorally in sameness, groupness, and commonality. Similarly, the Afrocentric paradigm focuses on collective identity, spirituality, and an affective approach to knowing (Schiele, 1996). African values and behaviors stand in sharp contrast with European values of competition, individuality, and difference. African values are expressed in strong kinship bonds (Hill, 1971; Leigh & Green, 1982) and an emphasis on religion and spirituality (Boyd-Franklin, 1989).

Although Boyd-Franklin (1989) affirms that "there is no such thing as *the* Black family" (p. 6), she and others (e.g., Leigh & Green, 1982) describe several patterns that characterize many African American families. For one, families extend beyond nuclear arrangements to include informally adopted children, friends ("aunts" and "uncles"), and distant and closely related biological kin. Children may be raised by grandparents or in multigenerational households. The paternal relatives of a child in a mother-headed, single-parent family may be an important component of the family kinship system. Kinship networks are cooperative and interdependent.

Some writers describe the flexible family roles that are apparent in many African American families (Boyd-Franklin, 1989; Hill, 1971; Sue & Sue, 2008). The employment of both black women and black men has resulted in sex roles that tend to be egalitarian and family organization that is cooperative (Leigh & Green, 1982). During times of crisis, the extended kinship system can be mobilized to assume absentee roles (Hines & Boyd-Franklin, 1982). Children are socialized to be assertive and independent and are valued for themselves rather than for their ability to manipulate the physical world (Leigh & Green, 1982).

Religion or spirituality is frequently cited as a source of strength among African Americans (Boyd-Franklin, 1989; Hines & Boyd-Franklin, 1982; Hill, 1971; Leigh & Green, 1982; McAdoo, 1987; Sue, 2006). Rooted in the African experience and oppression during slavery, religion and religious institutions provide structures for meaning, emotional expression, affiliation, and political organization. The church is a place in which African Americans can feel at home, reach out for spiritual support, express deep feelings, and receive acceptance. A source of meaning beyond the material world, religion is a counterforce that provides hope for change. Although most of the organized religions with which African Americans are affiliated are Christian, some are Muslim.

African American culture has been and continues to be influenced by racism. In nineteenth-century mental health history, practitioners describe a "mental illness" called *drapetomania*—the uncontrollable urge on the part of slaves to escape their situation (Suite et al., 2007). A twentieth-century version of pathologizing African Americans is misdiagnosis, discussed earlier in this chapter, which contributes to mistrust (Suite et al., 2007). Today African Americans are overrepresented among those with "high need" of mental health services—the homeless, the incarcerated, those exposed to trauma, and those with substance abuse problems (DHHS, 2001).

INDIGENOUS CONCEPTS OF HEALTH, MENTAL HEALTH, AND MENTAL ILLNESS   African American concepts of mental health and mental illness are influenced by those of the dominant white culture and by religious beliefs. As U.S. citizens, African Americans have been socialized to accept mainstream biomedical concepts (Jackson, 1981) and to use mainstream health and mental health services. For some, however, religion provides a primary system of meaning for human experiences. Some African Americans explain their psychological symptoms in religious or folk terms and view using the formal treatment system negatively (Hines & Boyd-Franklin, 1996).

CULTURE-SPECIFIC SYNDROMES   One of the culture-specific syndromes that is seen in African Americans and persons of Caribbean background is called *falling out* or *blacking out*. It is characterized by sudden collapse, paralysis, and inability to speak or see. Hearing remains unimpaired and eyes are open during these episodes (Jackson, 1981). Another is *rootwork*, which attributes maladies to evil forces (APA, 2000).

ILLNESS BEHAVIOR   African Americans use informal and formal supports to assist them with mental health problems. Historical and ongoing discrimination create distrust of mainstream services; thus, during times of crisis, they are likely to turn to friends, family, neighbors, and religious resources for help (Hines & Boyd-Franklin, 1996; Suite et al., 2007). African Americans who use mainstream mental health services may hesitate to be open with clinicians. Past experience with the public assistance, child welfare, and court systems has taught blacks to be wary (Boyd-Franklin, 1989). Accordingly, their resistance may be viewed as a strength (Boyd-Franklin, 1989).

Some research indicates that African Americans have fewer sessions of psychotherapy than whites and that they leave treatment prematurely (DHHS, 2001). Thus, quality as well as quantity of contact needs to be improved. If the clinician is not African American, he or she should acknowledge this difference and explore potential racial barriers early in their work together (Hines & Boyd-Franklin, 1996).

IMPLICATIONS FOR PRACTICE   Mental health problems experienced by African Americans must be seen in the context of their socioeconomic status and the suffering they have endured in a predominantly white society. Although the cultural values and adaptations to the macro system that African Americans have made are sources of strength, they vary from patterns of white Americans of European descent who usually have dominant roles in mental health organizations. Unless clinicians of other ethnicities come to understand and appreciate the differences and strengths of African Americans, they are likely to rely on inappropriate values and stereotypes in their treatment of blacks.

Social workers should consider the differences among African Americans based on national origin, religion, education, and economic status. Some recent immigrants from Africa have had horrific experiences that should be explored after a relationship is established. Those from the Caribbean and other parts of Latin America are from diverse cultures. The heterogeneity among African Americans and the complex families and modes of mutual assistance and self-help within black communities call for a systems approach to assessment and treatment. The family system and the diverse sources of support within the nurturing and sustaining systems should be identified. Clients should be helped to build supports and to eliminate obstacles to their individual and collective betterment. To counteract the effects of discrimination, clients should be helped to use their own inner resources as well as community resources to attain goals of their own choosing that are consistent with their values. They should be assisted to be instrumental in developing and effecting solutions to identified problems. Furthermore, African Americans should be encouraged to organize politically to attain solutions to collective problems.

American Indians and Alaska Natives

American Indians and Alaska Natives are thought to have emigrated from Asia by crossing the Alaskan land bridge some 20,000 years ago (Kitano, 1985). At the time Columbus came to the "New World," some 1,000 tribes and millions of people were scattered across the continent (Blanchard, 1987). Others lived throughout Central and South America. These indigenous populations presented a formidable barrier to European conquerors, who thought that they had "discovered" a new land. The Europeans dealt with the American Indians by engaging in warfare with them, trading goods, entering into treaties with them, and depriving them of sources of their livelihood. In the process, a large proportion of American Indians were killed and others fell prey to deception and diseases and were introduced to alcohol.

After the United States was founded, public policies that undermined American Indians' cultures were implemented. These included the displacement of American Indians from their land, the creation of reservations, sending American Indian children to American-style boarding schools, and land redistribution (Kitano, 1985). The status of American Indian tribes as nations within a nation has created jurisdictional confusion over land, civil rights, and child placement for a number of generations (Johnson, 1982). The loss of land, tribal unity, and cultural identity has had a long-range impact on those American Indians who have survived.

Whereas the American Indians were colonized by Western Europeans, the Alaska Natives became subjects of the Russians, who required that the native Inuit and Aleut people hunt for furs (DHHS, 2001). After the United States purchased Alaska in 1867, Alaska Natives were subjected to U.S. law. Although reservations were established in the last decade of the nineteenth century, it was not required that Alaska Natives move there (DHHS, 2001). Policies changed in the 1970s when oil deposits were discovered on the North Slope of Alaska and there was a desire to clear that area to build the Alaska Pipeline. Alaska Natives were organized into corporations and were allowed to control millions of acres of land and close to a billion dollars (DHHS, 2001). Stockholders were restricted to those who were born by or before 1971, thus restricting the rights of those born afterward (Weaver, 2007).

Today, based on specific criteria, the Bureau of Indian Affairs recognizes some 564 American Indian and Alaska Native tribal groups (U.S. Department of the Interior, 2010). In addition, there are nonrecognized tribes (Trimble & Clearing-Sky, 2009). According to a special report on AIANs based on data from the 2000 U.S. Census but issued later (Ogunwole, 2006), their population consists of 2.4 million persons who identified exclusively with AIANs and 4.3 million persons if one includes those who identify with the former and another racial type. As suggested, they are culturally and racially diverse. Overall, about 72 percent speak only English in their homes, with the others either bilingual or primarily speakers of another language (Ogunwole, 2006). They are diverse with respect to religion, language, political structure, and social structure (Weaver, 2007). Although more than a third lives in federal reservations or trust lands or Alaska Native village statistical areas, 64 percent live outside these areas (Ogunwole, 2006).

American Indians and Alaska Natives have diverse family structures with some families that are matriarchal and others that are patriarchal (Sue & Sue, 2008). The extended family tends to be the basic family unit, with grandparents and other biological and nonbiological relatives included in the family (Sue & Sue, 2008; Sutton & Broken Nose, 2005). They tend to be accepting of lesbian, gay, bisexual, transgender, and queer persons, referring to them as *two-spirit people*. Caregiving is a significant role for two-spirit people (Evans-Campbell, Fredriksen-Goldsen, Walters, & Stately, 2007).

American Indians and Alaska Natives differ in their knowledge and identification with their native cultures and levels of assimilation (Weaver, 2007), resulting in diverse family styles. Red Horse (1988) described the *traditional* type as one in which the native language is preferred, the extended kinship system organizes community life, the land is revered, and the native religion is practiced. *Neotraditional* families are similar to the traditional ones, except that they may have adopted another religion, such as Christianity, and some prefer Spanish. *Transitional* families retain native values, language, and extended kinship ties in their intimate lives but adopt the customs and language of outsiders in their contacts with the wider community. If they live in an urban area, they try to bridge the gap by making frequent trips to their homeland. *Bicultural* families prefer English, live in nuclear units, and convert to other religions. Nevertheless, the adults may know their native language and religion and have an awareness of the sacredness of the land. *Acculturated* families associate primarily with nonnatives and retain few Indian values. A revival of traditional values, traditions, and language and criticism of the U.S. institutional system characterize the *panrenaissance* families. Social workers should assess the degree to which AIANs identify with their traditional culture and be sensitive to potential acculturation conflicts (Sue & Sue, 2008).

Disproportionate numbers of AIANs have low incomes and suffer from poverty. In 2000, the median family income was $28,919 for men and $22,834 for women (Ogunwole, 2006). At that time, the poverty rate was 25.7 percent for individuals (Ogunwole, 2006). Labor force participation for AIAN men was about 66 percent and for women, 57 percent (Ogunwole, 2006). About 80 percent had a high school education or more (U.S. Bureau of the Census, 2006). Over 20 percent of the families were headed by women without a spouse present (Ogunwole, 2006).

When one compares AIANs with other Americans, one finds numerous health disparities. AIANs have a lower life expectancy and die at higher rates from alcoholism, diabetes, tuberculosis, homicide, unintentional injuries, and suicide (DHHS, 2010). Their primary behavioral health problems are alcohol abuse, co-occurring substance abuse and mental disorders, and post-traumatic stress disorder (DHHS, 2001).

CULTURAL VALUES AND NORMS   Although the diversity among AIAN tribal groups makes it difficult to arrive at a set of values that applies to all groups, there are a few prominent themes. Among these are *holism*, *harmony*, and *community*. In contrast with the normative view among white Americans who perceive person and environment as separate entities, AIANs enculturated in their own traditions find unity and continuity among natural, supernatural, and human phenomena (Anderson & Ellis, 1988; Kunitz & Levy, 1981; Lewis, 1985; Nofz, 1988). They feel connected to their families, peers, and forebears and the land, which is held sacred (Nofz, 1988; Red Horse, 1988). Their sense of attuneness or harmony with the natural world extends to bodies of water, animals, and plants (Sutton & Broken Nose, 2005).

American Indians and Alaska Natives tend to value the welfare of the group over individual achievement. They are obligated to share their resources with their families and clans (Nofz, 1988; Sutton & Broken Nose, 2005). Because of these values, their children are in the untenable position in public schools that emphasize individuality and competition (Anderson & Ellis, 1988). American Indians avoid conflict or confrontation. They value privacy and do not like it when outsiders interfere with their lives (Lewis & Keung Ho, 1975; Trimble, Manson, Dinges, & Medicine, 1984). Unfortunately, behavior that is in keeping with their culture is frequently perceived by outsiders as passivity, shyness, and lack of ambition (Anderson & Ellis, 1988). On the other hand, they view the efforts of therapists to elicit personal experiences, thoughts, and feelings as intrusive or inappropriate (Lewis & Keung Ho, 1975; Trimble et al., 1984). American Indians value listening; silence is a form of communication (Sutton & Broken Nose, 2005).

American Indians have extended families of biological and nonkin relatives who socialize the young into the culture (Red Horse, 1980b). With the movement of the American Indian population to cities, many families are separated from each other geographically. Yet they do form communities within cities and return to their childhood homes for special ceremonies (Red Horse, 1980b). Although the American Indian population tends to be young, the elders occupy a position of respect in the community (Red Horse, 1980a). Grandparents are particularly important (Sutton & Broken Nose, 1996). Some AIAN cultures feel strongly connected to their ancestors (Weaver, 2007).

INDIGENOUS CONCEPTS OF HEALTH, MENTAL HEALTH, AND MENTAL ILLNESS American Indians' cultures do not distinguish between health and mental health. Consistent with their holistic view of the person and the environment, American Indians view disturbances in their mental health in relation to other aspects of their lives as well as the cosmos (Trimble et al., 1984). The Navajo Indians see physical and mental illness as manifestations of disharmony in nature that may represent the intrusion of supernatural forces or some other external cause. The disharmony could be caused by a breach of a taboo, an intrusion of spirits, witchcraft, or an etiological agent, such as an animal or the wind (Kunitz & Levy, 1981). Ghosts, spirits of the dead, and witchcraft are thought to be capable of interfering with the living.

CULTURE-SPECIFIC SYNDROMES A number of psychiatric syndromes are specific to AIANs. One of these syndromes, *pibloktoq*, or arctic hysteria, is a dissociative episode followed by seizures (APA, 2000). This syndrome is common among female Alaskan Eskimos. Another, characterized by fainting and preoccupation with death, is called *soul loss*. Here the soul, which enters the body at birth and leaves at death, appears to be departing the body (Kunitz & Levy, 1981). On the other hand, *spirit intrusion* is a form of possession by ghosts, evil spirits, or demons that is manifested by symptoms of agitated depression, somatization, and hallucinations. AIANs may experience a range of behavioral and somatic symptoms as a result of *taboo breaking*. When they violate taboos against forms of sexual expression (e.g., incest), murder, and other forbidden behaviors, they may become afflicted with what outsiders consider mental illness (Trimble et al., 1984). An additional syndrome associated with American Indian tribes is *ghost sickness*, which is characterized by a preoccupation with a person who died or with death and is manifested by symptoms of fainting, bad dreams, loss of appetite, and hallucinations (APA, 2000).

ILLNESS BEHAVIOR   Illness behavior is consistent with the degree of assimilation of the AIANs' family. Accordingly, one would expect individuals from traditional and neotraditional families to make use of herbal remedies and participate in ritual healing ceremonies; transitional families to utilize indigenous and mainstream methods; but bicultural and acculturated families to rely principally on U.S. institutional care (Red Horse, 1988).

Among the AIANs, there are persons and groups who serve as healers. They may be shamen, medicine persons, traditional healers, or clergy (for Christians), who provide culturally congruent forms of help. Some healers provide herbal remedies; others engage afflicted persons in healing ceremonies. Healing by medicine people may be spiritual or physical (Sutton & Broken Nose, 2005). At times clinicians will make referrals to native healers.

IMPLICATIONS FOR PRACTICE   Mental health practice with AIANs within the mainstream mental health system should be consistent with the values and behaviors of the individual's particular tribe or community and his or her degree of assimilation with mainstream U.S. culture. Some writers believe that American Indians view family therapy as interference, whereas group treatment that is focused and task-centered is in keeping with the peer group orientation of American Indians (Lewis & Keung Ho, 1975; Nofz, 1988). Other writers have been able to implement culturally sensitive family treatment with middle-class American Indians (Attneave, 1982).

In treating individuals from AIAN cultures who have problems with alcohol, special attention should be given to the cultural component of drinking. For American Indians, drinking tends to be a peer-group phenomenon that is associated with comradeship and solidarity rather than an individual means of escape (Anderson & Ellis, 1988). For some, drinking may be a way of overcoming shyness or their marginal social status (Anderson & Ellis, 1988; Nofz, 1988). Alcohol treatment in groups can use the peer group to promote cohesion without use of alcohol as a catalyst. Similarly, the cultural context of another social problem, suicide, should also be recognized (Davenport & Davenport, 1987). The clinician should inquire about the characteristics of the client's tribe and his or her preferred language and determine with which culture(s) the client identifies (Sutton & Broken Nose, 2005). Treatment of post-traumatic stress disorder, which may be the result of child abuse or violence, also requires sensitivity to the individual's culture and the meaning of the violence to the individual, family, and community. Consultation with tribal leaders or indigenous social workers may help non-AIAN social workers advocate for social justice in a way that is culturally congruent.

Asian Americans and Pacific Islanders

During the mid-nineteenth century, Asian immigrants (primarily single Chinese men) entered the West Coast of the United States for reasons similar to those of the white immigrants from Europe who were arriving—to improve their economic situation (Kitano, 1987). They worked as miners, railroad workers, domestic servants, and laborers in manufacturing industries. Few started families because of the shortage of Chinese women and the enactment of antimiscegenation laws. Because they accepted low wages, their presence aroused the rancor of whites (the "yellow peril") who were competing for the same jobs (Kitano, 1985). Discrimination against the Chinese was expressed in the passage of Chinese Exclusion Acts in 1882 and 1902 and the later Immigration Act of 1924.

From 1890 to 1924, however, Japanese were allowed to immigrate to Hawaii and the United States with their families (Kitano, 1985). Although they and their children became acculturated, they, too, suffered from discrimination. During World War II, racism directed at the Japanese

reached hysterical proportions, culminating in the placement of Japanese Americans in intern-
ment camps. Other Asian populations that have come to the United States are the Filipinos,
Koreans, Pacific Islanders, and Southeast Asians, whose immigration was facilitated
by the Immigration Act of 1965 and subsequent public policies. The Southeast Asians were
refugees from Vietnam, Laos, and Cambodia who sought asylum during the wars and political
changes that ravaged their lands (Kitano, 1987). Others came to seek educational and work
opportunities.

Asian and Pacific Island Americans consist of persons who have cultural roots in East Asia
(Japan, China, Korea), Southeast Asia (Indonesia, Vietnam, Cambodia, Laos, Thailand, the
Philippines, Burma), and the Pacific Islands (Guam, Samoa, Hawaii, Tonga). Individuals from
South Asia (Pakistan, India, Sri Lanka) are also considered Asian Americans (Kuramoto,
Morales, Munoz, & Murase, 1983). The Chinese, Filipinos, and Asian Indians are the most nu-
merous Asian Americans (U.S. Census Bureau, 2002). The population of Asian/Pacific Islanders
is about 13.5 million (U.S. Census Bureau, 2005), with over half residing in California, New
York, and Hawaii (U.S. Census Bureau, 2002).

Besides their varied national origins, specific ethnic groups are internally diverse.
Furthermore, they differ in their levels of acculturation and degree of their integration into the
dominant U.S. culture (DHHS, 2001). Refugees from Southeast Asia who had traumatic experiences prior to or en route to the United States are at high risk for post-traumatic stress disorder
and other disorders (DHHS, 2001). The discussion that follows focuses primarily on Asian
Americans whose roots are in East and Southeast Asia or are from the Pacific Islands.

CULTURAL VALUES AND NORMS   Although there is much diversity among Asian American
and Pacific Island American cultures of origin, several values and cultural norms are common.
Some of these are derived from the eastern religions of Confucianism, Buddhism, and Taoism,
but they may be intermixed with Christianity for those who have converted or are highly assimilated into U.S. culture. The interrelated values that will be emphasized here are family continuity, filial piety, avoidance of shame, and self-control.

The family is a fundamental source of values for Asian and Pacific Island Americans.
Among those of East Asian origin, the family links individuals with their ancestors on the
paternal side and ensures the perpetuation of the family's good name (Shon & Ja, 1982). In
keeping with these goals, families tend to be hierarchical, male dominated, and highly
structured (Shon & Ja, 1982; Sue & Sue, 2008). Children are obligated to exhibit filial piety,
that is, they are to be deferential, obedient, and loyal to their families (Ho, 1981). Grandparents
and parents are afforded a great deal of respect and authority. Above all, family members must
avoid shaming the family, the welfare of which supersedes the pursuit of individual goals
(Ishisaka & Takagi, 1982). Asian Americans and Pacific Islanders are sensitive to appearances;
if personal problems or behaviors that are discrepant with family and community expectations
come to be known to others, the Asian American feels shame and loses face (Ho, 1981).
Perpetrators of such behaviors not only disgrace themselves but also dishonor the family.

Compared with white Americans, African Americans, and Hispanics, Asian
Americans/Pacific Islanders have a higher percentage of families (82 percent) living in married
couple households with or without children living at home (Kreider & Elliott, 2009).
Furthermore, they have the lowest proportion of mother-headed single family households (5 percent) (Kreider & Elliott, 2009).

Asian Americans value self-control and emotional restraint (Ho, 1981; Sue & Sue, 2008).
Families expect members to control their emotions and avoid antisocial behavior. Asians who

subscribe to these values regard them as a sign of maturity (Ishisaka & Takagi, 1982). Indeed restraint may be viewed as a cultural strength, in that it promotes qualities of self-discipline, patience, and diligence, which are instrumental in achieving success in American society. It is not, however, consonant with prevailing models of mental health treatment that require emotional expression.

INDIGENOUS CONCEPTS OF HEALTH, MENTAL HEALTH, AND MENTAL ILLNESS Traditional Asian medicine embraces a holistic concept of health, mental health, and treatment (Marsella & Higginbotham, 1984). Mind, body, and spirit are thought to be a unity rather than separate systems. Health is equated with harmony or balance (Gould-Martin & Ngin, 1981). Traditional Chinese conceive of illness (mental or physical) as a disharmony between two life forces, *yin* and *yang* (Kleinman, 1980). Life forces, such as the wind, can disrupt the balance by entering the body during periods of vulnerability (Gould-Martin & Ngin, 1981). Indigenous healing methods aim to restore internal harmony as well as the unity between the person and the environment, which is as extensive as the Cosmos.

Cultures of Asia and the Pacific have developed three explanations of the origins of behavioral dysfunction (Ishisaka & Takagi, 1982). The *social explanation* places responsibility on untoward circumstances, such as a death, marital conflict, or job loss. The position of victimization rather than individual responsibility is highlighted—evoking sympathetic responses, advice, and release from ordinary responsibilities from others. The second explanation, *moral*, arises when a person has violated values that the community regards as sacred. For the most part, these involve forsaking family obligations and prescribed modes of conduct. Community elders, priests, and family members intervene in response to these transgressions. The third explanation is *organic*. Asian cultures accept physical or somatic explanations and symptoms as part of life. Asian Americans have an easier time accepting somatic explanations than Western theories that blame the individual or family for dysfunctional behaviors (Ishisaka & Takagi, 1982).

Asians attach a great deal of stigma to mental illness, which invokes thoughts about family curses, witchcraft, and other supernatural forces (Marsella & Higginbotham, 1984). To avoid shame, Asians limit their concept of mental illness to the most severe psychotic problems (Kleinman, 1980). Not unusual, they present psychological problems with somatic complaints (DHHS, 2001; Sue & Sue, 2008). Symptoms that would be considered expressions of nonpsychotic mental health problems in Western cultures tend to be treated by health professionals or indigenous healers (Kleinman, 1980).

CULTURE-SPECIFIC SYNDROMES A number of syndromes of dysfunction that are prevalent among groups of Asian origins have been described in the literature. Among these are the following.

Amok is an outburst of aggression that is particularly prevalent among Southeast Asian (especially Malaysian) men. It begins with a period of brooding and can eventuate in an act of homicide (APA, 2000). Later the amoker experiences exhaustion and amnesia and may commit suicide. The expression, *running amok*, derives from this syndrome (Favazza, 1985; Westermeyer, 1985).

Koro is an attack of anxiety associated with sexual organs. Men develop an intense fear that their penis is shrinking and receding into the stomach and that the result will be death. Women have similar fears centering on their nipples and vulva (APA, 2000). Koro is seen primarily in Asia, but has been reported in the West (Favazza, 1985; Westermeyer, 1985).

Latah is a startle response that is precipitated by a mild but sudden stimulus. The individual obeys and imitates the speech of others, regardless of the consequences. A syndrome of women of Southeast Asia, it has also been identified among the Bantu of Africa, the Ainu of Japan, and Malaysians (APA, 2000; Favazza, 1985; Westermeyer, 1985).

Hwa-byung (or *wool-hwa-byung*)—translated from Korean as "anger syndrome" because it appears to be suppressed anger—is characterized by fatigue, dysphoric affect, insomnia, anorexia, generalized aches and pains, and other symptoms (APA, 2002). A similar syndrome, *neurasthenia*, is found among Chinese (Lin & Cheung, 1999).

ILLNESS BEHAVIOR   Asian Americans and Pacific Islanders use mental health services at a lower rate than the other major racial/ethnic groups (DHHS, 2001). Such findings should not, however, be interpreted to mean that mental health problems are not prevalent or that Asian Americans do not need help (Crystal, 1989). Illness behavior is partially a function of the historical segregation and exclusion of Asian Americans from the mainstream, which made it necessary for ethnic communities to rely on each other and on indigenous resources to manage mental health problems. Moreover, cultural attitudes emphasize the primacy of families and extended networks as caregivers of members with mental health problems. Only when problems are serious and the family reaches its limits will they use external resources (Lee & Mock, 2005). Lack of English proficiency, together with a shortage of providers who speak the same language; absence of health insurance; lack of familiarity with psychotherapy; and stigma and shame may also contribute to low utilization (DHHS, 2001; Sue & Sue, 2008).

Asian American communities have their own healers, herbalists, physicians, acupuncturists, spiritual healers, and bone setters who provide culturally relevant help (Lin & Cheung, 1999). Some Asian Americans treat themselves at home with herbs, which can be purchased in ethnic neighborhood herb shops (Gould-Martin & Ngin, 1981). Other home treatments include special foods, tonics, and patent medicines (Kleinman, 1980). Asian Americans may contact indigenous or Western-style physicians, as well as sacred healers, before they are willing to see a psychiatrist (Kleinman, 1980).

IMPLICATIONS FOR PRACTICE   Mental health practice with Asian Americans and Pacific Islanders should be in keeping with their cultural values and concepts of mental illness. The clinician should be an authority figure who respects the roles and relationships in the client's family. Demands that the client express emotions and that they direct anger at family members are inappropriate. On the other hand, therapy that emphasizes self-control, will power, and avoidance of disturbing thoughts may be helpful (Lee, 1982). Asian American clients tend to be receptive to a therapist's taking an active role in structuring sessions and providing guidelines on the kinds of responses they should provide (Hwang, Wood, Lin, & Cheung, 2006; Lin & Cheung, 1999). The clinician should be aware that psychological problems are a source of stigma and may be expressed somatically. Furthermore, clinicians should recognize that Asian Americans may interact with others in ways that are in accord with cultural norms of proper behavior when, for example, they avoid eye contact (Toupin, 1981). Asian Americans have responsibilities to their families that continue throughout their lives. Intergenerational connections should be viewed as a strength.

Many Asian American communities have developed their own mutual assistance organizations that address the social, economic, and cultural needs of the community. These self-help organizations have arisen from needs that are not met by the larger community. Social work clinicians who work with Asian Americans should become familiar with the particular organizations that are available in the communities in which their Asian American and Pacific Islander clients live and link clients with these organizations when the clients' needs are consistent with the services offered by these organizations.

The diversity among Asian Americans and Pacific Islanders calls for knowledge specific to each group. Particular attention should be given to the circumstances around immigration, identification with the original culture, and the extent of assimilation and integration into mainstream U.S. culture. Asian Americans/Pacific Islanders commonly present problems over acculturation, parent–child issues, and trauma and have symptoms of somatization, dissociation, anxiety, and depression. Clinicians should be attentive to vague symptoms that do not fit into *DSM* categories; they may be culture-bound syndromes (Lin & Cheung, 1999).

Hispanics/Latinos and Latinas

The European conquerors began settlements in the New World in the sixteenth century. Whereas the French, English, Dutch, and Swedish settled in the eastern and northern sections of what is now the United States, the Spanish conquered Mexico and subsequently penetrated the natives' land, culture, and language, and married indigenous Indian women. In keeping with the pattern of expansion that was normative among Europeans at that time, the Spaniards moved into what is now the southwestern part of the United States. Mexico gained its independence from Spain in 1821.

The United States acquired Texas and the southwestern territories from Mexico during the Mexican American War, which ended in 1848, and through the Gadsden Purchase of 1853. At the time of the purchase, the land was occupied by a diverse population of persons of Spanish or Mexican descent, American Indians, and *mestizos* (mixed people of Indian and Spanish origins). Although the Mexicans had been granted rights of citizenship through the treaty that had been signed, in the ensuing years, Anglo Americans took over the land and secured dominance by controlling the economic, political, and educational institutions (Gibson, 1987). Nevertheless, immigrants from Mexico continued to flow into the Southwest and other parts of the United States where they were able to work. In addition, undocumented immigrants from Mexico and Central America penetrated the Mexican–American borders. Other Hispanic groups, such as Cubans, Dominicans, Salvadorans, and Ecuadorians, migrated in search of economic opportunities and political asylum. Puerto Ricans are U.S. citizens.

The term *Hispanic* was created by the federal government to describe people from South America, Central America, North America, the Caribbean, and others whose origins are Spanish (Castex, 1994). This designation is problematic because it draws attention to the conquering nation rather than the indigenous people. Furthermore, it obscures distinctions among people from different countries. Several additional terms are used to refer to persons of Mexican background—Mexicans, Mexican Americans, and Chicanos. Some Hispanics prefer to be called *Latino* (masculine) or *Latina* (feminine). Here the terms *Hispanic* and *Latino/Latina* are used interchangeably. Although many Hispanics/Latinos speak Spanish as their primary language, substantial numbers are bilingual or predominantly English speaking, and some speak other languages. Hispanics are multihued—black, brown, red, yellow, white, and various mixtures—and multiethnic. They are also heterogeneous in their lifestyles, cultural identification, politics, social class, education, sexual orientation, and occupations.

According to a 2004 American Community Survey Report, there are 40.5 million Hispanics of any race, comprising 14.2 percent of the United States' population (U.S. Census Bureau, 2007). These figures are probably an underestimate because of an unknown number of undocumented immigrants who enter the United States. Hispanics are the most populous and the fastest growing ethnic group in the United States. It is projected that by the middle of the twenty-first century, they will constitute 24 percent of the entire population (U.S. Census Bureau, 2004). Their fertility rate is high, with 75 out of 1,000 Hispanic women of childrearing age (compared with 50 out of 10,000 white women) who gave birth in the year prior to the American Community Survey (U.S. Census Bureau, 2007). Some 19 percent of the households are maintained by women with no husband present (U.S. Census Bureau, 2007). As it was shown in Table 6.1, Hispanics' poverty rate is around 23 percent. In 2004, 28 percent of Hispanic Americans were foreign born and noncitizens and 11 percent who were born elsewhere became naturalized citizens. Among Latinos in the United States, close to two thirds are of Mexican origin and the next highest group is Puerto Rican (U.S. Census Bureau, 2007). Although Hispanics live throughout the country, close to half reside in California and Texas, with seven other states (Florida, New York, Illinois, Arizona, New Jersey, Colorado, and New Mexico) having the next highest concentrations (U.S. Census Bureau, 2007).

CULTURAL VALUES AND NORMS Latinos have certain values that permeate their cultures. Primary among these is *respeto* (respect), which is accorded to one's parents, grandparents, elders, oneself, and others (Galan, 1985). Individuals are accorded respect on the basis of their inner qualities rather than their possessions—a form of individualism called *personalismo* (personalism) (Bernal, 1982; Garcia-Preto, 2005). Nevertheless, they do value hierarchy, especially within the family. Families tend to be patriarchal with traditional sex role expectations. Men are expected to be strong, hardworking, and dominant; women, passive, virtuous, nurturing, and self-sacrificing (Galan, 1985; Garcia-Preto, 2005; Sue & Sue, 2008). The terms *machismo* and *marianismo* capture respective male and female sex role ideals. Financial pressures have made it necessary for women to participate in the labor market.

Hispanic families include biological and unrelated persons, who provide companionship and support to each other. Children have unrelated godparents who function as substitute parents and advisers to the family. Families tend to be large, cohesive, and interdependent. The term *familismo* captures the strong emotional bonds and interdependence within the family and three-generational families (Falicov, 2005). The cultural value associated with interdependence is collectivism, the idea that the group needs and goals are to be given priority over individualistic aspirations (Ruiz, 2005).

INDIGENOUS CONCEPTS OF HEALTH, MENTAL HEALTH, AND MENTAL ILLNESS AND THEIR CAUSATION Most of the Hispanic cultural groups do not distinguish between health and mental health (Delgado, 1977; Schreiber & Homiak, 1981). Like the AIANs, they have a holistic view of the mind and body. When disorders that would be viewed as "psychiatric" in mainstream U.S. culture are viewed as folk illnesses, they are treated by folk healers or with folk remedies and/or by physicians or mental health professionals. Whichever sources are used, attention to the person as a whole, rather than a specific system, is in order (de la Rosa, 1988).

Mexican Americans have a concept of illness and disease that is sometimes called the *hot/cold theory* (Schreiber & Homiak, 1981). Rooted in the early Greek balance of humors theory, it views illness (mental or physical) as a state of disequilibrium caused by excessive exposure to heat or cold. Various internal and external objects, as well as emotional experiences, are classified as either hot or cold. For example, water and certain foods are considered cold; the sun and herbal teas are classified as hot. Treatment consists of neutralizing the excessive condition by drawing it off or consuming its opposite.

Among Puerto Ricans, *spiritism* is a prevalent belief. This is based partially on the Roman Catholic idea of a duality between material and spiritual worlds. One form of spiritism, *santeria*, is Nigerian in origin (Berthold, 1989). Adherents of spiritism believe that disembodied spirits of divine or deceased beings attach themselves to individuals at the time they are born and continue to influence their lives (Berthold, 1989; de la Rosa, 1988; Harwood, 1981b). Good spirits, such as one's guardian angel, help and protect individuals and influence their reaching higher goals. On the other hand, bad spirits can instigate problems either on their own or at the request of a living person who recruits them to engage in sorcery. The workings of malevolent spirits can result in physical or mental ailments (Harwood, 1981b).

CULTURE-SPECIFIC SYNDROMES   Some culture-specific syndromes are found among Hispanics. Latinos from the Caribbean are susceptible to *ataques de nervios* (nervous attacks). These are characterized by crying spells, uncontrollable shouting, seizure-like fainting episodes, dissociative experiences, and a general feeling of being out of control, with symptoms often occurring after a stressful life event (APA, 2000). Another syndrome that occurs with frequency among Hispanics is *susto*, fright, which occurs in response to an event that purportedly causes the soul to leave the body (APA, 2000). It has symptoms of anxiety disorders, somatoform disorders, and depression, such as diarrhea, loss of appetite, restlessness, sadness, sleep disturbances, and feelings of low self-esteem (APA, 2000). In an ethnographic study that compared illness discourses of African American, Puerto Rican, and white participants, Alverson and colleagues (2007) recognized that Puerto Ricans attributed the onset of their problems with "nervios" to the actions of others in their lives and saw this as having troubles rather than a mental illness. Furthermore, they did not like talk therapy but were receptive to taking medication.

ILLNESS BEHAVIOR   Latinos are less likely than whites to obtain mental health treatment from specialty or primary care providers (Cook, McGuire, & Miranda, 2007). Cook et al. attribute the lower utilization to lack of insurance and lack of knowledge about the effectiveness of treatment. These factors, as well as somatic presentations of symptoms and the use of cultural idioms to express distress, may contribute to the underrecognition of depression in the formal mental health system (Lewis-Fernández, Das, Alfonso, Weissman, & Olfson, 2005).

With respect to informal systems, Hispanics seek support from the family system, the church, merchant and social clubs, and folk healers (Delgado & Humm-Delgado, 1982). The family system provides emotional support, baby-sitting services, and home remedies (over-the-counter drugs, herbs, etc.) to persons with health or mental health problems. Another supportive system is the church, the Roman Catholic Church being the most prominent. Merchant and social clubs provide information, supplies, and social contacts that are culturally congruent. Hispanics will sometimes go to a botanical shop *(botanica)*, where herbs and objects that are needed in healing ceremonies are sold, advice about illnesses is given, and referrals to folk healers are made. Referrals are also made through personnel of the *bodega* (grocery store) (Delgado & Humm-Delgado, 1982).

The fourth system consists of folk healers, which have different names and functions for different Hispanic groups. Puerto Rican Americans go to spiritists for help with anxiety or somatic symptoms that have no organic cause (Delgado, 1978). Spiritists may recommend that clients participate in a healing ceremony that is attended by family members, mediums (persons who have the power to communicate with spirits), and others with infirmities. During the ceremony, candles are lit, prayers are read, the cause is discovered, and a spiritual cleansing is enacted. Spiritism, however, is not the only form of folk healing. Those Puerto Ricans and Cubans who practice *santeria* engage in its healing ceremony. Another type of folk healer is the herbalist, who recommends herbs in keeping with the hot/cold theory. A third type of healer found in Hispanic communities is the *curandero*, who views illness as the result of alienation from the Roman Catholic Church. The curandero's treatment aims to bring the individual closer to the church and its teachings (Delgado & Humm-Delgado, 1982).

IMPLICATIONS FOR PRACTICE   Latino clients, in consultation with the family system, use indigenous and/or mainstream mental health services. Because of a tendency to focus on somatic complaints, some Hispanics may use the health care system when the mental health care system may seem to be more appropriate. Those who do use the mental health care system should be provided with culturally congruent treatment. Delgado (1988) finds commonalities between folk healing and psychodrama that make it feasible to incorporate aspects of spiritism into group work treatment. He recommends that group leaders be authoritative, that the membership be diverse, and that activities rather than only verbal expression be emphasized. Similarly, Berthold (1989) sees parallels between spiritist healing and psychoanalytic treatment. The invocation of invisible spirits and causes in spiritism is not unlike the mobilization of unconscious forces and the ego in psychoanalysis. Both systems "work the cause" and restore individual functioning.

EVIDENCE-BASED PRACTICE WITH PERSONS OF DIVERSE CULTURAL BACKGROUNDS

One of the findings of the Surgeon General's supplementary report, *Mental Health: Culture Race, and Ethnicity* (DHHS, 2001), was that randomized controlled studies of interventions either excluded or included small numbers of participants who were from diverse cultures, and that data were not analyzed according to ethnicity. Thus, there were insufficient data by 2001 to support the evidence-based interventions and practice guidelines that have been found effective for the majority population. A review of psychosocial intervention research with diverse populations up to 2005 found that two evidence-based treatments (EBTs) for depression (cognitive-behavioral and interpersonal therapies) seem to be effective with African American and Latino populations (Miranda et al., 2005). These treatments are described in Chapter 8.

Because research continues to be limited, there is a continued need for intervention studies on diverse cultural groups. As Hwang (2006) outlined, practitioners today have three options: (a) implement existing EBTs as they are, (b) adapt EBTs so that they are more congruent with clients' cultures, or (c) develop new EBTs for specific cultural groups. Considering the first option culturally inadequate and the third costly, Hwang proposed a model for adapting psychotherapy to Asian Americans (option b) that involves building cultural bridges such as using familiar cultural terms and becoming familiar with the culture-specific ways in which clients express distress. Other authors have endorsed this type of approach with other groups (Conner & Grote, 2008).

Questions remain, however, about the compatibility between the paradigms of evidence-based practice (EBP) and cultural competence. Whitley (2007) sees EBP as "modernist" in its commitment to the idea that knowledge progresses incrementally and can be advanced through the use of scientific technologies such as standardized measures, and sees cultural competence as linked to multiculturalism and postmodernism, which recognize the value of differences and favor qualitative approaches to research. Aisenberg (2008) advises a shift in thinking away "from a monocultural, Eurocentric framework and from a narrow, positivist perspective on knowledge gathering and dissemination" to one that is responsive to diverse cultures (p. 305). He recommends that researchers form collaborative partnerships with ethnic communities to ensure interventions and community involvement in interventions that are culturally tailored. The adaptations should use culturally appropriate language and "incorporate cultural values, customs, and traditions into the content of the intervention" (p. 304). Miranda et al. (2005), too, recommend increasing research on cultural adaptations to evidence-based interventions.

Summary and Deconstruction

This chapter presented salient concepts, themes, and patterns relevant to understanding and working with clients from diverse racial, ethnic, and cultural groups. It discussed sociological and anthropological concepts and examined illness behavior and cultural disparities. The chapter focused particularly on African Americans, American Indians/Alaska Natives, Asian/Pacific Islanders, and Hispanics/Latinos—who are constructed as "other" in the United States. Although each group is itself multicultural and multiracial, some general characteristics of each group were described. From a postmodern perspective, this knowledge is a potential resource but one should avoid essentializing individuals and groups. Every individual needs to be seen in his or her multiple diversities.

Cultural information can contribute to ethnic sensitivity and cultural competence, but this is not enough. Clinical social workers need to reflect on their own ethnicities and their attitudes toward their own culture(s) and people who are different. Although most social workers are white, few contemplate their white racial identity and what it means to have privileges based on an accident of birth. Those social workers who are of African American, American Indian or Alaska Native, Asian, or Latino descent may be of mixed racial and ethnic background, including white. They are likely to have feelings about these categories. Although this chapter did not directly address other differences (e.g., religion, social class, gender, sexual orientation, and disability), these, too, enter into cross-cultural behavioral health practice. Regardless of one's cultural background, one identifies with varying degrees of positive and negative feelings with one's own cultural group(s).

The concept of cultural competence, however, has its limitations. A neutral term, it obscures racism, a widespread, contentious issue in the United States and elsewhere. In addition, the term has come to encompass a variety of differences—age, ability, sexuality, religion, gender, and nationality, among others (Abrams & Moio, 2009). By equalizing oppressions, it can have the effect of encouraging color blindness rather than antioppressive practice (Abrams & Moio, 2009). Beckett and Macey (2001) express additional concerns about the concept of multiculturalism, particularly as it is viewed in Great Britain, where the focus is on racism. They believe that by highlighting race, it underestimates the injuries caused by sexism and homophobia, as well as the intersections with race, gender, and sexual orientation. As a result, serious social problems such as female genital mutilation, coerced arranged marriages, and domestic violence among culturally diverse groups are ignored.

References

Abrams, L., & Moio, J. A. (2009). Critical race theory and the cultural competence dilemma in social work education. *Journal of Social Work Education, 45*(2), 245–261.

Aisenberg, E. (2008). Evidence-based practice in mental health care to ethnic minority communities: Has practice fallen short of its evidence? *Social Work, 53*(4), 297–306.

Alarcón, R. D., Becker, A. E., Lewis-Fernández, R., Like, R. C., Desai, P., Foulks, E., et al. (2009). Issues for DSM-V: The role of culture in psychiatric diagnosis. *Journal of Nervous and Mental Disease, 197*(8), 559–560.

Alegría, M., Canino, G., Ríos, R., Vera, M., Calderón, J., Rusch, D., et al. (2002). Inequalities in use of specialty mental health services among Latinos, African Americans, and non-Latino whites. *Psychiatric Services, 53*(12), 1547–1555.

Alessandria, K. P. (2002). Acknowledging white ethnic groups in multicultural counseling. *The Family Journal: Counseling and Therapy for Couples and Families, 10*(1), 57–60.

Alverson, H. S., Drake, R. E., Carpenter-Song, E. A., Chu, E., Ritsema, M., & Smith, B. (2007). Ethnocultural variations in mental health discourse: Some implications for building therapeutic alliances. *Psychiatric Services, 58*(12), 1541–1546.

American Anthropological Association. (1998, May 17). Statement on "race." Retrieved April 3, 2010, from http://www.aaanet.org/stmts/racepp.htm

American Psychiatric Association. (1994). *Diagnostic and statistical manual of mental disorders* (4th ed.). Washington, DC: Author.

American Psychiatric Association. (2000). *Diagnostic and statistical manual of mental disorders* (4th ed., text rev.). Washington, DC: Author.

de Anda, D. (1984). Bicultural socialization: Factors affecting the minority experience. *Social Work, 29,* 101–107.

Anderson, M. J., & Ellis, R. (1988). On the reservation. In N. A. Vacc, J. Wittmer, & S. B. DeVaney (Eds.), *Experiencing and counseling multicultural and diverse populations* (2nd ed., pp. 107–126). Muncie, IN: Accelerated Development.

Attneave, C. (1982). American Indians and Alaska Native families: Emigrants in their own homeland. In M. McGoldrick, J. K. Pearce, & J. Giordano (Eds.), *Ethnicity and family therapy* (pp. 55–83). New York: Guilford Press.

Beckett, C., & Macey, M. (2001). Race, gender and sexuality: The oppression of multiculturalism. *Women's Studies International Forum, 24*(3/4), 309–319.

Bernal, G. (1982). Cuban families. In M. McGoldrick, J. K. Pearce, & J. Giordano (Eds.), *Ethnicity and family therapy* (pp. 187–207). New York: Guilford Press.

Berthold, S. M. (1989). Spiritism as a form of psychotherapy: Implications for social work practice. *Social Casework, 70,* 502–509.

Blanchard, E. L. (1987). American Indians and Alaskan Natives. In A. Minahan (Ed.), *Encyclopedia of social work* (Vol. 1, pp. 141–150). Silver Spring, MD: National Association of Social Workers.

Bosmajian, H. (1974). *The language of oppression.* Washington, DC: Public Affairs Press.

Bourjolly, J., Finley, L., Pernell-Arnold, A., Sands, R. G., Solomon, P., & Stanhope, V. (2006–2007). Unpublished format for a multicultural assessment, based on Finley (1995), Finley & Shake (2000), & Finley (2005).

Boyd-Franklin, N. (1989). *Black families in therapy: A multisystems approach.* New York: Guilford Press.

Brodkin, K. (1998). *How Jews became white folks and what that says about race in America.* New Brunswick, NJ: Rutgers University Press.

Brown v. Board of Education of Topeka, Kansas, 348 US 8861 (1954).

Castex, G. M. (1994). Providing services to Hispanic/Latino populations: Profiles in diversity. *Social Work, 39,* 288–296.

Chestang, L. (1976). Environmental influences on social functioning: The Black experience. In P. S. J. Cafferty, & L. Chestang (Eds.), *The diverse society: Implications for social policy* (pp. 59–74). Washington, DC: National Association of Social Workers.

Conner, K. O., & Grote, N. K. (2008). Enhancing the cultural relevance of empirically-supported mental health interventions. *Families in Society, 89*(4), 587–595.

Crystal, D. (1989). Asian Americans and the myth of the model minority. *Social Casework, 70,* 405–413.

Cook, B. L., McGuire, T., & Miranda, J. (2007). Measuring trends in mental health care disparities, 2000-2004. *Psychiatric Services, 58*(12), 1533–1540.

Crissey, S. R. (2009). *Educational attainment in the United States: 2007.* Current Population Reports, P20-560. Washington, DC: U.S. Census Bureau. Retrieved September 10, 2010, from http://www.wwwcensusgov.zuom.info/prod/2009pubs/p20-560.pdf

Davenport, J. A., & Davenport, J., III. (1987). Native American suicide: A Durkheimian analysis. *Social Casework, 68,* 533–539.

Delgado, M. (1977). Puerto Rican spiritualism and the social work profession. *Social Casework, 8,* 451–458.

Delgado, M. (1978). Folk medicine in Puerto Rican culture. *International Social Work, 21,* 46–54.

Delgado, M. (1988). Groups in Puerto Rican spiritism: Implications for clinicians. In C. Jacobs & D. D. Bowles (Eds.), *Ethnicity and race: Critical concepts in social work* (pp. 34–47). Silver Spring, MD: National Association of Social Workers.

Delgado, M., & Humm-Delgado, D. (1982). Natural support systems: Source of strength in Hispanic communities. *Social Work, 27,* 83–89.

Dougherty, R. H. (2004). Reducing disparity in behavioral health services: A report from the American College of Mental Health Administration. *Administration and Policy in Mental Health, 31*(3), 253–263.

Evans-Campbell, T., Fredriksen-Goldsen, K. I., Walters, K. L., & Stately, A. (2007). Caregiving experiences among American Indian two-spirit men and women: Contemporary and historical roles. *Journal of Gay & Lesbian Social Services, 18*(3/4), 75–92.

Falicov, C. J. (2005). Mexican families. In M. McGoldrick, J. Giordano, & N. Garcia-Preto (Eds.), *Ethnicity and family therapy* (3rd ed., pp. 229–241). New York: Guilford Press.

Favazza, A. R. (1985). Contributions of the sociocultural sciences: Anthropology and psychiatry. In H. I. Kaplan & B. J. Sadock (Eds.), *Comprehensive textbook of psychiatry* (4th ed., pp. 247–265). Baltimore, MD: Williams & Wilkins.

Finley, L. (2005). Multicultural diagnosis and assessment. In L. Finley & A. Pernell-Arnold (Eds.), *Partners reaching to improve multicultural effectiveness: Workforce training curriculum to reduce racial and ethnic disparities.* Rockville, MD: Substance Abuse and Mental Health Services Administration.

Finley, L. Y. (1995). *When cultures meet curriculum.* Philadelphia: Medical College of Pennsylvania and Allegheny Health Sciences.

Finley, L. Y., & Shake, M. A. O. (2000). *Multicultural diagnosis and assessment module.* Hartford, CT: Department of Mental Health and Substance Abuse Services, Office of Minority Affairs.

Flaskerud, J. H. (2000). Ethnicity, culture, and neuropsychiatry. *Issues in Mental Health Nursing, 21,* 5–29.

Galan, F. J. (1985). Traditional values about family behavior: The case of the Chicano client. *Social Thought, 11*(3), 14–22.

Garcia-Preto, N. (2005). Puerto Rican families. In M. McGoldrick, J. Giordano, & N. Garcia–Preto (Eds.), *Ethnicity and family therapy* (3rd ed., pp. 243–255). New York: Guilford Press.

Gibson, G. (1987). Mexican Americans. In A. Minahan (Ed.), *Encyclopedia of social work* (Vol. 2, pp. 135–148). Silver Spring, MD: National Association of Social Workers.

Gould-Martin, K., & Ngin, C. (1981). Chinese Americans. In A. Harwood (Ed.), *Ethnicity and medical care* (pp. 130–171). Cambridge, MA: Harvard University Press.

Grier, W. H., & Cobbs, P. M. (1968). *Black rage.* New York: Bantam Books.

Harwood, A. (Ed.). (1981a). *Ethnicity and medical care.* Cambridge, MA: Harvard University Press.

Harwood, A. (1981b). Mainland Puerto Ricans. In A. Harwood (Ed.), *Ethnicity and medical care* (pp. 397–481). Cambridge, MA: Harvard University Press.

Hatzenbuehler, M. L., Keyes, K. M., Narrow, W. E., Grant, B. F., & Hasin, D. S. (2008). Racial/ethnic disparities in service utilization for individuals with co-occurring mental health and substance use disorders in the general population: Results from the National Epidemiologic Survey on Alcohol and Related Conditions. *Journal of Clinical Psychiatry, 69*(7), 1112–1121.

Helms, J. E., & Cook, D. A. (1999). *Using race and culture in counseling and psychotherapy: Theory and process.* Boston: Allyn and Bacon.

Hill, R. B. (1971). *The strengths of Black families.* New York: National Urban League.

Hines, P. M., & Boyd-Franklin, N. (1982). Black families. In M. McGoldrick, J. K. Pearce, & J. Giordano (Eds.), *Ethnicity and family therapy* (pp. 84–107). New York: Guilford Press.

Hines, P. M., & Boyd-Franklin, N. (1996). African American families. In M. McGoldrick, J. Giordano, & J. K. Pearce (Eds.), *Ethnicity and family therapy* (2nd ed., pp. 66–84). New York: Guilford Press.

Ho, M. K. (1981). Social work with Asian Americans. In R. H. Dana (Ed.), *Human services for cultural minorities* (pp. 307–316). Baltimore, MD: University Park Press.

Hopps, J. (1982). Oppression based on color. *Social Work, 27,* 3–5.

Hopps, J. G. (1987). Minorities of color. In A. Minahan (Ed.), *Encyclopedia of social work* (18th ed., Vol. 2, pp. 161–171). Silver Spring, MD: NASW.

Hwang, W.-C. (2006). The psychotherapy adaptation and modification framework: Application to Asian Americans. *American Psychologist, 61*(7), 702–715.

Hwang, W.-C., Wood, J. J., Lin, K.-M., & Cheung, F. (2006). Cognitive-behavioral therapy with Chinese Americans: Research, theory, and clinical practice. *Cognitive and Behavioral Practice, 13,* 293–303.

Ignatiev, N. (1995). *How the Irish became white.* New York: Routledge.

Ishisaka, H. A., & Takagi, C. Y. (1982). Social work with Asian- and Pacific-Americans. In J. W. Green (Ed.), *Cultural awareness in the human services* (pp. 122–156). Englewood Cliffs, NJ: Prentice-Hall.

Jackson, J. J. (1981). Urban Black Americans. In A. Harwood (Ed.), *Ethnicity and medical care* (pp. 37–129). Cambridge, MA: Harvard University Press.

Johnson, B. B. (1982). American Indian jurisdiction as a policy issue. *Social Work, 27,* 31–37.

Jones, B. E., & Gray, B. A. (1986). Problems in diagnosing schizophrenia and affective disorders among Blacks. *Hospital and Community Psychiatry, 37,* 61–65.

Kamya, H. A. (1997). African immigrants in the United States: The challenge for research and practice. *Social Work, 42,* 154–165.

Kasl, S. V., & Cobb, S. (1966). Health behavior, illness behavior, and sick role. *Archives of Environmental Health, 12,* 246–266.

Kitano, H. H. L. (1985). *Race relations* (3rd ed.). Englewood Cliffs, NJ: Prentice-Hall.

Kitano, H. H. L. (1987). Asian Americans. In A. Minahan (Ed.), *Encyclopedia of social work* (Vol. 1, pp. 156–171). Silver Spring, MD: National Association of Social Workers.

Kleinman, A. (1980). *Patients and healers in the context of culture.* Berkeley: University of California Press.

Kleinman, A. (1988). *The illness narrative: Suffering, healing, and the human condition.* New York: Basic Books.

Kreider, R. M., & Elliott, D. B. (2009). *America's families and living arrangements: 2007.* Current Population Reports, P20-561. Washington, DC: U.S. Census Bureau.

Kroeber, A. L., & Kluckhohn, C. (1952). *Culture: A critical review of concepts and definitions.* New York: Vintage Books.

Kung, W. W. (2003). Chinese Americans' help seeking for emotional distress. *Social Services Review, 77,* 110–133.

Kunitz, S. J., & Levy, J. E. (1981). Navajos. In A. Harwood (Ed.), *Ethnicity and medical care* (pp. 337–396). Cambridge, MA: Harvard University Press.

Kuramoto, F. H., Morales, R. F., Munoz, F. U., & Murase, K. (1983). Education for social work practice in Asian and Pacific American communities. In J. C. Chunn II, P. J. Dunston, & F. Ross-Sheriff (Eds.), *Mental health and people of color* (pp. 127–155). Washington, DC: Howard University Press.

Lee, E. (1982). A social systems approach to assessment and treatment for Chinese American families. In M. McGoldrick, J. K. Pearce, & J. Giordano (Eds.), *Ethnicity and family therapy* (pp. 527–551). New York: Guilford Press.

Lee, E., & Mock, M. R. (2005). Asian families: An overview. In M. McGoldrick, J. Giordano, & N. Garcia-Preto (Eds.), *Ethnicity and family therapy* (3rd ed., pp. 269–289). New York: Guilford Press.

Leigh, J. W., & Green, J. W. (1982). The structure of the Black community: The knowledge base for social services. In J. W. Green (Ed.), *Cultural awareness in the human services* (pp. 94–121). Englewood Cliffs, NJ: Prentice-Hall.

Lewis, R. (1985). Cultural perspectives on treatment modalities with American Indians. In M. Bloom (Ed.), *Life span development* (2nd ed., pp. 458–464). New York: Macmillan.

Lewis, R. G., & Keung Ho, M. (1975). Social work with American Indians. *Social Work, 20,* 375–382.

Lewis-Fernández, R. (2009). The cultural formulation. *Transcultural Psychiatry, 46*(3), 379–382.

Lewis-Fernández, R., Das, A. K., Alfonso, C., Weissman, M. M., & Olfson, M. (2005). Depression in US Hispanics: Diagnostic and management considerations in family practice. *Journal of the American Board of Family Medicine, 18*(4), 282–296.

Lim, R. F., & Lin, K. M. (1996). Cultural formulation of psychiatric diagnosis. Case No. 03. Psychosis following Qi-Gong in a Chinese immigrant. *Culture, Medicine and Psychiatry, 20,* 369–378.

Lin, K. M., & Cheung, F. (1999). Mental health issues for Asian Americans. *Psychiatric Services, 50*(6), 774–780.

Lum, D. (Ed.). (2007). *Culturally competent practice: A framework for understanding diverse groups and justice issues* (3rd ed.). Belmont, CA: Thompson Brooks/Cole.

Marsella, A. J., & Higginbotham, H. N. (1984). Traditional Asian medicine: Applications to psychiatric services in developing nations. In P. B. Pedersen, N. Sartorius, & A. J. Marsella (Eds.), *Mental health services: The cross-cultural context* (pp. 175–197). Beverly Hills, CA: Sage Publications.

McAdoo, H. P. (1987). Blacks. In A. Minahan (Ed.), *Encyclopedia of social work* (18th ed., Vol. 1, pp. 194–206). Silver Spring, MD: National Association of Social Workers.

McGoldrick, M., Giordano, J., & Garcia-Preto, N. (Eds.). (2005). *Ethnicity and family therapy* (3rd ed.). New York: Guilford Press.

McGuire, T. G., & Miranda, J. (2008). New evidence regarding racial and ethnic disparities in mental health: Policy implications. *Health Affairs, 27*(2), 393–403.

Miranda, J., Bernal, G., Lau, A., Kohn, L., Hwang, W.-C., & LaFromboise, T. (2005). State of the science on psychosocial interventions for ethnic minorities. *Annual Review of Clinical Psychology, 1,* 113–142.

Nadeem, E., Lange, J. M., Edge, D., Fongwa, M., Belin, T., & Miranda, J. (2007). Does stigma keep poor young immigrant and U.S.-born Black and Latina women from seeking mental health care? *Psychiatric Services, 58*(12), 1547–1554.

National Association of Social Workers. (1996/1999/2008). *Code of ethics of the National Association of Social Workers.* Retrieved January 23, 2010, from http://www.socialworkers.org/pubs/Code/code.asp?print=1

Nobles, W. W. (1976). Black people in white insanity: An issue for Black community mental health. *Journal of Afro-American Issues, 4,* 21–27.

Nofz, M. P. (1988). Alcohol abuse and culturally marginal American Indians. *Social Casework, 69,* 67–73.

Ogunwole, S. U. (2006). *We the people: American Indians and Alaska Natives in the United States.* Census 2000 special reports. Washington, DC: U.S. Census Bureau. Retrieved September 10, 2010, from http://www.census.gov/prod/2006pubs/censr-28.pdf

Parsons, T. (1964). *The social system.* New York: Free Press.

Pinderhughes, E. (1982). Afro-American families and the victim system. In M. McGoldrick, J. K. Pearce, & J. Giordano (Eds.),*Ethnicity and family therapy* (pp. 108–122). New York: Guilford Press.

Plessy v. Ferguson, 163 US 537 (1896).

President's New Freedom Commission on Mental Health. (2003). *Achieving the promise: Transforming mental health care in America. Final report* (DHHS Publication No. SMA 03-3832). Rockville, MD: U.S. Government Printing Office.

Red Horse, J. G. (1980a). American Indian elders: Unifiers of Indian families. *Social Casework, 61,* 490–493.

Red Horse, J. G. (1980b). Family structure and value orientation in American Indians. *Social Casework, 61,* 462–467.

Red Horse, J. G. (1988). Cultural evolution of American Indian families. In C. Jacobs & D. D. Bowles (Eds.), *Ethnicity and race: Critical concepts in social work* (pp. 86–102). Silver Spring, MD: National Association of Social Workers.

de la Rosa, M. (1988). Puerto Rican spiritualism: A key dimension for effective social casework practice with Puerto Ricans. *International Social Work, 31,* 273–283.

Ruiz, E. (2005). Hispanic culture and relational cultural theory. *Journal of Creativity in Mental Health, 1*(1), 33–55.

Sands, R. G., & Nuccio, K. (1989). Mother-headed single parent families: A feminist perspective. *Affilia, 4,* 25–41.

Sadock, B. J., & Sadock, V. A. (2007). *Kaplan & Sadock's Synopsis of psychiatry: Behavioral sciences/clinical psychiatry* (10th ed.). Philadelphia, PA: Wolters Klumer Lippincott Williams & Wilkins.

Schiele, J. H. (1996). Afrocentricity: An emerging paradigm in social work practice. *Social Work, 41,* 284–294.

Schreiber, J. M., & Homiak, J. P. (1981). Mexican Americans. In A. Harwood (Ed.), *Ethnicity and medical care* (pp. 264–336). Cambridge, MA: Harvard University Press.

Shon, S. P., & Ja, D. Y. (1982). Asian families. In M. McGoldrick, J. K. Pearce, & J. Giordano (Eds.), *Ethnicity and family therapy* (pp. 208–228). New York: Guilford Press.

Snowden, L. R., & Yamada, A.-M. (2005). Cultural differences in access to care. *Annual Review of Clinical Psychiatry, 1,* 143–166.

Steinberg, M. D., Pardes, H., Bjork, D., & Sporty, D. (1977). Demographic and clinical characteristics of Black psychiatric patients in a private general hospital. *Hospital and Community Psychiatry, 28,* 128–132.

Sue, D. W. (2006). *Multicultural social work practice.* Hoboken, NJ: John Wiley & Sons.

Sue, D. W., & Sue, D. (2008). *Counseling the culturally diverse: Theory and practice* (5th ed.). New York: John Wiley & Sons.

Suite, D. H., La Bril, R., Primm, A., & Harrison-Ross, P. (2007). Beyond misdiagnose, misunderstanding and mistrust: Relevance of the historical perspective in the medical and mental health treatment of people of color. *Journal of the National Medical Association, 99*(8), 879–885.

Sutton, C. T., & Broken Nose, M. A. (1996). American Indian families: An overview. In M. McGoldrick, J. Giordano, & J. K. Pearce (Eds.), *Ethnicity and family therapy* (2nd ed., pp. 31–44). New York: Guilford Press.

Sutton, C. T., & Broken Nose, M. A. (2005). American Indian families: An overview. In M. McGoldrick, J. Giordano, & N. Garcia-Preto (Eds.), *Ethnicity and family therapy* (3rd ed., pp. 43–54). New York: Guilford Press.

Takeuchi, D. T., Uehara, E., & Maramba, G. (1999). Cultural diversity and mental health treatment. In A. V. Horwitz & T. L. Scheid (Eds.), *A handbook for the study of mental health: Social contexts, theories, and systems* (pp. 550–565). Cambridge, UK: Cambridge University Press.

Toupin, E. S. W. A. (1981). Counseling Asians: Psychotherapy in the context of racism and Asian-American history. In R. H. Dana (Ed.), *Human services for cultural minorities* (pp. 295–306). Baltimore, MD: University Park Press.

Trimble, J. E., & Clearing-Sky, M. (2009). An historical profile of American Indians and Alaska Natives in psychology. *Cultural Diversity and Ethnic Minority Psychology, 15*(4), 338–351.

Trimble, J. E., Manson, S. M., Dinges, N. G., & Medicine, B. (1984). American Indian concepts of mental health: Reflections and directions. In P. B. Pedersen, N. Sartorius, & A. J. Marsella (Eds.), *Mental health services: The cross-cultural context* (pp. 199–220). Beverly Hills, CA: Sage Publications.

U.S. Bureau of the Census. (2009). *Income, poverty, and health insurance coverage in the United States: 2008.* Current Population Reports, P60-236. Washington, DC: U.S. Government Printing Office.

U.S. Census Bureau. (2002). *The Asian Population: 2000. U.S. Department of Commerce, Economics and Statistics Administration.* Retrieved May 13, 2010, from http://www.census.gov/prod/2002pubs/c2kbr01-16.pdf

U.S. Census Bureau. (2004). *U.S. Census Bureau News. More diversity, slower growth.* Retrieved May 14, 2010, from http://www.census.gov/Press-Release/www/releases/archives/population/001720.html

U.S. Census Bureau. (2005). *Asian/Pacific American Heritage Month.* Retrieved May 13, 2010, from http://www.census.gov/Press-Release/www/releases/archives/facts_for_features_special_editions/004522.html

U.S. Census Bureau. (2007). *The American community—Hispanics: 2004.* American Community Survey Reports. Retrieved May 14, 2010, from http://www.census.gov/prod/2007pubs/acs-03.pdf

U.S. Census Bureau. (2008). *B02-1.Race-universe: Total population. 2008 American Community Survey 1-Year Estimates.* Retrieved May 10, 2010, from http://factfinder.census.gov/servlet/DTTable?_bm=y&-context=dt&-ds

U.S. Department of Health and Human Services. (1999). *Mental health: A report of the Surgeon General.* Rockville, MD: U.S. Department of Health and Human Services, Substance Abuse and Mental Health Services Administration, Center for Mental Health Services, National Institutes of Health, National Institute of Mental Health.

U.S. Department of Health and Human Services. (2001). *Mental health: Culture, race, and ethnicity—A supplement to mental health: A report of the Surgeon General.* Rockville, MD: U.S. Department of Health and Human Services, Substance Abuse and Mental Health Services Administration, Center for Mental Health Services.

U.S. Department of Health and Human Services, Indian Health Service. (2010). *HIS fact sheets: Indian health disparities.* Retrieved May 11, 2010, from http://info.ihs.gov/Disparities.asp

U.S. Department of the Interior. (2010). *Bureau of Indian Affairs.* Retrieved May 12, 2010, from http://www.bia.gov/WhoWeAre/index.htm

Wang, P. S., Lane, M., Olfson, M., Pincus, H. A., Wells, K. B., & Kessler, R. C. (2005). Twelve-month use of mental health services in the United States: Results from the National Comorbidity Survey Replication. *Archives of General Psychiatry, 62*, 629–640.

Weaver, H. N. (2007). Cultural competence with First Nations Peoples. In D. Lum (Ed.), *Culturally competent practice: A framework for understanding diverse groups and justice issues* (pp. 254–275). Belmont, CA: Thomson Brooks/Cole.

Wells, K., Klap, R., Koike, A., & Sherbourne, C. (2001). Ethnic disparities in unmet need for alcoholism, drug abuse, and mental health care. *American Journal of Psychiatry, 158*(12), 2027–2032.

Westermeyer, J. (1985). Psychiatric diagnosis across cultur boundaries. *American Journal of Psychiatry, 142*, 798–8

Whitley, R. (2007). Cultural competence, evidence-ba medicine, and evidence-based practices. *Psychi Services, 58*(12), 1588–1590.

Whitley, R., Kirmayer, L. J., & Groleau, D. (Understanding immigrants' reluctance to use health services: A qualitative study from N *Canadian Journal of Psychiatry, 51*(4), 205–2(

Feminist Mental Health Practice

*The actual distress or dysfunction about which an individual initiates
therapy is thus seen not as pathological per se, no matter how much it
impairs a person's functioning, but most likely [is] a response to being
immersed in toxic patriarchal realities.*

—BROWN, *FEMINIST THERAPY*, 2010, P. 5

Despite incremental progress over the last 30 years, gender equity has not been achieved in the United States. In 2009, women's median weekly earnings were about 80 percent of that of men, with Latina and African American women having the lowest earnings (Institute for Women's Policy Research [IWPR], 2010). The gender gap was evident in most occupations regardless of whether men or women are more prevalent or whether there is an even mix of women and men in these fields (IWPR, 2010). With 31 percent of female-headed households impoverished (Wait, Proctor, & Smith, 2009), women continue to suffer from the "feminization of poverty" (Pearce, 1979). Besides having disparate income and poverty, women are subject to violence at home, at work, and elsewhere. According to a large national survey, women are experiencing intimate partner violence (IPV), rape, stalking, and physical injury during a violent incident to a greater extent than men (Tjaden & Thoennes, 2000a, 2000b). These experiences, as well as sexual harassment and human trafficking, are exceedingly detrimental to women's mental health.

This chapter describes feminist theory and practice and uses a feminist lens to discuss issues that adversely affect women's mental health. It describes several schools of feminism, psychological theories that depict women, gender differences in types of psychiatric disorders, and feminist practice. To illustrate how women's mental health problems are related to violence, the chapter discusses IPV and human trafficking. It also describes ways of intervening with women affected by trauma. The chapter begins by discussing different types of feminism.

FEMINIST THEORETICAL PERSPECTIVES

During the fourth quarter of the last century, feminism emerged as a significant political and social force in the United States and other parts of the world. In the United States, it is referred to as the "second wave" of feminism, following (after a long pause) the "first wave" that took place from the middle of the nineteenth century to the 1920s (Kinser, 2004). The second U.S. wave grew out of the civil rights movement of the 1950s and 1960s. It was given an impetus when middle-class, white women began to meet in consciousness-raising groups in which they became aware that the dissatisfaction they were experiencing individually was related to norms and ideologies that supported male dominance (i.e., "the personal is political"). Through a reflective, interactional process, they came to realize that stereotypical ideas about femininity (passive, dependent, emotional), women's bodies (ideally thin), and women's "place" (in the home) were consequences of patriarchy. Women participating in this process became aware that their disadvantaged positions in the political and occupational arenas, lack of power in intimate relationships, as well as their smaller physical size and strength, constrained their ability to achieve the autonomy and the opportunities they wanted to have.

A number of women also participated in political organizations that were emerging, such as the National Women's Political Caucus and the National Organization of Women. These groups, as well as many others, focused on issues such as the Equal Rights Amendment, reproductive freedom, rape, and domestic violence. Although these organizations were nominally open to lesbians and women of diverse races and ethnicities, nonheterosexual, nonwhite, working-class women tended to feel unwelcome. Furthermore, the latter constituencies did not have the same need to have their consciousnesses raised, as they were already aware of their marginal status. Still some of these women echoed Sojourner Truth's protest, "Ain't I a woman?" (hooks, 1981). The tendency of white women to speak about women as if they were all white and middle class has remained a sensitive issue among feminists today.

Feminism is not a single, monolithic theory or perspective; there are numerous feminist philosophical positions, frameworks, and theories. Nes and Iadicola (1989) clarified for social workers three orientations that were prominent in the 1980s—liberal, socialist, and radical. In her social work text on feminist theories, Saulnier (1996) added lesbian, postmodern, and global feminisms and others. Other writers described the expanding feminist approaches to wider audiences (e.g., Gonda, 1998; Jagger & Rothenberg, 1993; Mills, 1998; Tong, 1998).

Brown (2010) situated feminist psychological perspectives into four historical eras within the feminist movement of the last fifty years. Because the major feminist theoretical approaches fit best into Brown's first, second, and fourth stages, these will be used as an organizing framework here. The last of these stages is referred to elsewhere as "third-wave feminism" (Kinser, 2004).

No-Difference Feminism (1960s to early 1980s)

During this era, two types of feminism—reformist (or liberal) and radical—were prominent (Brown, 2010). *Liberal feminists* sought equal opportunities and rights for women within the existing political system. Believing that gender roles were limiting, liberal feminists considered men and women more or less the same (Tong, 1998). Their political agenda was to advance legislation to further equal rights. *Radical feminists* also minimized gender differences, but they attributed the sex/gender problem to the system of patriarchy, which they wish to see transformed (Brown, 2010; Tong, 1998).

In addition, Marxist, socialist, and lesbian feminisms were prominent during this period. *Marxist feminists* attributed the subordinate status of women to the capitalistic economic system, whereas *socialist feminists* emphasized both the economic and the patriarchal systems (Tong, 1998). Feminists of both of these persuasions advocated system changes. *Lesbian feminists* viewed both heterosexuality and patriarchy as systems of oppression that they wished to have overturned (Saulnier, 1996). In emphasizing the distinctiveness of lesbians, lesbian feminists anticipated the next stage.

Difference/Cultural Feminism (mid-1980s to mid-1990s)

Brown's (2010) second stage affirms that there *are* differences and that these differences should be acknowledged. Gilligan's (1982) book, *In a Different Voice*, epitomizes the new focus on gender differences. The Stone Center's "relational self" as characteristic of women (Surrey, 1991) is another example (Brown, 2010). (The ideas of Gilligan and the Stone Center will be discussed in a later section of this chapter.) In family therapy, feminist therapists recognized that a therapist's neutrality can undermine women who are in a disadvantageous position (Walters, Carter, Papp, & Silverstein, 1988).

A feminism that upholds differences is called *cultural feminism*. In patriarchal societies, men define their experiences, positions, and perspectives as the normal and legitimate ones and the experiences of women (and other disenfranchised groups) as "other" (de Beauvoir, 1968). As a result, women's identities are "overdetermined" by men whose constructions incorporate their own masculinist self-interests, fears, and misogyny (Alcoff, 1997). In response to this, cultural feminists have attempted to define themselves in their own terms. Cultural feminists view women as different but their constructions are positive; for example, they view "woman's passivity as her peacefulness, her sentimentality as her proclivity to nurture, her subjectiveness as her advanced self-awareness, and so forth" (Alcoff, 1997, p. 331). The problem with the cultural feminist approach is that it assumes that there is a universal female essence while it discounts the way in which the larger culture produces this and inscribes it on women's subjective identities (Alcoff, 1997).

Not mentioned by Brown (2010), two other schools of feminist thought fit into this category—feminist standpoint epistemology and black feminist standpoint. *Feminist standpoint epistemology* is a method of inquiry that takes the perspective of women as subjugated subjects as its starting point (Smith, 1987; Swigonski, 1994). It asserts that women have special insights that stem from their everyday experiences in their particular social location. Swigonski extends this approach to all oppressed populations, as all oppressions are interlocking. *Black feminist standpoint* recognizes the unique position of African American women. As Collins (1991) described it, "Black feminist thought consists of specialized knowledge created by African-American women which clarifies a standpoint of and for Black women. In other words, Black feminist thought encompasses theoretical interpretations of Black women's reality by those who live it" (p. 22). The reality Collins was referring to was black women's experience with racism, sexism, and classism.

Multicultural, Global, and Postmodern Feminisms (the twenty-first century)

The feminisms in this period serve as a corrective of the perspectives of previous eras that focused primarily on the perspectives of white middle-class women and/or assumed a unity that was not present. The first of these, *multicultural feminism* arose out of the exclusion of people of diverse cultures in the larger society and within the feminist movement. The melting pot ideology, defined in Chapter 6, as well as assumptions of white feminists that their perspective was universal, generated a reaction from the voices that had been disregarded (Tong, 1998). African American feminists such as Collins (1991) and hooks (1981) discussed the intersection between race, gender, and class. In particular, they created space for discussion about behaviors of black men toward black women such as sexual harassment and IPV (Tong, 1998).

Global feminism looks at the effects of colonialism or imperialist policies on the part of the First World toward the Third World (Tong, 1998). Primarily concerned with economic and political issues, its priorities are different from those of First-World feminists (Tong, 1998). Global feminists look at the struggles of women in parts of the world that have been affected in different ways by colonialism, fundamentalist religion, and culture (Saulnier, 1996). It recognizes differences in wants and needs of women in different locations and that their perspectives may diverge from that of Western feminists. For example, women in some countries may embrace a low-wage job because they need the job and realize that it will provide them with autonomy (Tong, 1998).

Postmodern feminism is critical of universal theories and the assumptions of objectivity, rationality, and neutrality in modern (post-Enlightenment) thought. According to postmodernism, categories that are presented as universal are social constructions (not *essences*) that are embedded in a particular social, cultural, or historical context and reflect power relations. Thus, when white, middle-class women talked about women and feminism in the 1970s, they were talking about women like themselves rather than those of diverse racial/ethnic groups, social classes, sexual orientations, and (inter)nationalities. Although different constituencies of women share certain problems, differences in where they are positioned in society produce multiple, diverse perspectives. Postmodern feminism recognizes and highlights this diversity (Sands & Nuccio, 1992). It is critical of binary categories such as male–female and black–white, in which one category is privileged and the other is devalued or considered peripheral. Moreover, these pairs are viewed as oppositional and mutually exclusive (Grosz, 1989). With respect to gender, binary categories promote the idea of opposite sexes that are very different from each other. Deconstruction is the method postmodern feminists use to derail this way of thinking and reveal underlying biases. (A related, new theoretical development that embraces the antiessentialism of postmodernism as well as intersectionality theory [the intersection between race, gender, and class] and critical race theory and practice is *critical race feminism*, which comes out of legal studies [see, e.g., Wing, 2003].)

As explained in Chapter 1, postmodernism is useful as a critical tool because it points out the limitations of perspectives that essentialize characteristics that are constructed. On the other hand, postmodernism is problematic because it assumes a universe in which one cannot define anyone or anything. If one cannot define *woman*, for example, how can one work for social change in the status of women? In this chapter, it is assumed that one can talk about women and other categories but that such categories are neither singular nor fixed in time.

The theories that have been discussed are the major schools of feminist thought. Most feminist theories take a critical stance toward gender inequality and embrace social changes that eradicate the subjugation of women and advance social justice. Because sexism has been such a pervasive aspect of social, political, and economic life, it is also reflected in psychological theories.

FEMINIST CRITIQUE OF PSYCHOLOGICAL THEORIES

Many of the psychological theories that have been traditionally used to guide mental health practice have constructed women as "other." Among the most problematic of these are Freud's psychoanalysis, Erikson's psychosocial theory, and Kohlberg's theory of moral development.

Feminist critiques of these theories have resulted in alternative ways of thinking about women's and men's psychological development.

Traditional Psychological Theories

FREUD Much of the early feminist criticism of human behavior theories was directed at Freud. According to his psychoanalytic theory, women are "anatomically inferior" because they lack a penis. This suggests that men represent the normal way of being and women are deficient (i.e., "other"). Similarly, Freud posed that women experience penis envy—when what they really envy is man's freedom, not his penis (Chodorow, 1978). In addition, Freud believed that women were masochistic and had underdeveloped superegos.

Freud's theory focused on sexual repression. He believed that infants and children were sexual; that unresolved psychosexual issues stemming from childhood contribute to adult psychopathology—particularly neuroses. Nevertheless, trauma suffered during the early years of life could be overcome through a corrective, psychoanalytic, therapeutic relationship.

Among the women Freud theorized about was one he referred to as Anna O. This educated, intelligent woman, a patient of his friend, Josef Breuer, was later identified as Bertha Pappenheim, one of the world's first social workers (Stewart, 1985). Freud initially believed that her hysterical symptoms and defenses were a means of protecting her from an awareness of sexually traumatic experiences that occurred during her childhood. Subsequently, Freud reinterpreted this, concluding that the sexual content represented fantasies about a parental figure. Later scholarship proposed that the "fantasies" were actual experiences of childhood sexual abuse (Masson, 1984). The attribution of real events to the imagination is a way of invalidating women's lived experiences.

Freud's genetic theory posed that there are developmental stages, which begin with infancy, that lay the foundation for later life. Of these (oral, anal, phallic, latency, genital), the phallic or oedipal stage was particularly important. During this period, boys are enamored of their mothers and develop a rivalry with their fathers, fearing that their fathers will castrate them. Boys resolve the oedipal complex by relinquishing their amorous feelings toward their mothers and identifying with their fathers. Freud hypothesized that women undergo a similar conflict in the opposite way. During the phallic stage, the female child becomes aware that she does not have a penis, blames her mother, and shifts her affection to her father (desiring to possess his penis or have his baby). She resolves the conflict by recognizing that it is hopeless to possess her father and identifies with her mother.

Feminist scholars have raised questions about Freud's interpretation of the preoedipal experiences of girls. Chodorow (1978) argues that girls' attachment to their mothers is continuous during and beyond the preoedipal and oedipal stages; that although girls form an attachment to their fathers, they do not break off from their mothers. Furthermore, girls' attachment to their mothers emphasizes relational qualities and is more prolonged and less differentiated than the mother–son relationship. Consequently, the boundaries between mothers and daughters may become blurred.

Chodorow is representative of feminist psychoanalytic thinkers in the United States and abroad who continue to find value in psychoanalytic ideas but wish to correct the misinterpretation of women in the theory. Many of these theorists identify with object relations theory, which in itself is a development of psychoanalysis. Object relations theory emphasizes the relationship between the self and others and the formation of personality patterns from the relational field (Hockmeyer, 1988). This is in contrast with classical psychoanalysis, which gives primacy to drives.

ERIKSON   Erikson expanded Freud's developmental theory to encompass the entire life course. Erikson's (1968, 1980) well-known psychosocial theory poses that there are eight life stages—trust versus mistrust, initiative versus guilt, autonomy versus shame and doubt, industry versus inferiority, identity versus role diffusion, intimacy versus isolation, generativity versus stagnation, and integrity versus despair. The stages unfold in sequence according to a ground plan that Erikson called the *epigenetic principle.* In this theory, Erikson recognized the interplay of biological, psychological, social, cultural, and historical factors in the unfolding of individual lives. Erikson saw this pattern as universal.

Some of Erikson's writings have presented difficulties for feminists. On the basis of his work with children at play, Erikson (1968) concluded that boys are oriented toward performance in "outer space," whereas girls concentrate on interiority, or "inner space." These descriptors mirror men's and women's anatomy as well as their respective activity and passivity. This interpretation of men's and women's essences, based on observed stereotypical behavior of children, seems to contradict the sociocultural, contextual tenets of his theory. Feminists have argued with Erikson about the inner space/outer space dichotomy, which he has defended (Erikson, 1974).

A further difficulty in Erikson's theory has to do with the sequencing of his life stages for women. Erikson places the stage of identity versus role diffusion before intimacy versus isolation. Research by Douvan and Adelson (1966) found that girls address intimacy before identity issues. Furthermore, Gilligan (1982) argues that the issues of intimacy and identity are intertwined for women. Erikson's universal stages seem to be based on men's life cycle.

KOHLBERG   Kohlberg was a cognitive developmental psychologist in the tradition of Piaget who developed stages of moral development. He studied children and adolescents, predominantly boys, of a range of social classes. Kohlberg came up with a sequence of developmental stages encompassing three levels—preconventional (self-serving), conventional (respecting societal norms), and postconventional (emphasizing values and principles). In his early work, there were six stages (two per level); later he relinquished the sixth stage (Crain, 1985).

Kohlberg proposed that his stages were universal, hierarchical, and sequential. One moves from the lowest level of moral development to higher stages, from the simple to the complex. Few people reach the highest stage. Each stage represents a significantly different way of thinking.

Kohlberg's stage theory was challenged by Gilligan (1982), who noticed that most of Kohlberg's subjects were boys and that when girls took the same moral development tests boys were given, girls achieved lower scores. Rather than accept the conclusion that women were morally inferior or deficient, Gilligan explained that girls do not perform as well as boys because women make moral judgments based on relational considerations rather than abstract ideas about justice. She posed that there was a (feminine) ethic of caring and responsibility that contrasted with a (masculine) ethic of justice reflected in Kohlberg's work. Criticizing Freud, Erikson, Kohlberg, and Piaget, Gilligan cited the work of several women theorists (Loevinger, Horner, Chodorow) to support her position. Gilligan pointed out that because of their fear of fusion, men have difficulty with intimacy, and conversely, because of their fear of separation, women have difficulty with autonomy. Gilligan (1982) may have motivated Kegan to develop theory and practice that account for differences between the two ethics (or "voices") that she described in her seminal work.

KEGAN   Kegan's (1982) developmental psychological theory incorporates the developmental stages of Erikson, Loevinger, Piaget, and Kohlberg while it responds to Gilligan's critique of her predecessors. Kegan proposed an evolving self that is engaged in a dynamic process of constructing and reconstructing its self and self-other relationships. The individual moves through interlocking stages (called incorporative, impulsive, imperial, interpersonal, and interindividual), always seeking a balance between the needs of the self and the desire to relate to others. Kegan's interindividual balance encompasses yearnings for both intimacy and autonomy, which he considers a lifelong conflict. He states that acknowledging both aspects of the evolving self corrects developmental theories that overemphasize autonomy and responds to feminist concerns about the importance of human attachments (Kegan, 1982). Kegan's "natural therapy" helps individuals use crises to create new meanings and, thus, achieve a new balance.

Feminist Concepts and Theories

In search of theories that attach importance to women's psychology, women have conducted research and developed concepts and theories that are more consistent with their experiences as women. These will be discussed next.

BELENKY ET AL. Cognitive developmental theory was also the basis for the research of Belenky, Clinchy, Goldberger, and Tarule (1986), whose *Women's Ways of Knowing* expanded on some of the issues that Gilligan identified. These authors conducted in-depth qualitative interviews with 135 women in high schools and colleges representing women who were advantaged and disadvantaged economically and who were ethnically diverse, and 45 women who worked with clients seeking support in social agencies in their role as parents. The analysis of transcribed interviews revealed five epistemological positions that the women participating in the study took: silence (voiceless, controlled); received knowledge (accepting knowledge from others but not creating one's own); subjective knowledge (conceiving of knowledge privately); procedural knowledge (learning and using procedures to communicate knowledge); and constructed knowledge (recognizing that all knowledge is contextual, seeing that one can create knowledge, and integrating subjective and objective ways of knowing). This project gave support to the notion that the metaphors of voice and silence captured women's experiences. "We found that women repeatedly used the metaphor of voice to depict their intellectual and ethical development; and that the development of the sense of voice, mind, and self were intricately intertwined" (Belenky et al., 1986, p. 18).

RELATIONAL-CULTURAL THEORY Gilligan's emphasis on connectedness also reverberated at the Stone Center at Wellesley College, where Miller (1986) and other feminist thinkers and therapists had been developing what came to be known as the relational self or self-in-relation theory (Jordan, Kaplan, Miller, Stiver, & Surrey, 1991). As these authors explained, "relational growth" is "the organizing factor in women's lives" (p. 1) and has some applicability to the lives of men. Stone Center writers are particularly interested in the mother–daughter relationship, the development of empathy and mutuality, and empowerment. Like Gilligan, they are critical of developmental theorists which view autonomy as the hallmark of human development. The therapy that they espouse helps women pursue relational (as well as other) goals and develop in their connections to others.

In their initial years of development, Stone Center theorists espoused a difference/cultural type of feminism. In stating that women are relational, they were saying that women have an inherent essential womanness. Rather than recognizing differences among women, they universalized. This changed starting with the Stone Center's edited volume, *Women's Growth in Diversity* (Jordan, 1997), which describes the self in more fluid terms and includes chapters on racial identity, lesbian relationships, and ways in which marginalized groups are shamed. The Stone Center now supports a relational-cultural perspective.

Relational-cultural theory (RCT) expands upon self-in-relation theory by encompassing diverse races, ethnic groups, and cultures and men. It gives emphasis to connections, particularly growth-fostering relationships, relational competence, and the impact of disconnection (Jordan & Hartling, 2002). The therapy involves mutual empathy, mutual empowerment, the voicing of nondominant perspectives, and transformation (West, 2005). RCT recognizes power differentials, such as those that occur in relationships between heterosexual men and women, between lesbians, and between the therapist and client. A therapy that began with concern with the individual woman, it has evolved so as to encompass social change:

> More recently, Relational-Cultural theorists have included in their thinking the notion that power-over arrangements form the bedrock of western socio-political and economic structures, and that these arrangements must be engaged not only on behalf of individual development, but on behalf of a social action imperative. Empowerment, seen in this context, extends beyond a strengthening of the individual self to collective strategies of resistance. (West, 2005, p. 109)

Implications for Feminist Practice

The previous discussion of psychological theories demonstrates how difficult it is to arrive at a common understanding of women. The psychoanalytic paradigm, accepted by some clinicians, constructs woman as "other." Newer psychologies acknowledge the centrality of relationships in women's lives, but they tend to essentialize women.

There is a need for a feminist social work practice that includes feminist values and is sensitive to differences among women, among men, and between individual men and women. Some feminists have found that a narrative approach, which encourages women to tell their stories and reconstruct them during therapy, is empowering (e.g., Laird, 1989). Narrative therapy addresses power discrepancies and externalizes problems that mental health professionals tend to consider individually generated (White & Epston, 1990). As discussed, relational-cultural therapy also addresses power differences.

Ideally a feminist practice would include the following characteristics:

1. partnerships rather than hierarchy in the worker–client relationship;
2. support for the client's expressing her voice, however different it may be from the voices of others;
3. support of the client's strengths and resilience;
4. recognition and addressing of gender-based power dynamics in therapeutic, couple, and family relationships;
5. promotion of the client's self-actualization and development through relationships, work, spirituality, art, and/or other meaningful areas of life;
6. encouragement of clients to develop relationships of mutuality with others;
7. respect for, and appreciation, and support of cultural differences;
8. avoidance of sexist language;
9. acknowledgment of the economic, political, and social issues that adversely affect women (e.g., employment discrimination, low wages, lack of child care, sexual harassment on the job, difficulties collecting child support);

10. fostering of women's empowerment, particularly their self-determination, sense of personal control, resistance to injustice, and self-advocacy;
11. advocacy for public issues that support women's empowerment;
12. consideration of the social context before constructing a diagnosis of psychopathology. (cf. Ault-Riche, 1986; Brown, 2010; Hare-Mustin, 1984; Land, 1995; Libow, 1986; Van Den Bergh, 1995)

Increasingly, feminists and feminist therapists have been acknowledging that feminism and feminist therapy are not restricted to women. Men can be feminist therapists and clients of feminist therapists. Defining feminism as "a movement to end sexism, sexist exploitation, and oppression," hooks (2000, p. viii) asserts in the title of her book, *Feminism Is for Everybody*. Dominance and control of some members of society of others create injustice for all. Thus, the goals of feminist therapy to empower clients and undermine power inequities (Brown, 2010) contribute to the welfare of all.

Mental health systems, however, have norms and practices that challenge feminist social work practice. For example, diagnosis is a sensitive issue to feminist therapists, who see diagnosing as nonegalitarian and disempowering (Brown, 2010). To gain perspective on the distribution of mental illness in the population, clinical social workers need to become familiar with findings of epidemiological research on gender differences in the prevalence of psychiatric disorders.

EPIDEMIOLOGICAL FINDINGS ON GENDER AND MENTAL ILLNESS

Although the *DSM-IV-TR* (American Psychiatric Association [APA], 2000) outlines specific criteria for each diagnosis, some diagnoses are more prevalent among women, whereas others are more common to men. The National Comorbidity Survey (NCS) of U.S. citizens from ages 15 to 54 identified some of these gender differences (Kessler et al., 1994). Considering the disorders as groups (e.g., "any anxiety disorder"), affective (mood) and anxiety disorders are more prevalent among women, whereas substance abuse/dependence is more widespread among men. In addition, the antisocial personality disorder is more prevalent among men (Kessler et al., 1994). Within the category of affective disorders, major depression and dysthymia are substantially higher for women than men, whereas having a manic episode (a symptom of bipolar disorder) is not differentiated by gender. Women have substantially higher prevalence rates of all the anxiety disorders, whereas men have higher rates for all the substance use disorders.

Another finding of the NCS is that lifetime prevalence of any disorder for all participants is 48 percent and the twelve-month prevalence is 29.5 percent (Kessler et al., 1994). These figures reflect comorbidity (having two or more disorders) by some of the participants. The NCS found that women had higher lifetime and twelve-month rates of prevalence than men for three or more concurrent disorders (Kessler et al., 1994). This gender discrepancy, like others, may be attributed to women's willingness to report and the culture's willingness to hear about their symptoms of mental illness. The difference may also be explained by the idiosyncratic way in which diagnoses of mental illness are constructed.

An international epidemiological study that was part of the World Health Organization's World Mental Health Survey Initiative came up with similar results across countries (Seedat et al., 2009). The study sample included adults from five countries that were classified as developing and ten countries that were considered developed. The findings on gender differences were that, compared with men, women had a significantly higher lifetime risk for major depressive disorder and any mood disorder and a higher risk of all anxiety disorders. Compared with women, men had a higher lifetime risk of all externalizing disorders (e.g., attention-deficit/hyperactivity disorder, intermittent explosive disorder) and all substance disorders (alcohol and drug abuse or dependence; any substance disorder). An additional analysis of the same data that looked at the interaction between gender and age cohort shed an interesting light on the findings. The higher odds for women having major depressive disorder and for men having intermittent explosive disorder and substance disorders were less pronounced for women and men, respectively, in younger cohorts in most of the countries. The narrowing of differences in major depression and substance abuse was more pronounced in countries that have greater gender role equality. The narrowing was attributed to increased gender equality, which can protect women from depression but can increase their risk of substance abuse (Seedat et al., 2009).

VIOLENCE PERPETRATED AGAINST WOMEN

According to the epidemiological studies that were discussed, women are more likely than men to experience depression or anxiety. At times the emotions and thoughts that women present and become constructed as symptoms of mental disorders are associated with violence. This section will discuss two types of violence perpetrated against women—IPV and human trafficking. These situational problems can precipitate new symptoms or exacerbate preexisting mental health problems.

Intimate Partner Violence

Intimate partner violence refers to the intentional use or threats of using physical and/or sexual violence as well as acts, threats, or coercive tactics that cause psychological or emotional harm to a victim (Salzman, Fanslow, McMahon, & Shelley, 2002). Although women are more likely than men to be victims, the official Centers for Disease Control (CDC) definition recognizes that men and women can be victims and/or perpetrators. The CDC definition includes violence between past and present married couples, cohabitating heterosexual couples, same-sex couples, and boyfriends and girlfriends (Salzman et al., 2002).

Intimate partner violence involves acts of aggression that is usually perpetrated by a stronger person against a weaker one. An assertion of power, it is a prototype of sexism and misogyny. Although some women affirm that they love the person who abuses them, it is difficult to understand how feelings as disparate as love and violence can commingle. Whether the violence involves battering or rape or intimidation, IPV is predicated on the belief that women are not valuable. To the extent that violence is promoted or overlooked by others, society is implicated.

The National Violence against Women Study (Tjaden & Thoennes, 2000c) found that close to 25 percent of the women surveyed said that they had been raped or assaulted by a spouse, partner, boyfriend, girlfriend, or date during their lifetime. This percentage was more than three times of that reported by men. When assaulted, women were more likely to be injured than men. About 18 percent of the women had been raped at some time during their lives with over half of these occurring before they were 18 years old (Tjaden & Thoennes, 2000a). A past history of rape or physical assault increased the risk of injury during their most recent episode. Among those of diverse cultural backgrounds, American Indian/Alaska Native and African American men and women reported more violent victimization than the other cultural groups (Tjaden & Thoennes, 2000c).

Women acquire a variety of mental health symptoms in relation to IPV. Those that are frequently reported in the literature are post-traumatic stress disorder (PTSD), depression, suicidality, and substance abuse (Afifi et al., 2009; Leiner, Compton, Houry,

& Kaslow, 2008; Rodríguez, Valentine, Son, & Muhammad, 2009). Ethnically diverse women who have experienced IPV, however, are often reluctant to use mental health services. Some of the barriers that have been identified have to do with the view within some cultures that one should keep the violence secret and the fear of being labeled mentally ill (Rodríguez et al., 2009). Other barriers include language issues, financial constraints, and mistrust based on a history of trauma perpetrated against the ethnic group (Bryant-Davis, Chung, & Tillman, 2009).

Women tend to use the informal help-seeking system until the violence becomes severe (Ansara & Hindin, 2010). Nevertheless, they are fearful for themselves and their children and worry about the future. If they are physically hurt, they may go to an emergency room or clinic where a health or mental health professional might inquire whether there was abuse. Afraid to implicate their partner, some women will construct a fabricated account of what happened. Despite the belief that women leave abusive relationships because of their children, one study found that being a mother tended to prolong women's remaining with their partners (Vatnar & Bjørkly, 2010). Walker (1979) outlined a cycle of violence that is typical of violent relationships. Following an abusive incident, the partner shows remorse and treats the woman solicitously. After a while, however, the partner's tension increases gradually. During this period, the woman avoids saying or doing anything that she thinks might precipitate another episode; she walks on eggshells. Then another incident occurs. This time the woman may seek safety with a family member or a shelter. In either case, it is highly likely that she will return to the batterer. Whether her reasons for returning are based on economic dependence, emotional attachment, or fear, this pattern of leaving and returning can be frustrating to social workers trying to protect women who are at risk of being severely injured or even murdered.

Social workers come across women and men who are subjected to violence in a variety of settings. Besides agencies that specifically serve this population (e.g., battered women's shelters, victim services, crisis centers), clinics, primary care settings, and emergency rooms are where the injured go for medical help. Murphy and Ouimet (2008) recommend that women in these settings have routine screenings for IPV, and that social workers conduct assessments and screenings, advocate for the women, and train health care professionals about the dynamics of IPV. Social workers working in mental health settings will likely be treating women for trauma-related symptoms, such as PTSD, depression, substance abuse, and suicidal thoughts. It is important that issues around IPV be explored. Finally, treatment of perpetrators should be a priority. Even if the injured partner leaves the relationship, the behavior is likely to be repeated in relation to a new partner.

The next example of violence perpetrated against women is human trafficking. This is an international issue as women (as well as children) are transported across the world. Women who are trafficked are involuntarily subjected to torture, rape, exploitation, and prostitution.

Human Trafficking

Feminist discourse about sex trafficking and prostitution is contentious. As Jeffreys (2009) describes it, the dominant approach, which is taken by socialist feminists and most other scholars, is to view prostitution as "sex work," which is a legitimate way to support oneself. The other perspective, that of radical feminists, is to view prostitution as violence perpetrated against women. As Jeffreys explains, radical feminists consider this violence "because it ignores the pleasure and personhood of the woman whose body is used, and she disassociates emotionally from her body to survive" (p. 318).

Human trafficking refers to the use of deception, coercion, or force toward men, women, and children to recruit, transport, and/or retain them to work in the sex trade or other industries with minimal or no remuneration. A form of slavery, it exists throughout the world. The term is associated with transporting people across national borders but trafficking can occur within a given country. Whether the trafficking occurs within a country or through smuggling from one country to another, at some point those who are trafficked are placed in situations where they are forced to work as prostitutes, domestic servants, sweatshop laborers, agricultural workers, and other occupational roles (Logan, Walker, & Hunt, 2009). Human trafficking is considered highly profitable industry (Schauer & Wheaton, 2006).

It is difficult to obtain a full picture of the extent of this phenomenon in the United States, as the activities are designed to be hidden. It is thought that most of the people who are trafficked are immigrants whose undocumented status contributes to their vulnerability (Logan et al., 2009). Those most susceptible to being recruited live in poverty, want a better life, and believe false promises that they will obtain genuine jobs (Logan et al., 2009). Once they are situated, they are treated abusively. They may be told, for example, that they had to repay their employer for the cost of transportation, putting them in the position of debtors. Humiliation, beatings, and rape may be used to coerce women and girls to work as prostitutes (Hodge, 2008). They may live in enclosed living quarters in isolated locations from which it is difficult to escape.

There are some legal protections in the United States for victims of human trafficking. The Trafficking Victims Protection Act (TVPA) of 2000 (Pub. L. No. 106-386), which was reauthorized in 2003, 2005, and 2008, enables victims to become eligible for benefits and services. After being certified eligible, they can obtain housing, job training, health care, and other services (U.S. Department of Health and Human Services, n.d.[a]). However helpful this act may be, it is difficult to locate human trafficking victims unless they escape or come to the attention of social service or health professionals for other reasons. Professionals may be uninformed about human trafficking and how to identify people in this situation (Sigmon, 2008). Some clues to identify victims of trafficking are the following:

1. Evidence of being controlled
2. Evidence of an inability to move or leave job
3. Bruises or other signs of battering
4. Fear or depression
5. Non-English speaking
6. Recently brought to this country from Eastern Europe, Asia, Latin America, Canada, Africa, or India
7. Lack of passport, immigration or identification documents. (U.S. Department of Health and Human Services, n.d.[b])

A number of obstacles, however, prevent victims from asking for assistance. Among them are the following: (a) they may be traumatized or experience a lack of control as a consequence of repeated sexual assaults, physical abuse, and threats; (b) they are afraid that they or their children will be beaten or killed if they try to escape; (c) they do not trust the police or other authorities; (d) they are afraid of being deported; (e) language and cultural barriers; (f) lack of knowledge about alternatives, physical and social isolation; and (g) shame (Logan et al., 2009; Sigmon, 2008).

Because the health, mental health, and social service communities have been slow in recognizing human trafficking, intervention approaches are not well developed. Initially, the needs to be addressed would be for safety, housing, financial benefits, and health care. Support, advocacy, and help becoming certified would be part of the early work. Considering that it is likely that the client is an immigrant, a culturally competent approach is in order (see Chapter 6). After the crisis abates, evidence of trauma may become prominent.

Trauma as a Response to Violence

Trauma can be viewed in two ways: (a) an event or a set of occurrences that arouses intense, disturbing emotions, such as the attacks on the World Trade Center and the Pentagon on September 11, 2001, and (b) as a subjective experience. As a subjective experience, it is not necessarily pathological. When the traumatic experience becomes overwhelming, substantially interferes with psychosocial functioning, and meets other criteria, the diagnosis of PTSD may be given. There is increasing evidence that traumatic experiences produce physiological reactions, even when there is no bodily harm (Rothschild, 2000). Epidemiological studies throughout the world have found that even though men are more likely than women to experience trauma, PTSD is more prevalent among women than men (Breslau, 2009). In one study, women formerly hospitalized at trauma center hospitals had a significantly greater risk of poorer outcomes than men (Holbrook, Hoyt, Stein, & Sieber, 2002).

In her classic book, *Trauma and Recovery*, psychiatrist Judith Herman (1992b) synthesized research on men traumatized by war or political captivity and women who have been sexually or physically abused. She stated there that because it is difficult for bystanders to acknowledge the pain of those who have been traumatized, and victims themselves are often silenced by their perpetrators and social norms that define some of their experiences as unspeakable, little sustained interest has been given to survivors of trauma. Herman noted that it took organized political movements (e.g., by Vietnam veterans and women's organizations) to draw public attention to the needs of individuals who have endured traumatic experiences.

Herman (1992b) observed three themes common to individuals who are subjected to psychological trauma. The first theme is *terror*, the overwhelming fear of danger, harm, or death. Terror occurs at the time of the focal event but remains in a fragmented form afterward. Individuals with PTSD experience hyperarousal (high sensitivity to signals of danger) as a means of protection against such events in the future. Although they do not think about the traumatic event constantly, frightening memories of the episode intrude on and interrupt their everyday lives. Some individuals unconsciously reenact traumatic experiences. Terror is also characterized by emotional constriction or numbing in which individuals become detached from others and from themselves. Herman described a "dialectic of trauma" in which there are swings between intrusion and constriction.

The second theme Herman (1992b) identified is *disconnection*, a rupture in the relationship between the victim and others. The traumatic event impairs the individual's sense of self, which in turn undermines self-confidence and basic trust. When trust is compromised, relationships with others and faith in God are affected. The nature of the event and individuals' capacity for resilience determine the level of psychological damage (Herman, 1992b). Individuals who are relatively young and have preexisting psychiatric disorders may be more vulnerable than others (Herman, 1992b). In the aftermath of the traumatic event, they need protection from others and a safe environment. Safety is particularly problematic for women who live with their abuser. Those who have supportive partners, family members, and friends can be helped to find a safe place in which to recuperate and people who will listen to them, accept them compassionately, and help them mourn. Public attitudes toward people in their situation and the responsiveness of the legal system to reported crimes also enter into the issue of disconnection (Herman, 1992b).

Captivity, the third theme, is a dimension of trauma that applies to situations that occur repeatedly over time in which the perpetrator has control over the victim (Herman, 1992b). The victim may be physically restrained (e.g., a prisoner of war), or she may feel imprisoned because psychological, economic, social, and legal dependencies keep her subjugated. The perpetrator exercises coercive control over the victim's mind so that she thinks the way he wants her to think. Some of the techniques used to achieve this are issuing threats (against the victim or others), outbursts of violence, arbitrary enforcement of trivial rules, supervision of the victim's physical activities (eating, sleeping, etc.), the use of intermittent rewards, and the destruction of personal attachments (creating isolation). These methods foster increased reliance on the perpetrator and ultimately total surrender of the self (Herman, 1992b). According to Herman (1992b), the *DSM* diagnosis of PTSD does not accurately describe survivors of captivity, who, in contrast with individuals exposed to a single event, are repeatedly traumatized over time. She suggests a new category, Complex PTSD, for experiences such as these (Herman, 1992a, 1992b).

Herman's Recovery Model

Although Herman (1992b) does not call her model feminist, the intervention (or recovery) program that she recommends is in keeping with the parameters of feminist practice described earlier. Although it is discussed here because of its sensitivity to violence perpetrated against women, Herman's model applies to survivors of incest, political imprisonment, and war trauma, who may be men or women. Recovery is predicated on a relationship between the therapist and client that empowers the client and promotes her connections with others. The client is in charge of her own recovery; the therapist bears witness to the abuse and fosters the process of healing. The therapist retains professional neutrality while joining with the survivor in asserting that the crime that was committed was immoral (Herman, 1992b). The therapist is sensitive to and handles the survivor's transference and his or her own countertransference. The parameters of the therapeutic contract are discussed, including the responsibilities of each party, the expectation of honesty and openness, and mutual commitment to the survivor's recovery.

Herman (1992b) describes three stages of recovery—the establishment of safety, remembrance and mourning, and reconnection with ordinary life. These follow from her description of the characteristics of trauma summarized earlier, as well as her synthesis of the stages of treatment of hysteria, combat trauma, multiple personality disorder, and complicated PTSD described by others. These stages do not necessarily progress in a linear sequence. The first, *the establishment of safety*, has several components. To begin with, the problem should be assessed and named. Giving the survivor's experiences a name—even a psychiatric diagnosis—can be liberating to a person who is overwhelmed by feelings she does not understand. Next, the survivor should be helped to regain control and restore her safety. She may feel out of control in her thinking, bodily functions, and interpersonal relationships. She can be helped with her thinking through the development of trust in the therapeutic relationship and can be assisted with behavioral strategies (e.g., relaxation exercises) and medication. If there are physical injuries, these should be given medical attention. Sufficient sleep, exercise, and a proper diet can also help her restore her bodily functions. She should be helped in finding a safe environment in which to live, a task that usually involves mobilizing support from individuals other than the perpetrator and persons who are likely to undermine her recovery. But even if the survivor continues to have contact with the perpetrator, she can be helped to develop a safety plan in the event of another episode (Herman, 1992b).

During the second stage, the focus is on *remembrance and mourning*, and the survivor tells her story (Herman, 1992b). Herman advises against exploring traumatic memories during the first stage, when the survivor is fragile and feels vulnerable. When ready, the client should be asked to tell the story as fully and completely as possible, including her feelings, images, and bodily sensations. The purpose of doing this is to objectify it and give it a reality that can eventually be integrated into the person's life (Herman, 1992b). Relating the story takes time because there is much resistance and repression that protect painful, sometimes humiliating, memories. The process begins with a review of the survivor's life before the traumatic event or situation and the set of circumstances that preceded it. The clinician takes the role of "an open-minded, compassionate witness, not a detective" (Herman, 1992b, p. 180) or investigator. It is possible that the survivor's "narrative truth" will not be consistent with the "historical truth" (Spence, 1982). The clinician follows the client's lead, exploring the survivor's everyday experiences and the memories she already has. When painful memories are revealed, sufficient time is left in the therapeutic interview for the individual to decompress from the telling.

Mourning takes place in the aftermath of telling of the story (Herman, 1992b). There are many losses to mourn—the self, attachment to the perpetrator, bodily integrity, and other losses. During this period, the survivor may have fantasies of retaliation against or forgiveness of the perpetrator or may wish for some kind of compensation. The relinquishment of these fantasies is part of the process of mourning and may enable the survivor to extricate herself emotionally from the perpetrator. During this period, the clinician "bears witness" while holding the survivor responsible for her own recovery (Herman, 1992b). Although mourning is painful, it does facilitate the return of emotional energy and involvement with others.

The third stage, *reconnection*, pertains to rebuilding the self and a personal life (Herman, 1992b). At this time, the survivor revisits safety issues addressed in the first stage (her body, her physical environment, etc.), but now she expends increased energy outward toward others, empowering herself in the process. One task involved in this stage is facing fear. This can be done by taking a class in self-defense, participating in a wilderness excursion, and/or confronting family members and/or the perpetrator. Another task is to come to terms with valued aspects of herself and building a new self from these. She sheds her victim identity and celebrates her survivor identity (Herman, 1992b). An important task of this stage is to reconnect with others—deepening previous relationships with family members, friends, and the therapist and creating new ones. Consistent with Erikson's stage of generativity versus stagnation, she becomes concerned about the next generation, including her children, if she is a parent. At this point, some survivors become active in social causes such as the battered women's movement and may speak out publicly about their experiences. Although resolution of the trauma is never complete, the survivor who works through the issues that have been described is able to live a fulfilling life with control, confidence, satisfying relationships with others, and feelings of well-being (Herman, 1992b).

Assessment of Herman's Model

Although Herman's (1992b) recovery program does not call itself feminist, it is in keeping with this approach. Its focus on recovery, healing, and survival is relevant to clinical social work practice with women exposed to IPV and abuse associated with being trafficked. It also applies to men who are exposed to violence and other disturbing events. Herman's model is sensitive to clients' loss of power in the past and, accordingly, respects their efforts to assume control over their own lives at their own pace. It supports clients' development of insight, connections with others, and self-confidence. It uses a narrative approach in helping the client construct and reconstruct the past and paves the way for a reconstructed empowered self in the future.

Evidence for Herman's model, however, is sparse. Herman and Schatzow (1987) described a group intervention in which women survivors of incest were able to recover and validate their traumatic memories. Herman (1992a) compiled evidence for the syndrome, Complex PTSD, which describes the experiences of people who have had repeated and prolonged exposure to trauma. Courtois and Ford's (2009) edited book, *Treating Complex Traumatic Stress Disorders: An Evidence-Based Guide*, provides a more extensive research base. We turn next to examining evidence-based practices and PTSD.

Evidence-Based Practice

Reviews of research on interventions with men and women with acute stress disorder (ASD) (APA, 2000) and PTSD have identified a number of treatment approaches that are supported by research evidence. ASD is diagnosable in the early stages—when symptoms are present from two days to four weeks; after that, PTSD is a possible diagnosis (APA, 2000). Several other symptoms must be present to meet criteria for these disorders.

Table 7.1 lists recommended principles guiding evidence-based psychosocial intervention with persons with ASD. According to the Practice Guidelines of the American Psychiatric Association (2004), as well as social work practice wisdom, it is important that clients feel safe and supported and can trust the clinician before they disclose personal difficulties. If the individual is in physical danger (e.g., following a beating) or is particularly vulnerable (e.g., brought into an emergency facility after being raped), the clinician should demonstrate sensitivity and gentleness. Psychological debriefing (also called critical-incident stress debriefing) is no longer recommended as a first response to people in acute stress (Marmar & Spiegel, 2010). Marmar and Spiegel recommend brief cognitive-behavioral therapy (CBT) for ASD.

There are more empirically supported psychosocial treatments for PTSD, with most involving CBT and/or techniques associated with CBT. In an extensive review, Ponniah and Hollon (2009) recommend the following:

- Most efficacious
  - Trauma-focused CBT
  - Eye movement desensitization and reprocessing (EMDR)
- Possibly efficacious
  - Stress management involving stress inoculation training
  - Hypnotherapy
  - Interpersonal psychotherapy
  - Psychodynamic therapy

The trauma-focused CBTs that they reviewed emphasized exposure and/or cognitive restructuring and were provided in individual and group formats. Similar findings for the most efficacious intervention were found in a review of meta-analyses of CBT (Butler, Chaplin, Forman, &

TABLE 7.1	Principles Guiding Evidence-Based Interventions with Clients with Acute Stress Disorder

- Restore sense of safety
- Quickly establish a therapeutic alliance
- Provide information
- After the objective danger and perceived threat dissipate, allow ventilation of feelings
- Diffuse guilt
- Facilitate social support
- Reinforce the importance of taking care of oneself

Source: Based on Marmar & Spiegel (2010).

Beck, 2006). The reviewers of the meta-analysis for PTSD observed "that both trauma-focused CBT and EMDR specifically address the PTSD sufferers' troubling memories of a traumatic event and the personal meanings of the event and its consequences" (Butler et al., 2006, p. 26). The Practice Guidelines of the American Psychiatric Association (2004) and the 2009 update (Benedek, Friedman, Zatzick, & Ursano, 2009) support the use of EMDR and CBTs that include exposure.

Post-traumatic stress disorder applies to a wide variety of stressors—including witnessing other soldiers getting shot, getting beaten, being raped, and surviving a fire. Some stressors are short and intense; others are prolonged and injurious. Most evidence-based interventions are not specifically adapted to specific stressors. Furthermore, they are not adapted to particular cultures or genders. There are a few psychotherapies for women with co-occurring traumatic experiences and substance abuse but only one model has empirical support (Najavits, 2009).

Case Studies

1. Corina Gomez is 17 years old and has lived in a small town in a Southern U.S. state for two years. She was smuggled to the United States from Guatemala after her parents agreed to sell her to a man known as Ernesto. Ernesto had told Corina's parents that she would be placed with a nice family that would ask her to do housework and some child care. As it turned out, the family consisted of parents, grandparents, and five children, who lived in a large home on a rural farm. Corina was asked to clean, cook, and take care of the family's children. At times she was also required to work on the farm. She had to work days and evenings, had no time off, and was not paid. Exhausted, she did not complain until the grandfather in the family began to molest her. When she resisted, he beat her brutally. Frightened, she ran away. She was picked up by the police, who brought her to an emergency room of a nearby hospital. If you were the emergency room social worker, what would you do?

2. Laura Williams is a 20-year-old woman who was serving in the U.S. military in Afghanistan for a year when she was raped by a soldier in her unit. When she complained about this to her superior officer, he checked with the soldier involved, who said that it was a consensual relationship. The officer decided to take no further action. Subsequently Laura was gang-raped by several soldiers in her unit. This time, Laura sought medical help, as she was bruised. Still the officer refused to take any action. When Laura became pregnant, she sought a medical leave, which was granted. When she got home, she developed terrifying nightmares, flashbacks, and other symptoms of traumatic stress. If you were the intake social worker, how would you handle the first interview? What kinds of social supports would she need? How would you work with her therapeutically?

Summary and Deconstruction

Feminist social work practice requires awareness of the status and vulnerabilities of women in contemporary U.S. society. As suggested, some of the symptoms that women present in behavioral health settings derive from poverty, underemployment, and physical abuse. Careful assessment of a woman's situation should determine whether the problem lies in the person, the situation, or relationships. The woman may need housing, financial help, a job, or a friend rather than psychotherapy or psychopharmacology.

Traditional approaches of individual, family, and group therapy tend to be hierarchical and, thus, patriarchal. Women and other groups whose voices have been silenced need to have relationships of partnership and equality in which to heal. In particular, they need therapeutic relationships, therapies, and communities that help them to control their own lives and make their own decisions.

This chapter has focused primarily on feminist practice with women. Although it attempted to be fair-minded in asserting that feminist therapy can be conducted by or with men, it overlooked other sectors of the population. These include, but are not limited to gays and lesbians, trans-men and trans-women, persons with visible and invisible disabilities, the aging, and persons with diverse racial, ethnic, and cultural identities. Furthermore, it did not acknowledge the multiple identities that people have and the multiplicities within specific categories.

For example, just as there are many feminisms and many versions of womanness, so are there multiple masculinities. Many, perhaps most, men fall short of the ideal of masculinity in U.S. society that is valorized by the media and applauded by movie audiences. Some men fall short of the ideal of masculinity of their particular ethnic subculture as well. The discrepancy between the ideal and actual may propel some men to engage in aggressive acts in which they demonstrate their power over women or the society that constructs standards they find impossible to meet. Substance abuse and externalizing disorders, which are more frequent among men than women, are characterized by exaggerated expressions of masculinity and sexism.

Like women, men are diverse. There are male secretaries, ballet dancers, hair dressers, and interior decorators, as well as executives, military men, athletes, and politicians. Although men in the former group are frequently constructed as feminine or gay, they are men who live out different versions of masculinity. Like women, they are affected by dominant constructions of gender.

Social constructions of masculinity are evident in behavioral health settings in which, it is often observed, it is difficult to engage men in treatment. Many men seem to believe that asking for help that requires revealing of one's inner feelings and weaknesses is demasculinizing. This is so regardless of the gender of the clinician. Being a client is feminine. Unless social workers and other clinicians address men's feelings about being male clients, they are likely to meet a great deal of client resistance.

Work with men and women in the mental health field demands sensitivity to gender issues, knowledge of theories as they apply to women and men, and familiarity with alternative approaches to psychotherapy. In the case of treatment of persons with PTSD, some interventions have strong evidential support, whereas others (e.g., Herman's model) are compatible with feminist (and social work) values. Emerging internet interventions are potential alternative treatments (Benight, Ruzek, & Waldrep, 2008). Application of these strategies can enhance women's and men's capacities to function, thrive, and make their own unique contribution to society.

References

Afifi, T. O., MacMillan, H., Cox, B. J., Asmundson, G. J. G., Stein, M. B., & Sareen, J. (2009). Mental health correlates of intimate partner violence in marital relationships in a nationally representative sample of males and females. *Journal of Interpersonal Violence, 24*(8), 1398–1417.

Alcoff, L. (1997). Cultural feminism versus post-structuralism: The identity crisis in feminist theory. In L. Nicholson (Ed.),*The second wave: A reader in feminist theory* (pp. 330–355). New York: Routledge.

American Psychiatric Association. (2000). *Diagnostic and statistical manual of mental disorders* (4th ed., text rev.). Washington, DC: Author.

American Psychiatric Association. (2004). *Practice guideline for treatment of patients with acute stress disorder and posttraumatic stress disorder.* DOI: 10.1176/appi.books.9780890423363.52257

Ansara, D. L., & Hindin, M. J. (2010). Formal and informal help-seeking associated with women's and men's experiences of intimate partner violence in Canada. *Social Science & Medicine, 70,* 1011–1018.

Ault-Riche, M. (1986). A feminist critique of five schools of family therapy. In M. Ault-Riche (Ed.), *Women and family therapy* (pp. 1–24). Rockville, MD: Aspen.

de Beauvoir, S. (1968). *The second sex.* New York: Modern Library.

Belenky, M. F., Clinchy, B. M., Goldberger, N. R., & Tarule, J. M. (1986). *Women's ways of knowing: The development of self, voice, and mind.* New York: Basic Books.

Benedek, D. M., Friedman, M. J., Zatzick, D., & Ursano, R. J. (2009). *Guideline watch (March 2009): Practice guideline for the treatment of patients with acute stress disorder and posttraumatic stress disorder* (pp. 1–12). DOI: 10.1176/appi.books.9780890423479. 156498

Benight, C. C., Ruzek, J. I., & Waldrep, E. (2008). Internet interventions for traumatic stress: A review and theoretically based example. *Journal of Traumatic Stress, 21*(6), 513–520.

Breslau, N. (2009). The epidemiology of trauma, PTSD, and other posttrauma disorders. *Trauma, Violence, & Abuse, 10*(3), 198–210.

Brown, L. S. (2010). *Feminist therapy.* Washington, DC: American Psychological Association.

Bryant-Davis, T., Chung, H., & Tillman, S. (2009). From the margins to the center: Ethnic minority women and the mental health effects of sexual assault. *Trauma, Violence, & Abuse, 10*(4), 330–357.

Butler, A. C., Chapman, J. E., Forman, E. M., & Beck, A. T. (2006). The empirical status of cognitive-behavioral therapy: A review of meta-analyses. *Clinical Psychology Review, 26,* 17–31.

Chodorow, N. (1978). *The reproduction of mothering: Psychoanalysis and the sociology of gender.* Berkeley: University of California Press.

Collins, P. H. (1991). Defining Black feminist thought. In *Black feminist thought: Knowledge, consciousness, and the politics of empowerment* (pp. 19–40). New York: Routledge.

Courtois, C. A., & Ford, J. D. (Eds.). (2009). *Treating complex traumatic stress disorders: An evidence-based guide.* New York: Guilford Press.

Crain, W. C. (1985). *Theories of development: Concepts and application* (2nd ed.). Englewood Cliffs, NJ: Prentice-Hall.

Douvan, E., & Adelson, J. (1966). *The adolescent experience.* New York: Wiley.

Erikson, E. H. (1968). *Identity: Youth and crisis.* New York: Norton.

Erikson, E. H. (1974). One more time the inner space: Letter to a former student. In J. Strouse (Ed.), *Women and analysis* (pp. 320–340). New York: Grossman.

Erikson, E. H. (1980). *Identity and the life cycle.* New York: Norton.

Gilligan, C. (1982). *In a different voice.* Cambridge, MA: Harvard University Press.

Gonda, C. (1998). Lesbian theory. In S. Jackson & J. Jones (Eds.), *Contemporary feminist theories* (pp. 113–130). New York: New York University Press.

Grosz, E. (1989). *Sexual subversions.* Boston: Allen & Unwin.

Hare-Mustin, R. T. (1984). A feminist approach to family therapy. In P. P. Rieker & E. H. Carmen (Eds.), *The gender gap in psychotherapy: Social realities and psychological processes.* New York: Plenum Press.

Herman, J. L. (1992a). Complex PTSD: A syndrome in survivors of prolonged and repeated trauma. *Journal of Traumatic Stress, 5*(3), 377–391.

Herman, J. L. (1992b). *Trauma and recovery.* New York: Basic Books.

Herman, J. L., & Schatzow, E. (1987). Recovery and verification of memories of childhood sexual trauma. *Psychoanalytic Psychology, 4*(1), 1–14.

Hockmeyer, A. (1988). Object relations theory and feminism: Strange bedfellows. *Frontiers, 10,* 20–28.

Hodge, D. R. (2008). Sexual trafficking in the United States: A domestic problem with transnational dimensions. *Social Work, 53*(2), 143–152.

Holbrook, T. L., Hoyt, D. B., Stein, M. B., & Sieber, W. J. (2002). Gender differences in long-term posttraumatic stress disorder outcomes after major trauma: Women are at higher risk of adverse outcomes than men. *Journal of Trauma Injury, Infection, and Critical Care, 53*(5), 882–888.

hooks, b. (1981). *Ain't I a woman: Black women and feminism.* Boston: South End Press.

hooks, b. (2000). *Feminism is for everybody: Passionate politics.* Cambridge, MA: South End Press.

Institute for Women's Policy Research. (2010, April). *Fact sheet: The gender wage gap by occupation, IWPR #C350a.* Retrieved May 20, 2010, from http://www.iwpr.org/pdf/C350a.pdf

Jagger, A. M., & Rothenberg, P. S. (1993). *Feminist frameworks* (3rd ed.). Boston, MA: McGraw-Hill.

Jeffreys, S. (2009). Prostitution, trafficking and feminism: An update on the debate. *Women's Studies International Forum, 32,* 316–320.

Jordan, J. V. (Ed.). (1997). *Women's growth in diversity: More writings from the Stone Center.* New York: Guilford Press.

Jordan, J. V., & Hartling, L. M. (2002). New developments in relational-cultural theory. In M. Mallou & L. S. Brown (Eds.), *Rethinking mental health and disorder: Feminist perspectives* (pp. 48–70). New York: Guilford Press.

Jordan, J. V., Kaplan, A. G., Miller, J. B., Stiver, I. P., & Surrey, J. L. (1991). *Women's growth in connection: Writings from the Stone Center.* New York: Guilford Press.

Kegan, R. (1982). *The evolving self: Problem and process in human development.* Cambridge, MA: Harvard University Press.

Kessler, R. C., McGonagle, K. A., Zhao, S., Nelson, C. B., Hughes, M., Eshleman, S., et al. (1994). Lifetime and 12-month prevalence of DSM-III-R psychiatric disorders in the United States: Results from the National Comorbidity Survey. *Archives of General Psychiatry, 51,* 8–19.

Kinser, A. E. (2004). Negotiating spaces for/through third-wave feminism. *National Women's Studies Association Journal, 16*(3), 124–153.

Laird, J. (1989). Women and stories: Restoring women's self-constructions. In M. McGoldrick, C. Anderson, & F. Walsh (Eds.),*Women in families: A framework for family therapy* (pp. 427–450). New York: W. W. Norton.

Land, H. (1995). Feminist clinical social work in the 21st century. In N. Van Den Bergh (Ed.), *Feminist practice in the 21st century* (pp. 3–19). Washington, DC: NASW Press.

Leiner, A. S., Compton, M. T., Houry, D., & Kaslow, N. J. (2008). Intimate partner violence, psychological distress, and suicidality: A path model using data from African American women seeking care in an emergency room. *Journal of Family Violence, 23,* 473–481.

Libow, J. (1986). Training family therapists as feminists. In M. Ault-Riche (Ed.), *Women and family therapy.* Rockville, MD: Aspen.

Logan, T. K., Walker, R., & Hunt, G. (2009). Understanding human trafficking in the United States. *Trauma, Violence, & Abuse, 10*(1), 3–30.

Marmar, C. R., & Spiegel, D. (2010). Posttraumatic stress disorder and acute stress disorder. In G. O. Gabbard (Ed.), *Gabbard's treatments of psychiatric disorders* (4th ed., p. 3). DOI: 10.1176/appi.books.9781585622986

Masson, P. (1984, February). Freud and the seduction theory. *Atlantic Monthly,* 33–60.

Miller, J. B. (1986). *Toward a new psychology of women* (2nd ed.). Boston: Beacon Press.

Mills, S. (1998). Post-colonial feminist theory. In S. Jackson & J. Jones (Eds.), *Contemporary feminist theories* (pp. 98–112). New York: New York University Press.

Murphy, S. B., & Ouimet, L. V. (2008). Intimate partner violence: A call for social work action. *Health and Social Work, 33*(4), 309–314.

Najavits, L. M. (2009). Psychotherapies for trauma and substance abuse in women: Review and policy implications. *Trauma, Violence, & Abuse, 10*(3), 290–298.

Nes, J. A., & Iadicola, P. (1989). Toward a definition of feminist social work: A comparison of liberal, radical, and socialist models. *Social Work, 34,* 12–21.

Pearce, D. (1979). The feminization of poverty: Women, work, and welfare. *Urban and Social Change Review, 2,* 28–36.

Ponniah, K., & Hollon, S. D. (2009). Empirically supported psychological treatments for adult acute stress disorder and posttraumatic stress disorder: A review. *Depression and Anxiety, 26,* 1086–1109.

Rodríguez, M., Valentine, J. M., Son, J. B., & Muhammad, M. (2009). Intimate partner violence and barriers to mental health care for ethnically diverse populations of women. *Trauma, Violence, & Abuse, 10*(4), 358–374.

Rothschild, B. (2000). *The body remembers: The psychophysiology of trauma and trauma treatment.* New York: Norton.

Salzman, L. E., Fanslow, J. L., McMahon, P. M., & Shelley, G. A. (2002). *Intimate partner violence surveillance: Uniform definitions and recommended data elements, version 1.0.* Atlanta, GA: Centers for Disease Control and Prevention, National Center for Injury Prevention and Control. Retrieved May 23, 2010, from http://www.cdc.gov/ncipc/pub-res/ipv_surveillance/intimate.htm

Sands, R. G., & Nuccio, K. (1992). Postmodern feminist theory and social work. *Social Work, 37*(6), 489–502.

Saulnier, C. F. (1996). *Feminist theories and social work: Approaches and applications.* New York: Haworth Press.

Schauer, E. J., & Wheaton, E. M. (2006). Sex trafficking into the United States: A literature review. *Criminal Justice Review, 31*(2), 146–169.

Seedat, S., Scott, K. M., Angermeyer, M. C., Berglund, P., Bromet, E. J., Brugha, T. S., et al. (2009). Cross-national associations between gender and mental disorders in the World Health Organization World Mental Health Surveys. *Archives of General Psychiatry, 66*(7), 785–795.

Sigmon, J. N. (2008). Combating modern-day slavery: Issues in identifying and assisting victims of human trafficking worldwide.*Victims and Offenders, 3,* 245–257.

Smith, D. E. (1987). *The everyday world as problematic: A feminist sociology.* Boston, MA: Northeastern University Press.

Spence, D. P. (1982). *Narrative truth and historical truth: Meaning and interpretation in psychoanalysis.* New York: W. W. Norton.

Stewart, R. L. (1985). Psychoanalysis and psychoanalytic psychotherapy. In H. I. Kaplan & B. J. Sadock (Eds.), *Comprehensive textbook of psychiatry/IV* (4th ed., pp. 1331–1365). Baltimore, MD: Williams & Wilkins.

Surrey, J. L. (1991) The self-in-relation: A theory of women's development. In J. V. Jordan, A. G. Kaplan, J. B. Miller, I. P. Stiver, & J. L. Surrey (Eds.), *Women's growth in connection: Writings from the Stone Center* (pp. 51–66). New York: Guilford Press.

Swigonski, M. E. (1994). The logic of feminist standpoint theory for social work research. *Social Work, 39*(4), 387–393.

Tjaden, P., & Thoennes, N. (2000a). Full report of the prevalence, incidence, and consequences of violence against women: Findings from the National Violence against Women Survey. Washington, DC: National Institute of Justice. Retrieved from http://www.ncjrs.gov/pdffiles1/nij/183781.pdf

Tjaden, P., & Thoennes, N. (2000b). Prevalence and consequences of male-to-female and female-to-male intimate violence as measured by the National Violence against Women Survey. *Violence against Women, 6*(2), 142–161.

Tjaden, P., & Thoennes, N. (2000c). Extent, nature, and consequences of intimate partner violence: Findings from the National Violence against Women Survey. Washington, DC: National Institute of Justice. Retrieved from http://www.ncjrs.gov/pdffiles1/nij/181867.pdf

Tong, R. (1998). *Feminist thought: A more comprehensive introduction* (2nd ed.). Boulder, CO: Westview Press.

U.S. Department of Health and Human Services. (n.d.[a]). *Trafficking Victims Protection Act of 2000 fact sheet.* Retrieved May 23, 2010, from http://www.acf.hhs.gov/trafficking/about/TVPA_2000.pdf

U.S. Department of Health and Human Services. (n.d.[b]). *Identifying and interacting with victims of human trafficking.* Retrieved May 24, 2010, from http://www.ccc-aht.org/Resources/identify_victimssserv.pdf

Van den Bergh, N. (Ed.). (1995). *Feminist practice in the 21st century.* Washington, DC: NASW Press.

Vatnar, S. K. B., & Bjørkly, S. (2010). Does it make any difference if she is a mother? An interactional perspective on intimate partner violence with a focus on motherhood and pregnancy. *Journal of Interpersonal Violence, 25*(1), 94–110.

Wait, C. D., Proctor, B. D., & Smith, J. C. (2009). *Income, poverty, and health insurance coverage in the United States.* Retrieved May 25, 2010, from http://www.census.gov/prod/2008pubs/p60-235.pdf

Walker, L. (1979). *The battered woman.* New York: Harper and Row.

Walters, M., Carter, B., Papp, P., & Silverstein, O. (1988). *The invisible web: Gender patterns in family relationships.* New York: Guilford Press.

West, C. K. (2005). The map of relational-cultural theory. *Women & Therapy, 28*(3/4), 93–110.

White, M., & Epston, D. (1990). *Narrative means to therapeutic ends.* New York: W. W. Norton.

Wing, A. K. (Ed.). (2003). *Critical race feminism: A reader* (2nd ed.). New York: New York University Press.

Evidence-Based Practice with Depressed Clients

According to the Substance Abuse and Mental Health Services Administration, in 2005 and 2006, an annual average of 67.4 percent of adults aged 18 or older who experienced a past year major depressive episode (MDE) received treatment for depression in the past year, i.e., saw or talked to a medical doctor or other professional about depression and/or used prescription medication for depression. Among adults aged 18 or older with past year MDE who received treatment for depression in the past year, 69.4 percent reported both talking to a professional and using medication, 23.8 percent reported talking to a professional but not using medication, and 6.7 percent reported using medication but not talking to a professional.

—SUBSTANCE ABUSE AND MENTAL HEALTH SERVICES ADMINISTRATION, *THE NATIONAL SURVEY ON DRUG USE AND HEALTH REPORT*, 2008, P. 1

Depression is a common and heterogeneous mood disorder that affects approximately 15 million American adults age 18 and over, or about 7 percent of the U.S. population in a given year (Kessler, Chiu, Demler, & Walters, 2005). Major depressive disorder (MDD) is the leading cause of disability in the United States for persons aged 15 to 44 (World Health Organization, 2004). It is also more prevalent in women than in men (Kessler et al., 2003).

Depression is characterized by sadness, irritability, lack of energy or interest in life, slowed movements, pessimism, feelings of worthlessness, guilt, morbid thinking, and changes in patterns of eating and sleeping. It is associated with chronic medical disease and disability, psychiatric comorbidity, and mortality. Depression increases the risk of heart attacks and is a frequent complicating factor in diabetes, stroke, and cancer, and studies show that depression is a contributory factor to fatal coronary disease (May et al., 2009). The economic costs associated with depression are estimated to be about $83 billion per year (National Institute of Mental Health [NIMH], 2006).

Depression as a mental disorder should be distinguished from the "blues" and "down days" or feeling "down in the dumps," which are common human experiences that are associated with stressors, disappointments, losses, and changes that are a part of daily life. Usually these feelings follow an event or interaction that is inconsistent with one's expectations or hopes. Feelings like these fade on their own or are relieved when one comes to terms with the situation or takes assertive action. Depressive symptoms can be considered manifestations of a mental disorder when they are experienced with great intensity and frequency, when they have a prolonged course, when they interfere with psychosocial functioning, and when they cluster with other symptoms.

As Table 8.1 shows, depressive symptoms occur on multiple domains. Furthermore, there are many kinds of depression and each individual puts his or her own unique inscription on it. Social scientists and clinicians, however, have found that classifying the disorders helps in the development and implementation of effective interventions. The *DSM-IV-TR* (American Psychiatric Association [APA], 2000) provides such a classification.

The diagnoses in the *DSM-IV-TR* (APA, 2000) that include marked symptoms of depression are mood disorder due to a general medical condition, substance-induced mood disorder, bipolar I disorder, bipolar II disorder, cyclothymic disorder, MDD, schizoaffective disorder (depressive type), dysthymic disorder, and adjustment disorder with depressed mood—to say nothing of the not otherwise specified (NOS) versions of these disorders, and bereavement. In addition, there are diagnoses of depression in the appendix of the *DSM-IV-TR* that are sometimes incorporated in the NOS category—minor depressive disorder,

TABLE 8.1	Symptoms of Depression
Type of Symptom	**Description**
Biological	Decreased or increased appetite, changes in sleeping patterns (hypersomnia, insomnia, early morning wakening), decreased libido, diminished energy
Cognitive	Worthlessness, hopelessness, self-depreciation, self-blame, guilt, pessimism, incompetence, deprivation, expectation of failure or punishment
Affective (mood)	Sadness, dejection, downcast, suffering, disinterest, irritable
Behavior	Slowed or diminished activity, withdrawal from usual activities, excessive sleeping, crying, passivity, decreased interpersonal/social behavior

premenstrual dysphoric disorder, recurrent brief depressive disorder, and mixed anxiety-depressive disorder. Two of the diagnoses (mood disorder due to a general medical condition and substance-induced mood disorder) are based on etiology; some are based on history of a manic, mixed, or hypomanic episode (e.g., bipolar I and II and cyclothymic disorders); and others are based on chronicity (dysthymic and cyclothymic disorders) (APA, 2000). Within many of the mood disorders are specifiers (denoted by "x" digits) that describe the severity, chronicity, onset, special features, and other characteristics of the most recent (e.g., severe with psychotic depression, postpartum onset, and atypical features) and recurrent episodes (e.g., seasonal pattern) (APA, 2000).

The *DSM-IV-TR* distinguishes between *unipolar* disorders, which are characterized by low moods, and *bipolar* disorders, which generally have highs and lows. This chapter will focus on the treatment of two unipolar illnesses—MDD without psychotic features and dysthymic disorder—in which neither is complicated by substance abuse. The psychotherapeutic treatments that will be described are for depressions that are in the mild to moderate range of severity. Individuals with severe or recurrent MDDs may benefit from the interventions for persons with serious mental illness that are described in Chapters 11 and 12. Because the two depressive disorders that are the focus of this chapter have a high rate of comorbidity with other psychiatric disorders (Kessler, Abelson, & Zhao, 1998), their treatment plan should take other comorbid disorders into consideration. Those with concurrent substance abuse disorders may respond to some of the interventions described in Chapter 13.

We will now proceed to describe MDD and dysthymic disorder. Next, biological aspects, social dimensions, and psychosocial theories will be explained. A discussion of late-life depression, cognitive therapy, interpersonal therapy, problem-solving therapy, medication issues, and alternative ways of healing will follow.

MAJOR DEPRESSIVE DISORDER

Major depressive disorder is the most common and serious of the depressive disorders and has been extensively studied. The *DSM-IV-TR* describes MDD as a mood disorder within at least one two-week episode of illness in which there is either a depressed mood or a loss of interest in daily activities (anhedonia). These are the two cardinal (signal) symptoms of MDD. Symptoms must represent a change from previous daily functioning and are not the consequence of a general medical condition, alcohol, or drugs (prescribed or street drugs). As shown in Box 8.1, the *DSM-IV-TR* stipulates that five or more of the following symptoms must be present during an episode.

Major depressive disorder is further delineated by four domains: chronicity (if an individual meets full criteria for at least two years), recurrence (the number of separate episodes that an individual has had), severity (mild, moderate, severe), and remission status. If the individual meets the criteria of a mixed episode (symptoms of manic and depressive episodes) or the person has these symptoms as a result of a recent loss (bereavement), the episode is not considered a major depressive one. Individuals may have single or recurrent episodes of MDD (APA, 2000). As indicated, MDDs may be accompanied by psychotic features. If there are psychotic symptoms, the clinician needs to determine whether one of the major psychotic disorders (schizophrenia, schizophreniform disorder, schizoaffective disorder, delusional disorder, or psychotic disorder NOS) is more appropriate (APA, 2000).

Box 8.1

Symptoms of Depression

1. Depressed mood most of the day, nearly every day, as indicated by either subjective report or observation made by others
2. Markedly diminished interest or pleasure in all, or almost all, activities most of the day, nearly every day
3. Significant weight loss when not dieting or weight gain
4. Insomnia or hypersomnia nearly every day
5. Psychomotor agitation or retardation nearly every day
6. Fatigue or loss of energy nearly every day
7. Feelings of worthlessness or excessive or inappropriate guilt nearly every day
8. Diminished ability to think or concentrate, or indecisiveness, nearly every day
9. Recurrent thoughts of death, recurrent suicidal ideation without a specific plan, or a suicide attempt or a specific plan for committing suicide

Source: Printed with permission from the American Psychiatric Association (2000, p. 356), with parenthetical examples and notes omitted.

DYSTHYMIC DISORDER

Dysthymic disorder (or dysthymia) consists of a pattern of chronic depression that persists for at least two years (APA, 2000), but is less severe than MDD. As Box 8.2 shows, according to the *DSM-IV-TR*, two or more of the following symptoms must be present while depressed.

As with MDD, other diagnoses should be considered before dysthymic disorder—particularly substance abuse, a general medical condition, schizophrenia, manic episodes, and others. Dysthymic disorder may have an early (before age 21) or late (age 21 or older) onset (APA, 2000).

Although diagnostic criteria for MDD and dysthymic disorder appear to distinguish them, their features do overlap. Researchers have estimated that 75 percent of individuals with dysthymia meet criteria for at least one major depressive episode, also referred to as double depression (Keller et al., 1995). Those with dysthymia who have depressive episodes tend to have longer periods of depression and spend less time fully recovered (Klein, Schwartz, Rose, & Leader, 2000).

Box 8.2

Symptoms of Dysthymia

1. Poor appetite or overeating
2. Insomnia or hypersomnia
3. Low energy or fatigue
4. Low self-esteem
5. Poor concentration or difficulty making decisions
6. Feelings of hopelessness

Source: Printed with permission from the American Psychiatric Association (2000, p. 380).

DEPRESSION IN OLDER ADULTS

*Depression is one **of the** most common mental health **disorders** among older adults.* It is a frequent cause of psychological distress in later life and significantly decreases quality of life. The U.S. population continues to grow older and the need for the social work field to provide assistance with mental health needs associated with later life will be critical. This will be especially apparent between the years 2015 and 2030, when older adults (65 or more years) will account for 20 percent of the total population, up from 13 percent in 2000 (U.S. Bureau of the Census, 2000). Moreover, currently less than 3 percent of older adults seek mental health care in the United States (Blazer, 2002). Added to this trend is the increasing proportion of minority older adults including African Americans, Latino, and Asian Americans (Arean et al., 2005; Gellis & Taguchi, 2003).

Prevalence estimates of major depression in general, relatively healthy, community elderly samples are low, ranging from 1 percent to 4 percent overall, with higher prevalence among women (Kessler et al., 2003). The prevalence rate for dysthymia is about 2 percent; although for minor depression, estimates are higher, ranging from 4 percent to 13 percent, with the same pattern of distribution across gender, race, and ethnicity (Blazer, 2002; Kessler et al., 2005). In comparison with the general older population, estimates of major depression in medically ill elderly are high, ranging from 10 percent to 12 percent, with an additional 23 percent experiencing significant depressive symptoms (Koenig, Meador, Cohen, & Blazer, 1988). In medically ill elderly receiving home health care, estimates of 13.5 percent were reported for major depression (Bruce et al., 2002). Rates of clinically significant depressive symptoms among medically ill elderly range from 10 percent to 43 percent (Steffens et al., 2000).

Depression with physical illness increases levels of functional disability, use of health services, and health care costs. It also delays or inhibits physical recovery. Common medical illnesses known to be associated with depression include heart disease, stroke, hypertension, diabetes, cancer, and osteoarthritis (Gellis, 2009). Late onset, unipolar depression is characteristic of suicides in later life (Conwell, Duberstein, & Caine, 2002). Older suicide victims often have had late onset undetected or untreated depressions, although typically they have had contact with their primary care provider prior to their death (Uncapher, 2000). This may reflect high levels of comorbid illness and/or fears of dependency or pain. Effective treatments for late-life depression are available including pharmacological and psychosocial interventions (e.g., cognitive-behavioral, problem-solving, and interpersonal therapies) that are discussed later in this chapter.

MULTIPLE RISK AND ASSOCIATED FACTORS

Epidemiological and Social/Environmental Factors

Several national epidemiological studies funded by the National Institutes of Health (NIH) have provided important data that widen our understanding of the prevalence and incidence of depression disorders. These include the 1980s Epidemiological Catchment Area (ECA) Study, the 1990s National Comorbidity Survey (NCS) and its replication (NCS-R) (2001–2002), and the National Epidemiologic Survey on Alcohol and Related Conditions (NESARC). In the latter study, the prevalence of twelve-month and lifetime *DSM-IV* MDD was 5.28 and 13.23 percent, respectively (Hasin, Goodwin, Stinson, & Grant, 2005). Studies have identified various risk factors for MDD including being female, middle-aged; Native American; separated or divorced; widowed; and having a low income, whereas for Hispanics, African Americans, and Asians, the risk was reduced (Hasin et al., 2005).

These large-scale epidemiological studies of groups at risk for depression have found that the lifetime prevalence for women is approximately twice that of men (Boyd & Weissman, 1986; Regier et al., 1988), although in the NCS, the proportion was slightly lower (21.3 percent for women and 12.7 percent for men) (Kessler et al., 1998). Similar female/male prevalence ratios have been documented across different ethnic groups and countries (Weissman et al., 1996). The higher rate for women can be explained by prevailing biological theories including hormonal differences, stress, and childbirth (when the onset is postpartum) (Noble, 2005; Sadock & Sadock, 2007). It may be that the rates for men and women are comparable, but men manifest depression in their higher rate of substance abuse and trouble with the law (Weissman & Klerman, 1977). Depression increases with age up to 65, after which it decreases (Regier et al., 1993; Weissman & Myers, 1978); however, minor and subthreshold depression is significantly higher in older adults (Gellis, 2009). The ECA Study found no significant differences by ethnic or racial group (Regier et al., 1993).

Risk factors most likely causally related to MDD across epidemiological studies are being female, prior history of depression, being divorced or separated, poor general health, major adverse life events, and low socioeconomic status (Kaelber, Moul, & Farmer, 1995). Factors that most plausibly protect people from major depression are being employed, advanced education, financial stability, and strong social support systems (Kaelber et al., 1995).

Biological Aspects

Evidence of a biological basis for depression comes from genetic and psychopharmacological research. Studies of genetic factors have found a higher percentage of depression among relatives of persons with depression than in the general population (Klerman, 1988). Studies of twins have revealed that identical twins have a rate of concordance for major mood disorders that is two to five times the rate for fraternal twins (McGuffin & Katz, 1989). The limited number of adoption studies has yielded inconclusive results relevant to unipolar illness (DeRubeis, Young, & Dahlsgaard, 1998).

Past research has suggested that several neurotransmitters—serotonin, dopamine, histamine, and norepinephrine—are associated with mood disorders (Sadock & Sadock, 2007). More recently, research has moved to the study of neural circuits, neurobehavioral systems, and more complex neuroregulatory structures (Sadock & Sadock, 2007). Brain neuroimaging research suggests that the subgenual prefrontal cortex of the brain may be involved in depression (Andreasen & Black, 2006). Considering the tentativeness of this research, it is likely that biological, psychological, and social dimensions are intertwined.

Psychological Aspects

Various psychological theories provide explanations for the development of depression including psychoanalytic theory, cognitive theory, attachment theory, learned helplessness, behavioral (learning) theory, and problem-solving theory. According to *psychoanalytic theory*, depression indicates disturbances in the oral stage of human development (Hirschfeld & Goodwin, 1988). Persons who have had conflictual experiences during this period (e.g., through the death of a parent or dysfunctional patterns of communication) may be fixated in this stage. As adults, such individuals continue to be dependent on others to meet needs that were not sufficiently satisfied during the first couple of years of life. Later experiences of loss or perceived loss threaten their ego integrity. On the other hand, persons who have not been orally deprived may regress to the oral stage in response to a loss. Regardless of whether fixation or regression is involved, the depressed individual suffers from the loss of an introjected object (Freud, 1917). During uncomplicated bereavement (mourning), the depressed person grieves, reliving past experiences and letting go of the lost object "bit by bit" to free energy for the development of new relationships. If the loss is complicated (melancholia), the individual will have ambivalent and angry feelings toward the internalized object and, thus, toward the self. If suicidal, the individual will want to obliterate the self/object. The melancholic person has a more difficult time breaking loose of the lost object than the mourner (Freud, 1917).

Beck's *cognitive theory* of depression is another contemporary framework for understanding depression. One principal assumption is that depressed persons have cognitions that represent misinterpretations of their experiences and depressogenic assumptions (Beck, Rush, Shaw, & Emery, 1979). The cognitions are represented in a *cognitive triad*—a view of oneself as inadequate, a tendency to interpret experiences in relation to others negatively, and a negative view of the future—and in cognitive thought structures (schemas) that categorize personal experiences. The depressed person uses inappropriate schemas based on faulty assumptions to interpret daily life events. In cognitive therapy, these distorted beliefs are examined, challenged, and replaced by more accurate and realistic ones (Beck et al., 1979). (See Chapter 3 on cognitive theory.)

Attachment theory has also been used to explain reactions to object loss. Based on observations of mothers and infants, as well as ethological research, Bowlby (1969) posed that there is a human instinct to adapt to one's environment, which is expressed initially in attachment to maternal figures and later in relationships with others. Attachment behavior is expressed in efforts to be in close proximity to a specific object; closeness arouses feelings of security, whereas separation arouses anxiety. During the developmental process, young people relinquish their attachment to parents as principal love objects and form relationships with peers (Weiss, 1982). In adulthood, love relationships based on attachment provide a source of meaning, security, and comfort (Marris, 1982). Loss is a disruption of the attachment process. Grief work entails the relinquishment of the lost object and the restoration of meaning (Marris, 1982).

Another explanation uses the concept of *learned helplessness*. Based on Seligman's (1975) experimental work with dogs, which became passive after experiencing exposure to shock under conditions from which there was no escape, the theory poses that helplessness (and the accompanying belief that one lacks control over one's environment) is learned. When opportunities to escape are presented to someone who has been exposed to harsh, unpredictable demands, the response is passivity. Learned helplessness explains the behavior of abused spouses who are paralyzed in their situations. It is also an analogue to depression.

According to *behavioral (learning) theory*, depression is a motivational deficit, which is associated with a lack of social skills and a low level of self-generated activities that produce positive reinforcements (Rosenhan & Seligman, 1984). Without sufficient reinforcements, individuals do not feel motivated to act. Instead they become passive and feel depressed. Behavioral therapy aims to enhance social skills, increase the activity level, increase reinforcement, and promote assertiveness.

According to *problem-solving theory*, psychological distress constitutes maladaptive or ineffective behavior leading to symptoms of depression (Nezu & D'Zurilla, 1989). Within this theoretical approach, "psychological distress is seen as a function of the reciprocal relationships among two types of stressful life events (i.e., major negative life events and daily personal problems), negative emotional states, and problem-solving coping" (Nezu, 2004). These stress variables are continuously changing in severity, frequency, and intensity over time. Problem-solving theory comprises two general, but partially independent, processes—problem orientation and problem-solving style (D'Zurilla, Nezu, & Maydeu-Olivares, 2004). *Problem orientation* involves the set of generalized appraisals and emotional reactions concerning problems in living, as well as one's ability to successfully resolve them. It can either be *positive* (e.g., viewing problems as opportunities to benefit in some way; perceiving oneself as able to solve problems effectively), which serves to enhance subsequent problem-solving efforts, or *negative* (e.g., viewing problems as a major threat to one's well being; overreacting emotionally when problems occur), which functions to inhibit attempts to solve problems.

The psychological theories relevant to this chapter on depression are cognitive-behavioral, interpersonal, and problem solving. We turn next to research using such theoretical approaches to psychotherapy with and without medication.

Research on Psychotherapy

Psychosocial treatments have been demonstrated to be effective among adults and older adults, particularly those who reject medication or who are coping with low social support or stressful situations. Based on NIH consensus statements, the Surgeon General's Mental Health report, and literature reviews, evidence-based approaches including structured cognitive-behavioral (CBT), interpersonal (IPT), and problem-solving (PST) treatments are effective alternatives or adjuncts to medication treatment (Gellis, 2009; Lebowitz et al., 1997; U.S. Department of Health and Human Services, 1999).

Although many kinds of psychotherapies are used to treat depression, with and without pharmacotherapy, three evidence-based practices will be detailed and two will be illustrated. Cognitive, interpersonal, and problem-solving therapies have been chosen because of the robust research evidence of their effectiveness and their compatibility with the managed care expectations that depression interventions be short term. Still, it is recognized that many practitioners use other therapies such as psychodynamic approaches. Before considering one of these or other psychotherapies, the clinician should complete a thorough assessment of the client's mental status and current life stressors. Often depression is related to a stressful life situation that may be remedied through crisis intervention and the mobilization of environmental supports if the situation warrants. Furthermore, the client should be screened for substance abuse, which can complicate treatment (see Chapter 13). A thorough physical examination is advised to determine whether a medical condition may be causing the depression. Clients who are suicidal should be assessed for hospitalization.

EVIDENCE-BASED PRACTICE: COGNITIVE OR COGNITIVE-BEHAVIORAL THERAPY

Cognitive therapy, as described here, was developed by Aaron Beck and his associates (Beck, 1976; Beck et al., 1979), but its roots go back to Plato (Karasu, 1990). The therapy is predicated on the idea that automatic thoughts and images (cognitions) precipitate depression and other symptoms of emotional disturbance. Automatic thoughts are "specific subvocalizations or self-statements that occur automatically and without conscious effort" (Sacco & Beck, 1995, p. 333). Treatment is directed at changing distorted, maladaptive, inaccurate cognitions to more adaptive ones. Sometimes called cognitive-behavioral therapy, the treatment uses behavioral as well as cognitive strategies. Table 8.2 compares the cognitive, interpersonal, and problem-solving approaches that are discussed in this chapter.

Although cognitive therapy does not preclude biological or developmental explanations or the use of medication (Beck, 1976), it is concerned principally with the thought patterns or schemas that underlie depression. A life experience, such as a loss, can activate latent schemas (e.g., attitudes about loss) that developed earlier in life. A person with unipolar depression is likely to interpret later life events in ways that emphasize the negative aspects, ignore the context, and reflect poorly on the individual. Selectively attending to those elements of the situation that coincide with depressogenic schemas, the individual construes the situation in a partial way,

TABLE 8.2	Major Features of Three Evidence-Based Psychosocial Practices for Treating Depression		
Feature	**Cognitive Approach (CBT)**	**Interpersonal Approach (IPT)**	**Problem-Solving Approach (PST)**
Major theorists	Plato, Adler, Beck, Rush	Meyer, Sullivan, Klerman, Weissman	Aristotle, D'Zurilla, Goldfried, Nezu
Concepts of pathology and etiology	Distorted thinking: dysphoria due to learned negative views of self, others, and the world	Impaired interpersonal relations: absent or unsatisfactory significant social bonds	Dysfunctional or ineffective problem solving contributes to avoidance or impulsivity-carelessness styles that produce negative outcomes
Major goals and mechanisms of change	To provide symptomatic relief through alteration of target thoughts; to identify self-destructive cognitions; to modify specific erroneous assumptions; to promote self-control over thinking patterns	To provide symptomatic relief through solution of current interpersonal problems; to reduce stress involving family or work; to improve interpersonal communication skills	To develop new coping skills and solutions to solving daily living problems; to develop new problem-solving orientation and style
Primary techniques and practices	Behavioral/cognitive: recording and monitoring cognitions; correcting distorted themes with logic and experimental testing; providing alternative thought content; homework	Communicative/environmental: clarifying and managing maladaptive relationships and learning new ones through communication and social skills training; providing information on illness	Behavioral/cognitive: establish realistic goal; generate/evaluate solution options; choose solution that best achieves desired goal; implement chosen solution in real world; homework
Therapist role/ therapeutic relationship	Educator/shaper: positive relationship instead of transference; collaborative empiricism as basis for joint scientific (logical) task	Explorer/prescriber: positive relationship/transference without interpretation; active therapist role for influence and advocacy	Directive role/educator: advocates optimistic attitude toward solving life problems; collaborative and rational in nature

Source: The columns, "Cognitive Approach" and "Interpersonal Approach," were from Karasu (1990). Printed with the permission of the American Psychiatric Association. The column, "Problem-Solving Approach," was developed by Gellis (2009).

without considering the whole (Beck et al., 1979). The following are examples of maladaptive explanations of a brief exchange between two coworkers at the coffee pot one morning:

Conversation:

AL: Hi Bob. How ya' doing?

BOB: Pretty good. How are you?

AL: Ok. Gotta go. (rushes off)

Bob's maladaptive explanations of Al's rushing off:

Al doesn't like me.

Al doesn't like me anymore.

I wonder what I did wrong.

An accurate assessment of this situation reveals that Al greeted Bob with warmth and friendliness. Yet Bob viewed the interaction as a reflection of Al's negative feelings toward him. Alternative explanations for Al's behavior are (a) Al had an appointment or a meeting; (b) Al needed to prepare for a busy day of work; and (c) Al went to the coffee pot for coffee, not to socialize. Essentially Al's reasons had nothing to do with Bob. The negative interpretation was a reflection of Bob's schemas.

Persons who are depressed are prone to make inaccurate interpretations of their experiences. Automatic negative thoughts intervene between life events and emotional responses, creating a negative bias. Depressed persons view life events that would ordinarily be viewed as undesirable, disappointing, or neutral as catastrophes. Convinced that their perception of reality is the same as reality (Beck, 1976), they feel pain associated with their own biased interpretations. Soon they become preoccupied with themes of rejection, inadequacy, and failure and blame themselves for unfortuitous experiences. As the depression deepens, the depressive themes predominate and reality testing becomes impaired (Beck, 1985).

The Therapeutic Relationship

Beck's cognitive therapy is implemented through a collaborative relationship between the clinician and the client. The therapist fosters those conditions that facilitate the development of a relationship and which are described in Rogerian therapy—warmth, genuineness, accurate empathy (Beck et al., 1979). Much attention is given to developing rapport and building trust. Although cognitive therapy emphasizes cognitions, emotions are important as well. The client is given the opportunity to express feelings and the clinician accepts the feelings the client shares.

Although the relationship is a partnership, the roles of clinician and client are different. The cognitive therapist may be viewed as a teacher, the client as a learner. The clinician explains cognitive theory to the client, provides structure to the sessions, asks questions about the client, and assigns homework. Before proceeding with the therapeutic work, the clinician explains that they will be working together to develop hypotheses and test them out (Hirschfeld & Shea, 1985). The clinician assumes an active role in identifying problems, in focusing on specific issues, and in the implementation of cognitive and behavioral techniques (Beck, 1985). The client is expected to describe feelings, cognitions, and behaviors, to work at revising inaccurate thoughts, and to carry out assigned activities and homework.

The Nature of Cognitive Therapy

Cognitive therapy is brief, present oriented, and focused. The time period varies from ten to twenty-five weeks (Jarrett & Rush, 1989). After termination, some clients continue in four or five "booster" sessions (Sacco & Beck, 1995). Although cognitive therapy can be implemented in couple and group formats (Jarrett & Rush, 1989), the individual approach will be described here.

Cognitive therapy employs the scientific method that is used in research. Throughout the process, information is gathered, hypotheses are tested, and logical conclusions are drawn. The clinician and the client examine thoughts and interpretations and create and evaluate experiments clients perform in their daily lives that test hypotheses. The client is encouraged to discard ideas that are illogical and do not reflect observed reality.

Hypotheses and experiments provide insight into underlying depressogenic assumptions and rules (Beck et al., 1979), which also can be tested. Beck identified several "silent assumptions" (Sacco & Beck, 1995, p. 339) that are related to depression:

1. In order to be happy, I have to be successful in whatever I undertake.
2. To be happy, I must be accepted by all people at all times.

3. If I'm not on top, I'm a flop.
4. It's wonderful to be popular, famous, wealthy; it's terrible to be unpopular, mediocre.
5. If I make a mistake, it means that I am inept.
6. My value as a person depends on what others think of me.
7. I can't live without love. If my spouse (sweetheart, parent, child) doesn't love me, I'm worthless.
8. If somebody disagrees with me, it means he doesn't like me.
9. If I don't take advantage of every opportunity to advance myself, I will regret it later. (Beck, 1976, pp. 255–256)

The goals of cognitive therapy are to promote relief of depressive symptoms and to prevent a recurrence (Beck et al., 1979). Subjectively, the client should have enhanced feelings of satisfaction and well-being. These goals are achieved by teaching the client to: "(a) learn to identify and modify his faulty thinking and dysfunctional behavior and (b) recognize and change the cognitive patterns leading to dysfunctional ideation and behavior" (Beck et al., 1979, p. 75).

The Process of Cognitive Therapy

Beck and his associates describe a process in which the strategies and methods vary over time. Prior to admission to treatment, they perform a preliminary evaluation of potential clients. The evaluation includes a history of the current difficulty, past history, a mental status examination, and a battery of tests. Among the tests that are used are the Schedule of Affective Disorders and Schizophrenia, the Hamilton Rating Scale for Depression, the Hopelessness Scale, the Scale for Suicide Intentionality, the Minnesota Multiphasic Personality Inventory, the Spielberger State-Trait Anxiety Scale, and the Beck Depression Inventory (Beck et al., 1979).

THE FIRST INTERVIEW During the first interview, attention is initially given to establishing rapport, inquiring about the client's expectations of therapy, and eliciting attitudes toward the self, the clinician, and therapy. On the basis of information that was gathered during the preliminary evaluation and observations about the client's mental status that are made in this session, the clinician identifies complaints ("I do not see any reason to go on") and transforms them into target symptoms (suicidal thoughts) or problems (difficulty completing school work) (Beck et al., 1979). When more than one symptom or problem is identified, potential targets are prioritized on the basis of the distress they arouse in the client and their amenability to treatment. The clinician and the client come to a negotiated agreement about the symptom or problem that will be focal.

The clinician devotes considerable time during the first session to educating the client about cognitive therapy. The cognitive theory of depression and intervention techniques (see next section) should be explained. In addition, the client is encouraged to read psychoeducational materials or use self-help material that provides information about cognitive therapy (Wright, Thase, & Beck, 2009). Particular attention is given to the client's responsibility to perform homework assignments between sessions. The clinician inquires about the client's activity level and asks the client to keep a record of the activities that he or she performs between this session and the next. Before this interview concludes, the client's feelings about the interview are elicited (Beck et al., 1979).

THE SECOND INTERVIEW During the second interview, the client is again encouraged to share feelings about the first session, but is also invited to raise questions about the reading material or the process. The clinician answers the client's questions and responds to questions. In addition, the homework assignment on activities is reviewed. If the client appears to be having difficulty getting motivated to be active, the clinician and the client together develop a schedule of activities to be performed by the client. The client is given the homework assignment of rating each activity performed with respect to degree of mastery and pleasure (Beck et al., 1979).

Sometime during the first few interviews, the clinician presents the client with a "case formulation" or conceptual explanation, which serves as a framework for the therapeutic process (Sacco & Beck, 1995, p. 333). Throughout therapy, sessions are structured. They begin with the clinician and the client developing an agenda of what they wish to accomplish during the session (Beck et al., 1979). This usually includes the client's summary of experiences since the last session and a review of the homework assignment. Issues and concerns pertaining to the previous session can also be raised. The client and the clinician together identify problems and negotiate about which ones will be addressed in the session. The client chooses among strategies suggested by the clinician (e.g., role playing, refuting automatic thoughts) for looking at targeted problems in the session. Sessions also include an elicitation of the client's feelings, summary statements by the clinician, and a description of the next homework assignment (Beck et al., 1979).

In each session, the client is asked about depressive symptoms and about events that have occurred since the previous meeting. The clinician responds to the reported experiences by inquiring about the client's feelings, thinking, and behavior. During these discussions, the client reveals distorted thinking that is associated with life events. The clinician begins to point out the relationship between the client's negative cognitions and depression (Beck et al., 1979).

MIDDLE PHASE During the middle phase of intervention, attention is given to automatic thoughts that are associated with disturbing feelings (sadness, anxiety, and lack of interest in life). Clients may be asked to perform homework assignments in which they record the circumstances related to these feelings, that is, the precipitating event and cognitions. It is customary for clients to record the situations, automatic thoughts, and emotional responses in multicolumn charts. During the sessions, clients are questioned about aspects of the situations they describe (orally or in the charts) that they may have excluded. This is because persons who are depressed frequently construct their experiences narrowly, omitting dimensions that do not conform with their negative schemas. The clinician challenges the client's distorted thinking and presents alternative explanations based on a comprehensive consideration of evidence. In addition, the clinician elicits (during the sessions and in homework assignments) rational alternative explanations from clients, which can be incorporated as an additional column for their charts. Other techniques are used to help clients identify dysfunctional cognitions and restructure them. Clients are given further information about the relationship between their feelings and depressogenic assumptions. At times, clients are asked to test out their assumptions in assigned activities to be performed between sessions.

CONCLUDING SESSIONS As therapy draws to a close, the client is given more responsibility for initiation of the agenda, homework assignments, and setting goals. Cognitive and behavioral techniques are used to anticipate and practice rational strategies of interpreting experiences. Depending on the client's progress, attention can be given at this time to changing maladaptive schemas (Wright et al., 2009). During the last few sessions, the client is prepared for termination and for retaining the benefits of thinking constructively in the future. Client and clinician discuss issues the client is likely to face in the future and strategies with which to handle them.

Methods of Cognitive Therapy

Cognitive therapy employs an array of cognitive and behavioral methods and procedures, some of which are used throughout therapy and others that vary in relation to the severity of the depression and the stage of therapy.

COGNITIVE METHODS Although cognitive techniques are implemented throughout therapy, the nature of these techniques varies over time. In the beginning, the clinician uses a didactic approach to explain what automatic thoughts are and how they affect emotions and behavior (Beck et al., 1979). Then the client is helped to *identify automatic thoughts* in his or her daily life. The client may be given a homework assignment to keep a record of events and associated negative cognitions and emotions that occur between sessions. This assignment, as well as specific examples that the client offers during sessions, can be used as a basis for a *discussion of cognitive errors*. The client and the clinician together look at the facts and the client's interpretation of the event and *generate alternative explanations*. Such a logical examination can result in *distancing* oneself from one's experience (becoming more objective) and in shifting responsibility from the client to another source (*reattribution*). The client can learn how to modify negative cognitions through a homework assignment in which automatic thoughts and alternative explanations are listed, or through a process of questioning and presenting modified interpretations during the session (Beck, 1985; Beck et al., 1979).

During the course of therapy, *hypotheses* that underlie a client's behavior are identified and *tested empirically*. For example, Mrs. Dell, who was depressed and slightly overweight, spent little time outside her home. She explained that she only shops for groceries early in the morning because later in the day, when the store is crowded, people stare at her large body. The hypothesis the clinician formulated was, "Because you are depressed, you expect other people to view you in a negative way." This woman was asked to shop at various times and keep track of the number of people who stared at her each time she shopped. She discovered that whatever time she went, very few people stared at her.

BEHAVIORAL METHODS If the client is severely depressed, behavioral strategies are used early in the process. Clients who are so depressed that they cannot get out of bed, for example, are helped to become more active through the use of *activity schedules* and *graded task assignments* (Beck et al., 1979). At first the clinician makes the client write up a schedule of daily activities. If the client does not appear to be sufficiently active, the clinician and the client develop a schedule of hourly activities that expand upon the client's usual repertoire. New and more demanding activities are added gradually over time (graded task assignments). Clients are also asked to keep a record of activities that are accomplished and to grade them on a scale from 0 to 5 according to the degree of pleasure (P) and sense of mastery (M) that are experienced (Beck et al., 1979, 1985).

Other behavioral techniques complement cognitive strategies (Beck et al., 1979). *Role playing*, with the clinician and the client taking the roles of parties described by the client, makes visible the difficulties a client is having in a social interaction. Identified problems are often related to automatic thoughts. In addition, *cognitive rehearsal* helps clients prepare mentally for the performance of tasks the client anticipates will be difficult. With this technique, the client is asked to imagine performing a task, step by step. In walking through the situation, the client identifies obstacles and thinking patterns that impede accomplishment of the task. The cognitive rehearsal is repeated until the obstacles are overcome in the imagination. Then the client is asked to perform the task in real life. In addition, *diversion* techniques are used. The client is encouraged to become distracted from painful emotions by engaging in other activities, focusing on environmental stimuli, and imagining pleasant scenes.

Case Example

Maxine Brown is a 45-year-old married woman who entered therapy saying that she was so far down and could not get up. She reported a loss of appetite, sleeping excessively, and a lack of energy. Mrs. Brown said that she was having difficulty getting motivated to take care of all the people who needed her and felt like a failure as a wife and stepmother. The client related that she has been married to Mr. Brown for a year and that everything was "perfect" until Mr. Brown's 16-year-old son Todd moved in with them four months ago. Todd leaves his dirty clothes scattered throughout the house, uses foul language, and expects Mrs. Brown to pick up after him. Mrs. Brown said that instead of feeling love for Todd, she resents him.

Mrs. Brown said that she could hardly manage her responsibilities before Todd moved in. She has a part-time job as a bookkeeper, is principal caregiver for a sick uncle who lives alone in an apartment Mrs. Brown cleans, and has homemaking responsibilities. Mrs. Brown explained that Mr. Brown takes care of the lawn and home repair but considers housework "woman's work." Although the client usually keeps up with the housework, since Todd moved in with them, she has let the laundry and cleaning accumulate. She has been going to work regularly, but she does not work as quickly as she used to.

When asked how Todd came to live with them, Mrs. Brown said that his mother arranged this with Mr. Brown several months ago. Apparently Todd's mother was planning to remarry and the relationship between Todd and her gentleman friend was not good. When asked if she was involved in the decision to take Todd, she said that her husband did not ask her; he acted as if they had no choice. When asked how she felt about not being asked, Mrs. Brown said she felt slighted. She said that she would have agreed to take Todd if she were asked, because Mr. Brown had an obligation to his son, but she would have liked to have been part of the decision. Mrs. Brown said that she has a great deal of resentment built up inside because after she struggled for 15 years as a single parent, her own children are independent and she was looking forward to married life as a couple without parental responsibilities. She wondered if she was a selfish person.

During the preliminary evaluation and the first interview, the clinician established that Mrs. Brown had a diagnosis of MDD, single episode. The client reported that there were previous times in her life when she felt depressed, but she has always been able to "snap out of it." According to the Beck Depression Inventory, Mrs. Brown was mildly to moderately depressed. She showed strengths in her continued functioning at home and at work.

In the first session, the client and the clinician (a social worker) identified several problems and target symptoms. They agreed that she had problems communicating her feelings to her husband, difficulty setting limits with her stepson, and problems managing her responsibilities. Target symptoms were sadness, lack of motivation, anger, and lack of interest in eating. She had vague suicidal thoughts but no intention to kill herself. The client and the social worker agreed that Mrs. Brown's difficulty getting motivated to perform her responsibilities and the anger that Mrs. Brown felt but did not express would be the target symptoms initially. The client was asked to bring an hourly schedule of her daily activities to the next session.

At the beginning of the next session, the clinician and Mrs. Brown developed an agenda for this meeting. They would review the client's homework, discuss events of the past week, and explore the target symptoms they had discussed last time. When Mrs. Brown handed the schedule to the social worker, she mentioned that she did not feel that she accomplished very much during the past week. Nevertheless, the clinician observed that Mrs. Brown's schedule was packed. The client spent most of her time cooking, cleaning, taking care of others, or at work, and she spent little time resting or engaging in recreational activities. When asked what else she thinks she should have accomplished, Mrs. Brown said that she did not clean her uncle's kitchen, did the laundry only twice a week, and did not clean her stepson's room, although it was a mess. This led into a discussion of events in her life during the last week. Mrs. Brown said that she felt better after the last interview and that since then she has become more aware of her anger. She said that she resents cleaning up after her stepson; therefore, she puts off the task of cleaning his room. She also has resentment toward her husband for agreeing to have his son come and toward Mr. Brown's former wife for sending him here. Mrs. Brown said that she feels tired as well as resentful. The social worker then asked the client to explain her expectations of herself in relation to Todd. Mrs. Brown said that she expects herself to feel love toward Todd and to care about him as she cared about her own children. She believes that she has an obligation to take on the responsibility of mothering him without resenting it. She views this as something she owes her husband, who is the principal wage earner. The social worker asked Mrs. Brown if she thought she could force herself to feel love if she did not feel this emotion. Mrs. Brown supposed that she could not, but blamed herself for not being able to love Todd. She said that she wished that she were not so angry at Todd; that maybe she could feel love if she did not feel anger. The social worker questioned Mrs. Brown's reasoning about feeling love.

SOCIAL WORKER:	What makes you think you must love Todd?
MRS. BROWN:	If I'm his stepmother, I should love him.
SOCIAL WORKER:	You can be a stepmother to him without feeling love.
MRS. BROWN:	How can I? If I didn't love him, I'd be a cruel stepmother.
SOCIAL WORKER:	It sounds as if you believe that you need to love him in order to treat him well—that if you didn't love him, you'd be cruel.
MRS. BROWN:	I'm not cruel and I don't hate him, but I don't especially like him either. I think I could like him better if he would cooperate.

The social worker and the client then discussed Mrs. Brown's resentment of Todd's lack of cooperation further. This led into the following discussion:

SOCIAL WORKER:	Can you be more specific and tell me what you are angry at Todd about?
MRS. BROWN:	He doesn't seem to be in the least concerned about me and all the work he has created for me. He doesn't make his bed or clean his room. He doesn't bring his dishes to the table.

	He doesn't do the laundry. My girls took care of their own rooms and they used to help me with the dishes. Todd doesn't do anything.
SOCIAL WORKER:	It sounds as if you believe he has responsibilities around the house and he isn't doing his part.
MRS. BROWN:	Yes.
SOCIAL WORKER:	I wonder if you have communicated this to him.
MRS. BROWN:	I never had to tell my girls; they just knew. I keep waiting for Todd to volunteer to do something but he seems to expect to be waited on. He should know he has responsibilities.
SOCIAL WORKER:	It looks as if he does not know. He can't read your mind. Now that he's living with you, so it's up to you to tell him what the rules are.
MRS. BROWN:	You mean I should tell him what I want him to do around the house?
SOCIAL WORKER:	Yes, tell him what you expect of him. Regardless of how you feel about him, you have the right to have expectations of him.

The homework that was assigned after this session had two parts. The first assignment was for Mrs. Brown to communicate her expectations of Todd to both her husband and Todd. It was important for Mrs. Brown to explain to her husband that she could not assume responsibilities that should be Todd's. In addition, Mrs. Brown was to continue to record her activities, but was to rate them in terms of the pleasure she received. Meanwhile she was encouraged to do more activities that she enjoyed.

Next time Mrs. Brown reported satisfaction in how the conversation with Todd went. She told him that he was responsible for cleaning his room, setting the table, and washing the dishes. He complained but said he would go along with what she wanted. She said that her husband questioned her decision to have Todd set the table and wash the dishes, but when she told her husband that Todd's lack of cooperation was contributing to her depression, he supported her. Mrs. Brown rated all her activities in the low end of the scale in pleasure, except for an hour a day she took to watch TV, which she rated 3 (on a scale that went from 0 to 5).

During the next few sessions, Mrs. Brown reported feeling satisfied that Todd was cooperating. Nevertheless, she still felt depressed. The social worker identified some of the client's beliefs that seemed to be problematic for her. Mrs. Brown believed that she had to be a perfect housekeeper and that she had to take care of whatever was asked of her by family members. Her depressogenic assumption was "in order to be happy, I have to be successful in whatever I undertake" (Beck, 1976, p. 255). During one session, the following conversation took place:

SOCIAL WORKER:	What do you think would happen if you did not do all of the chores you usually do next week?
MRS. BROWN:	I would feel like a failure.
SOCIAL WORKER:	What do you think would happen to the work you did not complete?
MRS. BROWN:	I would probably get it done the following week.

SOCIAL WORKER:	So it is possible that you can do fewer things than you usually do?
MRS. BROWN:	I could do less. But whatever I do get done does not seem to be enough.
SOCIAL WORKER:	How can you tell what's "enough"?
MRS. BROWN:	When I'm exhausted, I know I've done enough. I usually work until am exhausted.
SOCIAL WORKER:	What do you think would happen if you stopped working on chores before you reached the exhaustion point?
MRS. BROWN:	I don't know; I've never done that.
SOCIAL WORKER:	Perhaps we can work this into your homework assignment for this week.
MRS. BROWN:	I'd be willing to try that.

With this and other homework assignments, Mrs. Brown recognized that she did not have to work as hard as she was working; that she could accomplish smaller amounts of work at a given time, yet leave time to engage in activities that are pleasurable. With her stepson doing his share, she had more positive feelings toward him. As she approached termination, she began to think of ways in which she could obtain help from a homemaker home health aide for her uncle. During the last few sessions, she discussed her reluctance to share her feelings about Todd's coming to live with them when her husband first brought up the topic. She recognized that she had the distorted belief that she was not allowed to express her feelings when they deviated from what she thought were her husband's expectations. Mrs. Brown expressed confidence that she could improve her relationship with her husband as well as her own sense of well-being by breaking this unstated rule. In the last interview, Mrs. Brown reported that she and her husband had a discussion about chores around the house and that they agreed to distribute the household tasks more equitably and to go out to eat once a week. She said that she has learned to pace herself better and was no longer depressed.

As this case illustrates, cognitive therapy can be used to help depressed individuals who have distorted ideas to change their thinking and behavior. A short-term therapy with a record of effectiveness, it can promote relief from painful emotions and dysfunctional ways of thinking about oneself, others, and the future. A therapy that is guided by scientific reasoning, it promotes logical thinking, which can be useful in problem solving. Such an approach is appealing to clinicians who value intellectual processing and to clients who are capable of learning to examine their beliefs.

MINDFULNESS COGNITIVE THERAPY

New research is emerging on mindfulness-based cognitive therapy (MBCT) with empirical support (Grepmair et al., 2007; Ma & Teasdale, 2004). This type of approach is based on the theoretical framework of the cognitive vulnerability model of depression relapse (Teasdale et al., 2000). The model posits that an individual can reduce the risk of depressive relapse by increasing his or her awareness of negative thinking at the actual time of reoccurrence or potential relapse. The individual can be trained in and practice inward monitoring or mindfulness, that is, meditation, breathing, body scanning, listening to sounds, teaching concentration, and focusing skills (Thompson & Waltz, 2007). MBCT can assist the client to be more focused and aware of thoughts though somewhat removed from it in a decentralized way. Typically, MBCT is taught in eight weekly group sessions that run from two to three hours (Teasdale et al., 2000). In each session, formal meditation practices are taught and practiced that are designed to increase concentration and decouple the individual from the formal thoughts, feelings, and sensations. Daily homework is provided on skill practice and use in daily life to increase awareness of problem situations and how the individual is affected.

EVIDENCE-BASED PRACTICE: INTERPERSONAL THERAPY

Interpersonal therapy was developed by clinicians and researchers associated with the New Haven–Boston Collaborative Depression Project (Weissman & Klerman, 1989). It has been tested on nonbipolar depressed persons, using comparison groups treated with medication, alternative therapies, and placebos. There is considerable empirical evidence supporting its efficacy (de Mello, de Jesus, Bacaltchuk, Verdeli, & Neugebauer, 2005; Weissman & Klerman, 1989; Weissman, Markowitz, & Klerman, 2000).

Interpersonal therapy for depression is predicated on the idea that depression develops in an interpersonal and social context (Klerman, Weissman, Rounsaville, & Chevron, 1984). Theoretically, IPT is rooted in the psychobiological framework of Adolf Meyer (see Chapter 2) and the interpersonal theory of Harry Stack Sullivan. Meyer viewed psychiatric disorders as the outcome of attempts to adapt to the environment; Sullivan was interested in the interactions *between* people (Weissman & Klerman, 1989). The team responsible for the development of IPT also acknowledged the contributions of other theorists (e.g., Frieda Fromm-Reichmann and Silvano Arieti) who looked at the social and interpersonal dimensions of depression.

This therapy recognizes that depression derives from many sources and has diverse forms of expression. A number of causes—genetics, environmental stress, personality characteristics, and early life experiences—"combine in complex ways to produce the etiology and pathogenesis of depression" (Klerman et al., 1984, p. 38). Similarly, depression may be manifested differently in different clients. The proponents of this therapy use the medical model when they define depression as an illness and allow clients to assume the sick role (Klerman et al., 1984; Weissman et al., 2000). Although medication may be used, the focus of psychotherapy is social.

Interpersonal therapy is a brief, focused, present-oriented, time-limited form of treatment (Klerman et al., 1984; Weissman et al., 2000). The weekly psychotherapy usually lasts twelve to sixteen weeks, during which one or two problems related to an individual's current interpersonal relationships and life situation are addressed. No attempts are made to alter the personality structure or promote insight into intrapsychic conflicts, defenses, and the transference. Early life experiences, dysfunctional behaviors, and distorted cognitions are viewed in relation to current interpersonal relationships rather than as problems in themselves (Klerman et al., 1984). Developed originally as an individual therapy, it can also be used with couples, in group, and in telephone formats (Weissman, Markowitz, & Klerman, 2007).

The Therapeutic Relationship

The relationship between the clinician and the client in IPT is developed along the lines established by Rogerian therapy, that is, the therapist is warm and nonjudgmental and communicates unconditional positive regard (Klerman et al., 1984; Weissman et al., 2000). A positive transference is left alone; discord between the client and the clinician is compared with problematic interpersonal relationships in the client's life. The clinician is more active in IPT than in ego psychological treatment. Nevertheless, the client is responsible for making changes. The clinician assumes the role of client advocate and provides support, reassurance, and optimism to promote the client's efforts to change (Klerman et al., 1984).

The Intervention Process

Interpersonal therapy is implemented over three phases, each of which encompasses specific activities. At all times work is directed at achieving the goals of IPT—reduction of depressed symptoms and improvement of interpersonal functioning. The content of these phases that will be summarized hereafter is adapted from Weissman et al.'s (2007) *Clinician's Quick Guide to Interpersonal Psychotherapy* as well as the earlier source book (Klerman et al., 1984).

During the *initial phase* of one to three sessions, the client describes the symptoms and the interpersonal context of his or her life, a diagnosis is made, and a treatment contract is developed. Before a diagnosis is made, a client is referred to a physician to discern whether a medical condition is producing the depression. Meanwhile the clinician gathers information about the client's history, symptoms, and current functioning. The team that developed IPT recommends the use of the Hamilton Rating Scale for Depression to guide the review of symptoms with the client. This scale includes questions that probe for a depressed mood, feelings of guilt, insomnia, suicidal ideations, somatic anxiety, psychomotor retardation, sexual symptoms, weight loss, and the like. If the symptoms are consistent with a diagnosis of depression (and a medical condition is ruled out), the clinician links the symptoms with a diagnostic label and informs the client that he or she is depressed.

The clinician then proceeds to educate the client about depression. This includes the nature of depression, its course, and means of treatment. Facts about its prevalence in the general population, distribution among men and women, and the effectiveness of treatment should be explained. The clinician should convey optimism about prospects for recovery. At this point, the client is given permission to adopt the sick role, which allows the client to be excused from some social role obligations while seeking treatment. Next the client may be referred to a psychiatrist for an evaluation for medication.

During the initial phase, information is gathered and an assessment is made of the interpersonal context of the client's life. The clinician can start by asking the client to explain what was happening in his or her life when the symptoms began. The client is asked to identify and describe relationships with significant persons (family members, friends, coworkers), recent life events (infidelity, laid off from a job), and contexts (home, work) that constitute the contours of the person's life. The clinician encourages the client to talk about conflictual interpersonal relationships and interactions and about expectations of each party in a relationship. The client is asked to identify positive and negative aspects of relationships and how these relationships might change. Although the emphasis is on current relationships and life situations, the client may also talk about important past relationships.

Discussions about the interpersonal context should facilitate the identification of major problem areas. The developers of IPT identified four issues that predominate in clients with depression. These are grief, interpersonal disputes, role transitions, and interpersonal deficits. The clinician and the client try to arrive at a mutual decision about one or two primary issues that will become the focus of treatment. To do this, the clinician promotes the client's awareness of the relationship between symptoms of depression and interpersonal issues.

The initial phase concludes with the clinician providing an oral summary of the problem, an explanation of the concepts of IPT, and the development of a treatment contract. First, the clinician communicates an assessment of the major problems and how they are related to the interpersonal context of the client's life. For example, Tom Smith, a 35-year-old, recently separated man, was told:

> You seem to be depressed about being apart from your wife and children. You are living alone now, and you seem to be feeling lonely. It is clear that you do not want to lose your family and you are hoping that your wife will change her mind. Your wife, however, is acting as if she wants a divorce. You seem to be confused about what to do—try to win her back or come to terms with a divorce.

Some clients may have difficulty grasping the relationship between their mood and the interpersonal context of their lives. Instead they may blame themselves for their problems. These clients need to be told that life is made up of people and that the way relationships go affects feelings. Similarly, the lack of significant relationships can interfere with one's happiness. As one clinician put it, "Relationships are complicated; they cause problems. On the other hand, not having relationships is also difficult."

The explanation of concepts of IPT includes practical aspects (short-term, weekly one-hour sessions, fees, rules about cancellation and missed appointments) and expectations. The client is given the responsibility to use the sessions to review relationships and bring up current issues and feelings, including feelings about the therapeutic relationship.

The treatment contract consists of an oral agreement on the major problems and on two or three goals to be reached during therapy. These goals should be related to the problems and should be realistic and achievable within the short time span of treatment. For example, the 35-year-old man described earlier had problems in all four areas (grief, interpersonal disputes, role transitions, interpersonal deficits). The contract, however, was to work on limited goals:

1. Understand the circumstances and disputes that led up to the separation (interpersonal dispute).
2. Determine whether the disputes between his wife and him can be repaired (interpersonal dispute).
3. If the marriage cannot be repaired, grieve over the loss of previous roles (husband, live-in father) and come to terms with and assume new roles (single man, visiting father) (role transition).

During the *intermediate phase*, the problem areas and related goals are addressed, and at the same time attention is paid to the client's depressive symptoms. Efforts are made to engage the client in treatment. During therapy, the client is encouraged to understand the relationship between symptoms and interpersonal problems. As Table 8.3 indicates, the intervention goals and strategy during the intermediate phase are related to the problem area.

If the issue is grief, the client is helped to mourn by reviewing life with the lost person up to and following the loss, exploring feelings, and establishing new relationships. When role transition is the problem, the client is encouraged to discuss the advantages and disadvantages of the previous and new roles, mourn the loss of the old role through the expression of feelings, and develop a positive attitude, supports, and skills that are consistent with the new role. As for interpersonal disputes, the history, stage of dispute, and discrepant role expectations are discussed and actions are taken to reconcile or resolve the problem. If the client has interpersonal

TABLE 8.3	Implementation of Interpersonal Therapy during the Intermediate Phase	
Problem	**Goals**	**Strategies**
1. Grief (over a death)	**1.** Facilitate mourning process. **2.** Help the patient reestablish interest and relationships to substitute for what has been.	**1.** Review depressive symptoms. **2.** Relate onset of symptoms to death of significant other. **3.** Reconstruct the patient's relationship with the deceased. **4.** Describe the sequence of events and consequences of events just prior to, during, and after the death. **5.** Explore associated feelings (negative as well as positive). **6.** Consider ways of becoming involved with others.
2. Role transitions (change from one situation and associated role to another)	**1.** Mourn and accept the loss of old role. **2.** Help the patient to regard the new role as more positive. **3.** Restore self-esteem by developing a sense of mastery regarding demands of new roles.	**1.** Review depressive symptoms. **2.** Relate depressive symptoms to difficulty in coping with some recent life change. **3.** Review positive and negative aspects of old and new roles. **4.** Explore feelings about what is lost. **5.** Explore feelings about the change itself. **6.** Explore opportunities in the new role. **7.** Realistically evaluate what is lost. **8.** Encourage appropriate release of affect. **9.** Encourage development of a social support system and of new skills called in a new role.
3. Interpersonal disputes (conflicts)	**1.** Identify dispute. **2.** Choose plan of action. **3.** Modify expectations or faulty communication patterns to bring about a satisfactory resolution.	**1.** Review depressive symptoms. **2.** Relate symptoms' onset to overt or covert dispute with a significant other with whom patient is currently involved. **3.** Determine stage of the dispute (renegotiation, impasse, dissolution). **4.** Understand how nonreciprocal role expectations relate to dispute (issues, different expectations and values, options, likelihood of finding alternatives, resources). **5.** Are there parallels in other relationships (benefits, assumptions)? **6.** How is the dispute perpetuated?
4. Interpersonal deficits	**1.** Reduce the patient's social isolation. **2.** Encourage formation of new relationships.	**1.** Review depressive symptoms. **2.** Relate depressive symptoms to problems of social isolation or unfulfillment. **3.** Review past significant relationships including their negative and positive aspects. **4.** Explore repetitive patterns in relationships. **5.** Discuss patient's positive and negative feelings about therapist and seek parallels in other relationships.

Source: From Klerman et al. (1984). Reprinted by permission of Perseus Books, Inc., Publishers, New York.

deficits, the goals are to reduce social isolation and develop new relationships through a review of past relationships, identification of repetitive interpersonal patterns, and a discussion of parallels between the interaction with the therapist and relationships in the client's personal life. For Smith, the intermediate phase went as follows:

Mr. Smith explained, tearfully, that he and his wife were happy during the first ten years of their marriage, although there had been hard times. Last year, when he became unemployed, his wife took a job at a local warehouse, her first job. Although she claimed that she loved her job, Mr. Smith thought that she "changed for the worse" since working. She went out drinking after work with her new friends (while he babysat) and lost interest in housework. Meanwhile Mr. Smith had trouble finding a new job. Finally he located a well-paying job as a truck driver. When he told his wife that she no longer had to work, she refused to quit her job. In the past few months, they were increasingly distant. Their sex life was minimal and they hardly saw each other (he worked days and she worked nights). Mr. Smith said that he wants his old Cindy back, but the new Cindy does not seem to want him. He suspected that she was having an affair.

In the course of therapy during the intermediate phase, Mr. Smith recognized that his wife had changed over the years from a dependent "girl" to a woman who wanted more independence. He, however, wanted their relationship to stay the same. He also recognized that his wife was not satisfied with his unsteady pattern of working and wanted security. He expressed willingness to change himself by changing his expectations of the relationship.

Nevertheless, Mr. Smith's efforts to meet with his wife to discuss his willingness to change were unsuccessful. Mrs. Smith blocked his calls with an answering machine and did not return his messages. When he picked up the children for visits, a relative or friend greeted him at the door. His letters were not answered, except for a brief note advising him that all communications should be handled through her attorney. Mr. Smith heard rumors that she was going out with her boss. Finally Mr. Smith was served with divorce papers.

The accumulation of circumstances led Mr. Smith and the clinician to believe that it was not possible to resolve the interpersonal dispute between Tom and Cindy Smith; that divorce was inevitable. At this point he began to grieve the loss of Cindy and his role as husband and live-in father. Mr. Smith cried during therapy sessions and reported early morning wakening, loss of appetite, and feelings of depersonalization. He was referred to a psychiatrist for an evaluation for medication, which was prescribed. Meanwhile Mr. Smith shared his feelings about not having a wife and not sharing a home with her and the children; he had a difficult time being alone. He reported having great love for his wife, even though she did not seem to love him. He said that having a wife and family to go home to gave him a purpose for living and people to work for. Further exploration of his feelings, however, led to his expression of anger and anguish. He felt that he had been a devoted husband who was "dumped" when someone more affluent came along. He felt rejected sexually (and as a man) and longed for his wife's affection.

Nevertheless, Mr. Smith continued to work as a truck driver. Toward the end of the intermediate stage, he and the clinician discussed ways he could be a visiting father. He came up with such ideas as taking the children camping, on picnics, and to the zoo. He also (working through a lawyer) negotiated a visitation plan that included dinner a couple of evenings a week and overnight visits on weekends. In addition, Mr. Smith considered other ways to fill up his empty evenings, such as visiting his father and siblings (who had been making efforts to reach out to him), becoming involved in a local church, and joining Parents without Partners. Mr. Smith said that he did not feel ready to go out with other women at this time. Although he still reported sadness over the loss of his wife and the family as he knew it, he recognized that it was possible to build a new life in the future.

Early in the *termination phase* (during the last three or four sessions), the client is told that therapy will be ending shortly. The client is given the opportunity to express feelings about termination and about the therapist. The clinician helps the client grieve over the impending loss while at the same time assuring the client that he or she is capable of coping independently. The remaining time is used to evaluate the gains made in treatment and to prepare for the future. At times issues of loss that were present during treatment are replayed:

> Upon hearing that he had only four sessions left, Mr. Smith expressed sadness and feelings of hopelessness. At this point, the clinician reviewed with him the issues of loss that he has been facing and difficulties he has been having in being alone. Mr. Smith expressed gratitude to the therapist for being there and tried to convince her to extend the sessions beyond the twelve that had been agreed upon. The therapist noted that there were parallels in his wanting the therapy to last and his unwillingness to accept the impending divorce from his wife. Mr. Smith described himself as a "needy guy who doesn't see the handwriting on the wall." When asked how he felt about termination, the client expressed feelings of rejection. After a couple of sessions, however, he recognized that the therapy was supposed to be twelve weeks and that he had benefited from it. Mr. Smith said that although he felt bad about the divorce and about termination, he felt challenged at having a chance to rebuild his life as a single man. He reported joining a support group for single adults at a nearby church and increased contacts with his children, father, and siblings. Hopeful for a better future, he no longer was depressed.

Methods of Interpersonal Therapy

In IPT, the clinician uses a number of methods.

EXPLORATION   This method elicits information about the client's problems and symptoms through directive and nondirective questioning and responses. Nondirective techniques include open-ended questions, nonverbal or minimal communication ("uh huh"), encouraging the client to continue to talk, inviting the client to expand on ideas that are presented, and the use of silence as an encourager. Directive techniques include asking questions related to specific symptoms and interpersonal relationships.

ENCOURAGEMENT OF AFFECT   This method promotes the expression and experience of painful emotions. The clinician elicits the client's feelings ("how did you feel about that?") and responds by accepting the client's pain. This is especially useful in work with clients who have difficulty identifying and expressing their feelings. For clients who are overwhelmed with affect, the client should be helped to control feelings.

COMMUNICATION ANALYSIS   This method analyzes communication breakdown, especially in problems involving interpersonal disputes. The clinician asks the client to describe in detail specific incidents of faulty communication. Together they identify ambiguous messages, false assumptions, and indirect methods of response. Alternative interpretations and responses are suggested.

CLARIFICATION   The clinician attempts to get the client to rethink a previous statement and, thus, arrive at a deeper understanding of what has been said. This can be achieved by paraphrasing a client's message, asking the client to rephrase his or her own words, examining the implications of what a client has said, or drawing attention to unusual beliefs and inconsistencies between messages.

BEHAVIOR CHANGE TECHNIQUES   These techniques encourage behavior changes that are discussed or modeled during therapy to be enacted in the client's interpersonal behavior in everyday life. These are implemented through directive techniques, such as limited setting, giving suggestions or advice, providing information or education, modeling, and provision of direct assistance; decision analysis; and role playing. Therapeutic efforts to assist the client in the resolution of problems are predicated on the client's willingness to assume responsibility for his or her own actions. Accordingly, directive techniques are used cautiously in such a way to preserve the client's autonomy. With decision analysis, the client examines alternative solutions to a problem and probable consequences of each option. The clinician offers ideas about solutions and helps the client think through the alternatives, but the client makes decisions. With role playing, the clinician plays the role of a person in the client's life with whom the client is having a problematic relationship. This technique is used so that the clinician can assess the nature of the problem and the client can learn more constructive communication strategies.

USE OF THE THERAPEUTIC RELATIONSHIP   Although IPT does not emphasize the development of a transference, the client is encouraged from the beginning to share positive and negative feelings about the clinician and the therapeutic process. Moreover, if the client interacts with the clinician in distorted ways, the clinician will discuss these patterns with the client. Distortions in the client–therapist relationship are of diagnostic value; they suggest ways in which the client interacts with others. The clinician's acceptance of the clients' feelings about the clinician provides an opportunity to correct distortions and deal with sensitive issues in relationships.

In the case that was described in this chapter, several of these techniques were used. Exploratory techniques were used in the initial and intermediate phases to determine what was going on in Mr. Smith's life, who his significant others were, and whether repair of the marital dispute was possible. When Mr. Smith provided this information in a distorted way ("she's changed for the worse"), clarification techniques were used to determine what and who had changed and why. When the client realized that there was no hope of reconciliation, he began to grieve. The clinician encouraged him to express feelings, which were primarily sadness, loneliness, anger, anguish, and longing. Mr. Smith also felt the loss of his wife as a sex partner and felt that his masculinity had been challenged by a competitor. Mr. Smith was encouraged to change his behavior through a discussion of options that were available to him as he made the transition to the roles of visiting father and single adult. The therapeutic relationship was used in the end to help Mr. Smith deal with the separations in his life.

Interpersonal therapy encompasses perspectives and strategies employed by clinical social workers. First, it gives the social field the primary focus of attention, which is consistent with the person-in-situation perspective used in social work. Second, it focuses on relationships, which are critical in working with depressed women. Third, it includes stages of intervention and techniques that are widely used in the field. Research studies have found that interpersonal psychotherapy is efficacious not only with adults who are acutely depressed but also with depressed geriatric and HIV-positive clients (Hinrichsen, 2008; Markowitz & Weissman, 1995).

Interpersonal therapy is particularly compatible with the biopsychosocial conceptual framework of this book. First, it recognizes that depression has a biological base. Where appropriate, clients are offered the opportunity to take medication and assume the sick role. Second, it recognizes the social environmental context in which human problems arise and psychological problems that contribute to becoming frozen in social roles. IPT recognizes that there are multiple forces that influence the development and creation of problems. Its emphasis on the social context differs from the emphasis on cognition that is evident in the approach that will be discussed next. The major treatment manual for IPT is Weissman et al.'s (2000) *Comprehensive Guide to Interpersonal Psychotherapy.*

EVIDENCE-BASED PRACTICE: PROBLEM-SOLVING THERAPY

Problem-solving therapy for depression is based on a model of depression that characterizes social problem solving (SPS) as serving both mediating (e.g., Kant, D'Zurilla, & Maydeu-Olivares, 1997) and moderating (e.g., Nezu & Ronan, 1988) roles regarding the relationship between stressful life events and depression. Problem solving has been defined as the cognitive-behavioral process by which a person attempts to identify or discover effective or adaptive means of coping with stressful problems encountered during the course of everyday living (D'Zurilla & Nezu, 2007). In this context, it involves the process whereby individuals attempt to direct their coping efforts at altering the problematic nature of a stressful situation itself, their reactions to such situations, or both. Table 8.4 illustrates the therapeutic process of PST for late-life depression based on the work of Gellis and colleagues (2007, 2008) and Nezu and D'Zurilla (1989) for their work on adult depression. PST can range from six to twenty sessions and may last from thirty to sixty minutes depending on the setting and population served. Sessions are structured using the five steps of problem-solving and cognitive techniques delineated in Table 8.4. The PST therapist utilizes the therapeutic relationship to guide the client toward positive problem-solving current life stresses. Chapter 3 provides further details on problem-solving therapy for depression.

Problem-solving conceptualization suggests that depression can result as a function of deficiencies, or decreased effectiveness, in these problem orientation and problem-solving style dimensions (Nezu, 2004). For example, depressed individuals are often characterized by a negative orientation, having little confidence in their coping skills to deal with stressful problems, often believing that problems are insurmountable, frequently blaming themselves for causing the problem, and being depressed when problems arise. Collectively, negative beliefs decrease the client's motivation to engage in any meaningful coping attempts. One's ability to effectively define and formulate problems and to set realistic goals are also decreased when depressed, thus, making it very difficult to identify effective solutions. Often depressed individuals set unrealistically high goals and when they are not completed, frustration, blame, and decreased motivation are likely to occur. Depressed individuals also tend to generate both fewer and less effective alternatives to problem situations. The depressed client may also have difficulty carrying out a solution plan due to specific behavioral and social skill deficits. The depressed client may be distraught with the coping attempt and may feel that the personal goals have not been achieved.

TABLE 8.4 Problem-Solving Therapy Sessions for Depression

Session	Content
1 Identify Problems Develop Goal	Orient and introduce problem-solving therapy for depression (adopt positive attitude toward problem solving); explain connections between daily problems, stress, mood, and pleasurable events; review causes, symptoms, medications, and treatments for depression; identify and define nature of stressful problems in daily living; identify patient coping responses; realistic goal setting for relief of problem; orient to and choose two pleasurable activities (daily scheduling); set homework activity; obtain permission to contact and update primary care physician; brief telephone contact with patient during week as reminder to complete homework and pleasurable activities
2 Brainstorm Alternative Solutions	Review homework; review log of pleasurable activities; review symptoms; review coping responses to problem; identify problem-solving style; review goals; generate many alternative solutions; identify/choose one or two solutions based on criteria—realistic, achievable, cost, effort (predict outcome effectiveness and consequences); instruct patient to try out chosen solutions with action plan and monitor outcome; troubleshoot any difficulties; set homework; choose/schedule two pleasurable activities each day; brief telephone contact during week as reminder to complete homework and pleasurable activities
3 Review Advantages (pros) and Disadvantages (cons)	Review homework; review performance outcome for chosen solution; teach patient to reward self for efforts in attempted problem solving; review log of pleasurable activities; review symptoms; review goal and alternative solutions if solution was less than successful, or examine new problem and renew goals; brainstorm alternative solutions; choose one or two solutions (predict consequences—pros/cons); try solutions with action plan and monitor and evaluate outcome; troubleshoot any difficulties; set homework; choose two pleasurable activities; brief telephone contact during week for homework reminder; review patient progress with assigned homecare provider
4 Decide and Choose Solution(s)	Review homework; review performance outcome for chosen solution; patient rewards self for efforts in attempted problem solving; review log of pleasurable activities; review symptoms; review goal if solution was less than successful, or examine new problem and renew goals; generate alternative solutions; choose a solution (predict consequences) based on criteria—realistic, achievable, cost, effort; try solution with action plan, monitor, and evaluate outcome; set homework; troubleshoot any difficulties; choose two pleasurable activities; brief telephone contact during week as reminder to complete homework and pleasurable activities
5 Try Out Chosen Solution(s) Action Plan Monitor	Review homework; review performance outcome for chosen solution; patient rewards self for efforts in attempted problem solving; review log of pleasurable activities; review symptoms; review goal if solution was less than successful, or examine new problem and renew goals; generate alternative solutions; choose a solution (predict consequences); try solution with action plan, monitor, and evaluate outcome; set homework; troubleshoot any difficulties; choose two pleasurable activities; prepare patient for clinical termination; review PST-HC steps; brief telephone contact during week for homework reminder; review patient progress with homecare provider
6 Evaluate Review Skills Closure	Review homework; review performance outcome for chosen solution; patient rewards self for efforts; review log of pleasurable activities; review symptoms; review goal if solution was less than successful, or examine new problem and renew goals; generate alternative solutions; choose a solution (predict consequences); try solution with action plan, monitor, and evaluate outcome; set homework; troubleshoot any difficulties; choose two pleasurable activities; clinical termination with patient; review PST-HC steps and wrap-up; review progress with patient and homecare provider

Problem-solving therapy, then, is geared to teach clients specific skills to (a) enhance their positive problem orientation, (b) decrease their negative orientation, (c) improve their rational problem-solving ability, (d) decrease their tendency to be avoidant, and (e) minimize their tendency to be impulsive and careless when attempting to cope with stressful problems in living. In addition, the PST model is effective as it specifically targets the skills of solving daily living problems and self-efficacy. Through modeling and reinforcement of cognitive and behavioral skills, PST can also increase adults and older adults' sense of self-competence and self-efficacy in taking responsibility for day-to-day management of their lives and for reducing and minimizing the negative emotional and physical effects of any diagnosed medical problems. Improved problem-solving and coping skills along with resulting self-efficacy are potential active components thus likely to buffer against the effect of risk factors on depression. Strengthening self-efficacy by allowing clients the experience of successfully dealing with and thus overcoming specific problems can be a primary strategy for preventing and reducing depression among adults and older adults.

MEDICATION

Clinical social workers frequently work with clients who may need or are already receiving antidepressant medication. Because of the many effective drugs that are now available to treat depression, it is important to have some knowledge of these medications, their characteristics, and side effects.

Antidepressant Medication

Antidepressant medication is used to treat the biological and psychological symptoms of depression. Medication is not required for everyone who is depressed. Among those who need this intervention, different individuals benefit from different medications. It should be noted that there is a high rate (35 to 50 percent) of patient nonresponse to the first antidepressant medication prescribed, and thus, it is important to try other medications taking into consideration the patient's demographics and medical history (Olfson, Marcus, Tedeschi, & Wan, 2006). However, no immediate medication response should also signal to the clinician that one does not need to automatically change the medication if it is not working within less than a month (Papakostas, Perlis, Scalia, Petersen, & Fava, 2006). For example, for those depressed patients taking selective serotonin reuptake inhibitors (SSRIs), it may take up to five weeks to experience a positive response from the medication.

Some of the same drugs used to relieve depression also help anxiety disorders (see Chapter 9) and depression associated with schizophrenia and schizoaffective disorder (see Chapter 12). Similarly, some medications used to treat other disorders (e.g., antipsychotics, mood stabilizers, and antianxiety agents) are used to supplement or augment the effects of antidepressants—a strategy known as *polypharmacy*. The medications that will be described here treat primarily moderate to severe unipolar depression—particularly major depression and dysthymia.

Several classes of antidepressant medications have been developed including SSRIs, dopamine–norepinephrine reuptake inhibitors, serotonin–norepinephrine reuptake inhibitors (SNRIs), tricyclics and tetracyclics, and monoamine oxidase inhibitors (MAOIs). Individual clients respond differently to different medications but some individuals do not respond to any. Each of these drugs may take up to three to five weeks to effect a therapeutic response (Nemeroff & Schatzberg, 1998). Table 8.5 provides an outline of the major groups with the generic and trade names of specific drugs and their adverse side effects listed.

TABLE 8.5	Antidepressant Medications	
Group/Generic Name	**Trade Name**	**Side Effects***
Selective serotonin reuptake inhibitors (SSRIs)	Prozac	Nausea, diarrhea, constipation, appetite loss, headache, somnolence, dizziness, sweating, sexual difficulties, low sodium state.
	Paxil	
fluoxetine	Zoloft	
paroxetine	Celexa	
sertraline	Lexapro	
citalopram		
escitalopram		
Alternative antidepressants		Similar to SSRIs; also sweating
venlafaxine	Effexor	Headache, insomnia, nausea
bupropion	Wellbutrin	Dry mouth, nausea, fatigue
duloxetine	Cymbalta	Sedation, orthostatic hypotension
trazodine	Desyrel	Headache, nausea, dry mouth
nefazodone	Serzone	Somnolence, dry mouth, increased appetite
mirtazapine	Remeron	
Tricyclics and tetracyclics	Tofranil	Sedation, anticholinergic effects, seizures, orthostatic hypotension, sexual dysfunction, weight gain, amenorrhea, cardiovascular effects, overdose. Sudden withdrawal can cause anxiety.
imipramine	Elavil, Endep	
amitriptyline	Surmontil	
trimipramine	Sinequan, Adapin	
doxepin	Norpramin	
desipramine	Aventyl, Pamelor	
nortriptyline	Vivactil	
protriptyline	Ludiomil	
maprotiline	Asendin	
amoxapine		
Monoamine oxidase inhibitors (MAOIs)	Marplan	Eating certain foods can produce a tyramine-induced hypertensive crisis. Adverse interactions with other drugs. Orthostatic hypotension, edema, weight gain, insomnia, sexual dysfunction, blurred vision, sweating, dry mouth, overdose.
	Nardil	
isocarboxazid	Parnate	
phenelzine		
tranylcypromine		

*Except for the alternative antidepressants in which a sample of specific side effects was listed for each antidepressant, the side effects listed apply to each group in general.

Source: Based on Cowen (1998); Nemeroff & Schatzberg (1998); Sadock & Sadock (2007).

SELECTIVE SEROTONIN REUPTAKE INHIBITORS Selective serotonin reuptake inhibitors are, according to depression treatment guidelines, the first line of treatment and have become the drugs of choice by physicians (Andreasen & Black, 2006). These medications are commonly known as Zoloft, Prozac, Paxil, and Celexa, to name a few. They are designed as an antidepressant and antianxiolytic combination. They are currently recommended because they are at least as effective as the older tricyclic antidepressants (TCAs) but are safer and have less serious side effects. They produce fewer anticholinergic effects, less sedation, and little weight gain or orthostatic hypotension. There are, however, adverse side effects for SSRIs as well, but some of these can be reduced by decreasing the dosage (Nemeroff & Schatzberg, 1998). There is a debate about whether SSRIs are as effective as other drugs in the treatment of severe depression (Cowen, 1998).

ALTERNATIVE ANTIDEPRESSANTS   In recent years, a number of additional second-line antidepressant drugs have been introduced including dopamine–norepinephrine reuptake inhibitors and selective SNRIs (SSNRIs). These medications may be used for patients who have had an unsuccessful response with SSRIs or with a personal or family history of positive response to these drugs. Venlafaxine (also known as Effexor), currently most commonly used, is an SSNRI that has the advantage of not producing anticholinergic and sedating effects. It also appears to be particularly effective with individuals with severe depression (Nemeroff & Schatzberg, 1998). Bupropion (also known as Wellbutrin), a dopamine–norepinephrine reuptake inhibitor, does not produce orthostatic hypotension, anticholinergic effects, cardiovascular effects, sedation, or sexual dysfunction (Nemeroff & Schatzberg, 1998). Two other drugs listed on Table 8.5, trazodine and nefazodone, are structurally related to each other. Trazodine has fewer side effects than TCAs, has less severe cardiac effects, and is less likely to produce sexual dysfunction than SSRIs (Cowen, 1998). On the other hand, it has the disadvantages of orthostatic hypotension, excessive sedation, nausea, and dizziness (Cowen, 1998; Nemeroff & Schatzberg, 1998).

TRICYCLIC ANTIDEPRESSANTS   Tricyclic antidepressants are the third line of antidepressant medications. These drugs have a similar chemical structure and effect on the neurotransmitter amines. The first of these compounds that was developed is imipramine (Tofranil). Others include amitriptyline (Elavil), trimipramine (Surmontil), doxepin (Sinequan), desipramine (Norpramin), nortriptyline (Aventyl), and protriptyline (Vivactil). (Clomipramine, which is used to treat obsessive-compulsive disorder, is also in this group of antidepressants.) *Tetracyclic antidepressants* (e.g., maprotiline and amoxapine) have a chemical structure that is similar to that of TCAs.

Although there is little difference in effectiveness among the tricyclics and tetracyclics, they have different associated side effects. Amitriptyline, doxepin, and trimipramine are the most sedating; desipramine and proptriptyline are the least sedating (Sadock & Sadock, 2007). The sedating effect, however, may be desirable because it improves sleep. The tricyclics vary, too, in associated *anticholinergic effects*, that is, symptoms such as dry mouth, retention of urine, constipation, and blurred vision. The most anticholinergic are amitryptyline and trimipramine; the least anticholinergic are desipramine and maprotiline (Sadock & Sadock, 2007). TCAs also produce *orthostatic* (or postural) *hypotension*, that is, a lowering of blood pressure when one changes one's position, which can be a problem for older adults, who may fall and fracture themselves as a consequence. Other side effects are listed in Table 8.5. A major risk is overdosing.

MONOAMINE OXIDASE INHIBITORS   Although effective in treating depression, MAOIs pose health risks and have serious side effects and thus are less commonly used. Persons who take MAOIs are advised to avoid certain foods and beverages (e.g., aged cheese, smoked food, chocolate, wine, beer, fava beans) that are high in tyramine content. Consumption of these products can precipitate a hypertensive crisis (sweating, dizziness, high blood pressure) that may be life-threatening. Early indicators of an impending crisis are headaches, nausea, and vomiting. MAOIs have additional adverse effects such as orthostatic hypotension, weight gain, sexual dysfunction, and edema, which need to be frequently monitored (Sadock & Sadock, 2007).

ANTIDEPRESSANTS AND WOMEN   Even though a disproportionate number of women suffer from depression, their unique needs have generally not been taken into account in the development of antidepressant drugs. Women have special concerns about weight gain, amenorrhea, and medication during pregnancy. Social workers whose women clients are on medication can encourage them to discuss their concerns over these issues with psychiatrists and inquire about alternative medications. Although research is scant, it appears that taking tricyclics toward the end of pregnancy can cause anticholinergic side effects in the mother and child (Miller, 1996). More research has been conducted on the effects of women taking fluoxetine. Studies show that taking this medication after the first trimester is associated with no increase in malformations in the newborns (Miller, 1996).

ANTIDEPRESSANTS AND OLDER ADULTS   There have been over thirty randomized placebo-controlled clinical trials as well as many comparative trials (das Gupta, 1998; Salzman, Wong, & Wright, 2002) documenting the safety and efficacy of antidepressant treatment among older adults. Among elderly people, there has been one trial in relatively old medically ill patients, randomizing nortriptyline and a placebo (Katz, Parmelee, Beaston-Wimmer, & Smith, 1994). This trial generally showed efficacy of nortriptyline but with side effects including orthostatic hypotension. One large efficacy study of fluoxetine 20 mg showed efficacy but a relatively low response rate (Tollefson, Rampey, Beasley, Enas, & Potvin, 1994). Among late middle-aged and elderly patients with coexisting cardiovascular disease, it was demonstrated that fluoxetine was equivalently effective to nortriptyline but with fewer cardiovascular side effects (Roose et al., 1997). Since the SSRIs are just as effective as the older TCAs, their use in treatment in late-life depression may result in improved outcomes due to their lower side effect profile.

INSTRUMENTS USED TO ASSESS AND MONITOR DEPRESSION

A number of clinical tools and rapid assessment instruments are used to assist in the diagnosis of depression and to monitor treatment progress for adults and older adults. Some of these lend themselves to evaluations of treatment outcomes. The following instruments are suggested. Those preceded by an asterisk are included in Fischer and Corcoran's (2007) *Measures for Clinical Practice and Research: A Sourcebook*. References are given in parentheses for instruments found elsewhere. Unless indicated, these are completed by the client.

Beck Depression Inventory (Beck, Ward, Mendelson, Mock, & Erbaugh, 1961)

*Geriatric Depression Scale (Sheikh & Yesavage, 1986)

Hamilton Rating Scale for Depression (completed by clinician) (Hamilton, 1960)

Patient Health Questionnaire-9-item (Kroenke & Spitzer, 2002)

Cornell Scale for Dementia (Alexopoulos, Abrams, Young, & Shamoian, 1988)

COMPLEMENTARY AND ALTERNATIVE THERAPIES

The major interventions that were described in this chapter are professionally directed and have been found effective in clinical research trials. But from a client's perspective, other remedies may be more immediately satisfying and helpful. Individuals who are depressed may seek alternatives that do not have the sanction of professionals but hold promise and seem to work for others.

Currently there are a number of herbal remedies that consumers use to treat depression that can be purchased without a prescription. The most well known of these is St. John's wort or *Hypericum perforatum.* Research by the NIH found that the substance was of minimal benefit in treating major depression of moderate severity and no more effective than placebo (Hypericum Depression Trial Study Group, 2002). However, St. John's wort may benefit individuals with milder forms of depression (Linde, Berner, & Kriston, 2008). The problem with using an unregulated substance such as this is that there is variation in purity, content, and strength among the various brands on the market and it is not clear how much of which brand an individual should take. Furthermore, these substances may have unknown side effects and/or interact with prescribed medications. Other alternative ways of treating depression are exercise and light therapy (for seasonal affective disorder).

Case Study

Mrs. Dagostino is a 77-year-old female living alone in her own apartment. She lost her husband two years ago to cancer. About three years ago, she was diagnosed with cardiac disease. She has frequent medical appointments that tire her out, and she is on eight different medications. Transportation has been a problem for her because she does not drive. She has not had much energy and feels isolated but she states that she makes do with what she has. She does not feel that there is anything wrong and does not want to be a burden. She worries about her apartment and how disheveled it has become. Her daughter Pat decided to bring her mother to the social worker at the senior family services center for the following reasons:

During the past two months:

1. Mrs. Dagostino complains of back pain and she is not sleeping well nor is she eating well.
2. She is not remembering things as well as she used to.
3. She has difficulty concentrating and making decisions.
4. She worries about paying her bills on a limited income.
5. She stopped playing cards with her social group.
6. She is not interested in seeing friends or going out.
7. She related that things would be better if she were not around, "not a burden to my daughter," but she is not suicidal.

Summary and Deconstruction

This chapter began by distinguishing between ordinary mood changes and depressions that are socially constructed as psychopathological. It then reviewed the varied symptoms and complex classification of depressions. Clearly there is no "essential" depression; there are *depressions.* Depressions are heterogeneous, as are the individuals who experience them. For the clinician, however, knowledge of the types of depression can inform their implementation of interventions.

This chapter described three evidence-based psychotherapies used for the treatment of individuals with mild to moderate depression. These are short term, so they are compatible with requirements under managed care arrangements. All are focused, present oriented, and structured. CBT attends principally to distorted ideas that are associated with depression. IPT includes education about depression and focuses on one or two issues. PST focuses on developing skills in solving daily life problems related to psychological distress. Medication may be used concurrently with these psychotherapies.

Medication is commonly prescribed by psychiatrists and physicians to provide symptomatic relief of depression. This chapter reviewed the various types that are currently available—SSRIs, tricyclics and tetracyclics, MAOIs, and alternative antidepressants.

Individuals differ in their response to different drugs and some do not respond to any. Although the newer drugs appear to have fewer side effects, questions still remain about the appropriateness of these drugs for pregnant and lactating women and older adults.

Although professionals feel responsible for treating individuals who present with depressed feelings, some individuals prefer to treat themselves. Indeed some individuals recover through herbal remedies and other ways of coping that they have developed through experience or from prior therapy.

References

Alexopoulos, G., Abrams, R., Young, R., & Shamoian, C. (1988). Cornell Scale for Depression in Dementia. *Biological Psychiatry, 23*(3), 271–284.

American Psychiatric Association. (2000). *Diagnostic and statistical manual of mental disorders* (4th ed., text rev.). Washington, DC: Author.

Andreasen, N. C., & Black, D. W. (2006). *Introductory textbook of psychiatry* (4th ed.). Washington, DC: American Psychiatric Publishing.

Arean, P., Ayalon, L., Hunkeler, E., Lin, E., Tang, L., Harpole, L., et al. (2005). Improving depression care for older minority patients in primary care. *Medical Care, 43*(4), 381–390.

Beck, A. T. (1976). *Cognitive therapy and the emotional disorders.* Madison, CT: International Universities Press.

Beck, A. T. (1985). Cognitive therapy. In H. I. Kaplan & B. J. Sadock (Eds.), *Comprehensive textbook of psychiatry/IV* (pp. 1432–1443). Baltimore, MD: Williams & Wilkins.

Beck, A. T., Rush, A. J., Shaw, B. F., & Emery, G. (1979). *Cognitive therapy of depression.* New York: Guilford Press.

Beck, A. T., Ward, C. H., Mendelson, M., Mock, J., & Erbaugh, J. (1961). An inventory for measuring depression. *Archives of General Psychiatry, 4,* 561–571.

Blazer, D. (2002). *Depression in late life* (3rd ed.). New York: Springer.

Bowlby, J. (1969). *Attachment.* New York: Basic Books.

Boyd, J. H., & Weissman, M. M. (1986). Epidemiology of major affective disorders. In G. L. Klerman, M. M. Weissman, P. S. Appelbaum, & L. H. Roth (Eds.), *Social, epidemiologic, and legal psychiatry* (pp. 153–168). New York: Basic Books.

Bruce, M., McAvay, G., Raue, P., Brown, E., Meyers, B., Keohane, D., et al. (2002). Major depression in elderly home health care patients. *American Journal of Psychiatry, 159,* 1367–1374.

Conwell, Y., Duberstein, P., & Caine, E. (2002). Risk factors for suicide in later life. *Biological Psychiatry, 52*(3), 193–204.

Cowen, P. J. (1998). Psychopharmacology. In A. S. Bellack & M. Hersen (Eds.), *Comprehensive clinical psychology* (Vol. 6, pp. 136–161). Amsterdam: Elsevier Science.

De Mello, M. F., de Jesus, M. J., Bacaltchuk, J., Verdeli, H., & Neugebauer, R. (2005). A systematic review of research findings on the efficacy of interpersonal therapy for depressive disorders. *European Archives of Psychiatry Clinical Neuroscience, 255,* 75–82.

DeRubeis, R. J., Young, P. R., & Dahlsgaard, K. K. (1998). Affective disorders. In A. S. Bellack & M. Hersen (Eds.), *Comprehensive clinical psychology* (Vol. 6, pp. 339–366). Amsterdam: Elsevier Science.

D'Zurilla, T. J., & Nezu, A. M. (2007). *Problem-solving therapy: A positive approach to clinical intervention* (3rd ed.). New York: Springer Publishing.

D'Zurilla, T. J., Nezu, A. M., & Maydeu-Olivares, A. (2004). Social problem solving: Theory and assessment. In E. C. Chang, T. J. D'Zurilla, & L. J. Sanna (Eds.), *Social problem solving: Theory, research, and training* (pp. 11–27). Washington, DC: American Psychological Association.

Fischer, J., & Corcoran, K. (2007). *Measures for clinical practice and research: A sourcebook* (4th ed., Vols. 1 and 2). New York: Oxford University Press.

Freud, S. (1917). Mourning and melancholia. In J. Strachey (Ed.), *The standard edition of the complete psychological works of Sigmund Freud* (Vol. 14, pp. 243–258). London: Hogarth Press and Institute of Psychoanalysis.

Gellis, Z. D. (2009). Evidence-based practice in older adults with mental health disorders. In A. Roberts (Ed.), *Social work desk reference* (2nd ed., pp.843–852). New York: Oxford University Press.

Gellis, Z. D., McGinty, J., Horowitz, A., Bruce, M., & Misener, E. (2007). Problem solving therapy for late life depression in home care elderly: A randomized controlled trial. *American Journal of Geriatric Psychiatry, 15*(11), 968–978.

Gellis, Z. D., McGinty, J., Tierney, L., Burton, J., Jordan, C., & Misener, E. (2008). Randomized controlled trial of problem-solving therapy for minor depression in home care. *Research on Social Work Practice, 18*(6), 596–606.

Gellis, Z. D., & Taguchi, A. (2003). Depression and health status among community-dwelling Japanese American elderly. *Clinical Gerontologist, 27,* 23–38.

Grepmair, L., Mitterlehner, F., Loew, T., Bachler, E., Rother, W., & Nickel, M. (2007). Promoting mindfulness in psychotherapists in training influences the treatment results of their patients: A randomized controlled double-blind study. *Psychotherapy and Psychosomatics, in Medical Settings, 76,* 332–338.

das Gupta, K. (1998). Treatment of depression in elderly patients: Recent advances. *Archives of Family Medicine, 7,* 274–280.

Hamilton, M. (1960). A rating scale for depression. *Journal of Neurological and Neurosurgical Psychiatry, 23,* 56–62.

Hasin, D., Goodwin, R., Stinson, F., & Grant, B. (2005). Epidemiology of major depressive disorder: Results from the National Epidemiologic Survey on Alcoholism and Related Conditions *Archives of General Psychiatry, 62,* 1097–1106.

Hinrichsen, G. A. (2008). Interpersonal psychotherapy for late life depression: Current status and new applications. *Journal of Rational-Emotive Cognitive-Behavioral Therapy, 26,* 263–275.

Hirschfeld, R. M. A., & Goodwin, F. K. (1988). Mood disorders. In J. A. Talbott, R. E. Hales, & S. C. Yudofsky (Eds.), *Textbook of psychiatry* (pp. 403–441). Washington, DC: American Psychiatric Press.

Hirschfeld, R. M. A., & Shea, M. T. (1985). Affective disorders: Psychosocial treatment. In H. I. Kaplan & B. J. Sadock (Eds.), *Comprehensive textbook of psychiatry/IV* (pp. 811–821). Baltimore, MD: Williams & Wilkins.

Hypericum Depression Trial Study Group. (2002). Effect of Hypericum perforatum (St. John's wort) in major depressive disorder: A randomized controlled trial. *Journal of the American Medical Association, 287*(14), 1807–1814.

Jarrett, R. B., & Rush, A. J. (1989). Cognitive-behavioral psychotherapy for depression. In American Psychiatric Association, *Treatments of psychiatric disorders: A task force report of the American Psychiatric Association* (Vol. 3, pp. 1834–1846). Washington, DC: American Psychiatric Association.

Kaelber, C. T., Moul, D. E., & Farmer, M. E. (1995). Epidemiology of depression. In E. E. Backham & W. R. Leber (Eds.), *Handbook of depression* (2nd ed., pp. 3–35). New York: Guilford Press.

Kant, G. L., D'Zurilla, T. J., & Maydeu-Olivares, A. (1997). Social problem solving as a mediator of stress-related depression and anxiety in middle-aged and elderly community residents. *Cognitive Therapy and Research, 21,* 73–96.

Karasu, T. B. (1990). Toward a clinical model of psychotherapy for depression, I: Systematic comparison of three psychotherapies. *American Journal of Psychiatry, 147*(2), 133–147.

Katz, I. R., Parmelee, P., Beaston-Wimmer, P., & Smith, B. (1994). Association of antidepressants and other medications with mortality in the residential-care elderly. *Journal of Geriatric Psychiatry and Neurology, 7*(4), 221–226.

Keller, M. B., Harrison, W., Fawcett, J. A., Gelenberg, A., Hirschfeld, R. M., Klein, D., et al. (1995). Treatment of chronic depression with sertraline or imipramine: preliminary blinded response rates and high rates of undertreatment in the community. *Psychopharmacology Bulletin, 31*(2), 205–212.

Kessler, R. C., Abelson, J. M., & Zhao, S. (1998). The epidemiology of mental disorders. In J. W. Williams & K. Ell (Eds.), *Advances in mental health research: Implications for practice* (pp. 3–24). Washington, DC: NASW Press.

Kessler, R. C., Berglund, P., Demler, O., Jin, R., Koretz, D., Merikangas, K. R., et al. (2003). The epidemiology of major depressive disorder: results from the National Comorbidity Survey Replication (NCS-R). Journal of the American Medical Association, *289*(23), 3095–3105.

Kessler, R. C., Chiu, W. T., Demler, O., & Walters, E. E. (2005). Prevalence, severity, and comorbidity of twelve-month DSM-IV disorders in the National Comorbidity Survey Replication (NCS-R). Archives of General Psychiatry, *62*(6), 617–627.

Klein, D. N., Schwartz, J. E., Rose, S., & Leader, J. B. (2000). Five-year course and outcome of dysthymic disorder: A prospective, naturalistic follow-up study. *American Journal of Psychiatry,157*(6), 931–939.

Klerman, G. L. (1988). Depression and related disorders of mood (affective disorders). In A. M. Nicholi, Jr. (Ed.), *The new Harvard guide to psychiatry* (pp. 309–336). Cambridge, MA: Belknap Press of Harvard University Press.

Klerman, G. L., Weissman, M. M., Rounsaville, B. J., & Chevron, E. S. (1984). *Interpersonal psychotherapy of depression.* New York: Basic Books.

Koenig, H., Meador, K., Cohen, H., & Blazer, D. (1988). Depression in elderly hospitalized patients with medical illness. *Archives of Internal Medicine, 148*(9), 1929–1936.

Kroenke, K., & Spitzer, R. (2002). The PHQ-9: A new depression diagnostic and severity measure. *Psychiatric Annals, 32*(9), 509–515.

Lebowitz, B. D., Pearson, J. L., Schneider, L. S., Reynolds, C. F., Alexopoulow, G. S., Bruce, M. L., et al. (1997). Diagnosis and treatment of depression in late life: Consensus statement update. *JAMA, 278,* 1186–1190.

Linde, K., Berner, M. M., & Kriston, L. (2008). St. John's wort for major depression. *Cochrane Database for Systematic Reviews, 2,* CD000448. Retrieved from http://www2.cochrane.org/reviews/en/ab000448.html

Ma, S., & Teasdale, J. (2004). Mindfulness-based cognitive therapy for depression: Replication and exploration of differential relapse prevention effects. *Journal of Consulting and Clinical Psychology, 72,* 31–40.

Markowitz, J. C., & Weissman, M. M. (1995). Interpersonal psychotherapy. In E. E. Backham & W. R. Leber (Eds.), *Handbook of depression* (2nd ed., pp. 376–390). New York: Guilford Press.

Marris, P. (1982). Attachment and society. In C. M. Parkes & J. Stevenson-Hinde (Eds.), *The place of attachment in human behavior* (pp. 185–201). New York: Basic Books.

May, H., Horne, B., Carlquist, J., Sheng, X., Joy, E., & Catinella, P. (2009). Depression after coronary artery disease is associated with heart failure. *Journal of the American College of Cardiology, 53,* 1440–1447.

McGuffin, P., & Katz, R. (1989). The genetics of depression and manic-depressive disorder. *British Journal of Psychiatry, 155,* 294–304.

Miller, L. J. (1996). Psychopharmacology during pregnancy. *Primary Care Update for OB/GYNS, 3*(3), 79–86.

National Institute of Mental Health. (2006). Questions and answers about the NIMH Sequenced Treatment Alternatives to Relieve Depression (STAR*D) study—background. Retrieved March 15, 2010, from http://www.nimh.nih.gov/health/trials/practical/stard/backgroundstudy.shtml

Nemeroff, C. B., & Schatzberg, A. F. (1998). Pharmacological treatment of unipolar depression. In P. E. Nathan & J. M. Gorman (Eds.), *A guide to treatments that work* (pp. 212–225). New York: Oxford University Press.

Nezu, A. M. (2004). Problem solving and behavior therapy revisited. *Behavior Therapy, 35*(1), 1–33.

Nezu, A. M., & D'Zurilla, T. J. (1989). Social problem solving and negative affective states. In P. C. Kendall, & D. Watson (Eds.), *Anxiety and depression: Distinctive and overlapping features* (pp. 285–315). New York: Academic Press.

Nezu, A. M., & Ronan, G. F. (1988). Stressful life events, problem solving, and depressive symptoms among university students: A prospective analysis. *Journal of Counseling Psychology, 35,* 134–138.

Noble, R. E. (2005). Depression in women. *Metabolism Clinical and Experimental, 54*(Suppl. 1), 49–52.

Olfson, M., Marcus, S., Tedeschi, M., & Wan, G. (2006). Continuity of antidepressant treatment for adults with depression in the United States. *American Journal of Psychiatry, 163,* 101–118.

Papakostas, G., Perlis, R., Scalia, M., Peterson, T., & Fava, M. (2006). A meta-analysis of early sustained response rates between antidepressants and placebo for the treatment of major depressive disorder. *Journal of Clinical Psychopharmacology, 26,* 56–60.

Regier, D. A., Boyd, J. H., Burke, J. D., Rae, D. S., Myers, J. K., Kramer, M., et al. (1988). One-month prevalence of mental disorders in the United States. *Archives of General Psychiatry, 45,* 977–986.

Regier, D. A., Farmer, M. E., Rae, D. S., Myers, J. K., Kramer, M., Robins, L. N., et al. (1993). One-month prevalence of mental disorders in the United States and sociodemographic characteristics: The Epidemiologic Catchment Area study. *Acta Psychiatrica Scandinavica, 88,* 35–47.

Roose, S., Glassman, A., Attia, E., Woodring, S., Giardina, E., & Bigger, T. (1997). Cardiovascular effects of fluoxetine, in depressed patients with heart disease. *American Journal of Psychiatry, 155*(5), 660–665.

Rosenhan, D. L., & Seligman, M. E. P. (1984). *Abnormal psychology.* New York: Norton.

Sacco, W. P., & Beck, A. T. (1995). Cognitive theory and therapy. In E. E. Backham & W. R. Leber (Eds.), *Handbook of depression* (2nd ed., pp. 329–351). New York: Guilford Press.

Sadock, B. J., & Sadock, V. A. (2007). *Kaplan & Sadock's Synopsis of psychiatry: Behavioral sciences/clinical psychiatry* (10th ed.). Philadelphia, PA: Wolters Klumer Lippincott Williams & Wilkins.

Salzman, C., Wong, E., & Wright, B. C. (2002). Drug and ECT treatment of depression in the elderly, 1996-2001: A literature review. *Biological Psychiatry, 52*(3), 265–284.

Seligman, M. (1975). *Helplessness: On depression, development, and death.* New York: W. H. Freeman.

Sheikh, J., & Yesavage, J. (1986). Geriatric Depression Scale (GDS): Recent evidence and development of a shorter version. *Clinical Gerontologist, 5,* 165–172.

Steffens, D., Skoog, I., Norton, M., Hart, A., Tschanz, J., Plassman, B., et al. (2000). Prevalence of depression and its treatment in an elderly population: The Cache County study. *Archives of General Psychiatry, 57*(6), 601–607.

Substance Abuse and Mental Health Services Administration, Office of Applied Studies. (January 3, 2008). *The national survey on drug use and health report—treatment for past year depression among adults.* Rockville, MD: Author.

Teasdale, J., Segal, Z., Williams, J., Ridgeway, V., Soulsby, J., & Lau, M. (2000). Prevention of relapse/recurrence in major depression by mindfulness-based cognitive therapy. *Journal of Consulting and Clinical Psychology, 68,* 615–623.

Thompson, B., & Waltz, J. (2007). Everyday mindfulness and mindfulness meditation: Overlapping constructs or not? *Personality and Individual Differences, 43,* 1875–1885.

Tollefson, G., Rampey, A., Beasley, C., Enas, G., & Potvin, J. (1994). Absence of a relationship between adverse events and suicidality during pharmacotherapy for depression. *Journal of Clinical Psychopharmacology, 14*(3), 163–169.

Uncapher, H. (2000). Physicians are less likely to offer depression therapy to older suicidal patients than younger ones.*Geriatrics, 55,* 82.

U.S. Bureau of the Census. (2000). *Current population survey.* Washington, DC: U.S. Government Printing Office.

U.S. Department of Health and Human Services. (1999). *Mental health: A report of the Surgeon General.* Washington, DC: U.S. Government Printing Office.

Weiss, R. S. (1982). Attachment in adult life. In C. M. Parkes & J. Stevenson-Hinde (Eds.), *The place of attachment in human behavior* (pp. 171–184). New York: Basic Books.

Weissman, M. M., Bland, R. C., Canino, G. J., Faravelli, C., Greenwald, S., Hwu, H-G., et al. (1996). Cross-national epidemiology of major depression and bipolar disorder. *JAMA, 276,* 293–299.

Weissman, M., & Klerman, G. L. (1977). Sex differences and the epidemiology of depression. *Archives of General Psychiatry, 34,* 98–111.

Weissman, M., & Klerman, G. L. (1989). Interpersonal psychotherapy. In American Psychiatric Association, *Treatments of psychiatric disorders: A task force report of the American Psychiatric Association* (Vol. 3, pp. 1863–1884). Washington, DC: American Psychiatric Association.

Weissman, M. M., Markowitz, J. C., & Klerman, G. L. (2000). *Comprehensive guide to interpersonal psychotherapy.* New York: Basic Books.

Weissman, M. M., Markowitz, J. C., & Klerman, G. L. (2007). *Clinician's quick guide to interpersonal psychotherapy.* New York: Oxford University Press.

Weissman, M. M., & Myers, J. K. (1978). Affective disorders in a U.S. urban community: The use of Research Diagnostic Criteria in a community survey. *Archives of General Psychiatry, 35,* 1304–1311.

World Health Organization. (2004). *The World Health Report 2004: Changing history, Annex Table 3: Burden of disease in DALYs by cause, sex, and mortality stratum in WHO regions, estimates for 2002.* Geneva: Author.

Wright, J. H., Thase, M. E., & Beck, A. T. (2009). Cognitive therapy. In R. E. Hales, S. C. Yudofsky, & G. O. Gabbard (Eds.), *The American Psychiatric Publishing textbook of clinical psychiatry* (5th ed.). Washington, DC: American Psychiatric Publishing.

Evidence-Based Practice for Clients with Anxiety Disorders

"I worry so much I can't control it and I become so fearful that I think everything will fall apart. Sometimes, I feel like I am going to die." "This fear comes over me, and I get short of breath. My heart pounds, and I think that I'm going to die." "I feel very nervous around other people, and I try to avoid having any attention called to me." "I can't get these thoughts out of my head, and they make me very anxious." "Ever since the accident, I can't stop thinking about it."

—COMMON STATEMENTS FROM PERSONS WITH ANXIETY

Anxiety is a state of tension and apprehension that is an uncomfortable but ordinary human response to a threatening situation (Kaplan & Sadock, 1998). Experienced viscerally as well as psychologically, it is a concomitant of thinking, feeling, and behavior. In the face of unknown, unfamiliar situations, anxiety can provide a warning of danger that can help an individual mobilize resources to meet the threat. When one confronts larger questions about the meaning of the cosmos, the purpose of existence, and one's own mortality, one is likely to experience existential anxiety.

Anxiety becomes described as a psychiatric disorder when the emotion is experienced with great frequency and intensity, when it interferes with psychosocial functioning, and when the response is out of proportion to the stimulus (Kaplan & Sadock, 1998). Although persons who suffer from anxiety disorders usually are not psychotic and can form relationships and function in social roles, many are unable to work or participate in community life without overwhelming discomfort. As the quotations that open this chapter suggest, clients experience anxious experiences differently. This chapter is about different types of anxiety disorders and clinical interventions that are used to treat some of them. Symptoms vary for different anxiety disorders but symptoms common to all are irrational fear and dread. The four most common anxiety disorders (excluding simple phobias) are generalized anxiety disorder (GAD), panic disorder (PD), social anxiety disorder (social phobia), and post-traumatic stress disorder (PTSD).

Anxiety disorders also commonly occur with other mental and physical disorders including alcohol and other substance abuse. Anxiety disorders have a high prevalence and associated disability thus represents a high cost to society. The annual cost of anxiety disorders in the United States is approximately $42 billion for which more than half of the direct and indirect costs involve nonpsychiatric medical treatment (Greenberg et al., 1999).

According to the National Comorbidity Survey Replication (NCS-R) Study completed between 2001 and 2003, over a twelve-month period, the prevalence of any anxiety disorder for adults was about 18 percent (Kessler, Chiu, Demler, & Walters, 2005) in the United States, and over a lifetime, it was 29 percent (Kessler, Berglund, et al., 2005). Among the groups of psychiatric disorders, the lifetime rates were highest for anxiety disorders and next for mood disorders at 21 percent (Kessler, Berglund, et al., 2005). This epidemiological study found that anxiety disorders were more prevalent among women than men. The NCS-R also found that the odds of having an anxiety disorder are greater for individuals with low income and education (Kessler, Chiu, et al., 2005).

Consistent with the integrative biopsychosocial framework of this book (see Chapter 3), anxiety disorders are heterogeneous. There are many types of anxiety disorders and differences among individuals with each type. Some symptoms such as panic attacks and agoraphobia can occur in different types of anxiety disorders (American Psychiatric Association [APA], 2000). Some individuals have more than one anxiety disorder or both an anxiety disorder and another psychiatric disorder such as depression. As Table 9.1 shows, anxiety disorders are characterized by a variety of concurrent biological, cognitive, emotional, and behavioral symptoms. The next section provides an overview of the various types of anxiety disorders.

TABLE 9.1	Symptoms of Anxiety
Type of Symptom	**Description**
Biological	Perspiration, heart palpitations, dyspnea, fainting, nausea, muscular tension, shakiness, flushing, gastrointestinal disturbances, insomnia, dizziness
Cognitive	Worry, apprehension, anticipation of danger or doom; thoughts about contamination, going crazy, or dying; irrational fears; preoccupied by and ruminating about repetitive themes; thoughts of embarrassment, humiliation
Emotional	Keyed up, fearful, on edge, irritable, terrified, "nervous"
Behavioral	Hypervigilant, jumpy, tremors, pacing, avoidance behavior

ANXIETY DISORDERS AND OLDER ADULTS

Epidemiological evidence suggests that anxiety is a common and major problem in later life, yet this has received less attention than depressive disorders. Anxiety disorders are often associated with common age-related medical and chronic conditions such as asthma, thyroid disease, coronary artery disease, dementia, and sensory loss (Diala & Muntaner, 2003). Anxiety in later life has been identified as a risk factor for greater disability among older adults (Bowling, Farquhar, & Grundy, 1996). Researchers and practitioners are beginning to recognize that aging and anxiety are not mutually exclusive; anxiety is as common in the old as in the young, although how and when it appears is distinctly different in older adults. Additionally, there is a need for more research applying existing evidence-based treatments to older adults experiencing late-life anxiety (Mitte, 2005).

Recognizing an anxiety disorder in an older person poses several challenges. Aging brings with it a higher prevalence of certain medical conditions, realistic concern about physical problems, and a higher use of prescription medications. As a result, separating a medical condition from physical symptoms of an anxiety disorder is more complicated in the older adult. Diagnosing anxiety in individuals with dementia can be difficult. For example, agitation typical of dementia may be difficult to separate from anxiety; impaired memory may be interpreted as a sign of anxiety or dementia, and fears may be excessive or realistic depending on the person's situation.

Epidemiology of Anxiety Disorders in Later Life

Although anxiety disorders, like most psychiatric conditions, may be less common among older adults than younger people, epidemiological evidence suggests that anxiety is a major problem in late life (U.S. Department of Health and Human Services, 1999). The NCS-R, which entailed interviews with nearly 6,000 people nationwide, reported a lifetime prevalence rate of 15.3 percent for *DSM-IV*-diagnosed anxiety disorders in older respondents over age 60 (Kessler, Berglund, et al., 2005). Another study, which surveyed approximately 500 community-dwelling, triethnic elders, reported prevalence rates of 11.3 percent in blacks, 12.4 percent in Hispanics, and 21.6 percent in non-Hispanic whites age 75 and older (Ostir & Goodwin, 2006). Myers et al. (1984) report a six-month prevalence of anxiety disorders in late life ranging from 6.6 percent to 14.9 percent across three Epidemiological Catchment Area (ECA) sites. Comparable data from the Netherlands indicate a prevalence of 10.2 percent (Beekman et al., 1998). Anxiety disorders overall appear to be the most common class of psychiatric disorders among older people, more prevalent than depression or severe cognitive impairment (Kessler, Chiu, et al., 2005).

Phobias and GAD account for most anxiety disorders in late life (Beekman, van Balkom, Deeg, van Dyck, & van Tilburg, 2000; Le Roux, Gatz, & Wetherell, 2005). Empirical reviews summarized the prevalence of specific anxiety disorders in older community-based epidemiological samples as follows: phobias, including agoraphobia and social phobia, 0.7 to 12.0 percent; GAD, 1.2 to 7.3 percent; obsessive-compulsive disorder (OCD), 0.1 to 1.5 percent; and PD, 0.0 to 0.3 percent (Alwahhabi, 2003; Beekman et al., 1998, 2000). Prevalence of GAD in older adults was estimated at 1.9 percent in the ECA samples and 7.3 percent in a Dutch sample (Beekman et al., 2000; Blazer, 1997). Among people 55 years of age and older, Douchet, Ladouceur, Freeston, and Dugas (1998) found that 12.8 percent meet criteria for GAD. By comparison, ECA prevalence rates for older adults were 1.8 percent for major depression, 2.8 percent for dysthymia, and 4.9 percent for severe cognitive impairment (Regier et al., 1988).

The Case of Subthreshold Anxiety

Clinically significant anxiety, including the presence of symptoms that do not meet full diagnostic criteria for a specific disorder, is common among older adults and may be as high as 20 to 29 percent (Davis, Moye, & Karel, 2002; Lenze et al., 2005). This includes anxiety symptoms associated with common medical conditions such as asthma, thyroid disease, coronary artery disease, and dementia, as well as adjustment disorders following significant late-life stressors such as bereavement or caregiving. There is also controversy over whether the prevalence of anxiety has been accurately determined in older adults, because *DSM-IV* criteria may not apply as well, anxiety symptoms may be expressed as somatic features or behavior changes (e.g., aggression, assaultive behaviors), and the clinical presentation of anxiety in late life may be more likely to include depressive symptoms (Beck & Averill, 2004; Diefenbach & Goethe, 2006).

TYPES OF ANXIETY DISORDERS

The *DSM-IV-TR* (APA, 2000) describes several categories of anxiety disorders and the specific criteria necessary for their diagnosis. The major categories are as follows.

Post-traumatic stress disorder is an anxiety reaction to an event that threatens the life or bodily integrity of oneself or someone with whom one is closely associated. The individual may experience the event directly or witness or hear about it. The person with PTSD will relive the event (cognitively and emotionally), have nightmares or flashbacks, act as if the event were recurring, or experience distress in the face of stimuli that are reminders of the event.

Over a twelve-month period, PTSD affects about 3.5 percent of adults, affecting about 7.7 million Americans age 18 or older (Kessler, Chiu, et al., 2005; National Institute of Mental Health [NIMH], 2008). It can occur at any age including childhood (Margolin & Cordis, 2000). According to NIMH, PTSD is more likely to occur in women than men, and it is comorbid with depression, substance abuse, or other anxiety disorders (Regier, Rae, Narrow, Kaelber, & Schatzberg, 1998). Like PTSD, an *acute stress disorder* is a reaction to a traumatic event, but the duration is between two days and one month.

Generalized anxiety disorder is a pervasive, chronic condition rather than one that occurs in spurts like PD. GAD affects about 6.8 million adults (Kessler, Chiu, et al., 2005; NIMH, 2008) and about twice as many women as men (Kessler et al., 1994). Individuals with GAD worry excessively about situations or circumstances that are not, on the surface, threatening. Irrational thinking is accompanied by numerous symptoms of anxiety including worry and tension. GAD is diagnosed when an individual worries excessively about various daily living problems for at least six months and cannot control the worry. Symptoms include difficulty concentrating, startles easily, cannot relax, trouble sleeping, fatigue, headaches, muscle aches, irritability, sweating, and nausea, to name a few.

Panic disorder is a real psychiatric illness that can be effectively treated. It is experienced by approximately 6 million adults or 2.7 percent of the adult population in a twelve-month period (Kessler, Chiu, et al., 2005; NIMH, 2008) and is over twice as common in women as men (Kessler et al., 1994). PD is characterized by unexpected panic attacks—periods of heightened emotion that are frightening and uncomfortable—and anticipatory anxiety about their recurrence (APA, 2000). According to the *DSM-IV-TR*, at least four of a list of thirteen somatic and cognitive symptoms must be present to consider episodes of anxiety as panic attacks. Among these symptoms are heart palpitations, sweating, trembling, sensations of shortness of breath, fear of losing control, chest pain, or chills (APA, 2000). The combination of physical symptoms and the cognition of impending death lead some sufferers to emergency rooms believing that they are having a heart attack.

Panic disorder is frequently comorbid with depression, alcoholism, or drug abuse (Regier et al., 1998). Although for some individuals PD is a discrete experience, for others panic occurs hand in hand with agoraphobia. The frequency of the convergence of these two conditions led researchers to hypothesize that the emergence of spontaneous panic is a conditioning event that is a precursor to the development of agoraphobia (Klein & Gorman, 1987). Subsequently, the person's agoraphobia revolves around the fear of having another panic attack. In an analysis of data from the ECA Study, PD coexisting with agoraphobia was found in about one third of the cases of PD (Markowitz, Weissman, Ouellette, Lish, & Klerman, 1989). According to the NCS-R Study, the correlation between agoraphobia and PD is 0.64 (Kessler, Chiu, et al., 2005).

Agoraphobia is a fear and avoidance reaction to being in a place or situation from which there is no perceived way of getting assistance (APA, 2000). Like any phobia, it is an irrational fear of a situation or object confrontation, which results in overwhelming anxiety. To prevent anticipated anxiety, persons with agoraphobia avoid the situation that is associated with the reaction. Those who also have panic attacks may fear having a panic attack in the designated situation. The *DSM-IV-TR* describes *agoraphobia without a history of panic disorder* (APA, 2000).

Individuals with agoraphobia cope with their situation in a variety of ways. Some stay home all the time—a strategy that is incapacitating and further reinforces the fear of leaving the house. Others go out but limit their activities. These individuals may go to public places in the company of others or endure the discomforting anxiety to accomplish needed activities. Agoraphobics who go out alone will go out of their way to avoid the situations that disturb them; for example, a person afraid to drive on highways will use side streets. Others cope by using chemical substances.

Two other types of anxiety disorders are *social phobia* and *specific phobia*. *Social phobia* is an irrational fear of being in a situation in which one is expected to perform or may be observed by others. The person with a social phobia is especially sensitive to anticipated ridicule, embarrassment, or humiliation. Examples of situations that are problematic to persons with this disorder are speaking in public, eating in a restaurant, and using public lavatories. *Specific phobias* are associated with particular objects or situations. Social and specific phobias may have co-occurring panic attacks.

An additional type of anxiety disorder is *OCD*, a disabling condition that intrudes on thinking and behavior. OCD affects about 2 million adults or 1 percent of the adult population in a twelve-month period (Kessler, Chiu, et al., 2005; NIMH, 2008) and the disorder can be comorbid with depression, eating disorders, or other anxiety disorders. It appears in males and females in equal numbers and frequently appears in childhood, adolescence, or early adulthood (Robins & Regier, 1991).

Obsessions are persistent, irrational, egodystonic thoughts, impulses, or images, usually of an unpleasant nature, that take over the consciousness of a person with this disorder. They usually convey thoughts about contamination, sex, or aggression and are accompanied by self-doubt. Compulsions are irrational, stereotyped, ritualistic behaviors, which are attempts to counteract the obsessions. Examples include constant handwashing, cleaning, and checking. Compulsions are time consuming and repetitive; thus, they interfere with the accomplishment of more constructive activities. Acting out compulsions brings release but little pleasure, whereas resisting compulsions arouses anxiety. According to the *DSM-IV-TR*, either obsessions or compulsions are required for a diagnosis of OCD (APA, 2000), yet the two may co-occur.

In addition to these disorders, the *DSM-IV-TR* describes *anxiety disorder due to a medical condition* and a *substance-induced anxiety disorder.* Some medical conditions that produce symptoms of anxiety are hypoglycemia, congestive heart failure, chronic obstructive pulmonary disease, and encephalitis (APA, 2000). Likewise alcohol, cocaine, caffeine, and other substances can precipitate anxiety symptoms (APA, 2000). A medical evaluation should assess whether a medical condition or chemical substance is etiologically involved.

EXPLANATORY THEORIES

Although the various types of anxiety disorders that have been described have much in common, there are many differences among them. Furthermore, there are different scientific traditions associated with each of them. Rather than discussing the scientific findings that are associated with each type, this section will provide an overview of various theoretical explanations pertaining to particular anxiety disorders. In keeping with the integrative biopsychosocial perspective of this book, biological, social, and psychological explanations are intertwined. For a given individual with a particular disorder, different strands among each of the following aspects may be relevant.

Biological Aspects

Genetic studies suggest but do not prove that anxiety disorders are inherited. With respect to PDs, twin studies have revealed a higher concordance rate between monozygotic than dizygotic twins (Torgersen, 1983). Furthermore, first-degree relatives of persons with PD have a high risk of having the same disorder (Weissman, 1990). General anxiety disorder and obsessive-compulsive symptoms are also common among first-degree relatives of individuals with these particular disorders (Andreasen & Black, 2006). Nevertheless, specific genetic markers for anxiety disorders have not been identified. Trends among first-degree relatives can be explained by social learning.

Brain imaging studies suggest that there are abnormalities in the structure and function of the brains of some individuals with anxiety disorders (Sadock & Sadock, 2007). Further evidence that anxiety disorders are brain diseases comes from the medications that are effective in reducing symptoms. These medications suggest that the neurotransmitters norepinephrine, serotonin, and GABA play a role in the generation of anxiety disorders (Sadock & Sadock, 2007). Later in this chapter, antianxiety medications that are currently used to treat anxiety disorders will be described.

Social Dimensions

Stressful life events may play a role in precipitating panic attacks, although prospective research is needed because most studies have elicited information about life events from clients who were in the throes of their disorders (Barlow, 1988). The social dimension seems pertinent when there is agoraphobia along with panic symptoms because individuals with agoraphobia avoid situations based on their meaning in a social context. PTSD and acute stress disorder are, by definition, caused by social stressors such as war, rape, physical or sexual abuse, and assault. The high rate of anxiety disorders among women may be a consequence of living in a patriarchal society in which women are vulnerable to threats from the outside world and experience conflicts over remaining dependent versus becoming autonomous (Kaschak, 1992).

According to an analysis of data from the ECA Study of a community sample (Markowitz et al., 1989), participants who met diagnostic criteria for PD (of whom 70 percent were female and 75 percent were white) scored relatively poorly on several measures of quality of life. These included subjective ratings of physical and emotional health, substance abuse, suicide attempts, impaired social and marital functioning, financial dependence, and use of treatment facilities. The findings on persons with PD were comparable with those on persons with major depression but distinct from persons with neither panic nor major depression. The unusually high rate of suicidal ideations and suicide attempts among persons with PD was confirmed in another analysis of the same data (Weissman, Klerman, Markowitz, & Ouellette, 1989).

Psychological Theories

A number of psychological theories explain the etiology and expression of anxiety. Many of these theories are specific to particular kinds of anxiety disorders (e.g., phobias, OCD). To reduce the complexity and specificity of these theories, general statements will be made about each theory.

PSYCHOANALYSIS   Freud viewed anxiety as both normal and a potential source of neurotic development (Brenner, 1955). Normal anxiety provides a signal to the organism so that it can protect itself from harm. Pathological anxiety is associated with id instincts that cannot be held in check by the ego defenses. Because the anxiety has nowhere to go and must be expressed, it takes the form of neurotic symptoms. Anxiety neuroses (cf. GAD), phobic neuroses (cf. agoraphobia and other phobic disorders), and obsessive-compulsive neurosis (cf. OCD) represent channels for the expression of unacceptable id impulses.

Freud and later ego psychology theorists attributed the development of neuroses to failure to resolve early developmental issues. Phobias, for example, are associated with conflict in the oedipal stage, particularly castration anxiety, whereas obsessive-compulsive neurosis is traceable to conflicts during the anal stage. Phobias and panic attacks have also been attributed to difficulty mastering the task of separation-individuation (Hollander, Liebowitz, & Gorman, 1988).

EXISTENTIAL THEORY   Existential theory explains anxiety as a fact of life. Anxiety arises when one recognizes the beauty, wonder, and tragedy of life. Camus's (1991) image of Sisyphus pushing a boulder uphill only to see it fall down after it reaches the top captures the absurdity of life's struggles when one knows that death is inevitable. Existential theory explains Freud's normal anxiety but not the severe symptoms one sees in some of the anxiety disorders.

BEHAVIORAL THEORY   According to learning theory, anxiety is a response (a behavior) that is learned in association with a painful situation. Afterward the conditioned response to this situation generalizes to other situations. This maladaptive behavior can become further reinforced by the behavior of significant others, who condone it or provide support, which then provides the person with maladaptive behavior with what are called *secondary gains*, which perpetuate the anxious response. Although this pattern appears to be insidious, it can be reversed by altering the contingencies. Behavioral methods of therapy such as systematic desensitization and in vivo exposure have been very successful in the treatment of anxiety disorders.

COGNITIVE THEORY   Cognitive theory poses that anxiety is a normal emotion that is needed for survival. A person with an anxiety disorder feels anxious upon misperceiving a situation as dangerous. Interestingly, such a person ignores environmental cues indicating that the same situation is safe (Beck, 1985). In the face of perceived threat, the autonomic nervous system becomes activated, motoric activity ensues (fight, flight, faint, or freeze), and faulty cognitions and problematic emotions are triggered. Accordingly a situation that is inherently neutral is *catastrophized*. Cognitive therapy techniques such as imagery and cognitive restructuring can be helpful in the treatment of persons with anxiety disorders.

Recent conceptualizations of anxiety disorders are biopsychosocial, with treatments aimed at the biological symptoms, cognitions, and behaviors. The various interventions that will be described sequentially are based on cognitive and behavioral theories.

COGNITIVE-BEHAVIORAL TREATMENT OF ANXIETY DISORDERS

In today's managed care environment, brief, evidence-based, measurable, and effective treatment modalities are advantageous. Cognitive-behavioral treatment can extinguish (or reduce the intensity of) disturbing symptoms of anxiety over a short period of time. Some of the interventions that are used to treat anxiety disorders will be described next. The first three are used principally with persons with phobias and OCD.

Systematic Desensitization

Systematic desensitization was developed by Joseph Wolpe and described in *Psychotherapy by Reciprocal Inhibition*, which was published in 1958. His ideas are developed further in a subsequent book (Wolpe, 1982). Wolpe applied his method of psychotherapy to adults with a spectrum of phobic conditions. His approach is predicated on the principle of reciprocal inhibition; that is, one can weaken neurotic anxiety by countering it with a competing stimulus. The strategy employed is to use a stronger stimulus to inhibit a weak form of the neurotic anxiety. Wolpe recommended as the stronger stimulus deep muscle relaxation, which produces a physical effect that is the opposite of anxiety. Relaxation diminishes the impact of anxiety-provoking scenes the client is later asked to imagine.

Systematic desensitization is carried out in four steps (Wolpe, 1982). First, the client is introduced to the Subjective Anxiety Scale. The clinician asks the client to give his or her worst experience of anxiety a rating of 100 and the state of absolute calmness a score of 0. In addition, the client is asked to rate his or her current state somewhere in between 0 and 100. Wolpe describes these ratings as *suds* (subjective units of distress).

Next the client begins training in deep muscle relaxation. Wolpe's exercises are based on those developed by Jacobson (1938), but Wolpe's exercises are taught to the client in a period of six weeks, whereas Jacobson's exercises took fifty or more sessions. The client is taught to contract and relax specific parts of the body, from head to toe, in incremental steps over time. The client is told, for example, to contract the fists, to feel the tension in the fist, hand, and forearm, and then to release the contracted fist and relax. (An abbreviated program of progressive relaxation of this kind is described by Craske & Barlow, 2006.) In addition, the client is expected to practice relaxation ten to fifteen minutes twice a day at home (Wolpe, 1982).

During the third stage, the clinician, with the help of the client, constructs a hierarchy of anxiety-producing events (Wolpe, 1982). A tentative list of items to include derives from the social history, results of instruments administered to the client prior to treatment, and discussion between the client and the clinician. Items are grouped together by theme (a) to determine which are relevant to treatment (e.g., items suggesting agoraphobia, acrophobia, and claustrophobia are relevant; objective fears about getting pregnant are irrelevant) and (b) to develop separate hierarchies, each related to a different theme. The client is asked to give a suds rating to each item listed under each theme and to give a rationale for these ratings. From this information, the clinician constructs a hierarchy of discrete, evenly spaced items for each theme (Wolpe, 1982). The following is an example of such a series, with suds scores listed in parentheses:

1. Being home alone, watching TV (10)
2. Walking down the block with my spouse (20)
3. Walking down the block alone (30)
4. Taking the bus with my spouse (40)
5. Taking the bus alone (50)
6. Going to the grocery store early in the morning (60)
7. Going to the grocery store on Friday afternoon (70)
8. Going to a shopping mall (any time) (80)
9. Going downtown during the week (90)
10. Going to the state fair on opening day (100)

The next step is the implementation of the desensitization procedure (Wolpe, 1982). This can be initiated in the third or fourth session, following relaxation training. After the client comes to a deep state of relaxation and eyes are closed, the clinician inquires how relaxed the client is. If the client says 0, the clinician offers a control scene, such as having the client imagine a pleasant, calm, sunny, summer day. If this does not produce anxiety, the clinician begins with the lowest-ranking scene from one of the lists of hierarchies and has the client imagine it. The client signals that the scene is being contemplated by raising a finger. After five to seven seconds, the clinician asks the client to stop and to provide a suds rating. Sometimes presentation of the same scene twice results in a lower rating the second time. Relaxation is implemented in between scenes, with the intervals between scenes being ten to thirty seconds. Subsequent sessions begin with items that have low ratings but are above 0 (Wolpe, 1982).

Flooding and Implosive Therapy

Flooding is a behavioral treatment technique that was introduced after systematic desensitization. Like its predecessor, flooding requires that the client imagine anxiety-provoking scenes. In flooding, however, the client does not get into a relaxed state prior to implementation of the procedure. Treatment consists of the clinician describing in great detail a scene that is highly anxiety provoking for the client. *Implosive therapy* is similar to flooding in its use of graphic images of disturbing scenes to extinguish anxiety. With implosive therapy, the clinician adds themes based on psychoanalytic insights into the client's early experiences to the scenes described during flooding, resulting in a more intense experience than that in flooding.

In Vivo Exposure

The principle that explains the effectiveness of systematic desensitization, flooding, and implosive therapy is that *exposure to what one fears reduces anxiety.* The methods that have been described thus far rely on cognitive processes (imagination) to extinguish anxiety. More recently, it has been recognized that in vivo (real-life) exposure is more readily translated into behaviors related to the client's life. In vivo exposure can be used to treat phobias (agoraphobia, social phobia, simple phobias) and OCDs.

In vivo exposure may be *prolonged* or *graduated* (O'Brien & Barlow, 1984). With prolonged exposure, the client faces the feared situation in an intense form (high on the hierarchy) early in treatment and for long periods of time. As such, prolonged exposure is akin to flooding. With graduated exposure, the client is exposed to situations that arouse little anxiety first. The client progresses over time to more threatening situations. Graduated exposure bears some resemblance to systematic desensitization but is carried out in a natural context.

The distinction between prolonged and graduated exposure highlights the significance of the dimensions of duration and intensity in relation to in vivo exposure. Research comparing these dimensions is equivocal. Some research suggests that sessions of two hours or more are more effective than shorter sessions (e.g., Stern & Marks, 1973). Nevertheless, clients who have been treated with prolonged in vivo exposure were more likely to drop out of treatment than those who were treated on a graduated basis (Barlow, 1988). Furthermore, prolonged exposure has the disadvantage of adversely affecting the interpersonal system (Barlow, 1988).

In vivo exposure can be implemented with various degrees of participation by the clinician. At one end of the continuum, the clinician directs and implements treatment from an office (e.g., exposing the client to snakelike objects and snakes in the office). Another approach is for the clinician to accompany the client to places in which the client will be exposed to disturbing stimuli (e.g., walking outside, around the clinic building). In the treatment of agoraphobia, some clinicians will accompany and provide support to small groups of clients taken to shopping malls for several hours at a time (Barlow, 1988). An alternative is for the clinician to set up a program of activities for the client to carry out independently in the community between sessions. In some cases, the clinician will promote the implementation of such a program by making home visits and involving a spouse or partner of the client (Mathews, Gelder, & Johnston, 1981). At the far end of the continuum is in vivo exposure that is carried out autonomously by clients through self-help manuals (e.g., Weakes, 1968, 1972) or client-run self-help groups.

Response Prevention

This is a method of blocking the performance of rituals by persons with OCD. As it is described by Turner and Beidel (1988), response prevention is a means to prevent reinforcement (and, thus, continuation) of anxiety reduction through repeated, ritualistic behavior. Accordingly, the client is deterred from carrying out a compulsion. In doing so, professional staff do not use physical force; instead they intervene by distracting, redirecting, or coaxing a client not to perform the ritual. Furthermore, they do not block the client from culturally normative activities, such as showering once a day or washing hands after handling dirt. Turner and Beidel use a combination of flooding (exposure to the feared stimulus) and response prevention in their treatment program for persons with OCD.

Thought Stopping

This cognitive technique is a means of interrupting the occurrence of intrusive or irrational thoughts. It is used to treat persons with GAD and OCD. It is implemented as follows. First, the client is asked to discuss and give an example of a situation in which the unwanted thoughts are present (Mahoney, 1974). Then the clinician has the client imagine being in that situation again and having those thoughts (Rimm & Masters, 1974). After the client indicates the presence of such thoughts, the clinician shouts, "Stop!" Startled, the client stops focusing on the previous thought. Exposed to this method of conditioning repeatedly, clients learn to recognize and subvocalize "stop" to themselves, thus interrupting their own thoughts. Because this method has weak empirical support (Mahoney, 1974; Turner & Beidel, 1988), it tends to be used as an adjunctive rather than as a principal treatment method.

Cognitive Restructuring

With cognitive restructuring, anxiety-producing thoughts are identified, challenged, and replaced with more accurate thoughts. At first the client is helped to recognize irrational automatic thoughts that accompany anxiety. This is facilitated by the assignment of homework in which experiences of anxiety are recorded and described (what happened, what the client was thinking, how the client was feeling). During therapy, the clinician challenges the rationality of the client's thoughts. For example, a client who left a party soon after arriving, when she experienced anxiety, noted that she saw someone she had gone out with previously and whom she liked but who never asked her out again. She believed that if they were to have a face-to-face encounter at the party, it would be "awful." The clinician had the client explore the many possibilities their encounter might have brought (including his asking her out again) and explained the difference between possible and probable outcomes (cf. Ellis, 1962). This client was encouraged to develop alternative ways of thinking and responding that she might have had to the occasion (e.g., people who date are bound to meet people they have dated in the past; even though she was uncomfortable seeing this man, she could still enjoy the party; one way to reduce her anxiety would have been to talk to him right away "to get it over with"; even if he does not want to talk to her, she is a worthwhile human being who has a right to be at the party and enjoy herself). Cognitive methods of treating anxiety disorders are discussed in depth by Beck, Emery, and Greenberg (1985).

Stress Inoculation Training

Stress inoculation training is a form of cognitive-behavioral therapy that helps clients develop skills in coping with stress (Meichenbaum, 1985). It engages clients as collaborators in the collection of data from their everyday experiences that arouse stress and in the selection of strategies to cope with stress. Clients learn to identify maladaptive thoughts, solve problems, regulate emotional responses, and implement coping skills. Stress inoculation can be used with a wide spectrum of populations in clinical and community settings. It incorporates many of the cognitive and behavioral techniques that were described previously (relaxation training, graded exposure, identifying automatic thoughts, modeling), as well as problem solving. Stress inoculation training can be implemented with individuals, couples, and groups.

The preceding section reviewed a variety of cognitive and behavioral methods that are used to intervene with individuals with different kinds of anxiety disorders. Many of these methods go back to the 1950s. In recent years, systematic treatment procedures for particular kinds of anxiety disorders have been developed. Several of them use or adapt several of the methods that were discussed; for example, stress inoculation training is used in treatment of PTSD (Calhoun & Resick, 1993). Social skills training, which is used with adults with severe mental illness, is also helpful in the treatment of social phobia (Barlow, Esler, & Vitali, 1998). The next section will summarize one of these treatment protocols as an example of an evidence-based practice for treating PD with and without agoraphobia.

EVIDENCE-BASED PRACTICE: COGNITIVE-BEHAVIORAL TREATMENT FOR PANIC DISORDER AND PANIC DISORDER WITH AGORAPHOBIA

The cognitive-behavioral treatment for PD and panic disorder with agoraphobia (PDA) that is described here (Craske & Barlow, 1993, 2008) is predicated on a biopsychosocial perspective. Barlow (1988) proposed a biopsychosocial process in which the inborn alarm system that is ordinarily activated under stress becomes susceptible to responding to "false alarms" that become conditioned responses. PD is "a learned fearfulness of certain bodily sensations associated with panic attacks," and agoraphobia is "a behavioral response to the anticipation of such bodily sensations or their crescendo into a full-blown panic attack" (Craske & Barlow, 1993, p. 1). According to the cognitive hypothesis (Beck et al., 1985), panic attacks first arise from tension from life problems that leave the individual with feelings of helplessness. When bodily or mental sensations associated with tension recur, the individual interprets them as signs of imminent catastrophes that threaten his or her life or well-being. The misinterpretation generates increased anxiety and sensations that can result in a panic attack (Salkovskis, 1998) and worry about the recurrence of such an attack (Barlow, 1988). Individuals with a family history of PD may be more physiologically vulnerable to reacting to internal stimuli in this way (Craske & Barlow, 1993).

Craske and Barlow's model is built on an understanding of anxiety, panic, agoraphobia, and several related concepts. Immediate anxiety is understood as *fight-flight response* to perceived danger; it is the organism's attempt to protect itself and prepare for action. In the face of a threat, the autonomic nervous system becomes activated. This system has two subsystems—*sympathetic* and *parasympathetic*. The sympathetic system, which prepares the body for action, triggers heart and blood flow, increases breathing, and stimulates sweating. The parasympathetic system protects the body by restoring it to its normal state. Persons with panic attacks fear the bodily sensations that occur when there is a fight-flight response. These sensations may be the outcome of stress, overbreathing *(hyperventilation)*, hypervigilance to normal bodily changes, or interoceptive conditioning. *Interoceptive conditioning* is a form of conditioning in which panic responses are stimulated by subtle bodily sensations that occur out of awareness of the individual (Craske & Barlow, 1993). Such sensations can become conditioned by association with normal activities that produce anxiety, for example, exercise or drinking coffee (Craske & Barlow, 1993). When individuals cannot identify a cause for their panicky feelings, they devise an explanation ("I'm dying," "I'm going crazy") or blame themselves (Craske & Barlow, 1993). Agoraphobia is a flight response to bodily states that precipitate panic attacks. (For a more detailed explanation of this process in the form of a handout that can be distributed to clients, see Craske & Barlow, 1993.)

The cognitive-behavioral therapy for PD/PDA aims to educate clients about their symptoms, correct misinterpretations of bodily symptoms, provide breathing retraining, and implement exposure exercises. Table 9.2 summarizes the major components of this intervention.

Note that the treatment can be implemented in an outpatient or inpatient facility or in the client's natural environment. This is a short-term intervention, compatible with the call for brief therapy by managed care entities. The authors report that 80 to 100 percent of clients are free of panic attacks by the end of treatment and that most of them maintain these gains for at least two years (Craske & Barlow, 1993).

Assessment

Before implementing such an intervention, a thorough assessment is required. The clinician conducts an in-depth interview with the client in which a history is taken of the presenting symptoms over time, and information is gathered about other life circumstances that may be relevant. Craske and Barlow use the Anxiety Disorders Interview Schedule—Revised (DiNardo & Barlow, 1988) to clarify the diagnosis. In addition, they ask the client to provide information on the panic attacks and to have a medical evaluation to rule out medical conditions. The clinician administers some behavioral approach tests on activities the client identifies as difficult and rates the client's anxiety at intervals. Self-report inventories are used for treatment planning and to assess changes during therapy (see, e.g., the Anxiety Sensitivity Index, Reiss, Peterson, Gursky, & McNally, 1986).

TABLE 9.2	Cognitive-Behavioral Treatment for Panic Disorder and Panic Disorder with Agoraphobia

Aims
Provide information about anxiety, panic attacks, hyperventilation
Change misinterpretations of bodily symptoms
Provide breathing retraining; modify cognitions
Provide repeated exposure to frightening internal cues and external situations

Settings
Outpatient clinic
Natural environment
Inpatient facility

Assessment
In-depth interviews
Screening instruments, behavioral tests
Medical evaluation
Client self-report information on panic attacks
Behavioral approach tests

Treatment Components
Education about anxiety, panic, cognitions, various treatment strategies, and self-monitoring
Cognitive restructuring
Breathing retraining
Applied relaxation
Interceptive exposure
Situational exposure

Number of sessions
10–15

Format
Individual sessions
Involvement of significant other toward end of treatment

Source: Based on Craske & Barlow (2008).

Treatment Components

The following treatment strategies are used to reduce panic and agoraphobic symptoms.

 Cognitive restructuring is used to identify inaccurate and irrational ideas that the client associates with the symptoms. These cognitions may be unproven hypotheses that explain their feelings. As with Beck's cognitive therapy for depression, these cognitions are challenged (particularly overestimating the danger and catastrophizing) and tested in between-session homework assignments. Accurate cognitions replace the inaccurate ones. Cognitive restructuring is integrated into the other treatment components.

Breathing retraining is instituted to address hyperventilating, described by 50 to 60 percent of clients who are treated for PD (Craske & Barlow, 1993). At first clients are asked to breath rapidly and deeply (i.e., to reproduce hyperventilation) for a minute and a half while standing. Then they are asked to what extent symptoms like these occur when they are anxious. Clients are provided didactic information about hyperventilation (described as overtaxing the body) and are retrained to breathe through their diaphragm rather than chest muscles and to control their breathing by keeping a count of the number of times they inhale and thinking, "relax," while they exhale.

Applied relaxation is training in progressive muscle relaxation. It is used to counteract muscular tension that occurs during panic attacks (Craske & Barlow, 1993). Clients are trained to contract and relax various parts of the body, one part at a time.

Interoceptive exposure aims to weaken the link between bodily cues and panic reactions by inducing feared experiences in such a way that the fear response does not occur (Craske & Barlow, 2008). Procedures such as running in place, breathing through a narrow straw, and shaking one's head from side to side are used to induce panic-like sensations. Clients are exposed to these experiences gradually and increasingly to acclimate them to biological sensations that had previously produced fear.

Situational exposure is something like the in vivo exposure that was described earlier. To deal with agoraphobia that is associated with some PDs, the client is exposed gradually and repeatedly to feared external situations such as malls or subways. Situational exposure weakens the link between context-related cues and anxiety and panic reactions (Craske & Barlow, 1993).

Intervention Sequence

Treatment is generally provided on an individual basis, with the option of incorporating a significant other, especially during the last few sessions. Although Craske and Barlow (1993) describe fifteen sessions, they indicate that panic symptoms can be controlled in ten. Telch et al. (1993) reported a significantly high level of effectiveness of a similar intervention using an eight-week group format.

SESSIONS 1 AND 2 During these introductory sessions, the client's education about anxiety and panic attacks begins, and the purpose and nature of treatment are explained. The physiology of anxiety and panic is described and the concepts of hypervigilance and interoceptive conditioning are introduced. The client is asked to describe the situations in which he or she experiences panic attacks. In addition, the expectations that the client is responsible for monitoring his or her own progress and for practicing assigned homework activities are conveyed. The client is asked to keep a record of his or her daily moods, the intensity of the client's anxiety, and the particular symptoms the client experienced.

SESSIONS 3–5 In session 3, the client is asked to hyperventilate and then breathe slowly until the symptoms diminish. Hyperventilation and breathing control are then explained. Breathing control exercises begin in session 3 and continue in the next two sessions. The client is asked to practice diaphragmatic breathing for ten minutes twice a day as homework. The relationship between breathing control and cognitions is introduced in session 3 with cognitive restructuring occurring in the next two sessions. In session 4, it is suggested that the client overestimates the consequences of panic; in session 5, cognitive structuring is extended to catastrophizing. Homework assignments for sessions 4 and 5 are to monitor the client's own overestimating and catastrophizing and to continue breathing exercises.

SESSIONS 6–9 After reviewing cognitive restructuring principles conveyed in the previous sessions, the focus moves to interoceptive exposure. In session 6, the concept of interoceptive conditioning is revisited, and a rationale for interoceptive exposure is given. Avoidance (characteristic of agoraphobia) is explained as a consequence of bodily sensations that are viewed as frightening. The clinician then introduces some interoceptive exposure exercises to assess the client's response, measured on a scale from 0 to 8. Examples of exercises are running in place, holding one's breath, spinning in a swivel chair, and breathing through a narrow straw. The results of these exercises are used to establish a hierarchy of activities for future practicing. In sessions 7 and 8, the client integrates breathing control and cognitive restructuring with interoceptive exposure. The exercises performed in the previous level are redone starting with those that had a low rating. When the client signals feeling an uncomfortable bodily sensation, he or she is asked to remain with the feeling another thirty seconds. The clinician helps the client, too, with cognitions that impede a more prolonged exposure ("What would happen if you ran in place another thirty seconds?"). After doing these during clinical sessions and as homework for a couple of weeks, interoceptive exposure is extended to naturalistic tasks that the client avoids because they stimulate bodily sensations (session 9). Examples of these are running up steps, drinking coffee, engaging in strenuous physical exercise, and driving with the windows closed. The client rates his or her anxiety reactions and lists them in hierarchical order. Cognitions associated with these experiences are elicited and restructured. The client is asked to select two items from his or her list to practice three times each.

SESSIONS 10–11 During session 10, the homework assignment is reviewed and situational exposure is discussed. With the latter, the focus is on situations that are associated with agoraphobia, that is, situations the client avoids out of fear of anxiety and panic. Situational exposure is explained as a means to obtain control over feared events or situations and is distinguished from interoceptive exposure, which emphasizes bodily sensations. If appropriate, a significant other can be brought into treatment in session 11 at which time the procedures and their rationale are explained to that person. During this session, the significant other is asked to explain how the client's disorder has affected their life together, and strategies are developed to engage this person's help as a coach. The client, significant other, and clinician then develop a hierarchy of activities that comes out of the client's daily life to which to apply situational exposure. The couple choose one activity among these to practice three times during the next week.

SESSIONS 12–15 The last few sessions, held with the client and significant other, involve the review of practice assignments and cognitions associated with carrying these out, exploring and addressing difficulties, and planning new assignments. Interoceptive exposure is integrated with situational exposure by having the client monitor his or her bodily sensations while engaging in situational exposure. The last few sessions are held on a biweekly basis.

Evaluation

Panic disorder and PDA are frightening and disabling conditions that interfere with social functioning and the quality of one's life. The preceding treatment protocol offers an effective remedy to this condition. It may be implemented in an office or hospital setting, in a client's residence, or another natural setting. The intervention may be the only treatment, or it may be used in tandem with prescribed medication (Craske & Barlow, 1993).

This clinical procedure requires that the clinician be knowledgeable about cognitive therapy, the dynamics of panic and agoraphobia, and the specific procedures summarized earlier. It is recommended that anyone who wishes to use this manualized protocol with clients should read further about cognitive therapy and the Craske and Barlow (1993) approach, and practice the specific procedures under supervision.

The cognitive-behavioral intervention that has been highlighted here focuses primarily on the anxiety symptoms and, to a lesser extent, on the personality of the individual who is suffering. Some of the clients with whom social workers work have life situations that can be better addressed with an approach that integrates ego psychology with cognitive-behavioral therapy. The following section presents an example of an individual with panic symptoms who was treated by a social worker who used an integrative approach.

Case Example

Integrated Methods

Harold Rogers is a 22-year-old, single man who complained of stress when he was first seen at an outpatient service of a community hospital. He reported having difficulty sleeping, weight loss, poor appetite, recurrent episodes of heart palpitations, chest pains, difficulty breathing, and dizziness. These experiences were occurring at least once a week in the past month in a variety of contexts—when he was alone in the car on his way to work, at work, and when he was home alone. With these disturbing symptoms, he wondered whether he was "going crazy." Upon awakening in the morning, he had thoughts of staying home from work, but he went to work anyway.

Mr. Rogers was unable to provide much information about his family background during the first interview because he experienced heart palpitations when he was asked. He did say that during the last year his parents "threw him out of the house" and "forced" him to support himself. They said he was a "bum" who sat around the house during the day, went out at night, and did not work. The client coped by at first moving in with his sister for a couple of months and getting a job and later moving in with his woman friend. He also mentioned that two months ago he had a benign tumor removed from his back. Several months ago, he added, two close friends died—one of cancer, the other in a car accident. Mr. Rogers said that when he developed the tumor, he thought that he might have cancer, too. The client said that he thinks about death a great deal and is afraid to be alone.

Mr. Rogers is a high school graduate who was working on a construction crew, building houses. The few "attacks" he has had at work occurred when he was on the roof. He reported feeling dissatisfied that this was a "lowly job" with no future. Some day he would like to have his own business as a photographer. He has thought about looking for another job but has not made any efforts to do so. He said that he has had little contact with his parents since they threw him out; he does see his older brother and sisters and has a number of friends. He reported having a good relationship with the woman he was living with (Margaret Tyler); nevertheless, she does occasionally put pressure on him to make a commitment and he does not want to get married. He also mentioned that Margaret has made his life comfortable: she cooks, cleans, and picks up after him.

Preliminary Assessment

This 22-year-old, employed, single man developed panic attacks during a year of many stressful life events. Not only did he experience a "forced" separation from his parents, he took a job that he perceived as "lowly," lost two close friends, and also had a medical condition that turned out to be benign. In addition, the woman he is living with, who provides much comfort, wants more of a commitment than he is willing to give. Thrust into a world that is uncertain, demanding, and insecure, he feels anxious. He appears to desire to escape from his current situation (by not going to work or fantasizing about another job) and has anxiety about being alone, but he has not developed an overt phobia. The theme of loss and separation predominates, with unresolved issues surrounding his separation from his parents. He seems to have some dependent traits and does not seem to reciprocate in relationships. His strengths include his working, living independently, ability to maintain relationships, and the willingness to ask for help. His symptoms of anxiety are compounded with mild depression. His *DSM-IV-TR* diagnosis is as follows:

Axis I:	300.01	PDA (moderate)
Axis II:	799.90	Diagnosis deferred
Axis III:	Benign tumor removed	
Axis IV:	Psychosocial and environmental problems: forced emancipation, changes in living situation, new job, deaths of two friends, medical problem	
Axis V:	GAF = 60 (current)	
	GAF = 75 (highest level past year)	

Treatment Plan

To treat PD, two strategies will be pursued. First, the client will be taught relaxation exercises in the office and will be assigned homework to practice these daily. Second, the client will be scheduled to see the staff psychiatrist. In view of his panic and concomitant mild depression, the use of an SSRI will be discussed with the doctor. Although the primary diagnosis is PD without agoraphobia, he is at risk of developing agoraphobia or a specific phobia (fear of heights). To prevent this from occurring, the clinician will advise the client "not to give in to the urge to avoid going out." In addition, activities involving his going out with his woman friend to pursue his hobby (photography) will be assigned.

Development of the Case over Time

Mr. Rogers was seen weekly for three months. Initially, treatment centered on his symptoms. During his consultation with the psychiatrist, it was learned that he drank beer occasionally (but not excessively) and was not eager to take medication that precluded these activities. The client, social worker, and psychiatrist agreed that medication was not necessary at this time, and they would pursue other strategies first. The social worker strongly encouraged Mr. Rogers to continue to face his fears by going to work and getting out. He practiced the relaxation exercises at home and at work. As planned, he and Margaret took expeditions in which he took photographs.

Meanwhile, the client became better able to talk about his past and his family situation. He revealed that when he was six, his father died of a heart attack at home. Soon afterward the client refused to go to school. He said that his mother took him to a child guidance center for treatment; eventually he returned to school. Mr. Rogers said that he has always been close to his mother and feels protective of her. Three years ago, however, she married a man who seemed to resent him, the only child at home. Mr. Rogers expressed anger toward the stepfather, who, he thought, convinced his mother to throw him out of the house. When asked whether he would like to return to them, he said no, and he thought it was time that he was on his own. Mr. Rogers said, however, that he did miss his mother. When asked about his not seeing her, he said that he supposed that he was angry at her, too. The client spent a number of sessions expressing feelings toward his father who died when he was six, his stepfather, and his mother. He said that after his father died, he had a fear of losing his mother, even though he realized that she was in good health. As the youngest child, he had his mother's attention much of the time and he enjoyed that. In therapy, his belief that he was "entitled" to being taken care of indefinitely by his mother was challenged as irrational and childish, and cognitions supporting his parents' right to live as they want and his responsibility to support himself were substituted. At this point, the client began to become aware of his reluctance to leave the nest and be on his own. This was followed by the expression of feelings of guilt about having been inconsiderate of his mother (as well as awareness that he may be taking advantage of Margaret). When asked what he thought he might do with his feelings, he said that he would like to reestablish a relationship with his mother as an independent adult. A couple of sessions were spent planning how he might initiate contact with her and rehearsing his visit with her. The client saw his mother alone at her home on one occasion, when he apologized for his past behavior and expressed the desire to be part of the family again. She accepted his feelings and invited him to bring Margaret with him to dinner the following week.

As these separation issues were worked through, the symptoms of anxiety and depression waned and the panic attacks disappeared. Still the client expressed dissatisfaction with his job and ambivalence toward Margaret. The client continued to pursue his hobby as a photographer and planned to sell some of his photographs to a publisher. When it was suggested that he and Margaret be seen together, he said that he did not want her to get involved in his personal problems. Termination was precipitated by his taking a job in a photography shop in a distant city. He said that the job paid less than his current job, but it was a "white-collar job."

In this case, a combination of methods was used. At first attention was given to the distressful symptoms. Relaxation exercises were implemented in the office and assigned for practice at home. In addition, the client was encouraged to continue to face stressful situations (in vivo exposure) and to go out on photography excursions that were in keeping with his interests. When the client was ready, ego-modifying treatment in which he reflected on patterns that arose in the past was used. It was learned that separation anxiety was a long-standing issue with him; that he had a school phobia following his father's death when he was a child. The client was given the opportunity to express feelings about his loss of his father as a child and his loss of his mother's complete attention when she remarried. He expressed anger at his mother and stepfather; yet he had the desire to reconcile with them. Cognitive therapy was used to help him recognize that his feelings of entitlement were irrational and inappropriate for him at this point in his life. The client was encouraged to reconnect with his mother and stepfather and was helped to do so through behavior rehearsal of his first meeting with his mother. Soon afterward, he was able to separate from his woman friend and simultaneously pursue a job that was in tune with his life goals.

Although the specific cognitive-behavioral treatment procedure for PD described earlier or the integrated approach described here work, some clients are not receptive to either strategy, or they participate in therapy while using alternative means of coping with anxiety. The following section reviews some of these.

RELIABLE INSTRUMENTS USED TO ASSESS AND MONITOR ANXIETY

The following instruments are useful in assessing and monitoring anxiety symptoms and measuring outcomes. Those found in Fischer and Corcoran's (2000) *Measures for Clinical Practice* are denoted with an asterisk; other sources are indicated in parentheses. All are completed by the client unless otherwise indicated.

Hamilton Anxiety Rating Scale (Hamilton, 1959)

Clinical Anxiety Scale (Snaith, Baugh, Clayden, Husain, & Sipple, 1982)

Yale-Brown Obsessive-Compulsive Scale (administered by clinician) (Goodman et al., 1989)

*Zung's Self-Rating Anxiety Scale

*Social Avoidance and Distress Scale

MEDICATION USED TO TREAT ANXIETY DISORDERS

Over the years, a number of drugs have been tested and used to treat anxiety disorders. Although these medications do not cure the disorders, they do relieve distressing symptoms, making it possible for clinicians to treat problems with psychotherapy. The drugs that have been used have varying cost–benefit ratios, which clients need to weigh before agreeing to pharmacotherapy. Major drugs that have been reported to be effective in the treatment of anxiety disorders will be discussed in the following section. Table 9.3 lists the drugs used for anxiety disorders by type and indicates their respective trade names.

Selective Serotonin Reuptake Inhibitors

A group of relatively new antidepressants that has demonstrated effectiveness in treating anxiety disorders is the selective serotonin reuptake inhibitors (SSRIs), discussed in Chapter 8. SSRIs have been found effective in treating PD and social phobia (Thuile, Even, & Rouillon, 2008), OCD (Rauch & Jenike, 1998), and PTSD (Davidson et al., 2005). One of the better known SSRIs for treating OCD is fluvoxamine (Luvox). SSRIs have the advantage of a low profile of adverse side effects. They usually take anywhere from four to six weeks before symptoms start to diminish. SSRIs are usually started at low doses and then are gradually increased, based on treatment guidelines usually developed by the APA, until they have a beneficial effect. They are, however, costly; less expensive generic versions have not, as yet, appeared on the market. Effexor (Venlafaxine), a drug related to SSRIs, is commonly used to treat GAD.

Tricyclic Antidepressants

During the past four decades, tricyclic antidepressant medications have been used to treat anxiety. These are an older generation of antidepressants than the SSRIs and work just as well for anxiety disorders except for OCD. However, they have many more side effects than the SSRIs. The drug that has been tested the most is *imipramine* (Tofranil), a tricyclic. This drug has been shown to be effective in treating PD and anticipatory anxiety associated with agoraphobia

TABLE 9.3	Medications Used to Treat Anxiety Disorders	
Group/Examples		**Trade Name**
Selective serotonin reuptake inhibitors (SSRIs)		
fluoxetine		Prozac
fluvoxamine		Luvox
paroxetine		Paxil
sertraline		Zoloft
citalopram		Celexa
Tricyclic antidepressants		
imipramine		Tofranil
amitriptyline		Elavil
desipramine		Norpramin
nortriptyline		Pamelor
doxepin		Sinequan
clomipramine		Anafranil
Monoamine oxidase inhibitors (MAOIs)		
phenelzine		Nardil
Atyical antidepressant		
venlafaxine		Effexor
Benodiazepines		
clonazepamn		Klonopin
lorazepam		Ativan
alprazolam		Xanex
diazepam		Valium
Azapirones		
buspirone		BuSpar

(Mavissakalian & Perel, 1989; Zitrin, Klein, Woerner, & Ross, 1983). Research indicates that it takes a high dose to treat agoraphobia but a moderate dose to treat PD (Mavissakalian & Perel, 1989). Furthermore, imipramine helps reduce nightmares, flashbacks, panic attacks, and mood disturbances in persons with PTSD (Horowitz, 1989). Other tricyclic antidepressants that are used to treat PD and agoraphobia as well as PTSD are Elavil, Norpramin, Pamelor, and Sinequan. These drugs have the advantage of reducing anxiety while at the same time they do not pose a threat of dependence. The disadvantages of tricyclics and their side effects (sedation, postural hypotension, anticholinergic effects, etc.) were described in Chapter 8.

Clomipramine (Anafranil) is a tricyclic that is used principally in the treatment of OCD. Although clomipramine does not eliminate obsessions and compulsions entirely, it does reduce preoccupation with obsessions and ritualistic behavior (Insel & Zohar, 1987). Like other tricyclics, clomipramine takes several weeks to produce changes; when the medication is withdrawn, the disorder reasserts itself (Stahl, 2009).

Monoamine Oxidase Inhibitors

Another antidepressant medication that is used to treat anxiety disorders is the monoamine oxidase inhibitors (MAOIs), particularly *phenelzine* (Nardil). Like imipramine, it treats panic and phobic anxiety. Moreover, the MAOI is effective in the treatment of social phobias and atypical depression with panic attacks (Liebowitz, 1989), as well as PTSDs with panic attacks (Horowitz, 1989). However therapeutic, the MAOI requires restriction of certain foods and drink (e.g., smoked food, aged cheeses) and medications (e.g., antihistamines) (see Chapter 8). In addition, certain side effects are associated with this group of drugs (e.g., hypotension, sexual difficulties). For these reasons, other medications are preferred for the treatment of panic and agoraphobia.

Benzodiazepines

Benzodiazepines are anxiolytics (antianxiety agents) that have historically been used to treat anxiety. Among the drugs in this group are *chlordiazepoxide* (Librium), *diazepam* (Valium), *clorazepate* (Tranxene), *oxazepam* (Serax), *alprazolam* (Xanax), and *lorazepam* (Ativan). Some of these drugs (e.g., Serax and Ativan) have a short half-life; that is, they are eliminated from the blood rapidly. Others have an intermediate half-life (e.g., Xanax), and others have a long half-life (e.g., Valium, Tranxene, and Librium) (Salzman, 1989). The two short-half-life drugs, Serax and Ativan, which do not have active metabolites and long-acting benzodiazepines with active metabolites that are prescribed in small doses and over increased intervals, are recommended for older adults (Cloos & Ferreira, 2009).

All these drugs have a calming effect. Furthermore, they produce sedation, promote sleep, and have some muscle relaxant and anticonvulsive effects (Cloos & Ferreira, 2009). The sedative effects may or may not be desired. Sedation causes drowsiness and slows reactions, which can interfere with the operation of machinery. This effect is compounded if the client uses alcohol or takes antihistamines (Cloos & Ferreira, 2009). A serious problem with these drugs is that, over time, they are addictive. Persons successfully treated for panic attacks, for example, can, upon withdrawal, experience *rebound panics*, recurrences that are more intense than those that were experienced previously. For these reasons, short-term use with minimal therapeutic doses (Salzman, 1989) and slow withdrawal (Barlow, 1988) are recommended.

Because the onset of the effects of benzodiazepines is rapid (especially Valium and Tranxene), these drugs are amenable to use for symptomatic relief of acute anxiety reactions (Cloos & Ferreira, 2009), such as those seen in an emergency room. Moreover, they have been found to be effective in the treatment of GAD, PTSD, and PD (Cloos & Ferreira, 2009; Horowitz, 1989; Noyes, Chaudry, & Domingo, 1986).

Alprazolam (Xanax) has been particularly effective in the treatment of PDs and associated phobic anxiety (Sussman & Klee, 2005). This drug appears to be less sedating than the other benzodiazepines. In addition, it has antidepressant effects on recipients, regardless of whether or not they have a secondary depression (Sussman & Klee, 2005). Research emanating from the Cross-National Collaborative Panic Study on approximately 500 subjects found that those who took alprazolam had a significantly higher rate of improvement in panic attacks, phobic fears, avoidance behavior, anxiety, and social disability than the control group on placebos (Ballenger et al., 1988). Improvement was evident after one week. Nevertheless, side effects that were treatment related were identified in another report by this research group (Noyes, Dupont, Pecknold, & Rifkin, 1988). These include fatigue, sedation, ataxia, amnesia, and slurred speech. These authors reported that the dropout rate among those who received the active drug was substantially lower (16 percent) than that of those who received the placebo (50 percent), a finding that suggests high acceptance of alprazolam.

Buspirone

Buspirone (BuSpar) is an antianxiety agent that is the equivalent of diazepam (Valium) but does not share many of the latter's drawbacks. Buspirone does not cause sedation, engender abuse or physical dependence, or act as an anticonvulsant (Eison & Temple, 1986). Accordingly, arousal, attention, and the capacity to act and react are preserved. Another advantage of buspirone is that it does not interact synergistically with alcohol (Eison & Temple, 1986); thus, it may be useful for persons with a history of substance abuse (Salzman, 1989). Nevertheless, buspirone does not act as quickly as the diazepam. Moreover, in some cases, lack of sedation may be viewed as a drawback. Buspirone seems to be useful in the treatment of GAD (Andreasen & Black, 2006).

Pharmacological Treatment

The aforementioned drugs are the major medications used to treat anxiety disorders. New drugs continue to be tested and introduced all the time. Moreover, some of the antidepressants that were discussed in Chapter 8 are sometimes prescribed together with some of the antianxiety medications that have been reviewed in this chapter. Table 9.4 lists specific anxiety disorders treated with drugs that have been shown to be effective in research studies.

These drugs provide symptomatic relief to those individuals who are willing to take them and who respond positively to them. Many clients who are given full information about the effects and risks associated with these medications will, however, refuse consent. Antidepressants have side effects that many individuals find troubling. Benzodiazepines can be addicting if taken over a long period of time and are not appropriate for persons with a history of substance abuse. Older adults are more sensitive to drugs and may have medical problems that complicate or preclude psychopharmacology (Banazak, 1997). Regardless of whether or not clients receive medication, they can benefit from psychotherapy. Therapy can assist in modifying negative anxious thoughts, emotions, and anxious behaviors troubling to the client that medication does not touch.

TABLE 9.4 Medication Used for Specific Anxiety Disorders

Disorder	Medications
Panic disorder with and without agoraphobia	SSRIs, TCAs (clomipramine and imipramine), MAOIs, benzodiazepines
Social phobia	SSRIs, benzodiazepines, atypical antidepressant (venlafazine)
Specific phobias	Do not appear to be responsive to drugs
Generalized anxiety disorder	Benzodiazepines, buspirone, venlafaxine
Obsessive-compulsive disorder	Clomipramine, SSRIs
Posttraumatic stress disorder	SSRIs, TCAs (imipramine, amitriptyline), MAOIs

Sources: Based on Cowen (1998), Rauch & Jenike (1998), Roy-Byrne & Cowley (1995), Sadock & Sadock (2007), Yehuda, Marshall, & Giller (1998).

Research on Medication and Psychotherapy

The relative effects of medication and psychotherapy in the treatment of anxiety have not been subjected to as extensive studies as those with respect to depression. Recent reviews of randomized trials using SSRI antidepressants for anxiety disorders have found encouraging results on social anxiety (paroxetine, sertraline, fluvoxamine, venlaxafine), PTSD (sertraline, fluoxetine), OCD (paroxetine, sertraline, fluoxetine, escitalopram), GAD (venlaxafine, escitalopram), and PD with or without agoraphobia (paroxetine, venlaxafine) (Thuile et al., 2008).

According to empirical evidence, the path to treatment for anxiety disorders likely suggests a more unified treatment approach based on new studies on emotional regulation and dysregulation, rather than a specific diagnostic category and associated diagnostic treatment protocols (Allen, McHugh, & Barlow, 2008). Cognitive-behavioral therapy treatment procedures for psychological disorders have many similarities: (a) changing emotion-focused cognitive schemas of individual-perceived thoughts based on daily life events, (b) preventing avoidance behaviors of negative internal or environmental triggers or cues, and (c) modifying emotion-based behaviors (Allen et al., 2008).

Some early research has focused on the relative merits of behavioral treatment and pharmacotherapy in the treatment of PD and agoraphobia. Particular attention has been given to testing Klein and Gorman's (1987) model of panic and agoraphobic development. These researchers posed that panic precedes and conditions the development of agoraphobia. Furthermore, they suggested that imipramine is able to treat the panic attacks but not avoidant behavior or anticipatory anxiety. One group of researchers found in a controlled study that there was significant improvement among all subjects given encouragement and instructions to practice in vivo exposure (to be explained in the next section) on their own, with those on imipramine rating higher clinically, depending on the dose of imipramine they had (Mavissakalian & Michelson, 1986). In another analysis, however, it was found that subjects who were not told to practice exposure benefited in relation to both phobic and panic symptoms. Here, too, a relation between medication dosage and the target symptoms was found (Mavissakalian & Perel, 1989). In another study in which behavior therapy with and without imipramine was compared with supportive therapy with imipramine, no differences were found among the various treatments (Klein, Zitrin, Woerner, & Ross, 1983). On the basis of these studies, it appears that *medication and exposure* (as well as support), separately or together, can effectively treat panic and anticipatory anxiety.

Craske and Barlow (2008) suggest that many patients are already on some type of psychotropic medication. Thus, it is essential that the individual is stable and on an appropriate medication dose so that psychotherapist can clearly identify the anxiety symptoms (Allen et al., 2008). Use of antianxiety medications does not appear to have a negative impact on treatment; however, research suggests that individuals who receive medication alone or cognitive-behavioral therapy augmented with medication tend to relapse (Barlow, Gorman, Shear, & Woods, 2000).

Pharmacological Treatment for Anxiety in Older Adults

In part because of the tendency for older adults to present to primary care physicians, anxiolytic medications, including benzodiazepines, are the most common treatment for late-life anxiety (Lenze et al., 2003). ECA data suggest that benzodiazepine use among elderly people is approximately 14 percent higher than the rates for younger adults (Swartz et al., 1991).

Benzodiazepine users are also more likely than nonusers to experience accidents requiring medical attention, due to increased risk of falls, hip fractures, and automobile accidents

(Tamblyn, Abrahamowicz, du Berger, McLeod, & Bartlett, 2005). Older patients taking benzo-diazepines are also more likely to develop disabilities in both mobility and activities of daily living (ADLs) (Gray et al., 2006). Benzodiazepines can impair memory and other cognitive functions (Wengel, Burke, Ranno, & Roccaforte, 1993). These medications can also cause tolerance and withdrawal, interactions with other drugs, and toxicity (Krasucki, Howard, & Mann, 1999).

Although safer medications, particularly SSRIs, are often used to treat anxiety in older adults, they can cause unpleasant side effects, and some older people prefer not to take them. Furthermore, SSRIs have not completely replaced benzodiazepines as a treatment for anxiety in older people (Keene, Eaddy, Nelson, & Sarnes, 2005). Safe and effective alternative treatments for anxiety, appealing to an older population, are clearly needed.

OTHER WAYS OF HEALING

Anxiety is a universal feeling that is not likely to be defined as a disorder unless it seriously interferes with everyday functioning and is identified as problematic by a professional. Through a social process of help seeking and finding, diffuse and uncomfortable feelings become reconstructed as symptoms of an anxiety disorder. Regardless of whether individuals experiencing these feelings seek professional help, many of them discover a number of ways of healing on their own.

One means of helping oneself heal, which was borrowed from Eastern religions, is meditation. Some individuals find that meditation clears their minds, relaxes their bodies, and reduces their stress. One version of this, transcendental meditation (TM), is practiced as follows:

> You begin by sitting in a comfortable position and silently repeating a word or sound over and over again. If a thought other than the meditative word comes to mind, you repeat the word or sound again. It has been said that the level of rest achieved by TM is deeper than sleep. (Phalen, 1998, p. 107)

Meditation may be a component of a lifestyle that includes eating a well-balanced diet (which may be low in fat content, macrobiotic, or vegetarian), getting ample sleep, practicing yoga, and exercising. By controlling these aspects of one's life and finding inner peace, one can become empowered to take charge of one's life.

Another means of healing oneself is through religion and spirituality. Religion offers a framework in which one's experiences can make sense; religious organizations offer support for this framework, a sense of community, and opportunities to pray. Whether one finds solace in group or individual prayer, or through one's own individual form of spirituality, one may find comfort, peace, and tranquility this way.

The previous chapter mentioned herbal treatment in relation to depression. There are also herbs that are reputed to treat anxiety. Two publications that describe these treatments are Foster and Tyler's (1999) *Tyler's Honest Herbal: A Sensible Guide to the Use of Herbs and Related Products* and Robbers and Tyler's (1999) *Tyler's Herbs of Choice: The Therapeutic Use of Phytomedicinals.* One should be cautious about these remedies, dosage, and how they may interact with prescribed drugs.

There are a number of organizations that provide information and help to individuals with anxiety disorders and their families. Among the national organizations are the Anxiety Disorders Association of America, the National Center for PTSD, the Obsessive-Compulsive Foundation, and the National Alliance for the Mentally Ill (which includes PD, PTSD, and OCDs among the major disorders they support). There are myriad support groups for individuals with anxiety disorders and their families in large cities and some smaller communities. In addition, there are many self-help books and tapes (as well as Web pages) that provide information about coping with anxiety.

Case Study

Cynthia Brown is a medium-tall, 30-year-old, married woman who reported that she weighed 160 pounds. She has an attractive face and dresses in such a way that she looks lighter than her stated weight. She said that her problems are of her own making: because she is ashamed of being overweight, she isolates herself. She stays home most of the time and avoids opportunities to go out. She has difficulty getting herself mobilized to go to the grocery store, usually waiting until they are out of food and she must go. The client expressed concern that she will be seen at the grocery store. Whenever her husband suggests that they go out together or with another couple, she finds a reason for them not to go out.

Mrs. Brown said that even though it looks as if she "prefers" to be at home, she does not do much when she is at home. She feels as if she spends all her time serving others—even the dog—but is not doing anything for herself. She and her husband, Jason, have a 3-year-old daughter, Amy; her husband has a son, age 12, from a previous marriage, who lives with them. Mrs. Brown believes that her husband gives more attention to his son than to their daughter. To compensate, she devotes herself to Amy. Even though Mrs. Brown has allowed Amy to go to a nearby nursery school, she worries about her the whole time Amy is in school. She is afraid that "something will happen to Amy."

Mrs. Brown said that she and Jason met at the time Jason was separated from his first wife. At that time Cynthia was thin and worked as a model. Jason told her that his first wife had a weight problem; that her weight contributed to their divorce. Mrs. Brown has some concern that her husband will reject her. She said that she knows her refusal to go out has been getting on his nerves, too. She mentioned that when they first met, her husband used to worry that other men would want her. Now she worries that her husband will be attracted to other women.

The social worker remarked that Mrs. Brown has described a number of problems—fears about leaving the house, worries about her daughter, a weight problem, and marital difficulties—and asked her what she wanted to work on. The client said that if she could get over her anxiety about leaving the house, she thinks that the other problems will resolve themselves.

Summary and Deconstruction

Although *anxiety* is an ordinary response to perceived danger and to awareness of the unknown, *anxiety disorders* are extraordinary. Inner tension becomes constructed as a disorder when the tension reaches a heightened level. In some respects, individuals with

anxiety disorders live more intensely than others, but in other respects, they suffer more and can become debilitated.

Anxiety disorders are heterogeneous and complex. All the anxiety disorders described in the

DSM-IV-TR are characterized by a set of biological, cognitive, emotional, and behavioral symptoms, many of which occur across types. With some anxiety disorders, individuals avoid certain kinds of situations (e.g., social phobias); with other disorders, they feel compelled to act in certain ways (OCD). With some disorders, the anxiety is concentrated and erupts (PD); with other disorders, the anxiety is diffuse (GAD). Individuals with anxiety disorders experience the same symptoms differently.

This chapter reviewed biological, psychological, and social explanations of anxiety disorders. Genetic explanations are not definitive. The numerous psychological theories attest to the heterogeneity of the disorders and individual differences; some explanations may fit more with some individuals' experience than others. The association of anxiety disorder with gender and socioeconomic class (income, education) raises questions about the role of stress in the generation of anxiety disorders.

This chapter described an evidence-based treatment for cognitive-behavioral treatment of individuals with PDA. However effective the program is, it is not appropriate for all clients and does not address some of the psychosocial and developmental issues that may be pertinent. Some clinical social workers combine and integrate different methods in their work with clients. A case example illustrated how ego psychology can be used together with exposure and cognitive restructuring.

Individuals with anxiety also design their own treatments from the options they discover on their own or in their own communities. Among these are meditation, yoga, exercise, herbal remedies, and living a healthy lifestyle. In addition, some clients and members of their families participate in support groups, read self-help books, and find "answers" on Web pages. Clinical social workers need to be cognizant that individuals' ways of coping include these methods as well as (or instead of) going to professionals.

References

Allen, L., McHugh, R. K., & Barlow, D. (2008). Emotional disorders: A unified model. In D. Barlow (Ed.), *Clinical handbook of psychological disorders* (3rd ed., pp. 216–249). New York: Guilford Press.

Alwahhabi, F. (2003). Anxiety symptoms and generalized anxiety disorder in the elderly: A review. *Harvard Review of Psychiatry, 11*(4), 180–193.

American Psychiatric Association. (2000). *Diagnostic and statistical manual of mental disorders* (4th ed., text rev.). Washington, DC: Author.

Andreasen, N. C., & Black, D. W. (2006). *Introductory textbook of psychiatry* (4th ed.). Washington, DC: American Psychiatric Publishing.

Ballenger, J. C., Burrows, G. D., DuPont, R. L., Lesser, I. M., Noyes, R., Pecknold, J. C., et al. (1988). Alprazolam in panic disorder and agoraphobia: Results from a multicenter trial. I. Efficacy in short-term treatment. *Archives of General Psychiatry, 45,* 413–422.

Banazak, D. A. (1997). Anxiety disorders in elderly patients. *Journal of the American Board of Family Practice, 10*(4), 280–289.

Barlow, D. H. (1988). *Anxiety and Its disorders.* New York: Guilford Press.

Barlow, D. H., Esler, J. L., & Vitali, A. E. (1998). Psychosocial treatments for panic disorders, phobias,

and generalized anxiety disorder. In P. E. Nathan & J. M. Gorman (Eds.), *A guide to treatments that work* (pp. 288–318). New York: Oxford University Press.

Barlow, D. H., Gorman, J., Shear, K., & Woods, S. (2000). Cognitive behavioral therapy, imipramine or their combination for panic disorder: A randomized controlled trial. *Journal of the American Medical Association, 283*(19), 2529–2536.

Beck, A. (1985). Cognitive therapy. In H. I. Kaplan & B. J. Sadock (Eds.), *Comprehensive textbook of psychiatry/IV* (pp. 1432–1438). Baltimore, MD: Williams & Wilkins.

Beck, A. T., & Emery, G., with Greenberg, R. L. (1985). *Anxiety disorders and phobias: A cognitive perspective.* New York: Basic Books.

Beck, J. G., & Averill, P. M. (2004). Older adults. In D. Mennon, R. Heimberg, & C.Turk (Eds.), *Generalized anxiety disorder: Advances in research and practice* (pp. 409–433). New York: Guilford Press.

Beekman, A., Bremmer, M., Deeg, D., van Balkom, A., Smit, J., de Beurs, E., et al. (1998). Anxiety disorders in later life: A report from the longitudinal aging study Amsterdam. *International Journal of Geriatric Psychiatry, 13*(10), 717–726.

Beekman, A., van Balkom, A., Deeg, D., van Dyck, R., & van Tilburg, W. (2000). Anxiety and depression in later life: Co-occurrence and communality of risk factors. *American Journal of Psychiatry, 157*(1), 89–95.

Blazer, D. G. (1997). Generalized anxiety disorder and panic disorder in the elderly: A review. *Harvard Review of Psychiatry, 5*(1), 18–27.

Bowling, A., Farquhar, M., & Grundy, E. (1996). Associations with changes in life satisfaction among three samples of elderly people living at home. *International Journal of Geriatric Psychiatry, 11*(12), 1077–1087.

Brenner, C. (1955). *An elementary textbook of psychoanalysis.* New York: Doubleday Anchor.

Calhoun, K. S., & Resick, P. A. (1993). Post-traumatic stress disorder. In D. Barlow (Ed.), *Clinical handbook of psychological disorders: A step-by-step treatment manual* (2nd ed., pp. 48–98). New York: Guilford Press.

Camus, A. (1991). *The myth of Sisyphus and other essays.* (J. O'Brien, Trans.). New York: Vintage Books.

Cloos, J. M., & Ferreira, V. (2009). Current use of benzodiazepines in anxiety disorders. *Current Opinion in Psychiatry, 22*(1), 90–95.

Cowen, P. J. (1998). Psychopharmacology. In A. S. Bellack & M. Hersen (Eds.), *Comprehensive clinical psychology* (Vol. 6, pp. 136–161). Amsterdam: Elsevier Science.

Craske, M. G., & Barlow, D. H. (1993). Panic disorder and agoraphobia. In D. Barlow (Ed.), *Clinical handbook of psychological disorders: A step-by-step treatment manual* (2nd ed., pp. 1–47). New York: Guilford Press.

Craske, M. G., & Barlow, D. H. (2006). *Worry.* New York: Oxford University Press.

Craske, M. G., & Barlow, D. H. (2008). Panic disorder and agoraphobia. In D. Barlow (Ed.), *Clinical handbook of psychological disorders* (3rd ed., pp. 1–64). New York: Guilford Press.

Davidson, J. R. T., Connor, K. M., Hertzberg, M. A., Weisler, R. H., Wilson, W. H., & Payne, V. M. (2005). Maintenance therapy with fluoxetine in posttraumatic stress disorder: A placebo-controlled discontinuation study. *Journal of Clinical Psychopharmacology, 25,* 166–169.

Davis, M. J., Moye, J., & Karel, M. J. (2002). Mental health screening of older adults in primary care. *Journal of Mental Health and Aging, 8*(2), 139–149.

Diala, C., & Muntaner, C. (2003). Mood and anxiety disorders among rural, urban, and metropolitan residents in the United States. *Community Mental Health Journal, 39*(3), 239–252.

Diefenbach, G. J., & Goethe, J. (2006). Clinical interventions for late-life anxious depression. *Clinical Interventions in Aging, 1*(1), 41–50.

DiNardo, P., & Barlow, D. H. (1988). *Anxiety Disorders Interview Schedule—Revised (ADIS-R).* Albany, NY: Graywind Publications.

Douchet, C., Ladouceur, R., Freeston, M. H., & Dugas, M. J. (1998). Worry themes and the tendency to worry in older adults. *Canadian Journal on Aging, 17*(4), 361–371.

Eison, M. S., & Temple, D. L. (1986). Buspirone: Review of its pharmacology and current perspectives on its mechanism of action. *American Journal of Medicine, 80*(Suppl. 3B), 1–9.

Ellis, A. (1962). *Reason and emotion in psychotherapy.* New York: Lyle Stuart.

Fischer, J., & Corcoran, K. (2007). *Measures for clinical practice: A sourcebook* (Vols. 1 and 2, 4th ed.). New York: Oxford University Press.

Foster, S., & Tyler, V. E. (1999). *Tyler's honest herbal: A sensible guide to the use of herbs and related products* (4th ed.). New York: Haworth Herbal Press.

Goodman, W. K., Price, L. H., Rasmussen, S. A., Mazure, C., Fleischmann, R. L., Hill, C. L., et al. (1989). The Yale-Brown Obsessive-Compulsive Scale. I: Development, use, and reliability. *Archives of General Psychiatry, 46,* 1006–1011.

Gray, S. L., LaCroix, A. Z., Hanlon, J. T., Penninx, B. W., Blough, D. K., Leveille, S. G., et al. (2006). Benzodiazepine use and physical disability in community-dwelling older adults. *Journal of the American Geriatrics Society, 54*(2), 224–230.

Greenberg, P., Sistitsky, T., Kessler, R. C., Finkelstein, S., Berndt, E., Davidson, J., et al. (1999). The economic burden of anxiety disorders in the 1990s. *Journal of Clinical Psychiatry, 60,* 427–435.

Hamilton, M. (1959). The assessment of anxiety states by rating. *British Journal of Medical Psychology, 32,* 50–55.

Hollander, E., Liebowitz, M. R., & Gorman, J. M. (1988). Anxiety disorders. In J. A. Talbott, R. E. Hales, & S. Yudofsky (Eds.), *Textbook of psychiatry* (pp. 391–443). Washington, DC: American Psychiatric Press.

Horowitz, M. J. (1989). Posttraumatic stress disorder. In American Psychiatric Association, *Treatments of psychiatric disorders: A task force report of the American Psychiatric Association* (Vol. 3, pp. 2065–2082). Washington, DC: American Psychiatric Association.

Insel, T. R., & Zohar, J. (1987). Psychopharmacologic approaches to obsessive-compulsive disorder. In H. Y. Meltzer (Ed.), *Psychopharmacology: The third generation* (pp. 1205–1210). New York: Raven Press.

Jacobson, E. (1938). *Progressive relaxation.* Chicago: University of Chicago Press.

Kaplan, H. I., & Sadock, B. J. (1998). *Synopsis of psychiatry* (8th ed.). Baltimore, MD: Williams & Wilkins.

Kaschak, E. (1992). *Engendered lives: A new psychology of women's experience.* New York: Basic Books.

Keene, M. S., Eaddy, M. T., Nelson, W. W., & Sarnes, M. W. (2005). Adherence to Paroxetine CR compared with Paroxetine IR in a medicare-eligible population with anxiety disorders. *American Journal of Managed Care, 11*(12, Suppl.), S362–S369.

Kessler, R. C., Berglund, P., Demler, O., Jin, R., Merikangas, K., & Walters, E. (2005). Lifetime prevalence and age of onset distributions of DSM-IV distributions in the National Comorbidity Survey replication. *Archives of General Psychiatry, 62*(6), 593–602.

Kessler, R. C., Chiu, W., Demler, O., & Walters, E. (2005). Prevalence, severity, and comorbidity of twelve month DSM-IV disorders in the National Comorbidity Survey Replication (NCS-R). *Archives of General Psychiatry, 62*(6), 617–627.

Kessler, R. C., McGonagle, K. A., Zhao, S., Nelson, C. B., Hughes, M., Eshlman, S., et al. (1994). Lifetime and 12-month prevalence of DSM-III-R psychiatric disorders in the United States: Results from the National Comorbidity Survey. *Archives of General Psychiatry, 51,* 8–19.

Klein, D. F., & Gorman, J. M. (1987). A model of panic and agoraphobic development. *Acta Psychiatrie Scandinavia, 76*(Suppl. 335), 87–95.

Klein, D. F., Zitrin, C. M., Woerner, M. G., & Ross, D. C. (1983). Treatment of phobias. II. Behavior therapy and psychotherapy: Are there any specific ingredients? *Archives of General Psychiatry, 40,* 139–145.

Krasucki, C., Howard, R., & Mann, A. (1999). Anxiety and its treatment in the elderly. *International Psychogeriatrics, 11*(1), 25–45.

Le Roux, H., Gatz, M., & Wetherell, J. L. (2005). Age at onset of generalized anxiety disorder in older adults. *American Journal of Geriatric Psychiatry,13*(1), 23–30.

Lenze, E., Mulsant, B. H., Mohlman, J., Shear, K., Dew, M. A., Schulz, R., et al. (2005). Generalized anxiety disorder in late life: Lifetime course and comorbidity with major depressive disorder. *American Journal of Geriatric Psychiatry, 13*(1), 77–80.

Lenze, E., Pollock, B., Shear, K., Mulsant, B., Bharucha, A., & Reynolds, C. (2003).Treatment considerations for anxiety in the elderly. *CNS Spectrum, 8*(12, Suppl. 3), 6–13.

Liebowitz, M. R. (1989). Antidepressants in panic disorders. *British Journal of Psychiatry, 155*(Suppl. 6), 46–52.

Mahoney, M. J. (1974). *Cognition and behavior modification.* Cambridge, MA: Ballinger.

Margolin, G., & Cordis, E. (2000). The effects of family and community violence on children. *Annual Review of Psychology, 51,* 445–479.

Markowitz, J. S., Weissman, M. M., Ouellette, R., Lish, J. D., & Klerman, G. L. (1989). Quality of life in panic disorder. *Archives of General Psychiatry, 46,* 984–992.

Mathews, A. M., Gelder, M. G., & Johnston, D. W. (1981). *Agoraphobia: Nature and treatment.* New York: Guilford Press.

Mavissakalian, M., & Michelson, L. (1986). Agoraphobia: Relative and combined effectiveness of therapist-assisted in vivo exposure and imipramine. *Journal of Clinical Psychiatry, 143,* 1106–1112.

Mavissakalian, M. R., & Perel, J. M. (1989). Imipramine dose–response relationship in panic disorder with agoraphobia. *Archives of General Psychiatry, 46,* 127–131.

Meichenbaum, D. (1985). *Stress inoculation training.* New York: Pergamon.

Mitte, K. (2005). Meta-analysis of cognitive-behavioral treatments for Generalized Anxiety Disorder: A comparison with pharmacotherapy. *Psychological Bulletin, 131*(5), 785–795.

Myers, J. K., Weissman, M. M., Tischler, G. L., Holzer, C., Leaf, P., Orvaschel, H., et al. (1984). Six-month prevalence of psychiatric disorders in three communities. *Archives of General Psychiatry, 41,* 959–967.

National Institute of Mental Health. (2008). Numbers count: Mental disorders in America. Retrieved April 17, 2010, from http://www.nimh.nih.gov/health/publications/the-numbers-count-mental-disorders-in-america/index.shtml#PTSD

Noyes, R., Chaudry, D. R., & Domingo, D. V. (1986). Pharmacologic treatment of phobic disorders. *Journal of Clinical Psychiatry, 47,* 445–451.

Noyes, R., Dupont, R., Pecknold, J., & Rifkin, A. (1988). Alprazolam in panic disorder and agoraphobia: Results from a multicenter trial II, patient acceptance, side effects and safety. *Archives of General Psychiatry, 45*(5), 423–428.

O'Brien, G. T., & Barlow, D. H. (1984). Agoraphobia. In S. M. Turner (Ed.), *Behavioral theories and treatment of anxiety* (pp. 143–185). New York: Plenum Press.

Ostir, G. V., & Goodwin, J. S. (2006). Anxiety in persons 75 and older: Findings from a tri-ethnic population. *Ethnicity & Disease, 16*(1), 22–27.

Phalen, K. F. (1998). *Integrative medicine: Achieving wellness through the best of Eastern and Western medical practices.* Boston: Journey Editions.

Rauch, S. L., & Jenike, M. A. (1998). Pharmacological treatment of obsessive compulsive disorder. In P. E. Nathan & J. M. Gorman (Eds.), *A guide to treatments that work* (pp. 358–376). New York: Oxford University Press.

Regier, D. A., Boyd, J. H., Burke, J. D., Rae, D. S., Myers, J. K., Kramer, M., et al. (1988). One-month prevalence of mental disorders in the United States. *Archives of General Psychiatry, 45,* 977–986.

Regier, D. A., Rae, D., Narrow, W., Kaelber, C. T., & Schatzberg, A. F. (1998). Prevalence of anxiety disorders and their comorbidity with mood and addictive disorders. *British Journal of Psychiatry, 34*(Suppl.), 24–28.

Reiss, S., Peterson, R., Gursky, D., & McNally, R. (1986). Anxiety sensitivity, anxiety frequency, and the prediction of fearfulness. *Behaviour Research and Therapy, 24,* 1–8.

Rimm, D. C., & Masters, J. C. (1974). *Behavior therapy: Techniques and empirical findings.* New York: Academic Press.

Robbers, J. E., & Tyler, V. E. (1999). *Tyler's herbs of choice: The therapeutic use of phytomedicinals.* New York: Haworth Herbal Press.

Robins, L. N., & Regier, D. A. (1991). *Psychiatric disorders in America: The Epidemiologic Catchment Area Study.* New York: Free Press.

Roy-Byrne, P., & Cowley, D. (1995). Course and outcome in panic disorder: A review of recent follow-up studies. *Anxiety, 1,* 151–160.

Sadock, B. J., & Sadock, V. A. (2007). *Kaplan & Sadock's synopsis of psychiatry: Behavioral sciences/clinical psychiatry* (10th ed.). Philadelphia, PA: Wolters Klumer Lippincott Williams & Wilkins.

Salkovskis, P. M. (1998). Panic disorder and agoraphobia. In A. J. Bellack & M. Hersen (Eds.), *Comprehensive clinical psychology* (Vol. 6, pp. 399–437). Amsterdam: Elsevier Science.

Salzman, C. (1989). Treatment with antianxiety agents. In American Psychiatric Association, *Treatments of psychiatric disorders: A task force report of the American Psychiatric Association* (Vol. 3, pp. 2036–2052). Washington, DC: American Psychiatric Association.

Snaith, R. P., Baugh, S. J., Clayden, A., Husain, A., & Sipple, A. (1982). The Clinical Anxiety Scale: An instrument derived from the Hamilton Anxiety Scale. *British Journal of Psychiatry, 141,* 518–523.

Stahl, S. (2009). *Stahl's essential psychopharmacology: The prescriber's guide.* New York: Cambridge University Press.

Stern, R., & Marks, I. (1973). Brief and prolonged flooding: A comparison in agoraphobic patients. *Archives of General Psychiatry, 28,* 270–276.

Sussman, J., & Klee, B. (2005). The role of high-potency benzodiazepines in the treatment of panic disorder. *Journal of Clinical Psychiatry, 7*(1), 5–11.

Swartz, M., Landerman, R., George, L., Melville, M., Blazer, D., & Smith, K. (1991). Benzodiazepine anti-anxiety agents: Prevalence and correlates of use in a southern community. *American Journal of Public Health, 81*(5), 592–596.

Tamblyn, R., Abrahamowicz, M., du Berger, R., McLeod, P., & Bartlett, G. (2005). A 5-year prospective assessment of the risk associated with individual Benzodiazepines and doses in new elderly users. *Journal of the American Geriatric Society, 53*(2), 233–241.

Telch, M. J., Lucas, J. A., Schmidt, N. B., Hanna, H. H., Jaimez, T. S., & Lucas, R. A. (1993). Group cognitive-behavioral treatment of panic disorder. *Behaviour Research and Therapy, 31,* 279–287.

Thuile, J., Even, C., & Rouillon, F. (2008). Long-term outcome of anxiety disorders: a review of double blind studies. *Current Opinions in Psychiatry, 22,* 84–89.

Torgersen, S. (1983). Genetic factors in anxiety disorders. *Archives of General Psychiatry, 40,* 1085–1089.

Turner, S. M., & Beidel, D. C. (1988). *Treating obsessive-compulsive disorder.* New York: Pergamon.

U.S. Department of Health and Human Services. (1999). *Mental health: A report of the surgeon general.* Washington, DC: Author.

Weakes, C. (1968). *Hope and help for your nerves.* New York: Hawthorne.

Weakes, C. (1972). *Peace from nervous suffering.* New York: Hawthorne.

Weissman, M. M. (1990). The epidemiology of panic disorder and agoraphobia. In J. C. Ballenger (Ed.), *Clinical aspects of panic disorder: Frontiers of clinical neuroscience* (Vol. 9, pp. 57–65). New York: Wiley.

Weissman, M. M., Klerman, G. L., Markowitz, J. S., & Ouellette, R. (1989). Suicidal ideation and suicide attempts in panic disorder and attacks. *New England Journal of Medicine, 18*(321), 1209–1214.

Wengel, S., Burke, W., Ranno, A., & Roccaforte, W. (1993). Use of benzodiazepines in the elderly. *Psychiatric Annals, 23*(6), 325–331.

Wolpe, J. (1982). *The practice of behavior therapy* (3rd ed.). New York: Pergamon.

Yehuda, R., Marshall, R., & Giller, E. (1998). Psychopharmacological treatment of post-traumatic stress disorder. In P. E. Nathan & J. M. Gorman (Eds.), *A guide to treatments that work* (pp. 377–397). New York: Oxford University Press.

Zitrin, C. M., Klein, D. F., Woerner, M. G., & Ross, D. C. (1983). Treatment of phobias. I. Comparison of imipramine hydrochloride and placebo. *Archives of General Psychiatry, 40,* 125–138.

A Framework for Intervention with Persons with Severe Mental Illness

> *Never in the history of America have we known so much about mental health and how to enable people with mental illnesses to live, work, learn, and participate fully in the community. Recovery from mental illness is now a realistic hope. Yet much of what we know is not accessible to the people who need it most.*
>
> —SUBSTANCE ABUSE AND MENTAL HEALTH SERVICES ADMINISTRATION, *TRANSFORMING MENTAL HEALTH CARE IN AMERICA*, 2005, P. 1

As the above statement indicates, this is a new era in the understanding and treatment of severe mental illness. In the past, clients with schizophrenia, major depression, and bipolar disorder would have been labeled *chronically mentally ill* and possibly placed in the back wards of psychiatric facilities for indefinitely long periods of time. Today the term *chronic mental illness* is considered pejorative (Bachrach, 1988; Jimenez, 1988) as it suggests that a psychiatric condition is permanent, irremediable, and hopeless. Now clients can expect to live fulfilling and productive lives in the community despite a mental illness.

The current climate of hope came about through changes in conceptualization, values, and knowledge about treatment. The concept of recovery and the principles of psychiatric rehabilitation provide a value-based orientation that is appropriate for working with persons with severe mental illness. Research has come up with models and concepts that give practitioners a framework for understanding serious mental illness. A further reason for optimism is the development of evidence-based methods of practice that are compatible with the concept of recovery and the principles of psychiatric rehabilitation. These psychosocial treatments increase the salutary effects of medication.

This chapter begins with a discussion of what is meant by *severe mental illness* and related terms that have replaced the term *chronic*. The *chronic* label originated in the medical practice of differentiating between acute and chronic illness. An illness is considered *acute* when there is a flare-up of symptoms that are expected to abate following treatment. In contrast, an illness is viewed as *chronic* when it is prolonged, persistent, and in some cases progressive. In addition to avoiding the latter term, this book uses *person-first* language. Accordingly, an individual will be described as "a person with schizophrenia," "an adult with a psychiatric disability," and other descriptors that do not equate the person with the illness (Estroff, 1987).

DEFINING SEVERE MENTAL ILLNESS

Psychiatric maladies previously described as chronic are now called *severe* or *serious mental illness* (SMI) or *severe and persistent mental illness* (SPMI). Generally, the term is used "to convey a history of serious acute episodes, psychiatric comorbidities, continuing residual disability, and high levels of medical and psychosocial need" (Mechanic, 2008, p. 5). Policy analysts and researchers have focused on three characteristics—diagnosis, disability, and duration (Bachrach, 1988; Goldman, 1984). The empirical literature, however, reveals inconsistency and disagreement on "the relevant diagnostic categories, the nature and degree of disability, the length of illness, and the relative importance of each" (Schinnar, Rothbard, Kanter, & Jung, 1990, p. 1602).

Legislation enacted in the last two decades of the twentieth century made it obligatory for the states to develop specific criteria for defining serious or severe mental illness. Under the Comprehensive Mental Health Services Plan Act (Pub. L. No. 99-660, 1986), which required that states develop plans for the implementation of community mental health services, states had to report target numbers of clients with SMI who would be served. To do this, they had to operationalize the concept of SMI. Subsequently, the federal government established guidelines to help states in this process. The ADAMHA (Alcohol, Drug Abuse, and Mental Health Administration) Reorganization Act (Pub. L. No. 102-321, 1992), which separated the federal agencies involved in research from those concerned with services, also established a block grant for community mental health services. Funds were allocated for adults with SMI and children with serious emotional disturbance (SED). This legislation required that the service-oriented Substance Abuse and Mental Health Services Administration (SAMHSA) develop a federal definition of severe mental illness (as well as SED) that could guide states in their implementation of the block grants. The following criteria were subsequently established:

1. Age 18 and over,
2. Who currently or at any time during the past year,
3. Have had a diagnosable mental, behavioral, or emotional disorder of sufficient duration to meet diagnostic criteria specified within *DSM-III-R*,
4. That has resulted in functional impairment which substantially interferes with or limits one or more major life activities. (SAMHSA, 1993, p. 29425)

The third criterion applies to successors to the *DSM-III-R* as well, but, according to the *Federal Register*, it excludes diagnoses of substance use disorders, developmental disorders, and *V*-codes, unless they co-occur with one of the included mental health disorders, and it includes the diagnosis of Alzheimer's disease. Furthermore, "All these [included] disorders have episodic, recurrent, or persistent features; however, they vary in terms of severity and disabling effects" (SAMHSA, 1993, p. 29425). The fourth criterion, functional impairment,

> is defined as difficulties that substantially interfere with or limit role functioning in one or more major life activities including basic daily living skills (e.g., eating, bathing, dressing); instrumental living skills (e.g., maintaining a household, managing money, getting around the community, taking prescribed medication); and functioning in social, family, and vocational/educational contexts. Adults who would have met functional impairment criteria during the referenced year without the benefit of treatment or other support services are considered to have serious mental illnesses. (SAMHSA, 1993, p. 29425)

The final report of the President's New Freedom Commission on Mental Health (2003) uses the same criteria for severe mental illness and the same definition of functional impairment.

State definitions that were to be developed after the publication of the federal criteria were expected to be consistent with the federal one, but they could vary. A study comparing the prevalence of SPMI in a clinical sample from West Philadelphia using the definitions established by ten states found a great deal of difference among them. The prevalence varied from 38 percent (using Hawaii's definition) to 72 percent (using Ohio's definition) (Rothbard, Schinnar, & Goldman, 1996). The diverse definitions reflect differences among the states and their respective political constituencies in their willingness to commit resources to a wide spectrum of individuals.

With respect to diagnosis, most states target psychotic disorders, such as schizophrenia and schizoaffective disorder, but they also include severe mood disorders, such as bipolar and major depressive disorders, which may or may not have psychotic features. Rarer psychotic disorders such as delusional disorder and shared psychotic disorder may also meet state criteria. Some states include borderline and other personality disorders when there is evidence of poor global functioning or when there is a co-occurring Axis I disorder. Organic psychoses, alcohol and drug dependence, and mental retardation are sometimes included as well (Schinnar et al., 1990). Table 10.1 describes the *DSM-IV-TR* diagnostic categories that guided the development of this chapter and those that follow. It is recognized, however, that a high level of functional impairment over a prolonged period of time along with other diagnoses (e.g., post-traumatic stress disorder, obsessive-compulsive disorder) can produce severe mental illness. Clients with these disorders can benefit from the same services as those for clients with other illnesses.

As for disability, some of the criteria states use to operationalize this concept are impaired activities of daily living and basic needs, limited and impaired performance in employment, impaired functioning in nonwork activities (e.g., leisure, homemaking), social behavior demanding intervention by the mental health system or courts, level of functioning as measured by the Global Assessment of Functioning (GAF) scale (Endicott, Spitzer, & Fleiss, 1976), and meeting eligibility criteria for Supplemental Security Income (SSI) or Supplemental Security Disability Insurance (SSDI) (Schinnar et al., 1990).

There is also variability in the use of duration as a state criterion. Some states have no duration criterion, whereas others consider the length of the illness or treatment (e.g., two years or

TABLE 10.1	Categories of Serious Psychiatric Disorders
Diagnostic Category	**Description**
Schizophrenia	Disturbance in cognitive and emotional functioning, including perception, language and communication, affect, speech, volition, and organized behavior. Characterized by positive symptoms (e.g., delusions or hallucinations), negative symptoms (e.g., flat affect, apathy), and/or disorganized behavior, as well as impaired occupational or social functioning. Symptoms must be present at least six months, including one month in which the symptoms are active.
Schizoaffective disorder	Disturbance in mood (depression, mania, or mixture of the two) with concurrent symptoms of schizophrenia.
Bipolar I disorder	Disturbance in mood in which there is a history of or current manic symptoms characterized by symptoms such as grandiosity, flight of ideas, and pressured speech. Often there is a previous or current episode of major depression or a mixed episode. Manic symptoms must be present at least one week for single episode. Should cause marked impairment in social or occupational functioning. May have psychotic features. Chronicity of two years applies to depressive episode only.
Bipolar II disorder	Disturbance of mood in which there is a history of or current episode of major depression and a history of or current hypomanic episode and no history of a full manic or mixed episode.
Major depressive disorder	Disturbance in mood characterized by at least two weeks of marked dysphoria, insomnia, loss of interest in life, lack of pleasure, and other symptoms that result in distress and impairment in social and occupational functioning. Described as chronic when it persists for two years.

Source: Adapted from American Psychiatric Association (2000).

more), the length of hospitalization (e.g., ninety days or more within a three-year period), the number of hospitalizations, the use of residential or partial hospitalization services, and/or the use of outpatient services (Schinnar et al., 1990).

Establishing their own definitions of SMI may work on the individual state level, but this practice makes it difficult to compare the population of persons with SPMI among states or to combine data across states. Epidemiologists working with national data have had to identify specific indicators to estimate the prevalence of severe mental illness in the United States. Combining data from the National Comorbidity Survey and the Baltimore Epidemiologic Catchment Area Study, Kessler et al. (1996) estimated that 4.8 million adults had SPMI and another 5.6 million had serious (but not persistent) mental illness in 1990. In a report that accounted for individuals living in homeless shelters, nursing homes, hospitals, correction facilities, and elsewhere, as well as those living in households in the community, Kessler et al. (1998) estimated that there are 12.2 million adults with severe mental illness in the United States.

Clinical social work practice with persons with severe mental illness is guided by a variety of theories, concepts, research findings, and philosophies. Although many of these developments arose from research on schizophrenia, the findings are applicable to other serious disorders as well. In addition to presenting this information, this chapter discusses psychiatric rehabilitation, community integration, and evidence-based and promising strategies for intervention with adults with severe psychiatric disabilities. Chapter 11 will provide information on community care, including case management and assertive community treatment (ACT), supported housing, supported employment, and a range of other community services. Chapter 12 will describe specific treatment strategies, such as psychopharmacology, illness management and recovery, and family psychoeducation.

RELEVANT PERSPECTIVES, CONCEPTS, AND MODELS

Biopsychosocial Perspective

Scientific research supports the assumption that the major psychiatric disorders—schizophrenia, bipolar disorder, and some major depressions—are brain diseases. As discussed in Chapter 3, genetic studies, neurophysiological findings, and responsiveness to medication provide evidence for this conclusion. Genetic studies of twins, one of whom was identified as having schizophrenia, have found higher rates of concordance between monozygotic than between dizygotic twins (Kendler, 1988). Studies of adoptees with schizophrenia spectrum disorders have found an unusually high prevalence of schizophrenia and spectrum disorders among natural relatives (Kendler, 1988). Similar results have been realized with respect to the genetics of unipolar depression and bipolar disorder (McGuffin & Katz, 1989). Furthermore, neurophysiological studies of the brain using sophisticated laboratory equipment have identified structural abnormalities among persons with schizophrenia, mania, and dementia (Andreasen, 1984; Andreasen et al., 1990; Taylor, 1987). The effectiveness of medication for schizophrenia, bipolar disorder, and major depression supports the role of neurotransmitters in the production and treatment of the disorder.

Recognition of a biological, neurophysiological, genetic explanation represents a marked departure from the past, when psychoanalytic and family communication theories about the development of serious psychiatric disorders predominated. Still the scientific evidence is incomplete. Some people do not respond to medication, whereas others respond with a reduction of some symptoms but not others (Schwartz, 1999). The high concordance rate between monozygotic twins is persuasive, but this does not explain why some cotwins do not develop the disorder. It is evident that psychiatric disorders are heterogeneous and complex and that biological causality does not apply to all disorders (Schwartz, 1999).

Meanwhile there is persuasive evidence that psychosocial interventions, in tandem with medication, reduce the relapse rate for persons with schizophrenia and related disorders. In a remarkable study by Hogarty et al. (1986) in which participants were randomly assigned to four conditions—medication combined with family psychoeducation, medication together with social skills training, all three interventions, and only medication—participants had the lowest relapse rate when they were assigned to all three conditions (0 percent) and this was followed by medication together with family treatment (19 percent) and medication plus social skills training (20 percent). Those who took medication alone had a 41 percent relapse rate. This study along with others along the same lines convinced the developers of the Patient Outcomes Research Team (PORT) study (discussed later in this chapter) to recommend a combination of psychosocial interventions and medication for persons with schizophrenia. Conceptual models that account for the onset of psychiatric disorders and relapses as well as environmental factors, including psychosocial interventions, will be discussed next.

Stress-Diathesis and Attention-Arousal Models

The *stress-diathesis* model—also referred to as the *vulnerability, stress-vulnerability, stress-vulnerability-coping-competence*, or *stress-vulnerability-protective* model (Liberman, 1982, 1988a, 1988b; MacKain, Liberman, & Corrigan, 1994; Zubin & Spring, 1977)—focuses on the individual with the disorder in relation to his or her internal and external processes. Although the model developed from research on schizophrenia, it has been applied to other serious mental illnesses (e.g., Grunebaum et al., 2006; Slavik & Croake, 2006). *Diathesis* refers to a biological predisposition (e.g., a family history of the same disorder) that makes one susceptible to the disorder. According to this model, schizophrenia arises in an individual with biologically based vulnerability, a low threshold for tolerating stress, and inadequate coping strategies. In the face of a biological, psychological, or socioenvironmental stressor, the predisposed individual has an initial episode or exacerbation of schizophrenia (Falloon & Liberman, 1983; Land, 1986). Empirical research shows that stress also affects the course of serious mood disorders (Hammen, 1995).

Relapse into illness seems to be related to several aspects of the stressful life experience. First, the episode is connected to the individual's perception of the dangerousness of the demand in relation to his or her ability to respond effectively (Jones & Fernyhough, 2007; Zubin & Spring, 1977). Second, the individual's coping ability and competence are relevant. *Coping ability* refers to the skill and initiative used to develop strategies to handle life situations; *competence* refers to the skills needed to succeed in assuming social roles in the contexts of everyday life (Zubin & Spring, 1977). In the face of an overwhelming stressor, coping can break down and in some cases result in an episode of a psychiatric disorder (Zubin & Spring, 1977). Persons who have a history of relatively high premorbid (prior to psychosis) functioning tend to adapt better to stress than those without such a history; if there is a breakdown, they are more likely to achieve a higher level of functioning than those with a poor premorbid history (Liberman, 1982).

Figure 10.1 is a visual representation of the stress-diathesis model. *Stressors* may be environmental or internal (biochemical, intrapsychic) events or processes that are perceived negatively and arouse anxiety and challenge the coping capacities of the vulnerable individual. Stressful life events such as moving or losing a family member are examples of environmental stressors. Alcohol and drugs are examples of internal stressors. Stressors are risk factors. Social supports provided by family, friends, neighbors, psychosocial rehabilitation programs, and other sources and competencies such as vocational skills, the ability to make friends, and other capacities serve as protective factors. Supports and competencies offer structure, strategies, confidence, and encouragement that can provide a buffer against stress (Pilisuk, 1982). When stressors and supports are in balance in a vulnerable individual, social functioning can be maintained.

A related model that elucidates vulnerability in relation to schizophrenia is the *attention-arousal* model (Anderson, Reiss, & Hogarty, 1986). According to this approach, the person with schizophrenia has a "core psychological deficit" (Anderson, Hogarty, & Reiss, 1980) in the ability to select, sort, filter, and evaluate stimuli. This deficiency results in diffuse responses and hyperarousal to stimuli, regardless of their relevance to a situation. The individual is affected by both internal and external stimuli (information), which make a demand for information processing. When the demands increase, the organism becomes distracted, inattentive, and aroused. The person with schizophrenia responds to these stimuli by maintaining a narrow focus of attention, missing the full picture. This produces a state of disintegration and sensory malfunctioning. In a state of high arousal, an individual can perceive and behave in dysfunctional ways (e.g., hallucinations, aggressive behavior). Medication can modify the internal conditions associated with arousal and attention deficits, thus reducing vulnerability; intervention with families can reduce

---

Vulnerabilities

Family history of severe mental disorder, genetic factors, early onset, low premorbid functioning, and/or abnormal neurological activity, which adversely affect cognition and set the stage for a high reactivity to stress.

Stressors (–) (Risk Factors)	Competencies and Supports (+) (Protective factors)
Life events that are perceived as threatening or demanding	Social skills
Unstable living situation	Supportive family and friends
Interpersonal conflict ("expressed emotion")	Medication use
Medical problem	Use of other mental health services
Substance abuse	Vocational skills
	Coping skills

FIGURE 10.1 The Stress-Diathesis or Stress-Vulnerability-Coping-Competence Model

excessive external stimulation. The attention-arousal model assumes that some, but not excessive, stimulation is desirable. Accordingly, social interaction that is low-keyed and nonintrusive facilitates psychosocial functioning, whereas intensive and demanding interaction can be deleterious.

The stress-diathesis and attention-arousal models suggest avenues for intervention that can be incorporated into social work practice. Clinical social workers can, for example, help clients with severe mental illness develop and use supports, enhance their coping skills, and change conditions in their living environments that are stressful. Furthermore, social workers can help clients take care of themselves by obtaining medical care, taking their medication as prescribed, and avoiding chemical substances. More will be said about the application of these models in Chapters 11 and 12. For now, we will look at one stressor that has been the subject of a great deal of research and controversy—expressed emotion.

Expressed Emotion

The *expressed emotion* (EE) construct developed from the research of Brown and his associates in England who conducted a series of studies on persons with schizophrenia who were discharged from the hospital to family and nonfamily settings (Brown, 1959; Brown, Carstairs, & Topping, 1958). When they determined that those male patients who lived with parents or wives had a higher rate of readmission to the hospital than those who lived with other relatives or in a community lodging, the researchers delved more deeply into the families' interactions.

Subsequently, Brown and colleagues found that family environments characterized by a high level of criticism, hostility, and emotional involvement—key indicators of EE—were associated with a patient's worsening or relapse and those environments characterized by a low level of these emotions had a better outcome (Brown, Birley, & Wing, 1972; Brown, Monck, Carstairs, & Wing, 1962).

Researchers' preferred means of assessing EE is the Camberwell Family Interview, an audiotaped open-ended individual interview (Hooley & Hiller, 1998). At a later time, the audiotapes are coded by trained raters who—based on the content and tone of voice—identify instances of critical comments, emotional overinvolvement (EOI), and hostility (Hooley, 2007). On the basis of the number of comments along these dimensions in relation to a threshold number, family members are classified as either high or low in EE (Hooley, 2007).

After Brown's initial work, other British researchers replicated and expanded upon his research, arriving at similar conclusion (Leff & Vaughn, 1981, 1985; Vaughn & Leff, 1976). These studies also looked at the role of medication and additional diagnoses. Since these early studies, research on EE has expanded further. In addition to schizophrenia, it has been applied to major mood disorders, anxiety disorders, eating disorders, and personality disorders (Hooley, 2007). Researchers have also assessed EE in other countries (e.g., Kottgen, Sonnischsen, Mollenhauer, & Jurth, 1984; Parker, Johnston, & Hayward, 1988; Wig et al., 1987) and among subcultures in the United States (e.g., Koneru & Weisman de Mamani, 2007). A meta-analysis of twenty-seven outcome studies of EE in families of persons with schizophrenia, schizoaffective disorder, mood disorders, and eating disorder confirmed that high EE in the family is associated with high relapse rates in all these disorders (Butzlaff & Hooley, 1998). Interestingly, EE was a stronger predictor of outcome for major mood disorders than for schizophrenia (Butzlaff & Hooley, 1998).

Research on EE has been stimulating to researchers but troubling to families of persons with schizophrenia and other serious disorders. Researchers have found in the family environment a construct (EE) that is consistent with hypotheses based on biological research that this population is vulnerable to stress and has difficulty processing complex information. On the other hand, families see this research as blaming them. The families' misgivings may be justified, as EE may be the consequence of the relationship between the client and family member or may be precipitated by the client's behavior (Hooley, 2007).

Nevertheless, research on EE does provide some guidance to clinicians. It alerts them to potential interpersonal stressors that can be modulated through intervention. Some family psychoeducational programs are designed to help families reduce criticism, hostility, and overinvolvement (e.g., Anderson et al., 1986). The focus on intervention with families with high EE should not, however, divert the clinician from the needs of *all* families with a relative with severe mental illness for support and education.

Expressed emotion draws attention to family interactions that, according to the stress-diathesis model, can be problematic to a person who is vulnerable. The other part of the model, however, consists of competencies and supports. Competencies and supports are incorporated in the concept of recovery to which we turn next.

RECOVERY

Recovery is a fundamental concept for working with persons with severe mental illness. It is a positive orientation that counters past impressions that severe mental illness is unremitting and untreatable. The idea is for consumers to establish goals for themselves that create meaning and purpose in their lives (Anthony, 1993). The concept of recovery is supported by ten longitudinal studies of persons with schizophrenia conducted in the United States and abroad, most of which found that about half of the patients recovered or improved (see Corrigan, Mueser, Bond, Drake, & Solomon, 2008). Embraced by consumers, family members, and service providers, recovery is now recognized as a guiding perspective in public policy. As recommended in the final report of the President's New Freedom Commission on Mental Health (2003), the focus of system change and intervention with persons with severe mental illness is to be on promoting recovery.

The concept of recovery has been defined in a variety of ways in the academic literature (Onken, Craig, Ridgway, Ralph, & Cook, 2007), by government entities, and by individual consumers. Here are some examples:

> Recovery from mental illness is not the same as cure. It means gaining control over one's life if not one's illness. It means living a useful, satisfying life even though symptoms may reoccur. (Anthony, 1992, p. 18)
>
> Recovery is the process of pursuing a fulfilling and contributing life regardless of the difficulties one has faced. It involves not only the restoration but continued enhancement of a positive identity and personally meaningful connections and roles in one's community. Recovery is facilitated by relationships and environments that provide hope, empowerment, choices and opportunities that promote people reaching their full potential as individuals and community members. (Recovery Advisory Committee, Philadelphia Department of Behavioral Health, Draft, FY 2007–2008 County Mental Health Plan, p. 3)
>
> [O]ver the years I have learned all different kinds of ways to help myself. Sometimes I use medications, therapy, self help and mutual support groups, friends, my relationship with God, my work, exercise, spending time with nature—all these things help me remain whole and healthy even though I have a disability. (Deegan, 1997)

Recognizing differences in the way this concept has been defined, the National Consensus Conference on Mental Health Recovery and Mental Health Systems Transformation (2004) came up with the following consensus statement based on the deliberations of expert panelists:

> Mental health recovery is a journey of healing and transformation enabling a person with a mental health problem to live a meaningful life in a community of his or her choice while striving to achieve his or her full potential. (National Mental Health Information Center, n.d.)

The consensus group also identified ten fundamental components of recovery. As Table 10.2 shows, these include self-direction, individualized and person centered, empowerment, holistic, nonlinear, strengths based, peer support, respect, responsibility, and hope. In essence, recovery recognizes the strengths, dignity, and rights of individual consumers to make choices, form relationships with peers, and take responsibility for their own well-being. It is both a goal and an ongoing process, with the process fluctuating over time. Service providers can help consumers recover by appreciating and building on their strengths and resiliences, by promoting self-direction and empowerment, and by recognizing that recovery encompasses multiple dimensions of individuals' lives.

The first, if not the foremost, component listed is *self-direction*. It highlights the importance of consumers' developing their own goals, managing their own illness, and determining their own pathway toward recovery. Consumers now run their own peer drop-in services and work as peer specialists in existing mental health agencies. They direct their own treatment and, if they wish, develop their own advance directives to assert how they wish to be treated if they need more intensive care (see Chapter 5).

The description of the second component in Table 10.2, *individualized and person centered*, calls attention to culture as an aspect of recovery. The culture may be an ethnic group such

TABLE 10.2	Fundamental Components of Recovery
Component	**Description**
Self-direction	Consumer determines his or her own life goals and pathway for achieving these goals. The emphasis is on individual control, self-determination, and choice.
Individualized and person centered	Pathways to recovery differ based on individual strengths and resiliences, preferences, needs, cultural background, and experiences. Recovery is both a journey toward wellness and an outcome of that journey.
Empowerment	Consumers have the authority to make choices among options and participate in decisions affecting their lives. They can organize with other consumers around their collective needs and aspirations.
Holistic	Recovery pertains to all aspects of the individual's life including his or her biopsychosocial-spiritual being, living situation, education, mental health, social networks, and family.
Nonlinear	The process of recovery begins with an awareness of possibilities and continues in a back and forth way.
Strengths based	Recovery values and builds on the capacities, talents, resiliences, coping abilities, and innate worth of the individual.
Peer support	Consumers develop mutually supportive relationships with other consumers in recovery, offering each other a sense of belonging, an important role, and community.
Respect	It is crucial that society, systems, and communities accept and appreciate consumers, eliminate discrimination and stigma, and protect their rights, and that consumers accept themselves.
Responsibility	Consumers are responsible for taking care of themselves and for their unique journeys toward healing, wellness, and recovery.
Hope	Consumers internalize the belief, fostered by family, friends, providers, and others, that they can overcome obstacles and have a better future.

Source: Adapted from the National Mental Health Information Center (n.d.).

as Puerto Rican American or a community of individuals who share a characteristic such as a sexual orientation or religion. The consumer's cultural group usually has a perspective on mental illness that affects the consumer's self-acceptance.

The focus on *strengths* in this conceptualization of recovery has been integral to social work practice for some time. It is particularly important to highlight the strengths of persons with SPMI, as competencies can be overlooked if providers focus on symptoms and deficits. Recognizing strengths is also part of a holistic and empowering orientation. It is incorporated in the strengths model of case management that is described in Chapter 11 and other interventions described in Chapters 11 and 12.

Although some authors report that the concept of recovery has been part of the self-help movement since the 1930s (Onken et al., 2007), credit needs to go to William Anthony, executive director of the Center for Psychiatric Rehabilitation at Boston University. Recovery is integral to psychiatric rehabilitation.

PSYCHIATRIC REHABILITATION

Rehabilitation is an approach to enhancing the functioning of persons with disabilities. *Psychiatric* rehabilitation was stimulated by medical programs for the physically disabled (Anthony, Cohen, & Cohen, 1984; Anthony & Liberman, 1986) and adapted to the needs of persons with severe mental illness. As such, psychiatric rehabilitation has had vestiges of a medical orientation. *Psychosocial* rehabilitation grew out of the consumer-run Fountain House (see Chapter 11), which emphasized consumer empowerment and peer-group support. Because these parallel movements and philosophies have converged in recent years, the terms *psychosocial* and *psychiatric rehabilitation* are used interchangeably here.

Psychiatric rehabilitation regards the serious mental health problems of consumers as disabilities (Corrigan et al., 2008). The focus is on expanding physical, psychiatric, and social functioning and unblocking obstacles so that consumers can achieve their life goals (Corrigan et al., 2008). This includes the abilities to perform activities of daily living, maintain a stable living arrangement, work, attend school, develop friendships, engage in recreational activities, and obtain medical, mental health, and social services. Anthony and Liberman (1986) recommended that helping professionals provide "the least amount of support necessary" (p. 542), so that clients will be helped to become as self-sufficient as they can. This help entails "systematic processes and interventions by which adults with severe psychiatric disorder are assisted in achieving full integration into communities of their choosing through environmental supports and modifications and personal skills and resource acquisition" (Solomon, Schmidt, Swarbrick, & Mannion, 2011). More will be said about community integration in the section that follows this one.

As originally conceived by Anthony et al. (1984), two kinds of interventions are fundamental to rehabilitation. These are client skills development and environmental resource development. Often psychiatric illnesses such as schizophrenia first appear in adolescence or young adulthood, by which time the individual has not sufficiently developed the vocational, social, and living skills that are needed to function relatively independently in the community. Schizophrenia is also associated with deficits in cognitive functioning. Regardless of the mental disorder, skills that facilitate social functioning can be taught or enhanced through programmatic interventions. Environmental resources that are related to client needs can also be developed.

Recovery is the centerpiece of psychiatric rehabilitation. The U.S. Psychiatric Rehabilitation Association (USPRA)—an organization of practitioners, agencies, educators, researchers, government entities, families, and consumers—defines psychiatric rehabilitation this way:

> Psychiatric rehabilitation promotes recovery, full community integration and improved quality of life for persons who have been diagnosed with any mental health condition that seriously impairs functioning. Psychiatric rehabilitation services are collaborative, person directed, and individualized, and an essential element of the human services spectrum, and should be evidence-based. They focus on helping individuals re-discover skills and access resources needed to increase their capacity to be successful and satisfied in the living, working, learning and social environments of their choice. (See USPRA at http:/www.uspra.org/i4a/pages/index.cfm?pageid=4124)

Over the years, numerous efforts have been made to delineate principles to guide the practice of psychiatric rehabilitation. The principles developed by Anthony et al. (1984), which are seminal, include the following:

1. The central focus should be on improving the capabilities and competence of the psychiatrically disabled person.
2. Psychiatric rehabilitation can help clients change their behavior within their relevant environments (e.g., residential, community, employment).
3. Improvement of vocational outcome is a central focus. This includes securing a job in the competitive market, working part time, holding protected jobs, working in transitional employment, or volunteer work.
4. Psychiatric rehabilitation can be implemented best when the clinician conveys an attitude of hope.
5. Psychiatric rehabilitation requires the management of dependence that is consistent with the client's needs.
6. The client is to participate in the rehabilitation process, including setting goals, making decisions about living arrangements, social activities, and treatment.
7. Psychiatric rehabilitation highlights the recovery process in which individuals learn to live with their illnesses.

The International Association of Psychosocial Rehabilitation Services (IAPSRS, now USPRA) developed its own core principles of psychiatric rehabilitation. They give a central role to recovery and include some of the components of recovery described in Table 10.2. They go beyond the principles of Anthony et al. by highlighting the role of culture and ethnicity in recovery, the principle of normalization, community integration, partnership with families, and the expectation that practitioners try to improve services. (The core principles can be downloaded from www.iaspsrs.org.)

Today psychiatric rehabilitation is achieved through a wide range of programs. Some are independent psychosocial programs such as Horizon House in Philadelphia, Thresholds in Chicago, Independence Center in St. Louis, and Portals House in Los Angeles, whereas others are affiliated with mental health centers (Corrigan et al., 2008). The programs have a number of offerings including, but not limited to, supported housing, case management, consumer drop-in programs, supported employment, social skills training, family intervention, and psychiatric and substance abuse treatment (Mueser, Drake, & Bond, 1997). Several of these interventions, now considered evidence-based practices, will be described in future chapters.

COMMUNITY INTEGRATION AND SUPPORTIVE SERVICES

Community integration is a "unifying concept providing direction and vision in community mental health for people with severe mental illness (SMI)" (Bond, Salyers, Rollins, Rapp, & Zipple, 2004, p. 569). The concept was implicit in the deinstitutionalization movement, which promoted the return of persons with severe mental illness to local communities (Mechanic, 2008), and is explicit in the report of the President's New Freedom Commission on Mental Health (2003) and the SAMHSA document, entitled *Community Integration for Older Adults with Mental Illnesses* (Center for Mental Health Services, 2004). Community integration is supported by the Supreme Court's 1999 decision in *Olmstead v. L.C. and E.W.*, which found that it was discriminatory under the Americans with Disabilities Act of 1990 to maintain individuals with disabilities in institutions when there are alternatives in the community (see Chapter 5).

Generally speaking, community integration refers to consumers' entering the daily life of natural communities as fully as possible. This means living in community residences, using recreational facilities, participating in educational activities, working, using transportation resources, and otherwise partaking of ordinary community life. Building on prior conceptualizations and research, Wong and Solomon (2002) identified three dimensions of the concept— physical, social, and psychological integration. Physical integration entails participating in activities, spending time, consuming goods, and using services outside one's residence, whereas social integration refers to social interaction with others in the community and involvement in social networks. Psychological integration has to do with the perception of membership in a community and the expression of emotional connection with neighbors. Connectedness was a salient characteristic identified by consumers in a qualitative study seeking to their perceptions of social integration (Ware, Hopper, Tugenberg, Dickey, & Fisher, 2007).

During the early years of deinstitutionalization, the main concern was that formerly hospitalized patients be housed and receive services that were the equivalent of those they had in institutions (Stroul, 1993). Initially residential alternatives and community resources were either lacking or inadequate to meet the needs of deinstitutionalized patients (Stroul, 1993). Another concern was that services that existed were fragmented (Turner & TenHoor, 1978). Recognizing gaps in community services, the National Institute of Mental Health initiated the pilot Community Support Programs (CSPs) in 1977 (Grob, 1994). The purpose was to help communities develop demonstration projects of comprehensive, coordinated services for adults with severe and persistent psychiatric disabilities for whom long-term semiskilled and skilled nursing home care was inappropriate (Turner & TenHoor, 1978).

The concept of *community support system* (CSS) was defined as a network of caring persons or services to help vulnerable persons with severe mental illness to develop their potential and meet their needs without being excluded or isolated from the community (Turner & TenHoor, 1978). In order for such a system to work, there was a need for a core service agency (e.g., a community mental health center) and a key person or persons who would be responsible for ongoing contact with clients (e.g., the case manager or team) (Turner & TenHoor, 1978). CSPs included an array of housing alternatives, mental health treatment facilities, client identification and outreach services, rehabilitation programs, health and dental care, income support and entitlement resources, crisis response services, peer support, and advocacy services (Stroul, 1993) that enhance the capacities of communities to meet the needs of persons with severe mental illness who live in the community.

As the CSS/CSP model evolved during the 1980s and early 1990s, it has undergone changes in conceptualization and emphasis (Moxley, 2002). First, the consumers and families have become more active in expressing their wants, needs, and goals, including recovery (Moxley, 2002). Second, disability and support are now viewed more broadly. Accordingly, attention is paid to "disabling situations or environments" and to support as "a source of energy useful to the promotion of personal development" (Moxley, 2002, p. 31). Other changes include strengths-based rehabilitation and an orientation toward outcomes (Moxley, 2002).

As with CSS/CSP, the concept of community integration has undergone changes in interpretation. This is the consequence of the determination of members of consumer movements that consumers not be segregated in mental health subcommunities. Bond et al. (2004) explain this by asserting what community integration is *not*:

Community integration is *not* immersion in worlds created and managed by mental health professionals, such as day treatment programs, sheltered workshops, group homes, and segregated educational programs. These settings are designed specifically to pull consumers into treatment and away from community life. The acid test in determining if community integration is realized is whether consumers are being steered toward a protected setting that is not part of the "regular community." (pp. 570–571)

As suggested, there are many barriers to community integration. In a multistage focus group study of the experiences of consumers in Norway, Granerud and Severinsson (2006) found that living with shame and fear of exclusion was the most prominent theme. Participants reported feeling lonely or neglected while they struggled to achieve equality in the job market, relationships, or other arenas. In a multicultural focus group study, Wong, Sands, and Solomon (2010) found that participants' concept of community had to do with feeling accepted (and its converse, rejected) and togetherness and that a number of indicators of personal identity, including ethnicity, sexual orientation, gender identity, and religious faith, are integral to the goal of community integration. Clearly stigma and discrimination enter into feelings of acceptance and the actualization of acceptance into the community.

The document, *Community Integration for Older Adults with Mental Illnesses* (Center for Mental Health Services, 2004), describes this population and the barriers they face. The report notes that adults 65 and older with SMI are at increased risk of suicide, substance abuse problems, comorbid medical conditions, and poverty. They are frequently placed in nursing homes because of a lack of alternatives in the community and fiscal barriers. Many of those who remain in the community are untreated. There is a shortage of health and mental health providers who are sufficiently skilled to work with this population (Center for Mental Health Services, 2004).

Social workers can foster community integration of adults of all ages by working on the community level to combat stigmatization and promote community acceptance. When they work with individuals, they can encourage them to develop friendships outside mental health programs, attend religious services if they are interested, and assume significant social roles such as employee or citizen (Farone, 2006). Practitioners can help consumers identify opportunities to work in mainstream organizations, in peer-run organizations, and as peer counselors in mental health agencies. They can foster consumers' recovery by supporting their managing their own symptoms and receiving mental health services (Farone, 2006). Services and resources that can contribute to this process are described in Chapter 11. Social workers can also advance consumers' recovering by implementing interventions that are evidence based or empirically supported.

EVIDENCE-BASED AND EMPIRICALLY SUPPORTED PRACTICES

Clinical social workers practicing with clients with severe mental illness work with the clients themselves and clients' family members in a community context. They use knowledge from intervention outcome studies as well as evidence-based practices and practices and knowledge acquired through practice experience (practice-based evidence). In the following three chapters, several evidence-based, empirically supported, and promising psychosocial interventions will be described and exemplary programs will be highlighted.

The selections made were informed by empirical and expert reports on meta-analyses, clinical outcome studies, and consensus treatment guidelines. In recent years, psychiatrists have been publishing consensus reports in which they recommend particular interventions at particular stages (e.g., first acute episode, continuing and maintenance treatment) for clients with particular diagnoses (e.g., schizophrenia, major depression, bipolar disorder), based on a review of research studies. Written largely by psychiatrists, the reports tend to put medication in the center and psychosocial interventions at the periphery. The revised 2009 Schizophrenia PORT report states that, in comparison with 1998, when the first PORT recommendations appeared (Lehman, Steinwachs, & Co-Investigators of the PORT Project, 1998):

> The most recent update of the PORT psychosocial treatment recommendations included 6 recommendations . . . we aimed to update the existing recommendations with more recent research. . . . These areas include cognitive remediation, peer- and consumer-based programs, first-episode psychosis and treatments for obesity and smoking cessation. Finally, while past PORT efforts have chosen not to review the literature related to treatments for co-occurring substance use disorders (SUDs), the overall importance and clinical impact of these problems and the volume of research caused us to reconsider that decision and to review this treatment area as well. Therefore, this PORT review of psychosocial programs updates reviews in 7 areas as well as adding 5 new areas of review. (Dixon et al., 2010)

Table 10.3 contains the recommendations on psychosocial interventions included in the PORT's updated report. It should be noted that for the psychosocial interventions the expert panelists' overall agreement on the strength of the evidence was high (rating of 6.3 on a scale from a low of 1 to a high of 7) but they rated the ease of putting the recommendations into practice relatively low (3.4 on a 7-point scale).

Consensus reports on schizophrenia, treatment guidelines, and meta-analyses are ongoing features of the psychiatric and psychological literature. Some journals that carry these reports are the *American Journal of Psychiatry*, the *Journal of Clinical Psychiatry*, and the *Journal of Clinical Psychiatry*. In addition, websites of the American Psychiatric Association and American Psychological Association offer gateways to this information. The websites of the National Association of Social Workers (http://www.socialworkers.org/) and the Council on Social Work Education (http://www.cswe.org/) also provide information and linkages to other sources.

Evidence-based practices are strongly supported numerous randomized controlled trials, meta-analyses, and other evidence (Bond & Campbell, 2008; Mueser & Drake, 2005; Mueser, Torrey, Lynde, Singer, & Drake, 2003). Those described as "promising" are supported by empirical evidence but not to the extent of those considered evidence based. Those practices that will be described in this book are the following:

1. ACT (Chapter 11)
2. Supported Employment (Chapter 11)
3. Supported Housing (Chapter 11)
4. Supported Education (Chapter 11)
5. Illness Management and Recovery (Chapter 12)
6. Family Psychoeducation (Chapter 12)
7. Integrated Dual Diagnosis Treatment (Chapter 13)
8. Motivational Interviewing (Chapter 13)

TABLE 10.3	Recommended Psychosocial Treatments from the Schizophrenia Patient Outcomes Research Team

Assertive Community Treatment

Systems of care serving persons with schizophrenia should include a program of assertive community treatment. This intervention should be provided to individuals who are at risk for repeated hospitalizations or have recent homelessness. The key elements of assertive community treatment include a multidisciplinary team including a medication prescriber, a shared caseload among team members, direct service provision by team members, a high frequency of patient contact, low patient-to-staff ratios, and outreach to patients in the community. . . .

Supported Employment

Any person with schizophrenia who has the goal of employment should be offered supported employment to assist them in both obtaining and maintaining competitive employment. The key elements of supported employment include individually tailored job development, rapid job search, availability of ongoing job supports, and the integration of vocational and mental health services.

Skills Training

Individuals with schizophrenia who have deficits in skills that are needed for everyday activities should be offered skills training in order to improve social interactions, independent living, and other outcomes that have clear relevance to community functioning. Skills training programs . . . typically include a focus on interpersonal skills and share several key elements, including behaviorally based instruction, role modeling, rehearsal, corrective feedback, and positive reinforcement. . . .

Cognitive Behavioral Therapy

Persons with schizophrenia who have persistent psychotic symptoms while receiving adequate pharmacotherapy should be offered adjunctive cognitive behaviorally oriented psychotherapy to reduce the severity of symptoms. The therapy may be provided in either a group or an individual format and should be approximately 4–9 months in duration. The key elements of this intervention include the collaborative identification of target problems or symptoms and the development of specific cognitive and behavioral strategies to cope with these problems or symptoms.

Token Economy Interventions

Systems of care that deliver long-term inpatient or residential care should provide a behavioral intervention based on social learning principles for patients in these settings in order to improve their personal hygiene, social interactions, and other adaptive behaviors. The key elements of this intervention, often referred to as a token economy, are contingent positive reinforcement for clearly defined target behaviors, an individualized treatment approach, and the avoidance of punishing consequences. . . .

Family-Based Services

Persons with schizophrenia who have ongoing contact with their families, including relatives and significant others, should be offered a family intervention that lasts at least 6–9 months. . . . Key elements of effective family interventions include illness education, crisis intervention, emotional support, and training in how to cope with illness symptoms and related problems. . . . In addition, a family intervention that is shorter than 6 months but that is at least 4 sessions in length should be offered to persons with schizophrenia who have ongoing contact with their families, including relatives and significant others, and for whom a longer intervention is not feasible or acceptable. Characteristics of the briefer interventions include education, training, and support. . . .

TABLE 10.3	Recommended Psychosocial Treatments from the Schizophrenia Patient Outcomes Research Team (*Continued*)

Psychosocial Interventions for Alcohol and Substance Use Disorders

Persons with schizophrenia and a comorbid alcohol or drug use disorder should be offered substance abuse treatment. The key elements of treatment for alcohol and drug use disorders for persons with schizophrenia include motivational enhancement (ME) and behavioral strategies that focus on engagement in treatment, coping skills training, relapse prevention training, and its delivery in a service model that is integrated with mental health care. . . .

Psychosocial interventions for Weight Management

Individuals with schizophrenia who are overweight . . . or obese . . . should be offered a psychosocial weight loss intervention that is at least 3 months in duration to promote weight loss. The key elements of psychosocial interventions for weight loss include psychoeducation focused on nutritional counseling, caloric expenditure, and portion control; behavioral self-management including motivational enhancement; goal setting; regular weigh-ins; self-monitoring of daily food and activity levels; and dietary and physical activity modifications.

Source: Kreyenbuhl, Buchanan, Dickerson, & Dixon (2010). By permission of Oxford University Press.

INSTRUMENTS USED TO ASSESS AND MONITOR SEVERE MENTAL ILLNESS

With severe mental illness, concern lies with psychosocial functioning as well as symptoms. The following is a list of instruments that can be used to assess and monitor psychosocial functioning and psychotic symptoms. As in the previous chapters, those instruments included in Fischer and Corcoran's (2007) collection are denoted with an asterisk.

*Auditory Hallucinations Questionnaire

*Scale for the Assessment of Negative Symptoms (administered by the clinician)

*Scale for the Assessment of Positive Symptoms (administered by the clinician)

Brief Symptom Inventory (Derogatis, 1975)

Quality of Life Interview (Lehman, 1988)

Summary and Deconstruction

This chapter began by explaining the optimism in today's recovery-oriented environment. This is evident in the movement away from pejorative language about "chronic" mental illness toward "person-first" terminology. Because of an increase in knowledge and the variety of treatments that are currently available, persons formerly relegated to the back wards of psychiatric hospitals can now have fulfilling lives.

The chapter then discussed mental health challenges that are socially constructed as serious, severe, or severe and persistent mental illness. The criteria generally used to arrive at this designation are diagnosis, disability (functioning), and duration. The diagnoses that are often included are schizophrenia, schizoaffective disorder, bipolar disorder, and major depression, which tend to have a long course or numerous recurrences. Some states include additional disorders in their definitions. Disability refers to impairment in social role functioning in capacities such as self-care, homemaking, and employment. Duration can be applied to the length of the illness or time in treatment. These criteria enable some individuals to be served while others are allowed to fall between the cracks.

Clinical social work practice with persons with severe mental illness is informed by a number of perspectives, models, and concepts. The stress-diathesis model describes the impact of stress and supports on a person with a biological vulnerability. Variations on this emphasize coping, competence, and protective factors. The attention-arousal model explains that when persons with schizophrenia become aroused by internal and external stimuli, they become distracted and find it difficult to process the information. EE in the family is a stressor that can create difficulty for the client. Families construe the term *EE* as family blaming, particularly when one considers that families are assuming a major burden of care for their relative.

The hallmark of today's mental health climate is the concept of recovery. Although the term suggests cure, it has come to mean developing one's own life goals, making choices, and living them out to the extent possible. A nonlinear process, recovery for one person is different from that of another. Recovery is integral to community integration and psychiatric rehabilitation.

The terms *psychosocial* and *psychiatric rehabilitation* have different historical roots, but today they have converged. They refer to the promotion of physical, psychiatric, and social functioning to the extent possible for the individual. They aim to promote and enhance recovery in line with consumer aspirations and goals. Clinical social workers motivated to intervene need to consider *not acting* before acting—so that consumers can direct their own recovery.

In order that recovery and psychosocial rehabilitation can take place, community integration is essential. Rather than separating individuals with SMI from the community in mental health programs or residences, social workers should foster their participation in the wider community. This does not negate the importance of CSPs such as supported housing and employment but it does alert practitioners to the importance of natural personal and community connections. At the same time some communities are concerned about segregating persons with severe mental illness, other communities, especially those in rural areas, lack community supports.

Among the programs that support clients are specific psychosocial interventions associated with positive outcomes that are recommended in the PORT study, meta-analyses, randomized controlled studies, and other research-based reports. Although these studies put psychopharmacological interventions in the center and psychosocial ones at the periphery, all these interventions are important. The next three chapters will highlight some of these strategies.

The concepts and strategies discussed in this chapter reflect both the dominance of the medical model and quantitative reasoning and the increasing empowerment of consumers and their families. Consumers portray their journeys as nonlinear but linear thinking guides the implementation of psychiatric treatment. Social workers navigate diverse, if not contradictory, discourses, using, modifying, and avoiding resources and strategies that the previous generation found essential.

References

American Psychiatric Association. (2000). *Diagnostic and statistical manual of mental disorders* (4th ed., text rev.). Washington, DC: Author.

Anderson, C. M., Hogarty, G. E., & Reiss, D. J. (1980). Family treatment of adult schizophrenic patients: A psycho-educational approach. *Schizophrenia Bulletin, 6,* 490–505.

Anderson, C. M., Reiss, D. J., & Hogarty, G. E. (1986). *Schizophrenia and the family: A practitioner's guide to psychoeducation and management.* New York: Guilford Press.

Andreasen, N. C. (1984). *The broken brain: The biological revolution in psychiatry.* New York: Harper & Row.

Andreasen, N. C., Ehrhardt, J. C., Swayze II, V. W., Alliger, R. J., Yuh, W. T., Cohen, G., et al. (1990). Magnetic resonance imaging of the brain of schizophrenia. *Archives of General Psychiatry, 47,* 35–44.

Anthony, W. A. (1992). A revolution in vision. *Innovations & Research, 1,* 17–19.

Anthony, W. A. (1993). Recovery from mental illness: The guiding vision of the mental health service system in the 1990s. *Psychosocial Rehabilitation Journal, 11,* 11–19.

Anthony, W. A., Cohen, M. R., & Cohen, B. F. (1984). Psychiatric rehabilitation. In J. A. Talbott (Ed.), *The chronic mental patient: Five years later* (pp. 137–157). Orlando, FL: Grune & Stratton.

Anthony, W. A., & Liberman, R. P. (1986). The practice of psychiatric rehabilitation: Historical, conceptual, and research base. *Schizophrenia Bulletin, 12,* 542–559.

Bachrach, L. L. (1988). Defining chronic mental illness: A concept paper. *Hospital and Community Psychiatry, 39,* 383–388.

Bond, G., & Campbell, K. (2008). Evidence-based practices for individuals with severe mental illness. *Journal of Rehabilitation, 74*(2), 33–44.

Bond, G., Salyers, M. P., Rollins, A. L., Rapp, C. A., & Zipple, A. M. (2004). How evidence-based practices contribute to community integration. *Community Mental Health Journal, 40*(6), 569–588.

Brown, G. W. (1959). Experiences of discharged chronic schizophrenic mental hospital patients in various types of living groups. *Milbank Memorial Fund Quarterly, 37,* 105–131.

Brown, G. W., Birley, J. L. T., & Wing, J. K. (1972). Influence of family life on the course of schizophrenic disorders: A replication. *British Journal of Psychiatry, 121,* 241–258.

Brown, G. W., Carstairs, G. M., & Topping, G. (1958). Post hospital adjustment of chronic mental patients. *Lancet, 2,* 685–689.

Brown, G. W., Monck, E. M., Carstairs, G. M., & Wing, J. K. (1962). Influence of family life on the course of schizophrenic illness. *British Journal of Preventive and Social Medicine, 16,* 55–68.

Butzlaff, R. L., & Hooley, J. M. (1998). Expressed emotion and psychiatric relapse: A meta-analysis. *Archives of General Psychiatry, 55,* 547–552.

Center for Mental Health Services. (2004). *Community integration for older adults with mental illnesses: Overcoming barriers and seizing opportunities* (DHHS Publication No. SMA 05-4018). Rockville, MD: Author.

Corrigan, P. W., Mueser, K. T., Bond, G. R., Drake, R. E., & Solomon, P. (2008). *Principles and practice of psychiatric rehabilitation: An empirical approach.* New York: Guilford Press.

Deegan, P. E. (1997). Recovery and empowerment for people with psychiatric disabilities. *Social Work in Health Care, 25*(3), 11–24.

Derogatis, L. R. (1975). *Brief symptom inventory.* Baltimore: Clinical Psychometric Research.

Dixon, L. B., Dickerson, F., Bellack, A., Bennett, M., Dickinson, D., Goldberg, R., et al. (2010). The 2009 schizophrenia PORT psychosocial treatment recommendations and summary statements. *Schizophrenia Bulletin, 36*(1), 48–70.

Endicott, J., Spitzer, R., & Fleiss, J. (1976). The Global Assessment Scale: A procedure of measuring overall severity of psychiatric disturbance. *Archives of General Psychiatry, 33,* 766–771.

Estroff, S. E. (1987). No more young adult chronic patients. *Hospital and Community Psychiatry, 38,* 5.

Falloon, I. R. H., & Liberman, R. P. (1983). Interactions between drug and psychosocial therapy in schizophrenia. *Schizophrenia Bulletin, 9,* 543–554.

Farone, D. W. (2006). Schizophrenia, community integration, and recovery: Implications for social work practice. *Social Work in Mental Health, 4*(4), 21–36.

Fischer, J., & Corcoran, K. (2007). *Measures for clinical practice: A sourcebook* (Vols. 1 and 2). New York: Oxford University Press.

Goldman, H. H. (1984). Epidemiology. In J. A. Talbott (Ed.), *The chronic mental patient: Five years later* (pp. 15–31). Orlando, FL: Grune & Stratton.

Granerud, A., & Severinsson, E. (2006). The struggle for social integration in the community—the experiences of people with mental health problems. *Journal of Psychiatric and Mental Health Nursing, 13,* 288–293.

Grob, G. N. (1994). *The mad among us: A history of the care of America's mentally ill.* Cambridge, MA: Harvard University Press.

Grunebaum, M. F., Ramsay, S. R., Galfalvy, H. C., Ellis, S. P., Burke, A. K., Sher, L., et al. (2006). Correlates of suicide attempt history in bipolar disorder: A stress-diathesis perspective. *Bipolar Disorders, 8,* 551–557.

Hammen, C. L. (1995). Stress and the course of unipolar and bipolar disorders. In C. M. Mazure (Ed.), *Does stress cause psychiatric illness?* Washington, DC: American Psychiatric Press.

Hogarty, G. E., Anderson, C. M., Reiss, D. J., Kornblith, S. J., Greenwald, D. P., Javna, C. D., et al. (1986). Family psychoeducation, social skills training, and maintenance chemotherapy in the aftercare treatment of schizophrenia: I. One-year effects of a controlled study on relapse and expressed emotion. *Archives of General Psychiatry, 43,* 633–642.

Hooley, J. M. (2007). Expressed emotion and relapse of psychopathology. *Annual Review of Clinical Psychology, 3,* 329–352.

Hooley, J. M., & Hiller, J. B. (1998). Expressed emotion and the pathogenesis of relapse in schizophrenia. In M. F. Lenzenweger & R. H. Dworkin (Eds.), *Origins and development of schizophrenia: Advances in experimental psychopathology* (pp. 477–468). Washington, DC: American Psychological Association.

Jones, S. R., & Fernyhough, C. (2007). A new look at the neural diathesis-stress model of schizophrenia: The primacy of social-evaluative and uncontrollable situations. *Schizophrenia Bulletin, 33*(5), 1171–1177.

Kendler, K. S. (1988). The genetics of schizophrenia and related disorders. In D. L. Dunner, E. S. Gerson, & J. E. Barrett (Eds.), *Relatives at risk for mental disorder* (pp. 247–263). New York: Raven Press.

Kessler, R. C., Berglund, P. A., Zhao, S., Leaf, P. J., Kouzis, A. C., Bruce, M. L., et al. (1996). The 12-month prevalence and correlates of serious mental illness (SMI). In R. W. Manderscheid & M. A. Sonnenschein (Eds.), *Mental health, United States, 1996* (pp. 59–70) (DHHS Publication No. SMA 96-3098). Washington, DC: U.S. Government Printing Office.

Kessler, R. C., Berglund, P. A., Walters, E. E., Leaf, P. J., Kouzis, A. C., Bruce, M. L., et al. (1998). A methodology for estimating the 12-month prevalence of serious mental illness. In R. W. Manderscheid & M. J. Henderson (Eds.), *Mental health, United States, 1998* (pp. 99–109) (DHHS Publication No. SMA 99-3285). Washington, DC: U.S. Government Printing Office.

Koneru, V. K., & Weisman de Mamani, A. G. (2007). Acculturation and expressed emotion in Caucasian, Latino, and Black relatives of patients with schizophrenia. *Journal of Nervous and Mental Disease, 195*(11), 934–938.

Kottgen, C., Sonnischsen, I., Mollenhauer, K., & Jurth, R. (1984). Families' high expressed emotion and relapses in young schizophrenic patients: Results of the Hamburg–Camberwell family intervention study II. *International Journal of Family Psychiatry, 5,* 71–82.

Kreyenbuhl, J., Buchanan, R. W., Dickerson, F. B., & Dixon, L. B. (2010). The schizophrenia Patient Outcomes Research Team (PORT): Updated treatment recommendations 2009. *Schizophrenia Bulletin, 36*(1), 94–103.

Jimenez, M. A. (1988). Chronicity in mental disorders: Evolution of a concept. *Social Casework, 69,* 627–633.

Land, H. M. (1986). Life stress and ecological status: Predictors of symptoms in schizophrenic veterans. *Health and Social Work, 11,* 254–264.

Leff, J., & Vaughn, C. (1981). The role of maintenance therapy and relatives' expressed emotion in relapse of schiz-ophrenia: A two-year follow-up. *British Journal of Psychiatry, 139,* 102–104.

Leff, J., & Vaughn, C. (1985). *Expressed emotion in families: Its significance for mental illness.* New York: Guilford Press.

Lehman, A. (1988). A quality of life interview for the chronically mentally ill. *Evaluation and Program Planning, 11,* 51–62.

Lehman, A. F., Steinwachs, D. M., & Co-Investigators of the PORT Project. (1998). At issue: Translating research into practice: The schizophrenia patient outcomes research team (PORT) treatment recommendations. *Schizophrenia Bulletin, 24*(1), 1–10.

Liberman, R. P. (1982). Social factors in the etiology of schizophrenic disorders. In L. Grinspoon (Ed.), *Psychiatry: 1982 annual review* (Vol. 1, pp. 97–112). Washington, DC: American Psychiatric Press.

Liberman, R. P. (1988a). Introduction. In R. P. Liberman (Ed.), *Psychiatric rehabilitation of chronic mental patients* (pp. xvii–xxii). Washington, DC: American Psychiatric Press.

Liberman, R. P. (1988b). Coping with chronic mental disorders: A framework for hope. In R. P. Liberman (Ed.), *Psychiatric rehabilitation of chronic mental patients* (pp. 1–28). Washington, DC: American Psychiatric Press.

MacKain, S. J., Liberman, R. P., & Corrigan, P. W. (1994). Can coping and competence override stress and vulnerability in schizophrenia? In R. P. Liberman & J. Yager (Eds.), *Stress in psychiatric disorders* (pp. 53–82). New York: Springer.

McGuffin, P., & Katz, R. (1989). The genetics of depression and manic-depression disorder. *British Journal of Psychiatry, 155,* 294–304.

Mechanic, D. (2008). *Mental health and social policy: Beyond managed care* (5th ed.). Boston: Allyn & Bacon.

Moxley, D. P. (2002). The emergence and attributes of second-generation community support systems for persons with serious mental illness: Implications for case management. *Journal of Social Work in Disability & Rehabilitation, 1*(2), 25–52.

Mueser, K. T., & Drake, R. E. (2005). How does a practice become evidence-based? In R. E. Drake, M. R. Merrens, & D. W. Lynde (Eds.), *Evidence-based mental health practice: A textbook* (pp. 217–241). New York: W. W. Norton.

Mueser, K. T., Drake, R. E., & Bond, G. R. (1997). Recent advances in psychiatric rehabilitation for patients with severe mental illness. *Harvard Review of Psychiatry, 5,* 123–137.

Mueser, K. T., Torrey, W. C., Lynde, D., Singer, P., & Drake, R. E. (2003). Implementing evidence-based practices for people with severe mental illness. *Behavior Modification, 27*(3), 387–411.

National Mental Health Information Center. (n.d.). *National consensus statement on mental health recovery.* Retrieved July 22, 2009, from http://mentalhealth.samhsa.gov/publications/allpubs/sma05-4129/

Onken, S. J., Craig, C. M., Ridgway, P., Ralph, R. O., & Cook, J. A. (2007). An analysis of the definitions and elements of recovery: A review of the literature. *Psychiatric Rehabilitation Journal, 31*(1), 9–22.

Parker, G., Johnston, P., & Hayward, L. (1988). Parental "expressed emotion" as a predictor of schizophrenic relapse. *Archives of General Psychiatry, 45,* 806–813.

Pilisuk, M. (1982). Delivery of social support: The social inoculation. *American Journal of Orthopsychiatry, 52,* 20–31.

President's New Freedom Commission on Mental Health. (2003). *Achieving the promise: Transforming mental health care in America. Final report* (DHHS Publication No. SMA 03-3832). Rockville, MD: U.S. Government Printing Office.

Recovery Advisory Committee, Philadelphia Department of Behavioral Health, Draft, FY 2007-2008 County Mental Health Plan.

Rothbard, A. B., Schinnar, A. P., & Goldman, H. (1996). The pursuit of a definition for severe and persistent mental illness. In S. M. Soreff (Ed.), *Handbook for the treatment of the seriously mentally ill* (pp. 9–26). Seattle: Hogrefe & Huber.

Schinnar, A. P., Rothbard, A. B., Kanter, R., & Jung, Y. S. (1990). An empirical literature review of definitions of severe and persistent mental illness. *American Journal of Psychiatry, 147,* 1602–1608.

Schwartz, S. (1999). Biological approaches to psychiatric disorders. In A. V. Horwitz & T. L. Scheid (Eds.), *A handbook for the study of mental health: Social contexts, theories, and systems* (pp.79–103). New York: Cambridge University Press.

Slavik, S., & Croake, J. (2006). The individual psychology conception of depression as a stress-diathesis model. *Journal of Individual Psychology, 62*(4), 417–428.

Solomon, P., Schmidt, L., Swarbrick, P., & Mannion, E. (2011). Innovative programs: Severe mental illness. In S.

Estrine, H. Arthur, R. Hettenbach, & M. Messina (Eds.), *New directions in behavioral health: Service delivery strategies for vulnerable populations.* New York, Springer Publishing Co.

Stroul, B. A. (1993). Rehabilitation in community support systems. In R. W. Flexer & P. L. Solomon (Eds.), *Psychiatric rehabilitation in practice* (pp. 45–61). Boston: Andover Medical Publishers.

Substance Abuse and Mental Health Services Administration. (1993, May 20). Definition of adults with SMI and children with SED. *Federal Register, 58*(96), 29422–29425.

Substance Abuse and Mental Health Services Administration, U.S. Department of Health and Human Services. (2005). *Transforming mental health care in America: The federal action agenda: First steps* (DHHS Publication No. SMA 05-4060). Rockville, MD: Author.

Taylor, E. H. (1987). The biological basis of schizophrenia. *Social Work, 32,* 115–121.

Turner, J. C., & TenHoor, W. J. (1978). The NIMH Community Support Program: Pilot approach to a needed social reform. *Schizophrenia Bulletin, 4,* 319–344.

Vaughn, C. E., & Leff, J. P. (1976). The influence of family and social factors on the course of psychiatric illness. *British Journal of Psychiatry, 129,* 125–137.

Ware, N. C., Hopper, K., Tugenberg, M., Dickey, B., & Fisher, D. (2007). Connectedness and citizenship: Redefining social integration. *Psychiatric Services, 58*(4), 469–474.

Wig, N. N., Menon, D. K., Bedi, H., Ghosh, A., Kuipers, L., Leff, J., et al. (1987). Expressed emotion and schizophrenia in North India. *British Journal of Psychiatry, 151,* 156–173.

Wong, Y. L. I., Sands, R. G., & Solomon, P. L. (2010). Conceptualizing community: The experience of mental health consumers. *Qualitative Health Research, 20*(5), 654–667.

Wong, Y. L. I., & Solomon, P. L. (2002). Community integration of persons with psychiatric disabilities in supportive independent housing: A conceptual model and methodological considerations. *Mental Health Services Research, 4*(1), 13–28.

Zubin, J., & Spring, B. (1977). Vulnerability—a new view of schizophrenia. *Journal of Abnormal Psychology, 86,* 103–126.

Evidence-Based and Best Practices with Adults with Severe Mental Illness in a Community Context

*A decade ago, for a book, I interviewed several hundred people
who had been institutionalized for mental illness and who had,
to varying degrees, recovered enough to return to the world most
of us live and work in. I asked them what had made the
difference, and they attributed their good fortune to many
things: medications, doctors, social workers, therapists, religion,
and various programs. But in all instances, they said that the key had
been a relationship—the presence in their lives of somebody—
professional, family, or friend—who believed in them, who talked with
them, and who was committed to staying with them for the duration.*

—NEUGEBOREN, "PERSONAL ACCOUNTS: MORE MAGIC BULLETS?, 2008

The previous chapter discussed the conceptual and philosophical bases for the care of persons with serious and persistent mental illness. Under today's model of care, a majority of these individuals live in the community where they receive varying amounts of help from physical and behavioral health, residential, vocational, financial, and other services. This chapter describes case management service delivery models, which are used by clinical social workers who work with this population in tandem with community resources and services. It also discusses a variety of resources that can help clients who want to use them. Some of these resources are not available in every community (there is an urban–rural differential), whereas others not mentioned are found in some locations. The goal here is to present a range of services and resources that are potentially beneficial to persons with severe mental illness. Those services that are evidence based or are models of best practices are highlighted.

The perspectives of clients (or consumers) and professionals may be different. Clients are likely to view resources in terms of their individual needs, aspirations, feelings, and recovery goals. Professionals may think in terms of the services that are available. This chapter will emphasize the professional perspective, keeping in mind that social workers are responsible for bridging the gap between their clients' recovery goals and the community's offerings (i.e., the social environment). To move in this direction, we will start with a narrative of a young man who became a client of the mental health system.

Case Scenario

Larry Leeds is a 20-year-old single man who lives with his parents in a small southern town that is 100 miles from a metropolitan area. His father owns and runs a corner grocery store; his mother works as a customer representative at a bank. Larry is the oldest of three children, all boys. The family is active in the local church.

Larry was a shy child who performed well in school until his junior year in high school, then his grades declined, and he became argumentative at home. Concerned about his "attitude," his mother discussed the problem with their family doctor, who recommended that the parents take Larry to the area's community mental health center for an evaluation. The staff there concluded that Larry was struggling with adolescent autonomy issues and referred him to their adolescent therapy group. Larry attended the weekly group for three months, during which his attitude at home did not change but his grades improved. Larry became friendly with a couple of young men in the group who introduced him to marijuana.

Early in his senior year, Larry became more belligerent at home and cut classes at school. He accused his father of being the devil and his mother of being a devil worshiper. He told his parents that he had special powers to ward off the devil and that they should keep out of his way. One day, while cleaning Larry's room, Mrs. Leeds discovered knives and a gun hidden in a closet. She called her husband and then the family physician, who again referred her to the mental health center. Angry that the center minimized his problems the year before, Mrs. Leeds wondered if a stronger approach was necessary. She and her husband decided to take Larry to the nearest hospital, where he was admitted to the acute psychiatric unit with a diagnosis of schizophreniform disorder.

Larry was hospitalized for a month and discharged with medication (Haldol). The family was told that it was suspected that he was using street drugs, which were exacerbating his psychotic symptoms. Larry was advised to avoid friends who use drugs, to take his medication as prescribed, and to return to high school. He was referred to a private psychiatrist thirty miles away for follow-up. Larry complied with this plan and completed high school.

The following year Larry attended a community college and lived at home. About halfway through the first semester, he had an argument with his academic counselor in which Larry accused his counselor of having a pact with the devil. After Larry struck the counselor, the police were called. Larry was taken to the psychiatric unit of the community hospital, where he was admitted for the second time.

During this episode, Larry was given the diagnosis of schizophrenia, paranoid type (provisional). The diagnosis was considered provisional because the extent of Larry's drug use was unknown. The hospital psychiatrists told the parents that drugs bring out the paranoid symptoms. Nevertheless, the doctors said that a diagnosis of schizophrenia was probable and told the parents that this is a serious and disabling illness. Again Larry was discharged on medication, which the parents were advised to administer. This time Larry was referred to the local community mental health center for follow-up.

Larry was assigned to both a psychiatrist and a therapist at the center. He was told that the sessions would be confidential and that no one would be provided with information about him without his consent. The therapist recommended that he participate in the day treatment program that was run by the center, but Larry refused. Larry said that he wanted to return to school and live on his own. The therapist tried to work with him to help him adapt his goals to his illness. After a while, Larry stopped therapy and refused to take medication. Within three months, he was rehospitalized. This time the diagnosis of schizophrenia, paranoid type was confirmed.

Larry's experience is not unusual. Like many young persons with severe mental illness and their families, neither he nor his parents were aware of the seriousness of his illness until there was a crisis. Then they responded by using the personal, familial, and community resources that were available. Because the onset of his symptoms was concurrent with his passage through adolescence and his use of street drugs, it was unclear what the nature of Larry's difficulty was.

Severe mental disorders are complex in their diagnosis, treatment, and aftercare needs. The specific illnesses and their expression are heterogeneous, requiring intervention approaches that are tailored to the individual client. Before deinstitutionalization, persons with serious mental illness were treated in hospitals, which provided a range of services under one roof. Today diverse, multiple, yet individualized services need to be available in the community.

Some communities, like the one in which Larry lives, have few resources. Yet, within a radius of 100 miles, other services are available. Elsewhere, perhaps in a more urban area, there may be many resources that it requires a systems expert, such as a case manager, to identify the appropriate supports and link the client with them. Intervention with persons with serious mental illness entails the coordination of mental health services, as well as vocational, housing, and entitlement programs. Furthermore, other human needs, such as health care, socialization, transportation, recreation, artistic expression, and spiritual development, and the needs of family members, are to be addressed.

RECOVERY ORIENTATION

Until recently, persons with severe mental disorders (e.g., psychotic disorders) were considered destined for lifelong deterioration. However, family and consumer advocacy movements began to examine and challenge this notion in the 1980s and 1990s while research demonstrated that a considerable proportion improve functioning with age (e.g., Harding, Brooks, Ashikaga, Strauss, & Breier, 1987). The concept of recovery, which is endorsed by advocacy groups and is central to professional intervention with this population, is not a goal or an end state but a process or a guiding principle (U.S. Public Health Service, 1999). As explained in Chapter 10, the 2004 National Consensus Statement on Mental Health Recovery that was developed through efforts of the Substance Abuse and Mental Health Services Administration (SAMHSA) states that mental health recovery is "a journey of healing and transformation enabling a person with a mental health problem to live a meaningful life in a community of his or her choice while striving to achieve his or her full potential" (2004). Recovery is a positive orientation that is inherent in case management approaches to service delivery for the seriously mentally ill. A recovery approach to clinical services involves consumers as partners in their treatment and setting their own personal goals.

This chapter describes community-based multifaceted service delivery approaches to clients with serious and persistent mental disorders. Not all such clients are young or have the diagnosis of schizophrenia, like Larry. Some have less serious diagnoses, yet are functionally disabled. Others have mental disorders that have periodic peaks, such as recurrent major depression and bipolar disorder. This chapter begins with the critical function of case management and proceeds with a discussion of the community services that are potential supports to clients. Among the variety of social and rehabilitative programs that are described, evidence-based and best practices will be underscored.

CASE MANAGEMENT AND COMMUNITY-BASED CARE

Case management (CM) is a generally accepted term that is used to describe the practice of coordinating a diverse set of services for clients and is frequently linked to the mental health field. It is a response to the complexity of the human service delivery system as well as the multiple needs of clients with severe mental illness who live in the community. Some CM models include the provision of therapy, whereas others only provide supportive counseling. CM is practiced in a number of other human service fields (e.g., addictions, aging, developmental disabilities, health care, and child welfare) and is not associated with a particular profession. Yet social workers are particularly well equipped to fulfill this role and apply diverse CM models and do so in various mental health settings.

The overarching goals of CM models are to (a) optimize client functioning to avoid hospitalization, (b) connect and sustain contact with services, (c) reduce the length of hospital stay when it occurs, (d) promote the highest level possible of client psychosocial functioning through rehabilitation, and (e) improve quality of life (Ellison, Rogers, Sciarappa, Cohen, & Forbess, 1995). A common framework for developing service objectives in CM include (a) continuity of care, (b) accessibility of services, (c) accountability of the services provided, and (d) efficiency of services (Baker & Intagliata, 1992).

According to the most current National Association of Case Management guidelines, there are three levels of CM (Hodge & Giesler, 1997). Level I is described as "the most intensive level of CM providing frequent and comprehensive CM support to the most severely disabled adults 24 hours per day, 7 days a week." Level II states, "CM provides a 24 hour, 7 day goal directed type of CM which is recovery and outcome oriented for people who wish to make regular progress in growth and rehabilitation." Level III "is the least intensive CM mode provided to people who are at present satisfied with their role or are largely able to self manage much of their progress. [It is] provided 40 hours per week with ongoing on-call for crisis intervention arrangements" (p. 26).

Case management is accomplished through the establishment of one pivotal relationship with a client (or, in some cases, a relationship with a team). The case manager helps the client obtain and use community resources that will facilitate his or her well-being and recovery. The agency auspices of case managers vary. The case manager may, for example, work out of an outpatient department of a psychiatric hospital; a psychiatric unit; a community mental health center; a local community-based office; a psychosocial rehabilitation program; or an adult protective service agency that serves the vulnerable aged, the physically disabled, and/or the severely mentally ill.

Functions of Case Management

The five basic functions of CM are (a) assessment, (b) planning, (c) linkage, (d) monitoring, and (e) advocacy. These functions are as follows.

1. *Assessment* is a comprehensive evaluation of the client's needs based on the client's history, diagnosis, strengths, resources, and difficulties. It requires the compilation of information from various sources (psychiatric hospital or unit, mental health center, family members, physician, psychosocial rehabilitation services that may have been previously used) as well as the client and client system. The assessment of a person with severe mental illness should be thorough, as treatment is holistic. It is recommended that case managers gather information about the client's situation and current needs in the following domains:

- housing
- physical health status and care (including use of health care services, diet, sleep, and exercise)
- mental health status, diagnosis, and needs for mental health services (medication, psychosocial rehabilitation, etc.)
- sources of economic support and ability to manage own money
- primary sources of emotional support (family, friends, service providers) and the quality of these relationships
- parental status (children cared for by client or someone else)
- personal hygiene and grooming
- socialization, recreation, and leisure time activities
- vocational, educational, and employment background and current status
- substance use and abuse
- involvement with criminal justice system and current status
- means of transportation, their accessibility, and the client's ability to use these means
- spiritual/religious orientation and needs

2. As part of the second function, *planning*, the case manager examines the client's situation in these domains and determines where needs are already met, where there are gaps, and where there is unrealized potential. On the basis of the assessment, a service plan that is tailored to the individual needs of the client is developed. In keeping with the principles of the community support system and social work values, the client should be an active participant in the development of the plan. In cases in which families are involved in the support of a client, and clients consent to their participation, inclusion of the family is valuable. Ideally the service plan is also developed collaboratively with representatives of the agencies that are included in the plan. The needs, services, and means of implementation should be delineated in measurable terms.

3. Case managers also assure that the client is *linked* with the appropriate community support services. To be able to do so, case managers should be knowledgeable about the existing resources, eligibility requirements, and how to access these sources of support. In working with individuals with mental illness, simply making a referral is not sufficient; means should be developed to facilitate the client's use of services. This may necessitate teaching and modeling for the client how to take the bus, mobilizing family members or volunteers to provide services, arranging transportation services, or perhaps the case manager escorts the client to the service.

4. The fourth function is *monitoring*. The case worker oversees the case to ascertain that the client is following through with the plan. If some aspect of the plan is not implemented, the case manager determines which obstacles might be interfering and tries to remedy them. If the client is carrying out the plan but the plan is not working, it may be that some aspect of the plan needs to be changed.

5. Another component of CM is *advocacy*. In fulfillment of this role, case managers act on behalf of clients to assure that clients' rights are protected and that they obtain services for which they are eligible. If clients are denied services or are mistreated in the community, case managers pursue informal and formal strategies to overcome obstacles to receiving services.

These five basic functions emphasize the administrative role of the case manager. They are particularly compatible with the generalist skills taught in social work bachelor's programs and in the first year of social work master's programs. When several direct service functions are added, the advanced skills of the clinical social worker come into play.

One of these additional functions is helping the client with *problem solving*. Living in the community, clients with serious mental disorders encounter everyday living problems and stressors with which they may have difficulty. The case manager works collaboratively with the client or client system by identifying the problem and breaking it down to manageable components, generating alternative solutions, promoting decision making, and evaluating the actions that are taken. The need for problem-solving activity arises in the process of monitoring the client over time. The problems may be personal, interpersonal, environmental, or a combination.

A related direct service function is *crisis intervention* (Lamb, Weinberger, & DeCuir, 2002). Crises are eruptions of stress in reaction to problems that cannot be managed using a person's usual coping mechanisms. Persons with serious and persistent mental illness are highly vulnerable to stress, which can arise within the individual or externally. Internal stressors are related to the disorder, which may produce an exacerbation on its own or be the result of a client going off the prescribed medication. External stressors such as poverty, eviction, interpersonal difficulties, problems on the job, and expressed emotion in the family—singly or in combination—can also arouse stress. Clients with severe psychiatric disorders may respond to stress in extreme ways; for example, they may threaten suicide, engage in violent behavior, or develop delusions or hallucinations (Flax, 1982). The case manager can provide support to the individual client, mobilize support from the family, intervene with persons who may be contributing to the problem, or call on community resources that can be used to resolve the crisis. This may require that the case manager make home visits, accompany the client to a psychiatric emergency service, or contact other support services in the community. In some cases, hospitalization is necessary. When a crisis occurs, the case manager may spend large blocks of time with a single client.

Consider the following crisis that occurred soon after Larry's third hospitalization, after which he was assigned a case manager.

April 4: John Martin, case manager, received a telephone call from Larry's mother, requesting that he meet with Larry. The case manager made a home visit, where he spent a couple of hours with Larry, and additional time with Larry and his parents together.

Larry told the case manager that he would like to have spending money, but his parents "won't let me apply for financial aid." (John recalled that during his first meeting with Larry, John told Larry about SSI.) Larry said that when he asks his parents for money, he feels like a child.

John figured out how much money Larry would receive with SSI, considering that he was living at home, and told Larry about Medicaid, for which he was also entitled. They discussed his right to receive benefits, but Larry was troubled by the prospect of going against his parents' wishes. John identified the following issues for Larry to consider: (a) Larry's respect for his parents' feelings and his fear of their disapproval; (b) his parents' coverage for him under their medical insurance at least until he is 21 years old; and (c) the amount of SSI he would receive versus his ability to earn the equivalent amount by doing chores for his parents, his grandparents, and neighbors.

During the family session, the case manager gave Mr. and Mrs. Leeds the opportunity to share their feelings about "not accepting welfare" and being responsible for Larry at least until he is 21 years old. John described the SSI program as an entitlement to which Mr. and Mrs. Leeds, as taxpayers, have contributed. Larry shared his feelings about being financially dependent on them and not having any spending money. He articulated his desire to live on his own and hold a job some day. At the conclusion of the session, the family agreed to the following:

a. Out of respect for his parents, Larry would not apply for SSI until he was almost 21 years old.
b. Larry's parents will pay him for performing three hours of yardwork weekly.
c. Larry will seek out similar jobs working for his grandparents and neighbors.
d. His parents will make efforts not to treat him like a child.
e. The case manager will work with Larry to make plans for services that will help him become more self-sufficient in the future, such as living in a group home.

Implicit in the functions that have been described is that the case manager provides a *supportive therapeutic relationship.* Although the establishment of a therapeutic alliance is central to all of social work practice, it is particularly important in working with persons with severe mental disabilities, who may be fearful, suspicious, or hostile toward others. These reactions may be a consequence of an illness that impairs their ability to establish relationships (Kantor, 1988) and/or a response to a new person. It is critical for the case manager to help the client overcome his or her apprehensions and form a therapeutic working alliance (Harris & Bachrach, 1988). The case manager can achieve this by conveying positive regard, attentiveness, and consistency; by engaging in activities together with the client; and by responding promptly to help the client with major and minor problems.

Another direct service function of the case manager is *working with the family* (Moxley, 2009). Many severely mentally ill persons live with their parents, spouses, siblings, or equivalent significant others. Even if the client lives apart from the family, emotional ties remain. The family can be a partner in the development and implementation of the service plan. Family members are able to provide key information about the client, identify signs of relapse, provide transportation, monitor the client's response to treatment, and assist with everyday problems. Moreover, the family can advocate for an individual member and for the corporate needs of clients. Despite the contributions families make, they are frequently excluded from consideration.

Clinical social workers who are employed as case managers call on their generalist skills in assessment, brokerage, case planning, and advocacy and on their clinical skills in the assessment of mental health problems and their treatment. Clinical social workers are trained to select interventions that are compatible with clients' needs, to use community resources, and to engage in client advocacy. We turn next to some intervention models social workers can use to work with clients with severe mental illness as case managers or members of a community mental health treatment team.

Case Management Models

During the last two decades of the twentieth century, numerous models of community care and CM for persons with severe mental illness were discussed and compared in the literature (see, e.g., Chamberlain & Rapp, 1991; Mueser, Bond, Drake, & Resnick, 1998; Solomon, 1992). Among these are the (a) broker, (b) rehabilitation, (c) strengths, (d) clinical, and (e) intensive case management models. As the following discussion will show, these models have some differences in philosophy, the depth of relationship with the client, and the client–case manager ratio. It is likely, however, that in the context of work with a particular individual in a particular situation, case managers operating from different models would act in similar ways.

1. The *broker* (or expanded broker or generalist) *model* is the most basic approach (Solomon, 1992). In this model, the case manager links the client with community resources and coordinates among different service providers (Mueser et al., 1998). The broker usually works from a central office and has a relatively high caseload (Solomon & Meyerson, 1997). Although the effectiveness research on this approach is inconclusive (e.g., Franklin, Solovitz, Mason, Clemons, & Miller, 1987), the broker model continues to be implemented widely.

2. The *rehabilitation model* "includes the functions of psychiatric rehabilitation to the functions of the broker case management model" and has an average (15–30) case manager to client ratio (Anthony, Forbess, & Cohen, 1993, p. 99). Person centered, it helps clients increase their functioning in the environments that they choose. CM that incorporates this model involves the use of a functional assessment, teaching of daily living skills, and the establishment of an overall rehabilitation goal (Anthony et al., 1993; Rogers, Anthony, & Farkas, 2006). The psychiatric rehabilitation model uses the *Choose-Get-Keep* approach of rehabilitation that was initially applied to vocational rehabilitation of persons with psychiatric disabilities and has since been applied to housing and educational settings (Anthony, Cohen, Farkas, & Gagne, 2002). Insufficient knowledge is available and empirical work needs to be done on the effectiveness of the rehabilitation model.

3. A third approach is the *strengths model*, which emphasizes the client's positive attributes and the community's resources. It is guided by the following six principles:

1. People with psychiatric disabilities can recover, reclaim, and transform their lives.
2. The focus is on individual strengths rather than deficits.
3. The community is viewed as an oasis of resources.
4. The client is the director of the helping process.
5. The case manager–client relationship is primary and essential.
6. The primary setting for our work is the community.

(Rapp & Goscha, 2006, pp. 55–65, passim)

This model is implemented through a collaborative relationship, an assessment of strengths, personal planning, resource acquisition, ongoing modification of the plan, and graduated disengagement (Rapp & Goscha, 2006).

4. A fourth model, *clinical case management*, posits that the case manager is a psychotherapist, who provides a relationship that encourages the client to change internally and grow (Roach, 1993). This is a development of Lamb's (1980) earlier conceptualization of the therapist–case manager, who is the client's primary therapist as well as a broker who links clients with resources. As a therapist, the clinical case manager helps clients interpret events accurately, teaches skills, and serves as a role model. This approach requires that the case manager be knowledgeable about object relations theory and have good clinical skills and training (Roach, 1993).

5. The fifth model, *intensive case management* (ICM), likely developed out of the Assertive Community Treatment (ACT) model (to be discussed later), where case managers work with clients who are heavy users of mental health services, have relatively small caseloads, and reach out assertively to clients to help them cope with community living (Corrigan, Mueser, Bond, Drake, & Solomon, 2008). Usually there is emergency, round-the-clock coverage. The ICM case managers generally have individual caseloads, but can work in teams. ICM has been vaguely defined in the field as meaning more "intense" than usual CM, suggesting more attention to the individual client.

One study (Jinnett, Alexander, & Ullman, 2001) examined the impact of the type of treatment setting (i.e., inpatient rehabilitation, day treatment center, community-based ICM program) and exposure to ICM services on the quality of life of 895 U.S. veterans with serious mental illness. Results demonstrated improvement in health, general, leisure, social and housing domains of quality of life. These findings are not explained by functional status or disease severity. The study did not find any effects of treatment setting on quality of life.

A review in the 1990s examined various models of community care for individuals with serious mental illness and reviewed the research on CM and included ACT model (Mueser et al., 1998). The report looked at seventy-five studies of CM using randomized controlled trial, quasi-experimental, and pre-post designs and included ICM and ACT. A majority of the research reviewed had been conducted on ICM and ACT models (Mueser et al., 1998). Randomized trial research on ICM and ACT demonstrated that these models improved housing stability and reduced the length of stay in the hospital, particularly for high service users (Mueser et al., 1998). The review also indicated that both models had moderate impact on improving symptoms and quality of life. Further, most of the research suggested that there was little impact of ICM and ACT on social functioning, arrest rates, time spent in jail, or vocational functioning, thus leading to inconclusive research on the effect of CM services on the seriously mentally ill (Mueser et al., 1998). In a more recent systematic review on CM models, Burns and colleagues (2007) concluded that ICM produces effective results when clients tend to have high hospital utilization rates.

Intensive case management has also been used as part of jail diversion programs for persons with serious mental illness. A recent review of the existing literature found mixed results on ICM outcomes (Loveland & Boyle, 2007). The authors concluded that ICM programs rarely led to reductions in jail or arrest rates over time. Generally, no significant differences were found between ICM programs and standard outpatient mental health services. However, ICM programs that had integrated substance abuse treatment into their program tended to be more effective at affecting rates of arrests and incarceration to some degree (Loveland & Boyle, 2007).

As CM continues to evolve and progress, the concept of recovery has become a fundamental principle in service delivery. A recovery orientation, according to Moxley (2009), includes a nondirective approach, client empowerment, and choice in all aspects of service delivery, answering existential questions about what is the purpose/aim of the client's life and how the client can achieve identified goals, an assumption of an active client/consumer, and an assumption that the community has numerous supports and resources to meet the client's goals. A case manager for whom a recovery orientation is fundamental can be viewed as a coach rather than a manager.

We turn next to the ACT model as an evidence-based practice for persons with serious and persistent mental illness. Although some authors classify ACT as a model of CM (e.g., Corrigan et al., 2008), we are viewing it here as a form of community care.

Assertive Community Treatment: An Evidence-Based Practice

Assertive community treatment is an approach to community care that spawned some of the CM models that have been discussed. As a program of direct service, the ACT program should be differentiated from CM models that grew out of it, such as ICM. During the 1970s, Leonard Stein (professor of psychiatry) and Mary Ann Test (professor of social work) of the University of Wisconsin developed a program in Dane County, Wisconsin, which was an alternative to hospitalization. "It was a comprehensive array of services that essentially transferred all the functions of the hospital to the community" (Solomon, 1999, p. 151). As the program evolved, it changed its name from Training in Community Living (TCL) to Program of Assertive Community Treatment (PACT) to Mobile Community Treatment (MCT) Program. These programs provided comprehensive, continuous care to clients with severe mental illness.

Assertive community treatment is an evidence-based practice model that grew out of the approach that was originally developed in the 1970s. It can be described as a comprehensive and intensive treatment program for individuals with serious and persistent mental illness who do not benefit from traditional outpatient or clinic-based services (Morse & McKasson, 2005). The basic principles of ACT include (a) the community is the primary locus of care, (b) treatments and supports must be comprehensive, (c) treatments and care must be flexible and highly individualized, (d) the team is the provider of treatment, and (e) the team is mobile in the community. ACT services focus on community integration of the client/consumer as well as assertive outreach to bring services to the client (SAMHSA, 2008). ACT programs provide continuous round-the-clock, time-unlimited support to its client/consumers of services.

The ACT program was adopted wholly or partially (in hybrid forms) by groups in other communities in the United States, Canada, England, and Australia. A large body of outcome research on ACT programs produced positive results, especially in the reduction of hospitalizations, reduction in symptom severity, and improved housing stability (Coldwell & Bender, 2007; Stein & Santos, 1998). The authors of the updated Patient Outcomes Research Team (PORT) study (Dixon et al., 2010) found strong evidence for ACT services and recommended the use of the ACT model as a system of community care for persons diagnosed with schizophrenia. SAMHSA (2010) has published an evidence-based practice kit to help communities develop such a program. Further information on ACT service guidelines is also available from the National Assertive Community Treatment Association. According to recent research reports, the ACT program is not a panacea for all clients, but is highly recommended for individuals who have repeated risk for hospitalization or are recently homeless (Coldwell & Bender, 2007; Nelson, Aubry, & Lafrance, 2007).

TABLE 11.1	The Assertive Community Treatment (ACT) Program

The desired outcomes of the ACT program are to:
- reduce the use of hospitalization
- increase quality and stability of community living
- normalize activities of daily living (e.g., employment)

The goals are to help clients:
- in their recovery through habilitation and community treatment (primary goal)
- maintain good physical health
- achieve a reduction in psychotic symptoms
- maintain normalized housing
- minimize involvement in the criminal justice and law enforcement systems
- acquire and maintain a job
- maintain a substance-free lifestyle
- meet additional individualized goals

The key features of the ACT program are as follows:
- a transdisciplinary team that shares a caseload of the same group of clients
- flexible service delivery
- fixed point of responsibility
- individually tailored treatment programs
- direct provision of services
- delivery of services in the client's natural environment (home, neighborhood, place of work)
- support in daily living skills
- assertive outreach and follow-up
- crisis intervention, problem solving, helping clients cope
- teaching clients skills in the environments in which they are to use them (in vivo services)
- small caseloads
- for consumers with the greatest need

Sources: Based on Stein & Santos (1998); Stein & Test (1982, 1985); Substance Abuse and Mental Health Services Administration (2008).

Table 11.1 outlines the major features of the ACT program. This will now be described as one of this book's examples of an evidence-based best practice.

In its original conceptualization, ACT had a multidisciplinary team functioning collectively as case managers, enabling the team to deploy workers efficiently when a number of clients are in crisis at the same time or when one or more team member is unavailable (Witheridge & Dincin, 1985). Today the same principle of group responsibility holds, but the teams are described as *transdisciplinary:* "Transdisciplinary teams blend the knowledge and skills of professionals from multiple disciplines. They transcend the typical provider-consumer relationship by giving consumers a decisive voice in *which* services they receive and *how* they receive them" (SAMHSA, 2008, p. 4). Transdisciplinary team processes include (a) the development of comprehensive assessments, (b) participation in development of consumer-centered treatment plans, (c) implementing and monitoring of treatment plans, (d) development of weekly consumer schedule based on consumer's treatment plan, (e) participation in daily team meetings, and (f) maintaining team communication logs (SAMHSA, 2008).

The major characteristics of the current ACT model are delineated below:

1. The primary responsibility of the ACT team members is for all services.
   - Staff consists of people experienced in psychiatry, psychology, nursing, social work, rehabilitation, substance abuse treatment, and employment.
   - Rather than referring people to multiple programs and services, the team itself provides the treatment and services a recipient needs.

2. Help is provided where it is most needed.
   - Program staff works with recipients in their homes, neighborhoods, and other places where problems and stress arise and support and skills are needed.

3. Help is provided when it is needed.
   - Rather than only seeing recipients a few times a month, program staff with different types of expertise can be in contact with people as many times a day as necessary.
   - Help & support are available 24 hours a day, 7 days a week, 365 days a year, if needed.

4. There is a shared caseload of ACT service recipients.
   - ACT staff members do not have individual caseloads. Instead, they share responsibility for the consumers served by their program team.
   - Each recipient likely gets to know multiple members of the team. If a team member goes on vacation, gets sick, or leaves the program, there are always other people the recipient knows to carry on.

5. Focused attention is on recipients' life needs.
   - Program staff members work closely with each recipient to develop a plan that helps the recipient reach his or her goals.
   - Staff members review each recipient's progress reaching those goals daily. If a recipient's needs change or a plan is not working, the team can respond immediately.
   - This careful attention is possible because the team works with only a small number of recipients-approx. 10 recipients for each person on the staff. (SAMHSA, 2008)

Teams have the advantage of providing continuous care for the client by anyone on the team. ACT teams meet on a daily basis, at which times clients are discussed, intervention strategies developed, and tasks distributed among the team. Clients are seen often and regularly in the community. The MCT Program in Wisconsin, designed specifically for difficult-to-treat, predominantly young clients, had two shifts of staff, who met daily between shifts and weekly as a total staff to give status reports on clients and coordinate their efforts (Stein & Diamond, 1985; Stein & Test, 1982).

The ACT model recognizes that clients with serious mental disorders have three disabling conditions that interfere with their social functioning (Stein & Test, 1985). These are (a) strong dependence needs, (b) a limited range of problem-solving or instrumental skills, and (c) the likelihood of developing psychiatric symptoms in the face of stress. These characteristics interfere with community living and create vulnerability to rehospitalization. On the other hand, the model recognizes that each client has strengths that are the basis for effective community functioning. To promote a client's functioning and prevent stress, the team assertively reaches out to clients to engage them and to keep them engaged in programs and in the community toward recovery. Clients who do not show up for appointments are sought out so that obstacles to their participation can be overcome.

With ACT, clients are also helped to become more independent. For some, this entails separation from parents by living apart from them. At the same time supports are provided for the client, structured visiting with parents is arranged, and the community is prepared to receive new residents ("Training in Community Living," 1983). In other cases, separation is not pursued. "Whether we separate patients from their families or not, we continue to work closely with families" (Stein & Test, 1982, p. 66).

One of the unique features of this model is in fostering the development of personal coping skills and strengthening activities of daily living while living in and being a citizen of the community. Accordingly, case managers reach out to clients in their homes and local communities. They may meet clients over coffee in the client's neighborhood, at a psychosocial rehabilitation program, or at the client's residence. The emphasis is on in vivo (real-life) assistance with ordinary daily activities in the same context in which they will be used. The team member models a skill (e.g., banking, shopping) where the skill is needed (e.g., a neighborhood bank, shopping center) and teaches the skill to the client. This approach differs from a program-based strategy in which the client is expected to learn a skill in one setting and apply it in another. In vivo assistance is consistent with the observation that many persons with severe and persistent mental illnesses have difficulties transferring learning from one situation to another (Stein & Test, 1982).

The ACT program is a community care service model that goes well beyond what is usually incorporated in CM programs. Stein (1992) notes that communities often expect individual case managers to do the work of a multidisciplinary team and serve as "glue" to fix a "fragmented nonsystem of public mental health care" (p. 173). He recommends that communities establish "continuous care teams" comprised of psychiatrists, psychologists, social workers, nurses, rehabilitation workers, and psychiatric technicians who specialize in difficult-to-treat clients, and that the staff–client ratio not be greater than 1:10. Stein (1992) recommends that ACT teams be available seven days a week. More stable clients can be cared for by less ICM teams.

Recent empirical work has extended the ACT model to other outcomes including addictions, employment, and subpopulations such as forensic clients. Several studies have examined ACT as an integrated treatment for individuals with serious mental illness and substance use disorders with mixed results (Essock et al., 2006). One modification in the ACT model is to integrate an addiction services specialist into the team. One study (Drake et al., 1998) found evidence of decreased substance use with an integrated ACT team, whereas other studies found no evidence for reductions in substance use (Essock et al., 2006; Morse et al., 2006). In forensic psychiatry, the goal of ACT is to reduce recidivism and promote engagement in treatment through the addition of a probation officer. Evidence for the impact of ACT programs among individuals with mental illness who also have a criminal background remain mixed (Chandler & Spicer, 2006; Lamberti, Weissman, & Faden, 2004).

ASSUMPTIONS UNDERLYING COMMUNITY CARE PRACTICE WITH PERSONS WITH SEVERE MENTAL ILLNESS

Community care with persons with severe mental illness is based on assumptions that are consistent with social work values and the perspectives of recovery and rehabilitation. These are as follows:

1. Persons with severe and persistent mental illness have the capacity to live in the community with appropriate supports.

2. Persons with serious mental illnesses have the capacity to grow, change, learn, improve, and recover.

3. Recovery, especially in the context of serious mental illness, embraces a hopeful vision for people who experience psychiatric disorders.

4. Such persons have strengths that can be developed and enhanced.

5. In a recovery framework, people who experience severe mental illness can live a life in which mental illness is not the driving factor for their lives.

6. Severe mental illness creates vulnerability to stress, dependence, and poverty that are exemplified in frequent crises.

7. In a recovery framework, service providers are called on to be a source of hope, support, and education, and partners with consumers on their journey through mental illness and accompanying outcomes.

8. For many persons with severe mental illnesses, learning is most effective when it takes place in the environment in which it is to be used; learning takes place gradually and in incremental steps.

9. Persons with severe and persistent mental illness have the right to participate in service planning and to make informed decisions on their own behalf.

10. Families/caregivers are partners in the rehabilitation and planning process, provided that clients consent to their help.

(SAMHSA, 2008)

These assumptions are predicated on the recognition that many individuals with serious mental illness recover or make substantial gains in their functioning, and, accordingly, that their potential for growth should be incorporated into treatment planning and implementation. In being optimistic about clients' capacity to learn and develop, the case manager recognizes and works with each client's strengths and capacities. Nevertheless, the vulnerabilities to stress and dependence should also be considered, so that when a crisis occurs, the case manager is ready to engage the client in problem solving to manage the situation.

The responsibility for the rehabilitation of persons with severe mental illness is shared among the client, the family (when available), the case manager, mental health services, other social service agencies, and the community as a whole. Clients are responsible for taking care of themselves. The community has a responsibility to respect the clients' rights, to accept them as citizens, and to respond to their needs. The case manager is in a critical position of mediating between the client and the community, yet also representing the client's interests.

In keeping with these assumptions, some of the key principles underlying quality practices in working with persons with serious and persistent mental illness are that:

- The nature and quality of the therapeutic relationship is critical.
- Quality practices are inclusive and continuous.
- Quality practices are individualized: matching services to the needs, strengths, preferences, and values of the recipient.
- Quality practices promote responsible partnerships via informed and shared decision making.
- Quality practices cannot be separated from quality practitioners.
- Quality practices are dynamic.
- Quality practices are outcome oriented and continuous.
- Quality practices are culturally competent.

(Suggested by New York State Office of Mental Health, 2008)

and include specific values for evidence-based practitioners in mental health:

- **Recovery:** As a unifying concept: creating and supporting services, practices, and policies that facilitate safety, hope, choice, and empowerment.
- **Partnership Building:** Meaningful and sustained quality is maximized through multistakeholder involvement.
- **Optimal Treatment:** Every single individual is entitled to receive mental health services that are evidence based and effective. Avoid the underuse, overuse, or misuse of services.
- **High Need:** Focus on the needs of the most seriously disabled and vulnerable population.

(Suggested by New York State Office of Mental Health, 2008)

In keeping with these guidelines, the following strategies are recommended:

1. Reach out assertively to clients in their natural environments on a regular and consistent basis, and at times of crisis.
2. Recognize clients' independence and support their recovery.
3. Teach life/social skills in the environments in which they are needed incrementally, supporting clients as they master each step.
4. Help clients obtain services and living situations that are consistent with their needs for recovery and autonomy. Decisions on housing should be guided by the clients' wishes and their capacity to manage in the new environment.
5. Assist clients to use resources available in their community.
6. Advocate for clients on the individual and community levels. This includes promoting the development of additional services that meet gaps in the existing mental health service delivery system and fostering work opportunities.
7. Help clients reduce hospitalization by addressing incipient problems at an early stage, intervening at times of crisis, and referring clients to services that are alternatives to hospitalization. Sometimes, though, hospitalization is necessary.
8. Conduct the CM role in keeping with social work values, with psychosocial rehabilitation goals, and within a recovery perspective. Be especially attentive to clients' rights to individualization, dignity, self-determination, and the least restrictive alternative; the principles of normalization, integration, and continuity of care; and clients' civil rights.
9. Develop constructive, collaborative relationships with families of persons with serious mental disorders.

COMMUNITY SUPPORT SERVICES AND RESOURCES

Persons with severe and disabling mental disorders can benefit from a variety of community services. The particular package of services that is appropriate for each client is related to the client's assessed psychosocial needs, the client's wishes and recovery goals, the client's financial status, and the resources available in the community in which the client lives. At times, the social worker will develop new services (e.g., initiate a new program for the mentally ill substance user through cooperative programming). The types of community services that will be discussed here are inpatient and outpatient treatment services, housing, crisis services, day treatment, vocational rehabilitation, consumer programs, health care, entitlements, and other services and resources.

Inpatient Treatment Services

Although current philosophy emphasizes treatment in the community, hospitalization is often needed on an emergency or intermittent basis for persons who are a danger to themselves or others and/or cannot take care of themselves. It is prompted by acute episodes and is sometimes used to regulate a client's medication. For a small number of clients, long-term hospitalization— or a structured, closed community treatment program that is the equivalent of hospitalization— may be the most appropriate option.

Inpatient care may be provided in local community hospitals, whether they are public, private, or university hospitals, or in Veterans Administration (VA) hospitals, or by the military. These hospitals usually have psychiatric units in which they treat persons who are admitted. Each hospital has its own admission procedures. In addition, some state psychiatric facilities continue to operate and care for clients on a long-term basis and manage forensic units in which they treat persons who are criminally committed. Hospitals vary, too, in the type of treatments they provide. Some offer primarily medication, whereas others have structured therapeutic treatment programs. Managed care entities may be consulted about admission and length of stay.

Outpatient Treatment Services

For persons with serious and persistent mental illnesses, outpatient behavioral mental health treatment is likely a necessity. Those with such mental disorders require a comprehensive, sustained program of care that deemphasizes traditional verbal psychotherapeutic approaches but is nonetheless therapeutic.

Clients who have been hospitalized should be linked with some type of community-based CM or outpatient mental health service prior to discharge. Joint planning before discharge between hospital social workers and community providers is helpful. Those who have never been hospitalized may be assisted by a case manager or other mental health professional to secure these services. Outpatient services are provided in a variety of settings, depending on the community and its range of services. ACT teams are one source, as are various types of CM services that may provide psychiatric rehabilitation, continuing day treatment programs, and community mental health centers. Many of these centers provide not only psychiatric supervision but also outpatient therapy, partial hospitalization (day treatment), emergency services, and other programs particularly targeted to the seriously mentally ill. Some communities have freestanding outpatient clinics in which medication is prescribed and supervised and CM is provided. Other areas have CM programs only. Still others have clinics that are associated with public hospitals, university hospitals, VA hospitals, ethnic-centered services, private practices, and behavioral health carve-outs.

Many persons with severe mental illness are on medication. Medication requirements within the hospital and the community may be different. Moreover, the need for medication may change over time. Many psychotropic drugs have side effects that need to be monitored by case managers, nurses, and/or psychiatrists. (Psychopharmacology will be given special attention in Chapter 12.)

Although most clients can benefit from some support, psychotherapeutic treatment should be offered on a selective basis to those clients for whom this is appropriate,. Structured approaches such as cognitive-behavioral therapy to reduce severity of symptoms (Dixon et al., 2010) can help clients manage daily living problems that may occur in the community.

An alternative to psychotherapy is participation in social skills training programs, especially in groups. With such training, clients can learn how to handle interpersonal problems and master effective social and vocational skills at the same time as they receive support from their peers. The most recent psychosocial recommendations from the 2009 Schizophrenia PORT indicates that individuals with schizophrenia who have skill deficits for everyday living should be offered skills training to improve interpersonal skills and independent community living (Kreyenbuhl, Buchanan, Dickerson, & Dixon, 2010). Social skills training is incorporated into the Illness Management and Recovery program that is described in Chapter 12. There is strong empirical support indicating that persons with serious and persistent mental illness can learn community living skills when provided with structured behavioral skills training (Kurtz & Mueser, 2008; Vauth et al., 2005).

For clients who are living with or are close to family/relatives, family-based service interventions are helpful. The 2009 Schizophrenia PORT recommends a family intervention that may last between six and nine months because such interventions have been found to significantly reduce relapse rates and rehospitalization in persons with severe mental illness (Kreyenbuhl et al., 2010). This evidence-based practice approach will also be discussed in Chapter 12.

Although the provision of medication is sometimes equated with treatment, intervention with the severely mentally ill encompasses the broad domain of adaptive living in the community. The relationship with the case manager, together with appropriate housing, psychosocial rehabilitation services, and natural supports all within a recovery perspective, can help sustain the client in the community.

Housing Options and Best Practices

The housing arrangements of persons with serious and persistent mental disorders are diverse. The kind of housing chosen and the neighborhood in which the housing is located are important to the client's well-being and may be related to their financial status since many clients have limited incomes.

The current best practice trend in housing for the seriously mentally ill is *supported housing* for clients to choose where they live and that arrangements be long term rather than transitional (New York State Office of Mental Health, 2006). This approach can create opportunities through development of a range of housing options, community support services, rent subsidies, and advocacy and brokering and CM services (Ridgway & Rapp, 1997). Supportive housing encompasses community support and psychiatric rehabilitation approaches within a recovery perspective. This approach is viewed as encouraging consumer empowerment and is rehabilitative in that clients gain skills in selecting, obtaining, and maintaining the kind of housing they want (Carling, 1993; Wong, Filoromo, & Tennille, 2007). Supported housing is housing that is integrated with the provision of community supports with the purpose of providing a cost-effective service while improving the lives of persons with serious mental illness. Some housing arrangements may be short term because a client's hospitalization or eviction interrupts a stable situation. Supported housing is not meant to replace existing housing options but to provide a wider array of services for the person with severe mental illness who is on the road to recovery. Some states have developed guidelines for implementation of supported housing (New York State Office of Mental Health, 2006). The Department of Housing and Urban Development (HUD) provides some housing assistance to low-income individuals and families who meet eligibility criteria (the "Section 8" program).

A recent literature review of housing models for persons with mental illness examined forty-four unique housing options that were described in thirty studies and were categorized as residential care and treatment, residential continuum, permanent supportive housing, and nonmodel housing (Leff et al., 2009). Residential care and treatment model housing was defined as board and care homes, group homes, community residences, halfway houses, and cooperative apartments. Residential continuum model housing was defined as high demand–high readiness housing that may overlap in their components with residential care and treatment models. This model is based on the notion that residents move from one housing model to another as they progress in their rehabilitation and recovery. Permanent supportive housing models provide staff support and treatment as needed in a "wraparound" service delivery concept. Nonmodel housing was defined in the Leff and colleagues (2009) study as those options for homeless persons that use short-stay or shelter beds. In this study, all models of housing in comparison with the non-model housing approach accounted for significantly greater housing stability. It was greatest for the permanent housing model. They also found that for reductions in psychiatric symptoms, only the residential care and treatment housing model differed from the nonmodel housing (Leff et al., 2009). Both permanent and residential care and treatment housing models were significantly greater in reduction in hospitalizations as compared with nonmodel housing.

Possible alternative housing arrangements are described next. These include living with one's family and in family care homes, commercial boarding homes.

LIVING WITH ONE'S OWN FAMILY   Many clients live with family members such as their parents, grandparents, sibling, spouse, children, or a significant other. These natural environments have the advantage of providing continuity and a potentially caring environment. However advantageous it may be for clients to live at home, the needs of families should also be considered. Families may become burdened with the care of a mentally ill member. Unless they are educated about mental illness and have sufficient supports of their own, it is likely that there will be a time when they will not be able to continue to care for their ill relative at home. Consider the following situation:

> When 50-year-old Molly first returned home to her husband after she was hospitalized for the sixth time, she slept all day and paced the floors at night. They shopped for food together, but her husband Ray did all the cooking and cleaning. Ray accepted his wife's condition because he was accustomed to it. When she began to accuse him incessantly of poisoning her food and going out with other women, however, Ray became angry. He was further disturbed by her refusal to bathe and take care of herself. Ray reached the limits of his tolerance and concluded that it was too difficult to continue to care for her. In desperation, he asked the case manager/social worker what other support services and potential housing alternatives were possible for Molly.

Before deciding on an alternative resource in the community, other arrangements can be explored. Other family members or a community service might provide *respite care*, a temporary place in which the client can stay while the primary caregiver rests or goes on vacation. Respite care is an underdeveloped but highly needed community resource (Zirul, Lieberman, & Rapp, 1989). Some communities provide nursing-home beds, board-and-care placements, or alternative residences for this purpose. Such programs can result in a reduction in subsequent hospital days for participating clients (Geiser, Hoche, & King, 1988). In this case, Molly was placed temporarily in a family care home, where her behavior and medication were closely monitored and a personal hygiene behavioral program was instituted. Meanwhile Ray had time to think about and problem solve about his needs and obligations with the help of a clinical social worker.

FAMILY CARE HOMES Family care or adult foster homes are some of the oldest existing forms of community care for psychiatric clients. In the ideal home, there are one to four clients who are integrated into a family setting and encouraged to develop habits of personal care and social skills. The caretaker, who is paid for services on a per-client basis, provides the client with bed and board and assures that the client receives physical and mental health care. The caretaker administers medication, takes the client to a mental health center for appointments, and gets the client ready for social rehabilitation programs.

Family care homes vary in size, atmosphere, and the autonomy available to clients. In some homes, the clients occupy a separate floor or wing from the family, thus comprising their own group. In other homes, the clients interact daily with children or grandchildren of the caregiver and participate in family activities such as meal preparation and gardening.

Family care homes are administered by VA hospitals, state hospitals, mental health agencies, or the private sector. Usually they are linked to the mental health delivery system in some way. Frequently social workers, nurses, and/or other mental health workers meet with clients and caretakers at the family care homes. During such visits, changing conditions of individual clients and the household can be observed and monitored. Family care homes are subject to state licensing laws.

SUPPORTED APARTMENTS These are autonomous living units, usually operated under the sponsorship of a hospital, agency, or social rehabilitation service. Certain apartments within an existing apartment complex are designated for client use, or certain buildings or blocks of apartments are used. The agency may own the housing units or lease the apartments or homes for the clients. In other cases, the agency's role is primarily consultative.

Clients residing in supported apartments usually share units with each other. Matches may be facilitated by mental health workers or preselected by clients. Because sharing an apartment brings individuals into close contact, care should be taken to ensure that apartment mates are compatible. Furthermore, clients should have skills in food preparation, house cleaning, cooking, and doing laundry. It is desirable that they be able to manage their own money and use public transportation.

Some communities have *specialized supported apartments* for clients with special needs. These apartments may serve parents with children, clients with dual diagnoses (mental illness and substance abuse or mental retardation/developmental disabilities), or individuals who had been incarcerated.

COMMERCIAL BOARDING HOMES Boarding, or board-and-care, homes are relatively large establishments, usually run for profit by nonprofessional proprietors. They, too, require licenses or certification, depending on the state. These facilities provide meals and shelter and administer medication. They offer less intimate contact and supervision than family care homes; ordinarily clients are free to leave the facility and wander about in the community. Generally, residents share rooms with other residents.

Payment for board-and-care homes comes from public transfer programs such as Supplemental Security Income (SSI) and Social Security. Most of the monthly allotment goes to the proprietor, but a small allowance is for the client. Because the margin of profit in such facilities is small, proprietors may be tempted to economize on food or deprive clients of their spending money.

Many boarding homes do not provide opportunities for socialization, rehabilitation, and social skills development. They are linked with the mental health system to the extent that the mental health worker or proprietor fosters the connection.

PERSONAL CARE GROUP HOMES These therapeutic residences help clients improve their skills in socialization and daily living. They provide a congregate living situation, structure, support, and on-site supervision. Group homes generally have rules that clients must honor if they want to stay. Although in the past group homes were primarily transitional facilities, today there are long-term group homes that do not "push" residents to move on (Carling, 1993).

TRANSITIONAL RESIDENCES These facilities, which also have on-site supervision, are available on a temporary basis. While living in these residences, clients may be required to enroll in a day treatment or vocational rehabilitation program, or hold a job while they receive psychiatric treatment. Staff members foster clients' development of skills in daily living so that with these supports clients can move to an autonomous living situation in the future.

STRUCTURED HOUSING AND REHABILITATIVE SERVICES Many communities offer a range of residential programs that are designed to be rehabilitative. For example, the Philadelphia Department of Behavioral Health and Mental Retardation Services (n.d.[a]) offers through contracted services long-term structured residential programs for clients who require treatment and rehabilitation in a controlled environment where there is a great deal of supervision. Long-term structured residences can become permanent placements for those who need it. Another structured residential program in Philadelphia is called a residential intensive therapeutic arrangement, which provides short-term, intensive residential treatment to clients age 18 and older who need a structured environment (Philadelphia Department of Behavioral Health and Mental Retardation Services, n.d.[b]).

24-HOUR CARE AND NURSING HOMES These facilities provide nursing and medical care as well as housing to individuals who need twenty-four-hour supervision. Generally, there are different levels of care, for example, skilled and intermediate. Although age is generally not a requirement for admission, these facilities may not welcome young clients with severe mental illness nor are they necessarily equipped to treat them (Carling, 1993). Nevertheless, they do provide a protective environment for older, fragile clients.

DOMICILIARY CARE HOMES *Dom care* homes are for persons determined to be disabled because of a physical or mental illness or frailties of old age who do not require hospitalization or nursing home care. Individuals who live in these homes usually require some supervision or assistance in performing activities of daily living.

SINGLE-ROOM OCCUPANCY HOTELS Some clients live in single rooms in hotels, a housing situation that has been given the acronym of SRO. These rooms are occupied primarily by poor people, usually welfare recipients. The single rooms may or may not have cooking facilities. Clients may have to use hot plates for preparing meals. Bathrooms are frequently shared. Conditions in these hotels are notoriously poor: they are unclean, cold, poorly maintained, and unsafe. Prostitution and drug dealing are rampant. Nevertheless, they are an improvement over the streets.

OTHER COMMUNITY RESIDENCES The varied U.S. communities in urban and rural areas have other kinds of facilities that are used for or adaptable to persons with severe mental illnesses. Many YMCAs and YWCAs, for example, have single rooms that are amenable to the severely mentally ill because they are quiet and private. These rooms may be available in a crisis or on a long-term basis. Some communities convert hotels and motels into residences for this population.

Some clients live in housing that is public or subsidized by the government. Apartments for elderly and disabled people, many of which have medical and social service personnel on the staff, can provide comfortable living quarters for the mentally disabled. It is incumbent on the social worker/case manager to identify such alternatives in the community.

INDEPENDENT LIVING   Some clients are able to live in the community on their own or with a roommate to share costs. These clients are sufficiently independent to assume their own leases, manage payment of the rent, keep the apartment reasonably clean, and prepare meals without a mental health professional supervising the arrangement. Persons who live independently still may be linked with the mental health delivery system. They may be attending a clinic and/or participating in a vocational rehabilitation program.

SHELTERS FOR THE HOMELESS   Homelessness is a social problem that is connected with unemployment, gentrification of urban areas, substance abuse, and family conflict, as well as mental health and other social policies. Substantial numbers of the homeless suffer from severe mental illness. Homelessness among the mentally ill may be the outcome of inadequate discharge planning, lack of available housing, client unwillingness to live in housing that is available, or eviction, among other factors. With little money, food, or social support—and poor coping skills—the homeless mentally ill are forced to fend for themselves. The "bag ladies" and "shopping-cart men" who are mentally ill are familiar sights in urban areas where they may be seen panhandling, eating others' leftovers, and collecting objects from garbage cans. It is not surprising that many of them are physically sick and that they are robbed, raped, and otherwise exploited.

Some individuals with severe mental illness are able to make their way from the streets to shelters for the homeless. Publicly run shelters accommodate large numbers of persons in open areas that provide little privacy or protection from theft or harassment. Shelters provide beds for a limited population, making it desirable for potential users to arrive early. Although they usually are not open during the daytime, some shelters offer social services or make referrals to appropriate mental health agencies and residences.

Some cities have alternative facilities that serve the same purpose as shelters for the homeless. Private organizations, often under religious auspices, run smaller, more personal facilities. Clients using these services may be allowed to stay longer than one night and may be helped to receive entitlements, obtain medication, and secure employment. Sometimes these facilities run their own programs of vocational rehabilitation (e.g., Goodwill Industries). Some shelters have accommodations for families.

A program that enables homeless consumers to avoid shelters is known as *Housing First*. In contrast with residential services that require that clients comply with demands such as receiving treatment for substance abuse, the Housing First approach is to help individuals and families obtain housing as soon as possible with few strings attached. Consumers are required to meet the terms of their lease agreement and are offered services that can be used as needed. More information about this program and where it is available may be obtained from the Website of the National Alliance to End Homelessness (http://www.endhomelessness.org/section/tools/housingfirst).

JAILS   Another housing alternative is the jail. Persons with mental illnesses may end up in the criminal justice system for a variety of reasons. Nevertheless, some individuals are treated for mental illness while incarcerated and receive CM services when they are released. Jail diversion court programs have been implemented with varying effects on recidivism and arrest rates.

Crisis Services

Persons with serious mental disabilities are sensitive to stress and subject to exacerbations of their psychiatric illnesses. In keeping with the requirement that treatment be the least restrictive, communities have developed a number of resources that are used to contain crises and avoid hospitalization. Among these are emergency services, crisis residences, and day hospitalization. At times, however, hospitalization is the most therapeutic alternative.

Emergency services are outpatient psychiatric units that are associated with general hospitals or mental health clinics. They treat persons who walk in or are brought in for treatment of acute psychiatric symptoms as well as stress-related reactions. Persons with severe psychiatric disorders may be escorted by family members, case managers, or the police. Police respond to a variety of situations but particularly to those in which clients are out of control, appear disoriented, or threaten violence.

Because emergency services do not operate on an appointment basis and, thus, may have an unpredictably full schedule, some units use a triage system in which all cases are screened briefly as soon as possible to determine which cases should be seen first and which require the services of a psychiatrist. Such systems are useful because many persons who use emergency services are not in crisis. Some users do not know of other community resources that can meet their needs more appropriately. Others' cultural styles make it more comfortable for them to ask for help for psychosocial needs from emergency services than from other community services.

Clients whose needs are perceived as urgent present florid psychotic symptoms, suicidal or homicidal behaviors, or aggression. Those who are brought in by the police tend to capture the immediate attention of staff. Case managers who accompany clients who are less visibly affected but are in emotional pain need to be assertive in requesting attention.

Emergency treatment varies according to the client's diagnosis and needs. Those with acute or extreme symptoms are screened to determine whether they meet the state's criteria for hospitalization. Those with acute psychotic symptoms are often given medication. Persons with anxiety, depression, confusion, and somatic symptoms that are related to stressful life events are helped through crisis intervention strategies.

Crisis intervention is a means of helping people under acute stress to restore their psychosocial functioning to the precrisis level at the very least. The emergency service worker must work very quickly to assess the seriousness of the problem and provide treatment. The worker does this by establishing rapport, asking the client about the precipitating event (the "last straw" that preceded the request for help) and hazardous conditions that created vulnerability to a crisis, and giving the client an opportunity to express painful emotions. In the course of hearing about the problem and the client's feelings, the emergency service worker makes an assessment and, in collaboration with the client, develops strategies to help the client solve the immediate problem. By connecting the client's symptoms with the causes of the problem and formulating a plan to address immediate issues, the worker helps the client restore cognitive functioning (Dixon, 1987).

At times emergency service workers intervene aggressively with violent or excited clients, placing them in lock-up rooms or putting them into restraints. Such measures, used for a limited amount of time and in conjunction with other means to help the client gain control (talking quietly and calmly to the client, medication), can be effective in the short term. Nevertheless, these emergency interventions present ethical dilemmas for social workers because they deprive clients of self-determination and their dignity. Under all circumstances, clinicians should first consider the least restrictive intervention.

Crisis residences provide temporary housing for persons with acute psychiatric problems. Alternatives to hospitalization, rather than shelters, they promote the remission of psychiatric symptoms, stabilization, and resolution of the problem that led to the acute state. The primary means of treatment are medication and crisis counseling. The goal is to restore the client to a previous level of functioning and to return the client to a suitable living arrangement in the community. Crisis residences have diverse admission criteria and limitations on the length of stay.

Crisis residential care may be provided in a separate facility (such as a crisis house) or in units within a community complex of residential facilities (such as purchased shelter in boarding houses or hotels). A study that compared client outcomes for those in a consumer-managed, unlocked crisis residential facility with those in a locked inpatient psychiatric facility found that those in the consumer-run residence showed more improvement in symptoms of psychopathology and in service satisfaction than those in the psychiatric facility (Greenfield, Stoneking, Humphreys, Sundby, & Bond, 2008).

Acute partial hospitalization is a kind of nonresidential care that is either a community-based alternative to complete hospitalization or a means of "stepping down" from hospitalization to community care. It may be run administratively by a hospital or an outpatient mental health center. Clients participate in an intense therapeutic program but return to their usual living quarters at night. These programs are usually time limited.

Partial Hospitalization

Partial hospitalization or day treatment provides structure, support, and activities that are found in total hospitals, and at the same time it enables the client to live in the community. It offers opportunities for socialization for persons who are likely to withdraw from others when they are left on their own. Furthermore, it provides consumers with a place to go and a means to broaden their activities, skills, and interests. In the course of the significant amount of time that is spent in these programs, staff are able to observe and monitor clients' adaptation to the community and prevent incipient problems.

Rosie (1987) described three types of programs: (a) day hospitals, which provide diagnostic and intervention services for persons with acute symptoms; (b) day treatment programs, which are used on a limited-time, goal-directed basis for clients whose acute symptoms are remitting, such as persons who are making the transition from the hospital to the community; and (c) day care centers, which focus on the maintenance or rehabilitation of severe psychiatric and psychogeriatric clients. Although these variations are not present or differentiated in every community, they do describe the kinds of programs that can meet the needs of persons with serious and persistent psychiatric disabilities.

Partial hospitalization programs may have their own facilities or may be situated in wings of hospitals or within behavioral health services. A minimum of a large community room and an office is needed. Self-contained programs situated in houses with comfortable living rooms, dining areas, kitchens, laundry facilities, showers, and group therapy rooms provide a naturalistic environment in which rehabilitation can take place. Such settings lend themselves to the teaching of skills in food preparation, laundry, housecleaning, and personal grooming. With sufficient space, clients can have some, but not constant, social interaction with others.

Partial hospitalization programs vary in structure. Some begin with community meetings in which clients plan daily, weekly, and special activities. Therapeutic group activities such as psychodrama, art therapy, medication adherence, and social skills training may be included. Outside experts such as nutritionists may be invited to meet with client groups. Programs that are under the aegis of managed behavioral care organizations tend to be tightly structured around therapy with limited time for informal socialization.

Training in activities required for daily living is incorporated in partial hospitalization programs. Clients' functioning levels should be assessed individually with the kinds of training offered consistent with the level of skill, comprehension, and disability of subgroups of clients. Furthermore, the topics should be relevant to the client's developmental stage and lifestyle. Some areas that can be addressed in activities training are living within a budget, using public transportation, meal preparation, shopping for clothes, housecleaning, dating, and personal grooming. Clients who are parents may benefit from sessions on child care. Clients who already have some of these skills can assist the staff in communicating and demonstrating these skills. Clients should have the opportunity to perform the skills after they are taught or modeled.

With today's emphasis on recovery, partial hospitalization programs are losing their attraction. This is because these programs have fostered the development of subcommunities of mental health clients who have become passive service recipients rather than active consumers. The federal plan to transform mental health care, which was the outgrowth of the report of the New Freedom Commission, is grounded in recovery and thus emphasizes client self-direction (U.S. Department of Health and Human Services, 2005).

Integrated Treatment for Schizophrenia and Substance Abuse: An Evidence-Based Practice

Studies have reported that between 20 and 75 percent of individuals with schizophrenia have co-morbid substance use disorders (Dixon et al., 1999; Tsuang, Fong, & Lesser, 2006). Substance use disorders increase the likelihood of poor medication adherence, and is associated with greater disability, lower functioning, increased hospitalizations, higher levels of depression and anxiety, greater housing instability, and increased involvement with the legal system (Compton, Weiss, West, & Kaslow, 2005; Margolese, Negrete, Tempier, & Gill, 2006). Integrated treatments for dual disorder clients use a variety of treatment services including CM, twelve-step programs, motivational interviewing cognitive-behavioral therapy, social skills training, behavior therapy, and family psychoeducation. Chapter 13 discusses this evidence-based practice.

Vocational Rehabilitation and Supported Employment Programs

Because work is a central life experience that can promote self-esteem and financial independence, provide structure, offer social opportunities, and facilitate community integration (Lehman et al., 2002), gainful employment is a goal of the psychosocial rehabilitation of clients with severe mental illness. Nevertheless, only 10 to 20 percent of clients are competitively employed at a given time (McGurk & Mueser, 2004). There are a number of barriers to employment, including policies around the use of Medicaid dollars, discrimination in hiring, personal discouragement, and a paucity of rehabilitation programs (Baron, 1999). Nevertheless, traditional and newer strategies of vocational rehabilitation and supported employment are available in some communities.

Vocational rehabilitation is a comprehensive program of "work therapy" that encompasses "work evaluation, training, guidance, and placement" (Jacobs, 1988, p. 247). It is also an important component of psychosocial rehabilitation. Clients can not only be helped to develop skills related to a particular line of employment; they can also be helped to use transportation to get to a job, arrive at a job on time, get along with others, and take orders from supervisors. Furthermore, they can be trained in ways to look for a job, develop a résumé, and handle an interview. Once they have found a suitable job, they can be helped to keep it (Bellack & Mueser, 1986).

Vocational rehabilitation follows from an assessment of a person's work skills (Jacobs, 1988). This is based on the individual's prior education and work history, observed behavior, and reports from previous employers, the client, or the client's family. The federal Office of Vocational Rehabilitation (OVR) has local affiliates that provide testing, counseling, training, and placement of persons with physical, developmental, and psychiatric disabilities who qualify. In some cases, this agency will pay for clients' college education or vocational training and for medical care required for rehabilitation. Nevertheless, this type of train-and-place model of vocational rehabilitation (including sheltered workshops, to be described next) has not been found to be successful in assisting persons diagnosed with schizophrenia to find and keep jobs in the market place (Bond, Drake, & Becker, 2008).

SHELTERED WORKSHOPS   A traditional approach to vocational rehabilitation is the sheltered workshop, which employs persons with severe and persistent psychiatric and other difficulties. Workshops enable clients to participate in low-pressure, noncompetitive work settings and learn basic vocational skills. Generally, the workdays are shorter than the usual eight hours; in some cases, clients may work only a few days. Sheltered workshops or their sponsoring organizations develop contractual relationships with industries for tasks such as cutting, sorting, and bagging items for retail sale. Clients are assigned particular jobs and are usually paid at a rate below the minimum wage.

Clients are trained to perform a variety of tasks and are encouraged to improve their performance. They are able to demonstrate progress and receive increased pay for performing more and more complicated tasks at a faster rate. Furthermore, clients benefit from the experience of getting to work on time, handling interpersonal relationships on the job, and using their time productively. For some clients, working in a sheltered workshop is a step toward competitive employment. Others maintain their workshop jobs for years. Sheltered workshops are segregated from the mainstream. Because integration and recovery are central to the philosophy of psychosocial rehabilitation, alternative strategies are often preferred.

THE CLUBHOUSE MODEL OF VOCATIONAL REHABILITATION AND SUPPORTED EMPLOYMENT

Fountain House, a social club founded in New York in 1948 by former psychiatric patients, is a member-run program of psychosocial rehabilitation in which work is central to its mission (Propst, 1988). The New York program has expanded tremendously since its inception and has spawned similar programs elsewhere. Today there are 334 clubhouse programs operating in 27 countries throughout the world that are linked through the International Center for Clubhouse Development (2008).

The clubhouses are organized around a *work-ordered day*, in which club members work along side staff in "work units" (Macias, Jackson, Schroeder, & Wang, 1999) and perform tasks that need to get accomplished. These include typing, answering telephones, running the cafeteria and coffee shop, giving tours, housecleaning, operating the duplicating machine, and data entry. Because the program is voluntary and members feel wanted and needed, motivation tends to be high. In the process of participating, members become aware of their abilities, learn new skills, and gain confidence (Propst, 1988).

Three vocational programs that are typical of most clubhouses are transitional employment (TE), supported employment (SE), and independent employment (IE), which operate on a continuum (McKay, Johnsen, & Stein, 2005). *TE* consists of temporary, part-time entry-level positions that are negotiated by clubhouse staff, who are responsible for their implementation. Job sites are developed by the clubhouse that provides on-site job training to the member-employee and covers the job when a member is unable to go to work (McKay et al., 2005). Members are paid the going rate for that job (minimum wage or above) for the number of hours they work. Participants in TE programs receive a great deal of support from the clubhouse staff as do those in the SE program. SE may be full or part time but is not temporary (McKay et al., 2005). The third vocational option, IE, provides support for full time. This program is available to those who aspire to and are capable of holding a competitive job and no longer need or do not require the support offered in the other options. Both SE and IE positions "belong" to the member (McKay et al., 2005).

SUPPORTED EMPLOYMENT: AN EVIDENCE-BASED PRACTICE   Supported employment, based on the individual placement and support (IPS) model (Becker & Drake, 2003, described in detail), emphasizes rapid placement in a competitive job based on the individual's needs and skills augmented with ongoing training and support from a job coach or job support case manager (Drake & Bond, 2008; Lehman et al., 2002). The evidence-based SE approach that is to be discussed here involves placing people on the job first and then provides the support and training they need, for example, by initially providing them with a job coach. The IPS model stresses the integration of employment and mental health services. When job placements are based on clients' preferences, job satisfaction, and tenure increase (Bond et al., 2008). Research on programs that help clients obtain and maintain jobs in the competitive market shows that program participants have a considerably higher rate of competitive employment and earn more money than individuals in comparable rehabilitation programs (Lehman et al., 2002; Mueser, Drake, & Bond, 1997; Twamley, Jeste, & Lehman, 2003). A continued focus on SE with its support enhancements is likely to expand beneficial outcomes to a wider range of individuals with schizophrenia.

Core components and basic characteristics on this evidence-based practice are provided in Table 11.2. The goal of SE is competitive employment. SE should be integrated with treatment, consumer choice should guide the process, a job search should ideally be started as soon as the consumer gives permission, and ongoing supports should be in place for success and maintenance (SAMHSA, 2009).

JOB CLUBS   Another empowering approach to work is participating in a job club. This is a program supported by rehabilitation staff, which places the responsibility for finding a job on clients (Jacobs, 1988). The clients devote full time to the program, which teaches job-seeking skills and provides resources (telephones, counselors, secretarial support, job leads, etc.) to help clients locate a job (Jacobs, 1988).

Supported Education: A Best Practice

Adults with serious mental illness who wish to pursue postsecondary studies may be eligible for participation in programs of supported education that may result in employment opportunities. This aspect of psychosocial rehabilitation provides supports to help participants consider their educational goals and pursue advanced education, thus, taking advantage of resources within a college or community college environment (Mowbray, Brown, Furlong-Norman, & Sullivan-Soydan, 2002). The varied programs that exist are located at educational institutions or at clubhouses, psychiatric hospitals, and mental health centers (Morrison & Cliff, 2007; Unger, 1997).

TABLE 11.2	Supported Employment (SE): An Evidence-Based Practice

Core Components

- SE programs help anyone who expresses the desire to work.
- Employment specialists help consumers look for jobs soon after they enter the program.
- Support from employment specialists continues as long as consumers want it.
- Jobs are seen as transitions.
- SE programs are staffed by employment specialists who are a part of a clinical treatment team.
- SE is individualized.

Basic Characteristics

- Employment specialists manage caseloads of up to 25 consumers.
- Employment specialists provide only vocational services.
- Each employment specialist carries out all phases of vocational service.
- Employment specialists are part of the mental health treatment teams with shared decision making.
- Employment specialists function as a unit.
- There are no eligibility requirements to enter the SE program.
- Vocational assessment is an ongoing process.
- The search for competitive jobs occurs rapidly after program entry.
- Employer contacts are based on consumers' job preferences.
- Employment specialists provide job options that are in a variety of settings.
- Employment specialists provide competitive job options that have permanent status.
- Employment specialists help consumers end jobs when appropriate and then find new jobs.
- Individualized follow-along supports are provided to employers and consumers with no time limitations.
- Vocational services are provided in community settings.
- Assertive engagement and outreach are conducted as needed.

Source: Substance Abuse and Mental Health Services Administration (2009).

The key components of the supported education model are similar to those in SE. Psychosocial rehabilitation strategies such as skill development, environmental support, goal development, and client choice are used (Mowbray et al., 2005). Research has found that a variety of methods of supported education are associated with subsequent enrollment in college or vocational training at six-month and twelve-month follow-up periods (Morrison-Dore, 2008; Mowbray, Collins, & Bybee, 1999). Individuals with psychiatric disabilities are generally satisfied with job support services and can complete college-level courses (Leonard & Bruer, 2007).

Peer Support Specialists: A Best Practice

Peer support includes services from persons who have experienced serious mental illness who offer services to clients based on their experiences as consumers within a recovery perspective. Peer self-help services may also be family-provided services to other family caregivers with a relative diagnosed with a serious mental disorder (e.g., NAMI, discussed later in this chapter). Peer specialists may be paid or volunteer. Peer support principles include social support, experiential knowledge, social learning through others with common problems, and increased self-awareness. Benefits for consumer providers of service include personal growth, increased potential for employment, mutual support, and potential reduction in hospital admissions. These services offer choices and options and enhance self-determination and recovery. Peer support specialists can teach coping and social skills that may be needed to increase resiliency (the ability to cope with life challenges) within a system focused on recovery (Solomon & Draine, 2001). Peer support specialists can also organize structured recreational activities based on preferences of clients/consumers and offer regular support and contact to engage the consumer in other mental health services (Min, Whitecraft, Rothbard, & Salzer, 2007). Peer support can be provided where community mental health services are offered including hospitals, consumer-operated drop-in centers, outpatient clinics, and psychosocial rehabilitation centers, to name a few (Chinman, Young, Hassell, & Davidson, 2006). Frequently, peer support services are offered by consumer-operated organizations in which a majority of the staff has a history of mental illness. Many mental health agencies, including psychiatric rehabilitation services, also offer peer support.

Evidence on peer support services is sparse (Solomon, 2004); yet the current trend is to consider it as an emerging best practice when provided as an adjunct to traditional mental health services, according to the 1999 Surgeon General's Mental Health report (U.S. Public Health Service, 1999). The report by the President's New Freedom Commission on Mental Health (2003) recognized peer support as an emerging best practice. The report recommended an increased presence for consumers with mental illness in providing services to their peers, particularly through consumer-run organizations.

Clubhouses, Drop-In Centers, and Consumer-Run Organizations

CLUBHOUSES   Consumers have developed and operated many of their own activities and programs. Among the first such program was Fountain House, mentioned in the earlier discussion of vocational rehabilitation programs. Clubhouse participants are called *members*, not clients, who belong to a community that values them. Clubhouses modeled along the lines of Fountain House are member-run programs of psychosocial rehabilitation. Besides the vocational programs that were described earlier, there are evening and weekend social activities and programs.

DROP-IN CENTERS   Another resource that is run by consumers is the drop-in center. Like clubhouses, these are places in which clients can feel at home, socialize, and give each other support. Centers vary in their administrative structure, focus, and times at which they are open. Usually there are paid staff as well as a core group of consumer volunteers who assure that the programs run smoothly (Kaufmann, Ward-Colasante, & Farmer, 1993).

OTHER CONSUMER-RUN PROGRAMS   A variety of other consumer-run services have emerged, and it is anticipated, others will follow. In their research, Solomon and Draine (1995) found that CM delivered by consumers was comparable with CM provided by nonconsumers in terms of specific outcomes.

FAMILY/CONSUMER ADVOCACY ORGANIZATIONS   Consumers and their families have also developed self-help and advocacy organizations to help them deal with the stigma of mental illness, the effects of the disease, and deficiencies in the mental health service delivery system. As persons who have "been there," they know what it is like to be mistreated or to have needs, wants, and rights that are not recognized by service providers. Those who call themselves *consumers* emphasize their rights as members of society to receive, evaluate, choose, and refuse services.

Consumers help each other solve problems individually and take actions collectively. They may give advice to other consumers about particular mental health services, psychiatrists, or social workers; work for the creation of new resources; disseminate information about medication; or lobby for a desired bill. Some of these groups are unique to a locality or state; others are part of a national network. Professionals may be allowed to join but not to vote. Increasingly, government entities are supporting consumer organizations.

NATIONAL ALLIANCE ON MENTAL ILLNESS   One of the most influential of the *family consumer groups* is the National Alliance on Mental Illness (NAMI) and its state and local affiliates. NAMI represents the interests of families of persons with severe psychiatric problems as well as the interests of consumers. On the local level, the group educates members and the public about mental illness, provides information about resources, promotes the development of better mental health services, and the like. Nationally, NAMI advocates for research and programmatic support for persons with serious and persistent mental illness. NAMI members are sensitive to and reject the historical trend of holding parents responsible for the development of mental illness in their children. NAMI views mental illness as a brain disease and engages in advocacy and supports research on biological treatments and biopsychosocial services. Clients and professionals can join NAMI.

Social worker case managers have a number of responsibilities in relation to consumer groups. First, they should become knowledgeable about the groups in their own community and inform clients and families about their existence, what they do, and the potential benefits (e.g., information, family education classes, social contacts, empowerment, a source of meaning). Second, social workers should get to know members of consumer groups and listen to their grievances. Some of their complaints can be addressed through mediation, advocacy, and brokerage. Third, social workers might want to join some of these groups.

Citizen Advocacy Groups

There are a few citizen advocacy groups whose constituencies include the general public, professionals, researchers, client consumers, and family members. One of the oldest such groups is the *National Mental Health Association*, now called Mental Health America, and its local branches. These organizations provide information on mental health topics, offer educational and support groups to consumers and families, and lobby for improved mental health legislation (Lefley, 1996). Another advocacy organization is the *Judge David L. Bazelon Center for Mental Health Law*, which is concerned with the civil liberties of persons with mental illness as well as their rights to housing, income support, and health care (Lefley, 1996). State Protection and Advocacy (P&A) Centers are legal services mandated by the federal Protection and Advocacy for Individuals with Mental Illness (PAIMI) Act to protect the rights of clients with disabilities through lawsuits and advocacy activity (Lefley, 1996).

Health Care

Compared with the general population, individuals with serious mental illness have a shorter life span and more medical problems (Bazemore, 1996). The early deaths are due to natural causes (e.g., heart disease, infection) and unnatural causes (e.g.; trauma, suicide) (Bazemore, 1996). The medical problems may be the consequences of poor health care. Because of difficulties in cognitive processing, distortions in self-awareness, and mistrust of outsiders, some persons with mental illness may not identify health problems or be unwilling to discuss them with others.

Many individuals with serious mental illnesses receive or are able to qualify for either Medicare or Medicaid; some have private health insurance or are eligible for VA benefits. Many states have contracted with managed care entities to administer health and behavioral health services to public sector clients. Veterans may be treated in VA facilities. Public and private sources of insurance cover the costs of visits to physicians, medication, and hospitalization, but, especially under managed care, they have their limits. Advocacy for those who do not qualify for medical services or are refused care may be effective.

Health care management should be part of the client's individual service plan. The client should be helped to maintain a balanced diet, live in a clean environment, and identify symptoms of health problems. The client should be linked with a doctor, clinic, or hospital in which ongoing and emergency health care are available. The client's teeth, eyes, ears, and feet may need the attention of specialists.

Women of childbearing age who are consumers may decide to use the services of a family planning clinic. They should be provided with information about birth control, sexuality, and childbearing. The impact of birth control pills on their physical and mental health, as well as the interaction between psychotropic medication and pregnancy and lactation (Mogul, 1985), should be discussed. Furthermore, women should be helped to protect themselves from situations that make them vulnerable to sexual exploitation.

Schwab, Drake, and Burghardt (1988) recommend that in dealing with health care providers, the case manager act as a *culture broker*. As such, the case manager should gain an understanding of the client's mental functioning; how the client perceives his or her body, symptoms, and the medical care system; and the composition of the client's social system, so that communication with a physician who does not understand the client's social world can be facilitated. Furthermore, barriers to receiving health care should be identified. Using personal observations and knowledge obtained from working with the client, the case manager can bridge the gap between the client's culture and the medical system, interpreting one to the other.

Entitlements

Serious and persistent mental illness entitles persons to a range of public benefits for which they must apply. Each entitlement has its own set of requirements, forms, and stipulations. The case manager should be familiar with the programs for which an individual may qualify, eligibility requirements, and application procedures.

If clients are not working or if they are underemployed, they may be eligible for some form of financial assistance. One can qualify for Social Security disability insurance on the basis of one's own work history and mental or physical impairment, or because one is a widow or a disabled child of a person with a work history. Those who qualify for Social Security are also eligible for Medicare. If the Social Security allotment is not sufficient or if the applicants turn out to be ineligible, they can apply for SSI and Medicaid. To qualify as "permanently and totally disabled" under Social Security or SSI, medical documentation must be provided. Other possible sources of financial assistance are VA disability pensions and local public welfare programs. Persons who have work histories might be eligible for disability or retirement insurance that was a fringe benefit where they worked, or unemployment compensation, if their job was terminated.

Another entitlement is food stamps. Those who are eligible for other forms of public assistance may also be eligible for food stamps. Some clients may qualify for food stamps only or for stamps on an emergency basis only. Certain restrictions apply; for example, they cannot be used to pay for cigarettes or alcohol.

With the burgeoning population of homeless, many soup kitchens and food banks/pantries have come into existence. Food kitchens provide one or two free meals a day, and food pantries supply applicants with canned goods, cheese, and other food items. Often these establishments are housed in churches or community centers. Shelters for the homeless also provide users with free meals. Clients in poor financial straits might also receive help from faith-based organizations.

Supports for Clients Who Are Parents

Although women with severe mental illness have a fertility rate that is at least equivalent to that of the general population (Saugstad, 1989), their needs as parents have been sorely neglected. Parenting is work and, thus, can be incorporated in a program of rehabilitation if a client needs help in this area (Nicholson & Blanch, 1994).

A few intervention programs have served mothers and their children. Among these are mother–baby units in hospitals; home care programs incorporating home visits; and intensive, community-based rehabilitation of parents and children (Oyserman, Mowbray, & Zemencuk, 1994). There are a limited number of supported residential programs for mothers and children (e.g., Sands, 1995); residential treatment programs for substance abusing mothers (including those with a mental health diagnosis) are more common. The Mothers' Project at Thresholds, a psychosocial rehabilitation program in Chicago, has expanded its work with mothers with serious mental illness to include those who are homeless as well (Hanrahan et al., 2005). A qualitative study of seven programs for parents and their children around the country found that although the programs are diverse, most provide CM and parent support, skills training, and education, and that some offer family therapy, child-focused interventions, and housing (Nicholson, Hinden, Biebel, Henry, & Katz-Leavy, 2007).

Support Networks

Most of the community resources that have been described comprise a *formal* network of supports that can be mobilized to help an individual client adapt to community life. Mental health services, programs of entitlement, and housing units are needed components of the formal system. Such services tend to be impersonal, however. Embedded in these services, however, are personal relationships that can emerge naturally and serve as more intimate helping resources.

Natural or informal supports are persons and groups that evolve over time and through everyday interactions. These are made up primarily of people who care—one's family, however one defines it, friends, neighbors, people with whom one prays, and coworkers. They also might include hairdressers, storekeepers, bartenders, landlords, and others with whom one interacts informally. The persons one meets in support groups and community programs can become part of the natural system of supports.

Research on the social networks of persons with severe mental health problems has found that this population tends to have small, dense networks that are composed primarily of kin and that the networks contain few clusters (groups of people who interact with each other) and lack reciprocity (Cutler, 1984). Considering that persons with schizophrenia and some of the other severe disorders withdraw from social relationships and are threatened by emotional intensity, their narrow social world is not surprising.

One of the responsibilities of the case manager is to help the client build and expand supportive social networks. Interpersonal relationships are important because they serve as a buffer against stress and involve the individual in meaningful participation in the community. The case manager can help the client develop social networks by increasing opportunities for relationships to develop. This can result from linking the client with social and recreational groups, encouraging the client to reconnect with persons who were meaningful to him or her in the past and to maintain those current social contacts who might become friends, promoting the client's use of psychosocial rehabilitation services, creating socialization groups, and supporting the client's participation in the world of work.

The family is an important social support for some clients. Within the family, however, the consumer defines it: the potential to care, give, and help is great and should be engaged. Nevertheless, one should also take care to modulate a client's dependence on them and encourage other relationships as well. Some communities have volunteer programs, such as Compeer, in which community people provide peer support and friendship to persons with severe mental disabilities. For clients who do not have kin, or do not have relatives who live nearby who are supportive, friends and service providers become the equivalent of a family.

Ethnic-Specific Behavioral Mental Health Centers

Clients who identify with an ethnic community that operates its own mental health services may feel more comfortable receiving help from their own group. Some of the larger cities have mental health or multiservice centers for different ethnic groups that are sensitive to the language and culture-specific needs of members of their constituencies. Staff members who speak the same language as the client and are familiar with the client's culture work there. Supports for other communities—for example, the hearing-impaired, gays and lesbians, and persons with AIDS—are also available in some behavioral health centers as well as nearby communities.

Case Study

Estrella and Juan Martinez, both 25 and Mexican Americans, live in a barrio in California. The couple met five years ago in a state psychiatric hospital, where they were both hospitalized with schizophrenia. After they were discharged, they set up housekeeping together for a while and married after Estrella became pregnant with their daughter, Lucia. Lucia is now four and Estrella is again pregnant. Although neither Estrella nor Juan works regularly, they have income from SSI as well as food stamps and Medicaid. (Occasionally, Juan is able to earn money doing odd jobs.) They have close ties with Juan's family in the barrio but do not socialize with anyone other than kin.

The Martinezes have had a bilingual Mexican American case manager who has helped them obtain aftercare services in a culturally sensitive mental health center. Furthermore, this case manager has acted as culture broker in arranging Estrella's prenatal care and Lucia's entry into a Headstart program. Two months ago, this case manager was promoted and replaced by a new case manager who does not speak Spanish and knows very little about the Martinezes' culture and about the needs of persons with schizophrenia. Around the same time, Juan's parents moved away and Estrella had a miscarriage. These stressors put the Martinezes at risk of decompensating.

How should the case manager intervene in this case to promote support and buffer stress in a culturally sensitive way? What community services might be helpful?

Summary and Deconstruction

The recovery perspective is central to the transformation of mental health care in the United States. This perspective is fundamental to community care for the seriously mentally ill population and includes self-determination, personal hope, a holistic and a strengths-based approach. This chapter described models of community care and CM of individuals with serious and persistent mental illness as well as a few evidence-based and best practices. CM is an administrative mechanism that uses an individual or team to support and monitor clients' community living. Although ACT began as a model of treatment, it has also been absorbed into the ICM model, which does not only provide treatment itself but links clients with services.

There are numerous models of CM that have been touted, but in practice it is likely that they operate similarly. Generally, case managers perform assessments, monitor clients' progress, develop individually tailored service plans, and link clients with services. Regardless of the model, case managers engage in some direct work with clients and link clients with services. Some models require that case managers be more actively engaged in outreach, rehabilitation, and treatment than others. Clinical case managers provide psychotherapy along with the other tasks.

Case management is particularly needed in communities in which there are many resources but little coordination. Clients and families may not be aware of the services that exist and their rights to use them. Some communities, however, have fewer resources or have resources that are not sensitive to the needs of the community's ethnic/racial groups. It is not enough to have services; services must be adapted to clients' needs.

This chapter described a variety of resources that are available in some communities. These include a range of supported housing/residential services, inpatient and outpatient treatment facilities, ACT, supported education, crisis services, partial hospitalization, peer support services, SE, and vocational rehabilitation. In addition, clients need health care, as they are at risk of having medical problems and are entitled to financial resources. Nevertheless, clinical social workers can err in *providing* too many services to service *recipients* and acting in a paternalistic way. Above all, there is a need for client-centeredness. Clients have their own recovery goals and have developed and operate many of their own organizations and services. These organizations provide opportunities for persons with severe mental illness to become empowered. Families have also developed and operate advocacy organizations and wish to have their voices heard, too.

References

Anthony, W. A., Cohen, M. R., Farkas, M., & Gagne, C. (2002). *Psychiatric rehabilitation* (2nd ed.). Boston: Boston University, Center for Psychiatric Rehabilitation.

Anthony, W. A., Forbess, R., & Cohen, M. R. (1993). Rehabilitation-oriented case management. In M. Harris & H. C. Bergman (Eds.), *Case management for mentally ill patients: Theory and practice* (pp. 99–118). Langhorne, PA: Harwood Academic Publishers.

Baker, F., & Intagliata, J. (1992). Case management. In R. P. Liberman (Ed.), *Handbook of psychiatric rehabilitation* (pp. 213–244). Boston: Allyn & Bacon.

Baron, R. C. (1999). The impact of behavioral managed care on employment programming for persons with serious mental illness. *International Journal of Mental Health, 27,* 41–72.

Bazemore, P. H. (1996). Medical problems of the seriously and persistently mentally ill. In S. M. Soreff (Ed.), *Handbook for the treatment of the seriously mentally ill* (pp. 45–66). Seattle, WA: Hogrefe & Huber Publishers.

Becker, D. R., & Drake, R. E. (2003). *A working life for people with severe mental illness.* New York: Oxford Press.

Bellack, A. S., & Mueser, K. T. (1986). A comprehensive treatment program for schizophrenia and chronic mental illness. *Community Mental Health Journal, 22,* 175–189.

Bond, G. R., Drake, R. E., & Becker, D. R. (2008). An update on randomized controlled trials of evidence-based supported employment. *Psychiatric Rehabilitation Journal, 31*(4), 280–289.

Burns, T., Catty, J., Dash, M., Roberts, C., Lockwood, A., & Marshall, M. (2007). Use of intensive case management to reduce time in hospital in people with severe mental illness: systematic review and meta-regression. *British Medical Journal, 335*, 336.

Carling, P. J. (1993). Supports and rehabilitation for housing and community living. In R. W. Flexer & P. L. Solomon (Eds.), *Psychiatric rehabilitation in practice* (pp. 99–118). Boston: Andover Medical Publishers.

Chamberlain, R., & Rapp, C. A. (1991). A decade of case management: A methodological review of outcome research. *Community Mental Health Journal, 27*, 171–188.

Chandler, D., & Spicer, G. (2006). Integrated treatments for jai recidivists with co-occurring psychiatric and substance use disorders. *Community Mental Health Journal, 42*, 405–425.

Chinman, M., Young, A., Hassell, J., & Davidson, L. (2006). Toward the implementation of mental health consumer provider services. *Journal of Behavioral Health Services and Research, 33*(2), 176–195.

Coldwell, C. M., & Bender, W. S. (2007). The effectiveness of assertive community treatment for homeless populations with severe mental illness: A meta-analysis. *American Journal of Psychiatry, 164*, 393–399.

Compton, M., Weiss, P., West, J., & Kaslow, N. (2005). The associations between substance use disorders schizophrenia spectrum disorders, and Axis IV psychosocial problems. *Social Psychiatry and Social Epidemiology, 40*(12), 939–946.

Corrigan, P. W., Mueser, K. T., Bond, G. R., Drake, R. E., & Solomon, P. (2008). *Principles and practice of psychiatric rehabilitation: An empirical approach.* New York: Guilford Press.

Cutler, D. (1984). Networks. In J. A. Talbott (Ed.), *The chronic mental patient: Five years later* (pp. 253–266). Orlando, FL: Grune & Stratton.

Dixon, L., Postrado, L., Delahanty, J., Janine, M., Fischer, P., & Lehman, A. (1999). The association of medical comorbidity in schizophrenia with poor physical and mental health. *Journal of Nervous and Mental Disease, 187*(8), 496–502.

Dixon, L. B., Dickerson, F., Bellack, A., Bennett, M., Dickinson, D., Goldberg, R., et al. (2010). The 2009 Schizophrenia PORT psychosocial treatment recommendations and summary statements. *Schizophrenia Bulletin, 36*(1), 48–70.

Dixon, S. L. (1987). *Working with people in crisis* (2nd ed.). Columbus, OH: Merrill.

Drake, R. E., & Bond, G. R. (2008). Supported employment: 1998–2008. *Psychiatric Rehabilitation Journal, 31*(4), 274–276.

Drake, R. E., McHugo, G. J., Clark, R. E., Teague, G. B., Xie, H., Miles, K., et al. (1998). Assertive community treatment for patients with co-occurring severe mental illness and substance use disorder: A clinical trial. *American Journal of Orthopsychiatry, 68*, 201–215.

Ellison, M. L., Rogers, E. S., Sciarappa, K., Cohen, M., & Forbess, R. (1995). Characteristics of mental health case management: Results of a national survey. *Journal of Mental Health Administration, 22*, 101–112.

Essock, S. M., Mueser, K. T., Drake, R. E., Covell, N. H., McHugo, G. J., Frisman, L. K., et al. (2006). Comparison of ACT and standard case management for delivering integrated treatment for co-occurring disorders. *Psychiatric Services, 57*, 185–196.

Flax, J. W. (1982). Crisis intervention with the young adult patient. In B. Pepper & H. Ryglewicz (Eds.), *The young adult chronic patient* (pp. 69–75). San Francisco: Jossey-Bass.

Franklin, J., Solovitz, B., Mason, M., Clemons, J., & Miller, G. (1987). An evaluation of case management. *American Journal of Public Health, 77*, 674–678.

Geiser, R., Hoche, L., & King, J. (1988). Respite care for mentally ill patients and their families. *Hospital and Community Psychiatry, 39*, 291–295.

Greenfield, T. K., Stoneking, B. C., Humphreys, K., Sundby, E., & Bond, J. (2008). A randomized trial of a mental health consumer-managed alternative to civil commitment for acute psychiatric crisis. *American Journal of Community Psychology, 42*, 135–144.

Hanrahan, P., McCoy, M. L., Cloninger, L., Dincin, J., Zeitz, M. A., Simpatico, T. A., et al. (2005). The Mothers' Project for homeless mothers with mental illnesses and their children: A pilot study. *Psychiatric Rehabilitation Journal, 28*(3), 291–294.

Harding, C. M., Brooks, G. W., Ashikaga, T., Strauss, J. S., & Breier, A. (1987). The Vermont longitudinal study of persons with severe mental illness, I: Methodology, study sample, and overall status 32 years later. *American Journal of Psychiatry, 144*, 718–726.

Harris, M., & Bachrach, L. L. (1988). A treatment-planning grid for clinical case management. In M. Harris & L. L. Bachrach (Eds.), *Clinical case management: New directions for Mental Health Services, no. 40* (pp. 29–38). San Francisco: Jossey-Bass.

Hodge, M., & Giesler, L. (1997). *Case management practice guidelines for adults with severe and persistent mental illness.* Ocean Ridge, FL: National Association of Case Management.

International Center for Clubhouse Development. (2008). *Annual report 2008.* Retrieved March 9, 2010, from http://www.iccd.org/documents/2008_AnnualReport_FINAL.pdf

Jacobs, H. E. (1988). Vocational rehabilitation. In R. P. Liberman (Ed.), *Psychiatric rehabilitation of chronic mental patients* (pp. 245–284). Washington, DC: American Psychiatric Press.

Jinnett, K., Alexander, J., & Ullman, E. (2001). Case management and quality of life: Assessing treatment and outcomes for clients with chronic and persistent mental illness. *Health Services Research, 36,* 61–90.

Kantor, J. (1988). Clinical issues in the case management relationship. In M. Harris & L. L. Bachrach (Eds.), *Clinical case management: New directions for Mental Health Services, no. 40* (pp. 15–27). San Francisco: Jossey-Bass.

Kaufmann, C. L., Ward-Colasante, C., & Farmer, J. (1993). Development and evaluation of drop-in centers operated by mental health consumers. *Hospital and Community Psychiatry, 44,* 675–678.

Kreyenbuhl, J., Buchanan, R., Dickerson, F., & Dixon, L. (2010). The schizophrenia patient outcomes research team (PORT): Updated treatment recommendations 2009. *Schizophrenia Bulletin, 36*(1), 94–103.

Kurtz, M. M., & Mueser, K. (2008). A meta-analysis of controlled research on social skills training in schizophrenia. *Journal of Consulting and Clinical Psychology, 76,* 491–504.

Lamb, H. R. (1980). Board-and-care home wanderers. *Archives of General Psychiatry, 37*(2), 135–137.

Lamb, H. R., Weinberger, L. E., & DeCuir, W. J. (2002). The police and mental health. *Psychiatric Services, 53,* 1266–1271.

Lamberti, J. S., Weissman, R., & Faden, D. (2004). Forensic assertive community treatment: preventing incarceration of adults with severe mental illness. *Psychiatric Services, 55,* 1285–1293.

Leff, S., Chow, C., Pepin, R., Conley, J., Allen, E., & Seaman, C. (2009). Does one size fit all? What we can and can't learn from a meta-analysis of housing models for persons with mental illness. *Psychiatric Services, 60,* 472–483.

Lefley, H. P. (1996). The effects of advocacy movements on caregivers. In H. P. Lefley (Ed.), *Family caregiving in mental illness* (pp. 167–184). Thousand Oaks, CA: Sage.

Lehman, A., Goldberg, R., Dixon, L., McNary, S., Postrado, L., Hackman, A., et al. (2002). Improving employment outcomes for persons with severe mental illnesses. *Archives of General Psychiatry, 59,* 165–172.

Leonard, E. J., & Bruer, R. A. (2007). Supported education strategies for people with severe mental illness: A review of evidence-based practice. *International Journal of Psychosocial Rehabilitation, 11*(1), 97–109.

Loveland, D., & Boyle, M. (2007). Intensive case management as a jail diversion program for people with a serious mental illness. *International Journal of Offender Therapy and Comparative Criminology, 51*(2), 130–150.

Macias, C., Jackson, R., Schroeder, C., & Wang, Q. (1999). Brief report: What is a clubhouse? Report on the ICCD survey of USA clubhouses. *Community Mental Health Journal, 35*(2), 181–190.

Margolese, H., Negrete, J., Tempier, R., & Gill, K. (2006). A 12-month prospective follow-up study of patients with schizophrenia-spectrum disorders and substance abuse: Change in psychiatric symptoms and substance abuse. *Schizophrenia Research, 83*(1), 65–75.

McGurk, S., & Mueser, K. (2004). Cognitive functioning, symptoms, and work in supported employment: A review and heuristic model. *Schizophrenia Bulletin, 70*(2–3), 147–173.

McKay, C., Johnsen, M., & Stein, R. (2005). Employment outcomes in Massachusetts clubhouses. *Psychiatric Rehabilitation Journal, 29*(1), 25–33.

Min, S., Whitecraft, J., Rothbard, A., & Salzer, M. (2007). Peer support for persons with co-occurring disorders and community tenure: A survival analysis. *Psychiatric Rehabilitation Journal, 30*(3), 207–213.

Mogul, K. M. (1985). Psychological considerations in the use of psychotropic drugs with women patients. *Hospital and Community Psychiatry, 36,* 1080–1085.

Morrison-Dore, M. (2008). Review of community treatment for youth: Evidence-based interventions for severe emotional and behavioral disorders. *Research on Social Work Practice, 18*(5), 526–527.

Morrison, I., & Cliff, S. (2007). Antonovsky revisited: Implications for mental health promotion practice. *International Journal of Mental Health Promotion, 9*(2), 36–46.

Morse, G., & McKasson, M. (2005). Assertive community treatment. In R. Drake, M. Merrens, & D. Lynde (Eds.), *Evidence-based mental health practice* (pp. 317–348). New York: Norton.

Morse, G. A., Calsyn, R. J., Klinkenberg, W. D., Helminiak, T. W., Wolff, N., Drake, R. E., et al. (2006). Treating homeless clients with severe mental illness and substance use disorders, costs, and outcomes. *Community Mental Health Journal, 42,* 377–404.

Mowbray, C. T., Brown, K. S., Furlong-Norman, K., & Sullivan-Soydan, A. (2002). *Supported education and psychiatric rehabilitation: Models and methods.* Columbia, MD: IAPSRS.

Mowbray, C. T., Collins, M., Bellamy, C., Megivern, D., Bybee, D., & Svilvagyi, S. (2005). Supported education for adults with psychiatric disabilities: An innovation for social work and psychosocial rehabilitation practice. *Social Work, 50*(1), 7–20.

Mowbray, C. T., Collins, M., & Bybee, D. (1999). Supported education for individuals with psychiatric disabilities: Long-term outcomes from an experimental study. *Social Work Research, 23,* 89–100.

Moxley, D. P. (2009). Case management in psychosocial rehabilitation. In A. R. Roberts (Ed.), *Social workers' desk reference* (pp. 770–777). New York: Oxford.

Mueser, K. T., Bond, G. R., Drake, R. E., & Resnick, S. G. (1998). Models of community care for severe mental illness: A review of research on case management. *Schizophrenia Bulletin, 24,* 37–74.

Mueser, K. T., Drake, K., & Bond, G. (1997). Recent advances in psychiatric rehabilitation for patients with severe mental illness. *Harvard Review of Psychiatry, 5*(3), 123–137.

Nelson, G., Aubry, T., & Lafrance, A. (2007). A review of the literature on the effectiveness of housing and support, assertive community treatment, and intensive case management interventions for persons with mental illness who have been homeless. *American Journal of Orthopsychiatry, 77,* 350–361.

Neugeboren, J. (2008). Personal accounts: More magic bullets? *Psychiatric Services, 59*(2), 143–144.

New York State Office of Mental Health. (2006). *Supported housing program implementation guidelines.* Retrieved February 8, 2010, from http://www.omh.state.ny.us/omhweb/rfp/2006/nyny_iii/shguidelines.htm

New York State Office of Mental Health. (2008). *Creating an environment of quality through evidence-based practice.* Retrieved February 8, 2010, from http://www.omh.state.ny.us/omhweb/EBP/

Nicholson, J., & Blanch, A. (1994). Rehabilitation for parenting roles for people with serious mental illness. *Psychosocial Rehabilitation Journal, 18,* 109–119.

Nicholson, J., Hinden, B. R., Biebel, K., Henry, A. D., & Katz-Leavy, J. (2007). A qualitative study of programs for parents with serious mental illness and their children: Building practice-based evidence. *Journal of Behavioral Health Services Research, 34*(4), 395–413.

Oyserman, D., Mowbray, C. T., & Zemencuk, J. K. (1994). Resources and supports for mothers with severe mental illness. *Health and Social Work, 19(2),* 132–142.

Philadelphia Department of Behavioral Health and Mental Retardation Services. (n.d.[a]). *Long term structured residences (LTSR).* Retrieved March 9, 2010, from http://www.dbhmrs.org/long-term-structured-residences-ltsr/

Philadelphia Department of Behavioral Health and Mental Retardation Services. (n.d.[b]). *Residential intensive therapeutic arrangements.* Retrieved March 9, 2010, from http://www.dbhmrs.org/residential-intensive-therapeutic-arrangements

President's New Freedom Commission on Mental Health. (2003). *Achieving the promise: Transforming mental health care in America: Final report.* Retrieved February 8, 2010, from http://www.mentalhealthcommission.gov

Propst, R. N. (1988). The clubhouse model and the world of work. *TIE Lines, 5*(2), 1–2.

Rapp, C. A., & Goscha, R. J. (2006). *The strengths model: Case management with people with psychiatric disabilities* (2nd ed.). New York: Oxford University Press.

Ridgway, P., & Rapp, C. A. (1997). *The active ingredients of effective supported housing: A research synthesis.* Lawrence: University of Kansas School of Social Welfare.

Roach, J. (1993). Clinical case management with severely mentally ill adults. In M. Harris & H. C. Bergman (Eds.), *Case management for mentally ill patients: Theory and practice* (pp. 17–40). Langhorne, PA: Harwood Academic Publishers.

Rogers, E. S., Anthony, W. A., & Farkas, M. (2006). The Choose-Get-Keep model of psychiatric rehabilitation: A synopsis of recent studies. *Rehabilitation Psychology, 51*(3), 247–256.

Rosie, J. S. (1987). Partial hospitalization: A review of recent literature. *Hospital and Community Psychiatry, 38,* 1291–1299.

Sands, R. G. (1995). The parenting experience of low-income single women with serious mental disorders. *Families in Society, 76*(2), 86–96.

Saugstad, L. F. (1989). Social class, marriage, and fertility in schizophrenia. *Schizophrenia Bulletin, 15,* 9–43.

Schwab, B., Drake, R. E., & Burghardt, E. M. (1988). Health care of the chronically mentally ill: The culture broker model. *Community Mental Health Journal, 24,* 174–184.

Solomon, P. (1992). The efficacy of case management services for severely mentally disabled clients. *Community Mental Health Journal, 28,* 163–180.

Solomon, P. (1999). The evolution of service innovations for adults with severe mental illness. In D. E. Biegel & A. Blum (Eds.), *Innovations in practice and service delivery with adults: The evolution of service innovations for adults with severe mental illness* (pp. 147–168). New York: Oxford University Press.

Solomon, P. (2004). Peer support/peer provider services: Underlying processes, benefits, and critical ingredients. *Psychiatric Rehabilitation Journal, 27,* 392–401.

Solomon, P., & Draine, J. (1995). The efficacy of a consumer case management team: 2-year outcomes of a randomized trial. *Journal of Mental Health Administration, 22,* 135–146.

Solomon, P., & Draine, J. (2001). The state of knowledge of the effectiveness of consumer provided services. *Psychiatric Rehabilitation Journal, 25*(1), 20–27.

Solomon, P., & Meyerson, A. T. (1997). Social stabilization: Achieving satisfactory community adaptation for the disabled mentally ill. In A. Tasman, J. Kay, & J. Lieberman (Eds.), *Psychiatry* (Vol. 2, pp. 1727–1750). Philadelphia: W. B. Saunders.

Stein, L. (1992). Perspective: On the abolishment of the case manager. *Health Affairs,* 172–177.

Stein, L. I., & Diamond, R. J. (1985). A program for difficult-to-treat patients. In L. I. Stein & M. A. Test (Eds.), *New directions for mental health services: The training in community living model. A decade of experience* (no. 26, pp. 29–39). San Francisco: Jossey-Bass.

Stein, L. I., & Santos, A. B. (1998). *Assertive community treatment of persons with severe mental illness.* New York: W. W. Norton & Co.

Stein, L. I., & Test, M. A. (1982). Community treatment of the young adult patient. In B. Pepper & H. Ryglewicz (Eds.), *New directions for mental health services: The young adult chronic patient* (no. 14, pp. 57–67). San Francisco: Jossey-Bass.

Stein, L. I., & Test, M. A. (Eds.). (1985). *New directions for mental health services: The training in community living model. A decade of experience* (no. 26). San Francisco: Jossey-Bass.

Substance Abuse and Mental Health Services Administration. (2004). National Consensus Statement on mental health recovery. Rockville, MD: Author. Retrieved February 8, 2010, from http://mentalhealth.samhsa.gov/publications/allpubs/sma05-4129

Substance Abuse and Mental Health Services Administration. (2008). Assertive community treatment: Training frontline staff (DHHS Publication No. SMA 08-4344). Rockville, MD: Author.

Substance Abuse and Mental Health Services Administration. (2009). Supported employment: Training frontline staff (DHHS Publication No. SMA 08-4364). Rockville, MD: Author.

Substance Abuse and Mental Health Services Administration. (2010). Evidence-based practices: Shaping mental health services toward recovery—assertive community treatment. Rockville, MD: Author. Retrieved February 8, 2010, from http://mentalhealth.samhsa.gov/cmhs/community-support/toolkits/community.com

Training in community living. (1983). *Practice Digest, 6,* 4–6.

Tsuang, J., Fong, T., & Lesser, I. (2006). Psychosocial treatment of patients with schizophrenia and substance abuse disorders. *Addictive Behaviors and Their Treatment, 5*(2), 53–66.

Twamley, E., Jeste, D., & Lehman, A. (2003). Vocational rehabilitation in schizophrenia and other psychotic disorders. *Journal of Nervous and Mental Diseases, 191*(8), 515–523.

Unger, K. V. (1997). Supported education: An idea whose time has come, II. *Journal of the California Alliance for the Mentally Ill, 8*(2), 5–7.

U.S. Department of Health and Human Services. (2005). *Free to choose: Transforming behavioral health care to self-direction* (DHHS Publication No. SMA 05-3982). Rockville, MD: Center for Mental Health Services, Substance Abuse and Mental Health Services Administration.

U.S. Public Health Service, Office of the Surgeon General. (1999). *Mental health: A report of the Surgeon General.* Rockville, MD: U.S. Department of Health and Human Services.

Vauth, R., Corrigan, P. W., Clauss, M., Dietl, M., Dreher-Rudolph, M., Stieglitz, R.-D., et al. (2005). Cognitive strategies versus self-management skills as adjunct to vocational rehabilitation. *Schizophrenia Bulletin, 31*, 55–66.

Witheridge, T. F., & Dincin, J. (1985). The Bridge: An assertive outreach program in an urban setting. In L. I. Stein & M. A. Test (Eds.), *The training in community living model: A decade of experience* (pp. 65–76). San Francisco: Jossey-Bass.

Wong, Y. I., Filoromo, M., & Tennille, J. (2007). From principles to practice: a study of implementation of supported housing for psychiatric consumers. *Administrative Policy in Mental Health and Mental Health Services Research, 34*, 13–28.

Zirul, D. W., Lieberman, A. L., & Rapp, C. A. (1989). Respite care for the chronically mentally ill: Focus for the 1990s. *Community Mental Health Journal, 25,* 171–184.

Evidence-Based Interventions for Individuals with Severe Mental Illness and Their Families

What seemed unique about the IMR groups was the shared journey of growing cohesiveness together with the learning and practicing of skills.

—ROE AND COLLEAGUES, "ILLNESS MANAGEMENT AND RECOVERY: GENERIC ISSUES OF GROUP FORMAT IMPLEMENTATION," 2007

In addition to the community-based approaches described in Chapter 11, there are a number of other evidence-based and promising interventions that enhance psychosocial functioning, moderate symptoms, and promote recovery. This chapter describes three psychosocial approaches to intervention—illness management and recovery (IMR), family psychoeducation, and cognitive rehabilitation—that help clients and their families cope with the impact of severe mental illness on their lives. IMR and family psychoeducation are considered evidence-based practices (Mueser, Torrey, Lynde, Singer, & Drake, 2003), and cognitive rehabilitation is considered promising (Bond & Campbell, 2008). In addition, this chapter provides information on psychotropic medication used to treat individuals with serious mental illnesses.

The chapter begins with a description of IMR, an evidence-based intervention directed at individuals with severe mental illness. Family psychoeducation for close relatives and friends is described next. This is followed by a discussion of cognitive rehabilitation. The chapter concludes with a review of medications that are used in conjunction with psychosocial interventions.

EVIDENCE-BASED PRACTICE: ILLNESS MANAGEMENT AND RECOVERY

Illness Management and Recovery is a structured, manualized psychosocial intervention that aims to help consumers gain control over their psychiatric symptoms while identifying and pursuing personal recovery goals (Mueser et al., 2006). It recognizes the individual's ability to understand his or her illness and make choices around living with it. It entails teaching skills such as management of symptoms, relapse prevention, effective use of medication, coping with stress, and connecting with others. IMR is also known as Wellness Management and Recovery (WMR; Rychener, Salyers, Labriola, & Little, 2009).

Two theoretical perspectives underlie IMR. One, discussed previously in Chapter 10, is the stress-vulnerability model. In IMR, the consumer learns how to reduce vulnerability and stress by learning about the illness, developing and practicing strategies to prevent relapse, and increasing social skills and social support (Mueser et al., 2006). The other perspective is the transtheoretical model, which is the basis for motivational interviewing. The transtheoretical model, developed by Prochaska and DiClemente (1984), posits that the motivation to change one's behavior occurs along a series of stages of change—precontemplation, contemplation, preparation, action, and maintenance—and that the intervention is to be consistent with the stage of the consumer's motivation. In IMR, motivational interviewing is used to help clients identify and pursue their recovery goals, linking the educational content of IMR to these goals (Gingerich & Mueser, 2005; Mueser et al., 2006). Motivational interviewing will be revisited in Chapter 13.

The values underlying the notion of "recovery" constitute core values of IMR. These include (a) hope for an improved quality of life; (b) recognition that consumers have expertise on their own experience of mental illness; (c) the right and ability to make personal choices; (d) collaborative relationship between practitioners and consumers; and (e) respect for consumers (Gingerich & Mueser, 2006).

Besides these theories and values, educational and cognitive-behavioral methods of intervention are used to implement IMR. These include psychoeducation, social skills training, behavioral tailoring, coping skills training, and relapse prevention (Mueser et al., 2002). In the context of IMR, *psychoeducation* refers to teaching consumers about their illness, its course, and its treatment, a process that is accomplished through didactic and interactive methods (Gingerich & Mueser, 2005). *Social skills training* is a cognitive-behavioral intervention in which consumers are helped with information processing, problem solving, and communication so as to become more effective in interpersonal relations (Bellack, 2004; Liberman et al., 1986). In IMR, *behavioral tailoring* is used to help consumers develop ways to use everyday cues to remind them to take their medication (Gingerich & Mueser, 2003). *Coping skills* for IMR are methods of managing the distress and severity of psychiatric symptoms that may occur (Gingerich & Mueser, 2003). *Relapse prevention* entails learning triggers and early warning signs of relapse so as to prevent a psychiatric episode (Gingerich & Mueser, 2003). Cognitive-behavioral strategies that are incorporated into the program include modeling, shaping, cognitive restructuring, coping skills enhancement, role playing, and homework assignments (Gingerich & Mueser, 2003).

Illness Management and Recovery consists of a set of illness management strategies, each of which has strong research support (Mueser et al., 2002). The strategies include psychoeducation, cognitive-behavioral approaches to medication adherence, social skills training, coping skills training, and relapse prevention. Studies evaluating the IMR package as a whole have produced promising results (Hasson-Ohayon, Roe, & Kravetz, 2007; Mueser et al., 2006; Salyers et al., 2009).

Format and Structure

Illness Management and Recovery programs can be administered individually or in a group format. The individual approach has the advantage of being able to adapt the pace to the consumer's needs, spending more time where needed and less time where the consumer has considerable knowledge, whereas the group mode allows for diverse client perspectives, provides multiple sources of feedback, constitutes a built-in environment for social support, and is more cost effective (Gingerich, Mueser, & Cunningham, 2006). Sessions are usually weekly, lasting forty-five minutes to an hour over four to ten months (Gingerich & Mueser, 2006). The program has a structured curriculum that is described in the toolkit that is available on the Substance Abuse and Mental Health Services Administration (SAMHSA) Website (https://store.samhsa.gov/product/ SMA09-4463).

The program consists of ten modules, with each topic addressed over three to seven sessions (Mueser et al., 2006). Initially, participants have one or more sessions in which they are oriented to the goals and expectations of the program. Information is collected on the consumer's daily routine, activities, relationships, spiritual supports, and knowledge, which can help in the formulation of recovery goals. The ten modules that follow orientation are addressed using motivational, educational, and cognitive-behavioral strategies that are described in the toolkit. The IMR module topics are the following:

1. *Recovery strategies.*   The consumer is engaged in a discussion about what recovery means to the consumer, what goals he or she would like to achieve, and plans to achieve goals.
2. *Practical facts about mental illness.*   The consumer and practitioner converse about symptoms of mental illness, causes, myths, and stigma. The specific illnesses included are schizophrenia, bipolar disorder, and depression.
3. *Stress-vulnerability model and treatment strategies.*   Consumers learn about the interaction between biological vulnerability and stress and ways in which various treatment options and management strategies can help them reduce their symptoms, prevent relapse, and accomplish recovery goals.
4. *Building social support.*   The focus here is on the benefits of social support, ways to strengthen or increase support, and improving social interaction skills.
5. *Using medications effectively.*   The benefits and side effects of medication are discussed and weighed. Those who decide to take medication are taught strategies such as behavioral tailoring to incorporate medication into their daily routine. The medications included are antipsychotic, mood-stabilizing, antidepressant, and antianxiety and sedative medications.
6. *Drug and alcohol use.*   Consumers are given an opportunity to talk about their substance use and learn about the interactions between substances and mental illness. They weigh the pros and cons of continued use and sobriety.
7. *Reducing relapses.*   Consumers examine past relapses and learn to identify triggers and early warning signs to help them prevent future relapses. The goal is for them to develop individual relapse prevention plans.

8. *Coping with stress.* Here the focus is on identifying signs of stress and developing strategies to prevent and cope with stress.

9. *Coping with problems and persistent symptoms.* Consumers learn the problem-solving approach and apply it to problems and symptoms. They learn strategies (especially relaxation techniques) to deal with common problems and symptoms.

10. *Getting your needs met in the mental health system.* Information is provided about mental health services and entitlements so that they can make choices that are compatible with their recovery goals. They also learn strategies to advocate for themselves. (Gingerich & Mueser, 2006; Mueser et al., 2006; SAMHSA, 2009b)

The sessions have a specific structure, which creates consistency and continuity between meetings. Clinicians strive to make sure that the consumer understands and retains learning. Assignments to be accomplished at home are given at the end of each session and are reviewed in the next meeting. These are related to the individual's personal recovery goals, the module topic, or both. For example, a consumer can work toward building social support (Module 4) and the personal goal of getting out more by going out with a friend during the upcoming week. The sessions are organized in the following structured format:

- Informal socializing and identification of major problems, if any;
- Review of previous session(s);
- Review of homework;
- Follow-up on recovery goals;
- Set agenda for current session;
- Teach new material or review material that was taught previously;
- Agree on new home assignment;
- Summarize progress made in current session. (Gingerich & Mueser, 2003, p. 13)

The time allotted for each of these activities may vary, depending whether there are individual or group sessions, but in either case, the most time is devoted to the topic, "Teach new material or review material that was taught previously" (SAMHSA, 2009a).

Originally, the IMR groups were designed to have a closed group admission policy. This has proved to be impractical because participants were not able to attend regularly, moved away, or participated in other activities that precluded attendance (K. Mueser, personal communication). Mueser now recommends that consumers who join ongoing groups be oriented to the format of the group and be required to go through the Recovery Strategies module, have a few recovery goals in place, and have a brief review of the previous session beforehand (K. Mueser, personal communication). He also recommends that two or more new members join the group together.

Box 12.1 provides a description of the experience of "Tony," a member of an IMR group. A composite of a number of IMR group members, he is described as a man in his late forties with a diagnosis of schizophrenia, paranoid type and a history of alcohol dependence (Roe et al., 2007). The example shows how a client can draw on learning from previous modules and apply it to a personal situation. Others in the group can benefit from hearing about one participant's experience.

Illness Management and Recovery is a state-of-the-art method of intervention that is in synchrony with the philosophy of recovery. It enables consumers to identify and pursue their own goals and deal with obstacles that may impede the realization of their goals. It is client

Box 12.1

Case Description of a Participant in an Illness Management and Recovery Group

Tony's initial recovery goal was to strengthen his hobbies, having noticed that with free, unstructured time, his anxiety level increased, which led to an increase in paranoid thoughts. Much of his paranoia involved concerns that the government would take away his financial support and that he would end up destitute and homeless. Tony's initial goal was to read more, which he enjoyed before he became ill. However, his attention would often wander, making it difficult for him to concentrate. Using the problem-solving attainment model, which emphasizes and helps structure an active solution-focused approach, Tony identified a first step of reading one magazine per week. Using Socratic questioning and input from the group, Tony decided that the goal was too ambitious, and he undertook a more modest initial step, reading one magazine article per week. This proved to be a better goal and it reinforced for him and for group members the importance of taking a "shaping" approach to goal attainment. Tony continued to work on recreational goals, including listening to his records again, which caused him pleasure.

Tony developed a new personal goal during Module 8, Coping with Persistent Problems and Symptoms. He reported that he became very anxious in the afternoons when he started to worry about his finances, his station in life, and his future. As Tony was quite distressed by these fears, part of a session was devoted to applying the problem-solving model to his concerns. Tony and the group members generated various strategies for managing the situation, some of which were feasible (e.g., using relaxation exercises to calm down) and others were not (e.g., having Tony take a class to distract him, which he could not afford). During this exercise, Tony was reminded of how stress can lead to relapse (Modules 3 and 7) and how social support can be an important buffer against stress (Module 4); therefore, when feeling anxious, Tony was to use a variety of coping strategies (e.g., relaxation, getting out of the house, calling a friend) that had been effective in the past. To make sure Tony would feel comfortable calling a friend, he performed a role play of it in group with another member playing the role of his friend.

Tony was moved that the group devoted time to addressing his concerns. Group members commented that the exercise helped them put into practice topics they had been learning.

Source: Roe et al. (2007). Reprinted by permission of Taylor & Francis Group, http://www.informaworld.com.

centered, providing clients with the cognitive and behavioral tools they need to take care of themselves and improve their quality of life. Social workers who favor a structured, didactic approach are likely to find this intervention suitable.

EVIDENCE-BASED PRACTICE WITH FAMILY CAREGIVERS

Families play a crucial role in the well-being of relatives with serious mental illness. Parents and relational partners are often the principal caregivers, providing physical, emotional, and financial support. Other kin and nonkin family members—grandparents, aunts and uncles, siblings, children, fictive kin, friends, clergy, and neighbors—may also offer emotional and instrumental support to persons with serious mental illness (SMI). Family caregivers look after their relative in the family's home, or they may live separately yet maintain contact on a regular basis and/or are available in case of an emergency. Viewed by social workers as members of the consumer's support system, family members also have needs of their own.

Recognition of the family as a resource represents a paradigm shift in the way families have been regarded in the past. When psychoanalytic and family communication theories were dominant, families of persons with SMI were pathologized. For example, Fromm-Reichmann (1948) put forth the concept of the "schizophrenogenic mother," which not only drew attention to deficient parenting but also blamed the mother. Similarly, family theorists assigned disparaging labels to family interactional patterns such as "marital skew" and "marital schism" (Lidz, Cornelison, Fleck, & Terry, 1957) and the "double bind" (Bateson, Jackson, Haley, & Weakland, 1956). Today's more enlightened paradigm illuminates the strengths and resilience of families and views them as partners.

This section begins with a discussion about how families may be affected by a relative diagnosed with a severe mental illness. Then three family interventions that workers can use or make referrals to are delineated, specifically (a) family psychoeducation, (b) family education, and (c) family consultation. One evidence-based family psychoeducation program in particular, McFarlane's multifamily group approach, will be described.

Impact of Serious Mental Illness on the Family

A family member's serious mental illness can be "a catastrophic stressor for families" (Marsh, 1998, p. 54). Behaviors that are unusual for the individual or for the family (e.g., argumentativeness, acting withdrawn or unmotivated, aggression, noisiness, poor personal hygiene, and lack of cooperation) disrupt the family system, compelling members to adapt to situations that may be confusing to them. The term *family burden* captures the strain families experience in coping with their ill relative's behaviors, the gap between his or her needs and the services that are available, and the onset and course of the illness (Riesser & Schorske, 1994; Wasow, 1994). Researchers have differentiated between *objective* and *subjective* family burden. Objective burden refers to effects that are concrete and observable, such as financial costs, whereas subjective burden encompasses personal feelings and emotional reactions to the family member's mental disorder (Corrigan, Mueser, Bond, Drake, & Solomon, 2008).

Families' emotional reactions reflect their uncertainty, confusion, social isolation, and grief. Unable to interpret the unusual behaviors they observe, they may feel bewildered or frightened. Some families avoid having to explain the situation to others by isolating themselves. They grieve for the life they had envisioned for their disabled member, who may have shown promise as a child (Hatfield, 1987), and for the family's perception of itself as a family (Marsh, 1998). The perceived loss is often complex, complicated by anger, guilt, shame, and the continued presence of the ill relative who is experienced as lost (Jones, 2004). Boss (1999) calls a loss such as this an *ambiguous loss*, where the person is physically present but psychologically absent.

Taking a cluster analytic approach, Perlick and colleagues (2008) identified three types of family caregivers of adults with bipolar disorder: (a) burdened, (b) stigmatized, and (c) effective, based on their stress appraisal and coping profiles. The *burdened* group exhibited the least adaptive coping styles, using a great deal of avoidance coping, and had lower subjective support and poorer health and mental health outcomes over time than the other clusters. Both the *stigmatized* and the *effective* groups used adaptive coping strategies, but the former had poorer self-care than the latter.

In recent years, increased attention has been given to positive aspects of caregiving, such as personal gratification and feelings of family solidarity (Corrigan et al., 2008; Lefley, 2009). Van Wijngaarden et al. (2003) suggest that the term *caregiving consequences* is a more neutral alternative to *family burden* in that the former accounts for diversity among families and cultures.

Family resilience, in which families expand their knowledge, coping skills, and competence, derive satisfaction in helping their relative recover, and engage in advocacy activities, can develop as a consequence of dealing with a family member's mental illness (Marsh, 1998).

Regardless of how families feel about caregiving, they frequently lack knowledge and information about mental disorders, medication, behavioral management strategies, and community services. Even if they are provided with a diagnosis, they may not know what the diagnosis means and they may not understand the long-term implications (Gantt, Goldstein, & Pinsky, 1989). In addition, they may experience frustration in their contacts with the mental health system (Marsh, 1998) and may find themselves assuming the role of case manager in a system that lacks resources and excludes them from the treatment process (Francell, Conn, & Gray, 1988). Altogether, they may be bewildered about the psychiatric disorder and at a loss about how to cope with their family member.

In response to their frustrations, some family members have joined organizations that both provide mutual support and advocate for the interests of families and their mentally disabled relatives. The National Alliance on Mental Illness (NAMI) is one organization through which families of relatives with serious and persistent mental disorders can advocate politically to make their needs, wants, and recommendations heard.

Clinical social workers can help relieve families of some of their burdens by listening to and addressing their concerns. Families are intrinsically involved in the care of identified clients and are a major source of support. Social workers can "tune in" to the situation of families and assess how family members relate to and affect each other. To address their needs and help consumers, a number of family interventions have been developed.

Family Psychoeducation

Family psychoeducation is an intervention in which families learn about their relative's mental illness and treatment and how they can cope with and help the ill family member and gain support for themselves. The particular approaches vary in format, participants, focus, theoretical perspective, and goals (Lefley, 2009). Family psychoeducation interventions take place in single family units, in multiple family group sessions, or in a combination; with or without the consumer present; at a clinic or the family's home; and over varying periods of time. They tend to be illness specific.

There are a number of approaches to family psychoeducation. The first-generation intervention models were developed in the 1980s within research programs investigating treatment of individuals with schizophrenia whose families had high expressed emotion (see Chapter 10). These models include crisis-oriented family therapy (Goldstein & Kopeikin, 1981), behavioral family management (Falloon, Boyd, & McGill, 1984), social intervention (Leff, Kuipers, Berkowitz, Eberlein-Fries, & Sturgeon, 1982), and psychoeducational family management (Anderson, Reiss, & Hogarty, 1986). These family intervention models, which were implemented in tandem with a regimen of medication for the client, have been found more effective in reducing clients' relapse rate than medication alone (Dixon & Lehman, 1995; Goldstein & Miklowitz, 1995).

Second-generation psychoeducational studies focused on identifying which components of the family treatments contribute to the client's remaining out of the hospital (Goldstein & Miklowitz, 1995). Moreover, these studies included families that were not high in expressed emotion and families of consumers with disorders other than schizophrenia. Miklowitz (2008), for example, has researched and developed a protocol for families of individuals with bipolar disorder. Another second-generation model is that of McFarlane (1990, 1994) and his associates (McFarlane et al., 1995), who developed the psychoeducational multifamily group approach. Research and implementation on this and other models have become widespread internationally, and some cross-cultural studies within the United States have been conducted (Lefley, 2009).

Analyses of the results of studies that have been mentioned and others have found that a variety of models of family psychoeducation are effective in reducing symptoms and relapse rates of clients (McFarlane, Dixon, Lukens, & Lucksted, 2003; Mueser, Drake, & Bond, 1997; Murray-Swank & Dixon, 2004). The components that are common to effective psychoeducation models include the following:

- Up-to-date information about the psychiatric disorder, its etiology and treatment;
- Up-to-date information on medications, including their treatment effects and side effects;
- Support for family members;
- Illness management (i.e., coping with symptomatic behaviors, identifying indications of decompensation and crisis management, etc.);
- Communication skills; and
- Problem-solving methods. (Lefley, 2009)

One of the recommendations of the updated Patient Outcomes Research Team (PORT) is that, where feasible, family interventions include illness education, crisis intervention, training in coping with illness symptoms and related problems, emotional support, and a duration of at least six to nine months (Kreyenbuhl, Buchanan, Dickerson, & Dixon, 2010).

Family psychoeducation is considered an evidence-based treatment for serious psychiatric disorders (Bond & Campbell, 2008; Mueser et al., 2003). The second-generation evidence-based model that is featured here is McFarlane's psychoeducational multifamily group (PMFG).

EVIDENCE-BASED PRACTICE: PSYCHOEDUCATIONAL MULTIFAMILY GROUP McFarlane's PMFG approach fosters the consumer's recovery by engaging the family and consumer in educational, supportive, and problem-solving activities. A structured program that is described in McFarlane's (2002) book, *Multifamily Groups in the Treatment of Severe Psychiatric Disorders*, and in a toolkit available for downloading on a Website of evidence-based practices from SAMHSA (https://store.samhsa.gov/product/SMA09-4423), it has been applied not only to families of persons with schizophrenia but also to families with members with bipolar illness, major depression, borderline personality disorder, and other conditions (described in McFarlane, 2002).

Empirical support for this approach to psychoeducation comes from a four-year study in Bergen County, New Jersey (McFarlane, 2002); the multisite New York State Family Psychoeducation Study (McFarlane et al., 1995); and the Family-Aided Assertive Community Treatment (FACT) Outcome Trials, which combined PMFG and ACT (McFarlane, 2002). The Bergen County study compared PMFG with psychoeducational single-family treatment and family-dynamic multifamily groups (FDMFG), finding that PMFG treatment resulted in the lowest patient relapse rate after four years, with FDMFG next (McFarlane, 2002). This study supported the critical role of multifamily groups, common to both PMFG and FDMFG, and their social network building function (McFarlane, 2002).

The New York State study was conducted at six public hospitals with a diverse population of consumers. Acutely psychotic hospitalized patients who either lived with or had frequent contact with their families were randomly assigned, following consent to contact families, to one of two interventions—PMFG or single-family treatment. Patients were given standard doses of antipsychotic medication, adjusted to maintenance levels by prescribing psychiatrists. The researchers found that for those families that received multifamily group psychoeducation, patients had a lower two-year relapse rate than those who had single-family treatment (McFarlane, 2002; McFarlane et al., 1995). (Leff et al. [1990], however, found no differences in their comparative study, but their interventions were somewhat different from McFarlane et al.'s [1995] study.)

The third example of empirical support, FACT, was a two-part study that focused on young men with complicating issues (adherence, dual diagnosis) whose families were randomly assigned to PMFG or crisis family intervention (CFI), with all patients simultaneously receiving ACT. Over a two-year period, both groups had improved outcomes with no differences in relapse rates and level of symptoms but young men from those families receiving PMFG had a significantly higher rate of employment (McFarlane, Dushay, Stastny, Deakins, & Link, 1996). The second part of the FACT study compared outpatients in FACT with those in conventional vocational rehabilitation in which there was a clinician who assisted with assessment and referrals and interceded when there was a crisis. Here, too, those randomly assigned to FACT had a significantly higher rate of employment (McFarlane, 2002).

McFarlane et al. (1995) built their approach on the first-generation work of Falloon et al. (1984) and Anderson et al. (1986), expanding them with multifamily groups. The PMFG model is predicated on the stress-diathesis model and, in particular, research highlighting the importance of social support and support networks as means to create an emotional environment for consumers that would moderate stressors and compensate for cognitive deficits such as those found in schizophrenia (McFarlane, 2002). It recognizes family burdens and the stigma that consumers and, through association, families face. The model seeks to create a therapeutic support system or "healing community" because of a tendency of consumers to have small social networks and for families to respond to stigma by isolating themselves (McFarlane, 2002, p. 37). It also seeks to reduce expressed emotion and improve communication within the family (McFarlane, 1990).

The PMFG model is implemented in three stages—(a) joining individuals and families; (b) educational workshop for families; and (c) multifamily group sessions that include the consumer. During the third stage, the focus is on problem solving. (McFarland [2002] describes four stages, breaking the third stage into two components, problem solving and social and vocational rehabilitation, but they will be combined here because problem solving is the modality used throughout.) The activities encompassed during these stages call upon the clinician using skills in relationship-building, teaching, and group leadership; being knowledgeable about mental illness and its treatment; and having a commitment to recovery. Clinicians regard their relationship with the family as a partnership and are more self-disclosing and willing to give advice than they might when conducting psychotherapy (McFarlane, 2002).

The stages of PMFG are described next. The following portrayal is based on both McFarlane (2002) and the SAMHSA family psychoeducation toolkit.

Stage 1: Joining.   The goal of this stage is to develop a working alliance with the family and consumer, obtain information about the family, and prepare them for stages that will follow. McFarlane's early research was with consumers hospitalized during an acute episode and their families. Clinicians connected with consumers while they were hospitalized and with family members separately, with each having at least three joining sessions, with meetings with families lasting one hour, and those with the consumer taking a half hour (McFarlane, 2002). Considering that hospitalization is often short and patients vary in their stability following discharge, the consumer may participate in some or all of these sessions or have individual sessions. Regardless of whether they meet separately or together, the clinician should connect with all family members, conveying a nonjudgmental attitude, empathy, and a willingness to advocate for the family and consumer. According to McFarlane's model, each of two clinicians joins with three or four different families who will get together in stages 2 and 3.

All the joining sessions begin with about fifteen minutes of small talk and end with five minutes of the same. Following informal chitchat, the *first joining session* begins with the clinician inquiring about the most recent psychiatric episode. He or she asks about the consumer's prodromal or precursor symptoms and changes in the consumer's behavior (e.g., decline in grooming) that preceded the psychotic episode. The clinician makes a list of these symptoms and asks about what seemed to precipitate the most recent episode. In addition, the clinician asks how the family coped with this episode, assuring them that their feelings are valid, inquires about treatment in the past, and briefly describes the PMFG.

During the *second joining session*, the clinician explores the family's feelings during past episodes. Assuming that rapport was established in the first session, the family is encouraged to express personal reactions and feelings, including feelings of grief and anger. In addition, the clinician inquires about the reactions of family members, friends, and the responsiveness of the mental health system and accepts the family's feelings and criticisms. Finally, the clinician asks about the family's social network, resources, and supports. Tools such as the genogram can be used to help identify relatives.

In the *third joining session*, the clinician continues to gather information about the family's social network, including work and school, and moves into identifying the strengths and resources of both the consumer and the family. Another task is to identify short-term and long-term goals of the consumer. These usually include symptomatic stabilization, relapse prevention, increasing social skills, and vocational goals, but they may include others. Next, the clinician prepares the family for the multifamily psychoeducational workshop and the groups that follow that. Specifics are given about the format, date, location, and goals of the workshop. The clinician inquires whether the family has any concerns and addresses those concerns. More joining sessions are scheduled if needed.

Stage 2: Multifamily Educational Workshop.   The educational workshop is modeled on the one originally developed by Anderson et al. (1986). Participants include members of six to eight families who were "joined," excluding the patient. This is offered on a single day or over a weekend. The major aim of the workshop is to impart factual, up-to-date information about the mental illness and its treatment and ways families can cope with their situations. Because this is the first occasion in which the family members who will participate in the multiple-family group meet, it has the additional purpose of promoting a supportive atmosphere and preparing participants for the groups. The subject matter that is covered in the workshops includes the following:

- Psychobiology of the specific mental illness
- Diagnosis
- Treatment and rehabilitation
- The course and prognosis
- Impact of mental illnesses on the family
- Relapse prevention
- Family guidelines (recommended ways for family members to interact with client to prevent relapse). (http://store.samhsa.gov/product/SMA09-4423)

Prior to the workshop, the leaders—the two clinicians who do the family "joining"—have numerous tasks: create a schedule of topics for the workshop, identify handouts that will be needed, arrange speakers if needed, identify videotapes to be used, and make arrangements to serve snacks and lunch. It is helpful to prepare a folder that contains the agenda, handouts that will be used in the presentation, and a list of resources (Sands & Solomon, 2003). Generally, the same clinician workshop leaders will conduct the multifamily group sessions that will follow the workshop (stage 3). A psychiatrist, psychopharmacologist, or nurse may be asked to speak about more technical biological topics, such as the way medications work, or this material may be presented by one or two clinicians who did the joining or through a videotape. In any case, the clinicians should be well informed about the mental illness as questions are likely to be asked later in the workshop or in the future. The clinicians should assume the leadership role even if speakers participate. It is recommended that leaders convey calmness, empathy, acceptance, and hope and that they do not press participants to speak if they do not wish to do so. At the same time, the leaders should create opportunities for participants to ask questions and raise concerns. Family members may, for example, have concerns about what it will be like to meet as a multifamily group that includes consumers.

During the workshop, families are introduced to the "Family Guidelines" that they are to use in relation to their family member. These include advice such as going slowly, establishing family routines, setting limits, and allowing family members to have space. The guidelines are predicated on the idea that having a family structure with a regular routine, rules, and reasonable expectations promotes stability and predictability. Expectations should be concrete and specific (e.g., wash the dishes every night). Workshop participants are told that the guidelines will be referred to in the multifamily group sessions as well. The workshop leaders review the guidelines one by one, linking them with the biological information that was presented earlier. Families can use these guidelines to manage their own stress-producing reactions (i.e., emotional expressiveness), to have realistic expectations, and to create comfort in the family environment.

In setting the tone during the joining sessions and educational workshop, clinicians need to be culturally sensitive. Members of some cultures may take longer than others to develop trust. Others will find it particularly challenging to modify their intense style of communication. Some may feel reluctant to discuss family matters with persons outside the family. For non-English-speaking families or families for whom English is their second language, a workshop and handouts in their first language are desirable. It is also advantageous to have a clinician from a similar culture. Clinicians should explore ways in which to adapt the model to different cultures.

Stage 3: Multifamily Group Problem Solving.   Stage 3 begins approximately two weeks after the workshop. The participants are the six to eight families that attended the workshop and the consumers who are affiliated with these families, as well as the two clinicians who led the workshop. The first three meetings are preparatory. Most of the remaining sessions are centered on problem solving. At times, however, meetings will be devoted to hearing an outside speaker or celebrating a holiday or special event. McFarlane (2002) recommends that meetings last an hour and a half and that they be held every other week for six months and monthly for at least another year.

The goals of the first two group sessions are to build a group that will be willing to share concerns based on having a common type of family situation. As in the early stages of group work, it is important to create comfort, ease participants' anxiety, and encourage participants to get to know each other and to bond. The leaders will want to promote a collaborative, supportive, accepting atmosphere.

The *first group session*, held around a table or sitting in a circle, begins with the leaders welcoming the group, explaining the format, and introducing themselves. When they describe themselves, they share personal information such as the ages of their children, their work experiences, their favorite books or movies, and their leisure-time activities. This provides a model for others' introductions. Because this is the first meeting, which should be positive, discussions about the consumer's illness, feelings about the illness, and topics that are likely to evoke shame or deep emotions are discouraged. Group leaders thank each person who speaks and point out commonalities between participants. No one is forced to share, but they are encouraged to say something. Another task of the first group meeting is to explain the rules. These include the expectation of attendance by all family members who interact regularly with the consumer, with the consumer given some leeway when he or she is symptomatic, feels vulnerable, or is intoxicated; confidentiality; no physical interaction during the sessions; maintain emotional control; share difficulties as they wish; and no interrupting. The first meeting concludes with a brief description of the next meeting.

The *second group session* begins with fifteen minutes of group socializing or chitchat and then moves into the topic of how mental illness has changed participants' lives. One of the leaders starts the process by talking about mental illness in his or her family, if that is the case, in a friend's family, or in the lives of families he or she has worked with. The leader can also talk about his or her feelings about working in this field or with families. Then others are asked to talk about how they have been affected by mental illness in the family. Group leaders thank participants after they speak and point out commonalities where they exist. They explain to the group that in future meetings they will be working on solving problems like some of those that were raised in this session. The meeting concludes with a ten-minute period of social talk around topics such as their plans for the weekend. Participants are reminded when the next meeting will take place.

The *third group meeting*, as well as future sessions, begins and ends with socialization. This is to foster the development of social skills. The primary focus of the third meeting is to introduce the group to the problem-solving method. The group is told that this will be the major activity of the group, and that it is important that they understand how this works. It is explained that initially group members will discuss how things have been going as a way to determine which problem to work on. Once one problem is chosen either by the leader or by the group, the problem-solving process begins. The leader explains that there are six steps of the problem-solving process and either distributes a handout or asks someone to record the steps on the blackboard or newsprint. The steps are as follows:

1. Define the problem
2. Generate solutions
3. Discuss advantages and disadvantages of each solution
4. Choose the best solution
5. Form an action plan
6. Review the action plan. (SAMHSA, 2009c, Module 4, p. 7)

The leader should explain each step of the problem-solving process and give examples. For instance, the leader could start by saying:

Sometimes when there is a difficulty in the family, it is hard to pinpoint exactly what the problem is. For example, last week Mrs. Smith spoke about being upset over

Todd's sleeping late in the morning. On the face of this, we do not know what about this behavior bothers Mrs. Smith, how Todd feels about it, how well Todd sleeps during the night, and so on. We will want to take some time during our sessions to figure out what exactly is bothering whom and what are the circumstances around the problem.

After the problem is defined (first step) by the family or consumer who shared it, the group brainstorms about possible solutions. During the second step, one does not evaluate the solutions; one simply develops a laundry list. The leader, coleader, or a group member lists the possible solutions on newsprint or another visible medium. The third step entails evaluation of each of the solutions, determining their advantages and disadvantages. The fourth step, choosing the best solution, is accomplished by the consumer and his or her family, who are encouraged to weigh the pros and cons. It is important that they "own" the solution as well as the problem. The fifth step is to develop a specific, detailed, written plan for addressing the problem. This includes specific tasks and who is responsible for which activities. To follow up on this, one of the practitioners will call during the week and the family will report the outcome at the next meeting.

During the *fourth and subsequent meetings* of the multifamily groups, the group engages in problem solving using the steps presented in the third meeting. The format for structuring problem solving is delineated in Table 12.1. As in previous sessions, the meetings begin and end with socialization or group chitchat about their everyday lives outside of the illness. Next is a process called the *go-around*, where participants talk about how things are going. During this twenty-minute period, family members bring up issues or problems with which they are dealing if they wish. The leaders acknowledge problems that are raised, convey empathy, and address the issues by using the Family Guidelines or suggesting an alternative approach. After the go-around, one of the group leaders or the group as a whole decides which problem should be worked on by the multifamily group. This can be the most pressing one, the one that can best be handled in a group setting, or one that is general enough to help others who may experience the same or a similar problem. As indicated in the table, decision making takes about five minutes. The centerpiece of the meeting is problem solving around the selected problem. This process calls for some participation of the entire group and some focusing on the consumer and his or her

TABLE 12.1 Structure of Psychoeducational Multifamily Group Sessions

Activity	Time Needed (minutes)
Socialization: social conversation with families and consumers as a group	15
Go around the room reviewing how things are going • Families share events and salient issues among families • Clinician responds to each	20
Selection of a single problem	5
Use six-step structured problem-solving process	45
Socialization	5
Total time	90

Source: Adapted from (SAMHSA 2009c).

family. As asserted by Yalom and Leszcz (2005), group members benefit from giving to others. The group goes through the problem-solving steps, coming up with a plan to deal with the problem. The group meeting concludes with socialization.

According to the PORT study and McFarlane's research, family psychoeducation is most beneficial to the consumer and family if it continues for nine months or more. This requires a high level of commitment on the part of participants and awareness, accrued over time, that the multifamily group is helpful. Another factor that may keep the group going is group cohesion (Yalom & Leszcz, 2005) and bonding, which develops through sharing a common problem and trusting others.

OTHER EVIDENCE-BASED MODELS OF FAMILY PSYCHOEDUCATION   Besides McFarlane's model, there are other second-generation models in which clinicians work with family units rather than with multiple family groups. For example, Mueser and Glynn's (1999) behavioral family therapy, built on the work of Falloon et al. (1984), begins with an assessment of the family's needs and proceeds to a behaviorally oriented family therapy that includes education and skills training in communication and problem solving. Also benefiting from the work of Falloon and his colleagues, Miklowitz (2008) adapted his family-focused treatment to the needs of consumers with bipolar disorder and their families. Miklowitz begins the process by joining with the consumer and family and conducting a functional assessment on the consumer and family. Next is the psychoeducational module, which extends over seven sessions. This is followed by communication enhancement training over seven sessions and problem solving over four to five sessions. There are two or three sessions devoted to termination and planning. Miklowitz's (2008) book serves as a treatment manual. This and other methods of family psychoeducation are, however, therapy for the consumer and family. Other approaches do not aim at treatment.

Family Education

No matter how effective family psychoeducational programs may be, family members have tended to view their fundamental assumption (expressed emotion) as family-blaming (Solomon, 1996). Over the years, family education has become decoupled from family psychoeducation. Educational workshops, organized by both professionals and families, provide a format in which family members can learn about the various psychiatric disorders, medication, and community resources and are encouraged to develop coping skills, including mutual support. These programs generally extend over a period of eight to twelve weeks, but they can be consolidated into day-long workshops (E. Mannion, personal communication). They are usually freestanding programs that are not part of the consumer's treatment (Solomon, 1996). Rather than focusing on helping families manage expressed emotion, they emphasize family strengths and resilience (Marsh & Lefley, 1996).

The Training and Education Center (TEC), a unit of the Mental Health Association of Southeastern Pennsylvania, has been offering workshops for family members, partners, and friends of adults with severe mental illness who live in the Philadelphia area. TEC originally offered a generic, ten-week family workshop, some of which has been incorporated into NAMI's family education program. TEC now offers workshops over a shorter span of time on specific topics such as:

- Promoting "Recovery" in a Loved One with Mental Illness (six weeks)
- Self-Care for Surviving Complicated Grief, Trauma & Burn-Out (four weeks)
- Finding the Right Balance when a Loved One Has Borderline Personality Disorder or Mood Swings– Based on Dialectical Behavior Therapy, an Evidence-Based Practice for BPD (eight weeks)

- Managing Your Anger When a Loved One Has a Mental Illness (six weeks)
- Living with Mental Illness in a Spouse or Partner (six weeks)
- Coping When a Relative with Mental Illness Refuses Treatment (six weeks) (http://www.mhasp.org/services/tec.html#mark)

NAMI sponsors its own family educational program. NAMI's Family-to-Family Education Program (FFEP) "uses a unique combination of healing, consciousness-raising, and empowerment" (Burland, 1998, p. 33) to help families understand and come to terms with caring for and supporting a mentally ill relative. Courses are taught over a period of twelve weeks by a pair of leaders, usually family members certified as trained family education leaders. Theoretically, the FFEP is based on trauma recovery and stress-coping concepts (Lucksted, Stewart, & Forbes, 2008). The program uses the technique of consciousness-raising to deflect blame from family members and help them heal from the trauma. The class concludes by encouraging participants to advocate and teaching them how to do so (Burland, 1998).

Family-to-Family Education Program's curriculum includes information about major psychiatric disorders (schizophrenia, bipolar disorder, borderline personality disorders, obsessive-compulsive disorder, panic disorder, and co-occurring addictive disorders); medications; the biology of the brain; recovery; evidence-based treatments that promote recovery; the subjective experience of mental illness; problem solving and communication; crisis management; self-care; community resources and supports; and advocacy (Lefley, 2009; http://www.nami.org/). The curriculum is similar to that used in family psychoeducation workshops but is more focused on the families' needs. Like evidence-based family psychoeducational programs, FFEPs are manualized (Dixon et al., 2004). FFEPs do not include consumers and do not charge participants (http://www.nami.org/). A quantitative evaluation of family participants who agreed to be interviewed at four different times demonstrated that FFEP was effective in reducing subjective burden, increasing knowledge about severe mental illness and the mental health system, and increasing empowerment (Dixon et al., 2004). A qualitative follow-up study found that participants gained new information and support, insights and acceptance, and new tools and skills for handling challenging situations, and experienced changes in behavior and feelings of control (Lucksted et al., 2008).

In addition to the family education programs that have been described, there are others including (a) the Three R's Psychiatric Wellness Rehabilitation Program offered at various hospitals and community centers in about thirteen states in the United States and in two cities in Canada; (b) Pebbles in the Pond in the state of Washington; (c) Bryce Hospital, the Alabama Model; and (d) Partnership for Recovery developed by Patricia Scheifler (Lefley, 2009). Information about these programs can be found in Lefley's book or by contacting the programs directly.

Family Consultation

Family consultation is an alternative or supplement to family psychoeducation or family education. The consultant, who may be a professional or family member, provides advice, guidance, and support to a family member or family unit on an as-needed basis (Solomon, 1996). A social worker who is working with the consumer, such as a case manager, a treatment team, or a social work practitioner who is not part of the consumer's treatment setting may serve as family consultant (Solomon, Bogart Marshall, Mannion, & Farmer, 2002). Usually the consumer is not included (Corrigan et al., 2008), but when the consumer is being discussed his or her consent is needed (E. Mannion, personal communication).

In contrast with family therapy and other clinical services, family consultation is not a form of treatment that aims to reduce dysfunction (Marsh, 1998). The relationship between the consultant and consultee is a collaborative one in which the family identifies concerns to be addressed (Marsh, 1998). As examples, the family may have issues around accessing resources, living arrangements, eligibility for entitlements, and other matters (Lefley, 2009). Education is part of the consultation if the family has concerns that require information such as medication (E. Mannion, personal communication).

Family consultation is usually short term. It can take place over one session or more with the frequency varying according to the family's needs (Marsh, 1998; Solomon et al., 2002). It may occur in person or by telephone. Consultation is a convenient form of help for families that find participation in family psychoeducation over an extended period of time is too demanding, for those with specific needs (Solomon et al., 2002), or for those who live in areas where there are not many alternatives. Edie Mannion, director of TEC at the Mental Health Association of Southeastern Pennsylvania, identified, from her experience, three skill areas that need attention by the consultant. First, the consultant needs to empathize with, normalize, and respond to the consultee's *feelings*. Second, *focusing* involves defining the problem clearly and specifically. Third, *finding* refers to identifying and exploring options (Solomon et al., 2002).

Although research on family consultation is limited, one study found that participants in family consultation gained increased self-efficacy following this intervention (Solomon, Draine, Mannion, & Meisel, 1996, 1997).

COGNITIVE REHABILITATION

Up until now this chapter has discussed treatments other than traditional individual psychotherapy. In general, intensive psychotherapy is not recommended for persons with schizophrenia. Nevertheless, some clients with this and other major mental disorders seem to benefit from individual and group therapy that is ego-supportive, structured, and reality based. Some of the psychotherapeutic approaches for depression discussed in Chapter 9 may be used with clients with major depression.

Because schizophrenia is characterized by cognitive deficits, cognitive approaches are promising as a means to intervene with clients with this disorder. One strategy, *cognitive rehabilitation*, aims to remedy deficits in information-processing skills such as vigilance, memory, recall, and conceptual abilities (Penn & Mueser, 1996) that are not helped by medication (Storzbach & Corrigan, 1996). Social functioning and problem-solving skills are requisites for social interaction and dealing with daily life stresses and problems. These skill sets are necessary for improved quality of life and for participation in supported employment opportunities for individuals with schizophrenia. Intervention methods such as positive reinforcement, repeated practice, semantic encoding, and the introduction of an incompatible behavior have been found effective for treating deficits in attention and memory and for limiting hallucinations and delusions (Storzbach & Corrigan, 1996).

Over the past two decades, the empirical literature has grown sufficiently to permit an examination of the outcomes of cognitive rehabilitation for schizophrenia to inform practice (Krabbendum & Aleman, 2003; Kurtz, Moberg, Gur, & Gur, 2001; Pilling et al., 2002; Twamley, Jeste, & Bellack, 2003). A recent meta-analysis found that cognitive rehabilitation produces moderate gains in cognitive functioning, and when combined with psychiatric rehabilitation, also improves functional outcomes (McGurk, Twamley, Sizter, McHugo, & Mueser, 2007). However, there remains uncertainty as to whether these improvements translate into meaningful gains in "real world" applications for personal care and social functioning among individuals experiencing serious mental illness. Controversy exists in the cognitive rehabilitation literature as to the gold standard for training methods. For instance, some recommend individual and group exercises, whereas others suggest computer-based training and some favor strategy coaching techniques with others advocating repeated practice drills (Kurtz et al., 2001; Twamley et al., 2003). Future treatment innovations and research should refine methods and indicate how generalizable such learning is.

The final topic addressed in this chapter is medication. Although social workers do not prescribe medication, they work in environments in which psychopharmacology is a fundamental form of treatment. Because clinical social workers observe clients in clinical and community settings, they are well positioned to assess the impact of medication on clients' functioning, provide education and support for medication adherence, and confer with psychiatrists when there is a possible need for a change or adjustment. Social workers cannot make these judgments without knowledge about medication and adherence issues.

ANTIPSYCHOTIC AND MOOD STABILIZING MEDICATION

Medication has increasingly become the standard (but not only) mode of treatment for persons with severe mental disorders. Psychotropic drugs are ordinarily used both to treat acute symptoms and to maintain the functioning of clients whose symptoms are not evident or are in remission. Medication is usually prescribed by psychiatrists who supervise the client's adherence over time. As case managers and therapists, clinical social workers work with and educate consumers; explore their feelings about and attitudes toward taking prescribed medication; observe side effects, signs of concomitant substance use or abuse, and adherence or nonadherence with the medication regimen; and decide whether and how to intervene when there is a problem.

Psychiatric assessments of consumers' medication needs take into consideration their physical health, individual and family health/mental health history, medication history, allergic reactions, age, sex, height, and weight, as well as findings from the mental status examination and diagnosis. Results of preliminary and intermittent physical examinations and laboratory and other tests guide the psychiatrist in the selection of appropriate drugs and in the monitoring of side effects. Research findings, clinical experience, and the drug responses of the individual also enter into decisions about which drugs to prescribe. The dosage is adjusted over time when the client's responses can be observed not only by the psychiatrist but also by the client, other mental health professionals, and those who interact with him or her on a regular basis.

Medication is used to ameliorate symptoms, which are expressive of a client's subjective state, reaction to environmental stressors, and mental disorder. Specific sets of symptoms that persist over time suggest diagnoses such as those described in the *DSM-IV-TR* (American Psychiatric Association, 2000). In turn, the symptoms and diagnosis suggest particular drugs or drug groups. Medications for depression and anxiety were discussed previously in Chapters 8 and 9. Those that are used to treat persistent psychotic and bipolar symptoms—antipsychotics and mood stabilizers—are described here. At times, antipsychotic medications are used to treat mood disorders and mood stabilizing agents are used to augment the treatment of psychotic disorders. The use of a combination of drugs is called *polypharmacy*.

Antipsychotic Medication

The drugs that are used to treat psychoses are known as antipsychotics or neuroleptics. Although psychotic symptoms are the primary target of these drugs, some also have a sedating effect. Antipsychotics are used to treat schizophrenia (all subtypes), schizoaffective disorder, schizophreniform disorder, delusional disorder, major depression with psychotic symptoms, and other disorders and are used on a short-term basis to manage acute episodes of mania (Sadock & Sadock, 2007). These drugs are capable of managing (but not entirely eliminating) hallucinations, cognitive disorganization, and agitation. Today, both first- and second-generation antipsychotics are prescribed.

FIRST-GENERATION ANTIPSYCHOTICS "First-generation," "conventional," or "typical" antipsychotic agents are used to treat schizophrenia and other disorders with psychotic symptoms. They are most successful in the management of *positive* (or florid) *symptoms*, which are overt expressions of unusual sensory experiences (hallucinations), disturbed thinking, and/or disorganized behavior. They are less effective with *negative* (or deficit) *symptoms* such as flat affect, poverty of speech, apathy, asociality, and/or impairment in attentionality (Andreasen, 1985). They also have some disturbing side effects.

The first of these drugs to be discovered was chlorpromazine (Thorazine). Other phenothiazenes (the name of the group of drugs of which this is an exemplar) include thioridazine (Mellaril), trifluoperazine (Stelazine), and fluphenazine (Prolixin). Some of the common first-generation antipsychotics are listed in Table 12.2.

These medications can also be distinguished by their *potency*. A high-potency drug is one in which a low dosage is sufficient to address targeted symptoms. The standard dosages of

TABLE 12.2 First- and Second-Generation Antipsychotic Medication

Group/Generic Names	Trade Names
First-Generation Antipsychotics	
Chlorpromazine	Thorazine
Fluphenazine	Prolixin, Permitil
Haloperidol	Haldol
Mesoridazine	Serentil
Molindone	Moban
Perphenazine	Trilafon
Thioridazine	Mellaril
Thiothixene	Navane
Trifluoperazine	Stelazine
Second-Generation Antipsychotics	
Amisulpride	Solian
Aripiprazole	Abilify
Clozapine	Clozaril/Leponex
Olanzapine	Zyprexa
Quetiapine	Seroquel
Risperidone	Risperdal
Ziprasidone	Geodon

Source: Based on Bentley & Walsh (2006); Mulsant & Pollock (2009); Sadock & Sadock (2007).

high-potency drugs such as Haldol and Prolixin (6–12 mg/day for maintenance therapy) are equivalent to standard dosages of low-potency drugs such as Thorazine and Mellaril (300–600 mg/day for maintenance therapy) (Lehman, Steinwachs, & Co-Investigators of the PORT Project, 1998). In other words, a low dosage of a high-potency drug is the equivalent of a high dosage of a low-potency drug.

Among the side effects of some of the first-generation drugs are sedation and extrapyramidal symptoms (EPSs). *Sedation* is a calming response, produced especially by the low-potency antipsychotics. Sedation helps control agitation, aggressiveness, mania, and irritability, an effect that, in some cases, is desired. On the other hand, sedation induces sleep, lowers awareness, and limits responsiveness—which can interfere with performance of everyday activities, work, and the operation of machinery. *EPSs* are disturbances in motor activity that are associated with blockage of dopamine receptors (Wittlin, 1988). Types of extrapyramidal side effects include parkinsonian symptoms, dystonias, akathisia, and neuroleptic malignant syndrome (Kamin, Manwani, & Hughes, 2000). These and other side effects are described in Table 12.3.

TABLE 12.3 Side Effects of First-Generation Antipsychotic Drugs

Side Effect	Description
Sedation	Calmness, drowsiness, tiredness, lowered awareness, and responsiveness.
Dystonias	Muscular spasms of the throat, neck, eyes, jaws, tongue, back, or whole body. These are seen frequently during the first few days of treatment, especially in young men.
Parkinsonian symptoms	Characterized by rigidity, shuffling gait, muscle stiffness, stooped posture, drooling, and a regular, coarse tremor.
Akathisia	Muscular discomfort, manifested by motor restlessness. The client is unable to sit still and appears agitated.
Akinesia	Reduced motor activity, listlessness, low spontaneity, and apathy.
Tardive dyskinesia	Involuntary movements, primarily of the face, tongue, mouth, and neck, but also of the extremities. These symptoms appear after prolonged use of neuroleptics.
Anticholinergic effects	Symptoms include dry mouth, blurry vision, urine retention, and constipation. Nausea and vomiting are other possible symptoms.
Postural hypotension	A lowering of blood pressure related to changes in one's position. It is manifested by fatigue, loss of balance, fainting, and falling.
Neuroleptic malignant syndrome	A side effect of antipsychotic medication that is life-threatening. Characterized by fever, akinesia, rigidity, delirium, dystonia, and abnormal behavior. On the surface, it looks like an acute form of schizophrenia.
Sexual and reproductive disturbances	These include difficulties having erections and ejaculating, low libido, breast enlargement, galactorrhea, and menstrual irregularities or amenorrhea. Together with additional side effects such as weight gain and skin disturbances, these symptoms can be especially disturbing to sexually active clients.

Source: Based on Baldessarini & Cole (1988); Cohen (1988); Sadock & Sadock (2007); Rifkin & Siris (1987); Wittlin (1988).

The prevention and treatment of side effects present a formidable challenge to psychiatrists. Prevention of tardive dyskinesia is facilitated by the use of low doses of antipsychotic drugs. Adjunctive agents, such as Cogentin, Benadryl, and Artane, are sometimes used to manage side effects, but these, unfortunately, have effects of their own (Bentley & Walsh, 2006). A further concern is possible severe drug–drug interactions (Sadock & Sadock, 2007).

First-generation antipsychotic drugs are usually administered orally but a few are given intramuscularly. Oral administration is respectful of clients' dignity, autonomy, and right to self-determination. Intramuscular "depot" preparations are long-acting solutions that are given to clients who have difficulty adhering to the prescribed medical treatment. Haloperidol (Haldol) and fluphenazine (Prolixin) can be administered intramuscularly (Sadock & Sadock, 2007). One of the second-generation medications, Risperdal, is also offered orally and intramuscularly (Sadock & Sadock, 2007).

SECOND-GENERATION ANTIPSYCHOTICS Psychopharmacological evidence-based research has produced a second generation of drugs that are also described as *atypical antipsychotics*. These drugs are reported to reduce the risk of extrapyramidal side effects, compared with their predecessors, and to be efficacious for schizophrenia and acute mania (Sadock & Sadock, 2007). The Clinical Antipsychotic Trials of Intervention Effectiveness (CATIE), which compared one first-generation antipsychotic (perphenazine) with several second-generation drugs, found that the first-generation drug perphenazine held its own in overall effectiveness compared with risperidone, quetiapine, and ziprasidone and in risk of tardive dyskinesia and was the most cost effective (Swartz et al., 2008). A meta-analysis of comparative studies of nine second-generation antipsychotics found some differences among them, with differences having more to do with positive than negative symptoms (Leucht et al., 2009).

One of the first of the atypical antipsychotics approved in the United States was clozapine. This medication is used largely for individuals who do not respond to standard antipsychotic medications. It does not produce the EPSs that are associated with the first-generation medications, and it appears to suppress tardive dyskinesia while a client is taking this medication (Sadock & Sadock, 2007). Furthermore, it seems to moderate negative as well as positive symptoms. On the other hand, clozapine poses the risk of agranulocytosis, which lowers white blood cell count needed to fight infections, and it can also cause seizures. To avert agranulocytosis, blood levels are monitored regularly (Sadock & Sadock, 2007).

Other second-generation antipsychotics have different strengths and side effects. For example, olanzapine, which surpassed a number of other medications in effectiveness in several studies (Leucht et al., 2009; Swartz et al., 2008), is associated with weight gain and metabolic effects. Risperdone has a low incidence of EPS when the dosage is low but produces side effects such as sexual dysfunction in men, weight gain, postural hypotension, and mild sedation (Marder, 1997). Aripiprazole (Abilify) is reported to represent an advance beyond the other second-generation antipsychotic medications in its somewhat different chemical composition, its effectiveness with neurocognitive functions, and its tendency to be nonsedating (Sadock & Sadock, 2007). Other second-generation antipsychotics are listed on Table 12.2.

IMPACT ON WOMEN AND OLDER ADULTS Antipsychotic medication has different effects on men and women (Seeman, 2004). For women, psychiatrists need to take into account their menstrual cycle, pregnancy status, lactation status, and age. Because women may be taking ancillary medication for mood problems and/or contraceptives, these drugs can interact with antipsychotics (Seeman, 2004). Research findings on the impact of antipsychotic drugs taken during pregnancy on the fetus are inconsistent (Wichman, 2009). If medication is withheld during that time, the mother's psychotic symptoms may interfere with her taking care of herself and her baby (Miller, 1991). Some psychiatrists suggest that women be prescribed lower doses during pregnancy, with the dose raised after delivery (Seeman, 2004). Others recommend that women be advised not to breast-feed while taking antipsychotics (Sadock & Sadock, 2007).

Older adults taking antipsychotic medication also require special attention. Because tardive dyskinesia is associated with long-term consumption of first-generation antipsychotics, older clients are at high risk or may already be afflicted with the condition. They face a risk of falling as a result of postural hypotonia, a side effect of some antipsychotics. Second-generation antipsychotics are being used increasingly for treatment of psychotic symptoms in late life (Rapoport, Mamdani, Shulman, Hermann, & Rochon, 2005). These drugs are efficacious in the treatment of schizophrenia and the psychological and behavioral symptoms of dementia and delirium (Mulsant & Pollock, 2009). There are differences among these drugs in the side effects, tolerability, and safety for older adults (Mulsant & Pollack, 2009). Older adults' physical health status (e.g., the presence of a cardiac problem) and other medications they are taking may preclude the use of certain antipsychotics. With older adults, care should be taken about drug interactions and dosage. The social worker should gather information on the use of prescribed medications, alcohol and other nonmedical drugs, over-the-counter drugs, and herbal preparations.

Overall, the geriatric psychiatry literature suggests (a) antipsychotic medication is effective in reducing psychotic symptoms in older adults with schizophrenia; (b) it is not clear that any drug or category of drugs is any more effective than any other; (c) adverse effects differ between the typical and atypical medications, with typical medication having increased EPS (particularly tardive dyskinesia) in older adults and atypical medication presenting an increased risk of elevated glucose and triglycerides; however, risk of death is not higher among users of atypical compared to typical antipsychotic medications; (d) doses may need to be lower among older adults, particularly among individuals with later onset of the disorder, and should be increased gradually; and (e) there is a need to individualize medication management of older adults due to differences in how drugs are metabolized and to the potential of concurrent medical conditions to cause or exacerbate harmful effects and the potential of drug interactions with medications used to treat these concurrent conditions.

Mood Stabilizing Agents

Mood stabilizing agents are used to treat bipolar disorder and other disorders with manic or hypomanic symptoms. They are also used as an adjunctive medication for other mental disorders. Table 12.4 presents the drugs that have been shown to be effective in the treatment of acute mania and, to some extent, for the depressive phase and in maintenance treatment (Keck & McElroy, 1998). For a long time, lithium was the standard treatment, but today several anticonvulsant drugs are also used as first-line treatments of bipolar I disorder (Sadock & Sadock, 2007).

LITHIUM Lithium is used to treat bipolar I disorder in the acute phase and prophylactically to prevent the recurrence of manic and depressive episodes. Sometimes lithium is used together with an antipsychotic agent during an acute bipolar I manic episode or with an antidepressant during an acute bipolar I depressive episode (Yatham et al., 2006). Lithium has been used with some success in the treatment of schizoaffective, cyclothymic, and bipolar II disorders (Sadock & Sadock, 2007).

Lithium is prescribed initially after a physical examination and laboratory tests. Maintenance on lithium requires regular monitoring of lithium levels and periodic laboratory tests. The purpose of checking lithium blood levels is to ensure that the client is receiving a

TABLE 12.4 Mood Stabilizers

Group/Generic Names	Trade Names
Lithium	
Lithium carbonate	Eskalith and Eskalith CR
	Lithobid (slow-release tablets)
	Lithotabs
	Lithonate
	Lithane
	Carbolith
Lithium citrate	Cibalith-S (syrup)
Anticonvulsants	
Carbamazepine	Tegretol
Valproate/valproic acid	Depakene
Valproate/divalproex sodium	Depakote
Oxcarbazepine	Trileptal
Lamotrigine	Lamictal

Source: Muzina, Elhaj, Gajwani, Gao, & Calabrese (2005); Mulsant & Pollock (2009); Sadock & Sadock (2007).

therapeutic dose and is avoiding toxicity. Among the symptoms of toxicity are dry mouth, severe episodes of diarrhea, vomiting, tremors, confusion, coma, poor coordination, slurred speech, and seizures (Cowen, 1998; Sadock & Sadock, 2007). Side effects include tremors of the hand, thirst, increased urine output, weight gain, cardiovascular changes, and acne (Cowen, 1998). Clients should be counseled to report their side effects immediately; social workers should observe bipolar clients' physical and mental states so that psychiatric intervention can be mobilized quickly if needed.

Although lithium is helpful to those individuals who respond to it, some individuals do not respond to it, have disabling side effects, or cannot take it because of concurrent health issues. Fortunately, there are other drugs that can be used.

ANTICONVULSANTS Several anticonvulsive drugs are now used alone or together with lithium or an antipsychotic as a first-line treatment for bipolar disorder in its acute phases (mania or depression) or for maintenance (Yatham et al., 2006). Carbamazepine appears to be comparable to lithium in its effect on acute mania, as a prophylaxis for depressive and manic episodes of bipolar I disorder, and for preventing relapses of bipolar II disorder (Cowen, 1998; Sadock & Sadock, 2007), but like lithium, carbamazepine has adverse effects and can produce toxicity. Among the adverse side effects are double or blurred vision, dizziness, drowsiness, cardiac effects, and gastrointestinal distress (Sadock & Sadock, 2007). There is a slight risk of agranulocytosis, and it can cause a disturbance in cardiac conduction in individuals with preexisting heart problems (Cowen, 1998). Blood needs to be monitored on a regular basis.

Valproate or valproic acid (also formulated as divalproex sodium) is another mood stabilizer, approved for the treatment of acute mania and mixed episodes associated with bipolar I disorder

(Sadock & Sadock, 2007). Divalproex sodium is considered a first-line maintenance treatment for bipolar disorder (Yatham et al., 2006). Common side effects of valproate include tremor, sedation, drowsiness, transient hair loss, and weight gain (Cowen, 1998; Sadock & Sadock, 2007).

The other drugs listed in Table 12.4 are less well studied but are, nevertheless, used to treat bipolar disorder. Oxcarbazepine is similar to carbamazepine in molecular structure but may be safer and better tolerated (Sadock & Sadock, 2007). Although research from small controlled trials supports its use to treat acute bipolar mania, more rigorous studies are needed (Muzina et al., 2005). Lamotrigene has been found successful in treating acute bipolar I depression and rapid cycling bipolar II disorder and in thwarting a recurrence of bipolar depression (Muzina et al., 2005).

IMPACT OF MOOD STABILIZERS ON WOMEN AND OLDER ADULTS Research on the use of lithium and anticonvulsant mood stabilizers during pregnancy suggests that there are risks to the mother and the unborn child, but findings are contradictory and inconclusive (Gentile, 2006). The risk to the infant appears to be highest in the first trimester (Burt & Rasgon, 2004). There is also concern that these drugs reach a nursing infant (Gentile, 2006; Sadock & Sadock, 2007). As with antipsychotic medications, the psychiatrist, together with the consumer, should weigh the costs and benefits (Gentile, 2006).

Mood stabilizing drugs pose risks to older adults as well. Lithium is considered efficacious in the treatment of acute manic episodes and as a prophylaxis for mania, while it also poses risk of toxicity (Mulsant & Pollock, 2009). Among the side effects of lithium that have been reported in the literature are cognitive and neuromotor impairments, cardiovascular effects, and disturbances in the thyroid function (Young, 2005). Older adults may better tolerate anticonvulsant drugs such as divalproex sodium (Mulsant & Pollock, 2009; Young, 2005). Comorbid medical conditions as well as interactions with drugs used to treat other conditions need to be considered (Young, 2005).

ADJUNCTIVE MEDICATIONS The mood stabilizers that were discussed have been used with each other (two at a time) or together with an antipsychotic or antidepressant drugs in the treatment of bipolar disorder. A meta-analysis of randomized controlled trials demonstrated that the combination of second-generation antipsychotics with mood stabilizers was more effective in the treatment of acute mania than treatment with only mood stabilizers (Scherk, Pajonk, & Leucht, 2007). Antipsychotics are sometimes used on a long-term basis for individuals who have recurrent episodes of mania that are not controlled with lithium. Antidepressants are used together with a mood stabilizer to treat clients with bipolar depression (Frances, Kahn, Carpenter, Docherty, & Donovan, 1998), but this is done cautiously because antidepressants can precipitate mania, hypomania, and rapid cycling (Prien, 1987). We turn next to the implications of knowledge about the medications that have been discussed for social work practice.

Implications for Clinical Social Work Practice

This review of medications prescribed for persons with psychotic and mood-fluctuating disorders provides a knowledge base for the social work practitioner. Social workers should become aware of research updates in medications, changes in medications that have been ordered by psychiatrists for clients, alterations in the client's behavior prior to and following medication changes, and contingencies that enter into the client's education and adherence with a medication regimen. Factors such as clients' attitudes toward taking medication, undesirable side effects, and the use of alcohol, street drugs, caffeine, and tobacco should be explored.

As members of the mental health team, social workers have a role in educating clients about and monitoring their adherence with prescribed drugs. As social workers with professional values of client self-determination, self-actualization, and respect for human dignity, clinical social workers must balance their commitment to positive client outcomes with a concern for clients' wishes and rights.

One obstacle to adherence may lie in the client's feelings or thoughts about taking medication. Medication may be perceived symbolically as a crutch or a reminder that he or she has a serious disorder. This feeling or thought may be particularly acute among persons with severe mental disorders, whose psychiatric illness seems interminable. Dependence on medication may reinforce feelings of helplessness and hopelessness; interfere with self-esteem and autonomy; and contradict sociocultural values about independence, self-sufficiency, and competence.

Some clients may have thoughts related to their psychiatric difficulties that affect their adherence to medication. For example, Mike, a young man with an obsessive-compulsive personality disorder as well as schizophrenia, would not take his medication on days in which he overslept. In exploring the reasons for his noncompliance, the clinical social worker discovered that the directions on the medication bottle said, "Take twice daily at 8 A.M. and 8 P.M.," and Mike concluded, "If I've slept late, I've blown it." In this case, the social worker had the psychiatrist change the written instructions to "twice daily" and counseled the client about taking each tablet at two different times.

Clinical social workers can encourage clients to talk about their feelings about medication to sort out the realistic and the unrealistic. For example:

> Susan, a 25-year-old musician, had the diagnosis of bipolar disorder for three years. She had her first manic episode during her senior year of college, which resulted in her taking a leave of absence. Later she returned to college and completed her degree.
>
> Susan expressed a number of concerns about lithium. For one, she felt that it interfered with her creativity. During manic episodes, she would stay awake into the night, composing music. She felt less creative on lithium. In addition, Susan found it embarrassing to come to the clinic, where she sat with clients who talked to themselves and exhibited bizarre movements.
>
> In talking with Susan, the social worker learned that Susan was frightened of the other clients and afraid that she would develop movements like theirs. When the side effects of schizophrenia were differentiated from those of lithium, Susan felt relieved. Only then did she admit that the music she composed when she was manic was not very good (she tape-recorded it once so she could listen to it later). In subsequent discussions, Susan recognized that her risk for recurrent episodes was high (three members of her family had the same disorder), and that lithium could protect her from interruptions in her career.

Clients also have subjective responses to the side effects of drugs. They may feel uncomfortable with the anticholinergic effects and self-conscious about obvious EPSs. Weight gain, skin eruptions, and sexual dysfunctioning may prompt some clients to take themselves off the medication. A social worker who listens attentively and probes for feelings may be able to problem solve with the client in an effort to effect a change in the medication. Options include a change in dosage, the introduction of medications for side effects, and a change in medication. Social workers can encourage clients to request medication changes and can offer to arrange appointments for that purpose and to sit in on appointments with psychiatrists. So long as it is acceptable to clients, the social worker can advocate and raise medication issues with the psychiatrist that clients may be reluctant to raise themselves.

Medication management is another issue that may arise in the process of working with a client. Many clients take their own medications as prescribed. Others are given medication by a family member, boarding home operator, or nurse. Medication may be in the forms of capsules, tablets, or liquid, or it may be administered intramuscularly. Clients who are given medication by others may feel controlled, dependent, or childlike.

With respect to clients' self-determination and dignity, self-administration is the most desirable alternative. Clients who have a history of nonadherence or abuse of medication, however, may not be given that option. Social workers can work with clients and client systems to promote the maximum self-determination feasible with respect to medication and develop with clients goals that reflect their wish for more control and independence. Tools such as calendars, daily checklists, medication packs, and charts can be developed. A tool that can help in the management of medication that also gives clients control is "My Portable Medication Record," a booklet that clients can take with them when they go to different treatment settings. It provides places for the client's medical insurance information, pharmacy, emergency instructions, the doctor's name, health issues, and hospitalizations, as well as documentation of the history of medications used and their effectiveness (Conn & Edwards, 1999). In addition, clients can be encouraged to keep medication in a place that is visible and to take the medication at the same time every day.

Sometimes social workers obtain information about clients that indicates that they are diverging from their treatment plan. The use of alcohol and street drugs, the sale of prescribed medication, hoarding of medication, and borrowing from or lending medication to others may result in adverse physical reactions or suicide. Concerns about these behaviors should be discussed directly and honestly with the client and the psychiatrist. Mental health team meetings are an appropriate forum for discussing ethical as well as treatment issues, and for the team to develop a common treatment strategy.

Summary and Deconstruction

This chapter described a number of strategies social workers and other professionals use to help clients and families improve their lives when a family member has a severe mental illness. The strategies are psychosocial and medical.

Although medication is prescribed by psychiatrists, social workers play a role in medication management through their observation of how clients use and are affected by medication. Antipsychotic drugs seem to control positive symptoms but have limited success with negative symptoms. The second generation of antipsychotics promised to have fewer deleterious side effects than the first, but both have side effects that need to be taken into consideration. Mood stabilizers can help individuals with bipolar and related disorders.

Still medication does not cure mental illness nor does it entirely eliminate symptoms. It cannot help individuals with their interpersonal and problem-solving skills.

Illness Management and Recovery helps consumers understand their illness, manage their symptoms, and improve their interpersonal and coping skills while pursuing their individual recovery goals. Psychoeducation, motivational interviewing, and cognitive and behavioral methods are used to help clients in either an individual or a group format. The program is structured, with modules on particular topics. Clinicians can consult the toolkit available through the SAMHSA Webpage that provides guidelines for the intervention.

Although individuals with severe mental illness tend to be constructed as "having" the disease, family members and others close to them experience the effects of the disease as well. Parents, who had other dreams for their children than those that were realized, are often the primary caregivers of their adult mentally ill children, even if they do not live in the same household. Likewise, siblings, spouses/partners, and children are affected by a family member's mental illness. Behavioral health professionals cannot expect families to continue to give care without receiving support for themselves.

The first generation of family interventions saw in the family a means to treat the identified client. Although these methods did succeed in educating families about their relative's illness and its treatment, they were not sufficiently family centered. Second-generation models such as that of McFarlane recognize families' needs to form a mutual support network while helping their family member. Alternatively families and professionals provide family *education*, rather than *psyc-*

hoeducation. NAMI sponsors a family education program that is led by trained family members.

These are some of today's leading evidence-based practices with individuals and families in which there is severe mental illness. Although in-depth psychotherapy is generally not recommended for persons with schizophrenia, some clients with severe mental illness can be helped with cognitive rehabilitation. Still, individuals and families develop their own ways of healing. Consumers struggle, with and without help, to create their own pathways to recovery, experiencing some hurdles along the road. Families, too, face challenges in caring for themselves while being there for their consumer family member. Because of the heterogeneity among people, a gap still exists to develop new client- and family-centered interventions that meet the needs of individuals who are suffering from severe mental illness and families who are living with its consequences.

References

American Psychiatric Association. (2000). *Diagnostic and statistical manual of mental disorders* (4th ed., text rev.). Washington, DC: Author.

Anderson, C. M., Reiss, D. J., & Hogarty, G. (1986). *Schizophrenia and the family.* New York: Guilford Press.

Andreasen, N. C. (1985). Positive vs. negative schizophrenia: A critical evaluation. *Schizophrenia Bulletin, 11*(3), 380–389.

Baldessarini, R. J., & Cole, J. O. (1988). Chemotherapy. In A. M. Nicholi, Jr. (Ed.), *The new Harvard guide to psychiatry* (pp. 481–533). Cambridge, MA: Belknap Press of Harvard University Press.

Bateson, G., Jackson, D., Haley, J., & Weakland, J. (1956). Toward a theory of schizophrenia. *Behavioral Science, 1,* 251–264.

Bellack, A. S. (2004). Skills training for people with severe mental illness. *Psychiatric Rehabilitation Journal, 27,* 375–391.

Bentley, K. J., & Walsh, J. (2006). *The social worker and psychotropic medication* (3rd ed.). Belmont, CA: Brooks/Cole.

Bond, G. R., & Campbell, K. (2008). Evidence-based practices for individuals with severe mental illness. *Journal of Rehabilitation, 74*(2), 33–44.

Boss, P. (1999). *Ambiguous loss: Learning to live with unresolved grief.* Cambridge, MA: Harvard University Press.

Burland, J. (1998). Family-to-family: A trauma-and-recovery model of family education. In H. P. Lefley (Ed.), *Families coping with mental illness: The cultural context* (pp. 33–41). San Francisco, CA: Jossey-Bass.

Burt, V. K., & Rasgon, N. (2004). Special considerations in treating bipolar disorder in women. *Bipolar Disorders, 6,* 2–13.

Cohen, D. (1988). Social work and psychotropic drug treatments. *Social Service Review, 62,* 576–599.

Conn, V., & Edwards, N. (1999). The portable medication record (PMR). *Psychiatric Rehabilitation Journal, 22*(3), 288–289.

Corrigan, P. W., Mueser, K. T., Bond, G. R., Drake, R. E., & Solomon, P. (2008). *Principles and practice of psychiatric rehabilitation: An empirical approach.* New York: Guilford Press.

Cowen, P. J. (1998). Psychopharmacology. In A. S. Bellack & M. Hersen (Eds.), *Comprehensive clinical psychology* (Vol. 6, pp. 136–161). Amsterdam: Elsevier Science.

Dixon, L., Lucksted, A., Stewart, B., Burland, J., Brown, C. H., Postrado, L., et al. (2004). Outcomes of the peer-taught

12-week family-to-family education program for severe mental illness. *Acta Psychiatrica Scandinavica, 109*(3), 207–215.

Dixon, L. B., & Lehman, A. F. (1995). Family interventions for schizophrenia. *Schizophrenia Bulletin, 21*(4), 631–643.

Falloon, I. R. H., Boyd, J. L., & McGill, C. W. (1984). *Family care of schizophrenia.* New York: Guilford Press.

Francell, C. G., Conn, V. S., & Gray, D. P. (1988). Families' perceptions of burden of relative care for chronic mentally ill relatives. *Hospital and Community Psychiatry, 39,* 1296–1300.

Frances, A. J., Kahn, D. A., Carpenter, D., Docherty, J. P., & Donovan, S. L. (1998). The expert consensus guidelines for treating depression in bipolar disorder. *Journal of Clinical Psychiatry, 59*(Suppl.), 73–79.

Fromm-Reichmann, F. (1948). Notes on the development of treatment of schizophrenia by psychoanalytic psychotherapy. *Psychiatry, 11,* 263–273.

Gantt, A. B., Goldstein, G., & Pinsky, S. (1989). Family understanding of psychiatric illness. *Community Mental Health Journal, 25,* 101–108.

Gentile, S. (2006). Prophylactic treatment of bipolar disorder in pregnancy and breastfeeding: Focus on emerging mood stabilizers. *Bipolar Disorders, 8,* 207–220.

Gingerich, S., & Mueser, K. (2003). *Illness management and recovery implementation resource kit.* Retrieved September 8, 2010, from http://download.ncadi.samhsa.gov/ken/pdf/toolkits/illness/16.IMR_Workbook.pdf

Gingerich, S., & Mueser, K. (2005). Illness management and recovery. In R. E. Drake, M. R. Merrens, & D. W. Lynde (Eds.), *Evidence-based mental health practice: A textbook* (pp. 395–424). New York: W. W. Norton.

Gingerich, S., & Mueser, K. (2006). *Illness management and recovery implementation resource kit.* Concord: New Hampshire-Dartmouth Psychiatric Research Center.

Gingerich, S., Mueser, K., & Cunningham, H. (2006). *Illness management and recovery group manual: A session-by-session guide.* Concord: New Hampshire-Dartmouth Psychiatric Research Center.

Goldstein, M. J., & Kopeikin, H. (1981). Short and long term effects of combining drug and family therapy. In M. J. Goldstein (Ed.), *New developments in intervention with families of schizophrenics* (pp. 5–25). San Francisco: Jossey-Bass.

Goldstein, M. J., & Miklowitz, D. J. (1995). The effectiveness of psychoeducational family therapy in the treatment of schizophrenic disorders. *Journal of Marital and Family Therapy, 21*(4), 361–376.

Hasson-Ohayon, I., Roe, D., & Kravetz, S. (2007). A randomized controlled trial of the effectiveness of the Illness Management and Recovery Program. *Psychiatric Services, 58*(11), 1461–1466.

Hatfield, A. B. (1987). Coping and adaptation: A conceptual framework for understanding families. In A. B. Hatfield & H. P. Lefley (Eds.), *Families of the mentally ill: Coping and adaptation* (pp. 60–84). New York: Guilford Press.

Jones, D. W. (2004). Families and serious mental illness: Working with loss and ambivalence. *British Journal of Social Work, 34,* 961–979.

Kamin, J., Manwani, S., & Hughes, D. (2000). Emergency psychiatry: Extrapyramidal side effects in the psychiatric emergency service. *Psychiatric Services, 51,* 287–289.

Keck, P. E., Jr., & McElroy, S. L. (1998). Pharmacological treatment of bipolar disorders. In P. E. Nathan & J. M. Gorman (Eds.), *A guide to treatments that work.* New York: Oxford University Press.

Krabbendum, L., & Aleman, A. (2003). Cognitive rehabilitation in schizophrenia: a quantitative analysis of controlled studies. *Psychopharmacology, 169,* 376–382.

Kreyenbuhl, J., Buchanan, R. W., Dickerson, F. B., & Dixon, L. B. (2010). The Schizophrenia Patient Outcomes Research Team (PORT): Updated treatment recommendations 2009. *Schizophrenia Bulletin, 36*(1), 94–103.

Kurtz, M., Moberg, P., Gur, R. C., & Gur, R. E. (2001). Approaches to cognitive remediation of neuropsychological deficits in schizophrenia: A review and meta-analysis. *Neuropsychological Review, 11,* 197–210.

Leff, J., Berkowitz, R., Shavit, N., Strachan, A. M., Glass, I., & Vaughn, C. (1990). A trial of family therapy versus a relatives' group for schizophrenia. *British Journal of Psychiatry, 157,* 571–577.

Leff, J., Kuipers, L., Berkowitz, R., Eberlein-Fries, R., & Sturgeon, D. (1982). A controlled trial of social intervention in the families of schizophrenia patients. *British Journal of Psychiatry, 141,* 121–134.

Lefley, H. P. (2009). *Family psychoeducation for serious mental illness.* New York: Oxford University Press.

Lehman, A. F., Steinwachs, D. M., & Co-Investigators of the PORT Project. (1998). At issue: Translating research into practice: The Schizophrenia Patient Outcomes Research Team (PORT) treatment recommendations. *Schizophrenia Bulletin, 24*(1), 1–10.

Leucht, S., Komossa, K., Rummel-Kluge, C., Corves, C., Hunger, H., Schmid, F., et al. (2009). A meta-analysis of second-generation antipsychotics in the treatment of schizophrenia. *American Journal of Psychiatry, 166*(2), 152–163.

Liberman, R. P., Mueser, K. T., Wallace, C. J., Jacobs, H. E., Eckman, T., & Massel, H. K. (1986). Training skills in the psychiatrically disabled: Learning coping and competence. *Schizophrenia Bulletin, 12*(4), 631–647.

Lidz, T., Cornelison, A. R., Fleck, S., & Terry, D. (1957). The intrafamilial environment of schizophrenic patients. II. Marital schism and marital skew. *American Journal of Psychiatry, 114,* 241–248.

Lucksted, A., Stewart, B., & Forbes, C. B. (2008). Benefits and changes for family to family graduates. *American Journal of Community Psychology, 42*(1–2), 154–166.

Marder, S. R. (1997). Risperidone (Risperdal). *The Decade of the Brain, 8*(3), 5–6.

Marsh, D. T. (1998). *Serious mental illness and the family: The practitioner's guide.* New York: John Wiley & Sons.

Marsh, D. T., & Lefley, H. P. (1996). The family experience of mental illness: Evidence for resilience. *Psychiatric Rehabilitation Journal, 20*(2), 3–12.

McFarlane, W. R. (1990). Multiple family groups and the treatment of schizophrenia. In M. I. Herz, S. J. Keith, & J. P. Docherty (Eds.), *Handbook of schizophrenia. Volume 4: Psychosocial treatment of schizophrenia* (pp. 167–189). Amsterdam: Elsevier.

McFarlane, W. R. (1994). Multiple-family groups and psychoeducation in the treatment of schizophrenia. *New Directions in Mental Health Services, 62,* 13–22.

McFarlane, W. R. (2002). *Multifamily groups in the treatment of severe psychiatric disorders.* New York: Guilford Press.

McFarlane, W. R., Dixon, L., Lukens, E., & Lucksted, A. (2003). Family psychoeducation and schizophrenia: A review of the literature. *Journal of Marital and Family Therapy, 29*(2), 223–245.

McFarlane, W. R., Dushay, R. A., Stastny, P., Deakins, S. M., & Link, B. (1996). A comparison of two levels of family-aided assertive community treatment. *Psychiatric Services, 47*(7), 744–750.

McFarlane, W. R., Lukens, E., Link, B., Dushay, R., Deakins, S. A., Newmark, M., et al. (1995). Multiple-family groups and psychoeducation in the treatment of schizophrenia. *Archives of General Psychiatry, 52,* 679–687.

McGurk, S., Twamley, E., Sizter, D., McHugo, G., & Mueser, K. (2007). A meta-analysis of cognitive remediation in schizophrenia. *American Journal of Psychiatry, 164,* 1791–1802.

Miklowitz, D. J. (2008). *Bipolar disorder: A family-focused treatment approach* (2nd ed.). New York: Guilford Press.

Miller, L. (1991). Clinical strategies for the use of psychotropic drugs during pregnancy. *Psychiatric Medicine, 9,* 275–298.

Mueser, K. T., Corrigan, P. W., Hilton, D. W., Tanzman, B., Schaub, A., Gingerich, S., et al. (2002). Illness manage-

ment and recovery: A review of the research. *Psychiatric Services, 53*(10), 1272–1282.

Mueser, K. T., Drake, R. E., & Bond, G. R. (1997). Recent advances in psychiatric rehabilitation for patients with severe mental illness. *Harvard Review of Psychiatry, 5,* 123–137.

Mueser, K. T., & Glynn, S. M. (1999). *Behavioral family therapy for psychiatric disorders* (2nd ed.). Oakland, CA: New Harbinger.

Mueser, K. T., Meyer, P. S., Penn, D. L., Clancy, R., Clancy, D. M., & Salyers, M. P. (2006). The Illness Management and Recovery program: Rationale, development, and preliminary findings. *Schizophrenia Bulletin, 32*(S1), S32–S43.

Mueser, K. T., Torrey, W. C., Lynde, D., Singer, P., & Drake, R. E. (2003). Implementing evidence-based practices for people with severe mental illness. *Behavior Modification, 27*(3), 387–411.

Mulsant, B. H., & Pollock, B. G. (2009). Psychopharmacology. In D. G. Blazer & D. C. Steffens (Eds.), *The American Psychiatric Publishing textbook of geriatric psychiatry* (4th ed.). Washington, DC: American Psychiatric Publishing. Retrieved August 13, 2009, from www.psychiatryonline.com

Murray-Swank, A. B., & Dixon, L. (2004). Family psychoeducation as an evidence-based practice. *CNS Spectrums, 9*(12), 905–912.

Muzina, D. J., Elhaj, O., Gajwani, P., Gao, K., & Calabrese, J. R. (2005). Lamotrigene and antiepileptic drugs as mood stabilizers in bipolar disorder. *Acta Psychiatrica Scandinavica, 111*(Suppl. 426), 21–28.

Penn, D. L., & Mueser, K. T. (1996). Research update on the psychosocial treatment of schizophrenia. *American Journal of Psychiatry, 153*(5), 607–617.

Perlick, D. A., Rosenheck, R. A., Miklowitz, D. J., Kaczynski, R., Link, B., Ketter, T., et al. (2008). Caregiver burden and health in bipolar disorder: A cluster analytic approach. *Journal of Nervous and Mental Disease, 196*(6), 284–491.

Pilling, S., Bebbington, P., Kuipers, E., Garety, P., Geddes, J., Martindale, B., et al. (2002). Psychological treatments in schizophrenia: II. Meta-analyses of randomized controlled trials of social skills training and cognitive remediation. *Psychological Medicine, 32*(5), 783–791.

Prien, R. F. (1987). Long-term treatment of affective disorders. In H. Y. Meltzer (Ed.), *Psychopharmacology: The third generation of progress* (pp. 1051–1058). New York: Raven Press.

Prochaska, J. O., & DiClemente, C. C. (1984). *The transtheoretical approach: Crossing traditional boundaries of therapy.* Homewood, IL: Dow Jones-Irwin.

Rapoport, M., Mamdani, M., Shulman, K. I., Herrmann, N., & Rochon, P. A. (2005). Antipsychotic use in the elderly: Shifting trends and increasing costs. *International Journal of Geriatric Psychiatry, 20*(8), 749–753.

Riesser, G. G., & Schorske, B. J. (1994). Relationships between family caregivers and mental health professionals: The American experience. In H. P. Lefley & M. Wasow (Eds.), *Helping families cope with mental illness* (pp. 3–26). Langhorne, PA: Harwood Academic Publishers.

Rifkin, A., & Siris, S. (1987). Drug treatment of acute schizophrenia. In H. Y. Meltzer (Ed.), *Psychopharmacology: The third generation of progress* (pp. 1095–1101). New York: Raven Press.

Roe, D., Penn, D. L., Bortz, L., Hasson-Ohayon, I., Hartwell, K., & Roe, S. (2007). Illness management and recovery: Generic issues of group format implementation. *American Journal of Psychiatric Rehabilitation, 10*, 131–147.

Rychener, M., Salyers, M. P., Labriola, S., & Little, N. (2009). Thresholds' Wellness Management and Recovery implementation. *American Journal of Psychiatric Rehabilitation, 12*(2), 172–184.

Sadock, B. J., & Sadock, V. A. (2007). *Kaplan & Sadock's synopsis of psychiatry: Behavioral sciences/clinical psychiatry* (10th ed.). Philadelphia, PA: Wolters Klumer Lippincott Williams & Wilkins.

Salyers, M. P., Hicks, L. J., McGuire, A. B., Baumgardner, H., Ring, K., & Kim, H.-W. (2009). A pilot to enhance the recovery orientation of assertive community treatment through peer provided illness management and recovery. *American Journal of Psychiatric Rehabilitation, 12*(3), 191–204.

Sands, R. G., & Solomon, P. (2003). Developing educational groups in social work practice. *Social Work with Groups, 26*(2), 5–21.

Scherk, H., Pajonk, F. G., & Leucht, S. (2007). Second-generation antipsychotic agents in the treatment of acute mania. *Archives of General Psychiatry, 64*, 442–455.

Seeman, M. V. (2004). Gender differences in the prescribing of antipsychotic drugs. *American Journal of Psychiatry, 161*(8), 1324–1333.

Solomon, P. (1996). Moving from psychoeducation to family education for families of adults with serious mental illness. *Psychiatric Services, 47*(12), 1364–1370.

Solomon, P., Bogart Marshall, T., Mannion, E., & Farmer, J. (2002). Social workers as consumer and family consultants. In K. Bentley (Ed.), *Social work practice in mental health* (pp. 230–253). Pacific Grove, CA: Brooks/Cole.

Solomon, P., Draine, J., Mannion, E., & Meisel, M. (1996). The impact of individualized consultation and group workshop family education interventions on ill relative outcomes. *Journal of Nervous and Mental Disease, 184*(1), 252–254.

Solomon, P., Draine, J., Mannion, E., & Meisel, M. (1997). Effectiveness of two models of brief family education: Retention gains by family members of adults with serious mental illness. *American Journal of Orthopsychiatry, 67*(2), 177–186.

Storzbach, D. M., & Corrigan, P. W. (1996). Cognitive rehabilitation for schizophrenia. In P. W. Corrigan & S. C. Yudofsky (Eds.), *Cognitive rehabilitation for neuropsychiatric disorders* (pp. 299–328). Washington, DC: American Psychiatric Press.

Substance Abuse and Mental Health Services Administration. (2009a). *Illness management and recovery: Training frontline staff* (HHS Publication No. SMA 09-4462). Rockville, MD: Center for Mental Health Services, Substance Abuse and Mental Health Services Administration, U.S. Department of Health and Human Services.

Substance Abuse and Mental Health Services Administration. (2009b). *Illness management and recovery: Practitioner guides and handouts* (HHS Publication No. SMA 09-4462). Rockville, MD: Center for Mental Health Services, Substance Abuse and Mental Health Services Administration, U.S. Department of Health and Human Services.

Substance Abuse and Mental Health Services Administration. (2009c). *Family psychoeducation: Training frontline staff* (HHS Publication No. SMA 09-4422). Rockville, MD: Center for Mental Health Services, Substance Abuse and Mental Health Services Administration, U.S. Department of Health and Human Services. Retrieved from http://store.samhsa.gov/product/SMA09-4423

Swartz, M. S., Stroup, T. S., McEvoy, J. P., Davis, S. M., Rosenheck, R. A., Keefe, R. S. E., et al. (2008). What CATIE found: Results from the schizophrenia trial. *Psychiatric Services, 59*(5), 500–506.

Twamley, E., Jeste, D., & Bellack, A. (2003). A review of cognitive training in schizophrenia. *Schizophrenia Bulletin, 29*, 359–382.

van Wijngaarden, B., Schene, A., Koeter, M., Becker, T., Knapp, M., Knudson, H., et al. (2003). People with schizophrenia in five countries: Conceptual similarities and intercultural differences in family caregiving. *Schizophrenia Bulletin, 29*, 573–586.

Wasow, M. (1994). Professional and parental perspectives. In H. P. Lefley & M. Wasow (Eds.), *Helping families cope with mental illness* (pp. 27–38). Langhorne, PA: Harwood Academic Publishers.

Wichman, C. L. (2009). Atypical antipsychotic use in pregnancy: A retrospective review. *Archives of Women's Mental Health, 12*, 53–57.

Wittlin, B. J. (1988). Practical psychopharmacology. In R. P. Liberman (Ed.), *Psychiatric rehabilitation of chronic mental patients* (pp. 117–145). Washington, DC: American Psychiatric Press.

Yalom, I., & Leszcz, M. (2005). *The theory and practice of group psychotherapy* (5th ed.). New York: Basic Books.

Yatham, L. N., Kennedy, S. H., O'Donovan, C., Parikh, S. V., MacQueen, G., McIntyre, R. S., et al. (2006). Guidelines update: Canadian Network for Mood and Anxiety Treatments (CANMAT) guidelines for the management of patients with bipolar disorder: Update 2007. *Bipolar Disorders, 8*, 721–739.

Young, R. C. (2005). Evidence-based pharmacological treatment of geriatric bipolar disorder. *Psychiatric Clinics of North America, 28*, 837–869.

CHAPTER

13

Clinical Practice with Persons with Co-occurring Substance Use and Serious Mental Illness

KATHLEEN J. FARKAS

Comorbidity constitutes a dizzying complexity rather than a unity.

—PIOTROWSKI, "COMORBIDITY AND PSYCHOLOGICAL SCIENCE: DOES ONE SIZE FIT ALL?" *CLINICAL PSYCHOLOGY: SCIENCE AND PRACTICE* (2007)

The pervasiveness of substance use, dependence, and abuse among clients across social work practice arenas is apparent. In mental health settings, social workers work not only with clients with substance use disorders but also with those with concurrent serious mental illnesses. Such dually diagnosed clients pose unique challenges to clinicians. This chapter provides a background for working with such clients and describes two evidence-based practices—motivational interviewing (MI) and integrated dual disorders treatment (IDDT).

Any time two separate disorders occur in one individual, the combination can be termed a co-occurring or a dual disorder. The terms *dual diagnosis* and *co-occurring disorders* refer to a diagnosis of substance abuse or dependence in addition to another Axis I disorder on the American Psychiatric Association's (APA) (2000) *Diagnostic and Statistical Manual of Mental Disorders* (*DSM*) multiaxial assessment framework. Studies conducted in clinical as well as community settings, using different measures and methodologies all have provided evidence of the co-occurrence of these two sets of disorders (Compton et al., 2000; DeLeon, 1989; Woody & Blaine, 1979). Co-occurring substance use disorders and mental illness complicate assessment and treatment efforts (Drake, Mercer-McFadden, Mueser, McHugo, & Bond, 1998), and there is a serious lack of services that address both substance use disorders and mental illnesses in an integrated fashion.

One of the reasons for the lack of integration is that mental health services and substance abuse treatment services have developed independently of each other. Mental health treatment developed along a medical model, whereas substance abuse treatment arose, in the United States, from a recovery support system. In the traditional mental health system or the traditional substance abuse treatment setting, co-occurring disorders are likely to be under-diagnosed and inadequately treated. Substance abuse treatment approaches that emphasize social interaction, self-reflection, or confrontation may be inappropriate and too difficult for people with severe mental illness, especially early in their treatment. Mental health treatment approaches built on the assumptions that substance use will end with the remission of mental health symptoms fail people with co-occurring substance dependence. Most social workers have been trained in either mental health or substance abuse treatment; social work training has typically not focused on the overlaps of mental health and substance use disorders. However, both clinical experience and advances in neurosciences, which highlight a biological base of addiction and mental illness, argue for an integrated approach to the assessment and treatment of co-occurring disorders (Pliszka, 2003; Spence, DiNitto, & Straussner, 2001).

Despite the separation of mental health and substance abuse treatment and training systems, mental health and substance use disorders have much in common (Ries, 1994). Both are chronic problems that require a lifelong recovery process. Proper assessment and treatment for both disorders target symptom abatement and remission, but the absence of symptoms does not indicate that the person is free of the underlying disorder. In fact, it is during periods of remission that some people with co-occurring disorders are tempted to discontinue medication, psychotherapy, and/or peer supports and then experience relapse. Despite efforts of advocacy groups, professionals, family members, and clients, there is still stigma associated with both mental disorders and substance use disorders. A dual diagnosis often compounds personal and social barriers for recovery. These barriers, as well as the nature of both mental and substance use disorders, can result in social isolation and the ability to interact in positive and productive ways with others in one's family and community.

This chapter begins by introducing the reader to terminology related to substance abuse and substance-related disorders and by describing the prevalence of substance abuse and co-occurring substance abuse and serious mental illness. Then clinical issues in the assessment and treatment of co-occurring disorders are described. Case examples are used to show the range of complex issues facing clients with dual disorders. After discussing different types of treatment models and the use of medication, the chapter describes two evidence-based treatment approaches—MI and IDDT.

TERMINOLOGY

Alcohol and Other Drug Use/Abuse/Dependence Continuum

Alcohol and other drug use can be classified on a continuum ranging from abstinence (no use) to social use (no problems) to misuse or abuse (with problems) to substance dependence (with many problems). Thinking in terms of a continuum is useful because it allows the social worker to explore alcohol and drug use, even if the client does not use alcohol or other drugs, as all behavior, including abstinence, is captured on the continuum. The continuum can be applied to the past month, the past year, or lifetime substance use. It can be applied to any or all drugs and provides a broad conceptualization for social workers to introduce a discussion of alcohol and other drug use into a clinical conversation.

Some substances are legally sanctioned and widely used in contemporary society. For example, ethanol (beverage alcohol) and nicotine (tobacco products) are commonly available psychoactive substances. Alcohol and tobacco products are legal substances for adults, but are restricted for those who are younger than age 21 (alcohol) and 18 (tobacco). Prescription drugs, legal with medical supervision, cause grave problems when used nontherapeutically and illegally. The National Survey on Drug Use and Health (NSDUH) uses the term *illicit drugs* to capture information on the use for the following substances: cocaine, hallucinogens, heroin, and marijuana, as well as the nonmedical use of prescription drugs (Substance Abuse and Mental Health Services Administration [SAMHSA], 2008).

Substance Abuse and Substance Dependence

Professionals use many terms to describe the psychological, social, and physical problems associated with alcohol and other drug use. Terms including alcoholism, drug abuse, problem drinking, and addiction can be found throughout the professional literature. The use of common terminology with standard descriptors and parameters is important to foster clarity and comparability in clinical communication. The APA's (2000) *DSM* offers definitions that capture the impact of consequences associated with alcohol and drug use.

Although there is controversy about the use of the *DSM* in social work (Eriksen & Kress, 2005; Kirk & Kutchins, 1994; Kutchins & Kirk, 1997), the terms *substance abuse* and *substance dependence* can add precision and accuracy without constricting social work practice to a rigid medical model (Gray & Zide, 2008). The *DSM* divides substance use disorders into the categories of substance abuse and substance dependence. Mall and Mall (2009) distinguish between the two in the following way: "substance abuse is described in terms of adverse social consequences" and "substance dependence is defined by physiologic and behavioral symptoms" (p. 66).

Substance abuse is excessive use of a drug not medically indicated and a pattern of recurrent and adverse consequences associated with that use. It is defined as "a maladaptive pattern of substance use leading to clinically significant impairment or distress" (APA, 2000, p. 199). Impairment or distress related to substance use must be found in at least one of the following criteria: failure to fulfill major role obligations; recurrent substance use in a physically hazardous situation; recurrent substance use legal problems and/or continued substance use "despite having persistent or recurrent social or interpersonal problems caused or exacerbated by the effects of the substance" (p. 199). There is room for interpretation on the number and/or severity of events that might define a *maladaptive pattern*, but the events and problems must occur within a twelve-month period to meet criteria for abuse. A single arrest for drunk driving or a domestic argument after an evening of drug use, for example, will not trigger a substance abuse diagnosis. However, careful questioning about either of these events may uncover a repetition of use and problems indicating a substance abuse diagnosis. Hasin, Grant, and Endicott (1990) have argued that substance abuse need not necessarily develop quickly into substance dependence, and some people continue to experience negative consequences related to substance use for many years, but not meet the criteria for substance abuse. Subthreshold alcohol and other drug use behaviors and consequences may also be problematic and should be carefully assessed and included in clinical reasoning and treatment patterns. The use of substances, even at subthreshold levels for a *DSM* diagnosis, may be clinically significant for persons with other Axis I diagnoses.

The *DSM*'s definition of *substance dependence* uses the idea of a "cluster of cognitive, behavioral, and physiological symptoms" related to alcohol and/or other drug use to characterize continued use despite significant problems (APA, 2000, p. 192). Meeting criteria for substance dependence may also include the presence of tolerance and withdrawal. *Tolerance* is present when the alcohol or drug appears to lose its effect; the person must use more to experience the desired effect. Tolerance is present if a person doubles his or her drinks within a given period, but does not feel drunk. *Withdrawal* is indicated by a specific set of symptoms that appear when the substance is not available. Taking a drink to settle a shaking hand or other physical symptoms related to alcohol use is an attempt to manage withdrawal. Tolerance and withdrawal are not necessary for a diagnosis of substance dependence, but only appear in the dependence category. If a person meets criteria for substance dependence, the diagnosis will be carried forward using course specifiers to further explicate length of symptom remission, environmental conditions, and pharmacotherapy. A diagnosis of substance dependence with the specifiers of full *sustained remission, in a controlled environment, and on agonist therapy* would be used to describe someone who had received a diagnosis of substance dependence in the past, but did not meet any criteria for substance dependence during the past twelve months, was incarcerated, and was on a regimen of methadone therapy.

Substance-Induced Disorders

The diagnostic picture is further complicated by the category of substance-induced disorders that are defined as "the development of a reversible substance-specific syndrome due to the recent ingestion of (or exposure to) a substance" (APA, 2000, p. 199). Substance intoxication and substance withdrawal fall into the category of substance-induced disorders. More difficult for diagnosticians are a litany of other substance-induced disorders including, but not limited to, substance-induced delirium, substance-induced amnesia, substance-induced psychotic disorder, substance-induced mood disorder, and substance-induced anxiety disorder. These disorders mimic the symptom patterns of a psychotic disorder, for example, except that the symptoms are attributable to the substance only. A differential diagnosis of a substance-induced disorder will require observation to determine the relationship between the substance use and the psychiatric symptoms.

PREVALENCE

Prevalence of Alcohol and Other Drug Problems

The NSDUH data, compiled by the SAMHSA (2008), provide information on alcohol and other drug use among community dwellers. Approximately half (51.1 percent) of all Americans over age 12 living in the community report that they had at least one drink of alcohol within the past thirty days. The rate of reported alcohol use increases at ages 12 to 13 (3.5 percent) until it peaks at 68.3 percent at ages 21 to 25 and 63.2 percent at ages 26 to 29. Lower proportions of older adults report using alcohol, with 47.6 percent of those age 60 to 64, and 38.1 percent of those of age 65 and older report using alcohol. Binge drinking is defined as five or more drinks on one drinking occasion, and 6.9 percent of the population age 12 and older reported binge drinking. Binge drinking is highest among those age 21 to 25 (45 percent) and somewhat lower among those age 26 to 34 (35.1 percent). Heavy drinking is defined as five or more drinks on one occasion on five or more days in the past thirty days, and 6.9 percent of the population aged 12 or over report heavy use (SAMHSA, 2008).

Approximately 20 million people report use of at least one illicit drug during the past thirty days. Among all illicit drug users, 72.8 percent report using marijuana (14.4 million people), and 53.3 percent of illicit drug users report using only marijuana. Illicit prescription drugs were used by 6.9 million people in the past thirty days. Other drugs reported were cocaine (2.1 million), hallucinogens (1 million), inhalants (0.6 million), and heroin (0.2 million) (SAMHSA, 2008).

Prevalence of Co-occurring Substance Use and Serious Mental Illness

Epidemiological studies have determined the prevalence of co-occurring substance use and mental illness. Most research and writing have focused on those disorders grouped in the *DSM*'s Axis I, including schizophrenia and other psychotic disorders, mood disorders, and anxiety disorders. Understanding prevalence and co-occurrence of substance use and mental health disorders is an important first step in clinical practice. Over the past few decades, there have been several community-based epidemiological studies that have assessed the prevalence of mental health and substance use disorders. Community samples are important because they include both treated and untreated persons and provide a more accurate accounting of the numbers of these disorders in the general population than research on those in treatment. The Epidemiological Catchment Area (ECA) Study, the first large-scale community study (Regier et al., 1990), documented the association among a variety of mental disorders and alcohol and other drug dependence. The National Comorbidity Survey (NCS) (Kessler et al., 1994), the NCS Replication (Kessler et al., 2005; Kessler & Merikangas, 2004), and the National Epidemiologic Survey on Alcohol and Related Conditions (NESARC) (Grant, Hasin, Stinson, Dawson, Chou, et al., 2005; Grant, Hasin, Stinson, Dawson, Ruan, et al., 2005; Hasin, Goodwin, Stinson, & Grant, 2005) have furthered the knowledge base on the dual disorders.

All three studies show an association between substance use disorders—both alcohol and other drugs—and the disorders listed on Axis I of the *DSM*. In their review of the evidence from these studies, Nunes and Weiss (2009) show that the presence of an alcohol or drug disorder doubles the odds of mood disorders, including major depressive disorder and dysthymia. These authors show greatly increased odds ratios for alcohol dependence (5.7) and other drug dependence (13.9) together with bipolar disorder using the NESARC data. Among the most commonly reported co-occurring mental health and substance use disorders is major depressive episode and alcohol use disorder (Kessler et al., 2003). Findings from the NSDUH combined 2004 and 2005 studies show the overall prevalence of depression: 7.6 percent of all adults aged 18 and older experienced a minimum of one major depressive disorder in the past year. NSDUH indicates that 8 percent of adults aged 18 and older reported an alcohol use disorder. The Ohio Substance Abuse and Mental Illness Coordinating Center of Excellence (Ohio SAMI CCOE) (2008) reports the degree of co-occurrence between substance use and mental disorders in that "one out of every two people with a severe mental illness will have a substance abuse disorder at some point in their lives."

CONCEPTUALIZATION, ASSESSMENT, AND TREATMENT OF CO-OCCURRING DISORDERS

Conceptualization

In reviewing the complexity of the relationship between substance use disorders and mental illness, Schuckit (2007) raises several broad questions related to comorbidity or co-occurrence. Are the two conditions separate and independent of each other? Does one disorder influence the

development of the second disorder? Has the second disorder developed in an attempt to minimize problems related to the first disorder? The responses to these questions have implications
for both assessment and treatment decisions. Social workers who were trained only in mental
health assessment and treatment may erroneously view substance use as a way to self-medicate
for psychiatric symptom relief. Those trained only in assessment and treatment of substance-
related disorders may view psychiatric symptoms as the result of substance use and assume that
abstinence will be an adequate treatment.

Several authors have presented conceptual frameworks to describe and treat co-occurring
disorders. Drake and Wallach's (2008) review focuses on four different conceptual models related
to research and treatment for substance use among people with serious mental illnesses. The four
research paradigms include the following: (a) neuro-science-pharmacology model; (b) cognitive-
behavioral model; (c) coercive treatment model; and (d) recovery environment model. The
neuro-science-pharmacology model argues that brain deficits or dysregulation in specific areas
of the brain give rise to mental illnesses. The authors cite Green, Noordsy, Brunette, and
O'Keefe's (2008) hypothesis that the impact of brain deficits is lessened by the use of alcohol
and other drugs. An additional hypothesis of the neuro-science-pharmacology model is that
drugs used to treat the brain deficits should also have an impact on the co-occurring use of alcohol and other drugs. Drake and Wallach (2008) review the empirical literature on the impact of
pharmacological treatments for schizophrenia, bipolar disorder, and major depressive disorder,
finding that these drugs have an inconsistent impact on substance use (Frye & Salloum, 2006;
Nunes & Levin, 2004; Singh & Zarate, 2006). The *cognitive-behavioral model*, in contrast to the
neuro-science-pharmacology model, emphasizes the role of psychotherapy over pharmacotherapy
and focuses on specific interventions including motivational interviewing and cognitive-
behavioral therapies in the treatment of co-occurring disorders. Drake, O'Neal, and Wallach's
(2008) review of the empirical literature does not provide robust support for the exclusive use of
this model to reduce substance use. The *coercive treatment model* rests upon the false assertion
that people with co-occurring disorders are violent and society must take action to protect public
safety through the incarceration and other criminal justice sanctions. Public policies driven by
this model have resulted in high rates of people with dual diagnoses in jail and prison populations and the vexing social problems of reentry and reintegration when they are released back
into the community. Drake and Wallach's (2008) review of studies of forensic assertive community treatment teams concludes that their impact on substance use among people with serious
mental illness is minimal.

The *recovery environment model* highlights the central role of social and environmental
forces in the development of substance use disorders among people with severe mental illness.
Social marginalization, alienation, and stigma push people with severe mental illness into inadequate housing and impoverished neighborhoods where drugs and alcohol are readily available
and widely used. The recovery environment model dictates more aggressive efforts "decreasing
environmental toxicity and increasing social and environmental protection and support for abstinence" (Drake & Wallach, p. 191). Evidence for the recovery environment model includes the
effectiveness of group interventions to reduce substance use (Drake et al., 2008) and of long-
term residential programming (Brunette, Mueser, & Drake, 2004).

Singer, Kennedy, and Kola (1998) used a four-quadrant model of co-occurring substance
use and mental disorders: (a) major mental illness and substance dependence; (b) major mental
illness and substance abuse; (c) less severe mental illness and substance dependence; and (d) less
severe mental illness and substance abuse to discuss treatment needs. The Center for Substance
Abuse Treatment (CSAT) (2005) Treatment Improvement Protocol (TIP) also sets forth a quadrant

High severity of AODA disorder and low severity of mental disorder	High severity of mental disorder and high severity of AODA disorder
Category III	Category IV
Low severity of AODA disorder and low severity of mental disorder	High severity of mental disorder and low severity of AODA disorder
Category I	Category II

FIGURE 13.1 Level of Care Quadrants

Source: Center for Substance Abuse Treatment (2005).

model based on relative symptom severity rather than diagnosis only and is shown in Figure 13.1. The acronym AODA in this figure stands for alcohol and/or other drug addiction.

Assessment Process and Tools

There are a number of excellent assessment tools for mental disorders and for substance use disorders. However, there is no one assessment tool recommended for the assessment of co-occurring disorders (CSAT, 2005). Most tools for assessment focus exclusively on either mental health disorders or substance abuse disorders. However, there are specific, integrated, assessment, and record-keeping approaches for working with drug and alcohol abusers in psychiatric settings (Orlin, O'Neill, & Davis, 2004). These authors suggest an integrated history that provides a detailed account of the onset of substance use, the onset of substance-related problem, and the onset of psychiatric symptoms, as shown in Table 13.1. This assessment form also asks specific questions about treatment history; periods of remission; triggers for return of symptoms/substance use; family history of illness(es); and family responses to client's illness(es). The client's perceptions of the positive and negative consequences of both substance-related disorders and psychiatric disorder are included in the interview. Social workers are also prompted to ask about the client's understanding of both disorders and to talk about any relationships he or she sees between the two. The client's perspective of his or her current strengths and capabilities, as well as his or her views on the need for treatment, provides additional information useful in negotiating treatment goals and resources. An integrated history provides a chronological pattern of mental health symptoms, medications, substance use, treatment, and social/environmental forces associated with both problems. Assessment in the treatment of co-occurring disorders is a continuous process and incorporates changes in the client's condition, preferences, and resources.

Orlin et al. (2004) suggest a companion drug diary to further explore the relationships between psychiatric symptoms and substance use. For this task, clients are asked to record the drug used, the amount of money spent on the drug, and the time of use (when and how long). For each day's drug use, clients are asked to complete the following sentence stems:

1. I knew I would use drugs today because:
2. Before I used I felt:
3. When I was using drugs I felt:
4. Afterwards I felt: (Orlin et al., 2004, p. 110).

Drug diaries are easy to use and are commonly used as a part of substance abuse treatment programming, especially the assessment stages of cognitive-behavioral approaches. A limitation of drug diaries is that people with some severe mental illnesses, including major depressive

TABLE 13.1	Integrated Assessment and History for Coexisting Disorders	
Areas of Assessment	Psychiatric Assessment	Substance Use/Abuse Assessment
Client's age of onset of symptoms	Age of symptoms and onset	Age of first use
Circumstances of symptoms	Description of symptoms	Age of first problems
Client's treatment history:	Hospitalizations and/or outpatient	Detoxification and/or inpatient, outpatient or twelve-step groups
Client's medication: Compliance history, side effects, patient's perception of helpfulness	List each medication: Side effect: Helpfulness:	List each medication: Side effect: Helpfulness:
Client's periods of remission of symptoms:	Times and circumstances when symptom free	Times and circumstances when not using or using less
Client's triggers for return of symptoms/substance use		
Family history of mental illness and/or substance use disorder		
Family's response to client's illness		
Client's understanding of illness		
Client's understanding of the relationship between mental disorder and substance use/disorder		
A. Positive consequences of the illness for the client		
B. Negative consequences of the illness for the client		
Client's understanding of the purpose of treatment		
Client's view on the importance of treatment		

Source: Adapted from Orlin et al. (2004).

disorder, bipolar disorder, and psychotic disorders, may not be able to complete a diary until their symptoms are under control and their medication side effects are minimized. Another limitation of drug diaries is that their use implicitly assumes clients will use substances during the week, which is a direct violation of abstinence-based treatment models. Sacks (2008) offers a brief overview of an integrated assessment process for co-occurring disorders and provides a list of standardized tools useful to the clinician working with this population. Integrated screening and assessment are fundamental to an integrated service approach to address both disorders and to enhance chances of treatment success and goal attainment.

Onset and Severity of Symptoms in the Assessment Process

Onset and severity of symptoms are key aspects in the assessment of co-occurring disorders. From the epidemiological evidence, we know that schizophrenia, bipolar disorder, and major depressive disorder are commonly diagnosed for the first time among people aged 18 to 29 (APA, 2000). The misuse of alcohol, prescription drugs, and illegal drugs is also high among younger age groups (SAMHSA, 2009). Therefore, there is a need for careful attention to the onset and severity of symptoms for both of these disorders, especially among young adults. At any age, substance use can mask or mitigate the severity of mental health symptoms. Substance use and abuse can also exacerbate the severity of the mental health symptoms or, in some situations, will result in symptoms that mimic psychiatric symptoms. Attention to only the mental health symptoms or only the substance-related symptoms is inadequate. Accuracy in diagnosis and treatment requires an understanding of the incidence of co-occurring disorders as well as the possible onset patterns and motivations for substance use.

The following five case studies illustrate specific patterns of symptom onset and severity and highlight some of the problems in the diagnosis of mental illness and substance use disorders.

1. Case of Michael: Alcohol and Psychotic Disorder

Michael began college at age 17 and did reasonably well in his school work in the first semester. He did have difficulty making friends but his family attributed that to Michael's usual routine of staying on his computer when he wasn't at class or at meals. He had great difficulty talking to people in person, but he developed and maintained e-mail and instant message contact with some of the other students in his residence hall. Periodically, Michael's roommate found him passed out on his bed with many empty beer cans littering the floor. It didn't seem that Michael was having any problems in school and his roommate did not see a reason for concern about his drinking or social interactions. During the winter semester, Michael suddenly stopped using his computer and wrapped it tightly in bubble wrap and duct tape to "keep evil out." He began to drink every night so that he was intoxicated most of the time. He told his friends that he was interested in "partying" all of the time, but he continued to stay in his room and drink alone. The resident assistant filed a warning on Michael for underage drinking in the residence hall, but he continued to drink heavily for several months. One afternoon, his roommate found him unconscious and called security for transportation to the health service. When Michael awoke in the hospital, he was agitated and repeatedly told the staff that "his thoughts were visible" and that he "needed to be shielded from external thought forces." The results of the toxicology screen showed Michael to have alcohol poisoning and he was kept in the hospital for observation to monitor for possible alcohol withdrawal symptoms.

Psychotic disorders include schizophrenia, schizophreniform disorder, schizoaffective disorder, delusional disorder, and psychotic disorders not otherwise specified (APA, 2000). In addition, major depression and bipolar disorder sometimes present with psychotic features. A large percentage of people with schizophrenia report lifetime substance use disorders (Hunt, Bergen, & Bashir, 2002; Ziedonis & Fisher, 1996). Onset of schizophrenia for men is typically earlier than for women, and Michael's social isolation and his distorted thinking are consistent with criteria necessary for the diagnosis of schizophrenia but these symptoms may also be attributable to heavy alcohol use. As Michael's symptoms intensified, alcohol was the method he used to lessen his discomfort and to mask and manage symptoms. The severity of his alcohol use resulted in withdrawal that may initially have delayed attention to an underlying psychotic disorder. The full diagnostic picture will not become evident until Michael's system is completely clear of alcohol and any other substances he may have ingested. Then his pattern of disturbed thinking and feelings of detachment can be evaluated as consistent with a psychotic disorder. The facts in Michael's case study indicate that he initially falls into category IV of the four quadrant model described in Figure 13.1: high severity of mental disorder and high severity of AODA disorder. The facts of the case suggest that Michael's use of alcohol is directly related to his efforts to relieve psychiatric symptoms. However, it is crucial that Michael receive a complete assessment for substance use disorder to document that assumption and to address the symptoms of alcohol use. Without assessment for alcohol abuse or dependence, Michael's dual disorder will only be partially addressed and he will be at increased risk for relapse. Any use of alcohol or other drugs would be contraindicated with the use of psychotropic medication. Reduced effectiveness and increased side effects of medication are common consequences of interactions between alcohol, other drugs, and psychiatric medications (Smelson et al., 2008). Michael is a good candidate for IDDT, an evidence-based treatment for co-occurring serious mental illness such as schizophrenia and substance use and abuse. IDDT is described later in this chapter.

Schizoaffective disorder is the combination of both psychotic symptoms and the symptoms of a major mood disorder. Substance use and schizoaffective disorder present a particularly difficult diagnostic challenge. Social workers must determine the onset of each set of symptoms—mood disturbances and thought disorders—and then determine the relationship of each to the substance use. Central nervous system depressants such as alcohol, opiates, and prescriptions of sedative drugs can mimic symptoms of depression. Stimulant drugs such as cocaine, methamphetamine, and medications for attention-deficit disorders can result in symptoms similar to mania or paranoia. The assessment period for dual disorders, therefore, must be long enough to determine the onset, extent, and relationships among the various symptom sets and the possible diagnoses for each. The following case illustrates the impact of the combination of substance dependence and schizoaffective disorder.

2. Case Example of Suzanne: Cocaine and Schizoaffective Disorder

Suzanne is a 32-year-old single woman who became homeless after the apartment building she lived in for twelve years was sold. Suzanne's former neighbors describe her as often moody and a little strange. Her neighbors said she would stay inside for months at a time and often seemed sad and depressed. Suzanne lived alone but insisted to her neighbors that she had a roommate who "butted into" her thoughts and was critical everything she did. When the apartment building was sold, Suzanne thought her only alternative was to live out on the streets. Suzanne met several other people who were homeless and began to spend time with a small group of younger men and women. Suzanne had used alcohol infrequently when she was in her apartment but had not used any other drugs. On the street, Suzanne was introduced to crack cocaine, and she began to use it to fit in with the other people on the street and to feel less sad and depressed. However, after she smoked crack cocaine with her friends, the voice of her "roommate" was harsh, and she criticized her for doing drugs and associating with bad people.

Suzanne's symptoms are consistent with schizoaffective disorder and she requires treatment for both the depressive and the thought disorder aspects of the diagnosis. Her cocaine use is most likely episodic and related to her current living situation. However, without intervention, her use of cocaine can be expected to continue and render her vulnerable for arrest and/or victimization on the street. The link between symptom management and substance use is common among people with mental disorders. Suzanne's case also illustrates how environmental changes can have widespread effects in the management of dual disorders. The next case portrays a combination of a substance and a mood disorder.

3. Case of Example of Jeanine: Alcohol and Depressive Disorder

Jeanine is an African American woman who began working in an advertising agency after high school. Her family used alcohol heavily while she was growing up and she began drinking as a young teen. She engaged in binge drinking in high school, but does not report any symptoms or problems associated with alcohol or other drug use. She describes herself as "a dark and moody type" and had been treated for a depressive disorder during adolescence. There is a drinking culture at her advertising agency and Jeanine often met her coworkers for a drink in the evening. Jeanine enjoyed these drinking occasions and quickly learned that she was able to drink four to five drinks in an evening without feeling adverse effects. To the contrary, she felt that alcohol allowed her to be more responsive and creative. As she gained more responsibilities at work, Jeanine began to have a couple of mixed drinks at home after work "to relax." When Jeanine was 25, her mother died after a long illness, and because of a weakening economy, Jeanine's work became much more stressful. About ten months after her mother's death, Jeanine was surprised at how sad she felt and how little she was able to sleep. She wasn't able to concentrate at work and she rarely ate more than one meal a day. She was now drinking at lunchtime "to help her cope with the afternoon" and to help her focus. She spent most evenings alone and had five or six drinks to help her sleep. She began to think about suicide as a way to escape her pain and had asked her doctor for sleeping medication.

Epidemiological studies show the overlap of depressive disorders and alcohol dependence. Data from NCS indicate that the prevalence of major depressive disorder is four times as likely among women with alcohol dependence as it is among women without alcohol dependence and three times as likely among men with alcohol dependence (Kessler et al., 1994). Jeanine's diagnostic picture is a complicated overlap of depression and substance dependence symptoms and triggering events in her life: sadness associated with her mother's death, increased alcohol intake, insomnia, lack of concentration, decreased interest in things she used to enjoy, suicidal ideation, and mounting stress at work. The pathway leading up to the onset is unclear: Did the depressive symptoms occur prior to increased alcohol use? Does she have an undiagnosed history of depression? Did increased alcohol use exacerbate an underlying depressive disorder or are the symptoms completely explained by an alcohol-induced mood disorder? What is the role of bereavement in her psychiatric distress? Only careful questioning on both mental health and substance use symptoms will reveal an accurate symptom pattern. If alcohol's role as a central nervous system depressant is not recognized, it is likely that the pattern of depressive symptoms will persist even with treatment. If only the environmental stressors are considered, an underlying substance use disorder will be missed. Without a careful assessment for substance use disorder, it is unclear if Jeanine symptoms meet criteria for alcohol abuse or dependence, but unchecked alcohol use will impede any treatment for depressive disorder and will exacerbate depressive symptoms. Jeanine's case most likely would be classified as category III (high severity of AODA disorder and low severity of mental disorder), based upon the findings of a clinical interview for substance use disorder in addition to depressive disorder and complicated bereavement. If Jane's depressive symptoms do not abate with the cessation of alcohol use, a more intensive mental health diagnosis is warranted.

We turn now to a case with a different combination of disorders. Stephen presents a separate set of symptoms and a long history of use, treatment, and relapse. Stephen's case illustrates how an underlying, untreated mental health disorder can repeatedly trigger relapse of substance use. The diagnosis of substance use disorders includes disruption in social activities such as job, school, or family life. Stephen's case shows that people with co-occurring disorders can function at high levels despite their illness and substance use.

4. Case Example of Stephen: Substance Use and Bipolar Disorder

Stephen's parents came to the United States as undocumented workers when he was 4 years old. He grew up in migrant camps but he excelled at school. A teacher helped him to become a U.S. citizen. Stephen started out as a car salesman at a local car dealership and did very well. One of the reasons for his success was that he had periods when he required very little sleep and had a lot of energy. He used these times to work on inventive advertising campaigns and to develop extensive professional networks for the dealership. He began to use alcohol heavily to help him sleep during those times. Stephen also experienced cyclical periods of depression and sadness and he turned to cocaine to help energize him. Despite his substance dependence, he built a successful business, was married to the mother of his three teen-aged children, and counted many friends and professional associates in his social circle. Stephen had a history of erratic and impulsive behavior that has always been associated with substance use. His wife reported that during an especially long period of depression and remorse he had talked about but not attempted suicide. He had been diagnosed with substance dependence early in his life, but had no mental health assessment or treatment. In his early thirties, Stephen sought treatment for his substance dependence. He became active in Twelve Step programs and was seen as a leader in the treatment community. Despite his devotion to recovery, Stephen had six serious relapses in the past twelve years. The last time Stephen entered treatment was after he drove to Las Vegas and lost over $400,000 at a blackjack table.

Stephen's story illustrates that a diagnosis of substance dependence earlier in life can be accurate, but the omission of a mental health assessment and diagnosis of a mental disorder contributes to relapse and continuing problems. Stephen's underlying pattern of depression and mania led to a co-occurring diagnosis of bipolar disorder, the symptoms of which continued to wreak havoc in Stephen's life despite his attempts to address his alcohol and drug dependency. The bipolar symptoms were attributed solely to his substance dependence and were undetected and untreated for over twenty years. The literature on the association of bipolar disorder and substance use disorder is growing (Cerullo & Strakowski, 2007). The symptoms of bipolar disorder can easily be masked as substance-induced impulses or depression. In his review of the relationship between bipolar disorder and substance use, Swann (2010) suggests a pharmacological treatment approach that addresses the shared neurologic mechanisms of both disorders.

Although mental disorders and substance use disorders can co-occur at any age, there is increasing attention to the needs of older adults (Blow, 1998; Farkas & Drabble, 2008). Depression, delirium, dementia, anxiety, and substance use disorders present with similar symptoms among older adults and diagnosis is complicated by the fact that alcohol and other drugs can have an increased effect in older people. Because of age-related metabolic and physical changes, even small amounts of alcohol or drugs can cause problems among older adults. The following case demonstrates the impact of co-occurring mental health and substance use disorders on an older adult.

5. Case Example of Donald: Co-occurring Disorders (in an older adult)

Donald, now 73, retired in his early sixties. He was an active volunteer at the community gardens in the summer and at the local elementary school in the winter. He described himself as a "social drinker" and typically drank every evening and sometimes during the afternoon watching sports with friends, a pattern that he had maintained since he was in his twenties. Donald's wife was concerned when she noticed he sometimes seemed confused in the evening and was not interested in getting up in the morning to volunteer. He told her that he didn't have the energy he used to. He stopped all of his volunteer work and now sits in the living room most of the day. Donald's physician suggested that he stop drinking any alcohol to see if that may have any impact on his mood.

For older adults, diagnosis is more complicated when professionals overlook alcohol or drug use as part of a mental health assessment. Donald's drinking pattern exceeds the National Institute on Alcohol Abuse and Alcoholism's guideline of a maximum of one drink a day or fourteen drinks per week for older adults. His drinking pattern would not be considered by most as heavy drinking; it is the effect and not the amount of alcohol that is central to the evaluation of problems in all age groups (National Institute on Alcohol Abuse and Alcoholism, 2005). Donald's symptoms of depression are serious, and alcohol may place a significant role in the severity of those symptoms. If his depressive symptoms lessened with abstinence, he would fall into category I (low severity of AODA disorder and low severity of mental disorder), but there is also the possibility that alcohol does not play a role in his symptom pattern and his diagnosis would be best explained by category II (high severity of mental disorder and low severity of AODA disorder). The expected increase in the population over age 60 in the next several decades necessitates continued efforts in diagnosis and treatment for co-occurring mental health and substance use disorders in later life (Bartels, 2006).

The preceding five cases all illustrate the complexity of co-occurring disorders. Aside from the importance of an integrated approach (Reedy & Hall, 2008), the research base is just beginning to shed light on which treatments are the most effective. Carroll, in her 2004 review of behavioral therapies for co-occurring disorders, points out that there are few rigorous studies of cognitive-behavioral therapy in the treatment of co-occurring disorders. Ostacher's (2007) review of medication therapy reiterates the importance of integrating psychosocial treatment with mental health services to improve compliance for psychiatric medications. Nunes and Levin (2004) echo Ostacher's point in their discussion of the importance of addiction treatment as well as antidepressant medication. Hesse's (2009) more recent review reiterates the promise of integrated treatments for co-occurring mental and substance use disorders, but cites the need for more rigorous and controlled studies.

Treatment Models

Treatment models for co-occurring substance use and mental health disorders can be classified as serial, parallel, or integrated (Ries, 1992). *Serial models* posit that substance use disorders and mental disorders must be treated separately and sequentially. The serial model most accurately pictures the traditional, separate development of mental health and alcohol and other drug treatment services. Serial approaches in mental health treatment required people to be free of alcohol and other drugs before entering into mental health therapy, so clients completed detoxification and then were admitted to the psychiatric service. Serial approaches consider mental disorders and substance-related disorders to be separate or to delineate one disorder as primary and one as secondary. Personnel in serial programs are trained in the assessment and treatment of either mental disorders or substance-related disorders. Communication between the two staff may exist, but is not extensive.

A *parallel treatment model* recognizes the relationship between the two disorders and provides some concurrent treatment. For example, a twelve-step meeting may be included as part of a mental health treatment program, or a therapeutic support group may be added to the schedule in an alcohol and other drug abuse treatment setting. There is awareness and agreement among both mental health and substance abuse treatment staff that the problems are related. A parallel treatment model may include some joint staff progress or discharge meetings, but treatment is separate and often uneven. Staff members in parallel treatment models are trained primarily in one area with some supplemental education about the other area.

Minkoff (1989), as well as Drake et al. (1998), defined a fully *integrated substance abuse and mental health treatment model* as including excellent coordination among highly trained staff who engage the client in work toward recovery goals for both substance abuse and mental disorders. A fully integrated treatment model provides services to address both disorders, and those services are provided by the same set of clinicians trained in assessment, intervention, and recovery. Two central principles of integrated treatment are increased accessibility to both types of treatment and improved individualization and clinical relevance for the client (Drake et al., 2008). Treatment integration should be the service system's responsibility rather than the client's. The literature includes models of integrated treatment set in addiction settings (Charney, Paraherakis, & Gill, 2001) and integrated models set in mental health facilities (Minkoff & Drake, 1991). The empirical literature has documented the merits of integrated service models in the treatment of dual diagnosis clients (Brunette et al., 2004; Drake, Mueser, Brunette, & McHugo, 2004; Mueser, Drake, Sigmon, & Brunette, 2005). A specific and well-developed treatment model, IDDT, to be described later in this chapter, provides an evidence-based approach for coexisting mental health and substance use disorders.

Use of Medications

Medication has been a mainstay of treatment for mental disorders for over fifty years and is generally accepted by both clients and practitioners within the mental health system. Developments in psychiatric medications have moved toward increased symptom control and decreased side effects. Integrated treatment models have fully accepted the use of medication for psychiatric problems within the framework of abstinence and sobriety. Alcoholics Anonymous (AA) supported the use of medication to treat psychiatric disorders beginning in 1984 (AA World Services) and supports heeding the advice of physicians and psychiatrists for treatment of mental illness. For some, the abstinence principle in AA has given rise to confusion about the use of psychiatric medications, and clients with co-occurring disorders may receive misguided advice to stop using medications or may hear such advice as support for their own desires to decrease or stop medication.

Research and treatment models using medication for substance use disorders are increasing. Pharmacotherapy has been accepted as standard treatment in detoxification and acute treatment for withdrawal symptoms. However, the use of medication as part of ongoing rehabilitation or maintenance in alcohol and other drug treatment is controversial for some. The Food and Drug Administration (FDA) has approved three medications to treat alcohol dependence: disulfuram

(Antabuse), acamprosate (Campral), and naltrexone (Revia and Vivitrol). FDA-approved medications for treatment of opiate dependence include methadone, naloxone, naltrexone, and buprenorphine. These medications work to control cravings and to manage risks of relapse. There is also an emerging evidence base on the effects of these medications on co-occurring psychiatric symptoms that is encouraging. Methadone maintenance therapy for opiate dependence as well as naltrexone therapy for alcohol dependence has been associated with decreased symptoms of depression (Nunes et al., 1998; Petrakis et al., 2007). Rychtarik, Connors, Dermen, and Stasiewicz (2000) found support among a sample of AA members for use of relapse-preventing medications. AA members reported that they had experienced some pressure from other AA members to stop taking medication to prevent relapse. Their conclusion is that AA philosophy may need to be updated to include these newer medications targeted at substance use disorders in addition to the long-standing principle to accept psychiatric medications prescribed and monitored by a physician.

Abstinence and Harm Reduction Approaches

The primary stated goal of alcohol and other drug abuse treatment in the United States is abstinence from all alcohol and other drugs. The goal of abstinence has been seen as an all-or-nothing outcome; either a person is abstinent or he or she is not. Relapse, however, is most often a part of the recovery process, requiring both clients and substance abuse treatment professionals to address substance use during the course of treatment. Harm reduction approaches provide a way to reduce a variety of negative consequences of alcohol and other drug use. For example, providing clean needles and safe-sex kits to sexually active intravenous drug users are well-documented harm reduction strategies to decrease HIV transmission (Lurie, Reingold, & Bowser, 1993). Abstinence from drug use is desirable, but not the primary goal of harm reduction approaches. In clinical practice, harm reduction ideas are familiar parts of public health policies and goal-setting strategies. In alcohol and other drug treatment settings, however, harm reduction approaches may be seen as controversial if they are not paired with a commitment to abstinence from all drugs and alcohol. It should be clearly understood that harm reduction approaches do not condone or encourage illegal drug use or problem-related use of alcohol (World Health Organization Expert Committee on Drug Dependence, 1993). A harm reduction approach can be consistent with abstinence-based recovery, especially when it is used with MI and stage-based treatment, one of two evidence-based practices that will be described next.

EVIDENCE-BASED PRACTICES WITH CLIENTS WITH DUAL DISORDERS

Motivational interviewing and IDDT are two evidence-based practices useful in clinical work to improve the lives of people with serious mental illness and substance use disorders. Both MI and IDDT are built upon the principles of Prochaska, DiClemente, and Norcross's (1992) transtheoretical theory of change. MI was developed for use in substance abuse treatment settings, and the approach has been adapted for use in many types of settings and for various applications of behavioral change (Miller & Rollnick, 2002). The evidence base for MI is therefore broad and not strictly limited to the population of people with co-occurring disorders (Chanut, Brown, & Dongier, 2005; Miller, Benefield, & Tonigan, 1993; Project MATCH Research Group, 1997). IDDT is an agency-based, multidisciplinary team approach that uses stage-wise assessment and treatment principles. The evidence base for IDDT is large and growing and is limited specifically to the population of people with schizophrenia and a co-occurring substance use disorder.

Motivational Interviewing

Motivational interviewing developed as a means to encourage change by recognizing that people approach change along a continuum and that effective treatment must take into account the stage of change for each individual (Miller & Rollnick, 2002). MI is build upon the transtheoretical model of change set forth by Prochaska and DiClemente (1983, 1984). The transtheoretical model is based upon a synthesis of psychological and sociological studies of the processes humans use to change their behavior or the behaviors of others. Prochaska et al. (1992) applied the transtheoretical approach directly to addictive behaviors and provided a framework for clinicians to help clients understand if and when they were reading, willing, and able to change. The stages of change include the following:

1. *Precontemplation:*   there is no serious intention of changing behavior now or in the forseeable future;
2. *Contemplation:*   there is awareness of a problem and some serious thinking about change, but no commitment to action;
3. *Preparation:*   there may have been some attempts to change but without success. There is serious thinking about change, but no action;
4. *Action:*   serious change occurs and significant time and energy is devoted to behavior change; and
5. *Maintenance:*   efforts are directed at consolidating gains, maintaining the changed behavior, and avoiding relapse. Success is defined as six months or more of the changed behavior. (Norcross & Prochaska, 2002; Prochaska et al., 1992)

Stages and processes of change are assumed to be voluntary. Prochaska et al.'s (1992) continuum includes a spot for those who are not convinced of any problem or need to change (precontemplation) as well as for those who are actively working toward change (action), and for those who have achieved change (maintenance). It is the client's view of the problem and his or her willingness and perceived ability to change that focuses assessment process.

The initial clinical task is to explore each client's stage-of-change ideas and to use those ideas to formulate goals appropriate to that stage. A stage-of-change approach eliminates the idea of "denial," replacing it with the stage of precontemplation. In a more traditional approach to treatment of substance use disorders, an assessment of "in denial of alcohol and other drug problems" might end the client's contact with treatment. Clients who do not acknowledge a problem or who are not interested in treatment programs, that is, clients in the precontemplation stage, can be engaged—whether it be in a working relationship with a staff person or by performing a concrete task that the client sees as important. The clinician, using the therapeutic processes associated with each stage (Prochaska et al., 1992), can work with the client to promote movement through the stages of change, encouraging, but not insisting upon action right away or at each session. The transtheoretical model assumes change is incremental and not necessarily linear in nature. As part of the process of change, people may slip back into a prior stage and stay at that level for a while before moving forward.

The transtheoretical approach paved the way for Miller and Rollnick's (2002) work on MI, which encourages clients to examine their reasons for change as well as their reasons to stay the same. MI embraces uncertainty about change as a normative, yet often unrecognized, aspect of the way humans change behaviors and attitudes. MI seeks to address ambivalence and uncertainty about change directly and to use a reflective, nonjudgmental, and objective process to foster decisions to change attitudes and behaviors.

As described by Miller and Rollnick (2002), there are four general principles to MI: (a) express empathy; (b) develop discrepancy; (c) roll with resistance; and (d) support self-efficacy. MI can be characterized as a client-centered approach and insists that clinicians develop a nonjudgmental and accepting stance toward clients, their problems, and their decisions. This *empathic approach* acknowledges the client's point of view as a valid response to his or her situation. Through the interview and listening process, the clinician would assist the client to weigh the pros and cons of his or her alcohol and drug use and develop a *sense of discrepancy* between desired goals and continued substance use. MI techniques teach the clinician to back away from challenging resistance and conflict. Clinicians trained in MI techniques will not let go of the work, yet will avoid open confrontation and a battle of wills with the client. The principle of *rolling with resistance* does not abandon the emphasis on change or supportive reasons for change. The client's point of view is acknowledged, but so are the discrepancies between the client's actions, current situation, and his or her stated goals. All are done in a supportive, encouraging, and nonjudgmental manner. Clinicians must convey the fact that change is possible and, indeed, probable for the clients. It is the clinician's optimism and belief in the client's ability to choose a change that encourages and sustains the change process. The *self-efficacy principle* entails supporting a client's steps toward change, however, small these steps might be. The client's confidence or his or her perception of self-efficacy to change is core to the overall MI stance. Martino, Carroll, Kostas, Perkins, and Rounsaville (2002) have revised MI principles and techniques specifically for work with people who have co-occurring substance abuse and psychotic disorders. These authors recommend simplifying open-ended questions and emphasizing affirmative statements. Psychiatric issues should be included in the personalized feedback and the discussion of decisions about alcohol and other drug use.

Joel's case presents the conflicts of facing many young adults who strive to build a life in the shadow of serious mental illness and presents an opportunity to discuss both MI and IDDT.

Case Example of Joel

Joel is 25 and first had an onset of psychotic symptoms when he was 20. He was diagnosed with schizophrenia and did well on a course of medication, psychotherapy, and peer supports for about three years until he moved from his parents' house. At the apartment building in which he lives, he has made a number of friends. Joel drinks with the friends and he uses marijuana and cocaine. He has been charged with disorderly conduct and public intoxication. He has told his case manager that he doesn't think that he needs medication and has been cutting down on his psychiatric medications on his own. He says that he uses alcohol or marijuana when he hears voices. He says he "feels normal" when he is with his new friends and likes to be included in their parties. He has been to AA meetings but says the meetings are too long and too hard to follow. Sometimes people at the meeting talk about medications as a bad thing and he uses that as support to cut down on his psychiatric medications. He says he "isn't an alcoholic" and doesn't have the same kinds of problems people in AA talk about. His case manager has no training in alcohol or other drug treatment and tells Joel to "just stop using drugs and alcohol." Joel is determined to be independent and to live "a normal life," which he feels includes going to alcohol and drug parties with his friends.

An MI approach to Joel's situation would engage him as one in precontemplation. Even in the face of legal consequences, Joel does not see any problem associated with his use of alcohol and drugs. He does not see a problem in decreasing his psychiatric medications. Joel's case manager, using MI techniques, would try to build their therapeutic relationship around Joel's interests in remaining independent in his apartment and in developing "normal" social relationships. The case manager would guide their conversation to highlight the discrepancies between Joel's goals and his behaviors and the possible consequences of his drinking on his living arrangement and his desire to live independently. An MI approach would help Joel to realize the links between his behaviors and his ability to live independently in the community. The clinician would support his self-efficacy to make positive choices as an independent person. The role of the environment and the extent to which Joel's new friends encourage him to act responsibly would also be addressed. Using a decisional balance approach, Joel and his case manager would develop a list of pros and cons for change and for staying the same or the status quo in Joel's life right now. Miller and Rollnick's (2002) model follows human nature; change will happen when the benefits of changing outweigh the costs of not changing. These decisional choices are unique to person and to situation. The constancy is in the clinician's use of the principles and in his or her nonjudgmental and optimistic stance.

As simple as the core principles are for MI, the training process is rigorous and thorough. While all clinicians can use the ideas and apply them in their work (Rosengren, 2009), there is a training program and certification process available through the Motivational Interviewing Network of Trainers (MINT) (see http://www.motivationalinterview.org/training/index.html).

In their meta-analysis of studies using MI approaches, Chanut et al. (2005) found that the results of MI approaches are not necessarily better than other methods of treating substance abuse and dependence, but that MI may provide positive results in less time than other approaches. While the reasons for the timing of the results are not clear, the authors speculate that the focus on client-centered goals and reduced resistance clear a path for behavior change. MI's established training guidelines and method to evaluate the integrity of the intervention's use will facilitate future evaluations of its effectiveness with various populations and settings.

Integrated Dual Disorders Treatment

Integrated dual disorders treatment is another evidence-based treatment approach for people with co-occurring severe mental illness and substance use disorders. The New Hampshire-Dartmouth IDDT model, developed by Robert Drake and his colleagues, is an integrative, multidisciplinary approach to assessment and treatment of mental health and substance use disorders (Drake et al., 1998; Mueser, Noordsy, Drake, & Fox, 2003). The elements of the IDDT model are shown in Table 13.2. The IDDT model is an agency-based approach that includes a multidisciplinary and collaborative team. The team provides a combination of pharmacological, psychological, and educational treatment. Family and social interventions are part of the IDDT service package as well as housing and employment resources. All IDDT team members are trained in the relationship between severe mental illness and substance use disorders. Team members work together to develop specific and targeted interventions for each client under their care. Stage-related interventions are seen as important in the development of specific goals and treatment plans and MI principles guide client and family interactions.

Integrated dual disorders treatment services are not bound by a specific service interval nor are they limited. Because both substance use disorders and severe mental illnesses are chronic in nature, IDDT services are available as needed. IDDT uses a comprehensive service management strategy and will assist clients to find suitable housing, employment, health care, and other needed

TABLE 13.2	Elements of Integrated Dual Disorders Treatment (IDDT)

Multidisciplinary Team includes a variety of disciplines including substance abuse specialist; counselor; physician or psychiatrist; nurse; employment specialist; housing specialist; and criminal justice specialist. Team leaders and case managers facilitate the team's communication with each other, the client, and the client's family and friends.

Stage-wise Interventions require using a transtheoretical model and the following stages of change: precontemplation; contemplation and preparation; action, and maintenance.

Access to Comprehensive Services allows the team to offer comprehensive services to meet needs of clients at each stage of change.

Time-Unlimited Services incorporate knowledge about the cycles of relapse and recovery common to both mental disorders and substance use disorders.

Assertive Outreach takes responsibility for active engagement and supportive relationship with clients and family members. IDDT team members are not limited to office contacts and work actively in the communities in which their clients live.

Motivational Interviewing principles guide all interactions with clients and family members. Communications are client-centered, goal focused, and supportive.

Substance Abuse Counseling promotes the development and practice of recovery skills.

Group Treatment provides opportunity to develop and expand supportive peer relationships and to promote social interactions and coping skills.

Family Psychoeducation includes developing partnerships with family and social supports. Family caregivers are actively engaged and may participate in specific family treatment programs.

Participation in Alcohol and Drug Self-Help Groups adds to social supports and relapse prevention. IDDT supports participation in Dual Recovery, Double Trouble, Alcoholics Anonymous, Narcotics Anonymous, Cocaine Anonymous, and Rational Recovery.

Pharmacological Treatment maximizes symptom reduction and minimized side effect and use of potentially addictive medications.

Interventions to Promote Health focus on prevention and treatment of chronic physical health problems as well as opportunities to increase health exercise and nutrition habits.

Secondary Interventions for nonresponders to substance abuse treatment are specific plans for those who do not respond to IDDT. These intensive interventions can include PTSD treatment, family interventions, medication to reduce drug craving, and intensive monitoring in partnership with the criminal justice system.

Source: Adapted from Ohio SAMI CCOE (2008). With permission of the Center for Evidence-Based Practices, Case Western Reserve University, Cleveland, Ohio.

community supports. In Joel's case, IDDT programming might assist in finding him a drug-free housing facility and facilitate his involvement in a social group or in a self-help group designed for those with coexisting mental health and substance use disorders.

In IDDT, different services are provided at different stages of treatment. IDDT teams use the term *stage-wise services*. The four stages of treatment in IDDT are engagement, persuasion, active treatment, and relapse prevention. The concept of stage-wise treatment requires clinical staff to understand the transtheoretical theory and processes of change, to assess accurately for the client's readiness for change and then to develop the treatment plan associated with the client's stage of readiness for change.

Clinicians working in an IDDT setting must be able to collaborate effectively with other professionals to ensure a well-functioning multidisciplinary team. In IDDT, a single team provides all mental health and substance abuse services. The stage-wise treatment principle means that clinicians must learn to assess the various stages of treatment and to provide those services most appropriate for the client's stage of change: precontemplation, contemplation, active treatment, and relapse prevention. In Joel's case example, the clinician would determine whether Joel perceived his alcohol and drug use to cause a problem in his life. If Joel did not see his use of alcohol and other drugs to be associated with any problems or concerns, the clinician would begin with the stage-wise interventions appropriate for precontemplation: engagement. The clinician would work with Joel to develop a trusting working relationship, to determine boundaries for the relationship, and to demonstrate genuine concern for his well-being. There is no confrontation or attempt at behavior change in the engagement phase. If Joel acknowledged his problems with alcohol and other drug use and he indicated an intention to change his behavior sometime in the future, the clinician assesses him to be in contemplation and uses the persuasion processes associated with that stage. Persuasion involves active listening and exploratory questions about Joel's views on how alcohol and other drug use might be related to his desire for friendship and social interactions would all be part of interventions associated with the contemplation stage. The clinician's goal is to engage the client and move with him or her to reach the active treatment stage when specific behavioral treatment can be initiated. Relapse prevention follows active treatment. The IDDT model does not assume all clients are ready to initiate active behavior change. In IDDT, all clients should be assessed for their readiness for change and all interventions pegged to that stage of change. Assessment steps and intervention processes in stage-wise treatment are directly derived from MI and applied in the multidisciplinary setting.

The IDDT model also emphasizes assertive outreach, comprehensive services, and a long-term approach to service delivery. Clinicians working in an IDDT model will be quick to pick up on any alcohol and substance use and will not wait for the problems to escalate into substance abuse or substance dependence. The comprehensive service perspective will allow the clinician to work with the client on issues including housing, employment, health care, and social networks. The comprehensive service approach further strengthens the ability of the multidisciplinary team to diminish barriers to care and fragmentation. The long-term approach to services mirrors the chronicity of both mental health disorders and substance use disorders. After clients have completed the steps in the plan of active treatment, the final phase of treatment is relapse prevention to provide follow-up and support for sustained behavioral success.

Peer support and self-help approaches are a mainstay of alcohol and other drug abuse treatment (Project MATCH Research Group, 1997). However, people with coexisting mental health and substance use disorders may find that some aspects of traditional self-help groups, such as AA, are not well suited for their needs. In Joel's case, typical AA meetings were "too long and too hard to follow." Special groups that address the needs of people with co-occurring disorders can provide a source of support from others who are experiencing similar problems (Cameron, 2007, 2009). These groups are called by various names (e.g., Dual Recovery Anonymous [DRA], MICA [Mentally Ill and Chemically Addicted] Support, Double Trouble in Recovery, and MIDAA [Mental Illness, Drug Addiction and Alcoholism]), but they share a common use of peer support principles and provide encouragement, knowledge, and social support from others who are experiencing similar problems. These specialized support groups make some modifications in self-help support groups to be useful to people with coexisting disorders (Orlin et al.,

2004). One of the adjustments, as indicated earlier, is a clear policy on the appropriate use of psychiatric and anticraving medications. Group members as well as any professional staff associated with the group need to have a uniform understanding of medication use within the context of mental health and substance abuse recovery. Abstinence continues to be a desirable goal, but the harm reduction philosophy is central as well. Group members should not be permitted to attend the group while under the influence of alcohol or other drugs of abuse, but a relapse is not reason for dismissal from the group. Relapse should be regarded as a treatment failure, not solely a client failure, and should be addressed with an increase in treatment intensity (Mee-Lee, 2001). Unlike the voluntary fellowship of AA, specialized groups like DCA, MICA, and MIDAA accept service referrals. Persons with coexisting disorders may need additional encouragement to attend and additional support to continue their participation with self-help groups. DCA, MICA, and MIDAA groups include other modifications such as a shorter format, more frequent meetings, and more directive information related to co-occurring disorders. Within the IDDT model, all staff members are trained in the use of twelve-step groups and will use the option of twelve-step support in the integrated treatment plan.

The advantages of the IDDT team model would become clear in Joel's case study. A multidisciplinary, cross-trained team would provide a comprehensive, integrated assessment of Joel's treatment and social needs. Expanded resources could be brought to bear to adjust any side effects of his medication, to secure an affordable drug-free living setting, and to increase his social circle and activities with support groups and other drug-free social events. Additionally, Joel's employment status would be assessed and the IDDT resources can promote a supported employment option for him to increase his income and independence and to decrease loneliness and free time. The MI approach would further support his desire to be independent and to help him make decisions about future drug and alcohol use and medication compliance. The evidence base for IDDT has been limited to severe mental illness, that is, psychotic disorders, but the approach has wide appeal for other types of co-occurring disorders.

Summary and Deconstruction

The term co-occurring disorders has been used in this chapter to discuss the needs of people with dual diagnoses of a serious mental disorder and a substance use disorder—either abuse or dependence. However, the term *co-occurring* has been restricted to a relative few mental disorders—schizophrenia and mood disorders including major depressive disorder and bipolar disorders. Certainly the severity and chronicity of these serious mental disorders and co-occurring substance use disorders warrant the attention of clinicians, policy makers, and researchers. The high rate of co-occurrence of these serious mental health disorders with substance use disorders indicates that social workers are likely to see such clients in their practice regardless of the setting. Budget constraints and the resulting stress on health and social services systems may in-

crease the numbers of clients with co-occurring disorders who seek help from agencies that traditionally did not expect to serve this population; thus indicating the importance of training in integrated screening and assessment methods for both disorders and understanding the various ways these disorders can be related.

However, the concept of co-occurring disorders is such a useful one that it can be applied to a far greater number of disorders including many of the anxiety disorders and the personality disorders. For example, substance abuse and misuse have long been shown to be associated with post-traumatic stress disorder and the co-occurrence of these two disorders increases the difficulty of assessment and treatment of both disorders (Kessler, Sonnega, Bromet, Hughes, & Nelson, 1995) and many of the same treatment models may apply. The concept of co-occurring disorders is one that can be used to improve services for people with other types of mental disorders and a co-occurring substance use disorder. One of the lessons of the current literature on co-occurring disorders is the need to address both disorders as important and worthy of assessment and treatment. Social workers, who are on the front lines in many mental health and community agencies, need training and supervision that features integrated screening and assessment techniques to address a range of co-occurring mental health and substance use disorders.

The current clinical practices associated with treatment of co-occurring disorders—MI and integrated assessment—have been shown to be effective with people who have severe mental illness and substance use disorders and have not been evaluated systematically

for use with the other disorders. The empirical base is sound, but limited to only a few mental disorders. In theory, these practices can be extended for use and evaluation with those who have less severity of symptoms and anxiety disorders. Treatment modules such as IDDT and the integration of medication with psychotherapy also have much to offer other populations, but the empirical base needs to be expanded to include other types of disorders. Advances in neuroscience will further our understanding of the similarities and differences between mental disorders and substance use disorders and can support innovation in social work assessment and treatment. Social work practitioners should accept these challenges and continue to collaborate with researchers and evaluators to add the clinical perspective and methods that enhance the well-being of clients with dual diagnoses and their families.

References

AA World Services. (1984). *The A.A. member medications and other drugs*. New York: Author.

American Psychiatric Association. (2000). *Diagnostic and statistical manual of mental disorders* (4th ed., text rev.). Washington, DC: Author.

Bartels, S. J. (2006). The aging tsunami and geriatric mental health and substance use disorders. *Journal of Dual Diagnosis, 2*(3), 5–7.

Blow, F. (1998). *Substance abuse among older adults*. Rockville, MD: U.S. Department of Health and Human Services, Public Health Service, Substance Abuse and Mental Health Services Administration, Center for Substance Abuse Treatment, Treatment Improvement Protocol Series (TIP).

Brunette, M. F., Mueser, K. T., & Drake, R. E. (2004). A review of research on residential programs for people with severe mental illness and co-occurring substance use disorders. *Drug and Alcohol Review, 23*, 471–481.

Cameron, A. (2007). Double trouble: Substance misuse, mental health and self-help. *Drugs and Alcohol Today, 3*, 25–28.

Cameron, A. (2009). Dual Recovery Anonymous (DRA) in the U.K. *Advances in Dual Diagnosis, 2*(3), 11–13.

Carroll, K. (2004). Behavioral therapies for co-occurring substance abuse and mood disorders. *Biological Psychiatry, 56*, 778–784.

Center for Substance Abuse Treatment. (2005). *Substance abuse treatment for persons with co-occurring disorders* (Treatment Improvement Protocol (TIP) Series 42, DHHS Publication No. SMA 05-3992). Rockville, MD: Substance Abuse and Mental Health Services Administration.

Cerullo, M., & Strakowski, S. (2007). The prevalence and significance of substance use disorders in bipolar type I and II disorder. *Substance Abuse Treatment, Prevention and Policy, 1*, 2–29.

Chanut, F., Brown, T. G., & Dongier, M. (2005). Motivational interviewing and clinical psychiatry. *Journal of Canadian Psychiatry, 50*(11), 715–721.

Charney, D. A., Paraherakis, A. M., & Gill, K. J. (2001). Integrated treatment of comorbid depression and substance use disorders. *Journal of Clinical Psychiatry, 62*(9), 672–677.

Compton III, W. M., Cottler, L. B., Abdallah, A., Phelps, D. L., Spitznagel, E. L., & Horton, J. C. (2000). Substance dependence and other psychiatric disorders among drug dependent subjects: Race and gender correlates. *American Journal of Addictions, 9*(2), 113–125.

DeLeon, G. (1989). Psychopathology and substance abuse: What is being learned from research in therapeutic communities. *Journal of Psychoactive Drugs, 21*(2), 177–188.

Drake, R. E., Mercer-McFadden, C., Mueser, K. T., McHugo, G. J., & Bond, G. R. (1998). Review of integrated mental health and substance abuse treatment for patients with dual disorders. *Schizophrenia Bulletin, 24*(4), 589–608.

Drake, R. E., Mueser, K. T., Brunette, M. F., & McHugo, G. J. (2004). A review of treatments for people with severe mental illness and co-occurring substance use disorders. *Psychiatric Rehabilitation Journal, 27*, 360–374.

Drake, R. E., O'Neal, E. L., & Wallach, M. A. (2008). A systematic review of psychosocial research on psychosocial interventions for people with co-occurring mental and substance use disorders. *Journal of Substance Abuse Treatment, 34*, 123–138.

Drake, R. E., & Wallach, M. A. (2008). Conceptual models of treatment for co-occurring substance use. *Mental Health & Substance Use: Dual Diagnosis, 1*(3), 189–193.

Eriksen, K., & Kress, V. E. (2005). *Beyond the DSM story: Ethical quandaries, challenges and best practices.* Thousand Oaks, CA: Sage Publications.

Farkas, K., & Drabble, L. (2008). *Advanced MSW curriculum in substance use and aging.* Council on Social Work Education, Gero-Ed Center. Retrieved on September 24, 2010, from http://depts.washington.edu/geroctr/mac/1_4substance.html

Frye, M. A., & Salloum, I. M. (2006). Bipolar disorder and comorbid alcoholism: Prevalence rate and treatment considerations. *Bipolar Disorders, 8*, 677–685.

Grant, B. F., Hasin, D. S., Stinson, F. S., Dawson, D. A., Chou, P., Ruan, J. W., et al. (2005). Co-occurrence of 12-month mood and anxiety disorders and personality disorders in the US: Results from the national epidemiologic survey on alcohol and related conditions. *Journal of Psychiatric Research, 39*(1), 1–9.

Grant, B. F., Hasin, D. S., Stinson, F. S., Dawson, D. A., Ruan, J. W., Goldstein, R. B., et al. (2005). Prevalence, correlates, co-morbidity, and comparative disability of DSM-IV generalized anxiety disorder in the USA: Results from the National Epidemiologic Survey on Alcohol and Related Conditions. *Psychological Medicine, 35*(12), 1747–1759.

Gray, W., & Zide, M. (2008). *Psychopathology: A competency-based assessment model for social workers* (2nd ed.). Belmont, CA: Thomson.

Green, A. I., Noordsy, D. L., Brunette, M. F., & O'Keefe, C. (2008). Substance abuse and schizophrenia: Pharmacotherapeutic interventions. *Journal of Substance Abuse Treatment, 34*, 61–71.

Hasin, D. S., Goodwin, R. D., Stinson, F. S., & Grant, B. F. (2005). Epidemiology of major depressive disorder: Results from the National Epidemiologic Survey on Alcoholism and Related Conditions. *Archives of General Psychiatry, 62*(10), 1097–1106.

Hasin, D. S., Grant, B., & Endicott, J. (1990). The natural history of alcohol abuse: Implications for definitions of alcohol use disorders. *American Journal of Psychiatry, 147*(11), 1537–1541.

Hesse, M. (2009). Integrated psychological treatment for substance abuse and co-morbid anxiety or depression vs. treatment for substance abuse alone: A systematic review of the literature. *BMC Psychiatry, 9*, 6. Retrieved on March 31, 2010, from http://www.biomedcentral.com/1471-244X/9/6

Hunt, G. E., Bergen, J., & Bashir, M. (2002). Medication compliance and comorbid substance abuse in schizophrenia: Impact on community survival 4 years after a relapse. *Schizophrenia Research, 54*, 253–264.

Kessler, R. C., Berglund, P., Demler, O., Jin, R., Koretz, D., Merikangas, K. R., et al. (2003). The epidemiology of major depressive disorder: Results from the National Comorbidity Survey Replication (NCS-R). *Journal of the American Medical Association, 289*, 3095–3105.

Kessler, R. C., Berglund, P., Demler, O., Jin, R., Merikangas, K., & Walters, E. (2005). Lifetime prevalence and age-of-onset distributions of DSM-IV disorders in the National Comorbidity Survey Replication. *Archives of General Psychiatry, 62*(6), 593–602.

Kessler, R. C., McGonagle, K., Zhao, S., Nelson, C. B., Hughes, M., Eshleman, S., et al. (1994). Lifetime and 12-month prevalence of DSM-III-R psychiatric disorders in the United States: Results from the National Comorbidity Survey. *Archives of General Psychiatry, 51*(1), 8–19.

Kessler, R. C., & Merikangas, K. R. (2004). The National Comorbidity Survey Replication: Background and aims. *International Journal of Methods in Psychiatric Research, 13*, 60–68.

Kessler, R. C., Sonnega, A., Bromet, E., Hughes, M., & Nelson, C. B. (1995). Posttraumatic stress disorder in the National Comorbidity Survey. *Archives of General Psychiatry, 52*(12), 1048–1060.

Kirk, S. A., & Kutchins, H. (1994). The myth of the reliability of the DSM. *Journal of Mind and Behavior, 15*, 71–86.

Kutchins, H., & Kirk, S. A. (1997). *Making us crazy: DSM: The psychiatric bible and the creating of mental disorders.* New York: Free Press.

Lurie, P., Reingold, A. L., & Bowser, B. (1993). *The public health impact of needle exchange programs in the United States and abroad* (Vol. I). San Francisco: University of California.

Mall, S. K., & Mall, G. D. (2009). DRINK TWO 6 PACK clarifies substance use. *Current Psychiatry, 8*(5), 66.

Martino, S., Carroll, K., Kostas, D., Perkins, J., & Rounsaville, B. (2002). Dual diagnosis motivational interviewing: A modification of MI for substance-abusing patients with psychotic disorders. *Journal of Substance Abuse Treatment, 23,* 297–308.

Mee-Lee, D. (2001). Persons with addiction disorders, system failures and managed care. In E. C. Ross (Ed.), *Managed behavior health care handbook* (pp. 225–266). Gaithersburg, MS: Aspen Publishers.

Miller, W. R., Benefield, R. G., & Tonigan, J. S. (1993). Enhancing motivation for a change in problem drinking: A controlled comparison of two therapist styles. *Journal of Consulting Clinical Psychology, 61,* 455–461.

Miller, W. R., & Rollnick, S. (2002). *Motivational interviewing: Preparing people for change* (2nd ed.). New York: Guilford Press.

Minkoff, K. (1989). An integrated treatment model for dual diagnosis of psychosis and addiction. *Hospital and Community Psychiatry, 40*(10), 1031–1036.

Minkoff, K., & Drake, R. (Eds.). (1991). *Dual diagnosis of major mental illness and substance disorder.* San Francisco: Jossey-Bass.

Mueser, K. T., Drake, R. E., Sigmon, S. C., & Brunette, M. (2005). Psychosocial interventions for adults with severe mental illnesses and co-occurring substance use disorders: A review of specific interventions. *Journal of Dual Diagnosis, 1,* 57–82.

Mueser, K. T., Noordsy, D. L., Drake, R. E., & Fox, L. (2003). *Integrated treatment for dual disorders: A guide to effective practice.* New York: Guilford Press.

National Institute on Alcohol Abuse and Alcoholism. (2005). Helping patients who drink too much: A clinician's guide, updated edition. Retrieved on September 30, 2009, from http://pubs.niaaa.nih.gov/publications/Practitioner/CliniciansGuide2005/clinciagnsguide.htm

Norcross, J. C., & Prochaska, J. O. (May, 2002). Using the stages of change. *Harvard Mental Health Letter,* pp. 5–7. Retrieved on March 18, 2010, from http://www.health.harvard.edu

Nunes, E. V., & Levin, F. R. (2004). Treatment of depression in patients with alcohol and other drug dependence. *Journal of the American Medical Association, 291,* 1887–1896.

Nunes, E. V., Quitkin, F. M., Donovan, S. J., Deliyannides, D., Ocepek-Welikson, K., Koenig, T., et al.(1998). Imipramine treatment of opiate-dependent patients with depressive disorders: A placebo-controlled trial. *Archives of General Psychiatry, 55*(2), 153–160.

Nunes, E. V., & Weiss, R. D. (2009). Co-occurring addiction and affective disorders. In R. K. Ries, D. A. Fiellin, S. C. Miller, & R. Saitz (Eds.), *Principles of addiction medicine* (4th ed., pp. 1151–1181). Philadelphia, PA: Wolters Kluwer, Lippincott, Williams & Wilkins.

Ohio Substance Abuse and Mental Illness Coordinating Center of Excellence. (2008). *Integrated dual disorder treatment: An overview of the evidence-based practice.* Retrieved on October 23, 2009, from http://www.ohiosamiccoe.case.edu

Orlin, L., O'Neill, M., & Davis, J. (2004). Assessment and intervention with clients who have coexisting psychiatric and substance-related disorders. In S. L. A. Straussner (Ed.), *Clinical work with substance-abusing clients* (2nd ed., pp. 103–124). New York: Guilford Press.

Ostacher, M. J. (2007). Co-morbid alcohol and substance abuse dependence: Impact on the outcome of anti-depressant treatment. *Psychiatric Clinics of North America, 30,* 69–75.

Petrakis, I., Ralevski, E., Nich, C., Levison, C., Carroll, K., Poling, J., et al. (2007). Naltrexone and disulfiram in patients with alcohol dependence and current depression. *Journal of Clinical Psychopharmacology, 27*(2), 160–165.

Piotrowski, N. A. (2007). Comorbidity and psychological science: Does one size fit all? *Clinical Psychology: Science and Practice, 14,* 6–19.

Pliszka, S. R. (2003). *Neuroscience for the mental health clinician.* New York: Guilford Press.

Prochaska, J. O., & DiClemente, C. C. (1983). Transtheoretical therapy: Toward a more integrative model of change. *Psychotherapy: Theory, Research and Practice, 19,* 276–288.

Prochaska, J. O., & DiClemente, C. C. (1984). *The transtheoretical approach: Crossing the traditional boundaries of therapy.* Malabar, FL: Krieger.

Prochaska, J. O., DiClemente, C. C., & Norcross, J. C. (1992). In search of how people change: Applications to the addictive behaviors. *American Psychologist, 47,* 1102–1114.

Project MATCH Research Group. (1997). Matching alcoholism treatment to client heterogeneity: Project MATCH posttreatment drinking outcomes. *Journal of Studies on Alcoholism, 58,* 7–29.

Reedy, A. R., & Hall, J. A. (2008). Treatment issues with substance abuse disorder who have mood or anxiety disorders. *Mental Health and Substance Use: Dual Diagnosis, 1*(1), 44–53.

Regier, D. A., Farmer, M. E., Rae, D. S., Locke, B. Z., Keith, S. J., Judd, L., et al. (1990). Comorbidity of mental disorders with alcohol and other drug abuse – results from the Epidemiological Catchment Area (ECA) Study. *Journal of the American Medical Association, 264,* 2511–2518.

Ries, R. K. (1992). Serial, parallel and integrated models of dual diagnosis treatment. *Journal of Health Care for the Poor and Underserved, 3*(1), 173–180.

Ries, R. K. (1994). *Assessment and treatment of patients with coexisting mental illness and alcohol and other drug abuse* (Treatment Improvement Protocol (TIP) Series 9, DHHS Publication No. SMA 95-3061). Rockville, MD: Substance Abuse and Mental Health Services Administration.

Rosengren, D. B. (2009). *Building motivational interviewing skills: A practitioner's workbook.* New York: Guilford Press.

Rychtarik, R. G., Connors, G. J., Dermen, K. H., & Stasiewicz, P. R. (2000). Alcoholics Anonymous and the use of medications to prevent relapse: An anonymous survey of members attitudes. *Journal of Studies on Alcohol and Drugs, 61*, 134–138.

Sacks, S. (2008). Brief overview of screening and assessment for co-occurring disorders. *International Journal of Mental Health and Addiction, 6*, 7–19.

Schuckit, M. A. (2007). Comorbidity of substance use disorders with psychiatric conditions. In J. B. Saunders, M. A. Schuckit, P. J. Sirovatka, & D. A. Regier (Eds.), *Diagnostic issues in substance use disorders: Refining the research agenda for DSM-V* (pp. 133–155). Arlington, VA: American Psychiatric Association.

Singer, M. I., Kennedy, M. J., & Kola, L. A. (1998). A conceptual model for co-occurring mental and substance-related disorders. *Alcoholism Treatment Quarterly, 16*(4), 75–89.

Singh, J. B., & Zarate, C. A. (2006). Pharmacological treatment of psychiatric comorbidity in bipolar disorder: A review of controlled trials. *Bipolar Disorder, 8*, 696–709.

Smelson, D., Dixon, L., Craig, T., Remolina, S., Batki, S., Niv, N., et al. (2008). Pharmacological treatment of schizophrenia and co-occurring substance use disorders. *CNS Drugs, 22*(11), 903–916.

Spence, R. T., DiNitto, D. M., & Straussner, S. L. A. (Eds.). (2001). *Neurobiology of addictions: Implications for clinical practice.* New York: Haworth Press.

Substance Abuse and Mental Health Services Administration. (2008). *Results from the 2007 National Survey on Drug Use and Health: National findings* (Office of Applied Studies, NSDUH Series H-34, DHHS Publication No. SMA 08-4343). Rockville, MD: Author.

Substance Abuse and Mental Health Services Administration, Office of Applied Studies. (2009). *The NSDUH Report: Concurrent illicit drug and alcohol use.* Rockville, MD: Author.

Swann, A. J. (2010). The strong relationship between bipolar and substance use disorder. *New York Academy of Sciences, 1187*, 276–296.

Woody, G. E., & Blaine, J. (1979). Depression in narcotic addicts: Quite possibly more than a chance association. In R. Dupont, A. Goldstein, & J. O'Donnell (Eds.), *Handbook of drug abuse* (pp. 277–285). Rockville, MD: National Institute on Drug Abuse.

World Health Organization Expert Committee on Drug Dependence. (1993). *WHO Technical Report Series (twenty-eighth report).* Geneva, Switzerland: World Health Organization.

Ziedonis, D. M., & Fisher, W. (1996). Medication-based assessment and treatment of substance abuse in patients with schizophrenia. *Direct Psychiatry, 16*(11), 1–8.

INDEX